W9-AHH-415

To Julia

Coded Letters, Concealed Love

I hope you enjoy this

Sora

Coded Letters, Concealed Love

The Larger Lives of Harriet Freeman and Edward Everett Hale

Sara Day

NEW ACADEMIA PUBLISHING

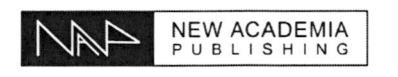

Washington, DC

New Academia Publishing 2014

Printed in the United States of America

Library of Congress Control Number: 2013954487
ISBN 978-0-9899169-3-6 paperback (alk. paper)
ISBN 978-0-9899169-6-7 hardcover (alk. paper)

New Academia Publishing
PO Box 27420, Washington, DC 20038-7420
info@newacademia.com - www.newacademia.com

Cover: Harriet Freeman drives Edward Everett Hale on the Dundee Road during one of his visits to her in Intervale, New Hampshire, August 1902. Hale Family Papers, Sophia Smith Collection, Smith College, Northampton, Massachusetts.

For Stephen, Gordon, and Colin,
and my dear mother Joan

Contents

List of Illustrations ix

Acknowledgments xiii

Introduction:
Love Letters and Coded Clues—the Untold Story 1

1. A Parish Call 11
2. The Freemans and the Hales 23
3. Panic, Church, and Science 51
4. Romantic Love 79
5. Loss and Liberation 109
6. The Protégés: Charlotte Stetson [Gilman], Helen Keller, and Others 133
7. Romance and Deception 145
8. Separations and Tragedy 173
9. The Toll of Depression 203
10. "For pity's sake" 233
11. An Adventurous Life 263
12. First Winters without Edward 297
13. Preservation and Conservation 323
14. Filling the Gap 337
15. Life after Edward 369

Epilogue: Concealing Is Revealing 395

Postscript 400

Notes 401

Bibliography 451

Index 457

List of Illustrations

Cover: Harriet E. Freeman driving Edward Everett Hale on the Dundee Road, White Mountains, New Hampshire, August 1902.

Edward Everett Hale, ca. 1859 12

Harriet E. Freeman and Helen Atkins, 1862 13

South Congregational Church, Union Park Street, Boston, ca. 1862-1869 15

Union Park, South End, Boston, 1860s 17

The Freeman family, 1860s 24

Emily Perkins Hale and Ellen Day Hale, ca. 1855 40

Susan and Edward E. Hale, ca. 1850 42

Summer home of Edward Everett Hale, Matunuck, Rhode Island, 1890s 57

Emily Perkins Hale, 1880s 62

Edward Everett Hale, 1880s 70

Letter, Edward Everett Hale to Harriet E. Freeman, September 29, 1884. 92

Hollis Street Church, Back Bay, Boston, ca. 1885 110

Harriet Freeman and Edward E. Hale in canoes on Wash Pond, Matunuck, 1887 120

Helen Keller and Anne Sullivan on Cape Cod, summer 1888 138

Helen Keller, Anne Sullivan, and Edward Everett Hale, ca. 1903 140

Charlotte Perkins Stetson (Gilman), Pasadena, California, ca. 1890 142

Sarah Jane Farmer with Swami Vivekananda and Edward Everett Hale, 1894 187

Edward Everett Hale in his study, 1890s 190

Hale family group on piazza of Red House, Matunuck, 1890s 199

E. Atkins & Company employees under old slave bell at Soledad, Cuba, 1895 204

Mohonk Lake Mountain House register, July 24, 1896 213

Marine Biological Laboratory students collecting specimens, 1895 219

Letter, Harriet Freeman to Edward E. Hale, April 12, 1897 228

Silas Weir Mitchell, 1890s 243

Edward Everett Hale at Mohonk Mountain House, June 1899 254

"Looking Backward," cartoon by Laura E. Foster, 1912 258

Amadeus Grabau, 1905 272

Edward Everett Hale and Harriet Freeman at Smith College, June 1902 279

Hales and family on the Matunuck beach, July 4, 1902 280

"At the Start, Ravine House," White Mountain hiking party, July 9, 1902 281

Harriet Freeman driving Edward Everett Hale, White Mountains, August 1902 284

Caroline and Ethel Freeman and Edward Everett Hale, Intervale, August 1902 285

Harriet E. Freeman, Intervale, August 1902 286

Delegates, American Forest Congress, Washington, D.C., January 2, 1905 326

Statue of Edward Everett Hale by Bela Pratt, Boston Public Garden 382

Acknowledgments

This entire project would not have been possible without the enthusiasm, encouragement, and support of philanthropist and historic preservationist Ken Woodcock. In one of those splendid serendipitous moments, and there have been many of them in the course of my research for this book, we were invited to an event by him and his wife Dorothy when he was embarking on a collaboration with the Pettaquamscutt Historical Society of Kingston, Rhode Island, to purchase and restore the former summer house of the Edward Everett Hale family in Matunuck, Rhode Island, where the Woodcocks have a summer home. I remembered that there is a significant special collection of letters between Edward Everett Hale and Harriet E. Freeman at the Library of Congress and that they had been described as "love letters" by Janice Ruth, formerly the women's history specialist of the Library's Manuscript Division and now the assistant chief. Ms. Ruth was one of my colleagues in editing *American Women*, the Library's women's history resource guide. The special collection had been acquired for the Manuscript Division in 1969 by the late John McDonough, a manuscript historian and dear colleague. Christopher Bickford, the director of the Pettaquamscutt Historical Society at that time, asked me if I would see if any of the letters were written from Matunuck and whether they threw light on the Hale house. The presence of code or, as I was to discover, a forgotten shorthand, in most of the three thousand letters convinced me to examine them more closely and translate the shorthand.

David Halaas, an historian and author with whom I had collaborated nearly twenty-five years ago on a major exhibition at the Library of Congress, advised me to put a previous book I was writing on hold in favor of getting to the bottom of a relationship that promised to have historical importance. I could not have guessed that this pursuit would last seven years. Dr. Halaas read almost every version of my drafts for an article, talks, and the book. I am extremely grateful for his encouragement and advice over the last several years and for his many helpful suggestions for improvements. Maida Goodwin, an archivist at the Sophia Smith Collection at Smith College, has been immensely helpful from the beginning of my research. With her knowledge of their Hale Family Papers, we were able to discover eighteen more of the Hale-Freeman letters. Because I was unable to spend a great deal of time in Northampton, she generously followed up on discoveries I made during two brief trips. In addition, her personal interest in botany and the White Mountains of New Hampshire, the shared passions of Hale and Freeman, have led me to Freeman letters at Harvard's Gray Herbarium, Freeman's activities with the Appalachian Mountain Club, and an album of photographs of one of Freeman's hiking excursions in the White Mountains, discovered and photographed by Randolph Mountain Club historians Al and Judy Hudson.

My first talk in Kingston, Rhode Island, in 2007 was attended by Dean Grodzins, a leading scholar of Unitarian history and author of a major biography of Theodore Parker. Dr. Grodzins subsequently commissioned me to write an article for the *Journal of Unitarian Universalist History*, which he then edited. His knowledge of nineteenth-century American and Unitarian history and his editorial skills added depth to my research and my article that I could not have achieved at that time without his guidance and encouragement. When he attended a talk I gave at the Boston Athenaeum in April 2013, Dr. Grodzins agreed to read my manuscript and subsequently made extraordinarily helpful suggestions which greatly strengthened the book.

With the publication of my article at the end of 2008, two more colleagues made initial and continuing contributions to my book. First, I heard from Fran O'Donnell, archivist at the Andover-Harvard Theological Library of the Harvard Divinity School. She told me that the Library had been given a significant collection of Hale materials amassed by a certain Harriet E. Freeman. Not knowing more about her at the time, they stored the collection. I followed up on her suggestion that I might travel to Cambridge to take a look and spent a week examining the voluminous articles, photographs, and inscribed books. The papers are now cataloged online as the Harriet E. Freeman Papers and the books have been transferred to the Library. Examining this collection convinced me that I had the makings of a book. Mary Chitty, a pharmaceutical librarian and taxonomist in Boston, former colleague, recreational historian, and longtime friend, also read my article and has made myriad contributions since then, including helping me track down Boston locations, generously inviting me to stay with her on two separate weeklong research trips to Boston, and reading and commenting on different drafts of my book and the final manuscript.

Joan Youngken, a colleague in research for the Hale House restoration and now curator of a private gallery celebrating the work of the artists in the Hale family, also read an earlier draft of my book. She contributed significantly to the Matunuck aspects of my book by drawing on her considerable knowledge of the Hale family. Lori Urso, the former director of the Pettaquamscutt Historical Society, consistently encouraged me to keep working on this demanding project by awarding me a generous research grant. Several descendants of Harriet Freeman's niece Helen Hunt Arnold have searched their family archives for photographs or other materials. Two of them, Holly Sawyer and Phoebe Bushway, found very rare photographs of Harriet Freeman. Mary Macomber Leue was close to another of Hattie's nieces, Ethel Hale Freeman, for many years until her death, and I have benefited from her memoir about her mother's relationship with Ethel and other insights about the Freeman family. Elizabeth Atkins helped me in my pursuit of Atkins family photographs. Catharina Slautterback, curator of prints and photographs at the Boston Athenaeum, drew my attention to an album of botanical watercolors made by Caroline Freeman, Harriet's mother, and this led me back to Mrs. Freeman's descendants for more information. Ms. Slautterback's unqualified support after she read my article undoubtedly added credibility to the invitation of Paula Matthews, former director of the Athenaeum, for me to speak about a controversial topic in the city where Edward Everett Hale remains revered in some quarters to this day.

I have been fortunate to have the guidance and support of Ralph Eubanks, until recently director of publishing at the Library of Congress and my boss for several years, who is now the editor of the *Virginia Quarterly*; of John Wright, a veteran agent for trade publishers in New York, who helped me fashion my first book proposal; and of Margery Thompson, who has had a long career editing scholarly books and spearheaded my more recent search for a university press, including fine tuning my various targeted proposals and capturing the essence and intention of my book in her letters of inquiry. But my timing was terrible, coinciding as it did with a significant retrenchment in print publishing in the face of New Media. Although the trade and university publishers eluded us, I learned a great deal from writing proposals and shaping the outline of the book, and was greatly encouraged by some of the positive comments made by acquisition editors who were intrigued by the subject but could not foresee a large enough market. Margery Thompson led me to New Academia Publishing which is publishing my book as one of their peer-reviewed academic imprints.

Throughout the seven years of research and writing, I benefited from the support and suggestions of colleagues in the Washington Biography Group. Linda Osborne, my former colleague at the Library of Congress, an accomplished editor and writer who worked for me forty years ago in her first professional research job after college, read my proposal and made helpful suggestions. Others who have read and commented on the article, book proposal, or parts of the book manuscript, or engaged in discussions about the subject matter with me, all of them longtime friends, include Heather Burke, Anne Burnham, Judith Gilmore, Mary Kopper, Philip Kopper, Susan Richardson, Barbara Mathias Riegel, Ruth Selig, and Marjorie Williams. Philip Kopper and Hugo Phillips devoted more time than I deserved to resolving technical challenges for this technically challenged writer, and Becky Lescaze offered moral support when I needed it most. Two freelance researchers, Eva Murphy in Boston and Anne Skilton in Chapel Hill, directed me to and/or copied, respectively, genealogical and probate information on the Freeman family, and Freeman's many letters to Professor Collier Cobb of the University of North Carolina. Members of the reference staff of the Manuscript Reading Room at the Library of Congress, who must have groaned as I appeared again and again over several years asking for the boxes containing the relatively obscure

Hale-Freeman letters, four at a time, were always courteous and helpful. If I have failed to name anyone who has helped me in whatever way, please accept my apologies and know that I am full of gratitude. And, finally, the masterly index was compiled by Amron Gravett.

Throughout these last seven years, my husband Stephen has been unfailingly encouraging and patient. Not only is he an excellent editor and sensitive sounding board but he has accompanied me on parts of my quest, staying with me at favorite Hale and Freeman meeting places, such as Mohonk Mountain House, just south of the Catskill Mountains of New York State, and Stonehurst, the former Merriman mansion in Intervale, New Hampshire, now a hotel, from which we explored the White Mountains. Twice I chose to spend weeks in the New York State Library in Albany rather than accompanying him to conferences in Hawaii. Only a researcher as obsessed as I have been to wade through the annual diaries and voluminous papers of Edward E. Hale Sr., including the related papers of his namesake son and biographer in that archive, could have turned down sipping mai tais in a suite overlooking a blue lagoon for Albany in November.

Sara Day
Washington, D.C.
Fall 2013

Introduction: Love Letters and Coded Clues—the Untold Story

When I described my seven-year odyssey to uncover the story behind 3,000 archived letters between Harriet E. Freeman and her longtime minister Edward Everett Hale, a married man, it is remarkable how often I was asked if I knew A. S. Byatt's Booker Prize-winning novel *Possession*. In fact, as a dogged researcher, Byatt's novel speaks to me and I must have read it several times. The witty contemporary narrative describes the quest of Roland Michell, an obscure postdoctoral research assistant, who finds in a book at the London Library, and guiltily purloins, drafts of a letter in handwriting he recognizes as that of the famous Victorian poet Randolph Henry Ash. He discovers that the letter was intended for a woman other than Ash's wife, a minor Romantic poet called Christabel LaMotte. With the help of a LaMotte scholar, Dr. Maud Bailey, Michell finds a hidden cache of the poets' letters. The author brilliantly invented letters, poems, and diaries "penned by" her fictional nineteenth-century lovers, stand-ins for Robert Browning and Christina Rossetti. So this illicit Victorian love story is told in their "own" words.

Despite some similarities, the story I have uncovered is real and is told in Hale's and Freeman's own words from their letters and other writings. In addition, they used a code to convey and conceal their most intimate feelings. Finding the Rosetta stone and translating those passages was a major breakthrough in understanding this relationship. As a celebrated author and reformer, the Reverend Hale's life and accomplishments are copiously recorded, but who was this woman Harriet E. Freeman? The letters provided numerous important clues and finding her passport, obituary, gravestone, and a family history was just the beginning. My published article about the relationship led me to a rich collection of articles by and about Hale, photographs of him, and copies of his books. Freeman had made this collection to commemorate the older man she adored. However, that collection gives little clue to her own adventurous life and considerable accomplishments, apart from Hale's grateful inscriptions in the many books they worked on together. Following Freeman's independent tracks took several more years but many would say that discovering Harriet Freeman is the real revelation.

Edward Everett Hale (1822-1909) was considered by his contemporaries to be a great and noble man, renowned for his kindness and optimistic spirit, a role model for America during a troubled era. It has been written of him that "Probably no man in America aroused and stimulated so many minds as Hale, and his personal popularity was unbounded." He was a leading Unitarian minister and social reformer, a preacher and lecturer, a prolific and popular writer, a mentor of the future president Theodore Roosevelt at Harvard, and chaplain to the United States Senate during Roosevelt's presidency. His eightieth birthday was celebrated with an unprecedented tribute by almost three thousand friends and admirers of "the Grand Old Man of Boston" in that city's new Symphony Hall on April 4, 1902. Today, if you visit Boston's popular Public Garden, you can find the impressive statue of Hale standing just inside one of the garden's principal gates, a reminder of his national reputation and celebrity during his lifetime.

During his last twenty-five years, however, Hale lived a double life. Ironically, the theme of double lives, or alter egos, was one of his favorite literary devices. Frederick Ingham was the harassed minister of Hale's first popular story "My Double and How He Undid Me" and reappeared in his most famous story "The Man without a Country" and several others. At one point, Hale even used the name Frederick Ingham as an apt concealer of his own double life.

From the first celebratory biography of Hale by his namesake son through two later biographies, the Hale marriage was described as successful, even cloudless. Hale was married to the former Emily Baldwin Perkins of Harvard, whose mother Mary Foote Perkins was born into the brilliant Beecher family. On the other hand, Hale's biographers mentioned his later life romantic partner, the much younger Harriet Freeman (1847–1930), only as his longtime literary amanuensis, assistant in his charitable works, and old friend—and, finally, not at all. And so Hale's impeccable reputation endured, with no hint of the human weaknesses that so often seem to accompany the qualities of charm, charisma, energy, and celebrity. But in 1969, eight years before publication of the last Hale biography, the Library of Congress acquired from a Freeman family descendant 3,000 of the Hale-Freeman love letters (1884–1909), partly written in code. Because interest in Hale had largely diminished, these letters remained unexamined for thirty-five years. Their significance became apparent only when the author began studying the letters in support of the restoration of the Edward Everett Hale summer house in Matunuck, Rhode Island, and succeeded in breaking the code the couple used to express their most intimate feelings.

Had this relationship been revealed at its height in the 1890s, the Reverend Hale might have experienced public disgrace similar to that faced by his wife's uncle, the Reverend Henry Ward Beecher, except that Hale did not have to contend with an enraged cuckolded husband who, in that notorious case, brought a civil suit against the famous minister and released the lovers' letters to the press. Charismatic leaders and celebrities seem to have a way of flying too close to temptation. In addition to Beecher, Charles Dickens was another nineteenth-century adulterous celebrity. According to his biographer Claire Tomalin, Dickens's affair with the young actress Ellen Ternan humiliated his wife, the mother of his ten children, and kept him in a state of high anxiety that the secret should not leak out to his adoring public. Emily Dickinson's brother Austin, an upstanding Amherst lawyer, carried on a torrid affair with the much younger Mabel Loomis Todd. Both were married but conducted their sexual assignations flagrantly in the Dickinson family dining room or upstairs in the Todd house. Today, one adulterous scandal seems to follow another, to the point of cliché. Some of these affairs have been extraordinarily blatant, while others have involved degrees of discretion but left trails of incriminating evidence, such as e-mails.

What kept the Hale affair out of the public eye was the couple's determination from the outset that they would avoid hurting or embarrassing their families or damaging Hale's position and reputation. As he had learned much from his uncle's scandal, Hale led Freeman, who had adored him since her teenage years, into a web of deception, including teaching her a forgotten shorthand and providing her with printed envelopes to conceal her letters from his family and colleagues. When suspicion and gossip occasionally arose, Hale and Freeman would cool speculation with lengthy separations made bearable by the long and frequent letters they wrote each other. After conducting this illicit affair for twenty years, Hale would not have been appointed chaplain to the United States Senate without the cover he received from his complicit family and his discreet and protective lover.

But can or should the Hale-Freeman relationship be compared to the sexually charged and generally short-term affairs that have brought down so many men, and not just in recent memory? Harriet Freeman was a remarkable woman in her own right, a woman of independent means and complex personality, with her own interests in botany, geology, the rights of American Indians, philanthropy, and travel. Her passion for nature and outdoor life led to her pioneering efforts in forest and wildlife conservation. She shared most of these interests with Hale, and it was he who encouraged her to study botany and geology. They became intellectual and temperamental soul mates at a time when his wife, who was not her husband's intellectual equal and shared few of his interests, had taken refuge in poor health and hypochondria, becoming too fragile and self-absorbed to keep up with her vigorous husband. Already working closely together, Hale and Freeman's emotional connection grew following the deaths of close family members.

Beyond the illicit affair, the Hale-Freeman letters provide an argument for a reexamination and reassessment of Hale's life and career, reminding this generation of readers of his deep moral leadership in issues such as immigration, religious tolerance, education, and world peace, issues that resonate even more urgently today. The letters provide insights into the couple's thoughts on religion, science, politics, and contemporary life, as well as a detailed chronology of Hale's activities, both private and public, after 1884, a period less examined by his biographers. They make it clear that his relationship with Harriet (Hattie) Freeman gave him the courage that seemed to have temporarily failed him in the face of grief and personal setbacks, reinvigorating his reformist energies and renewing his literary inspiration.

Meanwhile, Freeman's participation in efforts to establish or support scientific institutions that would open their classes or programs to women, her own scientific studies and participation in geological field trips, her financial support of impecunious geology students and teachers, and her activist role in bird and forest conservation made her a pioneer in overcoming prejudice against women in the sciences. Just as interesting were the backlashes against many of these progressive initiatives and Freeman's less admirable veer to the right in the face of uncontrolled immigration in the early twentieth century.

Hale's letters to Harriet Freeman began in earnest from his summer house in Matunuck, Rhode Island, during the months following their declaration of love for each other. Several years ago, that house was undergoing restoration, to be reopened as the Edward Everett Hale House, when I remembered a reference to Hale love letters in a resource guide I had edited for the Library of Congress. I agreed to take a look at the letters to see if any were written from Matunuck, and, if so, might they be informative about the house's history and original layout and furnishings, as well as the Hale family's summer life there. They proved valuable on all these counts, in fact the early letters fairly dance with Hale's love of the region's unspoiled beauty and his love for his children. But looking ahead to letters written in subsequent years, I noticed that parts were written in code. By now, I was intrigued but realized I could only understand the full nature of Hale and Freeman's relationship if I could break that code, which I recognized as an arcane shorthand.

Although Hale's letters dated from 1884, Freeman's letters do not appear in the correspondence until 1889. More cautious than Hale, she had instructed him to burn her letters, which he did, reluctantly, for the first five years of their correspondence. The special coded passages from them both grew longer as their relationship developed, reflecting periods of intense emotion and increased efforts to conceal the real content of the letters. With the help of Hale's instructions to Freeman and my "needle in the haystack" discovery at the Library of Congress of the 1832 shorthand manual referenced in one of his letters, I was able to translate the code—"Towndrow's terrible shorthand," as Hale called it. Their translated shorthand is given in this book in italics within angled brackets. By transcribing both the longhand and shorthand portions of the letters, arranging Harriet Freeman's many undated letters chronologically with the rest, and filling in the biographical details of this previously unknown woman, I was able to place their story in the context of their experiences and period and complete the essential parts of the puzzle of their relationship.

Freeman's emotional dependence on and devotion to Hale both brightened and darkened her life. In the late 1890s she succumbed to severe depression when, in the face of financial reversals, she felt forced to give up her comfortable Boston house, the "home away from home" she had made for him. Her letters to Hale during the year of her breakdown are heart-wrenching and emotionally revealing. Although she recovered both her equilibrium and her income to pursue an even more active and productive life, Hale's decision to accept nomination to become chaplain of the United States Senate at the age of eighty-one meant they saw far less of each other. Understandably, Freeman felt excluded from his life in Washington, where he wintered with his wife and artist daughter Nelly. The long letters written during Hale's last years (he died in 1909) are even richer in content and of broader historical significance as they discussed their joint efforts on behalf of forest preservation in New Hampshire's White Mountains, her other conservation efforts, their increasingly different reactions to the problems of unrestricted immigration, and his efforts on behalf of his long-term interests in international peace and arbitration and the education of African Americans. Hale was a people person, a man who knew just about everyone of interest during his long life and he liked to write Freeman vignettes and commentaries of his frequent encounters.

Following Hale's death, his secretary returned Freeman's letters to her at her request. She lived for another twenty-one years, busying herself with world travel, philanthropy, her study of botany and geology, and conservation, and continuing her talent for correspondence with others who shared her interests, especially with naturalists and scientists. And, judging by the notations on the envelopes and comments in letters to her nieces, she kept her true love alive by reading and rereading Hale's letters.

The Hale-Freeman letters, the principal evidence of their relationship, remained in the possession of members of the Freeman family until forty years ago. They sat in a white trunk that had passed quietly to Hattie's loyal, unmarried nieces after her death. In the early 1960s, following the death of Hattie's niece Ethel Hale Freeman (who was Edward Hale's goddaughter), Ethel's nephew and his wife found Hattie's and Edward's letters in that trunk in Ethel's West Newton house. Through a dealer, they first, unsuccessfully, offered the letters to the Houghton Library at Harvard and then to the Library of Congress, where they were accepted, arranged, and added as a special collection to its existing Hale Family Papers.

Apparently, Edward's granddaughter, writer Nancy Hale, was also unaware of the existence of the large collection of letters when she wrote to Hattie's great-niece in 1974, after meeting her at the memorial service for her mother Helen Hunt Arnold. Nancy explained that she had advised Helen to donate to Smith College some letters she had kept written by her grandfather Edward Hale to Harriet Freeman. She explained the "enormously compatible" friendship between their ancestors but had not thought that the shorthand in the letters might indicate more than that, even though some thought otherwise. In any case, she was certain that no one would be able to translate the "private, made up" shorthand, even if they wanted to. Hence, the full story of Harriet Freeman's and Edward Hale's love for one another remained concealed within the letters at the Library of Congress and Smith College Archives for three decades after being cataloged and made available for study.

Did Hattie and Edward ever wish their relationship known? On more than one occasion, Edward joked that they would need to catalog and index the letters in case anyone wanted to read them in future. And there is one suggestive sentence in Hattie Freeman's impressive obituary in the *Boston Evening Transcript* of December 30, 1930: "She was a prominent member of the South Congregational Church, popularly known as 'Dr. Hale's Church,' and she was closely associated with that widely known divine." At the time, however, few of the deceased's contemporaries were alive or able to notice or comprehend the clue to the secret affair buried within the details of her life of "enormous activity."

What is disturbing to contemporary eyes about the Hale-Freeman relationship is that Hale never publicly credited Freeman, his muse of twenty years and more, for all the assistance she gave him with his writing. In contrast, he gave his sisters Lucretia and Susan and his son and namesake, Edward E. Hale Jr., equal billing in their collaborations. In many letters and in shorthand inscriptions in books that he gave Hattie (which he often dedicated to "my co-author" or "from one of the authors to the other"), he did, however, acknowledge that he drew heavily on descriptive passages from her travel letters and collaborated with her on a variety of books, stories, articles, and sermons. The inscribed books now reside in the collections of the Andover-Harvard Theological Library at the Harvard Divinity School along with Freeman's collected articles by and about Hale and photographs of him.

It is difficult to ascertain how many of Freeman's stories or articles Hale published in his various magazines during the 1890s, since most appeared anonymously or under her initials. Beginning with the turn of the twentieth century, when fellow naturalist Emma Cummings accompanied her on botanical and geological field trips and foreign travels, Freeman published at least two accounts of their discoveries and adventures under her own name. More than likely, it was the illicit nature of Freeman's relationship with her famous soul mate and his family's discomfort with that fact that precluded his sharing credit with her.

An undeservedly forgotten figure, Harriet Freeman was a woman of intelligence, adventurous spirit, complex character, and strong views. Freed by her independent income, she might have achieved even more than she did had she not subsumed so much of her time and talent and expended so much emotional energy in supporting her "great man" as if he were her husband. But, despite suffering the inevitable indignities, loneliness, and miseries of being "the other woman," particularly in Hale's final years, Freeman's achievements and activities were extraordinary for a woman brought up in a time of circumscribed opportunities for women.

Hale and Freeman's hidden love story is a sharp reminder that little has changed in the realm of extramarital duplicity and its accompanying hypocrisy—except possibly in the degree of discretion they practiced and the web of family complicity that kept the affair from public knowledge. But their letters make an invaluable and fascinating contribution to our understanding of the social mores as well as the religious, intellectual, political, and scientific issues of the time. It is in this spirit that this book is written.

1

A Parish Call

Harriet (Hattie) Freeman was sixteen years old when, in October 1863, she was formally introduced by her mother to the family's minister, forty-one year old Edward Everett Hale. Hale was the Unitarian minister of the South Congregational Church in Boston's South End and was making his first call on the Freeman family, new parishioners who had recently moved to the neighborhood near the church. Greeted by Caroline Crosby Freeman, who was reclining on a sofa in the front parlor (indicative of her invalid state), Edward later recalled the warm and affectionate welcome she gave him. Caroline was only three years older than her minister. Her husband William Freeman was not at home that day but, following the visit, Hale noted in his journal, or daybook, the presence of one daughter and one son (Hattie's brother Fred was just nine at the time). Not surprisingly, the tall, striking, and charming man, whom she had first seen from afar two years before, made an immediate impression on an intelligent, shy, and romantic teenager. She would recall that her adolescent adulation for her charismatic minister led her so far as to bend down to kiss the steps on which he climbed to the church cupola. Twenty-one years later, Edward Hale wrote Hattie Freeman, "How little I knew that the one daughter was to be mine own."[1]

This beginning to their long relationship came against the dramatic background of the Civil War, when the Union's fortunes were at low ebb, despite the victory at Gettysburg that summer. Inspired by recent events, Hale had written a patriotic short story

Edward Everett Hale was twenty-five when Harriet Freeman was born. This photograph was taken about ten years later, around the time that the serious young minister accepted the call to minister to the South Congregational Church in Boston's South End.
Harriet E. Freeman Papers, bMS 273, Andover-Harvard Theological Library, Harvard Divinity School.

Fifteen-year-old Harriet Freeman and her five-year-old cousin Helen Atkins posed for this portrait in 1862, one year before the Reverend Hale called on the Freeman family in Union Park. The search for photographs of Hattie in which her face was not concealed was long and frustrating until one of Hattie's great-great nieces found this charming portrait of the young cousins in her parents' family archives.
Courtesy of Phoebe Bushway.

that appeared in the *Atlantic Monthly* the month after he called on the Freemans. "The Man without a Country" made him famous, but writing and editing were always his avocations, taking up a good deal of his time and energy.[2] He had become infuriated by fence-sitters or "Copperheads," Northern Democrats such as former United States Representative Clement Vallandigham who had expressed such violent dislike of President Lincoln and his Republican administration that he was banished behind Confederate lines. Vallandigham chose not to remain there and, returning north, was a candidate in 1863 for governor of Ohio. Edward hoped that his story would be published in time to affect the election.

Even though publication was delayed by a month (Vallandigham lost the election anyway), "The Man without a Country" brought Edward Hale to national attention. It concerns Philip Nolan, who, while on trial with Aaron Burr for conspiracy, shouts, "Damn the United States! I wish I may never hear of the United States again!" Taking him at his word, the court-martial condemns him "from that moment Sept. 23, 1807" never to hear his country's name again. Moved as a prisoner on board one U.S. naval vessel after another, Nolan "for that half-century and more" is "a man without a country." On his death bed, now a fervent patriot, he finally learns about his country's history since his punishment began.

The story's verisimilitude and the public temper during 1863, the year of its anonymous appearance in the *Atlantic*, made it popular. Totally unaware at the time of the effect that his hastily written short story would have on the Union's psyche and his own reputation, Hale had refocused his attention on his ministerial responsibilities, while exhorting his parishioners to support the Union cause in every possible way.

The church building where the Freemans worshipped was new. Not long after he took over as minister in 1856, Hale had concluded that the original South Congregational Church, completed on Castle Street in 1828, was inadequate for an increased mission of "neighborhood relief," and he worked with the church trustees to build a new church on Union Park Street. Designed by Nathaniel J. Bradlee in a combined Renaissance and Romanesque style with a unique belfry or cupola, it was dedicated in January 1862.

Nathaniel Bradlee's hand-colored proposed designs and final plans for the new South Congregational Church are in the collections of the Boston Athenaeum. The handsome red brick building, although shorn of its cupola and rose window and embellished with the ornaments of the Greek Orthodox Church whose home it has been for ninety years, still stands today.
Courtesy of the Trustees of the Boston Public Library/Prints.

Hattie's staunchly Unitarian parents were previously members of the Hollis Street Church, parent church of the South Congregational Church, when another charismatic minister, Thomas Starr King (1824-1864), rescued it from near collapse following a schism over temperance and antislavery issues. Like Edward Hale after him, the Reverend King became a close friend of the Freemans. When King was called to the Unitarian church in San Francisco in 1860 (he was credited with persuading California to remain loyal to President Lincoln and the Union), the Freemans began attending the South Congregational Church, still on Castle Street at that time; but their new house on Union Park was just a block and a half away from the church's new building on Union Park Street.

The new South End, where these churches were located, was built in the 1850s, after the filling of the South Cove marsh, to meet the demands of a rapidly growing population and in the hopes of offsetting the exodus of native Bostonians to the surrounding suburbs. The old South End was only a narrow isthmus of land, called "the Neck," connecting the town of Boston on the Shawmut Peninsula to the mainland. Hattie's grandfather William Freeman used to walk the road from his parents' house in Roxbury on the mainland to his work in the city along the barren Neck, which at its narrowest point was often under water during high tides. Once the landfill was complete, handsome brick and brownstone townhouses were erected to attract the mercantile class, many of them surrounding London-style squares.

Union Park was the residence of two Boston mayors and the grocery magnate S. S. Pierce, father of Hattie's childhood and lifelong friend Henrietta (Etta) Pierce. The Freemans and Pierces had bought their houses in the same year, 1861. Unusually for the time, No. 37 was purchased in Caroline Freeman's name with a mortgage secured by furniture, silver, and other valuables from her dowry, through her brother-in-law Elisha Atkins. Atkins was the Freemans' trustee and William Freeman's former business partner.[3] Like others in the square, the Freemans' elegant brick bow front and high stooped four-story townhouse was graced with walnut woodwork and elaborate fireplaces. In the middle of the small residential square

Judging by the size of the trees in the park and the style of the carriage, this rare photographic print of Union Park was made in the 1860s. *Courtesy of the South End Historical Society.*

was a garden with a lawn, fine elm trees, and two cast iron fountains, enclosed by an ornamental fence with attached gas lamps.

Unfortunately, the new South End was only briefly fashionable. Built as it had been on mortgages that largely failed during the Panic of 1873, it soon became a district of rooming and boarding houses and subdivided town houses, which eventually persuaded many wealthier residents, and the churches they attended, to move to the new, exclusive Back Bay area. Novelist William Dean Howells wrote of his protagonist in *The Rise of Silas Lapham*: "He had not built, but bought very cheap of a terrified gentleman of good extraction who discovered too late that the South End was not the thing, and who in the eagerness of his flight to the Back Bay threw in his carpets and shades for almost nothing."[4] But Hattie continued to live in that house for most of the next sixty years. Following her parents' deaths, she would make it a second home, even a "love nest," for her adored minister.

Edward Everett Hale's lifelong love of writing and editing and his connections to the literary, business, political, religious, and educational elite of Massachusetts and the nation had their origins in his childhood. His father owned Boston's leading daily newspaper, the *Boston Daily Advertiser*, and was a pioneer in introducing railroads to Massachusetts. His mother was the sister of Alexander and Edward Everett, both of whom rose to national prominence. The Everetts and the Hales were all staunch Unitarians closely associated with Harvard College. Writing was in the family's blood, and young Edward, who was intended for the ministry from childhood, was able to combine the pulpit and the pen. After ten years as minister to a new church in Worcester, he had been called to Boston's South Congregational Church.

In 1852 he had married Emily Baldwin Perkins of New England's famed Beecher and Perkins families. This was the year after her aunt Harriet Beecher Stowe, until then an obscure clergyman's wife, published the enormously popular and highly influential antislavery novel *Uncle Tom's Cabin*. Emily had been briefly engaged to future landscape genius Frederick Law Olmsted, and Edward renewed his acquaintance with her when she was deliberately staying away from her hometown of Hartford, Connecticut, with a cousin to avoid the short-lived social scandal resulting from breaking off her engagement. A young woman with many suitors, Emily seems to have had no doubt about her decision to marry this tall, intense young minister but their marriage was a surprising choice because of the doctrinal differences between his family and hers.

Hale was from a liberal wing of Congregationalism, the seedbed of tolerant Unitarianism. Meanwhile, Emily's grandfather was the firebrand Calvinist preacher, revivalist, and theologian Lyman Beecher, who, as early as 1817, had thrown down a gauntlet to the Harvard theologians who were denying the divinity of Christ. Beecher saw himself as attempting to break the Unitarian hold on Boston and reclaim it for the orthodox Puritan heritage when he served a congregational church in the North End from 1826-1832.

His son Edward Beecher was pursuing the same mission at Boston's Park Street Church. Of Lyman Beecher's seven minister sons, even the famously liberal-leaning preacher Henry Ward Beecher opposed Unitarianism. There was, therefore, a Montague and Capulet aspect to the Hale-Beecher Perkins union.

Emily Perkins was born on November 23, 1829. Her father was Thomas Clap Perkins, a prosperous Hartford lawyer, and she grew up in small-town comfort and privilege with two brothers, Frederick and Charles Perkins, and a sister Catherine (Katy Gilman, the future mother-in-law as well as aunt of her oldest brother's famous daughter, feminist Charlotte Perkins Gilman). A petite and very pretty young woman with velvet eyes, Emily was in the mold of her mother, Mary Foote Perkins, the only one of Lyman Beecher's daughters who, although intelligent and well-educated, kept strictly out of public life and submerged her own ambitions in the duties of a successful lawyer's wife and motherhood. Contrast this to the public and controversial careers of Mary Perkins's sisters, advice-book author, theologian, and educator Catharine Beecher (whom Mary had helped run her Hartford Female Seminary before she married); Harriet Beecher Stowe; and their half-sister, the suffragist Isabella Beecher Hooker.

Five and a half years before the Hales married, Hattie Freeman was born, on March 13, 1847, in a boarding house on High Street in Boston's North End run by a Mrs. Osborn, a friend of her mother Caroline Crosby Freeman. High Street was close to India Wharf where the shipping and trading company of William F. Freeman and Elisha Atkins was located (the fortunes of the Freeman and Atkins families would be intertwined throughout Hattie's life). But now Hattie's delighted father wrote to inform his wife's great-aunt at Pepperell near the New Hampshire border of his daughter's birth (Caroline Freeman's ancestral home was in Pepperell). The baby was baptized by the Reverend Dr. Francis Parkman, father of the eminent historian, at his church, St. Stephen's on Hanover Street, formerly the New North Church before it switched to Unitarianism.[5] Known today as Old St. Stephen's Church, its history reflects the dramatically changing demographic of its neighborhood. In 1862, it became a Roman Catholic church and two-time Boston mayor John F. "Honey Fitz" Fitzgerald and eventually his daughter Rose Fitzgerald Kennedy were baptized there. Rose Kennedy's funeral service was also conducted at this historic church.

The year of Hattie's birth was coincidentally the height of the Irish potato famine, which drove waves of impoverished and often infirm Irish Catholics to Boston's North End, making it one of the most crowded and deprived of the city's neighborhoods. That year alone, Boston was overwhelmed by 137,000 new arrivals from Ireland. These mostly unskilled immigrants crammed into filthy shacks and cellars along the Boston waterfront. This and the cholera epidemic of 1849 must have convinced the Freemans to move further south to Edinboro Street, in addition to its proximity to the original railroad station. William Freeman had taken over the Bemis dye works on the Charles River in Newton, an easy train ride from his new home. There he established the Boston Dyewood & Chemicals Company, although his headquarters office remained on India Wharf. In 1860, Freeman bought the Bemis textile mill and was a principal in founding the Aetna Mills "for the purpose of prosecuting the manufacture of woolen fabrics by both water and steam power" from the Bemis Dam.[6] Labor for the Mill was drawn from the ever increasing Irish immigrant population.

By the time Edward Hale called on the Freemans, he had been married for eleven years and had fathered a daughter and five sons (the first son died in infancy). The Hale family lived on busy Worcester Street in a house that was rapidly becoming too small for the still growing family. Following the family's move in 1869 to a spacious house, formerly a school, set in a large garden in Roxbury more than a mile away from the South Congregational Church, the Freemans often welcomed their minister to take lunch and rest at their house. Edward thus became a familiar figure at 37 Union Park, able to observe Hattie growing into maturity and to play a role in shaping her values and education. Over the next few years, Edward became widely known as a Unitarian leader, social reformer, and popular author—one of the moral voices of the corrupt and materialistic Gilded Age.

When she was twenty-four years old, in 1871, Hattie began working as a volunteer in Edward's church. That summer, she joined an expedition led by him to Waterville Valley in New Hampshire's

White Mountains. They would recall that their mutual attraction began as they shared a seat on a stagecoach to the mountains they both loved, the scene of many of their future rendezvous.

2

The Freemans and the Hales

By the early 1870s, Edward Hale was establishing a reputation well beyond Boston for liberal and reform leadership and literary accomplishment. Moreover, he was a member of a family and an ever widening circle of friends that included several nationally known figures. Thus his biography to that point easily overwhelms that of the obscure Harriet Freeman. But the "larger life" that she and Edward came to share was made possible by the generous income derived from the great success in business of both Hattie's father William Freeman and her uncle Elisha Atkins—and of Elisha's son Edwin. The Freemans' and the Atkins's stories are inextricably linked.

Hattie was born into old Colonial American stock. On her father's side, she was descended from Edmond Freeman who arrived at Plymouth from England in June 1635. He and nine others were granted land by Governor William Bradford and established the town of Sandwich on Cape Cod in 1639. Edmond Freeman was a leader of the settlement and an assistant to the governor but was "too liberal for the age," believing in religious toleration for Quakers and other persecuted sects. Edmond's son John, who married Mercy Prince, daughter of the governor of Massachusetts and granddaughter of Elder William Brewster (one of the founders of the Plymouth Colony who arrived in America on the Mayflower in 1620), became a large landowner in Harwich, later renamed

The Freeman Family
(Mary Ellen Freeman standing)

The prosperous merchant William Freeman and his wife Betsy posed with their adult children in about 1860. Hattie's father William F. Freeman is seated between his two sisters. Standing to his right is Mary Freeman Atkins, who was married to William Frederick's former trading partner Elisha Atkins. Seated on William Freeman's right is his brother Frederick, standing between the Freeman parents is their son Bradford, and seated at extreme right is their daughter Sara Maria. Another son, George, was a successful merchant in New York.
From Helen A. Claflin, A New England Family, 1956. Courtesy of Katharine Wrisley Claflin Weeks.

Brewster, and was prominent in public affairs. He was made Captain of the Colonial council of war during King Philip's war in 1675. In his will, he declared "freedom for my negroes" with "four acres of land, a horse, and a cow."[1]

Hattie's grandfather, William Freeman (1789-1870), was of the eighth generation of Freemans on Cape Cod. He was born in Brewster but moved with his mother and siblings to Roxbury on the outskirts of Boston when he was five, was apprenticed as a boy to a dry goods merchant, and soon built up his own trading and shipping firm. His son, Hattie's father, William Frederick Freeman (1817-1888, just five years older than Edward Everett Hale), spent several years as a young man living in Cuba, where he worked for Tate & Company, consigning cargoes of sugar and molasses to his father in Boston. His years in Cuba and at sea colored his outlook and memories for the rest of his life.

The bank failures of 1837 forced the senior William Freeman out of business, but he weathered the crash, investing instead in 1838 in the new trading partnership of his son William Frederick and family friend Elisha Atkins. William Freeman lent the two young men $2,500 each and turned over to them the ship "Charlotte" and the brigs "Adelaide" and "Neptune." They leased space on Boston's India Wharf and shipped household goods and provisions to Trinidad, Cuba, in exchange for sugar and molasses. In the meantime, the older William Freeman became a director of Boston's Commonwealth Bank and president of the Boston Wharf Company. In 1844, Atkins married his partner's sister Mary Freeman and William F. Freeman married Caroline Crosby Lewis (1819-1880) of Pepperell, Massachusetts, near the New Hampshire border.

Caroline was the oldest daughter of James Lewis (1785-1845), who graduated from Dartmouth in 1807 and read law in Groton, Massachusetts, where the Lewis family had moved when he was still a child. In January 1819, Lewis married Harriet Parker (1798-1875) of an old, established family in nearby Pepperell, where he practiced law. That year, Lewis built a stately Federal-style mansion opposite Pepperell's town hall and became a leading public citizen, at times representing his town as a Massachusetts representative and senator, earning him the local honorific "Squire Lewis." The Lewis's daughter Caroline was born in December 1819, was introduced to society, and then married William Frederick Freeman at the age of twenty-five. Caroline's younger sisters, Harriet and Mary, married, respectively, Boston lawyer and abolitionist Charles Mayo Ellis, who was a Harvard classmate of Edward E. Hale, and Francis A. Howe, son of a Pepperell minister, a physician educated at Amherst and Harvard and Columbia Medical Schools.[2] The sisters' brother Samuel Parker Lewis was another Harvard graduate and lawyer. The Pepperell ancestral home and its associations would figure strongly in Hattie Freeman's life. It became the Freemans' summer home when Caroline Freeman inherited it following her mother's death in 1875 (her father had died in 1845).

The firm of Atkins & Freeman grew steadily during the 1840s as the partners sent vessels to various ports in the Windward Islands, St. Thomas, and Jamaica, to Guatemala for cargoes of coffee, cochineal (the source of a crimson dye), and grenadilla wood (for making woodwind instruments and fine furniture), and to Rio de Janeiro for coffee to deliver to New Orleans. William Freeman the younger gradually became more interested in Central and South American dyewoods and sold his partnership share to Elisha Atkins in 1849, two years after his daughter Hattie's birth, in order to focus on manufacturing logwood extracts and dyes. Elisha then changed the name of his shipping and trading business to E. Atkins & Co.

Hattie's earliest childhood memories were of the Edinboro Street house. She probably attended a local public school before she was sent away to boarding school in Pepperell. For many years, she imagined that being sent away was a punishment for inviting her entire class from her school in Boston to her house on her birthday without first asking her parents. Perhaps her mother's fragile health made it difficult for her to cope with her head-strong daughter.[3] However, the Freemans may have been impelled to this decision as much by the 1859 Eliot School Rebellion resulting from tensions between Irish Catholic immigrants and the existing Anglo Protestant community in the North End over religious education in the schools, tensions which would continue to challenge the Yankee status quo.[4] In any case, Hattie was extremely unhappy at the school in Pepperell, an experience that caused her to stutter but also seems to have strengthened her resolve and independent spirit.

Perhaps to avoid the tensions in the city's public schools, the Freemans sent their son Frederic William (Fred), born in 1854, seven years after his sister (another daughter had died young), to school at the prestigious private Chauncy Hall. William Freeman, a strict but loving disciplinarian, apparently boosted his children's education by providing them with the best of nineteenth-century literature. He certainly fueled Hattie's lifelong passion for travel and adventure. He told her colorful stories of his years at sea, which she never tired of hearing, and, in 1862, when she was fifteen, she accompanied her father on a trip to Germany, Holland, and Belgium. Hattie was encouraged to learn the piano, to sing, and to paint in watercolors by her talented mother. It was considered an appropriate education for a marriageable daughter of her social class at that time but it gave little basis to or indication of the intellectual woman that she would become. Hattie, who always related primarily to her father's influence, seems to have been a restless, energetic devotee of outdoor life and an earnest autodidact from childhood while giving no credit to her mother for creative talents which more likely derived from her.

In the absence of documentation about her, Caroline Freeman could be stereotyped as just another domestically oriented, intellectually blinkered "good wife" of her generation. But the survival of two remarkable albums of her beautifully rendered watercolors and several scrapbooks of newspaper clippings and ephemera which she collected daily during the Civil War indicate a more complex person. The first album, donated by her descendants to the Boston Athenaeum, is a collection of her botanical watercolors; the second, which remains in private hands, is a folio of small landscapes (including mountains and lakes), animals, birds, and insects that she made for her daughter ("HEF from CCF"), calling it "Happy Hours." In 1870, William Freeman purchased a share in the Boston Athenaeum. The following year, he borrowed a number of books from the Athenaeum of which many of the titles related to his wife's and his daughter's shared interests in natural history and painting. These included books on plant life, the use of the microscope, North American insects, and one that was presciently titled *Art in the Mountains*.[5]

As Boston became a leading sugar market, Elisha Atkins, with the largest number of vessels in the sugar trade, became a very wealthy man. In 1869, he sent his son Edwin (1850-1926) to Cienfuegos, Cuba, to learn Spanish and the sugar business from the Atkins Company's agent rather than sending him to college. Edwin (Hattie's cousin Ned) spent the next fifteen winters there, working in the office of the Torriente brothers, Spanish owners of several sugar mills. The same year, Elisha Atkins became a director of the Union Pacific Railroad and head of its finance committee during the years it was being built and established. Elisha marked his success in business with the symbols of social stature, a hilltop estate in Belmont with magnificent views of Cambridge and the city to the south, and an imposing townhouse, designed by Nathaniel Bradlee, on the prestigious north or sunny side of Commonwealth Avenue, the grandest address in Back Bay.[6]

Like the South End, the Back Bay residential area was built on a marsh, in this case at the estuary of the Charles River to the west of, or behind, the Boston peninsula. Over a period of thirty years, this massive landfill project added some 450 acres to the original 783 acres of Boston's urban territory. Edward Hale's younger brother Charles, as state commissioner of public lands, was responsible for laying out the Back Bay. Various reasons were given for undertaking such an ambitious and expensive land reclamation project which involved excavating and transporting gravel in huge quantities from quarries by rail. The marsh had become dangerously polluted as a result of sewer outflow from the city and inadequate tidal flow for clearing it and there was no room to accommodate the dramatic population explosion resulting from mass immigration. Unspoken at the time, were the ongoing fears of the ruling elite of English Protestant descent that poor, uneducated Irish Catholics would soon hold the voting majority in a city where the wealthy no longer wished to live. Thus, the Back Bay development, with its defined boundaries, was deliberately designed to attract and retain wealthy buyers. Two of the Back Bay's original anchoring cultural institutions were the Rogers Building of the Boston Technical Institute (known as Boston Tech and later the Massachusetts Institute of Technology) and the Museum of the Boston Society of Natural History, both of which would figure prominently in Hattie's life.[7]

And so the Freemans and Atkinses, of seventh-generation Cape Cod stock, which had included several merchants and ships' captains, became nouveau riche industrialists with no family tradition of college education up to that time, while the Hales, college-educated professionals, were rarely free of financial anxiety, and even disaster.

Edward Everett Hale's great-uncle Nathan Hale was the Revolutionary War hero who famously declared before being hanged for spying by British troops: "I only regret that I have but one life to lose for my country." Edward's father, named for his martyred uncle, was the son of the Reverend Enoch Hale of Westhampton in western Massachusetts. The Hales were descended from Robert Hale who emigrated from England in 1626, settling in Charlestown. Educated at Williams College, Nathan Hale Jr. (1784-1863) first tried the law and teaching before settling on journalism. After moving to Boston, he became owner-editor for fifty years of the city's first daily and leading Whig newspaper, the *Boston Daily Advertiser*. He was also a passionate pioneer of railroads, directly responsible for the Boston and Worcester line and the purchase of its first steam engine from England. Young Edward's enduring love for railroad travel began when he and his siblings joined their father on early runs on the new line.

Edward's mother, Sarah Preston Hale (1796-1866), a scholar and talented linguist in her own right, was the younger sister of two of Boston's nationally famous sons, Alexander and Edward Everett, both Harvard graduates who had taken charge of her education following their parents' deaths. Alexander Everett (1792-1847), a diplomat, held posts in Russia, the Netherlands, Spain, and China. Edward Everett (1794-1865) was a Unitarian minister before he became a politician, president of Harvard College, governor of Massachusetts, United States minister in England, secretary of state, and a renowned orator. He is probably most remembered today, and even satirized, for his forgotten two-hour speech at Gettysburg, which immediately preceded Abraham Lincoln's immortal three-minute address. Everett's promising nephew and namesake was intended by his family for the ministry from childhood on.

Edward had three surviving older siblings, Sarah, Nathan, and

Lucretia, and three younger, Alexander, Charles, and Susan (four others died in childhood). But, of this large family, only Edward would marry and have children. In addition to her large brood, their intelligent, versatile, and energetic mother often helped her husband by translating European news reports and publications, while also writing occasional pieces for his newspaper. "To write a book for one of the Hales, was as natural as to breathe…[they] were all authors by instinct," alleged Van Wyck Brooks in *The Flowering of New England*.[8] And indeed journalism was in all their blood: Edward's older brother and sister, Nathan and Lucretia, and younger brother and sister, Charles and Susan, as well as Edward himself, all contributed to their father's newspaper and became writers and editors; Nathan and Charles launched short-lived magazines and Charles also became a politician. These siblings and Edward's children would collaborate with him on many literary and journalistic projects over the years.

The Hales knew just about everyone of note in Boston, and their small houses, first on School Street and then at No. 1 Tremont Street, were always the center of lively gatherings.[9] Daniel Webster and his family, for example, were neighbors and close family friends. Edward begged to be allowed to join his older siblings at the local dame school at the extraordinarily early age of two and was then a student at the prestigious Boston Latin School. But he always said that his real education took place at home.

Both parents had a genius for education, providing the boys with the tools for mechanical and scientific experimentation and all the children with a wealth of books. The family took many excursions into the countryside together, collecting botanical specimens for study at home. All the Hale siblings flourished in this stimulating and loving household.[10] An important figure in the Hales' family life was their devoted "Man Friday" Abel Fullum. This Yankee of convictions and ingenuity with a heart of gold, memorialized by Edward as the "last of the feudal vassals," took care of their neighbor's horses until Daniel Webster went to Washington to serve in Congress. The day Edward was born, Fullum allied himself with the Hale households and served them until his death in 1886.

Edward matriculated at Harvard at age thirteen, rooming his first year with his older brother Nathan, whom he worshipped.

Nathan was an upperclassman and member of a secret literary group Alpha Delta Phi (of which Edward became a proud and active lifelong member), some of whom edited Harvard's literary magazine *Harvardiana*. Since the group, which included poet James Russell Lowell—already an acknowledged genius—generally met in Nathan's rooms, it was a heady environment for an intellectually precocious teenager. Edward made lifelong friends at Harvard and remained close to his alma mater for the rest of his life but he always decried its lack of stimulus for young minds due to the rigidity of the educational system at that time. His friend Thomas W. Higginson, who was a freshman at the start of Edward's junior year, described Edward at that time as a "tall, slim young student who had, according to current report among the freshmen, sprung out of bed almost at the last stroke of the bell, thrown his clothes over the stairway, and jumped into them on the way down."[11] Edward was never known for sartorial elegance of dress, in fact exactly the opposite.

During Edward's college years in the 1830s (he graduated second in his class in 1839 behind future historian and educator Samuel Eliot and was named class poet), Unitarianism was already under attack by transcendentalists. He witnessed and, at the time, abhorred as ill-mannered toward his teachers, Ralph Waldo Emerson's notorious Divinity School Address in July 1838, in which Emerson attacked conservative, old school Unitarians for their unquestioning belief in the divinity of Jesus Christ and for their uninspiring teaching, dry of spirituality, devoid of self, and detached from contemporary concerns such as slavery. Emerson exhorted his audience to commune with nature and "dare to love God without mediator or veil."[12] Edward came to admire Emerson and the two men became good friends. Edward's literary biographer, John Adams, concluded that it was unclear when this change of heart came about but it was certainly in place by 1849. As a young minister in Worcester, Edward managed or sponsored a series of lectures Emerson gave there and, by 1855, Emerson began inviting Edward to stay at his house in Concord.

Although he never became a transcendentalist, Edward was influenced by their belief that religion was primarily a matter of personal intuition, emotion, and faith. Late in his life, he praised

Emerson as "the religious teacher who has done most for England and America, and is doing most for England and America today."[13] One of Edward's classmates, Charles Mayo Ellis, who became Hattie's uncle by marriage, wrote pseudonymously a pamphlet which has proved valuable to scholars of transcendentalism with its clear definition of its beliefs. Ellis was later an antislavery lawyer who defended his minister and lifelong friend, radical abolitionist and transcendentalist Theodore Parker, against contempt of court charges in the Anthony Burns fugitive slave case.[14]

Fed up with stultifying formal education and unwilling to burden his parents with the cost of three more years at the Harvard Divinity School, Edward studied for the ministry privately under the guidance of his pastor, working his way through an enormous reading list. At the same time, he spent four years reporting for his father's newspaper as "South American Editor" and sometimes on debates in the State House. He also wrote book reviews for the *North American Review* and tried his hand at teaching at the Latin School for a couple of years. Between his brother Nathan's and his parents' and uncles' wide-ranging intellectual, political, and business friends, he had contacts at the highest level and honed his burgeoning love of history in occasional evening constitutionals with historian George Bancroft, a transcendentalist.

After Edward resigned his teaching post, his college classmate William Francis Channing, son of Unitarian preacher William Ellery Channing, secured a position for him as junior assistant on the Geological Survey of New Hampshire during the summer of 1841. With their friend and classmate Samuel Longfellow, brother of the poet who was then teaching modern languages at Harvard, the young men traveled from place to place, culminating in the impressive feat of climbing the 6,288-foot-high Mt. Washington during a September thunderstorm. Edward was so enchanted by the autumn forests that he said "if there ever came a summer vacation when he did not want to go to New Hampshire he would know that he was physically out of order and should go for the benefits of outdoor life."[15] So began his lifelong love of the White Mountains, which came to be a particular bond between him and Hattie Freeman.

***

Following his successful trial sermon before the Boston Association of Ministers on October 24, 1842, Edward Hale became licensed to preach. Edward Everett wrote to his sister congratulating her son on his achievement, concluding, "I hope Edward will keep out of transcendentalism."[16] Quickly in demand as a supply preacher, young Edward received invitations to become the pastor of substantial congregations in Montreal and several New England towns, but he always answered that he was not ready. Indeed, he was still very young at age twenty-two. Since Unitarianism was wracked by controversy, his indecision is understandable. His apparent wavering between a literary life and the ministry has been of interest to Hale's biographers who have wondered if his failure to devote himself fully to either made him less effective than he might have been in both. However it seems to have been a period when he was forming his own point of view. Forty years later, emerging from a midlife crisis, Edward admitted in his letters to Harriet Freeman to feeling the same struggles between public service and a private life of writing. Yet he would always tell anyone who asked that he was primarily a minister, his writing only incidental to that calling.

Young Edward Hale's lifelong interest and involvement in national politics began in November 1844, when he was called to Washington, D.C., for what he thought would be a temporary engagement that lasted five months. That winter, as a substitute minister at First Unitarian Church (renamed All Souls Unitarian Church in 1877), he attended sessions of Congress almost daily as legislative reporter for his father's newspaper. Sixty-five years later, Edward remembered that he was in the crowd below the window of the Washington Post Office when the result of the presidential election in Maryland arrived via the new experimental telegraph from Baltimore.[17] Democrat James K. Polk of Tennessee won that state and ultimately beat the "Great Compromiser" Henry Clay of Kentucky, whose opposition to Texas's annexation, war with Mexico, and "Manifest Destiny" cost him the close election.

Edward, who had watched all the passionate debates, went to the Capitol on March 2, 1845, the morning after President Tyler signed the annexation resolution, and called Rufus Choate, a family friend, from his seat in the Senate Chamber. "I am going to Boston, Mr. Choate. What shall I tell my father?" The Massachusetts senator responded, "Tell him we are beaten, Mr. Hale...We have been beaten in a great battle."[18] The next morning, a disgusted Edward returned to Boston. There he wrote at lightning speed and had printed at his own expense a political pamphlet arguing for the remedy of encouraging non-slaveholding settlers to emigrate to the new state of Texas. "Northern energy has peopled and civilized southern countries before—may it not again?"[19] His appeal fell on deaf ears and, to mix metaphors, sank without a trace, but he was finding his voice and something like it would be proposed for Kansas.

A month after returning from Washington, Edward was a part time minister at the newly established Congregational Church of the Unity in Worcester, Massachusetts. Since the railway between Worcester and Boston was a family affair (the most successful of his father's many ventures into pioneering railroads in Massachusetts), it would be easy to travel home for Boston's social and cultural activities and to see his family. By good fortune, he lodged in the home of Mr. and Mrs. Moses Phillips. A publisher and bookseller, Mr. Phillips would soon be one of the founders of the liberal *Atlantic Monthly* and took a genuine interest in Edward's literary efforts while Mrs. Phillips became a warm surrogate mother to the young minister. That summer, he and William Channing climbed 5,268-foot Mt. Katahdin in Maine (as did Thoreau not long after). Harvard botanist Asa Gray had asked Edward (all the Hales were keen amateur botanists) to gather specimens of plants there for his herbarium and Edward was able to report to the Boston Society of Natural History that August that he had discovered "eight phanerogamous plants which are not found below that elevation."[20]

After a delay of a few months, the standing committee of the Church of the Unity was able to offer Edward fulltime employment, which he accepted enthusiastically. He was ordained minister there on April 29, 1846, three weeks after his twenty-fourth birthday. He quickly became an advocate for the poor, many of whom were the forced immigrants who disembarked from every ship arriving from Ireland following the potato famine that year. Poor French Canadians seeking work were also arriving en masse in New England. As an important railroad center, Worcester was one of the immigrants' stopover points on their way to the frontier. But most of Edward's parishioners were typical of a commercial town—manufacturers, merchants, and bankers.

Finding the demands of his Worcester ministry were not overwhelming at first, Edward discovered to his delight that he was able to pursue his many other interests, including writing, hiking in the White Mountains, giving papers at the American Antiquarian Society (which he continued to do until resigning in 1907), and gardening, particularly growing roses. From now on for almost sixty years, he would make the ministry a jumping-off place for innumerable activities, astonishing his contemporaries.

The 1850s were sad years for the Hale family. The loss of two of Edward's favorite siblings deeply shocked and distressed him. His younger brother Alexander, who was Edward's most intimate correspondent at this time, graduated from Harvard in 1849, moved to Pensacola as a government engineer, and was drowned in September 1850 as a volunteer member of a lifesaving crew attempting to rescue a sinking vessel. His oldest sister Sarah was never in robust health and became seriously ill that year. Edward sent her almost daily notes to cheer her up and even took her to Washington, hoping that a milder climate would save her life. She did not survive the return trip, dying in May 1851. Edward had already lost his childhood friend Edward Webster, his brilliant uncle Alexander Everett, and his closest friend in Worcester, railroad clerk Frederic Greenleaf.

Adding to the Hale family's troubles was the precarious state of their finances due to Nathan Sr.'s enthusiasm for railroads and his injudicious investments. Nathan Jr. was now carrying almost all the responsibility for the family newspaper while both his earlier magazine venture, the ambitious *Boston Miscellany of Literature and Fashion*, in which Edward published his earliest short stories, and younger brother Charles's new enterprise, *Today: A Boston Literary Journal*, lost money and were short-lived. Their mother Sarah begged Edward to accept an offer he had received to minister to the First Church of Boston and return to the saddened family fold but he had new reasons to stay in Worcester, which he appeared to conceal initially from his family. He had met his future wife Emily Baldwin Perkins and felt they would be happier away from Boston, at least for now.

Unitarianism was the nexus for Hattie and Edward's love story, and thus an important context to understand. "The Boston religion," as it was often called, was closely associated with the Harvard Divinity School, particularly following the election in 1805 of the liberal minister Henry Ware as Hollis Professor of Divinity. His election precipitated the controversy that was to divide the congregational churches of New England's Standing Order. In May 1819, the brilliant preacher William Ellery Channing (1780-1842) spelled out Unitarian beliefs clearly and powerfully in "Unitarian Christianity," a ninety-minute sermon delivered at an ordination in Baltimore. The new denomination was a liberal reaction to the orthodox Calvinism (Congregationalism) of the New England Puritans, particularly the latter's rigidly uncompromising, from the Unitarian point of view, doctrines of original sin, predestination, and eternal damnation. Unitarianism fundamentally differed from orthodox Protestant theology in its belief that only God possesses supreme Divinity. Instead of the Trinitarian view of God as Father, Son, and Holy Ghost, it advocated the unity of God, the New Testament teaching of Jesus Christ, the brotherhood of man, salvation by character, and the improvement of mankind through social reform. By the time Edward Everett Hale was born in 1822, the positions of the two branches of Congregationalism were clearly drawn and the next phase was separation. The American Unitarian Association was founded in 1825.

As mentioned, Hale became a minister during a turbulent time in Unitarian and national affairs. Orthodox Unitarian clergymen were under attack from within their denomination by abolitionist transcendentalists and by antislavery activists who castigated the denomination's failure to take on the nation's great sin of slavery. Theodore Parker, James Freeman Clarke, and Thomas Wentworth Higginson were among the increasing numbers of Unitarian ministers and intellectuals who actively preached in favor of abolition. In 1845, the Reverend Clarke presented "A Protest against American Slavery" at a meeting of Unitarian ministers in Boston and the petition was adopted and circulated widely to others for signatures. Although 173 ministers signed, about eighty, including the most influential ministers of the denomination, declined; young Edward Everett Hale was among the latter. This was undoubtedly due to the influence of his businessman father Nathan, of Massachusetts senator Daniel Webster, and of his uncle Edward Everett, former governor of Massachusetts, who was about to become president of Harvard. These men were willing to compromise in hopes of preserving the Union but also because, among their friends and constituents were the Unitarian Appleton and Lowell families, textile-mill owners who felt threatened by attacks on the southern cotton planters and their dependence on slave labor.

Other national Massachusetts politicians, notably former president John Quincy Adams, who subsequently served in the U.S. House of Representatives from 1831 until his death in 1848, and U.S. Senator Charles Sumner championed the civil liberties of abolitionists whom the South was attempting to silence. Sumner not only denounced the "barbarism of slavery" in the South but also racial segregation in the North. By 1848, the Northern Whig Party had split into factions (antislavery "Conscience" and "Cotton," representing business interests wishing to maintain good relations with the cotton-producing South). This marked the end of an era in Boston with most Whigs gradually moving into the new Republican Party and the rise of Democratic-ethnic politics. Even while he appeared to distance himself from the schisms over abolition, Edward was in fact in close touch and sympathy with many antislavery activists in Worcester, including Thomas W. Higginson.

Of more immediate concern to Edward E. Hale, as the minister of a parish in rapidly industrializing urban Massachusetts, was the sad condition of European immigrants, mostly Irish, who were arriving at East Coast ports in vast numbers but largely left to sink or swim. In 1852, he published a 64-page pamphlet, *Letters on Irish Emigration,* which he hoped would advocate action by the national government. "The State should stop at once its effort to sweep them back," he argued. "It should welcome them; register them; send them at once to the labor-needing regions; care for them if sick; and end, by a system, all that mass of unsystematic statute which handles them as outcasts or Pariahs." Westward migration, he felt, would not only increase economic prospects for the Irish but also lessen Yankee fears of a Papist revival in America.[21]

Always tolerant and large of spirit, but more pragmatic than radical, Edward saw a way of resolving the twin issues of immigration and slavery following the passage in 1854 of the Kansas-Nebraska Act, which shocked most New Englanders. Northern Whigs saw what they considered to be two essential politically binding agreements between North and South, the Missouri Compromise (1822) and the Compromise of 1850, being demolished by the Kansas Nebraska Act. The old compromises had, among other things, excluded slavery from vast tracts of western territory; the new act, pushed through Congress by Democrats, allowed local settlers in any given territory to decide if it would be slave or free. All western territories were now potential new slave states, at least in theory.

Edward began to see emigration to the western territories of Kansas and Nebraska as both a solution to immigration problems and a curb on the expansion of slavery. He enthusiastically supported Massachusetts Representative Eli Thayer in his proposal to create the Massachusetts Emigrant Aid Company to help Northern settlers, including new immigrants to the United States, move to the proposed territories of Kansas (which he and his family spelled "Kanzas") and Nebraska. There they were to establish the "free soil" population necessary to counter slave-holding settlers from the South. Thus, he was able to revive his ideas for Texas. Edward worked tirelessly for the Emigrant Aid Company, speaking all over New England on the subject, wrote antislavery articles, and compiled a handbook for emigrants, *Kanzas and Nebraska*.[22]

The Hale family's travails certainly influenced Edward to accept the call in 1856 to minister to the South Congregational Society, whose church was on the corner of Washington and Castle Streets in Boston's South End. His predecessor there was Frederic Dan Huntington. Huntington's ministry was successful, and during his fourteen years as minister, "the Church was full; its debt was paid; the charities were admirably administered; [and] the Sunday School was in perfect order."[23] Huntington formed the Board of Charities and the ladies' charitable South Friendly Society (1833). But, in 1856, he was appointed Plummer Professor of Christian Morals at Harvard College and preacher at the college chapel. Four years later, Huntington left the Unitarian church for the Episcopal Church and in due course was anointed Episcopal bishop of Western New York. This high-profile defection, caused in Huntington's case by his strong loyalty to Jesus Christ as Lord and Savior and his distress at the transcendentalists' attacks on Christ's uniqueness, led Edward to make what was for him a rare pronouncement of Unitarian beliefs in five doctrinal sermons to his new, young congregation.[24]

Before taking further initiatives which put him firmly in control of the minds and hearts of his new congregation, thirty-seven-year-old Edward leaped at the opportunity in the fall of 1859 to make his first trip to Europe. His uncle Edward Everett asked him if he would accompany his oldest son William, who had just graduated from Harvard, to Cambridge University to continue his studies there. Emily supported the idea as did Henry Kidder, head of the church's standing committee. During his "Ninety Days' Worth of Europe," as he would call the book he made from the letters he wrote to his family and to the *Daily Advertiser* (still edited by Charles Hale), Edward delivered his young cousin to Cambridge, met up with a Harvard classmate in London, and then made the "grand tour" through Europe with him. He reveled in the changing landscapes, the art galleries, and literary associations, and even took the time to seek out the brother of one of his family's maids when he was in Ireland.[25]

On his return, Edward threw himself into widening the scope of his church's activities. Concluding that the original SCC church, completed on Castle Street in 1828, was inadequate for an increased mission of "neighborhood relief," he worked with the church's trustees to build a new church on Union Park Street which opened its doors in 1862. When the Hales moved to Boston in 1856, they had one daughter, Ellen (Nelly, b. 1855). A son, Alexander, had died in infancy in 1853. Over the next thirteen years, Emily gave birth to seven more sons, Arthur (b. 1859), Charles Alexander (Charley, 1861-1868), Edward E. Jr. (Jack, b. 1863), Philip (Phil, b. 1865), Herbert (Bertie, b. 1866), Henry (Harry, 1868-1876), and Robert (Rob or Bob, b. 1869). The toll on her small frame (for example, Nelly weighed 11 pounds, 5 ounces at birth) must have been grievous.

Young Emily Hale was captured with her one-year-old daughter Ellen (Nelly) in a daguerreotype made by Edward Everett Hale himself in 1855. Unfortunately, this charming image is in very poor condition.
Hale Family Papers, Sophia Smith Collection, Smith College.

***

Until the Civil War, Edward's reputation was largely parochial and confined to Massachusetts but the war and its aftermath made him a national figure. Edward and his brother Charles, now speaker of the Massachusetts House of Representatives, were both extremely active in supporting the Union army through patriotic appeals in the *Advertiser* and speeches. Edward also wrote inspirational pieces for the *Atlantic,* made highly effective recruiting appeals from his pulpit and drilled young soldiers on Boston Common, served as a director of the United States Sanitary Commission, and even spent several weeks at the front in Virginia. The U.S. Sanitary Commission, a private volunteer relief agency chartered by the U.S. Government in June 1861, was founded and organized by its president, Unitarian minister Henry Whitney Bellows (1814-1882) to address the appalling conditions and loss of life in the soldiers' camps and on the battlefields. Many thousands of volunteers raised money, collected donations, worked as nurses, ran kitchens in army camps, administered hospital ships and soldiers' homes, made uniforms, and organized Sanitary Fairs across the Union states to support the Federal army with funds and supplies. Emily Hale's former fiancé Frederick Law Olmsted was the Commission's first executive secretary. Back home in Boston, the ladies of the South Friendly Society, led by Sarah Hooper, set up sewing machines in the church vestry to make clothes for the soldiers and sent off boxes of donated supplies to wherever they were needed.[26]

The Civil War years compounded Nathan Hale Sr.'s difficulties as his health failed. Edward and Charles Hale struggled together to shelter their parents and sisters from financial harassment and save the family business but Nathan Hale Jr., who managed the newspaper editorially with his father from 1841 to 1853, had retired to academic life as professor of mental and moral philosophy at Union College in Schenectady, New York. Charles retained editorial control in addition to his political career until his health broke down in 1861. Following their father's death in 1863, Charles and Edward agreed that it was time to sell the *Advertiser* to Messrs Chandler and Waters. Edward's connection with the *Advertiser* did not end with its sale but Charles and his sisters now sought other employment.

Edward Hale is shown here in a mid-1850s daguerreotype with his youngest sister Susan. The two were close for the rest of Hale's long life and collaborated on several children's travel books. A warm and unconventional personality, Susan was gifted with many friends and was a devoted aunt to her brother's many children.
Hale Family Papers, Sophia Smith Collection, Smith Archives.

In 1864, Charles became U.S. consul-general in Cairo, Egypt, where he remained until 1870, although the *Advertiser*'s new owners continued to hope that Charles would return to edit the newspaper he had struggled so hard to keep in the family. Lucretia Hale turned to writing to help earn a living. Susan Hale, likewise, helped support the family by teaching and writing.

Both of the Hale sisters were able to pursue more independent lives following their parents' deaths, beginning with an extended visit to their brother Charles in Cairo in 1867. Lucretia was one of six women elected to the Boston School Committee in 1874 and re-elected the following year—its first women members. Among her best known and best loved creations that began appearing in her many published short stories over the following decades was the Peterkin family, which she based partly on Hale family experiences and traits and Boston social life of the era. The stories were collected and published in book form as *The Peterkin Papers* (1880). Susan Hale, in addition to writing and lecturing, studied art in Paris and Germany, and gave lessons in watercolor.

The Reconstruction years, during which Edward became nationally known as a Unitarian leader and preacher, educational and social reformer, writer, editor, and lecturer, were busy and productive years for him. This was, after all, a period of profound social change in America. Reconstruction of the South following the war, industrialization, the raising of capital to build vast networks of railroads, the absorbing of relentless waves of impoverished immigrants, and displacement of native populations by westward migration, caused massive problems requiring initiatives in social reform and infrastructure innovations. The creation of unprecedented corporate and private wealth led to the inevitable human frailties of greed, corruption, and the excesses of the very rich during the so-called Gilded Age. Two major economic depressions, that began in 1873 and 1893, produced devastating bankruptcies and massive unemployment. Class conflict, labor unrest, and violent strikes were endemic.

Through his writings, sermons, lectures, and his personal example, Edward Everett Hale emerged as one of the moral voices of this troubled era. He threw himself into the avant-garde of social reform both through the charitable outreach of his own and other Boston churches and his support for reform efforts nationally. As a leader of the Soldiers Memorial Society, a successor to the Sanitary Commission, he was involved in efforts to promote the education of poor whites in the South through the establishment of free schools in Richmond, Virginia; Wilmington, North Carolina; and Charleston, South Carolina. He was also early in supporting the industrial education of former slaves, identifying most closely with the work of the Hampton Institute in Virginia. But he came to regret that he had not made a much greater personal commitment of time and effort to the cause, as he told Hattie in an 1890 letter: "If, in 1866, when the war was over, I had abandoned all other work, and thrown myself into the business of Southern Education...and I was tempted to do so, I seriously think this country would have been a different nation today."[27]

Instead of focusing on Southern education, Edward had turned his attention to reforming the ailing Unitarian church so as to bring it into the forefront of liberal thought and leadership. To achieve this ambition, he followed the lead and worked closely to support the vision of prominent Unitarian Henry W. Bellows, minister of the First Congregational Church of New York City (now Church of All Souls), and the founder of the U.S. Sanitary Commission. In the course of his work for that organization, Bellows had become convinced that, in the vast social transformation the country was experiencing, the opportunity existed for liberal Christianity to supplant evangelical Protestantism as the dominant religious force in the reunited nation. If Unitarianism was to compete for leadership of liberal Christian churches, then it would need a strong organization. Edward became Bellow's most effective collaborator in this effort. The other was transcendentalist James Freeman Clarke, pastor of the Church of the Disciples in Boston.

The American Unitarian Association (AUA), founded in 1825, was supported by individual, rather than church, memberships. The AUA's fundraising and outreach had always been weak and were increasingly stymied by theological disputes. On the one side were the Boston conservatives who insisted "that Christianity was of divine origin and sanction, and that Jesus Christ, though not a person of the Trinity, was divinely authorized to proclaim the way of salvation to erring men." On the other side, "Radicals," individualistic followers of Ralph Waldo Emerson and Theodore Parker, "were moving towards a wholly naturalistic interpretation of religion, which allowed no specially privileged place for Jesus."[28] Bellows sought to mediate and reconcile these differences so that the Unitarian body could organize more effectively by enlarging and strengthening the "broad church" group, as he called it, those in the middle ground between the conservatives and radicals. Resistance to an official statement of belief was so strong that it was decided to drop any discussion of it in the conference and focus instead on a "practical" statement of purpose.

Some six hundred clerical and lay delegates, representing more than three-fourths of the Unitarian churches in America, attended the April 1865 organizing conference in New York City. Clarke gave the opening sermon, which emphasized the possibility of wider cooperation if such cooperation were based on a concern for Christian action rather than doctrine. With Edward's help, Bellows worked tirelessly to prevent conservatives or radicals from splitting the convention and a draft constitution and bylaws consisting of a preamble and eight articles were passed. Edward concluded later in the *Christian Examiner* that what was important was that Unitarians had demonstrated they "were a singularly practical body; determined to have some organization, equally determined to have no creed."[29] The following year, Edward led the first official meeting of the newly created National Conference, in Syracuse, New York.

Even though Unitarian organization was now greatly strengthened, the so-called Radicals in the broad umbrella of Unitarianism, ranging from scientific theists to transcendentalists, felt excluded when the first National Unitarian Conference committed the denomination to the "Lordship of Christ." Some of these radicals organized the Free Religious Association, with its members making eloquent attacks on the more conservative views of clergy, the Bible, and the Christian faith. The group also attracted members from another group of American radical religious leaders, some Reform Jews, many of whom had emigrated from Germany in the 1840s and whose leader, Isaac Mayer Wise from Cincinnati, joined the Free Religious Association, hoping that the organization would become the vanguard of a combined secularized religious tradition among both Christians and Jews.

A number of appointments in 1866 confirmed Edward's position as a leader in the further rejuvenation of Unitarianism. He helped to form and became first president of the Suffolk Conference, comprising the Unitarian churches in the Unitarian heartland of Suffolk County, Massachusetts, including Boston. He remained president for twenty-five years and used his influence to arrange a distribution of the responsibility for the administration of charity among the different Unitarian churches of Boston. Location became the organizing principle behind the establishment of the Associated Charities which relieved the churches of some of their responsibilities. That year, he was elected to the Harvard Board of Overseers by the graduates (until 1875) and made a trustee of Antioch College in Ohio, both centers of Unitarianism; and, in the mid-1880s, he was appointed, along with Episcopalian Phillips Brooks (a distant cousin) and Alexander McKenzie, one of Harvard's preachers to the university. The last appointment demanded occasional appearances in chapel, preaching of the Sunday sermon, and six weeks of college residence each year as a counselor to the students, which he greatly enjoyed. Fortunately, Edward had inherited an already well-organized ladies' charitable outreach arm to the church, the South Friendly Society, and had built a staff of dedicated assistants who were proud of his larger work and who freed him from many of the usual parochial chores.

The search for consensus among many divergent groups came at a time of intellectual ferment arising from scientific discoveries, religious scholarship, and growing shifts in moral and religious attitudes. There was a crisis of faith in the face of cultural secularization.[30] Charles Darwin's controversial *Origin of Species* (1859), which Americans were soon studying and debating, introduced the British naturalist's theory of evolution through natural selection. This posed a direct challenge not only to the Bible's Book of Genesis, but also to mainstream Christianity itself, and marked the beginning of the still boiling creation-evolution controversy.

Harvard botanist Asa Gray (1810-1888), for whom Edward had collected specimens for his herbarium in 1846 and who remained a good friend, was the first important American scientist to champion Darwin's new theories in light of some of his own empirical research. However, Harvard zoologist-paleontologist Louis Agassiz (1807-1873), another of Edward's friends, was adamant in his belief in "special creation," that the Creator's hand is displayed strikingly in every era of world history. He vehemently dismissed Darwin as well as Gray's support of him in a series of increasingly bitter debates with Gray in 1860, a dispute that was soon broadcast on a more popular level in magazines such as the *Atlantic Monthly*.[31] Hattie Freeman, who was just thirteen when Gray's review of Darwin's *Origin of Species* appeared in the *Atlantic*, would become intensely interested in opposing theories of evolution.

As a Unitarian leader for more than fifty years, Edward's pragmatism and good humor provided valuable glue, helping to bring about reconciliation of the Unitarian factions in 1894, as shall be seen. But, unlike more conservative ministers, he invited radical ministers to preach in his church, shocking his Beecher relatives, notably Harriet Beecher Stowe. However, Edward's ambition for an intellectual and literary forum for his ideas for a Utopian "New Civilization" could not be realized until 1869 with the first edition of *Old and New*. The AUA loaned $8,000 and the publication was also partly funded by William B. Weeden, Edward's close friend since they met during the Civil War, a wealthy Providence, Rhode Island textile manufacturer, Unitarian, and historian, who became a regular contributor. The new publication partly subsumed the *Christian Examiner*, for which Edward had been joint editor with conservative transcendentalist Frederick Hedge, as well as contributor, for twelve years.[32]

The first edition of *Old and New* included chapter one of Edward's moralistic serial "Ten Times One is Ten," which ran for six months, was subsequently published in book form, and turned him into the leader of an international social service movement. The story tells how ten people, meeting at the funeral of a good man named Harry Wadsworth, realize that he has transformed each of their lives. They each are inspired to better the lives of ten others, who each improve the lives of ten more, and so on in a kind of chain reaction of benevolence that soon brings about a moral reformation of the world, including the end of war. The mechanism of this transformation is a rapidly expanding network of "Harry Wadsworth Clubs," with their four mottoes: "Look up and not down"; "Look forward and not back"; "Look out and not in"; and "Lend a Hand!" Hale's story inspired the formation of countless service clubs, including the Ten Times One, Harry Wadsworth, and Lend-A-Hand Clubs, the King's Daughters, and the Look-Up Legions.

Late in 1869, at the same time he was struggling to put together the first issue of *Old and New*, Edward moved his large family, including the new baby Robert, from their crowded house in the South End to a spacious house, formerly a school, with a columned façade and a large garden at 39 Highland Street in Roxbury. Although Roxbury had recently been annexed to Boston, it was a good mile and a half away from his church. In spite of a regular horse car service, it was no longer so easy to get home for lunch, so Caroline Freeman suggested to Edward that he treat their house on Union Park as a home from home, taking his lunches and naps there as often as he wished. Over the subsequent years, Edward became a familiar figure in the Freeman household. There is evidence in his inscriptions in the books Edward gave Hattie in 1868 and 1870, that he had seen a great deal of her and her family since he first called on them in 1863.[33]

In the meantime, Emily, just like her mother Mary Foote Perkins—the "quiet Beecher"—before her, was apparently content in the expected Victorian role of devoted wife and mother at home in Boston, leaving public life to her husband. For many years, this traditional division seemed to suit Edward too. Edward Jr., later asserted in his *Life and Letters of Edward Everett Hale* (1917) that their father was often absent from family life during the church season, either at the church, or at countless meetings, on lecture tours, or writing and editing in his home study and that he remembered his mother as the serene and steady anchor at home.[34] Emily was a loving wife and mother, and the letters Edward wrote to her, of which numerous examples are printed in *Life and Letters*, show that he regarded her for many years as an intelligent and trusted confidante. But, unlike Edward's own strong-minded, scholarly mother, for whom he retained a lifelong reverence, Emily clearly did not share her husband's intellectual interests, or his love of the outdoors, adventure, and constant travel. In the summer, when the church was closed, it was Edward's turn to lead a more active style of parenting while Emily spent more and more time resting. Constant childbirth and child-rearing and the effort of keeping up with her hyperactive husband had exhausted her.

The Hales' children do not seem to have remarked on the disparity of energy and interests between their parents but their granddaughter Nancy Hale, Philip's daughter, who was born just a year before her grandfather died, evidently heard this from her father, two surviving uncles and her aunt. In her enchanting memoir of her parents and the Hale family, she quotes herself as saying to her mother, "Grandpa was so dominating. It seems to me he wanted to be Jehovah and have everybody else do what he wanted. Look how exhausted Grandmamma was." And in a letter she wrote to Hattie Freeman's great-niece in 1974, Nancy declared, "My grandmother was something of an invalid, and never up to his strenuousness, and besides that not at all intellectual in spite of being a Beecher," as she contrasted her with the astonishingly active and strong-minded Hattie.[35]

During the winter of 1870-71, twenty-three-year-old Hattie Freeman was considering the suggestion made by Sarah Hooper, a relative of the Cape Cod Freemans and a senior member of the South Congregational Church, that she should begin working at the church. Judging by the business-like letter that Hattie wrote on her mother's behalf in September 1870 from the Freemans' summer residence at Oak Hill in Newton, she was already practiced at running her invalid mother's affairs. Caroline Freeman had asked Hattie to write to Edward because she wanted him to officiate at the marriage in her Union Park townhouse of her forty-six-year-old brother Samuel Lewis, a Harvard educated lawyer, to twenty-one-year-old Catharine Titus, a native of Detroit. "Both he & his lady live out of town," Hattie explained, "but find it more convenient to be married in the city, leaving the same P.M. for North Carolina, their future home. I trust you will have no engagement to interfere with it as it would greatly disappoint us all." She continued, "The lady is Episcopalian & would like that form of service. Some day next week that Mother is in town, she would like to see you."

This 1870 epistle is Hattie's first surviving letter to Edward and she concludes with a paragraph that already shows her love of outdoor life and culture: "We are all very happy here & shall remain the greater part of the fall of which I am so glad for I am never ready to return to the city. Father and I enjoy much riding in the saddle while Fred and I have long walks. My piano is also here & with my books I have many sources of enjoyment. We should all be so glad to see you here before we return. Yours aff. Hattie E. Freeman."[36]

3

Panic, Church, and Science

In the summer of 1871, the year she joined the volunteer staff of the South Congregational Church in Boston's South End, young Harriet Freeman was one of her much older minister's party on a church trip to Waterville Valley in New Hampshire's White Mountains. For some years, Edward had been taking his oldest children and some of the "elite," as he called the most faithful and active staffers and parishioners, to this beautiful valley to escape Boston's heat and spend part of the summer enjoying outdoor life there. This may have been the first time that Hattie joined the Hale party but she was well versed in the region's mystique and the Freeman family may have vacationed there, judging by a few mountain landscapes painted by Hattie's mother.

Now Edward and Hattie shared an outside seat on the stage coach that carried them the last part of the journey from Boston. She recalled that ride twenty years later in a combination of longhand and the shorthand he had taught her to convey their most intimate thoughts: "<u>I remember, you do not</u>, that on the stage ride up I sat next [to] you. It was either rainy or very warm, for we held up an umbrella. I held it, & you held my wrist for a better support. I remember even then that <*that touch of yours, your hand on mine gave my heart pleasure. That love was in my heart then hardly born. How little we knew then of what was before us [or] where the paths of life would lead us*>."[1] Edward replied that, on the contrary, he remembered that journey well, including feeling the same tug of attraction. He was evidently enchanted by the slim young woman's youthful enthusiasm for the outdoors, for natural history, and for mountain-climbing.

But what of Emily Hale on this trip? Tied at home with young children and, until 1869, perennially pregnant, she may not have joined trips to the White Mountains after one memorable summer holiday there when Nelly was a baby. In any case, home-loving Emily never shared the vigorous Hale family's enthusiasm for outdoor life and natural history. This seems to be confirmed in a letter Edward wrote Emily from Waterville in August 1868 in which he happily described the older children's riding lessons, their various climbing excursions, Nelly's fishing and his painting, and the presence of his sister Susan and members of his church family.[2]

Until a photograph of fifteen-year-old Hattie with her five-year-old cousin Helen Atkins surfaced in a Freeman family archive, describing Hattie's appearance was a challenge. This photograph (see p. 13) shows that she was not a conventional beauty, certainly in comparison to her pretty little cousin—but her unflinching gaze seems already to indicate her strong personality. She had dark hair worn up and parted in the middle, somewhat hooded grey eyes beneath assertive eyebrows, a prominent and rather hooked nose, and a neat figure. According to a later passport description, she was 5 feet 3 inches, short compared to the towering 6-feet-2-inch Edward but not for women of the time. The earnest, bookish, and musical young woman was shy and reserved with strangers, particularly those who did not share her interests. Self-conscious since her school days about an embarrassing stutter which, even in adulthood, caused her to trip over her words when racing to convey her enthusiasms, she was reluctant for years about public speaking. But she lit up in the company of like-minded friends and colleagues, who delighted in her intelligence, generosity, and zest for life.

By 1871, Hattie was already on the church's music committee; now she began to teach in the Sunday school, along with her friends and neighbors Etta and Hattie Pierce, daughters of the founder of the renowned high-end Boston grocer Samuel S. Pierce, Helen Kimball of the Massachusetts insurance fortune, and Edward's right hand man, William Howell Reed. Reed, who would marry Hattie's cousin Grace Atkins in 1887 and who, like his father David Reed before him, would become a leading figure in the South Congregational Church and Society and in the national Unitarian hierarchy, also taught in the Sunday school at this time.[3]

The first issue of *Old and New* was due to go to press the very month that the Hales moved to Roxbury. Edward was now juggling his pastorate, a large family, a cultural magazine with a bottomless thirst for copy, and preparing to give a series of Lowell Lectures sponsored by the Massachusetts Historical Society. He relied on his older brother Nathan, a very experienced editor and now a professor at Union College in Schenectady, to share the burden of editing and also contribute articles. Edward's letters to his younger brother Charles described the tireless effort he made in the first year of the magazine's existence and his hope that Charles would decide to lead the editing when he returned home from Egypt where he had been American consul for some years. But Charles, although a regular contributor, returned to politics (he was appointed assistant secretary of state under Secretary Hamilton Fish in Washington in February 1872—a short-lived appointment) and Nathan died in February 1871. Then, on November 5 that year, Frederick Wadsworth Loring, a promising young journalist and novelist, and protégé of Edward's, who was committed to future articles and a collaborative serial, "Six of One by Half a Dozen of the Other," for the magazine, was killed while on assignment for *Appleton's Journal*, along with five other men, by Yavapai warriors during a stagecoach robbery in Arizona. Other family members who did help Edward with the editing, and also contributed articles, were his older sister Lucretia and brother-in-law Frederick Perkins while Emily's famous aunt, Harriet Beecher Stowe, was a frequent contributor. When family and friends let him down on promised copy, Edward struggled to fill the empty pages with his own writings.

Two disasters beyond Edward's control contributed to the demise of *Old and New*. The first was the Great Boston Fire of November 1872, which consumed sixty-five acres of Boston's financial district and destroyed 776 buildings, including the warehouse in which the paper stock for the magazine was stored, resulting in direct and indirect losses of $3,000. Edward was in Chicago at the time of the devastating fire and did not arrive home until November 23 but noted in his journal before he left the major problems of transportation and commerce in Boston caused by an epidemic of horse flu that spread across North America that year. Boston's fire department was immobilized by the lack of horses. As a result, all of the fire equipment had to be pulled to the fire by teams of volunteers on foot. Although this is often cited as the leading cause of the fire growing out of control, the city commission investigating the fire found that fire crews' response times were delayed by only a matter of minutes. More damaging were the highly flammable buildings and materials stored within them and the lack of fire codes.[4]

The second disaster was the financial panic that began at the end of 1873. This dealt serious blows to the viability of a magazine which had failed to gain enough subscribers to ensure its success as a business venture. When the AUA at the end of 1872 withdrew from the enterprise, angered by Edward's inability to return their $8,000 loan, Edward thought he had a better chance of counteracting the dullness of the theological articles by Unitarian clergymen that the AUA demanded. But it was too often he who struggled to inject a lighter tone with his own writings, sometimes in his own name, often anonymously. In fact, a competing magazine had dubbed *Old and New* "All Hale" in a review of the first issue, an acid observation which increasingly became a reality.[5]

This was a time, during President Ulysses S. Grant's second administration, of flabbergasting corruption, an era dubbed by Mark Twain "the Gilded Age." The disease was at its worst in the burgeoning railroad industry. As a director and head of the finance committee of the Union Pacific Railroad since 1869, Hattie's uncle Elisha Atkins was caught up in the notorious Crédit Mobilier scandal exposed by the *New York Sun* in September 1872 during Grant's second run for the presidency. It was alleged that the Crédit Mobilier, set up to raise the funds to build the first 100 miles of the transcontinental line, was in fact a dummy construction company formed by the Union Pacific Railroad to provide profits to stockholders and directors from the building of the railroad. The Crédit Mobilier charged inflated construction costs to the UPRR which in turn charged the government double the actual costs. It was further charged that Representative Oakes Ames of Massachusetts had sold its stock to select U.S. congressmen who would use their political influence to benefit the company by helping to defeat legislation that would have regulated the Union Pacific Railroad's rates. The vice president and former House Speaker Schuyler Colfax and his successor as Grant's running mate Henry Wilson of Massachusetts; Secretary of the Treasury George S. Boutwell; James A. Garfield, chairman of Appropriations; Henry L. Dawes, chairman of Ways and Means; William D. Kelley, chairman of Civil Services; John A. Bingham, chairman of the Judiciary Committee; and Glenn W. Scofield, chairman of the Naval Committee, were among twelve congressmen implicated in this scandal.

In the face of the allegations, House Speaker James G. Blaine, who disclaimed any involvement in the affair, appointed a select Wilson Committee to investigate. Elisha Atkins appeared before this committee on January 25, 1873. According to the *New York Times*, he "testified that he was a stockholder in the Credit [*sic*] Mobilier, but never was a director: also, that he was a stockholder in the Union Pacific Railroad, and a member of the board of directors of that road." Atkins "produced the $2,000,000 note given by the Union Pacific Railroad Company to the Credit Mobilier, dated Aug. 4, 1869, and indorsed by Mr. Atkins, trustee" and "the appeal bond for $600,000 given to secure the judgment in the suit of the State of Pennsylvania against the Credit Mobilier."[6] He denied additional allegations. Massachusetts Representative Ames and New York Democrat James Brooks, a director of the Union Pacific, were found guilty.

While Atkins was never indicted or incriminated of wrong doing, the impact of the scandal on the Atkins and Freeman families must have been considerable. His biographer and apologist William Howell Reed wrote in 1890, when he had become Atkins's son-in-law, "Elisha Atkins was the financial head of the Union Pacific and its debt to the government was a headache for him…He was, as he said 'entirely occupied with the finances and in keeping the road out of bankruptcy.' The hostile legislation of the years laid heavier burdens upon him, probably, than upon any single member of the board. Whatever the legislation, it was always in effect a crippling of the finances of the road, and there were times when he carried mainly on his own shoulders its entire floating debt, amounting to millions of dollars."[7]

In the wake of this scandal and many others that were revealed as the economy began to collapse during the Panic of 1873, the Republican Party was resoundingly defeated in the midterm election of 1874. Thirsting for blood after sixteen years in the political wilderness, House Democrats launched more than fifty committees to investigate the corrupt Grant Administration. James G. Blaine, now House minority leader and the front-running contender for the Republican presidential nomination in 1876, was accused of using his position as Speaker to offer worthless bonds as collateral for a loan of $64,000 he had received from the Union Pacific Railroad and which he had never been asked to repay and then using his influence as Speaker to provide the railroad with a land grant.

Elisha Atkins was among Blaine's defenders, giving a letter to the press on May 29, 1876, addressed to the Hon. James G. Blaine: "I have read the charges against you in the New-York *Sun*...concerning the North Pacific matter, and also your reported remarks in regard thereto...I considered your action in that matter was simply from a disposition to do a friendly act; that you had no pecuniary interest whatever in the transaction...Elisha Atkins."[8] In the face of proof of his additional complicity, Blaine chose to stonewall his accusers with a dramatic and audacious performance in his own defense on the floor of the House on June 5, 1876. One month later, Blaine was appointed to the vacant Senate seat from Maine. Blaine's checkered past would play a part in denying him this and two subsequent runs for the presidency (1880 and 1884) and would continue to draw in members of both Edward's and Hattie's families for more than a decade.

Despite the worsening economic crisis, Edward and Emily traveled to Europe during the summer of 1873 with their friend and chairman of the SCS standing committee Henry Kidder (who undoubtedly paid for the Hales) and his family.[9] While in England, Edward was able to sign up some leading British writers, including novelist Anthony Trollope and philosopher-theologian and Unitarian minister James Martineau, to write for *Old and New*. Long interested in the persecuted Waldensian Protestant sect in twelfth-century France, Edward now conducted research about them in the

Rhone Valley around Lyons for his 87-page novella *In His Name*. He considered this small gem of an historical romance to be his "best story" and by 1880 it had sold 20,000 copies in the United States.

Leaving Emily with the Kidders, Edward returned early from Europe to move his children into the house in Matunuck, Rhode Island, that his intimate friend and generous benefactor William Weeden had built for the Hale family in the hope that they would attract more of intellectual and artistic Boston to summer in the region.[10] From then on, Edward, sometimes without Emily, who increasingly did not share his delight in the simple South County lifestyle, would spend part of every summer in that spacious house. It became a sanctuary and a source of inspiration not just to Edward but also to other creative members of his family, including his sisters Lucretia and Susan. There he established a special bond with

Edward Everett Hale's summer home was originally off-white but appears to have been painted barn red about 1890 when Edward changed his letterhead to read "Red House, Matunuck." The team that restored the house in the early 2000s returned it to its interior and exterior form and colors as they were in the 1890s. The house is now open to the public during summer months.

his children as they grew up, delighting to see how they thrived in the outdoors, and there he would do much of his writing over the next thirty-five years. As his son Edward described it: "Few hours in my father's life, at this time (1870-1880) can have been happier than those he passed on the beach at Matunuck, sitting on the sand after the bath, and talking with Mr. Weeden, Doctor Bellows, and Doctor Hedge."[11]

But, despite all his efforts, Edward could not save *Old and New*. In 1875, he was forced to sell his brainchild to *Scribner's Monthly*, although he retained the copyright to the issues already published, reaping considerable financial rewards from permissions to reprint and books based on serials. Hattie and all those who were close to him were aware of Edward's bitter disappointment. But the venture had given him "reputation and influence" and he now had "a body of twelve or fifteen thousand devoted readers who would buy a copy of anything which bore his name."[12]

In addition to the failure of *Old and New*, a sex scandal, a death, and a chronic illness, all involving members of his family, undoubtedly helped cloud Edward's normally optimistic outlook on life in the mid-1870s. The first, involving Emily Hale's uncle, the famous, charismatic preacher Henry Ward Beecher (1813-1887), must have served as a warning as Edward and Hattie were drawn to each other. Beecher preached wildly popular sermons at Plymouth Church in Brooklyn Heights, New York, from 1847 until his death in 1887. Dubbed "the Gospel of Love," these sermons were in stark contrast to the stern Calvinism of his father Lyman Beecher and his six brothers, all Congregational pastors. In 1872, feminist and radical reformer Victoria Woodhull, who, as an advocate of "free love," was enraged by what she saw as Beecher's hypocrisy in condemning her views, publicly accused him of adultery with his extremely religious parishioner Elizabeth Tilton. Her information was based on conversations she had had first with fellow suffragist Elizabeth Cady Stanton and then with Stanton's informant, Elizabeth's husband, the journalist Theodore Tilton. Tilton, an active supporter of woman suffrage, was formerly a close friend of and literary collaborator with Beecher.

Elizabeth Tilton had told her husband in 1870 that she had

gone too far in her relationship with Beecher. Tilton later said that Beecher and his wife "were years courting each other by mutual piety," and that Beecher assured her that theirs was "a high religious love," and that their sexual intimacy was as "natural and sincere an expression of love as words of endearment." Beecher's biographer Debby Applegate provides evidence that this was not the first time Beecher had committed adultery with a parishioner. The level of his self-indulgence and hypocrisy was astounding.

For a few years, the Tiltons and Beecher kept these accusations and denials between themselves and a few confidantes but, in July 1874, Theodore Tilton openly accused Beecher of seducing his wife and of committing adultery with her between late 1868 and early 1870. The Plymouth Church committee appointed by Beecher to investigate the charges found him innocent of wrongdoing but the public and the press insisted that a civil trial be held. Tilton sued Beecher for "criminal conversation" (adultery) and "alienation of affections" and released incriminating letters to the press, adding fuel to the scandal. All the more remarkable, then, that so many of Edward and Hattie's love letters survived.

During the "scandal summer" of 1874, the *New York Times* ran 105 stories and thirty-seven editorials about the sordid affair while less circumspect papers ran far more. The scandal fueled vast numbers of pamphlets, broadsides, cartoons, and doggerel, some of them pornographic, as well as cheap books. Even the *Boston Post* described the remarkable public frenzy for the latest news of "the Brooklyn war." The sensational trial ran from January to July 1875, when a mistrial was declared. Theodore Tilton's lawyer read several paragraphs of Nathaniel Hawthorne's *The Scarlet Letter* into the record to demonstrate that Beecher was the spitting image of the Reverend Arthur Dimmesdale. Elizabeth Tilton's constant confessions and retractions of guilt undermined her husband's case and Beecher's wife Eunice never blinked in her support of him, and neither did his sister Harriet Beecher Stowe.[13]

All of this was certainly deeply distressing to the Hales. Fond of their Uncle Henry, Edward and Emily undoubtedly supported him through his travails, which he survived, achieving a measure of redemption before his death. However, while he was in all other respects the most liberal of men, Edward's dislike of iconoclastic suffragists and other socially rebellious women probably originated with, or was cemented by, this case. Elizabeth Cady Stanton later admitted that the stature and momentum of the women's movement were severely damaged by its involvement in the scandal. Moreover, even though he favored freedom of the press and was never a prude, Edward was among the prominent citizens and leading social reformers who welcomed Anthony Comstock, long an intense enemy of Victoria Woodhull, when he arrived in Boston in the late 1870s seeking to establish the first outpost outside New York for his Society for the Suppression of Vice. Comstock had engineered the arrest of Victoria Woodhull and her sister after they published their exposé on October 28, 1872 of Beecher's affair with Elizabeth Tilton in their newspaper, *Woodhull & Claflin's Weekly*. The sisters were quickly released but the following year Comstock founded his New York Society for the Suppression of Vice and succeeded in persuading the U.S. Congress to pass the Comstock Law, which made illegal the distribution of "obscene, lewd, or lascivious" material and any information related to birth control or venereal disease.[14]

With the demise of *Old and New*, Edward decided that he would spend more of his time on historical research and writing. He now began work on what would become *Philip Nolan's Friends*, a novel set in Texas at the time of the Louisiana Purchase. He had been embarrassed by the revelation that the name of his protagonist in "The Man Without a Country" not only belonged to a known historical figure but that that man's politics and ultimately fatal heroics were the antithesis of the treasonous behavior he attributed to his fictional Philip Nolan. So, in early 1876, he and his twenty-two-year-old daughter Nelly, who would become a favorite traveling companion, set off for Louisiana and Texas to research the true story of Philip Nolan. In one of many interesting letters he wrote Emily during this lengthy journey, Edward described their stay at a plantation north of New Orleans with an energetic and cultivated sugar planter who was deeply engaged in converting the former slaves on his plantation to paid workers and voters. This very busy, hospitable man had five young sons and two daughters. Edward's description of his host's wife is telling: "Of course he could not approach these duties, but that he has a cheerful, active, intelligent, prudent, careful, spirited wife, who is also very pretty."[15] He did not add "just like you, dear."

Edward and Nelly returned from the South West in May to find that his oldest son Arthur and the second-to-youngest Harry were fighting a mortal battle with diphtheria. Arthur survived but the disease killed eight-year-old Harry, a beguiling, handsome child.[16] The Hale family was devastated and it may have been about this time that Emily's incipient depression (a Beecher characteristic) became more serious. From now on, Edward's brother Charles, suffering from the excruciating advanced stages of syphilis, was living at Highland Street, which only exacerbated Emily's tendency to take to her bed or flee to her Hartford family in the face of difficulties.

It must have been obvious to Hattie and the rest of Edward's friends and staff that he was weighed down with cares at home. Edward was now in his fifties and the most perceptive of his biographers, Jean Holloway, noticed a falling off in the creativity of his short stories, attributing it to a midlife crisis about the direction he had taken in life.[17] Evidence from Edward's letters to Hattie make it more likely that his malaise was due to Emily's increasing self-absorption and failure to provide a restful and supportive home life for her husband as he was feeling beleaguered by the demands of his parish and wider activities. Emily was becoming a hypochondriac, perhaps even a neurotic, as her letters increasingly indicate from this period on. She did not share her husband's intellectual interests, was happiest in the company of her own wider family and trusted old friends, and, despite their devotion to their children, the couple was drawing apart emotionally. Emily's nervousness may have begun with the many setbacks to the viability of Edward's magazine venture. She was, with good cause, perennially worried about the family's finances. It was she who, in Edward's absence, nursed two young sons through diphtheria, only to lose one of them. Finally, it is more than likely that Emily had also closed the bedroom door following the birth of their youngest son which, for a vigorous man like Edward, must have been especially hard. This may have made him vulnerable to an extramarital liaison, despite his moral compass.

* * *

By the time *Old and New* failed—a low point for Edward, for whom editing was bred in the bone—Hattie had begun to take dictation and assist with research on his sermons and literary and historical writings. Edward now cast around for a new and absorbing literary project. Already freed of onerous parish work by his devoted staff, including a lay pastoral assistant, the same William Howell Reed, who acted as church treasurer (Edward was always financially incompetent), he hired in 1876 a formidably competent and hard-working widow, Judith W. Andrews, to run the South Friend-

Emily Perkins Hale is shown here in early middle age and her rather tired face lacks the warmth of expression that her husband captured in his 1855 daguerreotype. Her braided hair and earrings are indicative of the care she took over her appearance and dress to the end of her life.
Hale Family Papers, Sophia Smith Collection, Smith College.

ly Society. Hattie, who had mainly worked in the Sunday school up to that point, now became more active in charitable outreach, visiting and finding support for impoverished widows and taking on the responsible role of treasurer, working in tandem with Mrs. Andrews. The two women grew close.

Although she gave much of her time to the church and charitable work, Hattie was determined to pursue her own interests in natural history. She had hoped to attend Vassar College but her father refused to let her go and asked Edward to support him in this decision, which he did.[18] Hattie was undoubtedly drawn to Vassar, as were so many other young women interested in science, by the presence on its faculty of astronomer Maria Mitchell, the best known woman scientist of the nineteenth century (Hattie was a life member of the Maria Mitchell Society). Vassar was founded in 1865 but already by the 1870s it had become a target of a backlash against women's increasing participation in medicine, science, and higher education. In 1873, Dr. Edward Clarke of Boston published *Sex in Education*, a scurrilous attack on women's higher education, which asserted (with examples allegedly from Vassar College) that women's health was being ruined by intensive study. According to Margaret Rossiter, historian of American women scientists, the charge, "[A]lthough quickly refuted by the Vassar physician… struck such a responsive chord of public opinion that it put the advocates of women's higher education on the defensive for at least a decade, though with no obvious impact on college enrollments."[19] With Hattie's mother a chronic sufferer from ill health, it is hardly surprising that her father strongly refused his scholarly daughter's wish to leave home for Vassar.

Hattie was thirsty for knowledge and Edward was to play an important role in guiding her into fields of study that mirrored his own interests. But Hattie also benefited from the efforts of three extraordinary Boston women who fought to further women's higher education during the Gilded Age: Anna Eliot Ticknor, Lucretia Crocker, and Ellen Swallow Richards. In the midst of ongoing controversy about the college-level education of women, the Women's Education Association of Boston, a group of wealthy and socially prominent Boston women (of which Hattie became a member) which opened many doors for women in that city in the 1870s and 1880s, petitioned the Harvard Corporation to consider granting degrees to women. The corporation, through Harvard President Charles W. Eliot, turned down the request and it was a further seven years before the Harvard "Annex" (a predecessor of Radcliffe College) was established.

At the same time, Anna Eliot Ticknor (1823-1896), the highly educated daughter of George Ticknor, Harvard's professor of modern languages and founder and first president of the Boston Public Library, decided to do something about women's education. She launched the Society to Encourage Studies at Home in 1873 from the library of her parents' Beacon Hill mansion. Several Boston women from backgrounds similar to Ticknor's volunteered to teach the courses. Anna Ticknor's cousin Samuel Eliot, a historian, educator, and philanthropist, and good friend of Edward's since college, agreed to serve as chairman. The "S.H.," as it was known, the first of the correspondence schools in America, was divided into departments. Harvard paleontologist Louis Agassiz had urged his wife Elizabeth Cary Agassiz to include science in the curriculum from the start and she made sure that it was. Hattie would study and then volunteer to teach in the Science Department, led initially by Lucretia Crocker, and then by Ellen Swallow Richards.[20]

As the first woman supervisor in the Boston Public Schools, appointed in 1876, Lucretia Crocker (1829–1886) pioneered the discovery method of teaching mathematics and the natural sciences during her decade-long tenure. Earlier, she founded the Women's Education Association and joined five other women (one of whom was Lucretia Hale) in their successful drive to be the first women elected to the Boston School Committee. However, Ellen Swallow Richards (1842-1911) was almost certainly the most influential on Hattie's quest for scientific study. Hattie worked for two years as an S.H. Correspondent under Richards, guiding the studies in botany and geology by mail of women living beyond Boston.[21] A graduate of Vassar, Ellen Swallow (later Richards) had applied to Boston Tech (MIT) to study for a graduate degree in chemistry in 1870 but was turned down purely because, according to her husband Robert Richards, a professor of engineering there, the chemistry department did not want a woman to earn its first graduate degree. Instead, Boston Tech admitted her as a candidate for a second bachelor's degree and as a "special student" who did not have to pay tuition.[22] After her marriage, Richards volunteered her services at Tech's "Woman's Laboratory," which she persuaded the Women's Education Association to support from 1876 to 1883. Hattie probably studied mineralogy, one of Richards' specialties, in that laboratory while she was also a student at Boston Tech's Teachers' School of Science.

In the meantime, the South Congregational Church was flourishing and its fiftieth anniversary was celebrated with due ceremonial on February 3, 1878. A large choir, under the direction of the church's brilliant choirmaster B. J. Lang, sang the introduction to Mendelssohn's Hymn of Praise and the event was commemorated by the publication of *Memorials of the History for Half a Century of South Congregational Church*. It was at this point that Edward began to print systematically his regular sermons in four series dating from 1879 to 1881. Hattie, to whom over the years he dictated more than half of his sermons and who undoubtedly made contributions to their content, assisted him in making these selections.

Edward now began reaping laudatory notices for his literary accomplishments, particularly for his imaginative short stories. A long article discussing his literary output thus far, noting his strong interest in historical research and describing his working methods, appeared first in the *Boston Herald* and was republished in May 1880 in the *New York Times*. The article's unnamed author mentioned that Edward sometimes dictated his already conceptualized work to an amanuensis (secretary). This was almost certainly Hattie Freeman.[23]

Spending as much time together as they did, it is not surprising that Edward and Hattie drew close. In fact, Hattie remembered that they began to acknowledge a special fondness for each other that same year, 1880, the year of her mother's final illness and death, when Hattie was thirty-three and Edward fifty-eight.[24] Naturally, as the Freemans' pastor and close family friend, Edward was a frequent caller during this difficult time. He dined with Hattie and her father on February 12, called on William Freeman on February 27, dined with them again on March 4, the day before Caroline Crosby Freeman died at the age of sixty, and conducted her funeral service in the Union Park house on March 8. In the ensuing weeks, he lunched frequently with the Freemans, an already well-established pattern. Edward made no mention of Hattie in his diary after April that year, indicating that she was probably at the summer house in Pepperell, but on June 7, he traveled to West Newton, most likely in Hattie's company, to christen Fred Freeman's two oldest children, Caroline and Frank. He baptized the third, Ethel Hale Freeman, on January 1, 1882, and agreed to be the baby's godfather. Hattie would become extremely close to her brother's children.

The cause of Caroline Freeman's early death can only be conjectured, since Edward made no note of it in his journal, contrary to his usual custom. He remarked some eighteen years later, when Hattie was suffering from severe depression, that both her parents "died insane." But Hattie made no comment about her mother's health problems, other than remembering a side trip she had wanted to make when she was in Florida with her mother the winter of 1878, but was unable to leave her mother alone. Caroline Freeman, whose "gentleness and affectionateness" Edward always remembered, was a talented artist and compiled several scrapbooks about the Civil War but she may have suffered from dementia in her final years.[25] If so, the psychological burden would have been largely Hattie's and the cap on her adventurous nature increasingly hard to bear.

The Lewises were evidently artistic but there may have been some instability in the family. Caroline Freeman's brother Samuel Parker Lewis, who had a fine singing voice but seems to have failed as a lawyer, died at Pepperell in November 1882. Samuel's far younger wife had divorced him and their young children were adopted by her new husband, another lawyer close to her in age. The fact that the Pepperell house was left to Caroline Freeman rather than to Samuel Lewis and that his young wife gained custody of their children and changed their names seems to indicate a compelling reason to escape him. Perhaps he was alcoholic, abusive, or mentally ill. The dissolution of marriage was still frowned on in America, particularly by religious denominations. Individual states were now considering restrictive legislation. Despite her fondness for reminiscing, Hattie never referred to her Lewis uncle after her 1870 letter, which seems to indicate her enduring estrangement from his memory.

This was a time of shared sorrow since Edward's youngest and last surviving brother Charles, his most intimate confidant, was now in the advanced stages of syphilis, an all too common affliction before antibiotics. Charles had never married and, as his health deteriorated, he came to live in the Roxbury house where his increasingly bizarre and embarrassing behavior distressed Emily and the children.[26] Of the three Hale brothers who had worked intermittently for their father's newspaper, the *Boston Daily Advertiser*, it was Charles who had worked hardest to keep the newspaper in the family following their father's bankruptcy caused by unfortunate investments, and then he went into politics. But family letters and Edward's journal indicate that Charles suffered his first breakdown in 1876 and first paralytic attack in June 1879. By July 1880, Charles Hale was a patient at a mental hospital in South Boston, where he died on March 2, 1882. Edward was already saddened by the death in late January of the Reverend Henry W. Bellows, another of his closest intellectual companions and longtime associates. Charles's well-attended funeral took place at the South Congregational Church but was led by his own minister.

In contrast to Charles, who had never recovered emotionally from being jilted by a fiancé, Edward was rich in human warmth and devotion. His journal records his many meetings with Hattie in 1881 and 1882. He regularly lunched with her, and he took drives with her, ostensibly to make parish calls, but often with pleasurable side trips to parks and the botanical garden. An expert driver, she would call for him in the Freeman buggy on Tuesdays and Wednesdays. Sometimes they took trips further afield, often accompanied by Hattie's companion Mary Cobb. For example, on May 9, 1881, he wrote in his diary: "To Hatty Freeman's. With her and Miss Cobb to Malden to see the Chaddock House. Thence to Middlesex Fells. Home at 6."[27]

Despite the frequency of their meetings, Hattie was just one of several female assistants or "girls of the church" as he referred to them, and Edward openly recorded their times together in his diary. On January 14, 1882, for example, he noted that he dropped his secretary Mary Edes off with Hattie while he continued his sleigh ride to call on a parishioner, then "Return to Hatty's who shows us wonderful things with her microscope." Certainly, he was becoming more and more dependent on her. Fond as he was of writing Valentine poems to all his female staff (he had been class poet at Harvard), his poem to Hattie that year says it all:

I went to see my Valentine
I took my bags as if to say
If pressed a little I would stay.
Alack alas! Ah! wo the day
My Valentine was gone.

Another sun has risen now:
Perhaps if I sit here
In the still precincts of my home
And to the door bell turn an ear
Perhaps an omen of the year
My Valentine will come![28]

Seventeen years later, when he was reporting on the progress of his autobiography, Edward wrote Hattie, mostly in the shorthand that he taught her when their relationship became intimate and illicit: "There is twice as much needed as I had supposed. It will come down to about 1882 and then <*it will end abruptly by saying about this time his guardian angel stepped into his life and began to take care of him. And after this time what she did not do for him is not worth telling about and the reader is respectfully referred to her. But what her name is this book will not tell*>. Who can it be?"[29]

Indeed, Edward's letters and his journal record Hattie's extraordinary generosity and care of him. She remembered years later that she gave him her first gift for his sixtieth birthday on April 3 that year. Edward was preparing to leave on a leisurely research trip in Spain for his long-planned, but never realized, "History of the Pacific Ocean and its Shores." There he planned to meet up with Nelly, who was studying art in Paris, and his sister Susan, who was traveling on the Continent. Hattie sent the Freemans' factotum George Whalley to the church with pink roses for her minister, his favorite flower. She always treasured the message he sent back with George: "Dear Hatty, I keep your messenger that I may say 'Thank you' and 'God bless you.' The roses are summer indeed, and for the kind thought that prompted the present which makes my journey easy instead of hard. You know how I bless you for such love, Always yours, Edw. E. Hale."[30] They spent several days together in April and May rearranging the book cases in his study and Hattie also worked on revising the old parish register. Before he sailed for Europe, Edward gave her one of the ten copies of *Ten Times One is Ten* intended for "the Ten persons nearest me in the work & pleasure of Life."[31]

To contemporary eyes, the older Edward Hale seems an unlikely object of romantic love. Although tall, slim, upright, and even handsome into his forties, his looks coarsened with age, becoming heavy set and stoop shouldered by his sixties. He was notoriously careless about his appearance—his large, domed head, canny eyes set deep in a tanned and deeply wrinkled face framed by a shaggy beard and unkempt hair that he often cut himself, shapeless clerical black attire, and favorite slouch hat made him an eccentric and picturesque figure, a veritable sage. But his personal magnetism, enthusiasm, humor, and charm inspired extraordinary devotion from those who worked and worshipped with him, and elicited comments from all who met him. In the pulpit and on the rostrum, his deep, gravelly voice was sonorous, but in conversation it was gentle. His kindness was legendary, and Hattie was captivated by the intense interest he took in her life and aspirations. Her feelings were strongly tinged with adulation for this by now nationally celebrated older man whose multifarious activities and friendships at the highest level of politics, religion, and culture began to seem more appropriate for a secretary of state than a Boston clergyman.

Always irritated by dullness or pretentiousness, Edward was, as he admitted in his letters, frankly bored by his wife Emily's preference for conventional, gossiping friends and relatives, particularly after their talented and lively children began leaving home. For someone whose own mother balanced intellectual engagement and a large family with admirable finesse, Edward was increasingly disheartened by his wife's weakness, her perennial illnesses, her lack of intellectual curiosity, and her increasing incompetence in running their two houses. In Emily's defense, she had been the privileged and protected daughter of a successful Hartford lawyer,

A cabinet photograph by James Notman shows Edward Hale as his writings and leadership in social reform were bringing him national fame in the 1880s. Hattie had photographic prints made of virtually every image of her "great man" and these are now archived with the rest of her copious documentation of his life and achievements.
Harriet E. Freeman Papers, bMS 273, Andover-Harvard Theological Library, Harvard Divinity School.

with many suitors. Her marriage to Edward was evidently a love match but it produced too many children and she had to manage on a clergyman's income a household which often included his unmarried siblings, members of her own army of relatives, and constant visitors. Besides, her domineering and demanding husband insisted on efficient servants and well-prepared food (his morning coffee had to be prepared "just so") while his arrivals and departures were always unpredictable. Exhausted and overwhelmed, Emily was a semi-invalid for at least the last thirty years of her life. To outsiders, the Hales' marriage of more than thirty years appeared serene: with her patrician white hair, impeccable matronly attire, soft voice, and flawless manners, Emily seemed the perfect foil for the hearty, humorous cleric. But, despite their devotion to their children, they had become in many ways an ill-suited couple.

And so Edward was drawn to this spirited younger woman, an amateur scientist who was physically and intellectually adventurous in the mold of his own enterprising family. She was a devoted disciple of his philosophy of worship and social reform and, moreover, she adored him. Edward's vigor into his late seventies was constantly remarked upon. Like Edward, Hattie was irritated by vacuous talk; she despised the vapidity, gabbiness, and lack of energy of many women of her class. "You know how little I care for women's ordinary talk & how much I care for the talk of men who know a great deal or who have had a wide & large experience," Hattie wrote a few years later.[32] But the tone of their correspondence was still not much different from the way he wrote to other members of his staff, including his regular amanuensis (the nineteenth-century term for secretary) Mary Edes.

From Madrid in early June, Edward replied to a letter from Hattie, "Twenty times since we came into Spain have I been tempted to write to you. There is so much that will interest and amuse you when you come: for come I am sure you will." After describing their visit to the Alhambra and other historic cultural sites, he wrote, "It was just like your own energetic and thoughtful kindness to send off the circulars to the Ten Times One people. What the great cause of 10 x 1 needs is a little fanaticism. We must not be too calm and reasonable in re-making the world."[33] A letter he wrote from Matunuck in September was still more businesslike than personal: "I have material enough for our September Circular, and I would send it to Rand & Avery, if I did not think you had some notes to add. If you have will you mail them to me here, if you can send by your Wednesday mail, or to Roxbury afterwards." He concluded with an invitation to the annual Unitarian conference that showed Hattie remained well within the bounds of his church family: "Come to Saratoga. Emily & I will take care of you." Indeed, the inscription he wrote in the copy of *In His Name* that he gave her for her birthday the following March betrayed no overtly romantic feelings.[34]

In the meantime, Hattie's Uncle Elisha Atkins and cousin Edwin Atkins were making money hand over fist, with even more prosperous times to come as they became the largest American property holders in Cuba. They had weathered very difficult times for Cuban planters due to increased competition from sugar beet, economic hardship due to the Ten Years War (an unsuccessful revolt against Spanish rule, 1868-1878), the abolition of slavery in Cuba slated to become final in 1886, and the need to borrow capital to update machinery. The Atkins Company began giving credit to many of the Cuban planters and mill-owners, taking control of properties by foreclosure and incorporating many of them into the largest, the Soledad plantation in Cienfuegos. Here Edwin Atkins built his modern *central*, or sugar factory. It is probable that their various land deals, many of which were completed before emancipation in 1886, made the Atkinses major slave holders. In a letter to his wife in January 1882, Edwin described an inspection trip he made to Soledad: "Imagine me in the centre of a crowd of over two hundred negroes, each of whom kneeled down on passing me, saying 'Your blessing, Master' and then formed into a line. They were all the way from two years old to one hundred. I was very glad to see how contented they were, as it was quite the contrary last year, when [Ramon] Torriente and I first came to the estate." He was referring to the dreadful condition of the slaves when he first visited the estate after he took it over and the major improvements he had already made to improve their wellbeing.[35]

But in November, 1999, an Atkins descendant, former U.S. Congressman Chet Atkins, led a family party for the extended family's first return to Cuba and to Soledad since it was nationalized by

Fidel Castro in 1961. For Chet Atkins at least, it was a confrontation with the realities of their ancestor's often ruthless business practices, particularly his handling of recently emancipated slaves on his property: "The Boston Unitarian didn't free his slaves until the last possible moment, because they were an asset on his books, and he [Edwin Atkins] wanted to be able to depreciate the asset," he told June C. Erlick, author of a comprehensive article about this Cuban trip and Atkins family history, who was at the time publications director at Harvard's David Rockefeller Center for Latin American Studies.[36]

In 1884, the year that he took official title to Soledad, Edwin Atkins made his first effort at influence in Washington and New York, meeting Secretary of State James G. Blaine at the Atkins Company offices in Boston when Blaine visited Atkins's father Elisha to discuss railroad business. Edwin made the argument to Blaine that reciprocity with Spain for Cuban sugar would open up extensive markets for U.S. exports. The Atkins Company had bought the Bay State Sugar Refinery Company in 1878, which they sold to Henry Havemeyer's Sugar Trust in 1892. The trust controlled 85 percent of the sugar business in the United States.[37]

Obviously, as Hattie's close relations increased their wealth and social stature, the fact that their daughter and niece was embarked on an illicit relationship with a married minister, whose wife and children they knew well, would have been considered reprehensible. As long as Hattie's father lived and her companion Mary Cobb accompanied her on her travels, she was protected from gossip. The considerable time she spent assisting her minister was all in a good cause. But whatever the state of Hattie's relationship with Edward was then or later, his family always came first, and Hattie seems to have accepted that.

On April 26, 1883, the Hales received a heart-stopping telegram to tell them that their beloved Nelly, who had stayed on in Paris to complete her art studies, was desperately ill with typhoid. In a fever of anxiety about her, they boarded the first available ship in Boston accompanied by faithful Judith Andrews. On the Atlantic voyage, Edward found he was missing Hattie and concluded a brief note to her written on board ship and postmarked in Ireland, "With all love always."[38] The Hales arrived in Paris on May 12 to find, to their great relief, that Nelly had passed the crisis, although she was still bedridden after four weeks of illness.

Early in June, Edward, Emily, and Nelly moved out to the leafy suburb of Saint-Germain-en-Laye for Nelly's convalescence. Edward, who had encouraged Hattie to study botany, wrote that he was enjoying walking in the great royal forest of Saint Germain and collecting wildflowers. In Paris, he had visited the Jardin des Plantes, "where, by the way, you will some day enter yourself as a student…But by this time, I imagine you establishing yourself at Pepperell," he remembered. "Pray try to arrange some time when you can come to Matunuck. Nelly improves so fast that she walked with me 15 minutes this morning." He concluded with further reference to their work together: "I advanced a good deal your & my studies on Drake, Magellan and the other discoveries and before many days I shall send to Alden for Harper, the fruit of the Pacific Ocean papers. To say the truth they ought all to be written on this side the ocean. The material is much more here than it is with you."[39] It seems that Hattie was now helping Edward with research. At the end of the month, the Hales sailed home to spend the summer in Matunuck with Susan Hale and the four youngest boys.

A brief letter Edward wrote from Matunuck to Hattie in Pepperell on July 20, 1883, makes reference to Hattie having been at Annisquam, a clue that she was studying marine biology that summer with Alpheus Hyatt (1838-1902), curator of the Museum of the Boston Society of Natural History and another life-changing mentor in her life. That year, perhaps at Hyatt's suggestion, she became an original subscriber to *Science,* along with leading Boston scientists, businessmen, physicians, and clergy, but very few women. Many of Hale's well-connected friends were behind the new science magazine: Daniel Coit Gilman, president of Johns Hopkins University and brother of Emily Hale's brother-in-law, as well as Alexander Graham Bell and Gardiner Greene Hubbard. Hattie was listed along with about fifteen other women, including Abby May and Lucretia Crocker, in the section of private Boston individuals. Most of the scientists Hattie and Edward knew at Harvard and Boston Tech were listed but only two ministers, James Freeman Clarke and Minot Savage. Hale was not listed.

Hyatt had been a student of paleontologist Louis Agassiz but the great scientist's reactionary position on evolution became intolerable to his most brilliant students. In May 1870, Hyatt was elected custodian of the Boston Society of Natural History and, in 1881, he became its curator. The same year he joined the BSNH, Hyatt organized the Teachers' School of Science where he gave courses of lectures on biology to the public school teachers of Boston. Between 1870 and 1902, when Hyatt died, more than 1,200 school teachers attended his lectures and those of other natural historians, such as geologists William O. Crosby and George Barton of the Boston Technical Institute, where Hyatt was also a professor. The Boston Society of Natural History, the Boston Tech, and the Teachers' School of Science became Hattie's intellectual homes where she attended lectures and formed many friendships with the staff, faculties, and her fellow students.

Although there are no letters or records to prove it, Hattie may have begun her studies with Hyatt during the late 1870s when women were first admitted to membership in the BSNH. In 1879, under the auspices of the Women's Education Association of Boston, Hyatt established a summer laboratory for the study of marine zoology at his country place at Annisquam, on the Massachusetts coast near Gloucester. After a few years, the Annisquam project was abandoned and the lab removed in 1888 to Woods Hole on Cape Cod as a permanent seaside summer school for teachers and researchers. The Woods Hole Marine Biological Laboratory was again initiated by the Women's Education Association, of which Hattie was certainly a member. Hyatt was the first president of the WHMBL's board of trustees while Hattie was a member of the Woods Hole Corporation, or general board, and reliable donor for twenty years from 1887.[40]

Hyatt's productive period began immediately after the publication of Darwin's *Origin of Species* and ended just before the rediscovery of Gregor Mendel's law of heredity; thus he was one of the leaders in the active discussion of evolution during that speculative period. Differing theories of evolution always fascinated Hattie and she liked to discuss these ideas with Edward in her letters. She had undoubtedly imbibed the views of British polymath Herbert Spencer who spent much of his career exploring the ramifications of the view "that the Universe and all things in it have reached their present forms through successive stages physically necessitated." Spencer's assault on the Christian world view was popularized in America by his disciple Edward L. Youmans who became, in 1872, the founding editor of *Popular Science Monthly*. Hattie would have been steeped in Spencer's theories in the pages of this magazine. Unfortunately, Hattie, like too many others interested in the pseudoscientific theory of eugenics as it evolved in the late nineteenth century, came to subscribe to a malign twisting of Darwin's phrase "survival of the fittest," which was actually coined by his friend Herbert Spencer.[41]

Another self-proclaimed disciple of Spencer in America was freelance writer and lecturer John Fiske. Hattie was so enthusiastic about Fiske's book *Destiny of Man Viewed in the Light of his Origin* (1884) that she gave a copy to Edward to read and discuss with her. Fiske, who was primarily a historian (and an expounder of Manifest Destiny), had applied himself to the philosophical interpretation of Charles Darwin's work. Edward devoured the book on a train trip to Washington, telling Hattie, "There, briefly, is the Religion you have heard me preaching almost since you can remember. See how clearly it fits in with Mr. Fiske's philosophy."[42] In March 1888, Hattie gave Edward the first volume of Darwin's *Origin of Species*, and in other letters she would bring to his attention the contrast between Agassiz's theory of creation and Lamarck's theory of evolution (to which Alpheus Hyatt subscribed) as well as the face-off between Agassiz and Asa Gray over Darwin's theory.

Swiss born zoologist and paleontologist Louis Agassiz (1807–1873), student of French naturalist and zoologist Georges Cuvier and famous for his groundbreaking works on marine fossils and the effect of glacial movements and deposits, came to America in 1846. As professor of zoology and geology at Harvard College, he established the university's Museum of Comparative Zoology and influenced a generation of American scientists with his emphasis on studying science directly from nature. Despite his own evidences for evolution described in his famous "Essay on Classification," Agassiz opposed Darwinism and believed that new species could arise only through the intervention of God. He debated bitterly with Harvard's Asa Gray over the theory of evolution.

* * *

Hattie was always happiest in the mountains and in early October 1883, writing to her at Pepperell, Edward told her he had seen her letter to his secretary, Mary Edes, in which she described her hiking trip in the Adirondacks. This was probably made with the Appalachian Mountain Club, of which she became a member in 1879, the earliest it was possible for women to do so. From now on, she took frequent trips with parties of club members. "Is there anything like the open-air?" Edward now asked her, before telling her that the Sunday school was about to reopen and he had resumed his duties as preacher to the 800 Harvard undergraduates: "But it seems as if I were never to see you again," he wrote, "I tried the door-bell at 37 one day, thinking some stray person might be there. But there was never a reply." He concluded this letter, "Give my love to your father, and to Miss Cobb if she is with you. And do write a line sometimes. Ever Yrs. E. E. Hale."[43]

When Hattie did return to Union Park in November, their pent-up longing to see each other blossomed into a new intimacy.

4

Romantic Love

As Edward traveled across Wisconsin in January 1884 toward his next engagement in Madison, his mind was on his youthful assistant who had come to mean so much to him. His writing made even more difficult to read than usual by the shaking of the train, he told her how much he had enjoyed finding her letters at his various stops on his western tour. This was his fourth and final year as chairman of the National Unitarian Conference, and he had traveled west in yet another attempt to persuade the ministers of the radical Western Unitarian Conference back into the Boston-based American Unitarian Association fold. Edward Hale and the leaders of the Western radicals, most particularly the dynamic Welsh-born Reverend Jenkin Lloyd Jones of Chicago's All Souls Unitarian Church, were discussing the possibility of founding a new school "for a broad catholic study of religion and its application to life."[1]

There is nothing in the tone of Edward's January letters to indicate that he and Hattie were now in love, even as his journal records the astonishing amount of time they were spending together. Following his return to Boston, they took advantage of Emily's two-week absence visiting her relations in Hartford to enjoy shared interests together, including visiting the "Horticultural and Bird Shows" one evening. But on March 7, in a letter to Hattie hand-delivered to Union Park, Edward made an astonishing declaration when recalling the first time he called on the Freeman family in the fall of 1863: "How little I knew that the one daughter was to be mine own," he wrote possessively.[2] On Hattie's side, there are no surviving letters to confirm her feelings, but her gifts to Edward were becoming more munificent: for Christmas she had given him a fur tippet and for his sixty-second birthday on April 3, she gave him a silver bowl. Edward concluded his letter of thanks for the bowl, "Always yrs with ever so much love EEH."[3]

Before Edward left in mid-May for another Western trip to Cleveland and Chicago, he and Hattie were together at least every other day. From Illinois, Edward replied to her last letter received at church before he left. "You give me more than I can send you," he wrote, "for you send me life, and youth and insight, and I only tell you facts: which is not a fair exchange." He compared their correspondence to that between Johann Wolfgang von Goethe (1749-1832) and Bettina von Arnim, a twenty-two-year-old woman who had developed a passion for the fifty-eight-year-old genius of modern German literature. Goethe, wrote Edward, "let this fresh wide awake girl write to him from a young woman's fresh insight, and fill up his old tank, while he gave nothing back to her. Such a letter as yours last night is of just that sort, and I write back to you that I enjoyed it, and am well, and am prospering, and I do not, as I ought unfold any of the mysteries to you."[4] The question of who got most out of their relationship would arise again and again in their letters over the next twenty-five years. Certainly, Edward delighted in Hattie's scientific studies. In late May, he spent two evenings at her house as she and other science-minded friends attempted to view the stars through her new telescope, although foiled by cloud cover.

By mid-June, with her father absent from home in Coney Island, where he was undergoing treatment for an unspecified mental affliction, most of his own family now at Matunuck, and Emily due to visit her Beecher relatives with her mother, both Hattie and Edward were in high anticipation of his visit to her in Pepperell. Astonishingly, he entered a quite full account of his three-day visit in his journal, even naming his hostess.[5] It was during this visit that Edward apparently kissed his assistant for the first time and gave her a ring which she cherished for many years until she lost it. According to Edward's memory eight years later of those seminal days together, they swore undying friendship, love, and support for each other and promised that neither would ever cause the other harm. In Edward's position as a minister and a married man and in a society ("Proper Boston") that placed the highest value on respectability, trust had to be at the basis of their changed relationship. While he would tell Hattie innumerable times over the years how much he wished he could spend more of his life with her, he never mentioned in the letters the option of divorcing his wife and giving up his profession to marry her (although he now began toying with the idea of retiring to spend more time writing and in the outdoors with her).

On June 20, Emily Hale wrote one of her cramped letters (she had a habit of using small folded sheets and filling up every available space, making her afterthoughts hard to read) to her husband from Peekskill, New York. She was staying with her mother Mary Perkins at Boscobel, the Henry Ward Beechers' opulent mansion and estate overlooking the Hudson River. It is clear from her opening comment that she was used to Edward, whom she called "Papa," disappearing off without giving clear indications of his intended whereabouts: "Your long letter from Matunuck made me feel as if I had found you again. You seemed to have gone off into infinite space that Thursday morning."[6] Emily surely could not have guessed at that point that her vigorous husband was beginning to wander down the same adulterous path that her Uncle Henry followed so disastrously fifteen years earlier.

The now illicit couple's letters began flying between their summer houses. The reason Hattie's letters are missing for the first five years of their affair is clear in the opening to Edward's first letter from Matunuck: "I got your nice letter Wednesday. I read it again and again, and then, as bidden, tore it up and put it in the fire: which was hard on me." Suffering from a complex about her limited education in the humanities at this stage of her life, Hattie had evidently told Edward that she felt "ignorant" in comparison to him, for he replied at length, making it clear how much he admired her many accomplishments and interests:

> If I were to say in New-York, that a Boston friend of mine played and sang so well that she could lead the Sunday School on occasion and could always play Beethoven to a friend who was tired, that she was so much interested in geology that she was the personal friend of the most

> distinguished men we have in that line, that she had made some study of entomology and that her drawings of moths and caterpillars were accurate enough to be of scientific value, that her English was so good, and her use of it so accurate that literary men liked to secure her service as an amanuensis because printers would then be sure about their copy, do you think those people would ask me whether this young woman knew when Lessing was born?

He did not mention her knowledge of botany, presumably because he still considered her to be his pupil in that subject.[7] Eighteen years later, Edward would accurately describe Hattie as "a highly educated woman."

On July 1, Emily wrote from Peekskill that her Uncle Henry was looking forward to seeing Edward and that Hattie Beecher, Henry's daughter-in-law, had told her that Beecher would tell Edward "things which prove that Blaine is a dishonorable man and why he's so disliked in New York."[8] Beecher had annoyed his parishioners at Brooklyn's Plymouth Church by refusing to support James G. Blaine, the anti-patronage Republican candidate for the presidency. Instead, Beecher defiantly threw his weight behind the Democratic nominee, Governor Grover Cleveland of New York, apparently relating the attacks against Cleveland for having fathered a child out of wedlock as a young man to his own experiences a decade earlier. At one point, he even shouted, "If every man in New York State tonight who has broken the seventh commandment voted for Cleveland, he would be elected by a 200,000 majority!" Beecher became manic in his defense of Cleveland's morality, which, according to one biographer, further convinced his critics of his own guilt, even as he himself chose to view Cleveland's election in November 1884 as a personal vindication.[9]

The Hales, as staunch Whigs and then Republicans, were dismayed, and presumably Edward was discomfited, by the reemergence of questions about his uncle-in-law's moral hypocrisy. Although Edward remained loyal to Blaine, Beecher's distaste for "the plumed knight" was shared by many Boston Brahmins. For example, James Freeman Clarke, horrified by widely publicized evidence of Blaine's guilt in the Crédit Mobilier scandal, swung his support from the Republican candidate to Cleveland. When Clarke and more of Edward's friends switched party, Edward was extremely upset.[10]

With Emily still absent in Peekskill, and perhaps even if she had been there, the Matunuck commissary was not up to the standard that the exacting paterfamilias expected. In early July, he caustically referred to the unimaginative food being served daily in the Red House: "We may come to the dinner hour without knowing what we are to eat. There is always ham in the house, and dried beef, but after you have had these three days, you do not hanker for them on the 4th. Yesterday, I brought in two blue fish and two lobsters in triumph, just as they were beginning to fry the ham."[11] The same day, Emily wrote again from Peekskill where she was nursing her usual variety of minor ailments: "I shall finish my fortnight on Friday and I know I must be needed at home. I am afraid of Nelly's getting tired out with the children and with Lucretia. I feel quite lazy at present from your accounts of everything. I have seen my old friend Dr. Tilden who is visiting mother, and he gave me some pills and advised me to drink buttermilk…And I also eat cracked wheat and do exercises…But my face ache has changed to a dead tooth, the other side of my mouth and was pretty bad for one day."[12] A medical specialist today might retroactively suggest a cause of Emily's ever changing array of symptoms. Was it an autoimmune disease, chronic fatigue syndrome, or acute hypochondria? Whatever it was, it was evidently very real to her.

It had become obvious that the perpetually malingering and often absent Emily could no longer cope with running two houses. The following year, Edward decided to remove the burden of housekeeping from his wife, turning those duties in the Roxbury house over to the always conscientious Nelly when she returned from an eight-month resumption of her art studies in Paris, and putting his sister Susan in charge of the Matunuck house. From 1885 until her health began to fail shortly before her death in 1910, Susan ran the summer house as a private hotel for the Hale family and a roster of friends, all of whom were charged for their stays. From then on, Emily appeared even less frequently at Matunuck.

Writing to Hattie on July 10 from Brunswick, Maine, where he had given a lecture on American leadership, Edward told her how much she was on his mind: "I am always on the edge of saying 'Hatty says this, or Miss Freeman thinks that,' and then I stop myself, or coolly take the suggestion for my own."[13] From Brunswick, he planned to "cross over" to Peekskill to see Henry Ward Beecher, a prospect that cannot have given him much pleasure in view of Beecher's outspoken and embarrassing endorsement of Grover Cleveland and attacks on Edward's good friend Blaine. But it must have been a brief visit for, by July 12, Edward was in Coney Island to give his annual sermon at Manhattan Beach. While he was there, he called on William Freeman. Hattie's brother Frederick had asked Edward if he would give him and Hattie an assessment of the progress of their father's medical treatment.

Fred Freeman, a charming and athletic young man who was educated at Chauncy Hall, a prestigious private high school in Boston, and then apprenticed to his father's business as a clerk, had married Harriet Mower Clark very young and was already the father of three young children (seven-year-old Carrie, four-year-old Frank, and three-year-old Ethel, who was Edward's goddaughter) with another baby due in November. The lively Freeman family lived in the Boston suburb of West Newton and Fred was now paymaster for the Waltham Watch Company in Watertown. The fact that Fred Freeman asked Edward to make this call indicates that he was finding his father as difficult to get along with as was Hattie.

It seems that William Freeman had suffered a grievous head injury in a carriage accident which had left him in constant pain and dramatically altered his temperament so that he was now depressed, unpredictable, indecisive, and even verbally abusive. Edward was accustomed to providing similarly delicate interventions for his parishioners, demands which were beginning to exhaust him. But the Freemans had always been more than kind and generous to their minister and Edward was only too aware of the effect of William Freeman's erratic behavior on Hattie. On July 14, he passed on his impressions to Hattie: "I have just finished a letter to your brother about your father…whom I saw yesterday. I will not go over the ground again, because I shall ask Fred to shew it to you, further than to say, that your father really seems to me better and to enjoy life more, and I have told him so: also, that so far as you can say he has any wish, it is to stay at Brooklyn, and that I should think he had better stay. Clearly enough he wishes that some one else would decide this for him, but that is a part of the disease."[14]

Telling Hattie that her father wanted her and her friend Etta Pierce to join him at Coney Island for two weeks, Edward strongly advised against it ("I have some right to take care of you") and Hattie stayed on at Pepperell.

Edward's letters to Hattie from Matunuck that summer were among the most romantic and poetic he wrote, and he thought of her constantly. He strove to explain his passion for the surrounding South County countryside, particularly the glaciated freshwater pond immediately behind the house, on which the Hales kept several boats. In many of his letters, he described his early morning paddle across the pond in a canoe, imagining Hattie sitting in the prow. He delighted in sharing with her his botanical discoveries, which he examined under his microscope, although he complained that it was an awkward procedure since he had to constantly adjust both specimen and microscope while needing to put on and remove his glasses (Hattie soon gave him a new microscope). She in turn sent him reports and drawings of her own botanical finds and answered his questions. Each time they compared notes on different samples, they referred each other to the bible of botanizing, Asa Gray's *Manual of the Botany of the Northern United States*, called simply "the Manual." Both Edward and Hattie were part of Gray's web of amateur botanist correspondents on whom he relied to supply him with samples of plants for his herbarium until his death in 1888.[15] Although it was Edward who suggested that Hattie take up botany, a pursuit he had enjoyed as a child with his parents and siblings and which he still shared with his sister Susan but not with his wife or children, Hattie's mother was a talented amateur botanical illustrator and must have taught those skills to her daughter. An excellent and diligent student, Hattie's knowledge already exceeded Edward's. But their botanical back and forth served to strengthen their bond.

Edward now began looking forward to a trip to Boston in late July to see and work with Hattie. He stayed with Judith Andrews in her house on Rutland Square for four nights from Saturday, July 26. With the Union Park house closed up for the summer, Hattie presumably also stayed with her colleague, good friend, and surrogate mother, whom she called "Marmee." After he and Hattie spent most of three days together, according to Edward's diary, he returned to Matunuck.[16] Again, it is astonishing to see how open Edward was in recording his meetings with Hattie but presumably he felt that no one would find anything strange in his meeting his longtime volunteer staffer and secretary for work. Perhaps only Judith Andrews was beginning to suspect there was more between them. In later years, she was to become a willing intermediary and enabler.

The morning after his return to Matunuck, Edward was already longing for his soul mate. "If I only had you here, I would take you across the pond, and make you go to the little pond, and then you should go in and get the pond-lilies while I advised serenely on the shore! And I wonder if you swim well. I teach them all to swim." Returning from his row one morning, he waxed his most poetic: "If I had had you [with me] I would have shewn you the loveliest world of webs in the grass dotted all over with fog beads. I would have shewn you azalea and wild roses and milk weed just peering through the fog on the sides of the pond, I would have shewn you the loveliest mysterious vista between the trees, down on the other pond, and I would have made you guess out the mysterious form of my old Indian, who is a vague strange shaped maple, of different colour from the trees around him."[17]

Edward was always most involved with his children during their vigorous summers together at Matunuck. He had asked all of them (the oldest sons, Arthur and Jack, were not there at the time) to join him in penning verses to celebrate the seventy-fifth birthday on August 29 of his old friend, the writer Dr. Oliver Wendell Holmes, but they were all too busy: "Nelly works her flesh off her bones. Phil is drawing his specimen drawing for admission to the Art-School in New-York. Berty has been building a catamaran. Bob with them is coaching Seth for the Latin school, and is the favorite model of both the artists. Throw in swimming every day, running two miles a day to keep up their muscle, and so on and so on, and you see there is no great room for verses."[18]

Edward's characterizations of two of his sons seem on the mark in light of their subsequent lives. Of Rob, or Bob, the youngest son, adored by the entire family, he wrote on the boy's fifteenth birthday on September 5: "He is a charming boy…I have never known him do or say a hateful thing. And when you wrote of sinlessness, I think I thought of him immediately. He would never say so. He governs himself with a very hard hand…I stopped just there to give him his 15 kisses, and I told him that he had never given me a moment's anxiety since he was born. Some day you must know all these boys better. That will be when you make a visit here."[19]

But the increasingly covert nature of their relationship made it unlikely that she would ever spend time vacationing with Edward's sons.

Bertie, the second youngest son, was to begin his freshman year at Harvard at the end of September: "Poor dear Berty," wrote his fond but often worried father on the eve of his athletic, carefree son's departure for Cambridge, "He is nothing but a child, and sometimes it seems to me that he will never be a man. Literally there is nothing he cannot do, and yet he seems to be as indifferent to achievement as the most unambitious dolt…He lives absolutely in the present, without imagination, and almost without plan. He is happy and will enjoy College Life, but it is hard to say whether it is worth any sacrifice to send him there. Eh bien! Nous verrons!"[20] The following summer, when the Hales received Bertie's first Harvard grades, which were abysmal, Edward could not contain his anger and disappointment. Apparently, Bertie, the ugliest but most convivial and amusing of the Hales' sons, had discovered partying in addition to his rowing. But Bertie would buckle down to his studies once he made up his mind to be an architect.

Both Edward and Hattie were extremely upset when they got their wires crossed about where they could next meet. In late August, he waited for her all day in the Public Library but she was expecting him at Pepperell. "My poor dear little darling girl: I have your sad letter," he wrote in response to her misery, "and tho' I had been dreading it, it grieves me more than I can tell you. I cannot bear to go back over the ifs and buts of those two days…I ought to have telegraphed Thursday night."[21] Now he wrote, "I really think the best thing will be for you to name some day between Sept. 11 and Sept. 22 for me to spend at Pepperell, and for you to be persuaded to go with our party to Saratoga on the 22nd of September. I shall probably dictate half of the Council Report to you. Perhaps you can be in Union Park on the 12th or the 13th."[22] This was to be his last report as chairman of the Council of the National Unitarian Conference in Saratoga.

At this stage, Edward seemed to have no trouble compartmentalizing his private and working relationships with Hattie. With the summer drawing to a close, he refocused on work—national, parochial, and literary. He told Hattie that he had written a long letter to Judith Andrews "about neighborhood Jewish work…I copied for her (having no staff) a list of one hundred and fifty families who live within a short half mile of the church…What I want to do is to try to create a 'neighborhood' feeling among these people." He then described his plans for drawing them in.[23] On September 1, he sent Hattie a sketch showing how he would like to extend, rearrange, and furnish his study at the church, with four staff members facing each other across two desks: "At each ten feet we will have a double writing table, and in each alcove a supplementary desk."[24]

A few days later, the gregarious and easily distracted minister exhorted, "Now you must help me this winter not to dabble in everything but to stick to my simple duty which is to consolidate the parish around our Church. And I must have time enough for solid writing…I mean to be at the office at church with the bale wire slipped off a great deal, and to make the place pleasant to stay in, so that I shall not rush off at the first moment. Do you know I think I am a good deal like one of those great buzzing flies, rushing madly round all the time, and wasting no end of face on what proves to be nothing at all." And yet, in the very same letter, he told her he was contemplating retiring soon: "If the Insurance comes all right (and the wretches do not write to me) I shall feel at liberty next spring to resign. And some things tempt me to do so. But this I say to nobody but to you."[25]

Emily was adamantly against Edward's talk of retirement, at least partly out of her fear of the increased financial insecurity at a time when they were still educating their youngest sons. On October 15, she wrote Edward from Matunuck where she was enjoying a restful fall visit (she would not have known that Edward had been trying to persuade Hattie to join him at Matunuck that month).

Emily worried that her husband had too much on his plate and wondered if he could give up half of his parish work to a colleague. Aware of her husband's restlessly ambitious nature, she reminded him that "Mr. Clarke [James Freeman Clarke] is ten years older than you, and yet in regular work and I know you have always felt about other people that their power and influence were much diminished by being unsettled, even if it had been by their own wish. And that they often lamented it afterwards." She felt that he had forgotten this drawback in his longing for relief. She urged him, as she had done before, to give up everything except parish duties. And then she made a plea which seems pitiful in light of Edward's growing wish to spend time and find relaxation with Hattie. "Don't any more look on your home as a place to be avoided, because you cannot rest there," she begged him. "You might find it a real resting place, if you only would…could be spared to." "I know what a burden the parish visits are," she concluded, "but if you are not pulled in a thousand other directions, and can make them your great duty, you would actually enjoy them."[26]

Emily's argument for her husband to restrict his activities to his parish work from now on can be contrasted with the distaste for parish calls which he expressed to Hattie a few weeks earlier in the context of Emily dragging him around to make their farewells in the Matunuck area. It also shows how Hattie sweetened those calls: "Now as you know I am not over-fond of making calls except on the elect. The way I like to do it is to have a nice girl come for me, scold me if I deserve scolding, but, in general encourage me, and, after we have made the first call, recollect that she has a mountain or an Oak tree about seven miles off which is much more important to be seen on that particular day than any calls to be made."[27] The "elect" in Edward's eyes were his most devoted and hardworking staff, the majority of whom were women.

That year, Edward had begun corresponding with Francis G. Peabody, a young professor in the Harvard Divinity School, about the possibility of joining him as associate minister. But Peabody declined the offer of serving under Hale on account of health problems.[28] He remained at the Harvard seminary, becoming the first professor of social ethics there and then dean, and was a close friend of Edward for the rest of the older man's life. Two years later, one of the Reverend Peabody's students, another Edward Hale but no relation, agreed after much persuasion by Peabody and Edward E. to join him at the SCC as associate minister. The younger Hale lifted much of the burden of parish duties off Edward's shoulders and the talk of retiring was not raised for another ten years.

As the church season began, Edward became more concerned about secrecy. After all, Hattie's father was with her at Pepperell and he had a tendency to open her letters. There would be several more weeks of letters before Hattie returned to Boston in early November. From Saratoga, where he was presiding over the Eleventh National Unitarian Conference, Edward wrote, "You make wonderful progress in short hand. You have conquered four of the most important signs and there are but about forty. Suppose you try a few more."[29] This was the first indication that Edward was teaching Hattie an arcane shorthand so that they could be secure in expressing their most intimate thoughts and feelings in their letters.

Edward soon made it clear why he had chosen this particular phonetic shorthand to conceal the reality of his and Hattie's changed relationship. The shorthand had been invented by an Englishman, Thomas Towndrow, who published a textbook of its symbols and rules in 1832. In the mid-1830s, he taught his shorthand to students such as the Hale brothers in Boston before moving to New York in 1838. But with the introduction to the United States in the 1860s of Isaac Pitman's far simpler and faster shorthand, "Towndrow's terrible shorthand," as Edward later called it, was soon forgotten. "My two brothers could read it," Edward told Hattie, "but I now know no one who can. I have written the same thing twice, once in long hand once in short hand, so you will see how to join the letters." Two days later, he wrote, "I am trying to find my old guide to short-hand. But all those books have mysteriously disappeared," signing off "*<you know I love you always>*. You will get used to those symbols."[30]

As Edward was leading a willing Hattie into a web of secrecy and deceit, his wife had written nervously to ask him if her widowed old mother, Mary Perkins, could come and live with them that winter since Mrs. Perkins' caregiver in Hartford, her daughter-in-law Lucy, was suffering from paralysis.[31] Mary Perkins, a sister of the scandalous womanizer Henry Ward Beecher, was no fool and Edward knew it.

Edward was far from retiring, either from his church or his involvement in civic affairs. On December 10, 1884, Hugh O'Brien, riding the Democratic wave that swept Grover Cleveland into the White House, was elected Boston's first Irish-born Catholic mayor. O'Brien, a successful businessman who had emigrated to America as a child with his parents in the early 1830s, proved to be an admirable steward of the city's fortunes: he lowered taxes, widened streets, established a commission that hired Frederick Law Olmsted to design the Emerald Necklace park system, and built the new Boston Public Library on Copley Square. But his election confirmed the longstanding Yankee fear that Irish Catholics, who by 1885 comprised 40 percent of Boston's population, outnumbering native-born Protestants, would take political control of their city. In fact there was now a landslide of control of other Massachusetts city and town governments to Irish Democrats and from now on the system of Irish neighborhood bosses blossomed.

Yankee upper class domination was threatened not only in local government but also in the Boston public school system. After decades of humiliation inflicted on Irish Catholic children by old stock Protestant teachers in the public schools, the Catholic Church had already begun an aggressive push to establish parochial schools.[32] A solution seemed to be to ramp up the education of recently arrived immigrants in the Yankee mold. Edward's friend Edwin Mead had already inaugurated the year before a program for educating children of Boston's immigrant-dominated North End. And in 1889, the Massachusetts Society for Promoting Good Citizenship was launched with Edward Everett Hale as president.[33] This was in addition to his increased leadership in charitable and reform enterprises.

Always giving out to others himself, Edward needed a woman's support and empathy and Hattie was only too happy to provide both, and much more, once she returned to Union Park in November. But, in December 1884, Emily chose to take yet another rest cure with her Perkins relations, this time in New Haven. Moreover, she had left her tiresome, strong-willed mother at home with Edward

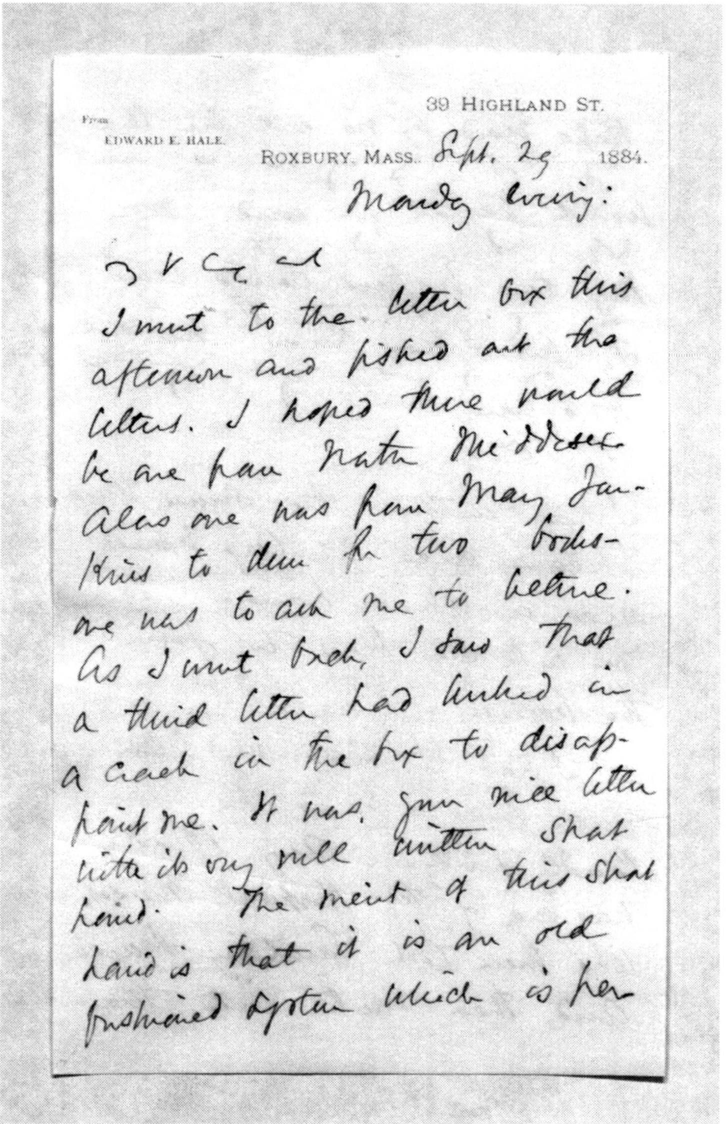

From
EDWARD E. HALE.

39 HIGHLAND ST.
ROXBURY, MASS. Sept. 29 1884.

Monday evening:

I went to the letter box this afternoon and fished out the letters. I hoped there would be one from Nathan Middlesex. Alas one was from Mary Jenkins to dun for two books. One was to ask me to lecture. As I went back, I saw that a third letter had lurked in a crack in the box to disappoint me. It was your nice letter written in very well written short hand. The merit of this short hand is that it is an old fashioned system which is her

Edward opened this letter with a rather paternal "<My dear little girl>." In fact, "my dear child" was his characteristic way of addressing all the women in his immediate circle. Even Hattie would become increasingly challenged by his difficult handwriting during the many years of their correspondence.

haps read by no one in the
world beside you and me.
My two brothers could read
it,—but I now know no one
who can.

I have written the same thing
twice—once in long hand
once in short hand—so
you will see how to join
the letters.

I had to read my letter
quick so as to go to the Amy
Bradly party. Amy Bradly
was one of the Hospital nurses,
who then took Sanitary service
and then went into the

Edward Everett Hale to Harriet E. Freeman, September 29, 1884.
Hale-Freeman special correspondence, Hale Family Papers, Manuscript Division, Library of Congress.

and Nelly. "I am really feeling better," she wrote, "and this is an excellent place for me. Tell mother that her hyosciamus, if that is the way to spell it, has really done me some good, in the way of calming me down, and I have slept till five o'clock, both nights." But four days later, she responded to his plea for her to return home: "Dear Papa, Your telegram has just come. And I have felt some doubts, but on the whole, I think I had better stay on here. They really want me to stay, and say I can help them."[34] Did Emily have any idea of the damaging effect that her frequent absences had on her relationship with her husband? But this was really a double standard. After all, Emily had put up with Edward's frequent and sometimes protracted absences for thirty years while struggling with their large brood.

Edward surely must have realized that his growing need for succor and support after all the years toiling for others had run him into direct conflict with his own declared principles. In 1881, three years before he and Hattie acknowledged their love but were already seeing a great deal of each other, Edward appears to have advocated in his sermon "The Unitarian Principles" (published by the American Unitarian Association) for "purity of life," which many would consider to be inimical to an extra-marital relationship. "From all these convictions," he wrote after describing them, "it follows as a matter of necessity that the Unitarian Church demands purity of character from those who belong to it. Strictly speaking, this is all that it demands. It asks for other things; but character is essential…Idle to preach the possible perfection of mankind, if the man who preach or the congregation who hear is satisfied with imperfection."[35]

But Edward never expressed any guilt to Hattie, at least in his surviving letters, nor did he ever use the word "adultery" in relation to his increasingly illicit involvement with her. His disarming charm and humor, his understanding of his own foibles and weaknesses, and nonjudgmental attitude toward human fallibility generally, makes it difficult to charge him with hypocrisy. But he was giving her the cliché justification for straying, telling her that she provided the essential ingredients that were missing in his long marriage, that she made it possible for him to bear all his responsibilities. As an example of his self-knowledge, while Hattie often seemed to pander to his vanity, encouraging him to boast about his successes, he briefly wondered the day after his return from the National Conference at Saratoga the previous September whether it was a crisis for himself and others that he had resigned from his Council chairmanship. His riposte was typical: "How little people know! I went to the front Monday night, because I was Chairman and had to welcome Stebbins & sit on the platform. Mrs. Frothingham, wife of one of our oldest ministers welcomed me, made room for me, and said 'My husband comes to the front because he is so deaf. Is that your reason?' It is a mighty good thing to be taught of how little account are your honours, such as they are."[36]

As Edward continued to think seriously about retiring from his ministerial duties to write fulltime, a lengthy profile of him by leading literary journalist and biographer William Sloane Kennedy appeared in the *Century Illustrated Magazine* of January 1885. Kennedy skillfully described his subject at the height of his powers, boosting his literary career with an enthusiastic appreciation of his talents as a writer, stylist, and historian. History was Edward's principal literary focus that year as he took much time off from the South Congregational Church for frequent trips to do research at the State Department in Washington, DC. He and his son Jack (Edward E. Hale, Jr.), a recent Harvard graduate now embarking on his own literary career, studied and copied the Benjamin Franklin papers that Edward Sr. had urged the government to purchase in 1882 and father and son collaborated in editing the two-volume *Franklin in France* (1886-1888). Edward's inscription in Hattie's copy acknowledges her considerable assistance in this ambitious project. In late November 1884, she, Mary Cobb, and Martha Brooks, an SCC colleague and close friend of the Hale family, had accompanied Edward to spend the day in Quincy, at Mrs. Charles F. Adams's invitation, to examine the correspondence between John Adams and Franklin.[37]

The first letter Edward wrote Hattie from Washington in early February shows the degree to which she cared for him and showered gifts on him. As he traveled by train from New York, he told her: "I could not but think that my valise came to me from you, my hand-bag from you, my portfolio from you <*and this was just as it should be as my heart and memory run back to you all the time*>."[38] Edward's Washington letters described his calls on many old friends, including historian George Bancroft, James G. Blaine, recently defeated for the third and final time in his bids for the presidency, and Senator George Frisbie Hoar. Edward became close to Hoar in Worcester, where the young Harvard-educated lawyer lived and practiced until he entered politics, first in Massachusetts and then in the U.S. House of Representatives from 1869-1876. Edward reminded Hattie that he had publicly recommended Hoar for election to the U.S. Senate in a letter he dictated to her in 1877 when visiting the Freemans at Pepperell. The two men became exceptionally close.

But the Hales' principal focus was the Franklin papers in the State Department Library where they spent six hours a day, including Sunday, selecting items to copy with the help of librarian Theodore F. Dwight, "an enthusiastic 10 x 1 man."[39] Apparently, they were racing to get the copying completed before the inauguration of the despised Grover Cleveland, fearing that a Democratic administration might deny them access to the papers, which did not happen. Returning to Boston on February 16, Edward was back in Washington a week later. "We had a good days work in the Department," he reported, "and I begin to see daylight there." After attending a reception and performing a reading of "Man without a Country," he concluded, "Ah well! There are but three days more here. I am like you. I am happy while I am at work."[40] Jean Holloway, his most insightful biographer, observed, "In Washington, even more than in Boston, Hale found the life of letters and the stimulation which he enjoyed."[41] It was a draw that would eventually carry him away from Hattie.

Edward's private and public lives were on an upswing that gave him renewed confidence but may also have made him temporarily careless of old friendships. That year, 1885, his intimate friend and major benefactor William Weeden was suffering the agonies of potential business failure and social isolation when his longtime partner in his woolen mills in Providence sold his shares to a New York firm. Weeden recalled in an unpublished reminiscence he wrote late in his life that Edward failed to respond to his agonized letter or offer any words of comfort or emotional support when the two men met subsequently at Weeden's home. Not surprisingly,

Weeden wrote that he thought less of Edward as a result. However, Weeden's letter may have been in response to Edward's request for a loan. Apparently, the Hales were finding that running the Matunuck house was too expensive at a time when they were paying for the college education of their younger sons. Emily had written to Edward in February asking him if he had informed Weeden that they might not be able to go to Matunuck that summer and if he could ask their friend and benefactor for a loan of a thousand dollars: "I suppose it would make things unequal between you, but it seems to me very unkind to a good friend like that not to let him help you in a thing that is so little to him, but weighs you and me down to the ground. He would have a right to be hurt, and he would be."[42] It is not known if Edward asked for a loan, but they did go to Matunuck as usual that summer. In any case, the timing was unfortunate.

Comments Edward made to Hattie many years later when Weeden was again tormented by business reversals indicate that he found his old friend had become a bore and old beyond his years and that he missed the "gay, impulsive young Idealist" he first came to know during the Civil War. This seems to give a lie to Edward's vaunted reputation for universal kindness and empathy and point to a flaw in his character. However, the Hales and the Weedens continued their relaxed summer socializing together and, when Weeden's mills were taken over by the American Wool Company in 1899, resulting in Weeden's resignation three years later, Edward wrote: "To me the sad thing is, that in the course of Consolidation of all the Wool Interests, William Weeden (aetat 70) has been bounced...He is notified that there is nothing for him to do. So he has to loaf round, glad to come up on my piazza and talk seedy politics, instead of making the clothes for 1/20 part of the people of America, as he once did."[43]

In mid-June, Hattie began her summer travels, probably accompanied by her longtime companion Mary Cobb. She botanized in the Pine Barrens surrounding Hammonton, New Jersey and the Jersey Cape, and in the Blue Ridge region near Deep Gap, North Carolina. She ended this excursion with what may have been her first stay at the Lake Mohonk Mountain House in the southern Catskills of

New York, which would be an important destination in future for both her and Edward, separately or together. Hattie proudly reported that she had found and collected forty-one species of flora unknown to her previously, checking them off in her Gray's Manual as she went. In the meantime, Edward and his secretary Mary Edes were working hard on the chores, including parish calls, that Hattie had laid out for them before she left. But he told her that he was increasingly worried about Mary, who was often seriously unwell.

The Hales escaped at last to Matunuck, which was now under Susan's management. "Everything is so lovely here!" he wrote exaltedly on arrival at the summer house. "Is it not a beautiful world, and why does the majority of Mankind prefer not to go into it any more than they can possibly help?" He continued in the shorthand that Hattie now thought of as the language of love, "<*Your letters are so nice that I want to stand on the house step and read them to the people as they pass by*>."[44] Knowing that the house could only be maintained with paying guests, Edward remarked in his diary "The only safety for Matunuck is to make on the 1st of June a rigid series of the guests and notify them when they are to come and when to go. The alternative is a crowded Hotel life through August." A few weeks later, he reported to Hattie, "Susy is passionately interested in her housekeeping and goes into it with all her heart. Of course this takes a great deal of care from Emily, and I think she will take more comfort here than she has ever done." In fact, Emily had written to Nelly in Paris on May 14, 1885, after she had been to see Susan in her Boston rooms: "I am so glad she has this Matunuck plan…she means to move her things down to Matunuck the first of June and really settle herself down there…And I hope I shall never keep house there again."[45]

Despite Edward's wish to avoid Boston that summer, his dental problems forced him to return there two or three times to have teeth pulled and to be fitted for false teeth and there were the inevitable funerals to be conducted. He and Hattie managed to meet up briefly in Boston on one of those visits but otherwise Edward's letters show him responding to all her questions about his summer life in Matunuck. He even included in one case his sketches of the first floor of the house and of the placement of furniture in his study. These floor plans, enclosed with Edward's letter of July 19, and his letters to Hattie describing family life in the house proved invaluable for the restoration by a team under the direction of the Pettaquamscutt Historical Society of the summer house, which was completed in early 2011 and opened to the public for the first time that summer as the Edward Everett Hale House. The restoration team followed closely the placement of furniture, particularly of Edward's desk and chair in front of the window with his back to the pond.[46]

Much of Edward's time that summer was spent making plans for his proposed new magazine *Lend a Hand.* Back at Roxbury briefly in mid-August to work with Mary Edes, he told Hattie, "I have been writing private letters to the people who ought to write for the Magazine, and am astonished to see how many there are."[47] It was also time for Edward's annual trip to Chautauqua, south of Lake Erie in northwestern New York State, to attend Recognition [commencement] Day for the graduates of the Chautauqua Literary and Scientific Circle four-year reading course. Founded to satisfy the hunger for knowledge in America after the Civil War, with an emphasis on religious belief, by 1885 the organization consisted not only of the main assembly grounds at Chautauqua, New York, but also nearly fifty assemblies in different parts of the country. Edward began submitting a series of articles called "A Course of Practical Ethics" that summer for the monthly *Chautauquan* magazine and laid out his proposed topics for Hattie, asking her and Mary Cobb for further ideas.[48] Writing to Hattie at the open window of his hotel overlooking Lake Chautauqua, he told her, "my only reason for being here, was to be ready for my first address tomorrow, at 8 a.m." He delighted that "A gentle mist on the lake gives that exquisite blue to the hills which makes the Italian lakes so beautiful…And I know that somewhere you are looking into the blue this lovely afternoon, and wherever that somewhere is, you are saying the same thing."[49]

Edward's oldest son Arthur met him at the station in New York on his return journey and they traveled on together to Matunuck. "Arthur has come on for his birthday," he wrote Hattie. "He is 26 today. He is the one of all my boys (save Rob) whom I understand most thoroughly." A Harvard graduate and talented pianist, Arthur had wanted a career in music but his father persuaded him to follow his grandfather into the railroad business. Edward reported that he had received extremely disturbing news about Mary Edes, who had not been well for some time and was now diagnosed with typhoid. A week later, he was in Boston to visit Mary and see what he could do to help her family: "She expressed an eager desire to see me. So they let me go in and see her for a minute. She does not look in the least sick…Per contra, the Doctor says her life hangs on a very thread, and he is giving brandy every two hours, a thing I have noticed they always do at the very last…Mary asked that your picture might be carried into her room where she could see it, and it is there."[50]

In the meantime, Edward and Hattie met briefly in Marblehead before he joined Emily to spend a few days with the Kidders at their house on a rocky point above the sea at nearby Beverly. Following the death of his first wife, their old friend had married the year before Elizabeth Huidekoper, daughter of the president of Meadville Theological College, of whom both Edward and Hattie would become extremely fond and admiring. They called her "The Princess." Writing from the Kidders, Edward teased Hattie in shorthand about an imagined consequence of their embraces in Marblehead: "You would hardly believe me if I told you that after I left you I had time to go to Dr. C[handler] <*to consult him about that funny wart if it be such on my lip. What would you say if I told you that he said it looked as if I had been kissed too much by some nice girl or as if I had permitted too much rough handling there. In point of fact*> no such thing happened for I <*did not have the time to go see*> him."[51]

Mary Edes seemed to rally for a while but, on September 15, Edward sent a brief note to Pepperell marked "At once, to be read first." "Dear Hatty," he scribbled, "It is all over. Mary died suddenly at half past ten…Emily was there last night and left some flowers… Dear dear child, how many pathetic stories of her unselfishness they begin to tell already. For each of which I could tell a hundred. I am only beginning to think that I could have guarded her against herself more, and that I ought to have done so. As you can guess I hardly know what I write."[52] Once again he wrote Hattie of his deep remorse that two of his secretaries (the first was Carry Tallant) had died while in his employ, while concluding, "<*Well darling I have you. And you are not jealous of them because they never were and never risk to be to me what you can be or are. I will try not to work you to death*>."[53] But again and again over the years, they would drive each other to exhaustion in marathon writing sessions.

Nelly arrived home safely from Europe in late September and was met in New York by her devoted father and oldest brother. After her eight months of art study in Paris, she would now uncomplainingly take on the yoke of housekeeping in her mother's place. In the meantime, her father and Hattie were looking forward to his autumn stay with the Freemans at Pepperell. Edward arrived there with a copy of his recently published *Stories of Invention told by Inventors and their Friends*, which he inscribed to Hattie, "To one of the authors from one of the others. Oct. 5, 1885. In memory of Watatick <*a matchless ride of fifteen miles and back on a perfect day*>."[54] The day after his return to Boston, a day of mundane frustrations in the church, he wrote, "but we had a perfect day yesterday, & Tuesday, & Monday, and we cannot have everything…So you see it was not all in vain that I went to Pepperell." The visit was evidently a customary fall visit to favorite parishioners and well chaperoned by William Freeman and Mary Cobb since Edward continued, "Emily was delighted with the flowers. The asters looked so so, but they have rallied charmingly today. I have planted the oaks, and let us hope our [his and Emily's] gr. Gr. Gr. Grandchild will play under them. I enclose 6 dollars, which I certainly owe. Tell your father I have not forgotten about the Alabama. I enclose the address of the Asylum."[55]

While Hattie lingered on in bucolic Pepperell with her father and Mary Cobb, Edward was hard at work setting up a new office for the Lend A Hand activities and editing the first issue of an ambitious new magazine, *Lend A Hand: A Record of Progress and Journal of Organized Charity*. A full decade had passed since he penned the last "Record of Progress" in the June 1875 issue of *Old and New* and the writing of the opening editorial for this new *Record of Progress*. He had spent months visiting, giving lectures to, and drumming up support from charitable organizations such as the Associated Charities in many cities, particularly Boston, New York, and Philadelphia, and now declared that he saw this magazine as "an organ for mutual communication." When Edward was away, Hattie had been closely involved with Mary Edes in editing and occasionally writing the magazine's short-lived predecessor, the *Circular for Ten Times One*, at the same time working hard to respond to requests from the many new charitable clubs that were forming in response to Edward's inspirational book, *Ten Times One Is Ten*.[56]

In late October, anticipating Hattie's imminent return to Boston for the winter, Edward remarked in a letter on Lend A Hand letterhead from its new office at 3, Hamilton Place, "You do not like this office much, nor the Magazine, but you will like to have a letter, I hope."[57] Hattie's negative feelings about his new venture came to be shared by the Hale family who felt that it dissipated Edward's energies and was a financial burden he could not afford. But for now Isabella Davis directed the activities and edited the reports of the burgeoning charitable clubs for young people while Mary Dickinson, president of the Women's National Indian Association, oversaw the "Women's Work for Women" department. Susan Hale served as a general editor, and Lucretia Hale wrote a weekly column on advances in Boston's public schools.

Edward himself contributed a monthly serial, "My Friend the Boss," in which the narrator's love interest, the admirable Mary Bell, bears a close resemblance to Hattie. Miss Bell, for example, is passionate about nature, particularly botany, and the narrator, who loves her unrequitedly, describes her as "not at first sight a beauty but of charm of expression and conversation that grew on everyone who came to know her." This and Edward's later serials, "Mr. Tangier's Vacation"—of which Hattie certainly wrote sections describing New England village life—and "Home Again," combined drama with serious discussion of social problems. A letter that Edward wrote Hattie from Coney Island in July seems to confirm that Hattie wrote parts of "Mr. Tangier's Vacation": "Yes, by all means read Mr. Tangier to Mary Cobb. If she understands that we are writing a novel together, she will understand why there is so much correspondence. The truth is that we shall make a very good double team. I am wretched in descriptions…in which you excel. Really we should make a team…I will give you permission to plug away on Mr. Tangier as long as you will. I shall be sure to like it, and the public will."[58]

* * *

At age thirty-eight, Hattie would have been considered to be an "unplucked blessing." If she ever received a proposal of marriage, she did not mention it in her letters. She was certainly in love with Edward all through her marriageable years. Despite the large surplus of women in Massachusetts due to heavy losses in the Civil War and the mass emigration west of many surviving young men, several of her cousins succeeded in finding husbands. On October 26, Hattie attended the wedding of her younger Atkins cousin, Helen, at her parents' Commonwealth Avenue mansion, to J. Rayner Edmands, a meteorologist in the Harvard Observatory. Perhaps Hattie had expressed some doubt about her cousin's choice of a groom because Edward now wrote her the day after her return to Pepperell, "<*Do you know, that when we received your cousin's card, it proves that Mr. Edmands is an old friend of Mrs. Hale, though I hardly knew him. She met him at Mt. Adams. She says he is thoroughly womanly, and she means that for a compliment*>."[59] Rayner Edmands and Hattie became allies in future years through their shared love of the Appalachian Mountain Club (of which he would be president in 1886), of hiking and camping in the White Mountains, and the impetus and financial support that each gave for the building of new graded trails there.

Instead of marriage, Hattie was on a path to becoming one of the strong-minded single Boston bluestockings and reformers made legendary in memoirs and fiction of the Gilded Age. For example, she was one of the women who, appalled by the suffering and mismanagement on Indian reservations, founded the Woman's National Indian Association (WNIA) to lobby for reform. She was a member from its inception in 1879 and would rise to become secretary of the Massachusetts branch in 1890. She and Mary Dickinson undoubtedly influenced Edward to publish reports from the Indian Rights Association, the WNIA, and from other Indian activists and observers in *Lend A Hand* in 1886, the year in which the reforms proposed and lobbied for in Congress that year resulted in the General Allotment Act (Dawes Severalty Act) of 1887. The IRA leaders, in the hope of ending U.S. government and tribal corruption and mismanagement in the running of Indian reservations and in the face of intense land pressure from white settlers and railroad interests, recommended allotting 160 acres of reservation land to each Indian family and opening up the surplus to white homesteaders. In the meantime, Edward published reports by the IRA's Washington lobbyist Charles C. Painter, by Indian activists such as anthropologist Alice C. Fletcher, and such observations on the ground as that submitted by Edward's former protégé at Harvard, young Theodore Roosevelt. Roosevelt's "Red and White on the Border" (*LAH*, February 1886) reported on relations between Indians and white cattlemen near his ranch on the Little Missouri River in the Dakotas.

In late May, Edward wrote to Hattie about the ongoing debate on general allotment as a solution to illegal land-grabbing. Hattie had evidently met with Suzette (Bright Eyes) LaFlesche, about the threat to seize the deeds to houses on her Omaha reservation, including her own family's house. It was LaFlesche who had inspired the Indian Rights Movement when she spoke in Boston's Faneuil Hall in December 1879, wearing native dress and a bear-claw necklace. Protesting the reservation system, LaFlesche thundered: "Did one Creator…intend that men created in his own image should be ruled over by another set of his creatures?" Among the many women who became her supporters, Helen Hunt Jackson (1830-1885) was inspired by her speech to write *A Century of Dishonor*, a book that cited injustices to the Indian peoples, and works of fiction about Native Americans including *Ramona*.[60] But despite all the good intentions of Indian sympathizers and reformers, the Dawes Severalty Act proved disastrous in the long run, leading to such spectacles as the Oklahoma land rushes of 1889-1890, and eventually depriving Indians of some 60 percent of their lands between 1887 and 1934, when allotment was ended.

In addition to his reform work and now his new magazine, Edward continued his usual frenetic life of ministering to his flock at the SCC, interspersed with travels by train to Washington and Philadelphia for continuing archival research for his book on the Franklin diplomatic papers. In late January 1886, he rushed to New York to see his close friend and colleague Henry Kidder who was dying from kidney failure. Kidder had traveled to New York to attend a dinner in honor of Thomas Baring, the British banker, for which his security firm, Kidder, Peabody & Co., was the American agent. But he was taken ill with uremia and was too sick to attend the dinner. The next day, Edward mailed a sad letter to Hattie at Bridgeport, Connecticut, as he traveled home: "I am afraid you will never see dear Kidder in this life again…I did not see him…Alas I fear it could have done no good…As you see I am pretty sad. But no one has had or has such friends as I." "<*I will be good and not forget that*>," he continued in shorthand, telling her that he knew she would support him in his grief (which Emily must have felt just as strongly).[61] At times like this, Edward certainly benefited from having, in effect, the emotional support of two wives.

Wherever he was, often on trains, Edward wrote long letters to Hattie, pouring out his love for her in lengthy shorthand passages and acknowledging the many thoughtful gifts she gave him. From Philadelphia in early February, he wrote, "Was it not wonderful that there was an extra box of those lovely prunes in the bag? How could they have got there," he asked archly. "I wish you would find out where I can buy them. I want to make a present of them to you…<*I am thinking all the time of your pretty verse that you want to belong to my inside life and not to my outside life*>," he continued in shorthand. "<*It is just what you are dear child. Do not think that I forget or can*>." "<*If only you were here now*>," he continued, although his immediate need seemed to be for her to copy five pages for him. The next day, he worried that he was taking up too much of her time: "<*I have sometimes been afraid that I was taking you away from your real favorite pursuits like your botany and your microscope in which you excel and which make you so far as they go the remarkable woman as you are in such affairs*>." "They are not the important affairs," he continued, somewhat patronizingly, "but they are important and it would be a shame if you should lose and I shall lose and everybody should lose the pleasure you take from them."[62]

Edward, always a highly social animal, loved to tell Hattie about all the dinners and receptions, many of them very grand, he was invited to wherever he went. But he would always let her know that he would give it all up for her company. In March, after describing a Cambridge dinner party he attended with Emily, he was anticipating his weekly drive with Hattie: "<*Yes I hope and believe it will be a pleasant day tomorrow and we will have a nice ride over the old roads*>. Surely it is time for decent weather. <*And you will have lots to tell me and I shall tell you the old story how you make me young and fresh and happy. God bless you my own child…*>"[63] And the day after his sixty-fourth birthday on April 3, he credited Hattie yet again with his renewed *joie de vivre*: "Think of it; how strange it is, that I seem to be just finding out how large and wonderful life is, and, tho I have always said that we are all linked together, higher powers and we ourselves I think I feel it more than ever. <*It is all bound up with my own Kit's care of me and love for me*>."[64]

In Mid-June, Hattie left for the Virginia Blue Ridge Mountains resort of White Sulphur Springs (precursor to the Greenbriers resort) with an Appalachian Mountain Club group. From Natural Bridge, on land once owned by Thomas Jefferson and described by him as "that most sublime of nature's works," she told Edward she would not be back in Boston until September 30, which evinced protestations from him. After the Blue Ridge Mountains, Hattie continued her summer with a week's stay at Tip Top House at the summit of Mt. Washington in New Hampshire, where she searched for botanical specimens before joining her father and Mary Cobb at Pepperell. One of Edward's letters to her there gives some hint of the challenges she was facing with her difficult and demanding father. She evidently felt keenly that he was holding her back and, as she approached her fortieth birthday, that life was passing her by: "I have your charming letter from Pepperell to my great joy," wrote Edward on July 16 from Swampscott, a summer resort for the wealthy on the North Shore of Massachusetts, where he and Emily were staying with the recently widowed Elizabeth Kidder and a party of her friends: "Indeed, indeed, as I read the short-hand close of it my whole heart goes out to you, as indeed it always does. I do know what you have to bear, and I wish so I knew how to help you bear it. <*But you are my own child and if my love and sympathy and hopes and prayers will help you you know you have them all*>. I like to think of you in your hammock reading and I hope you will get hold of some books that master you and make you fight yourself and your burdens and the passage of time."

Three days later, Edward was at Matunuck at last, telling Hattie, "I have a great weight off my shoulders having sent off yesterday 60 or 70 pages of copy. <u>The last</u>, my dear child, of the first volume of Franklin. There begins to be more Franklin and less of our text. So that 70 pages does not mean what it did when it was all in your hand-writing. Still it was a great deal of work. It is quite true that we have the second volume now on hand, but it is not quite so pressing."[65] Edward's long letters from Matunuck that summer describe country rambles, canoeing on the pond, bathing in the sea, and finishing up "The Boss" and other copy for the September *Lend A Hand*. They also refer again and again to his wish to buy her a plot of land nearby on which she could build a summer cottage!

That fall, Edward finally achieved the pastoral assistance he had been seeking. On September 15, he wrote Hattie "I had a nice visit from Mr. Edward Hale, whom you will like in spite of yourself." In the same letter, he told her that he arrived home late after a very busy day in Cambridge "to bid my dear Jack good-bye. The boy leaves home, practically forever…I should have been glad to give him all the last day, and this little hour before midnight was all." Thus one young Edward Hale left the family nest for graduate school at Cornell University as the other joined his father's church family. Harvard Divinity School graduate Edward Hale, who was no relation, was ordained as associate minister of the SCC on October 13. Four days later, young Hale preached his first sermon.

As Edward began to lean heavily on the energetic and highly competent Edward Hale, he was saddened by the prospect of losing the Hale family's devoted factotum Abel Fullum. On Christmas Eve, he received word that Fullum was mortally ill and went to see him at his lodgings in Roxbury. Two days later, Fullum died, apparently without suffering, and Edward made arrangements for his funeral and transportation of his body to his home town of Fitchburg. "There is no reason whatever to grieve that he is free from the burden of this tabernacle," wrote Edward the next day. "But he is all wrought in with all the past of my life, even from my boyhood, and all this came up together." He closed in shorthand, "<*You know how good and happy it makes me to think of you and to think of you always. Your own Kit*>."[66]

The following year, the certainties of Hattie's life began to crumble with a change of venue and an unforeseen tragedy. Both would begin to alter the dynamics of her relationship with Edward.

5

Loss and Liberation

For twenty-five years, since it was built on Union Park Street to Edward Everett Hale's specification and consecrated for his new congregation in January 1862, the South Congregational Church continued to serve the Unitarians of Boston's South End as a beloved neighborhood church. Its vaunted reputation for well-organized charitable outreach programs even preceded Hale's activist ministry and its location just a block away from Union Park made it particularly convenient for the Freeman family. But Boston's demographics were changing dramatically as the overcrowded city struggled to absorb unprecedented numbers of impoverished immigrants. Wealthy Unitarians left the South End in droves for Boston's Back Bay and the suburbs. At the same time, other denominations were drawing Unitarians into their churches, particularly the Episcopalians in response to the influence of Phillips Brooks, charismatic minister of Boston's Trinity Church on Copley Square and a distant cousin of the Hales. Phillips Brooks (1835-1893), who was born a Unitarian, was an even more towering figure than Edward Everett Hale in Boston's religious life, both as a preacher and physically (he was 6 feet 4 inches tall). In the beautiful new Trinity Church building, he preached Sunday after Sunday to large congregations. He was appointed Episcopal Bishop of Massachusetts in 1891, less than two years before his death.

The writing was on the wall. Church trustees decided to sell the Union Park Street church to a Jewish congregation and merge the South Congregational Society with the Hollis Street Society, from

The new Hollis Street Church opened its doors in the Back Bay in 1884 but became the South Congregational Church when the two societies merged just three years later.
Courtesy of the Trustees of the Boston Public Library/Prints.

which the SCS had broken away in the 1820s. Like the South Congregational, the Old Hollis Street Church had become stranded in the increasingly commercialized South End of Boston. In 1883-84, the Hollis Street Society built a massive and—to modern eyes—very ugly and overly ornate brick and terra cotta church building on the corner of Newbury and Exeter Streets at the heart of Back Bay, in the course of which it became heavily burdened with debt. This debt and an unfolding scandal would give the South Congregational Society trustees and the Unitarian Association the upper hand in merger negotiations.

The year 1887, one of dramatic change for the SCC, began with the twenty-fifth anniversary celebration of its opening on Union Park Street on January 7 and the usual busy schedule continued there for the next six months. As always, Edward was called away to many meetings and invitations to lecture outside Boston, but on January 12 he performed the marriage of Hattie's cousin Grace Atkins to his longtime right hand man in the church William Howell Reed, a fifty-year-old widower with a son.

It was an upsetting year for the wider Beecher clan. First, Charlotte Perkins Stetson, Emily's niece by the failed marriage of her older brother Frederick, had suffered a nervous breakdown following the birth of a daughter the year after her marriage. Her story and her connection to the Hales and indirectly to Hattie Freeman is told in chapter 7. The Beecher family received a further blow when Henry Ward Beecher suffered a stroke: "We hear by telegraph of Mr. Beecher's illness," Edward noted on March 5, a day when Hattie worked with him at his house on "The Human Washington," his address for the upcoming Chautauqua assembly in Florida. As reporters thronged the street outside the Beechers' Brooklyn house, the renowned and notorious preacher lapsed into a coma. Most of his surviving siblings attended his funeral on March 11 but his wife Eunice refused to allow his youngest half-sister, suffragist Isabella Beecher Hooker, to enter the house when Beecher lay dying or to attend the public funeral at Plymouth Church. Eunice, a bitter, grudge-bearing woman, would never forgive Isabella for her support of the attacks on her husband by Victoria Woodhull and other leaders of the women's rights movement in the 1870s and Isabella's belief in his guilt.[1]

Anticipating the worst, Emily may have traveled as far as Hartford with Edward on March 6 to support her mother, Mary Perkins, who was devoted to her brilliant but deeply flawed younger brother. From there, Edward wrote Hattie that he had written sixteen more pages of his novel "Mr. Tangier" on which they had been collaborating (it was published that year in serial form in *Lend A Hand*). After mailing them in Hartford, he pressed on to catch a steamer in New York for the beginning of his long planned trip to Florida. This was to be partly a vacation, with a commitment to preach and give two addresses at the Lake Weir Chautauqua at Ocala. Hattie had written notes folded into small triangles for Edward to open each day, in which she included information about the places he would be visiting and loving messages in shorthand. Toward the end of his trip, he told her, "Your letters have been charming <*and have done no end of good in making the railroad rides pleasant*>."[2] He wrote to her almost every day he was away.

When they reached Palatka, some of the party, including Edward, took a boat down the St. Johns River and then a train to St. Augustine. Everywhere Edward went in St. Augustine, he ran into people he knew from his extensive coverage of Indian Rights Association work in *Lend A Hand*. In the first volume alone, he had published articles by Herbert Welsh, co-founder and corresponding secretary of the Indian Rights Association, and Charles C. Painter, a principal in the IRA's Washington office, both of whom had traveled extensively inspecting the condition of Indians on reservations. Edward wanted to tour Fort Marion where "my dear Apache Indians" were imprisoned and received a pass from the commanding general to do so. "And then of course, I had only to say how glad we would be to see Maj. Bourke…when…Bourke and Herbert Welsh crossed the drawbridge and took us back again! He had just arrived, I think on some errand of mercy for Chatto and my other poor men. But this he could not tell me."[3]

During 1886, the U.S. government had sent five groups of Apaches from Arizona to Florida for incarceration. Of these 530 individuals, at least 475 were women, children, and noncombatants; fourteen, including Chatto, a Chiricahua subchief, were unjustly imprisoned having previously served as paid scouts for the U.S. Army, serving under Gen. Crook. Two of these scouts had made it possible to capture Geronimo. John C. Bourke, Captain of the U.S. Third Cavalry, was a famous Indian fighter, General Crook's right hand man, and author of such works as *On the Border with Crook*. The secret that Herbert Welsh could not tell Edward was revealed when, five days later, Welsh published his "Report of a visit to the Chiricahua Apache Indians at present confined in Fort Marion, St. Augustine, Florida," in which he argued that Fort Marion was entirely unsuitable to accommodate the 447 Indians currently confined there. Edward must have seen the more than a hundred tepees crowding the ramparts, where Indian women dried meat and cooked on open fires. Whether or not the Army was influenced by Welsh's report, on April 27, 1887, it decided to move these Apache prisoners of war to Mt. Vernon Barracks outside Mobile, Alabama. Without the permission or cooperation of relatives or friends, more than a hundred Apache children had already been sent to the Indian Industrial School at Carlisle, Pennsylvania.

Following Edward's return to Boston, he and Hattie managed to spend an astonishing amount of time together, but plans for their excursions sometimes went astray. On Fast Day, April 7, 1887, Edward wrote Hattie a note telling her that he had waited at his front window early the previous morning, hoping she would arrive for their Thursday morning drive "but no chargers and no Kit. I wanted so to call you out last night when I went away <*but was afraid of the watchful oversight of the others*>. I do not yet know whether you had your ride or not or whether your principles are too firm to let you ride today…<*you know I thought of you all the time and was sorry not to see you girded*> for battle."[4] Kit was a pet name Edward used for both Hattie and his daughter and just as often for himself. A week later, Edward returned from meetings in New York and Baltimore in time for his regular Tuesday outing with Hattie, ostensibly to make parish calls. Whatever their expectations were for the day, they were dashed: "To think of our plans being all knocked to pieces by a snow storm in spring. Ever since I saw you I have been padding around as a man has to do fighting against real & metaphysical gales. But when I remembered how patient and good you were I could not do else. And now, 8 p.m., I must put on a tail-coat and go to the Reception at the Vendome in Mr. Savage's honour."[5]

Edward liked to escape to the church cupola to avoid the constant demands on his time and patience. On Thursday, May 5, Hattie was at Pepperell for the day so Edward wrote her a note from this aerie where "no mortal in the world, excepting you, know where I am." Above his letter, he sketched the view made misty by an unseasonably hot day. "<*I got your pretty letter with all its praises this morning*>," he wrote, and then wondered why he did not pass on to her the nice things he was always being told about her.[6] But he did tell her the following week that his new young associate, the other Edward Hale, had remarked on the change he had noticed in Hattie: "I was so touched by something Mr. Edward said this morning. 'Do you know I did not understand Miss Freeman at first. Is she not much more cheerful than she used to be? When I first knew her I thought she was so much occupied for other people that she had not time to enjoy, but now she seems so cheerful and jolly.' I had the pleasure of telling him just the least bit about you, and what a wonderful woman you are. <*I did not tell him what a dear girl you are*>." In this letter, he mentioned that he had been to the AUA for the Carpenter meeting.[7]

Henry Bernard Carpenter (1840-1890) was the Irish-born pastor of the Hollis Street Church, and the plans had been for the two men to share the ministry of the merged churches—but this was not to be. As reported by the *New York Times* in February 1888, the Reverend Carpenter, a charming and brilliant if impractical man, an Oxford-educated lecturer and poet whose younger brother was the Bishop of Ripon, England, left his ministry in the wake of revelations that he was a bigamist. These came to light when the Reverend Brooke Herford of Boston's Arlington Street Church returned from a visit to England, also his native country, the summer of 1886. There a woman introduced herself, claiming she was Carpenter's wife and the mother of his two children and that they had never been divorced. Carpenter had come to America with his family in 1874 to evade an apparently trumped up moral charge made by his parishioners in Liverpool and in a final attempt to repair the brief, unhappy marriage for which both he and his wife had already signed legal separation papers. But the marriage was irreparable and his family returned to England soon after.

While he was rector of a Congregational Church in Bridgton, Maine, Carpenter married a local woman, Emma Bailey, assuring his new young wife's family what he apparently believed, that he was free to do so. Two years after he was called to the Hollis Street Church in 1878, the Carpenters had a son. Now, in 1887, as the Hollis Street Society trustees faced serious financial problems in the wake of building the expensive new church, they and the American Unitarian Association felt that a scandal would be ruinous so soon after its dedication. Unitarian lay leaders helped Carpenter to regularize his marital situation by obtaining a legal divorce in England and remarrying his second wife but calls for his departure may have had even more to do with the massive debt incurred by the Hollis Street Society under his leadership. The Carpenters left for "a rest" in Europe about the time the consolidation of the two churches took place in October 1887 and Bernard Carpenter was not expected to return to ministry.[8] But Edward would not be alone to shoulder his enhanced duties since young Edward Hale continued as associate pastor.

Facing the first of their annual summer separations in late May 1887, Edward accompanied Hattie to Worcester where she boarded a train for Asheville, North Carolina. There she was to join her teacher friend Parnell Murray and other students of natural history for riding and field trips in the nearby mountains. Mocking the Realist literary style advocated by his brother-in-law Frederick Perkins and practiced by such popular novelists as William Dean Howells and Alphonse Daudet, Edward described their parting in that documentary manner. "The train glided slowly away, gaining speed as it went. I waved my hand to her and she hers to me, and the man behind was very much amused by the tenderness of our parting. Then one column cut us apart for an instant; then we saw each other again. But, at last, the last column shut off her rather sad smile." He continued as he waited for the return train to Boston: "What did we say between 9 and 10.15 <*I hardly know*>. On the whole, I hardly care <*to remember the words*>. It is <*the spirit of the hour which made it pass by so fast and not the instructions which we gave to each other*>."[9]

Two days after seeing Hattie off at Worcester, Edward left town himself for Ithaca, New York, to visit his son Jack (Edward Jr.), now a graduate student of English literature at Cornell University. He had begun a letter to Hattie while waiting for his train at Albany but was interrupted by the very writer he mimicked in his Worcester letter, William Dean Howells, who sat down at his table, as he told Hattie later: "I cannot make you read his stories but you know I am very fond of them and of him…He talked most eagerly about Tolstoi, the Republican novelist: Tolstoi, having been a successful author, has gone back to his estates, and gone into peasant life, working with his hands, and touching elbows with his people. Howells is man enough to see the dangers of his own dilettante life, and was pathetic in his wish to really come into the people's life again."

Count Lev Nikolayevich Tolstoy (1828-1910), also known as Leo Tolstoy, the author of the epic novels *War and Peace* and *Anna Karenina*, renounced his aristocratic life for a life dedicated to Christian anarchy, social reform, and powerful criticism of the church, the state, and the law. His magnum opus *The Kingdom of God is Within You*, banned in Russia but published in Germany in 1894, summarized thirty years of his thinking and influenced the non-violent activism of Mahatma Gandhi and Martin Luther King Jr.

Howells did in fact turn to social reform writing in the 1880s but was Edward also referring to the novelist's sad personal life in this letter? Howells' wife Elinor and his daughter Winifred were both nervous invalids. Winifred, their eldest child, had been a neurotic since she was fifteen. At sixteen, in 1879, she had a severe breakdown. By the time Edward ran into Howells in Albany, Winifred was suffering from life-threatening anorexia and, the following year, Howells took her to Philadelphia to place her in the care of the celebrated neurologist Silas Weir Mitchell. Dr. Mitchell had developed the so-called "rest cure" to treat patients suffering from the widespread incidence of neurasthenia in the late nineteenth century, as will be seen.

His talk with Howells so excited Edward that he wrote from the Albany station to Emily describing the meeting. "Really, if I did what was wise I should spend this morning in writing in short hand in my note book, all he said and all I said, about Tolstoi's theories and the Saviour's wish." Unfortunately, he did not do this.[10] What Edward could not have known at that time was that Howells' departure in 1891 from increasingly reactionary Boston for tolerant, open-minded New York would mark the end of Boston's long reign as the literary capital of America. From that point on, Boston was in the late Indian summer of its intellectual leadership, leaving only, following the death of James Russell Lowell in 1891, Thomas Wentworth Higginson, Julia Ward Howe, and Edward himself of the older liberal writers.[11]

From Cornell, Edward wrote Hattie that Emily had decided to spend the summer at Roxbury with her ailing mother. Mary Perkins had become very frail following the shock of her brother Henry's death. But unlike Henry Ward Beecher and his parishioner Elizabeth Tilton, whose alleged sexual affair became one of the century's most notorious scandals, Edward and Hattie had generally observed convention during the comparatively uncomplicated early chapter in their romantic relationship. The boundaries would soon be breached, however, following a series of tragedies in Hattie's family.

On July 10, 1887, Hattie was climbing Mt. Adams in New Hampshire's Presidential Range of the White Mountains with Rayner Edmands, her cousin Helen's husband (Helen, who was pregnant, remained at home in Cambridge), when she received a telegram with the shocking news that her brother Fred had collapsed while playing tennis with his wife and another couple in West Newton. He died shortly after from a ruptured appendix. He was only thirty-three. His devastated sister traveled to West Newton as fast as the trains would take her. The next day, Monday, Edward was returning to Matunuck after preaching in Coney Island when he was met at Kingston by the news of Fred Freeman's death. Instead of going to Matunuck, he continued on the train to Providence where he wrote to and telegraphed the two Hattie Freemans. In his letter to his own Hattie sent to her sister-in-law's house, he offered her every support, although he was in the dark about the details: "You will have left word of all that I can do for you…Give my best love to her, and how I wish there were anything I could do for her, for those dear little children. What a happy family it has been!"[12] On Tuesday, Edward and Hattie's friend and neighbor Etta Pierce took the train to West Newton, where he conducted the funeral at the family's house. He then accompanied Hattie and her father to Pepperell, riding back to Boston the next day with Mr. Freeman, whose mental instability and depression since suffering head trauma in a carriage accident was surely greatly exacerbated by the sudden death of his son and heir.

Despite a frenetic schedule of summer lectures, Edward's letters show how attuned he was to Hattie's grief and misery. They had been discussing her first visit to Matunuck for some time before her brother's unexpected death but Susan had overbooked the house so that Edward once again advised Hattie to delay her arrival until they could spend more time together. In the meantime, he confirmed that he would arrive at Pepperell on August 17 so that Hattie and Mary Cobb could travel on with him to the next Chautauqua summer assembly, this time at East Epping, New Hampshire. His shorthand revealed Hattie's state of mind, trapped as she now was with her difficult father: "But <*my darling it so grieves me that you are*> not enjoying your own life <*which is the life of a nymph of the open air*> as you would have been but for this tragedy."[13]

Edward was expected to deliver the oration and confer awards on Chautauqua Recognition Day on August 18.[14] Leaving Pepperell early that day, Edward, Hattie, and Miss Mary were delayed at Nashua due to an accident on the line and were forced to travel via Manchester. They arrived in pouring rain just in time for Edward to confer the certificates. Returning via Manchester, "we missed our connection," noted Edward in his journal, and had to spend the night at the Windsor House in "a fourth rate bed in a third rate inn." He omitted the fact that Hattie and Mary must have stayed in the same hotel. The next morning, they arrived at Pepperell in time for breakfast, he and Hattie wrote together under the trees, they took a "beautiful ride" to the Nashua River, and Edward returned to Boston early the next morning.

Edward and Hattie were not apart for long. They traveled to Kingston together on August 25 where a wagon picked them up for the drive to Matunuck. Edward's journal lists a mix of work on correspondence and Franklin, walking, swimming, canoeing on Wash Pond behind the house, and reading to each other. Someone took a photograph of the two of them, sitting rather self-consciously in separate canoes moored alongside each other. Hattie had several copies made which she treasured for the rest of her life (see over).[15]

Her letters in later years often recall these happy days together. For example, in May 1892, she wrote, "I often think of the Sunday I was with you at Matunuck. We went to Mr. Weeden's parlor in the morning." It was a long established tradition for Edward to conduct an informal Sunday service for the Weeden and Hale households and their guests at Willow Dell, the Weedens' country house across the post road below the hill on which stood the Hales' house. Hattie remembered: "In the late afternoon I sat on a cushion at your feet on the front porch, while you read aloud to me a favorite sermon of Starr King's showing how unimportant (comparatively) in our real spiritual life was this transference to different conditions which we call Death...but now I remember the porch, the outlook over the flat to the sea, the fading light, & more than all, stronger than all else, the sense that I was close to you, that I was next to you, & in that was great sense of comfort & rest."[16]

Emily had known charming Fred Freeman from boyhood and, having lost two young sons herself, must have deeply sympathized with Hattie's overwhelming grief. She knew about Hattie's stay at Matunuck for Edward wrote her on August 29, "I think Hatty F enjoys her stay. She is very quiet in the house but takes long walks and comes home with great botanical novelties."[17] What he did not mention was that he accompanied Hattie on the long walks that day and every day of her stay. This and observing the two of them together probably confirmed Susan's growing suspicions about the true nature of her brother's relationship with his youthful assistant.

Four days later, back at Roxbury, Edward wrote to Hattie at Pepperell, "And did you not have nine perfect days? to stand out always on the calendar of visits? And will we not mark them with letters of gold?" He told her that he had met with her aunt Mary Atkins the day before: "I found she thought my plan for your father's taking a journey not <u>un</u>-feasible. She said that if we could persuade him that Elisha [Atkins, Hattie's uncle] needed a journey...or that it would be a kindness to take him, your father would take him: a suggestion which I thought pathetic and true. I know you will pooh-pooh at this, but it is to be thought of."[18] Edward's thoughts returned constantly to Hattie and their precious days together at Matunuck: "Everything you say about being in the open air pleases me, as you know it will, and everything you say about being happy

Hattie and Edward were photographed in adjoining canoes on Wash Pond during her late summer 1887 stay at Matunuck. This is the only image of the many that Hattie collected of Hale that includes her. However, her face is characteristically averted and the Reverend looks extremely displeased to have been caught by a camera with a possibly compromising companion. *Copy print in Harriet E. Freeman Papers, bMS 273, Andover-Harvard Theological Library, Harvard Divinity School.*

at Matunuck. Matunuck is for me a sort of temple consecrated to Nature, and when I am called away, as I am tonight, it makes me unhappy…as if I had no power to worship as I want to. I am glad to have you understand why and how it is that I am so jealous for it."[19]

Even as Edward geared up for his first winter as minister of the new church in Back Bay, he and Hattie were making plans for a brief vacation together to enjoy the fall colors in Bethel, Maine. In the meantime, Edward brought his new secretary Martha Adams down to Matunuck to begin work with him on Franklin and general correspondence, a canny cover for the purpose of Hattie's earlier visit. Martha would remain as Edward's secretary until 1900, when he retired as minister of the South Congregational Society and she married.[20]

But now, on September 14, as he was about to leave for a meeting about the leadership of the merged churches, he wrote Hattie,

"How curious it is that you should go back to Hollis St. Church where you began. For I suppose to-night will determine it. I am only anxious to save Mr. Carpenter's feelings."[21] Two days earlier, Emily had written Edward at Matunuck, "People asked me, coming out of church, about the Hollis St. matter. I hope, more and more, that it will be settled and should be very much disappointed if it fell through. The Herald says today that you and H.B.C. are to be joint pastors, that in an article correcting the many mistakes that have been made."[22] Edward seems to have confided the true situation to Hattie but not to his wife.

Kind as always, Edward had asked Bernard Carpenter to preach at the Newbury Street church on October 2, the first Sunday the merged congregations would meet there, but the compromised clergyman sent his successor a note to say he would not be able to preach as arranged. Edward grumbled to Hattie that, in her absence, he had no one to help him write a sermon but write it he did, in time to preach in Carpenter's stead. He also read Carpenter's touching note of explanation to the congregation. Edward reported the following day that the church was full to overflowing: "Every one was in good spirits, except Mr. Lyman Tucker [a devoted Hollis Street parishioner since the glory days of Thomas Starr King] who is heart-broken." But Edward was distressed by something his friend, the Episcopal minister Phillips Brooks, told him as they drove into town together that day: "He told me that Carpenter's brother, <u>Bishop of Ripon</u>, is the most popular of the young English bishops, and is a very distinguished man in '<u>The Church</u>' there. But he said, what I did not like, that when he <u>staid</u> with this gentleman at his house, or 'palace' as they call it, he never alluded to the fact that he had a brother in Boston, and that he, Brooks, did not even know it, till afterwards! There's drawing the line for you!"[23] That afternoon, he called on the departing cleric and Judith Andrews sent the Carpenters flowers.

Edward's sympathetic attitude to the Englishman's disgrace was typical of his humanity; in fact it may have been what he called "the tragedy" in his letters of early October 1887. But the Carpenter case throws the hypocrisy of Edward's own double life into even greater relief. He and Hattie had hoped to spend the first week of October in Bethel, but Edward remembered that he was already committed to preach in Saco that week. After a back and forth about when and how to meet, Edward wrote on his return from Saco, "I have been reading your letter once again. It is clear that I must decide some thing, and I decide that you start Monday morning from Pepperell…We will meet at the Grand Junction station in Portland, where the B&M cars meet that road. Let me have a line, at least, when you get this that I may be sure." Hattie had hoped to escape Pepperell for Bethel on Saturday but her father had returned from Cape Cod earlier than expected, further complicating her departure.

Whatever was going on with her father (at the very least, black depression and grief over the loss of his son, even violent rages, and all the while a failure to register Hattie's own feelings), it was causing Hattie enormous distress, as Edward's response in the same letter indicated: "…my mind goes back to your sufferings, and to my inability to help you. It would be so much better for your father, yes and for you, if some arrangement could be made like the old weather-glass, and when you were out he was in, and when he was out you were in. This I say, in the deepest sadness, and am only sorry if it seems trifling. Dear child, if in any way I can help you, be sure I will. Four days away in those mountains will be something: and after the first of November you have six plain months before you <*with certainly one person whom you love and can rely upon and with*> duties at least <*if not pleasures that will keep you from the one thought which makes life so nearly intolerable there*>."[24] Fred Freeman had shared the burden of their damaged father with his sister and both of them had asked Edward for his advice on how best to handle the difficult old man since his accident. Now Hattie felt the burden was hers alone and leaned even more heavily on her minister and intimate friend for counsel and support.

It must have astonished Edward's overworked staff, particularly his associate minister and new secretary, that he would depart on another vacation, however brief, right after taking on overwhelming responsibilities in the new church and having only just returned from his summer house. In fact, he himself felt guilty: "I certainly do not like to be away Sunday. Indeed, it seems some times to be wrong to be away in all the rush of new arrangements here. But I justify myself by saying that the world will never be so beautiful till twelve months more have gone by."[25] Hattie needed him desperately and he could not let her down. On Friday, October 7, the day after making final arrangements to spend the following week with Hattie in Maine, his daybook recorded the beginning of official business at the new church.

Judging by the aggrieved letter Edward wrote his wife from Bethel on October 11, Emily had been outspoken in her criticisms of what she saw as his abrogation of duty and fiscal irresponsibility. "I am sadly grieved that you think all this a waste of time or money," responded the deceiving husband. "I have talked of it all the summer as the wind up of the outings of the year. And when I planned it, I had no thought of the inconveniencies which appear now. Anyway, I will make the best I can of it, and know I can have a good time. Love to all from Papa."[26] Less than two weeks following the opening of the merged church, Edward Everett Hale's daybook was left blank for five days. It was not a good start. But on Sunday, October 16, he preached at the church and also wrote Hattie, "What a good time we had! I think of it every minute of every hour <*and I bless you every time I think of it*>. Tuesday morning I leave for Yonkers."[27]

No record has been found in Bethel of Edward and Hattie's brief stay in Bethel. Located in the foothills of the White Mountains in western Maine, the town today shows little evidence of its enormous popularity as a tourist town in the late nineteenth century. There were huge summer hotels around the Bethel Hill Common and guests could enjoy an unobstructed view of the mountains from the rooftop cupola of the Prospect Hotel. Edward and Hattie are more likely to have stayed in a discreet boarding house.

For the next two weeks, Edward and his staff were overwhelmed with work as they struggled to integrate the two congregations. Edward's letters cataloged endless meetings, parish calls, and difficult decisions. At Pepperell, Hattie played her part with Mary Cobb by organizing the records, parish lists, and correspondence of both churches, returning them in a large trunk to Boston where Martha Adams filed them. "Miss Adams, who arranged them in the drawer alphabetically was overwhelmed with admiration at such prowess. It shews her the standard she must aim at," wrote Edward gratefully. But, having noted that the hard-charging Judith Andrews was both exhausting herself and perhaps upsetting staff members from the former Hollis Street Church in her efforts to take charge, he urged Hattie in shorthand to be less driven and more accommodating when she returned to her job. "<*Your mission will be to make things run smoother and to keep life skipping and jaunty. You must not undertake to do everything but to be [flexible?] in that and willing to be forgiving and encouraging if everything does not get done.*>"[28] The daybook reports the resumption of Hattie and Edward's regular winter life of work together at the church, on the weekly sermons and his literary writings, and excursions together on Tuesdays and, whenever possible, Thursdays too.

On the first Tuesday in December, Edward noted his call on Hattie's ailing uncle, Elisha Atkins, presumably with Hattie, perhaps to discuss possible solutions to easing Hattie's burden with her frighteningly unpredictable father, Elisha's brother-in-law and former partner. Apart from that, there was a decision to be made about the future of the Aetna Mills. Atkins may already have been a major shareholder in William Freeman's flagship business since from now on the Mills came under the management of Atkins & Company, whose president was Elisha's son Edwin Atkins. The fact that Fred Freeman did not work there seems to indicate that the Atkinses already had a majority share.

Christmas is always tough emotionally for the lonely and the bereaved. Arthur and Edward Jr., arrived at the Roxbury house on December 19 but their father's joy in gathering his family for the holidays was blunted by his empathy for Hattie's deep sadness over the loss of her brother. He wrote to her on Christmas day, "The blot on my Christmas is that you are not happy. Your sad face went with me all day yesterday. We had a nice time all to ourselves Saturday [Christmas eve]."[29] For Christmas 1887 he gave her copies of his *History of the United States, written for the Chautauqua Reading Circles* (1887) and *In His Name*. He inscribed the first "To one of the authors from another Christmas 1887."[30] Many years later, Hattie reminded Edward of his kindness to her that first Christmas following her brother's death, and the gifts he chose to help allay her grief, including a "large dark red jar for which now for 21 yrs I have had an especial tenderness."[31]

On December 29, Hattie and the Freeman children accompanied Edward to an appointment at Rand, Avery & Co., his longtime printers and publishers, about the planned second volume of *Franklin in France*. "You will see me at 1.1/4," he wrote Hattie that morning. "I have the permit to visit the office."[32] Whether this was an appointment to check first proofs, an educational experience for the children or both is unknown, but Edward was becoming a surrogate father to the Freeman children who from now on were frequently in Hattie's care.

But now tragedy struck Hattie's family again. On New Year's Day, her cousin Helen Atkins Edmands gave birth to a baby girl with multiple complications and no hope of survival. The baby died a month later. A week after giving birth, Helen succumbed to scarlet fever. The loss of their youngest daughter and then her baby must have brought back to Elisha and Mary Atkins the horrors of losing three of their own children to infectious disease when they were very young. Helen had been particularly close to her father. Already frail from a bad fall, Elisha now suffered a stroke. Thus he was in no condition to help Hattie with her own father and he would die before the end of the year.[33]

Apart from a trip to Philadelphia and Washington in mid-January 1888 for continuing research at the American Philosophical Society and State Department archives for the second volume of *Franklin in France*, Edward remained in Boston throughout the winter and focused on his enhanced responsibilities in the new church. Despite the latest tragedy in her family, Hattie is likely to have attended the course of eight weekly evening lectures at Boston's Association Hall on behalf of the first season of the new Marine Biological Laboratory at Woods Hole. The lecturers included three of her favorite professors, William H. Niles of Boston Tech, George L. Goodale of Harvard, and, of course, Alpheus Hyatt.[34] As usual, Edward and Hattie saw much of each other at work and on their Tuesday excursions.

Edward was invited to participate in an Associated Charities conference in early March in Burlington, Vermont, organized by a group of civic leaders there. He caught a train to Burlington by way of Fitchburg, where Hattie and Mary Cobb joined him. As treasurer of the South Friendly Society and her sometimes role as Edward's secretary, Hattie's presence at the meeting would not have seemed remarkable. The three friends traveled on together through "beautiful country," talking on many subjects. What must Miss Mary have thought as her contemporary and longtime minister and her much younger family friend sat reading Arlo Bates's love sonnets to each other? There are indications in Hattie's letters at this time that Mary was jealous of the extra attention Hattie was receiving from their minister.

While Hattie is not mentioned in Edward's daybook record for the busy weekend in Burlington, the long letter he wrote her on a snowbound train to New York on March 13, her birthday, confirms that she was with him on the train journey to Burlington and that she had seen him onto his train for New York the day before.[35] A massive snowstorm was now blanketing the whole of New England. "I am pondering whether you have had better luck than I," he began: "We advanced, with long pauses, and various encouraging pulls about 60 miles from Rutland. But at half past seven, it was announced that all further progress was impossible, and we have spent the night in this same plush furnished car which you left me in…It is now six o'clock a.m. and our scouts report that the people at a store which has been discovered are doing their best to get breakfast for us…I think it very doubtful whether I arrive in New York in time for my reading." Hattie had given him the first volume of Darwin's *Origin of Species* and that had absorbed him so far. "If I had the second volume of Darwin I should be all right. Instead of that I shall have to write the 49th and 50th volumes of my own works. Fortunately I have paper enough!"

As he thought about Hattie's life on her forty-first birthday, Edward's words are those of minister, father, and lover, the supportive combination he felt she needed in the midst of her personal struggles: "You do not like to analyze yourself much…But you ought to know and to remember that you have been true to the gospel of the duty next your hand, 'Who worships God, shall find him,' and certainly you do manage to find fields of life, and chances, yours for angel-service, which nobody would have planned for you." He reminded her that he had good authority for this, "for as you know, I owe you inspiration and cheerfulness every day I live. I can write to you when I am buried in a snow-drift, and know you will be glad to read, or I can dream of you, when I am asleep, with a reasonable chance that you are dreaming of me." He knew how frustrated she was at not being able to live her own life and gently advised her to live day by day, concentrating on helping others. "I wonder if you had been sleeping in your rather forlorn car, on the summit between Rutland and the River," he continued, "for we hear just now that all New England is blocked. I am man enough to wish that you had had our comfortable car, which was much more fit for ladies, and we had had your harder quarters…I have not said that we have advanced 2 miles today, and are stuck in a drift worse than we were in before. The post-mark will shew you when & where I mail this."[36] The Great Blizzard of 1888 paralyzed the East Coast and caused 400 deaths. Edward and Hattie were lucky to escape so lightly.

But despite Edward's counsels of perfection, "angel-service" was never enough for Hattie; she was longing to escape to botanize in the mountains. When Edward was in Atlanta the next month for the Southern Conference of Unitarian and Other Christian Churches, Hattie wrote to him wondering whether or not she should embark on a two-month-long botanical field trip to the Colorado Rockies. She was loath to leave him for that long but he urged her to grab this opportunity, reminding her that he would be absent from Boston during much of those two months: "Both of us together will enjoy all you see and do in Colorado. It is a wholly new world, a flora above the clouds on Pike's Peak, new people & new things. You are not yourself, or rather you-and-I are not ourself, unless in a Life larger & larger. What you gain I shall gain, and shall gain it for always…So I have decided for you."[37]

On Edward's return to Boston, he called on William Freeman twice, ostensibly to urge him to let Hattie go to Colorado, and worked hard with Hattie and Martha Adams to complete the proofing and appendix of the second Franklin volume and organize the copy for Rand Avery. But in late April, he addressed a letter to Hattie to await her arrival in Colorado Springs as she traveled across the country. He gave her his addresses during May and advised her not to write to him at home, "but for necessity. If I am not at home, Mrs. Perkins would open it, and would ask unnecessary questions." Emily's mother, an intelligent and perceptive woman, seems to have been more suspicious of Edward's activities than was her daughter and the letters indicate that there was not a great deal of love lost between him and his mother-in-law. "I called to see your father yesterday," Edward told Hattie, "but he was just going down town with George so we gave up Bunker Hill till the afternoon, it took him quite out of himself. He was very companionable and pleasant & gave me a very pleasant hour & a half."[38] Would Hattie's father have been pleasant to his minister if he had known the extent of his involvement with his daughter?

In May, seven-year-old Helen Keller entered the lives of both Edward and Hattie, as described in the next chapter. Edward was enchanted by little Helen's evident intelligence and infectious *joie de vivre,* but he was also facing the loss of another close friend and colleague. He wrote Hattie that James Freeman Clarke was very weak and close to death. Then, two days later, he mourned: "Freeman Clarke is dead. You know that makes a bad break for me. He called me Edward & I called him James. There is now no minister for whom I care, older than I…Clarke I absolutely and thoroughly respect. Without seeing him a great deal, I loved him truly…Professionally, I am now left very much alone. But I like De Normandie & Bram. And this will bring us closer together…Mr. Edward I like & love, but we are years apart. So I shall very much <*fall back on you. Will you be my counselor adviser and friend*>"?

As Hattie prepared to begin the long train journey home from Colorado, she told Edward that she had climbed Pike's Peak, ridden on horseback a great deal, and by mid-July had collected 240 specimens of plants that were new to her. "Are you not glad that I taught you botany!" wrote Edward in response to that news.[39] His delight in her adventures is apparent in the many letters he wrote during her absence. But his reply to the news that she would not return home before July 1 indicates that the Hale family objected to the amount of time he had been spending with Hattie before her departure: "I can say definitely that I shall go to Matunuck June 28 and June 29. I shall stay there till I know you are in Boston. <*I had better not go to Pepperell at that time. I can tell you the reasons when you are come.*> Suffice it that they are reasons you will see the face of simply <*it would attract immediate attention and indignation at home*> and that I want <*for your sake as much as for mine to*> avoid."[40]

On July 2, Edward was relieved to report that he was now resting at Matunuck after a whirlwind of out-of-town engagements: "Briefly, the week was a very, very pleasant one, only lonely. It was immensely interesting to pass over that Vermont Central, and to be in Burlington, in this lavish loveliness of June, with the fresh memories of our March visit…Now there is no more speech-making until Weir's [*sic*]."[41] Nine days later, he wrote to her at Pepperell: "It really seems possible that Thursday night may find you in Pepperell. Really there is nothing to say but 'Joy-joy-joy'…Almost three months, think of that. It has never been so before." He had shown the dried forget-me-nots she had gathered "from the top of the world" to Susy who wanted to make a dress pattern of them, which they would call Hattie's "Pike's Peak frock." "But, oh dear," he sighed, "I cannot think of anything but that you are so near home. If only I were, as I ought to be at Albany to meet you, as I would gladly be if I dared, or could go there without being put in the newspaper." And he concluded teasingly, "<*You must not have such distinguished people anxious about you if you want them to come and meet you*>. I hope that does not provoke you."[42]

Edward was becoming a celebrity, recognizable by increasing numbers of the general public as a result of lengthy, illustrated profiles, as well as his own writings and lectures, featured in newspapers and magazines from New England to western frontier towns. From now on, Hattie would need to share him with an even wider constituency of admirers.

In mid-July, 1888, Emily Hale spent a week with her husband at the Chautauqua assembly at Weirs on Lake Winnipesaukee, New Hampshire, where he was to speak several times. Edward was then proposing to visit Hattie at Pepperell from July 25 to 30, a risky juxtaposition, before traveling to stay with his friends the Brams in Biddeford, Maine, where he attended yet another Chautauqua assembly. He was utterly exhausted the first two days after returning to Matunuck, writing to Hattie, "You are perfectly right in saying that I ought not to have made all these summer engagements. And I am as ready to promise as you are to beg that I will not make such another summer. But this year I have dear Phil's bills to pay and Berty's, so that I had to make both ends meet as I can…Now for three weeks of thorough rest here."[43]

If Hattie was chastising Edward for overbooking his time, she was not the only one. Emily must have observed the relentless pressures on him at Weirs and seems to have written him a loving letter, telling him she would join him in Matunuck a week earlier than he expected because he would be there. His response shows how quick he was to respond to any signs of affection from his self-absorbed wife: "As you say yourself, I like to have the care offered to me." He told her he would help her bear the burden of her difficult mother despite the old lady's "breaking every rule of the house," and concluded: "If you love me, that is enough. It is certain that I love you, and that with a tenderness which you do not yet understand or concur…But I am quite determined that another summer I will make few or none of these travelling engagements to speak." Edward also indicated in this letter that he expected some kind of appointment in London if Benjamin Harrison, the Republican candidate for the United States presidency, was elected. If so, it did not materialize. Sixteen years later, however, a high profile national appointment clarified the choice about which "wife" would accompany him away from Boston.[44]

But during that summer of 1888, there was no doubt for whom Edward yearned. In early August, as Hattie was leaving for a vacation in Brewster with her nieces and nephew, he quailed at the thought of having to leave Matunuck again for Chautauqua, little knowing that the very next day Hattie would receive word that her father had had another accident at Pepperell and was gravely ill. William Freeman lingered for several days and Edward agonized about whether or not he should leave for Chautauqua or race to Pepperell. Hattie's telegram telling him that her father had died on August 18 was not forwarded to him in Boston and Edward left for Chautauqua without knowing whether Freeman lived or died.

A week later, still at Chautauqua, Edward wrote the grieving and guilt-ridden Hattie, hoping she had returned to the children at Brewster: "You say you did not treat him well. You were an angel in comparison with me…And now the emancipation has come. Do you know I had imagined it a long, bitter, tedious waiting. I had even thought it would kill you and then, where should I be?" He continued, "All of a sudden, it came to me this morning. 'Why now, he has not that horrid button of bone pressing on his brain! Now he can see, and think, and remember, and love & plan, without that grinding oppression!'"[45]

Four days later, Edward wrote Hattie at Pepperell from Boston, where he had been able to see her briefly following his return from Chautauqua. "I shall go to Matunuck today," he told her. "I feel restless but much happier since I have seen you, and know how it all seems to you and how you fare."[46] In late September, he visited her at Pepperell, writing to her on his return: "I have looked back on Saturday and Sunday and Monday with perfect pleasure. We certainly left nothing undone which we ought to have done and the days each had its own mark to be remembered by…[a memory that] gives a new joy to all this winter that is before us. To be sure that we can help each other, and want to help each other, and that we have the good God as the third with us is everything."[47]

6

The Protégés—Charlotte Stetson [Gilman], Helen Keller, and Others

During 1887 and 1888, a young woman who would become the famous feminist intellectual Charlotte Perkins Gilman—the last of the brilliant Beechers—and a deaf-blind child, Helen Keller, both of them related to Edward, reached turning points in their lives. Charlotte had been turning to Edward Hale for advice since her childhood and her crisis was an avatar for what would befall Hattie a decade later. Helen Keller's plight had interested Edward and Hattie for some time before she arrived in Boston with her mother and her teacher Anne (Annie) Sullivan in May 1888.

Born in 1860, Charlotte Perkins was Emily Hale's niece, daughter of her oldest brother, writer and editor Frederick Beecher Perkins. He had left his family (Charlotte had an older brother Thomas) when the children were young and provided little support, so that they depended on the charity of relatives and friends, living, often at poverty level, in Providence, Rhode Island. Charlotte had no formal higher education apart from a year at the Rhode Island School of Design, but, like Hattie, she read voraciously (particularly the latest issues of *Popular Science Monthly*, which were sent to her in batches by her father and which gave considerable coverage to Herbert Spencer's interpretation of Darwinian evolution) and, in 1881, she began a course from the Society to Encourage Studies at Home.[1]

Charlotte had often stayed with the generous and welcoming Hales during her teenage years and even had a brief romantic attachment to her cousin Arthur. But she began to have doubts about marrying her fiancé, Providence artist Walter Stetson, after spending Thanksgiving 1882 with the Hales. She returned home depressed about the festive masquerade with play acting and dancing in the high-spirited Hale household. "I've outgrown this kind of fun," she told Walter, and claimed she no longer loved him. Although they went ahead with their wedding plans, it was a chilling first sign for Walter of Charlotte's emotional volatility.[2] Following the birth of their daughter the following year, Charlotte began to suffer from what we would now call severe postpartum depression. She spent a few months convalescing in Pasadena with her best friend Grace Channing and her family, who had recently moved there from Providence for the sake of Grace's health. Grace's father was Edward's college classmate and lifelong friend Dr. William F. Channing. Feeling much stronger after her months in California, Charlotte returned to Walter and Katharine but, by early 1887, she was suffering the symptoms of a severe nervous break-down.

In mid-February 1887, Edward called on neurologist Silas Weir Mitchell in Philadelphia, possibly to discuss his niece's declining mental health.[3] Mitchell was already well known to Edward through his literary work, and is thought to have treated at least one other member of the Beecher family. Three days after Edward's return from Philadelphia, Charlotte stopped by the Roxbury house. Edward was out but she noted in her diary that she had a long talk with her grandmother, Mary Perkins, before leaving to catch the train back to Providence.[4] An appointment was made for her to see Dr. Mitchell and she wrote a full description and chronology of her symptoms for him. Charlotte spent the entire month of May 1887 in one of Mitchell's sanitariums outside Philadelphia. Mitchell's famous "rest cure" treatment required bed rest, a milk diet, and total cessation of mental and physical activity. Although Mitchell was far from convinced that Charlotte was cured, there was no money to prolong her treatment, let alone spend up to a year convalescing in Europe which was what Mitchell generally advocated for his wealthier patients. According to an entry in Walter Stetson's diary, Mitchell advised her to return to her domestic duties and avoid too much brain work. But Helen Lefkowitz Horowitz, in her excellent study of Charlotte's formation and early years, has pointed out that Mitchell also advocated regular exercise as part of her recovery.

Meanwhile, Hattie wrote from Colorado Springs to her friend and mentor Alpheus Hyatt, curator of the museum of the Boston Society of Natural History. As later reported in the 1890 *Proceedings of the Boston Society of Natural History*, "a lady interested in the study of natural history [i.e., Hattie] expressed her desire to do something for the purpose of making the meaning of the exhibition collections more apparent to the public, especially to children...This matter has gone far enough to show, that if a regular office were made for this purpose and paid highly enough to secure a scientific man, or some person of sufficient scientific attainments, the results would amply repay the expenditure."[5] But Hattie did not think that Hyatt's first recommendation for this position could make the collections sufficiently interesting for children and hoped he would find someone more suitable.[6] Three years later, that perfect candidate appeared, a young Boston Tech geology student, Amadeus Grabau. Hattie and Edward would become important mentors to Grabau and later to his future wife Mary Antin.

At this point, also in May 1888, Helen Keller entered both their lives. Edward had become deeply interested in the welfare of his distant cousin's deaf-blind seven-year-old daughter, who was to begin studying at the Perkins School for the Blind. Helen, her mother Katharine Keller, and her teacher Annie Sullivan, herself a Perkins graduate, traveled in May from the Keller home in Alabama to Washington, D.C. There they called on President Grover Cleveland and Alexander Graham Bell, whose wife was deaf. It was Bell who had approached Michael Anagnos, director of the Perkins School, on behalf of the Kellers about finding an instructor for their seriously handicapped little girl. Edward wrote Hattie on May 31, "Little Helen Keller has come. I saw her mother and Annie Sullivan yesterday, Miss Mary [Cobb] is to see them today, and Emily and I will make a State call tomorrow. The mother is a pleasing person, glowing with happiness, as indeed she may be, in presence of a constant miracle."[7]

In early June, Edward described the Perkins School commencement, which Hattie and Mary Cobb had often attended in their roles as volunteers: "Our dear little Helen the light and life of the whole thing. Every now and then the exercises would be broken in upon with a coo-oo--oo of laughter from her, or a stream of kisses on Mr. Anagnos or Annie Sullivan, because Helen was quite too delighted to hold in. She read, very prettily, before the Assembly, Annie Sullivan interpreting. She fairly dances across the stage, life is such a joy to her…Did I tell you Annie always calls her 'Baby'?"[8]

The Hales held their "famous Helen Keller party," as Edward called it, at Highland Place, inviting five little girls to meet her: "Darling child, she fascinated us all," he wrote Hattie on June 9. He told her about the child's evident fascination as her fingers flew over a bas relief of Christ and John the Baptist, her questions, and his explanation of what she was feeling. Fifteen years later, when reviewing Helen Keller's autobiography, *The Story of My Life*, Edward described the extraordinary sensory and mental intelligence that Helen displayed as she felt the statuary in his house during this party: "It was in this interview that my personal intimacy with her began, and I am glad to say that it has continued ever since."[9] In his long letter describing the Keller party, Edward referred to Hattie's role in funding the journey of the "miracle worker," Annie Sullivan, from Boston to the Keller family in Alabama: "I always feel as if the whole success of the whole thing were yours. How little you thought when you sent your cheque for $30.00 for Annie Sullivan's summer vacation; and denied yourself a new bonnet, two pairs of gloves, three new lenses & four opera nights for it, that Helen Keller and a revolution of the Science of Education were to come from it!…(Did I tell you that M. Keller said the mother would have gone crazy if Helen had not been rescued)."[10]

In mid-June, Edward wrote to William Freeman at Pepperell and told him that he had received happy letters from Hattie in Colorado: "She says she has found a great many plants that are new to her…I heard indirectly from Miss Mary, at Brewster," he continued. "The little girl who is blind and deaf and dumb…is to go to Brewster with her mother. Their names are Keller. They are distant cousins of mine. I think Miss Mary arranged the plans and I am not sure but that they may go to her sister's house." Mary Cobb had found summer accommodation for the Kellers in the Elijah Cobb House there. Brewster was also the Freemans' ancestral home from the seventeenth century.

In 2007, a forgotten photograph of little Helen Keller and Annie Sullivan sitting in the garden of the Elijah Cobb House that summer resurfaced in a family collection donated to the New England Historic Genealogical Society of Boston.

The donor's mother had often stayed in the Elijah Cobb House during the summer as a child and she played with eight-year-old Helen there in July 1888, as did the Freeman children when they spent a holiday with Hattie in Brewster on her return from Colorado in July.[11] Toward the end of September, Helen and Annie visited the Freemans in West Newton. Hattie was evidently there too since she told Edward that she had invited Annie up to Pepperell for a brief holiday but Annie told her she was allowed no holiday by the Kellers. With Annie's help, Helen described her visit to her mother, who had returned to Alabama: "West Newton is not far from Boston and we went there in the steam cars very quickly. Mrs. Freeman and Carrie and Ethel and Frank and Helen came to station to meet us in a huge carriage. I was delighted to see my dear little friends and I hugged and kissed them. Then we rode for a long time to see all the beautiful things in West Newton. Many very handsome houses and large soft green lawns around them and trees and bright flowers and fountains."[12]

Edward would later publish several reminiscences about the young Helen, and Keller herself expressed her great fondness for him in *The Story of My Life* (1903), written with Annie Sullivan's help while Helen was a student at Radcliffe. But the Freeman family's role in Helen's Boston years is little known to her biographers. Helen remained in touch with Hattie's nieces for many years.

Meanwhile, Charlotte Stetson became even more depressed after returning to her husband in Providence, and, in late 1888, realizing that her spirits had almost entirely lifted during her 1885 stay in California, she departed again for Pasadena with some financial assistance from her friend Caroline Hazard's wealthy father. Rowland Hazard bought Charlotte's small property in Hartford and immediately lent her the money she needed. The Hazards of Peace

Holding a favorite doll and with Annie Sullivan beside her, Helen Keller sits on a chair under a bower in what was almost certainly the garden of the Elijah Cobb House in Brewster on Cape Cod. Hattie's companion Mary Cobb arranged for this holiday accommodation during the summer months following Helen's arrival in Boston and before she began her studies at the Perkins School for the Blind.
Courtesy of the New England Historic Genealogical Society, Boston.

Dale, Rhode Island, were all close friends of the Hales. Caroline Hazard would become president of Wellesley College in 1899, an appointment applauded by Edward despite his reservations about college education for women. This time, Charlotte took her small daughter Katharine with her, in a desperate bid for independence, hoping to support them both with writing and lecturing. Rather than staying with the Channings, she rented a cottage near their house. Walter Stetson, however, was not ready to give up on their marriage and he joined his wife and daughter in Pasadena in December 1888. During the year that he was there, Charlotte remained distant and Walter was thrown much into the company of Grace Channing. They fell in love with each other.

Edward Hale's connections to Charlotte Perkins Stetson resumed when he was staying with the Channings in Pasadena in early 1891. On March 10, he was interrupted while writing a letter to Hattie "by a visit from my niece Charlotte, Fred Perkins's daughter, a vivid, intense young woman of 30, who lives here. She wanted to read to me one of her Nationalist lectures which she is delivering here," he told Hattie, "and I wanted to hear it. I am afraid she is not physically strong enough to take up the role of a lecturer, as she wants to do. But she is awfully bright, & the lecture was telling and very much to the point." Charlotte was beginning to establish herself as a writer and lecturer and was writing plays with Grace Channing. Influenced by the socialist ideas of Edward Bellamy in his utopian novel *Looking Backward*—as was Edward—she had published her poem "Similar Cases" in the Bellamy-inspired *Nationalist* magazine in April 1890. The Hales had seen and admired this evolutionary poem about the "Eohippus," forerunner of the horse. During two rainy and very hot days in early June that year, Charlotte wrote her famous short story, "The Yellow Wall-Paper," which most scholars have interpreted as an indictment of her treatment three years earlier by Dr. Silas Weir Mitchell.

Charlotte narrated her story through the diary entries of a young wife and new mother suffering from "temporary nervous depression" while spending the summer in an old house leased for the summer. She has been confined by her domineering husband, John, and her brother, both physicians, to complete rest and a ban on writing and "fanciful thoughts" in the former children's nursery at

Edward appears to be congratulating Helen Keller, perhaps at a celebration of the publication of her autobiography. The photograph is inscribed to her by him and is dated January 1, 1903. Anne Sullivan's hair seems to be dressed for an important occasion.
Courtesy of the Schlesinger Library, Radcliffe Institute, Harvard University.

the top of the house. There the air is good but the window is barred. Writing her diary goes against her husband's proscription and, as she fails to improve, the narrator quotes her husband's warning. "John says if I don't pick up faster he shall send me to Weir Mitchell in the Fall." "I don't want to go there at all," she writes. "I had a friend who was in his hands once, and she says he is like John and my brother only more so!"

Banned from looking out of the window because she imagines that she sees people walking around the garden, she begins to focus on the room's ugly, yellow wallpaper with its over-wrought design. As she lies in bed at night, she imagines that she sees bars in the wallpaper and the figure of a woman struggling to get out. Increasingly, she identifies with the wallpaper-woman who she imagines escaping during the day and creeping around the garden and the room. During the last night before the family is due to leave the house, she thinks she sees the woman in the wallpaper begin to try and break out and she helps her by tearing the wallpaper off the walls. She has locked the door and thrown the key outside and refuses to allow anyone in the room. By now, she completely identifies with the wallpaper-woman, telling her husband when he breaks down the door, "I've got out at last...And I've pulled off most of the paper, so you can't put me back!" She is completely insane, reflecting Charlotte's greatest fear for herself.[13]

Charlotte knew she had written something very powerful and immediately sent the story to various literary friends and editors, including William Dean Howells, who sent it on to the editor of the *Atlantic Monthly*, but she had not succeeded in publishing it when she saw Edward in 1891. Edward visited Charlotte in her "little four roomed house, where she lives with her dear little girl, a charming child. She keeps house as her own servant, brings up her child by instinct, as she says, writes for a dozen magazines, and has written there eight lectures this winter." Edward continued his account for Hattie: "Physically she looks just like her mother, who is very pretty, and was a liar and fool—is now, I fear. But mentally and morally she is her father, Fred, over again, the brightest, best informed, and most absolutely impractical man I have ever had to deal with. He married a wife, because she wanted him to, & after the birth of 2 children found he could not live with her. Charlotte married a husband, whom she had steadily refused, simply because he wanted her to, and now, after the birth of this child, finds it better to have a continent between them. They are very fond of each other & write to each other every day."[14]

Edward's view of the breakdown of his brother-in-law's marriage to Charlotte's mother differs from accounts by many of Gilman's biographers who consider that Frederick Perkins cruelly abandoned his family and made little effort to support them. But Edward's empathy for both Fred Perkins, his onetime colleague on *Old and New*, and Fred's daughter demonstrates once again his tolerant attitude in the face of failed marriages while his admiration

Charlotte identified herself in this page proof photograph as sitting on the "steps of my little cottage." Despite her general dislike of domestic chores, she was trying to make a happy home in Pasadena for her little girl and was wearing the housekeeper's emblem, a white apron.
Charlotte Perkins Gilman Papers, Schlesinger Library, Radcliffe Institute, Harvard University.

for Charlotte shows his innate attraction to intelligent, free-spirited women (as long as they didn't behave rudely or aggressively). He may have helped her find a home for "The Yellow Wall-Paper" by persuading Edwin Mead, his successor as editor of the *New England Magazine*, to publish it. It appeared in the January 1892 issue and was met with mixed reactions. "The story could hardly, it would seem, give pleasure to any reader, and to many whose lives have been touched through the dearest ties by this dread disease, it must bring the keenest pain," wrote one critic, possibly a physician, to the *Boston Transcript*. It was his or her opinion that "such literature contains deadly peril" for those who were struggling with hereditary insanity. "Should such stories be allowed to pass without severest censure?"[15] Hattie Freeman, both of whose parents were mentally afflicted at the end of their lives, might have agreed with this opinion. It is not known if she ever read Charlotte's affecting story but Edward and Emily would certainly have done so.

When Charlotte initiated divorce proceedings against Walter in 1892, the press was often cruel in its denunciation of women like her who were renouncing marriage in favor of an independent, "self-sustaining" life. Edward and Hattie must have seen such headlines as the *Boston Herald*'s of December 20, 1892: "Nationalists on Marriage; Marital Relations Not a Part of Their Concern." Headlines elsewhere ranged from "Too Literary to be a Wife" (*Minneapolis Journal*) to the more tongue-in-cheek "His Tale of Woe. The Husband of Mrs. Stetson Unbosoms Himself…Her Plans for Bettering the Universe Annoyed Him. They kept Her Much Too Busy for His Comfort and Seriously Interfered with Domestic Affairs" (*Los Angeles Times*).[16] The dramatic increase in divorce and resistance of many college educated women to marriage were deeply troubling to the status quo. The newspapers did not report that Walter Stetson had fallen in love with Charlotte's close friend and literary collaborator, poet Grace Channing, whom he soon married. The three adults maintained a cordial relationship and Katherine Stetson spent most of the remainder of her childhood with her father and stepmother but remained close to her mother.

In 1900, Charlotte married her first cousin Houghton Gilman, who was seven years her junior. They had been childhood friends, often meeting at festive occasions at the Hales' house. A gentle, highly educated and cultured lawyer, Houghton was a frequent and very welcome summer guest in Matunuck over the years. Charlotte had reestablished contact with him when she was deep into researching and writing her great book *Women and Economics* (1898). Ironically, that was the year that Hattie became a patient of Dr. Silas Weir Mitchell at Edward's recommendation.

But for now, in 1889, Hattie and Edward were about to embark on the happiest and most intimate period of their long relationship.

7

Romance and Deception

Now that Hattie was orphaned, Edward evidently felt safer holding onto her letters. Her first surviving letter following her father's death, dated February 27 (although characteristically missing the year, 1889), captures her joy in her new found freedom: "Shall I write you of my day," she asked Edward, and then told him: "Down town all the morning. I went to Estes & Lauriats for Grace's present. & there saw a beautiful English work in two vols. on Alpine plants…I bought it for $7.00 with my hard-earned money from the botanical class…This afternoon I had a drive with Mr. Williams. Gypsy & Kasper harnessed doubled." Williams told her she was "too tender hearted" when she worried that Gypsy was too strong for Kasper. "We drove round a part of the Reservoir, where the roads were quite good," she wrote. "It was a fine mist all the way: & when we turned back towards the city, the easterly wind was pretty raw." She concluded, "*<I love you always more than you will ever believe>*."[1]

The next day, Edward traveled to Washington for the inauguration of President Benjamin Harrison. The sermon he delivered the day before the ceremony, at All Souls Unitarian Church on March 3, was a significant marker in what became one of his principal causes; he called for the first time for a permanent tribunal or international court of arbitration for peace to mark "the great victory of the Twentieth Century." He would live to see the establishment of a fledgling court at The Hague in the Peace Palace funded by Andrew Carnegie. But this effort, one of Edward's greatest interests in his final decades, failed to capture Hattie's imagination. Besides Edward, science, natural history, and outdoor life remained her abiding passions.

At last Hattie was free and had the income to live the life she had yearned for. William F. Freeman had left the Union Park house to his son Fred and had not changed his will. But on May 25, Fred's widow Harriet M. Freeman, with a substantial house of her own in West Newton, conveyed No. 37 to Hattie.[2] The spacious, well-furnished and appointed house which had been her home for eighteen years was now hers to run as she wished. In addition to the Freeman family's longtime handyman and driver George Whalley and their housekeeper and cook Mary Driscoll, Hattie hired young Sophie Russell as a maid. These two loyal, competent Irish Catholic women would serve her devotedly for more than thirty years. They made it possible for Hattie to run a most hospitable home, a comfortable and always welcoming sanctuary for Edward, removed from the constant, exhausting streams of parishioners and favor-seekers (he called them "map peddlers") at the church and his own house, as well as for her family and many friends. Much as she and Edward loved the country house in Pepperell, which Hattie now inherited, it may have represented for her at this stage too many years of parental servitude.

Following so many losses in their family the previous two years, the remaining Freemans and Atkinses drew closer. On March 1, 1889, Hattie told Edward she had spent the afternoon working at home on her slides. "Grace, Howell, Mrs. Reed & Aunt Mary came to tea…I showed them my butterflies, my microscope, & some slides with polarized light." Howell Reed wanted to borrow some of her specimens to show a friend who he said "was crazier than I."[3] On March 13, Edward recorded that he attended a high tea to celebrate Hattie's forty-second birthday that day with Grace and Howell Reed, Edwin and Katharine Atkins, Aunt Mary Atkins, Henrietta (Etta) Pierce (her close friend and neighbor), her companion Mary Cobb and her lodger Ida Noyes (principal of a kindergarten in Boston's North End), her sister-in-law Harriet Freeman, and her oldest niece Carrie.[4] As an example of how Edward was dividing his time between his two households, he welcomed "troops of friends" in his Roxbury house who came to fete him on his birthday on April 3, but then, as he noted in his journal, he "tried to go down town but stopped at the Freemans' and went no farther."

Edward was hard at work during 1889 reading the papers and letters of his old friend and longtime colleague, the Reverend James Freeman Clarke, at the request of Clarke's widow. Hattie recalled later how Clarke's daughter Lilian used to bring them hot oyster soup when they were working together on her late father's papers in his home study in Jamaica Plains. As the editor of Clarke's *Autobiography, Diary, and Correspondence* (1891), Edward "painstakingly deciphered, selected, and arranged fragments of autobiography and correspondence, composing connecting links and several chapters of narrative."[5] Writing from Matunuck in mid-April, 1889, Edward told Hattie: "I have had a good deal of J.F.C's correspondence here. I have a certain doubt creep on me whether he made the best he might have made of his life…He was actually buried by the petting & worship of a handful of people in the Indiana St. Church."[6] John Adams, Edward's literary biographer, called this "one of Hale's finest literary and scholarly achievements."

As a Transcendentalist, socially conscious minister of Boston's Church of the Disciples, major Unitarian leader, and scholar and author of twenty-eight books and over 120 pamphlets, whose career was remarkably similar to Hale's, Clarke was hardly idle. In fact, historians consider Clarke to be a more important leader and intellectual of the Unitarian denomination than Hale. Like Hale, he had discouraged intolerance and encouraged social reform, but his human rights advocacy included woman suffrage and university education for women, at which Edward balked, at least publicly. This was a characteristic position for more conservative clergymen at this time but astonishing for one as generally broad-minded as Edward Everett Hale.

Like James Freeman Clarke, the Reverend Joshua Young, the Freemans' minister at Groton near their Pepperell country house, was a supporter of women's rights and education. The same age as Edward, he was also a devoted friend and counselor to Hattie. "Do you know what an exalted opinion Mr. Young has of women!" Hattie wrote Edward on May 30 from Newport, Rhode Island, where she was part of a large party of women students on a geological walk along the cliffs led by Boston Tech Professor George Barton.[7] Scorning the gossipy chatter of some of the women in that party, which she felt was discourteous to their instructor, she recalled the Groton cleric's admiration for women of a more serious bent: "He thinks they are rapidly coming to the front in all matters of importance & that they will soon take on the lead, especially in church matters. It made me laugh when he tried to persuade me I belonged to this superior body."[8]

This was the year that Jane Addams, who attended a Unitarian church and ethical society while in Chicago, founded the secular Hull House settlement there and Frances Willard, a Methodist, was at the height of her powers as the leader of the Woman's Christian Temperance Union (WCTU), just to mention two of those extraordinary women, both friends of Edward. But, unlike those women, Hattie's talents and ambitions were often subsumed by her devotion to a demanding man. Characteristically, her letter glowed with happiness over a conversation with Edward the day before: "<*I think over and over again all that you said to me yesterday and how much we love each other*>."[9]

Joshua Young (1823-1904) was an exact contemporary of Edward but had been more radical in his anti-slavery activism before the Civil War. An ardent abolitionist, he was a conductor for the Underground Railroad following passage of the 1850 Fugitive Slave Law, both as a young divinity student in Boston and also, between 1852 and 1860, as pastor to the Unitarian church in Burlington, Vermont.[10] It was not surprising, therefore, that he was called to perform the funeral service on December 8, 1859, of fiery abolitionist John Brown at the remote Brown family farm at North Elba, a black community founded by Unitarian abolitionist Gerrit Smith on his land in the northern Adirondacks. Following Brown's execution in Charles Town, Virginia, for leading the raid on the federal arsenal at Harper's Ferry, his body was transported north by train to be buried at North Elba at his request.

Young's church was torn over the issue of slavery and he was forced to resign in the ensuing controversy. He took over the ministry at Groton near Pepperell in 1875 after years of wandering from parish to parish.[11] Two years later, in 1877, he was a grand chaplain for the dedication ceremony for the Soldiers and Sailors Monument on Telegraph Hill on Boston Common. Twenty-five thousand Civil War veterans marched six miles in a procession that ended on the summit, a spectacular event that Hattie must surely have witnessed. Edward Everett Hale is portrayed on that monument in a bas-relief commemorating the work of the U.S. Sanitary Commission. Young was certainly Hattie's confidant during troubled times and a letter she wrote him nine years later suggests that she may have confessed her love for Edward to him.

While Edward needed Hattie too intensely to give her up, he frequently expressed his admiration for her drive and competence and worried that he might be holding her back. When she spent a few days in mid-June with her recently widowed Aunt Mary at Belmont, she received two letters from Edward pondering her determined pursuit of advanced education in science. He mused about her wish to go away to Vassar and wondered how much she had resented his opposition to the idea at that time. He remembered how interested he was in her wish to understand her father's business and how he admired her determination to continue her education even if she was not permitted to go to Vassar. He also told her that Nelly had been equally eager to go to Antioch. "It is clear enough now," he continued, "that this car[ry]ing [*sic*] out of your own course, and creating, so to speak, your own teachers, have made you the interesting and independent woman you are, in a certain sense a leader and a person who has done much good to others like you who wanted to study who would never have forged out any such way."[12]

Bored as he had been by the rote learning practiced during his Harvard undergraduate days in the 1830s, Edward told Hattie how much he admired her determined pursuit of scientific knowledge. Referring to her recent declaration that she had hated school, where she had been upset and mortified by her stammering, he told her that he had forgotten that was ever a problem. Moreover, "if a girl who hated school & dodged it grows up to be like you…How clear it is that a great deal better could be done with most girls than is done. I think I shall make you put on paper your view of all this sometime. It is much more important that you should dictate your real autobiography to me, than that I should dictate my anecdotes of the outside of mine to you."[13]

Hattie's response to Edward's comments in view of his well-known opposition to university education for the women in his life might have been provocative and revealing but she either avoided the subject or that letter is missing. At this stage of their relationship, when her romantic love for him was mixed with a large helping of adulation, she appeared to avoid raising issues that might upset him, an attitude which gradually changed over the years. After all, she had promised to bring youth, energy, and fresh optimism into his life. So instead she wrote about her enjoyment of her stay with her Atkins relations: "It is a very warm day, but I am on the corner of the piazza, where it is as cool as it can be anywhere. There is no sound, save the singing of birds & humming of bees, & all is peaceful & quiet. It is years since I have been here for such a visit; & I said this morning at breakfast that I had not had a Sunday morning breakfast here since perhaps fifteen years ago when we were at Newton Highlands for several summers. Father & I used habitually to ride over horseback Sunday mornings. Going out to breakfast was a Cuban fashion that Father always liked & clung to throughout his life."[14]

In late June, Hattie wrote to Edward as she was waiting on the wharf in Eastport, Maine, to board the steamer for a brief vacation in Nova Scotia with her companions Mary Cobb and Hortense Dudley. Edward had seen them onto the coastal steamer in Boston and his last call on her at Union Park before they were separated for the summer was very much on her mind. She told him that she was reading a book on the Ice Age but her mind kept wandering back to the influence her minister had had on her, "Truly more than any other factor in my life…<*I keep saying to myself he loves me he loves me and I am so glad and happy in the thought that it is constant sunshine in my life. It is only the thought of the parting which must come for a little while…*>"[15]

Two days later, Edward wrote to tell her about the fiftieth reunion of his Harvard Class of 1839. At the last minute, he was asked to speak at the commencement dinner in place of class president Samuel Eliot, who was not feeling well, but Sam entertained the class to supper at his house that evening. "Your Mr. Watson was there," Edward reported, "and declared that he was very sorry he had never acknowledged the 'aphylum' and the other. They had both done well. He pretended it was because he had lost your address, but I gave him no mercy. He <u>has</u> shortia, and promised me a plant, which I shall give to you. He also promises me Bohemian Pluris, which he says delight in the seashore." Edward was referring to Sereno Watson, Asa Gray's longtime assistant and curator of the Gray Herbarium (Gray had died the year before), for whom Hattie had been collecting plants. Edward told her that he would see Watson again when he went to have tea with Sam Longfellow, another close college friend and groomsman at his wedding.[16] The history of the search for the very rare shortia and the part that Hattie would play in it will be told in chapter 11.

Hattie returned home in time to spend a precious half hour with Edward just before he left town with Emily and Nelly to attend the marriage of oldest son Arthur to Camilla Conner at her parents' country house in Cecil County, Maryland. Edward officiated, as he would at other of his sons' weddings. On the eve of leaving on the twelve-hour journey to Mohonk Mountain House to join her friend Miss Barr for two or three weeks, Hattie wrote Edward, who was now at Matunuck, "I used $3.75 out of the $18.00 I earned with my botany class in the purchase of Mr. Wright's North American Ice Age, which is now out. It is full of fascinating illustrations & I am eager to begin on it at once."[17] This is the second reference to her earnings from her botany class, although she never mentions where and to whom she gave those classes.

Mohonk Mountain House, a huge castle-like hotel perched on the cliffs above Lake Mohonk, just south of New York's Catskill Mountains, was founded by twin brothers Alfred and Albert Smiley in 1879. The Quaker Smileys, like Edward, were temperance advocates and they banned liquor, dancing, and card playing at their hotel. In 1883, Albert Smiley launched the Friends of the American Indian conferences there. The aim was to improve the living standards of American Indian populations and the meetings brought together government representatives of the Bureau of Indian Affairs and the House and Senate committees on Indian Affairs, as well as educators, philanthropists, and Indian leaders to discuss the formulation of policy. "How much do you know of this place & how much shall I tell you!" wrote Hattie, who had stayed there briefly in June 1884. "I really hope if you have another invitation to an Indian Conference here, you will come. It is worth while... for you to see a house carried on as this is; it would confirm your idea as to the possibility of a Kingdom of Heaven on earth." Although Edward did not attend an Indian conference there, as Hattie had hoped, he was a faithful attendee for many years of the annual Mohonk conferences on International Arbitration, giving the first major address there in 1895.

During this stay at Mohonk, Hattie was content to be on her own, relieved to be temporarily separated from the garrulous Mary Cobb: "Reading in these rustic summer houses among such charming surroundings is very pleasant. I am now reading with real pleasure Agassiz's Life & Letters, which I brought with me...You know I can never read anything of value in a room where Miss Mary is; because if she does not talk, I think every minute she is going to."[18]

Eleven days later, she wrote Edward at Weirs that she was about to leave the peace of Mohonk to continue her vacation in Saratoga, New York. "The Ice Age has contributed much to my enjoyment," she wrote. "I take it with me everywhere, to summer houses & in the boat. I have finished the physical geography part which interests me most & shall be ready to let you have it for August."[19] On July 31, she wrote from the United States Hotel at Saratoga Springs, where the weather was dreadful, finalizing plans for Edward to come to Boston from Matunuck to meet her: "I shall be back Saturday. You will come up Monday, as early as you can, & I will be at the house from three to four. And then we can have Tuesday morning as well. And I will not go to Brewster until Wednesday. <*I plan this all*> with reference <*to you: and please give me all the time you can for you do not know how much I want to see you and we never have time to tell each other all...*> Oh, <*how I long to see you*>."[20]

Hattie's letters from Brewster on Cape Cod, where she relaxed into a simple summer lifestyle near the beach with her nieces and nephew, show the joy she always felt in their company. The oldest, Caroline (Carrie), a kind and dutiful child, turned twelve that month, Frank was nine, Ethel Hale (Edward's goddaughter and already a studious child) was eight, and Helen, who was just a baby when her father died, was four. Between swimming, beach combing, and playing with the children, Hattie continued to study

Joseph Le Conte's account of Louis Agassiz's work and that of his American followers in comparison to the major British evolutionist Charles Darwin: "I can not understand Agassiz's position with regard to Evolution. He believes in the 'permanence of type.' So do the evolutionists, as far as I can see. Would it not be well if we were to have some serious reading together when we are together in Pepperell this fall. <*I think we should love and respect each other the more if we sometimes do so*>. Le Conte has one chapter on the position that Agassiz held to Evolution & just before his death, Agassiz wrote an article for the *Atlantic Monthly*, giving his own views. It was the first of a series, which he did not live to finish. Would you like to read them both with me?"[21] Edward would often credit Hattie with teaching him science and she can certainly be credited with opening his mind to the many theories of evolution that she studied.

Hattie begged Edward to visit them at Brewster but, in late August, Edward was entertaining another of his bluestocking friends at Matunuck. Sarah Jane Farmer was a rather more worldly woman than the love-sick Hattie of 1889, and likely the principal reason for his delaying a visit to Hattie at that time. None of Edward's surviving letters to Hattie that summer mention Farmer's visit but he wrote to Emily on August 28: "Miss Farmer drops entirely into our life, and does not have to be cared for. She was in her room writing, all the morning yesterday…It was a perfect afternoon for walking, and she enjoyed everything as much as I wanted her to do. She is a great talker, and as she has seen a great deal of the world, has very good stories to tell."[22] Farmer was a partner in a venture to open a resort hotel at her home in Eliot, Maine, three miles from Portsmouth, New Hampshire, on a site above the Piscataqua River made sacred by a gathering of Indian chiefs to smoke the pipe of peace. The Sarah Farmer Inn, built in 1889-90, was dedicated as Green Acre-on-the-Piscataqua and debuted with the 1890 season. She must have been full of enthusiasm for this project when staying with the Hales. In June 1892, Sarah had a vision of Green Acre as a place where various philosophies and religions could be taught. She also made it the last great bastion of Transcendentalism. Edward would become a regular lecturer there.

Perhaps Susan, harried by the endless round of visitors to the

Matunuck house and with the entire responsibility of housekeeping, resented the time Edward gave to this strong-minded bluestocking, who was there at Edward's invitation at a time when she and her brother were collaborating on a series of travel books for children, for she used a slur in referring to Farmer in a letter to "J.B.," thought to be her 26-year-old nephew Edward Jr. Although she usually called him Jack, Susan amused herself by making up pet names for her nearest and dearest. In this letter, she was describing the accounts for running the Matunuck house that summer, saying it had cost nearly $1,000 and that she had charged "poor Parber $350," considerably more than anyone else. She said she felt bad about "pinching him" for that much but he and his family were more expensive than others: "Of course his son Robert, his son [Arthur?], and daughter Camilla, his concubine Farmer and his lawful spouse are accounted to him."[23]

The words "concubine Farmer" are difficult to decipher but sure enough to mention, particularly since the sometimes caustic Susan was to refer to "the ex-concubine Harriett Freeman" in a letter to a friend nearly twenty years later. However, it was also a term that her nephews bandied light-heartedly in their letters about each others' and their friends' flirtations. Susan was a perceptive observer of people's foibles and characters and the tartness of her conclusions makes her letters enormous fun to read, but they must be read with caution. She was wrong about Sarah Farmer but she probably had a strong inkling even then that Hattie was far more than his literary amanuensis. Although brother and sister were very fond of each other, Susan was always clear-eyed about Edward's charm for intellectual women.

During her weeks at Pepperell, Hattie sought advice about selling the place that had been in her mother's family for three generations: "While Arthur was here," she reported about the assistance she received from a friend or relation, "he went with me to see the two men whom I thought best to consult in relation to the sale of this place. They both said it would have to be sold to some outside party. No one in town had money enough to take it. The chance of disposing of it as a country residence at this season of the year, is not great, & as the house should stand as it is until sold, it is not likely I shall have the work of pulling things to pieces this fall as I thought I might."[24] The Freeman children were staying with her but she had become very worried about little Helen who was running a high fever and coughing. Panicking when the local doctor proved to be incompetent, she decided on the spur of the moment to take Helen, a delicate child, home to her mother in West Newton, where the family doctor diagnosed bronchitis and immediately started treatment.

As Hattie had feared, Edward's visit to Pepperell was both delayed and shortened to a long weekend in mid-October. Hattie picked him up in the buggy at Ayer Junction on Friday and they drove as usual to call on local Unitarian friends. They spent all day Saturday canoeing on the nearby Nissitisset River together. Edward noted later in his journal, while not naming his hostess, that he dictated an account of this happy adventure, probably the next morning when "it rained like fury," for his "Tarry at Home Travel" column in the *New England Magazine*. His account, which was undoubtedly written in concert with Hattie, is redolent with their love of nature and pleasure in each other's company.

"Can man conceive anything more charming than this gliding on from reach to reach, in the midst of the glory of ten thousand colors, over the unrippled surface of the river, which reflects absolutely every form and tint?" Edward began:

> H. and I can never agree whether the forward seat or the seat aft is the better seat in the canoe. This disagreement in a voyage of discovery like ours is no inconvenience, for we need take but one boat and each can have his own way. For my part, at the prime of life, which is about sixty-seven years of age, I am well satisfied with what I have to-day. A heavy bearskin on the floor of the boat aft, a back devised by myself, the slope of which can be changed from time to time, the after thwart under my knees, and one's extended feet in the space between that thwart and the next, among the baskets and the shawls. H., on the other hand, who is younger, and inherits the straightness of back of I know not how many grandfathers and grandmothers, whose chairs are still preserved, prefers to sit as erect as they did on the

> foremost thwart, and pulls a strong paddle there. Now with two people who paddle as well as we do, you can do what you choose in the Nissitisset and you need not be at all tired.

As Edward dictated this account of nature lying on a sofa in Hattie's country house the next day, Hattie told him that it would only be entertaining if they included illustrations. Instead, the two of them painted word pictures of the bird and wildlife and abundant and colorful autumn foliage that they saw along the river banks and in the river itself as they paddled along for several miles. Noting a perfect spot for a picnic under a pine tree on the edge of a large meadow, they hauled the canoe out of the water, spread the bearskin on the ground and made a small fire of dead wood, cones, and twigs: "Now set the coffee can on the coals in the middle of the burning twigs. Open that basket and make scientific observations on the comparative worth, as a nutriment, of tongue sandwiches, hard-boiled eggs, rye biscuits, buttered, Seckel and Sheldon pears, diluted, as the case may require, with an infusion of *Caffea Mochaica* mixed in equal parts with *Caffea Javensis.*" On the leisurely paddle downstream, reported Edward, "as H. seemed to be in the mood for paddling, I let H. and the current do the work, while I did the advising and a fair part of the steering," a telling metaphor for their relationship at that point.[25]

In her first letter after Edward's departure for Boston, Hattie reported that the weather had turned glorious again: "It seems as if the sunshine were made double by the yellow leaves; & I feel as if living in a yellow world. Why do I not say 'How I wish you were here now, instead of on those grey days of Sunday & Monday'?" First, because she knew he did not like her dwelling on his absences but also because she was "too grateful for the joy I had <*when you were here*>." But she hated to think of him living in the city with "such meagre glimpses of the sky & the glories of the world. <u>Please, please</u>, do not spend all your time & strength in trying to set the whole world right," she begged him. "If those broken-winded old machines are breaking up in a natural way, let them go! Do not give your life in trying to save them <*you have hardly a right to offer your life as not your own. It is mine*>."[26]

The day after Edward left her, Hattie had an unexpected visit from Joshua Young, who asked her if she would consider accompanying him to the Unitarian Conference which was to be held in Philadelphia that year. His deafness was now so pronounced that he was nervous about traveling alone and needed someone to take notes for him at meetings. This request highlighted for Hattie her anomalous social position since her father's death and she asked Edward to advise her about the propriety of traveling to Philadelphia alone with her country minister, even suggesting that he ask Mrs. Hale for her advice on the matter! She may also have wanted to prompt a little jealousy. On the 25th, she wrote: "Mrs. Andrews writes me that Mr. Young & I are to be included in Mrs. Hooper's party of twenty-five, which goes to the Continental. Grace goes to the Colonnade. I…suppose I should just have the satisfaction of seeing her & seeing you by means of an opera glass across an immense building. I do not anticipate the least bit of pleasure seeing you under such circumstances; & yet I suppose it will be all different to me because I shall be conscious that you are there."[27]

During this conference, Judith Andrews, as the president of the Women's Auxiliary Conference, was the only woman elected to the National Conference Council. Perhaps this was what the Reverend Young had in mind when he told Hattie earlier in the year that women were coming to the forefront in all matters, particularly in religious leadership. The 1889 conference seems to have resolved many of the disagreements between the Ethical Unitarianism of the Western Conference and the Christian Unitarianism of the AUA. Several of the addresses showed a willingness to listen to and accommodate the ethical dissenters.[28]

Hattie was back at Pepperell by November 3. She had expected to meet up with Mary Cobb at the station in Boston but "Miss Mary" missed the train. Mary and Sophie had lit a blazing fire to welcome her on a cold afternoon and were looking very smart in their black dresses and white aprons. She had forgotten to tell Edward something "in the short time that I saw you, for there was so much else to <*say and my lips had so much else to do darling man*>." Elsewhere in this long letter, as it poured rain outside, she captured the ever increasing intimacy of their relationship: "I wonder what you are doing! You are in the study either lying on the sofa asleep under my shawl, or else stretched in the long chair, <*writing to me.*

How I wish we were together>. Either <*I were there or you were here shut in by all the storm…in each other's arms*> We should not care how long it rained then, should we? <*You will save all*> Thursday <*that we may be together…Be sure to give*> no engagements <*for that day because it will be the very last one we can be sure of being alone and having the house to ourselves*>."

Besides listing all the lectures and excursions she hoped they would attend together in Boston that winter, she also stated a rather more wifely intent: "<*I am going to try to make your life as easy as possible this winter and I am going to pet you and save you and help you and take care of you just as I should towards any which has a part of my own love my very very own.*>"[29] Ten days later, on the eve of leaving Pepperell for the winter, and perhaps for good, Hattie wrote: "I am nearly packed up. Two wagon loads have been carried to the depot to go by freight this afternoon. I have gone round to make my good bye calls."[30]

That winter, Edward and Hattie saw a good deal of each other at church and in public and private meetings but by early March 1890 Hattie was vacationing in Altamonte, Florida, with her widowed maternal uncle Frank Howe, a Newburyport physician, of whom she was particularly fond. However, the idle Florida resort lifestyle was not for her. Never one to waste time, Hattie's intolerance for boredom comes across in one of her Florida letters: 'I am glad I am not to stay here long. How one can stay here a winter, I do not understand. There is nothing to do but sit around, chat, crochet, read & play cards in the evening. I would sooner endure all the inclemencies of a northern winter, even if they killed me, for there I should the sooner enter Real Life: dawdling around here isn't Life."[31]

She and Dr. Howe returned via Louisville, Kentucky, where they stayed with his son, James Lewis Howe, a professor at the Polytechnic Institute. The younger Howe and his wife were Presbyterians so Hattie attended their church out of courtesy to them: "…such stuff as I heard," she complained. "Every time I go to an Evangelical church, I say I will never do it again…This man had no thought to his sermon. It was just save yourselves, Come to Jesus, be a thoroughgoing Christian & he yelled at us too. Such preaching really angers me: & it was an hour or two before I felt in a peaceful frame of mind."[32]

In the meantime, Edward was staying at the quiet, picturesque New Jersey shore resort of Island Heights with Nelly and an artist friend of hers. There the young women painted portraits of their landlady's daughter while Edward wrote 25 to 30 pages a day on the James Freeman Clarke book. Edward found that his immersion in James Freeman Clarke's life and papers made him increasingly introspective about his own life choices: "All this mulling over J. F. Clarke's diaries and letters make me ask myself, whether I have not wasted a great deal of my own life, in a good-nature, like his, which made me say yes to everything which came along," he wrote Hattie. "Or is this, perhaps, what Life is for, and what a Christian Minister is for, to Lend-A-Hand, as Clarke did and I have tried to do, where a hand was needed?" In September, Emily wrote from Pepperell, where she was taking yet another rest cure for her nerves accompanied by Nelly, expressing her anger at Mrs. Clarke's attempt to rewrite a portion of the Clarke book with some "friends of literary taste and experience." The Hales believed that William Lloyd Garrison had read the section on Clarke's antislavery initiatives and advised her to make revisions.[33]

Hattie now began the practice of treating each of her nieces and her nephew to special trips or travels with her. In early May, she took her eldest niece Carrie to stay with her in New York for a few days. Writing from the Victoria Hotel, she reported some rare personal indulgences: "We have had a hard rainy day; still, it has not been utterly lost to us. It did not rain as we went out, & we took a hansom…We spent the morning in gazing about in Stewarts, & in Tiffany's. I made my one purchase at the latter place. Now, don't think I am going into frivolities! I bought a piece of polished agatized wood, from Arizona. I think it beautiful & I am sure you will agree with me." They went to Vautine's, the great Japanese store, so that Carrie could buy small gifts for her family and friends with her allowance, and then to a matinee of "The Homestead."[34]

Hattie reminded Edward that only two weeks remained following her return when they could see each other before the Reverend Young came to stay with her for Anniversary Week. Then they would go their separate ways for the summer: "You will not make more engagements for that time than is really necessary. Especially, save Wednesday & Thursday after 12 N. We must crowd all our spring time into this short time <*for another parting comes so soon. Dearest love me trust me keep me and pray for me as I do for you*>."[35]

The Pepperell house was sold and Hattie now had to face the formidable hurdle of clearing out and distributing the accumulations of three generations, including an impressive library, eighteenth-century furniture, fine silver and paintings, and other treasures.[36] In early July, Edward responded sympathetically to her description of the emotionally wrenching task from Matunuck where he was reveling in his son Philip's company after his two years studying art in Paris. He was working hard on several commissioned articles and finishing up the Clarke book.

The following week, Hattie joined her nephew and nieces on Cape Cod. "I should so like to sit by, invisible, while you deal with the children before they go to bed," Edward wrote. 'How they will always look back to Brewster and Aunt Hatty, in all after life, as they look back on the foundations of their training. It is very edifying to me, to hear the boys dilate on something or other I told them in boyhood."[37] He scribbled another letter at 6 a.m. one morning because Philip wanted to paint his portrait "and this is the best hour two such busy people can select…You will be delighted to know that Phil has not said a word about hair-cutting, nor has anyone else, so that we can do as we please about it, when I am in town."[38] Locks of hair had a special significance for Victorian lovers (for example, George Armstrong Custer sent locks of his long blond hair to his wife Libby who saved them and, after his death, had them made into a wig). Edward would often refer to the "ear locks" he sent Hattie in small envelopes when they were separated over the years as the "last part of myself."[39]

Hattie maintained her cover as Edward's loyal assistant by occasionally writing letters to "Dear Mr. Hale" that he could share with his family. The Hales must have enjoyed the descriptive letter that she wrote about a visit to the Brewster Weir, although only Edward knew that it was really a siren call to tempt him to join her in Brewster. The fish weirs at Brewster were built by local fishermen each season and consisted of nets strung between sapling trees stuck deep into the sand. Visitors liked to ride out in horse-drawn wagons, as Hattie and the children did, to watch the men and teams of horses hauling out mackerel, whiting, pollock, and other marine life.[40] She took her description of the Brewster Weir further in her charmingly informative article published two months later in *The Look-Out: A Monthly Magazine* for young members of the Lend A Hand affiliated clubs. A born teacher, she wrote enchantingly for children. In May, her story "What Is It?" described the first time as a girl she observed a caterpillar become a chrysalis and then a butterfly. In July, her didactic article "Granite Hill" was printed in the same magazine, whose editor was longtime SCC staffer Minnie Whitman.

Edward's suggestion that the children would never forget their days at Brewster with "Aunt Hatty" was quickly corrected by Hattie, who told him they always called her "Aunt Harriet." But she agreed on the accumulation of childhood memories:

> I do give my whole time to them here, that they may have a good time. We have a great, wide open field all around the house, now just covered with the soft fuzzy heads of the rabbit clover. We had a game of tag there last night, though there is nothing I hate to do so much as to run. But it was delicious to see the freedom & grace of Ethel as she ran, her yellow curls coming out from the red flannel cape I had tied over her. You can have no idea what a joy it is to me to play for a short time that these children are mine; to have the care & direction of them. It is a wholly different thing to see them in their own home; where I can have no care of them. Much as I love & respect Hattie, when I have the children I want them without her. But I doubt if you can understand this."[41]

Hattie enjoyed just ten days at Brewster with the children before leaving on a Raymond excursion to Alaska with Judith Andrews. Edward noted in his journal on July 19 that he saw the "Alaska party" off at the Lowell Railroad Station that morning. In Montreal, the party switched onto the Canadian Pacific line, passing along the shores of Lake Superior to Winnipeg, then on to Victoria, British Columbia. En route from Montreal, Hattie wrote, "I wish you would keep my letters & give them back to me on my return as I have now my North Carolina letters. The time may come when I shall read them over with pleasure, for I write them with much more interest than I write in my journal, in which I can really only give headings." Considering Edward's great interest in her adventures, there are surprisingly few of Hattie's letters from this trip in the collection. One possibility is that Edward held on to them for his proposed but never completed history of the Pacific coast. However, he wrote to her at Yellowstone National Park on August 20, 1890, "I must get ready to give you back your letters. I shall do so, by copying into a book I have all the descriptions of all the journey across." He told her that he wanted to use them in his Norwegian story in *Lend A Hand*.

Again, Hattie expressed her disdain for frivolous women as she described those who would share their compartment during the long journey across Canada, calling one of them "flighty" and another a "fliberty [*sic*] gibbet, as so many women are."[42] She was equally critical of men who talked down to serious-minded women like her: "They would never talk to men in that silly way."[43] The next day, she wrote:

> I asked Mr. Holden some question last night about altitude & as the talk went on, I learned he had had a wide experience in balloon ascensions. I begged of him to take a seat in my section, & there for an hour he sat & told me stories of his balloon ascensions, of being carried out to sea & of being landed in the woods in Maine. Then he told me how marvelous the earth appeared as the shadows crept over it. He was once at an altitude of 10,000 ft. You know how little I care for women's ordinary talk & how much I care for the talk of men who know a great deal or who have had a wide & large experience…Do you know what a 'cantilever' bridge is? I do, and will tell you when I get home.[44]

Judith Andrews reminisced fourteen years later about the difference in Hattie's personality when she was in the company of people who shared her interests and enthusiasms: "How well I remember my surprise and delight in seeing your diffidence and reserve with strangers overcome by your enthusiasm over some geological formations, on that memorable trip of 1890. How plainly I recall one incident when you were talking with an elderly gentleman, your fingers nervously working with your watch chain, your eyes sparkling with excitement, and your words tripping over each other in your endeavor to talk rapidly, how interested was the listener, and how fearful you were afterwards that you had <u>bored</u> him!"[45]

Edward missed her terribly, as one letter begun at Roxbury and sent from Matunuck to Tacoma, Washington, makes quite clear: "Sixth day after my own child left and waved her hand so gracefully as the train swept away. Dreamed of her at night. Woke to count that this was the 6th day." From brushing his teeth with the toothbrush she gave him and washing with the sponge she gave him to packing for Matunuck with the valise and two bags she gave him, and then writing twelve letters that she would have written much better, everything reminded him of her. And then, when he had arrived at Matunuck, he continued, "Nap in the room she lived in when she was here. Made myself nice with the things from her dressing case. P.S. Went to bed and to sleep <*with her little prayer*>."[46]

This letter highlights Hattie's extraordinary generosity. Across the years, she showered expensive gifts, even furniture and clothing, on Edward and dispatched flowers, plants for their gardens, and hampers of fresh produce to the Hales, who were often in financial difficulties. Edward had many wealthy parishioners who were similarly generous but some of Hattie's gifts were astonishingly intimate, including a pair of Pepperell "under drawers." The nature of some of the gifts indicates that Emily Hale did not take sufficient care of her husband and Hattie was only too happy to fill this void. Apparently, these gifts to Edward did not escape Emily's notice, however, as her Christmas thank you letter to "Dear Miss Freeman" ten years later indicates: "It really seems as if you could not have given presents, of late, to any one out of this family. I keep seeing beautiful things in the study, and saying, 'Why, wherever did this come from?' till finally I am sure the answer will be 'Oh, Hatty always gives me this.'"[47]

As Hattie's closest counselor on the path she might take in her liberation, Edward thought of her when he paid a visit in August to Nathaniel (Nat) Kidder at the Milton estate he inherited from his father. Nat was one of three sons of his late friend Henry Kidder.

Edward's tour with young Nat of the beautiful gardens on the 18-acre estate surrounding his Italianate house and the lazy afternoon spent browsing his botanical library gave him an idea for Hattie's future: "I have found out what you are to do and how you are to live. You are to have a house a few miles out of Boston <*not beyond easy walking distance from me*> and you are to have a garden and a green-house. You will be perfectly happy, and that is what I want you to be, and you will be able to make all your friends happy and that is what you want to do."[48]

Edward told Hattie that he would take her to see the gardens when she returned to Boston. But Edward's dream of a convenient and yet discreet Arcadia was not to be. Hattie had decided to make 37 Union Park her permanent home and spend summers in the White Mountains or traveling abroad. That October, when Hattie was in the Berkshires and western Massachusetts enjoying the fall colors with Mary Cobb, Edward laid out for her a proposed schedule for their winter activities together that indicated he was hoping to spend more time with her than at home or on his church duties. He was trying to make the majority of parish visits before Christmas and had already decided to turn over to longtime staffer Minnie Whitman the editing of his *Lend a Hand* magazine.

Although Edward and Hattie had anticipated being together in Boston the entire winter of 1890-91, the winter sabbatical in California that Judith Andrews had been trying to arrange for her minister for some time became possible when several wealthy parishioners funded the trip. It would not be entirely a vacation because, as a member of the ministers' council of the National Conference, the trip would enable Edward to meet with California's Unitarian congregations and their ministers. On January 1, 1891, Edward wrote Hattie, "1890 was better than 1889. We will be cheerful and make of each day the best we can. No distance shall part us, and no custom of presence make us weary of each other. Truth 1st, Right with Truth: and Love with both." On the back of the envelope, he scribbled, "Unless something happens which I do not know, I will appear at 37."[49] In the meantime, the Hales received a letter from Arthur Hale informing them that Nelly, who was staying with him and his family in Philadelphia, was suffering from bronchitis. She would obviously benefit from spending the rest of the winter in California's mild climate with her father.

In reality, this was not a good time for Edward to leave his duties at the South Congregational Church. During the fall of 1890, Edward's hardworking associate, the other Edward Hale, received a call to become minister to a new Unitarian congregation in Orange, New Jersey. Edward tried hard to persuade "Mr. Edward" that he should not waste his talents in an obscure outpost. But on December 11, he noted in his day book: "I had a long talk with Edward, which must count as final, as he determines to go to Orange after Easter." Depending as he did on the younger man, Edward was very upset and appeared to have realized that the decision related to some fault of his own, most likely his abrogation of tiresome and tiring parish work. It was just as likely, however, that the young man, who was married, could no longer afford to share the senior minister's annual salary of $6,000. Edward noted in his journal on January 25, 1891, "We had an informal meeting of the Standing Committee, and determined to have a parish meeting to accept Edward's resignation."

The senior Edward began his long train journey to California via New Orleans and Texas at the beginning of February. He met up with Nelly in Marietta, Georgia, where she had been advised by her doctor to recuperate: "Here I found Nelly waiting at the station, as fresh as a rose, and with no signs of illness," he told Hattie in letter No. 3.[50] During the senior minister's lengthy absence, William Howell Reed, Judith Andrews, and Hattie determined to keep Edward well informed about activities at his church. Hattie described the younger Edward Hale's first sermon following the senior minister's departure and also gave a speech in the church suggesting ways to relieve young Hale of some of the excessive work which she and others felt might have contributed to his resignation, but it was too late to change his mind.

Writing on a train en route to Tucson, Arizona, Edward remarked of his associate, who was also a part time instructor in homiletics at Harvard: "Every word you write of his sermon interests and pleases me. I am conscious that I have learned a great deal from him intellectually, and I think I have gained from him orally & spiritually. Of this one must speak delicately whose moral and spiritual flame is as low as mine."[51] This seems to be a deeply revealing comment about his state of mind at that time—was it even an admission of guilt? Emily also reported that Robert had attended church and had heard "the very best sermon he has ever heard from him [Edward Hale]." She was feeling better "but the least thing upsets me." Rob was reading poetry to her. "He is the greatest comfort. I never knew a better son."[52]

Might Edward's young associate have noticed the too close relationship between the aging minister and his longtime staffer and parishioner? What would he have made of the passion and longing that Hattie poured out in her letters at that time? On February 25, for example, she wrote in longhand: "Shall I tell you how I slept last night? I had a green rug over me. I had a fur glove under my cheek; I had a little silver box in one hand, & a black croched [*sic*] ribbon in the other hand. Poor symbols of the reality, I grant. And yet they comforted me; & I clung to them as I had nothing else." Edward had given her all the treasures she described. A master of titillation, she then wrote, "I met Mr. Young in the street this morning. He put his arm around me & looked as if <*he wanted to kiss me. Do you care*?>" It seems that Hattie had a particular appeal for aging, married ministers. She concluded that letter in shorthand: "<*Good bye dearest. How many times have I lived over in*> thought <*the last hour that I passed in your arms*> & you <*told me what you had never said before that I was the*> breath <*of your life*>."[53]

As Hattie prepared to leave for a few days in Waterville, New Hampshire, with Martha Brooks, her friend and longtime colleague in the church, she wrote Edward the long, ardent letter tied with ribbons at the top in which she reminisced about the church trip there twenty years earlier when they sat on the outdoor seat of the stage coach and she thrilled to the touch of his hand as he helped her hold up an umbrella. Now from Waterville, she described three days of snowshoeing and tobogganing on wooded paths and open slopes around the base of Osceola Mountain with a group of men and women, all members of the Appalachian Mountain Club: "I had my first walk this morning with nine or ten others…it was a pretty sight, as we wound along in Indian file through the woods. The snow was all unbroken as we struck in…The hemlocks & spruce around us were all powdered with snow; & we heard a few stray chick-a-dees hopping in through the boughs." Reluctant to leave such natural beauty for Boston, she concluded, "I think with dismay of our dirty, slushy, muddy streets, of all the crowd, & so much that I hate in the city. But my occupations are there, & so I go back to them."[54]

By mid-March, Hattie's distress at Edward's long absence was palpable in her letters. Longing to join him for his last few weeks in California, she had suggested before Edward left that she might travel out there with her Uncle Frank Howe. She now admitted that "it was only a straw I grasped at in my unhappiness. It is not reasonable to do it. I doubt if Uncle Frank would leave home, it would be an expense & it would be so apparent here that I was tagging after you. I am not afraid, but I have too much pride. *<I must wait. It will seem a long time. But I must wait until you come back>*."[55] Two days later, having received Edward's account of all the writing he was doing on his *Life of Columbus* (he had Nelly doing research on Columbus in Washington archives when she was there in December and January) and the exhausting demands of Unitarian communities in Pasadena, Hattie reminded her intimate friend in a more wifely tone that he was supposed to be resting and enjoying the mild California climate: "Indeed, I think it is hardly fair or kind to your generous friends that you should be doing so much writing…Another thing that troubles me! You are not poking about enough in beautiful, out of the way, characteristic places; or you do not write me of them. You are seeing too much of the people & not enough of the country."[56]

Edward, meanwhile, wrote enthusiastically to his secretary Martha Adams about his wonderful outdoor life in the Ojai Valley.[57] In fact, it poured with rain during most of his stay there. He and Nelly were the guests of Edward's college friend William F. Channing in Channing's large, airy house in Pasadena with its spectacular views. Although he had graduated from medical school, Channing never practiced medicine. Instead, he had worked for ten years with Professor Moses G. Farmer, Sarah Jane Farmer's inventor father, in developing a fire-alarm telegraph. Then he invented a telephone that was bought by the Bell Telephone Company. He and his family had moved from Providence, Rhode Island, to Pasadena in 1885 for the sake of his wife and their daughter Grace's health.

Out of touch and not sure where Edward was, but knowing San Francisco was to be a high point of his California sabbatical, Hattie begged him not to go there without Nelly: "You will be awfully homesick & lonesome there with Dr. Stebbins & all the ministers; they will have receptions & receptions, & you will dine & make speeches, & lecture, & make calls, & wish for the time to come to start home. Reflect for one moment what awaits you here, & do come home for it rested & strengthened."[58]

Edward reassured Hattie once he had settled in with the Horatio Stebbinses in San Francisco: "You are to place me in a pleasant house, like a good Roxbury house on one of the high hills in New San Francisco [Berkeley]. Stebbins is, you know, an old and very dear friend. His (2nd) wife is a very pleasing woman, and they pet me & care for me as only you can do. We sleep late, I loaf in the house refused to visitors till 11.30 or 12, then I take a walk."[59] Nelly remembered more than twenty-five years later in *Life and Letters* that, while she stayed on at her cousin's ranch in the Ojai Valley, her father enjoyed his stay in San Francisco immensely. "My father gave lectures in the city and at Berkeley; he preached in the Unitarian Churches, he made many friends and enjoyed much."[60]

It was while he was staying with Horatio Stebbins that Edward fell off a verandah in the dark, causing a severe injury to his already damaged leg that plagued him for the rest of his days. His letters to Hattie often refer to the state of and treatments for his "sartorial muscle." In fact, he tended to regale her with intimate information about his bodily health, his "machine," as he called it. In addition to his gammy leg, he was often plagued by dental problems and gastrointestinal attacks ("my old problem"), which might be diagnosed today as irritable bowel syndrome. None of these problems of increasing age made Hattie love him any the less.

The letters exchanged between Boston and California show that Hattie was strong minded in her certainty of where she stood on the issues of naturalism versus traditional Christian symbolism. When he was staying in San Francisco, Edward dined at her suggestion with one of her favorite geologists, Joseph Le Conte, former pupil of Louis Agassiz at Harvard, who was now a professor of geology, natural history, and botany at the new University of California at Berkeley. Edward told Le Conte about a parishioner of his, "a naturalist of great learning and of equal courage," who, "knowing what we know of the anatomy of our species," so disapproved of seeing the image of a winged angel "in a Temple dedicated to the God of Truth"—it was in a stained glass window by John LaFarge commemorating Thomas Starr King in the South Congregational Church (formerly King's Hollis Street Church)—that "she was glad her back was turned to it." All the guests "applauded the sentiment heartily," Edward reported. "And I think it was Le Conte who said that was a parishioner worth having."[61] Hattie's reply indicated her naturalist theology and disbelief in biblical miracles. Reiterating her distaste for the angel ("this anomalous creature with wings"), she declared the image was "like shaking a red flag in my face for persons who have never studied natural law & know nothing of the absolute certainty of its workings, to say that that God can turn back the shadow on the dial, that He can make the sun stand still, that any child can be born without having a father, or that Life can come again into a dead body."[62]

Hattie made an appointment with young Edward Hale before his departure for spiritual advice about a personally troubling falsehood she had told relating to church affairs. She had signed "the Ritchie paper" as an act of kindness, which the younger Hale now told her she should not have done. Since Edward referred in his journal to a meeting with "Ritchie" and Goodrich at the Mechanics Bank on November 8, 1890, it appears that the Ritchie paper had something to do with the financial affairs of the South Congregational Church, perhaps relating to the mortgage. This may have been the confidential meeting that Hattie recalled in a 1904 letter to Edward: "When Edward Hale was Colleague, I went to him to see if he could explain to me why you did not always tell the Truth."[63] Perhaps she felt she was made to take the blame for the so-called Ritchie matter. All she told Edward at the time was that young Hale assured her she would be absolved of the care of souls in a future life. She trusted him enough to reveal an aspect of her own nature that she often discussed with her lover and mentor, her conviction that she was happiest in the natural world where she did not have to confront her ambivalence about segments of humanity (these appear to have run the gamut from gossiping Back

Bay society matrons to the sometimes unsavory slum dwellers she increasingly confronted in Boston's South End): "May I not have the vision [the knowledge of God] through the natural world, & must I get it only by loving Humanity, which I do not do?"[64]

Edward Hale was installed as the pastor of the First Unitarian Church of Essex County, New Jersey, on April 2. In October, his wife gave birth to their daughter Emily, who was to become T. S. Eliot's first and intermittent muse. Hers was a sad life. She twice expected to marry this difficult man, whom she first met when he was a Harvard student, and twice he chose other women, the first being a famously disastrous choice.[65] Edward Hale was not long in New Jersey; he returned to the Boston area in 1897 as minister of the First Church of Chestnut Hill in Newton, serving there until his death in 1918.

Although Hattie continued as treasurer of the South Church ladies' charities, despite the unfortunate "Ritchie affair," she began to spend less time working at the church so as to give more attention to her own scientific and philanthropic interests. Above all, she was now free to pursue a college-level education and had registered that year as a special student in biology (and would later take courses in geology) at Boston Tech, Class of 1895. On April 5, 1891, Hattie wrote to her mentor, Alpheus Hyatt, curator of the Museum of the Boston Society of Natural History, to confirm arrangements for employing one of his favorite geology students, Amadeus Grabau, as guide to the Society's collections: "I think Mr. Grabau ought to begin to act as Guide as early as the first of May…I know his means are very limited, & I have noticed his clothes looked very much worn. I think that for the reputation of the Society, that when acting as Guide, he should be better clad than I have usually seen him. If you can do it without hurting his feelings, will you see that he purchases a proper suit of clothes, & I will send you the amount for them. I…hope you can do for me, what I could not do myself."[66]

Hattie's patronage of and friendship with this young man with a brilliant future became one of her greatest pleasures and eventually a source of pride. She paid Grabau, a student at Boston Tech and then a graduate student at Harvard, an annual retainer to lead field trips and introduced him to Edward, who encouraged him to give lectures in the church and at Hale House, the settlement house (formerly the Tolstoi Club) established by Harvard undergraduates at Hale's suggestion. She also persuaded her Aunt Mary Atkins to award Grabau, son of a Lutheran minister in Buffalo, New York, her scholarship for a year of his studies.

Hattie now realized a dream of returning to Europe, which she first visited nearly thirty years earlier with her father. She sailed for England and Scotland in early July 1891 with Parnell Murray, a high school science teacher whom she met through her geology studies. From England, Hattie sent Edward detailed accounts of their experiences which he would use as a blueprint for his trip to the British Isles with Emily the following summer. On the eve of her voyage home in September, Edward wrote, "the long <*summer is at last ended. You have had a good time as I have had and we are as happy as we can be because we can see each other and tell each other everything*>."[67] But Hattie's Atlantic crossing coincided with the Unitarian conference in Saratoga, New York. Edward, a key player at the conference, sent a note from there to meet her on arrival on the *SS Britannica* in New York. At the close of the conference, the Reverend Brooke Herford of Boston's Arlington Street Church announced his retirement as council chairman and Edward was elected by his peers on the clergy council to take Herford's place as chairman.[68]

Edward's increased prominence made his relationship with Hattie even more risky. Even so, he wrote to her in shorthand on the eve of her return from Intervale: "<*I am always sure of your dear love and that you are willing to make sacrifices of every sort to make me happy and strong. You make me happy because you make me strong. I do think I have planned ways in which we can work together and love together so that you can help me and I hope I can you. You know I love you and you do me. Can I say more*>?"[69] Although this sounds almost businesslike, the emotional heat of the relationship seemed to reach a new level during the winter of 1891–1892 when they were both in Boston and seeing a great deal of each other.

8

Separations and Tragedy

If Hattie had forgotten that her man belonged to a vast constituency of admirers, then the celebrations of his seventieth birthday on April 3, 1892, jolted her back to reality. As *The Unitarian* proclaimed, "It is doubtful if any other living American writer or teacher is so widely known and loved as Dr. Hale."[1] Edward's birthday was on a Sunday that year: ironically, he preached on the "Victory of Love" and then, vigorous as ever, walked nearly all the way home. The next evening there was a party at the church with crowds of friends and presentations. "I really think a thousand people passed through those rooms in the course of the evening," he wrote Nelly, who was in San Francisco with her Aunt Susan, continuing with his description:

> Dear Mamma was not strong enough to go down, but I had Aunt Lucretia sitting by my side in receiving the guests… Mr. [George] Carpenter [chairman of the church's standing committee] presented to me from the parish an elegant great 'loving-cup' of silver…Mr. Reed read some specimen letters from seventy which had been received from seventy of my oldest and nearest friends. The first of these was from Dr. Furness, and the last from dear Helen Keller. By the way, Helen Keller was there herself, and I need not say was the centre of a great deal of attraction. She jumped up in my arms, and hugged me and kissed me and was full of real

> sympathetic interest in the occasion…I said to Mamma the next day there was not a functional moment about it all; the whole thing was pure affection from one end to the other.[2]

It was a busy, joyous early spring for the Hales as they prepared for Bertie's wedding to Margareta (Greta) Marquand on April 5. Bertie threw a dinner party for his ushers at Highland Street on April 1, "so that we were warned to make ourselves as scarce as possible," noted Edward in his journal, "and I went with Hattie Freeman to sup at her house. She and I took a little pull at the sermon also." The family gathered for the much anticipated wedding in the Unitarian Church at Newburyport. Once again, Edward co-officiated, this time with the local Unitarian pastor. The wedding breakfast was held at Curzon's Mill, the Marquand family's picturesque homestead at the junction of the Merrimack River and its last tributary before reaching the ocean. Twelve days later, the young couple sailed for Europe to begin their life together in Paris.

On April 18, Hattie and the Reeds were among the attendees at another celebration of Edward's seventieth birthday, a commemorative dinner at Boston's premier hotel, the Vendome. The dinner was preceded by a reception at which Edward was lionized: "all sort and conditions of men came to pay their respects," he noted in his journal for that day. "The best part of it was the very large attendance of Kings' Daughters and Lend a Hand Clubs. They would come in squads with their crosses on." Speeches following the dinner ranged across topics that recalled the many interests of his long life. "It was a beautifully kind and affectionate thing, from one end to the other. I enjoyed every moment of it. Dear Mamma did not feel strong enough to go; indeed, I begged her not to go, and I am glad she did not. But we have been talking it over, Bob, she, and I, all this (Tuesday) morning."[3]

Emily's absence from both the church and public celebrations of Edward's seventieth birthday is striking. Small wonder that Hattie felt that she was more of a partner and helpmate to Edward than was his own wife. In fact, the day book records his frequent visits to Hattie in Union Park during these weeks, ostensibly for work. But in early May, it was Emily, not Hattie, who accompanied him on a trip to Pepperell for four days of rest. Edward's journal entries noted good walks, gathering flowers, and a call on Dr. Babbidge (the Freeman family's retired minister in Pepperell).[4]

While Hattie continued to be enchanted with Edward, who, with a few telling exceptions, could do no wrong in her eyes, Susan felt that all the adulation was going to her brother's head. On May 10, she had just returned from an initially disappointing trip with Nelly to California, where a wealthy Unitarian friend of Edward's had promised, but failed to deliver, a course of lectures and where Nelly had hoped to sell some of her sketches.[5] Following a visit by her brother, Susan wrote an aggrieved letter to Jack, her favorite nephew, who was finishing up his doctorate at the university at Halle, Germany: "I find Parber very grumpy about Matunuck on account of his Bills there last autumn. In fact he was Cross as a Bear the only time I have seen him. I suppose a reaction after all his Homage; and I sometimes think he likes me as the only worm who wont turn he can lavish his Dark moments on…He said it was his usual fate to take the trouble to have a country house and then all his family refuse to live in it better shut it up etc etc etc."

After Susan told him she was going to be at Matunuck for the entire summer, that Jack was coming as soon as he could, Robert would be there most of the summer, and Lucretia for a total of ten weeks, "He then became very meeky, meeky, and said it was all right, he was glad etc." "I am sorry to tell about this," she told her nephew, who was obviously as clear-eyed about his distinguished father as she was, "for Parbar is really Glorious now in the eyes of all the World, & its more than ever a distinction to kling [*sic*] to him."[6]

More than likely, Edward's black mood was due to his imminent separation from Hattie and the ties of convention that made this necessary every summer. Edward had led Hattie to believe that he might be able to join her on a geological field trip to Mammoth Hot Springs in Yellowstone National Park led by Professor George Barton of Boston Tech, part of the geology curriculum she was now following there.[7] Hattie wrote that she was not surprised when Edward bowed out. But she might have been referring to her disappointment when she remarked: "It was very wretched & very bitter: & the bitterness came in the thought that you might have helped me & did not. I write this now in no anger, as you know but in a little sorrow, that you do not know how to help me over the hard places…I thought once I could tell you, but I believe it is something that cannot be taught."

Edward explained later, "with all other difficulties about my going with you, there was the great difficulty <*that it was with you*>… everybody <*in the parish or out of it*> would have known and said that Mr. Hale had gone off <*with Miss Freeman's party*>. I called it all the time Mr. Barton's party. But in <*the parish*> circles that would have deceived nobody."[8] Instead, the Hales had agreed to join their Marquand in-laws on a European vacation, with the prime objective of visiting their newly married children and their son Philip in Paris. George O. Carpenter, head of the SCC Standing Committee, had offered to pay for the Hales' holiday, following the tradition set by his predecessor Henry Kidder.

Emily had initially hesitated about leaving her old mother but was freed to accompany Edward when the Hartford relations took in Mrs. Perkins. Undoubtedly aware of gossip in the parish about her husband and Hattie Freeman, she must have realized the importance of accompanying her husband on this family vacation, as she expressed in a letter to Nelly, who was feeling waiflike in California after Susan returned to Boston. Emily made it clear that she and Edward longed for Nelly to return home, drawing a comparison to her growing realization of her own culpability in the emotional distancing of her marriage: "I have often thought that I had made a mistake, in urging Papa to go away, and stay away, without minding and that he did not really think I cared much, when the only thing I thought of was to keep from spoiling his pleasure, by making a fuss about it."[9]

In the meantime, dreading their separation, Hattie and Edward spent every moment they could with each other. Edward dictated many works in progress, including the first chapter of "A New England Boyhood," commissioned as a serial by *Atlantic Monthly*. On May 17, he noted in his diary one of their Tuesday outings together: "I went off on a charming lark, being one of the choice company on the top of the four-in-hand stage which drives every day to Wayland and back…I do not know when I have spent four hours more happily, and I really did not feel tired at all when I got home." The next day, he wrote: "Went down early to take tea with Helen Keller at Miss Freeman's and there the carriage called for me to take me to the meeting of the Law and Order League." And on Saturday, he noted, "caught Hattie Freeman and made her write nearly a writing-book full on the Perry Street Conference."[10] Then the annual Anniversary Week was upon them, and, as usual, Edward was distracted beyond endurance by its demands.

On the eve of leaving for the West, Hattie wrote Edward a number of letters to be opened each day as he crossed the Atlantic, pouring out her feelings for him. She wrote at least one while he was in her house: "I just heard your tread in the room above & now you are lying on the sofa upstairs, & I am conscious all the while, that if <*I wanted to I could run up stairs and open the door and say 'You must look up and kiss me, I can not live another moment without being in your arms and hearing your dear words of love*>.' But it will all be very different when you read this." Another, written immediately after Edward left her house for the summer, indicates the coolness of Edward's long marriage compared to the increasing sensuality of their affair: "<*I have been thinking of what you just told me that Mrs. Hale said to you long ago that she did not much like kisses. I am glad now I know that all you give are for me*>."[11]

Edward's letters to Hattie from Matunuck before he sailed for Europe with Emily are equally emotional and, in one case, astonishingly risqué. At first, he expressed relief to have escaped Boston, where his relentless schedule had driven him to nervous exhaustion. "What a pity that I cannot publicly say, <*I wish and propose to spend*> 4 <*out of the seven days in private with one chosen companion*>. All the bores and tramps must be satisfied with what they can suck of my life blood in the other 2 days. How would that do? Would they not all wonder who <*the companion was*>." But ten days later, missing her terribly, he wrote:

> The underlying principle is <*that I think of you almost all the time*>. I get horribly bored in this string of calling and letter answering. And <*I compare it all the time with what it would have been had you been here. Dear child of my heart*> I think <*of you all night and I think of you all day*> The <*twenty-seventh of August will come*> and we will find for ourselves <*a little*

> *white tent somewhere where*> rumours of oppression shall not reach us. It shall be our lodge in the midst of a wilderness. <*And there I will have you in my arms and it shall not be a hateful hurried dream*>.

The next day, Edward sent Hattie in shorthand a translation of a 2,000-year-old piece of Greek erotica which mirrored the myth of Achilles' rape of King Lycomedes' daughter. He wrote in his next letter that he would be very nervous until he heard she had burned it. Both letters missed her at several Western destinations and were eventually forwarded to Union Park.[12] Any of the many intimate letters that the couple dispatched to prearranged addresses could be intercepted. In fact, many were forwarded multiple times, as the envelopes show, and several were apparently lost altogether. Although the shorthand was intended to disguise their intimacies—now obviously physical—its very presence in the letters would excite curiosity.

The letters they wrote each other in June 1892 are among the most revealing about how each of them saw their relationship. There was no doubt about who had set the ground rules, as can be seen in Edward's letter addressed to Hattie at Butte, Montana (it was forwarded to the next address on her itinerary, in Idaho). She had reminded him of a date which had very special meaning for them both, June 17, the day at Pepperell when they made a serious commitment to each other and when he probably gave her the ring that she mentions several times in her letters. "I have taken great satisfaction in your recalling the date of June 17," he wrote, continuing:

> You were a year out, it was in 1884 and not in 1885. I do not wonder that the years seem fewer than they are. It is on the principle <*that time with you always passes much more quickly than any other time does*>...Seriously speaking that is about the date <*when all reserves were broken between us, so that*> we could trust <*each other entirely each sure that he or she might ask the other everything*> as I am so fond of saying of the highest confidence. Since these reserves were broken, each of us has been, in a way, emancipated <*for a good part of life if not for*

> *the whole*>. And I hope we are too sensible, both of us, not to accept half a loaf as better than none...For me, as you can see clearly enough, it is from that era <*that I began to grow insight again*> an experience which as you know, I am not the only person who observes, but which is spoken of by everybody.[13]

This letter, which seems to reemphasize the boundaries of their illicit relationship, reflects the fact that there was by 1892 growing parish gossip about them. Ten days earlier, Edward had reported that he and his sister Susan were questioned following a dinner party about the identity of that *other* woman, "not Mrs. Hale," with whom he was seen everywhere in Boston. He and Susan tried to throw off the scent by naming several women, including Hattie, working with him in the church. He concluded, with characteristic humor, "I shall have to make you wear a mask on alternate, or odd days, while I do on the even ones." Here Edward tried to dismiss the incredible risks he was taking, but he himself admitted at this time that the number of calls he made on Hattie at her house far exceeded those to any of his other parishioners: "Ah me! If each ring of mine at 37 could have taken one call off the list of 330 names which Edward [his former associate minister] left me as his legacy, how respectable would the appearance of that list be now!"[14] Susan Hale's complicity in the cover-up following the dinner party shows that she was at least concerned to protect her brother's reputation.

On June 29, Howell Reed sent Hattie an account of the Hales' departure for Europe that must have seemed bittersweet to her: "Mr. Hale was in overflowing spirits and as happy as he could be. There were several of our people to see him off and he received a sort of oration of welcome from many of the passengers whom he knew and who were glad of his company...A little after nine the ship moved grandly out of the dock amid the waving of handkerchiefs and adieus shouted backward and forward. Edward, Rob and I were on the end of the pier, and the Great Edward, towering above the feeble folk around him on deck, was scanning the faces eagerly to catch his last glimpse of his boys. I wish you could have seen his face light up as he saw them—it was a picture for a Kodac."[15]

* * *

Edward received a warm reception from Unitarians in London when he and his party arrived there in mid-July, after traveling in North Wales, the Lake District, and to Edinburgh. "[I]t is impossible to come to London without feeling the excitement of the place," he wrote Hattie at Union Park. "I should think it would wear them all out." Interesting though it all was, he closed his letter by reminding Hattie that more than half the time apart had now passed. "But when I get up in the morning <*particularly there is a sort of terrible feeling that the day*> will be dreadfully <*long without a sight of my little girl*>."[16]

Edward and Emily left the rest of their party to spend a quiet week in Devon together, continuing to track Hattie's path of the previous summer from her letters. Writing from Exeter, Edward told her that "Emily had had, or <*had fancied she had*> a sick turn there [in London] which required two visits from a Dr. James, an excellent fellow who takes care of the people in the hotel. With great skill, for which I respect & admire him, he made her understand <*that there was nothing in the world*> the matter with her. And we go on with a good deal of care thrown over-board."[17] Emily's perennial hypochondria and lassitude made her a tiresome, dispiriting companion for such an energetic, convivial man.

None of the many letters Hattie wrote to Edward in Europe, except those she composed beforehand, are in the collection. After Yellowstone, she apparently wrote a long letter from Banff in the Canadian Rockies before traveling home via Niagara. Meanwhile, the height of the Hales' European journey was their reunion with Philip, who had spent much of the last five years studying art in Paris at the Ecole des Beaux Arts and the Académie Julian and then with several American and European artists who were experimenting with Impressionism. Bertie had completed his architectural studies at the Ecole des Beaux Arts and now established an architectural practice in Paris, where he and Greta lived until 1895 and where their first two sons were born. After a few days in Paris, the large party of four Marquands and five Hales moved on to Giverny, "where Bert has the 60 francs house, and we will all spend a week together."[18] Although Claude Monet had been living in Giverny since 1883, he had only recently purchased the house and land where he would create his famous gardens and lily pond.

Edward made no mention of the great artist in his surviving letters to Hattie. Instead, he wrote again and again how he longed to be home and reunited with her. He reported that Emily, malingering as always, was too frail to write letters or to travel any distance, and the party had to progress in short stages back to Liverpool before boarding their steamship for Boston. He rushed to see Hattie almost as soon as they embarked in Boston.

Edward visited Hattie in Shelburne, New Hampshire, between September 12 and 15 after stopping off in Portland, Maine, to comfort his ailing friend, retired Unitarian minister Samuel Longfellow, youngest brother and biographer of poet Henry Wadsworth Longfellow. As usual, Edward justified his visit to Hattie by recording the work they did together: "We have done more than 40 pages in 2 days." He also sketched the views from the picturesque village of Gorham, they climbed the nearby crag together, and called on friends. As a token of thanks for Hattie's hospitality, he gave her a copy of his *East and West: A Story of New-Born Ohio*, published that year and inscribed "Harriet E. Freeman On an autumn visit to her new home Shelburne Sept. 14, 1892."[19]

Hattie's rental of a house in Shelburne and Edward's short visit marked the beginning of their many summer idylls in the White Mountains together. She was undoubtedly influenced in her choice of Shelburne on the Androscoggin River near the Maine border by the opinion of Thomas Starr King, her earliest minister, family friend, and author of the best of the guide books to the region. King had extolled the beauty of the Androscoggin Valley with its towering views of Mt. Adams and Mt. Washington.[20] But by the early 1880s, commercial logging companies were decimating the luxurious forests clothing the lower slopes and valleys of the mountains with rampant clear-cutting for the newly invented manufacturing of paper from wood pulp. During future visits, Hattie would begin complaining about the foul smell from the pulp mill at Berlin, a few miles north.

Edward and Hattie's confrontations with these ugly depredations, which also threatened several important watersheds, would convert them into passionate forest conservationists. Just four months after Hattie's return to Boston in October, an article in the *Atlantic Monthly* began to raise the alarm about the serious threat to

New Hampshire's natural beauty and ecology. Julius H. Ward marshaled some shocking facts, estimating that lumber operators were annually cutting approximately 600 million board feet of timber in the White Mountains and along the streams and rivers that ran into the Connecticut River. The Van Dyke brothers alone owned 100,000 acres of forested land in the White Mountains, including tracts on Mount Washington. "They have it in their power," Ward asserted, "to spoil the whole White Mountain region for a period of fifty years…and to bring about desolation."[21] Ward and other writers such as Charles S. Sargent, director of Boston's Arnold Arboretum, and historian Francis Parkman urged the state of New Hampshire to buy back private lands to create a state national park.

Edward's old friend Sam Longfellow died on October 3 and, in the hour after attending his funeral in Portland, Edward wrote Hattie his memories of the beginning of their long friendship at college: "I think we took to each other at once, two quiet boys, who did not care much for rough play, not at all for teasing or quarreling, and who did care for poetry, music, literature, drawing and flowers."[22] The latest of the couple's summer separations was coming to an end at last. As Hattie was packing up to return home at the end of the month, Edward exulted in her imminent arrival:

> Here you are in all the bustle of the last moment, tying up the cat and giving the keys to Mrs. Whitman. And I so tranquil at this desk, this prison which we call a home! Oh if we were both off for a last scramble on the Crag, with prospect of a fire and coffee. But next best will be furnace fire in your prison [to him a house was a prison compared to the outdoors]. The doorbell at 10.10. You will hide behind the door, <*and I shall kiss you and kiss you and kiss you till you*> really <*beg me not to do so any more and then*> I shall pretend to be good and shall begin all over again. It is only because I am Virtue and Decorum personified, with a large V and a large D, that I obey your orders, and that I do not appear at the station and stifle <*you with kisses in presence of*> all the henchmen.[23]

Edward was head over heels in love. Writing from Philadelphia in mid-November, the day after addressing the Unitarian Conference of the Middle States on "the duty of the Liberal Church in the Service of Man," he paid her one of his tributes, capturing what he most admired in her character and personality:

> Imagine me saying, that if in each considerable city there could be found a woman of genius, spirit and courage, with breath of clover, and wit and wisdom...if this woman were a brave horsewoman on a noble horse, a quick bright conversa, keeping people on their very best when with them, if she were a kind sympathetic visitor in the attics of the old women, if she were the life of children when they came about her; if she were absolutely of kin with Nature...if at the same time she knew how to enliven the most worried and tired of the workmen of that town, would put her head in his lap, or put her hand in his hand, and give life even to his most stupid days—imagine me suggesting this as the proper Sympathetic and philanthropic work of the Conference in cities. You can imagine also how it brought down the house, and how they all said 'Where, when, where.' But I would not tell.[24]

There was no doubt that Hattie had also become Edward's most confidential and trusted friend as well as lover. Just seven months earlier, he had told her, "You will forgive me if I say you are my only real counseller [*sic*]."[25] He had already lost a distressing number of his most intimate friends and contemporaries—he seemed to be forever conducting funerals—and now he was to lose another, with the premature death from diphtheria on January 23, 1893, of Phillips Brooks, his distant cousin, friend, and collaborator in social welfare. The longtime minister of Trinity Church, Brooks had been ordained as the Episcopal Bishop of Massachusetts just fifteen months earlier. "This was the day of dear Brooks's funeral," Edward noted in his journal on January 26, "and the town gave itself up to it very loyally. The stores were closed down town and Copley Square was resorted to by thousands and thousands of people... at half past eleven to Trinity, where all the Episcopal clergy of the state was invited, and where most of them were in full costume."[26] The charismatic Brooks had been extraordinarily successful in winning former Unitarians to his church: cultured Boston was almost entirely Unitarian in 1870 but by 1890 the percentage of Unitarians had dropped precipitously. For some, Unitarianism had become no longer Christian enough, both theologically and culturally; it was too outside the mainstream and too parochial.

Despite evidence that the nation's economy was tottering, plans continued for the World's Fair in Chicago to commemorate the four hundredth anniversary of the arrival of Christopher Columbus in the New World. In February 1893, several months before the exposition was due to open to the public, Edward traveled to Chicago with his railroad executive son Arthur. There he visited the Exposition grounds with three friends, one of whom was Charles Francis Adams Jr., former president of the Union Pacific Railroad. It is likely that the old friends visited the Transportation Building, then under construction, to provide some insights for its planned exhibits. Susan, Nelly, and Philip Hale were other family members who contributed time and artistry to the Columbian exposition.[27] In fact, Susan was invited on May 1 to the Fair's grand, if premature, opening, which was attended by President Cleveland and an estimated quarter of a million people.

But wherever Edward traveled and however much he was feted, his thoughts were never far from Hattie. Stuck on the back of an invitation to a luncheon in his honor on February 21 at Chicago's Union League Club is a poem written for Hattie:

> A chill fell on my heart today
> When she who holds it in her thrall
> Said, lightly, I shall be away,
> From June to sometime in the Fall.[28]

In the immediate aftermath of the fair's opening, trusts and banks began folding at an alarming rate and attendance plummeted. In addition to the terrifying economy, word was spreading that the fair, designed in large part by Daniel Burnham and Frederick Law Olmsted, was nowhere near completion, a fact that was confirmed by Hattie when she attended the Fair in late May with her cousins Grace and Howell Reed. "It is true that the exhibits are yet very incomplete," she told Edward. "In the Electricity [building] there is really nothing to see but packing boxes, & bales covered with cotton & paper & signs 'Hands Off.'" But she was dazzled by the beauty of the glistening white Beaux Arts buildings, the canals, and the lagoon. "There was too much wind for us to get any of the effects of reflection," Hattie wrote after their first day in the fair grounds. "But we lingered longest on the great lagoon where the beautiful buildings came to the water. The gondalas [*sic*] add much to the beauty, picturesque in outline & lovely in coloring."

While staying in the same Chicago boarding house with the Reeds, Hattie was able to observe Howell's demands on his much younger wife, causing her to remark that she herself would have little patience for the restrictions of such a marriage. And yet she mourned, as she always did, that she could not be with her own chosen companion: "Oh! Dear! I think it is cruel that I have to come one time, & you another: & that we cannot see this beauty together," she wrote sadly, a sentiment that she would repeat many times over the years. "We propose to return this evening to see the electrical display," she continued.[29] The effect at night of 200,000 electric lights ablaze on every building and walkway while giant searchlights swept the grounds was unprecedented. This display consumed three times more electricity than the entire city of Chicago.

But Hattie missed out on much by visiting the fair so early and returning to Boston before work was completed. By June 1, the temporary railroad tracks that scarred the lawns were removed and the large piles of boxes and unopened crates that Hattie remarked on were emptied and removed too. Most striking of all was the giant Ferris wheel, which did not make its first successful revolution until June 9, and the big cars still had to be hung. She did not know then that she would have another chance; she and Carrie would join Edward at the Fair for a week in late September, shortly before it closed.[30]

Following her return from Chicago, Hattie and Edward spent an idyllic few days together with Susan at Matunuck and then, judging only by a letter he wrote Emily from there, at Amherst with their mutual friend Professor Maynard at the Agricultural College.[31] Hattie then departed for a field trip of several weeks in the North Carolina Appalachian and Blue Ridge Mountains before the Hales gathered at Matunuck en masse for Jack's wedding on June 16 in Waterford, Connecticut, to Rose Perkins, daughter of a professor at Union College, Schenectady.[32]

Hattie's next destination that summer was Warsaw Salt Springs, forty-five minutes from Buffalo, New York—Amadeus Grabau's hometown—where she met up with him and her Brooklyn teacher friend Mary Dann. The two women could not have had a guide more expert than young Grabau in the geology and paleontology of upper New York State. Edward wrote on August 9 to thank her for her "wonderful geological letter…I am so pleased that the guide [Amadeus Grabau] pans out so well."

As usual, Hattie's letters from that summer's field trips are missing from the collection, most likely because she regarded them as a journal of her studies and kept them separately from most of her more personal letters. But she had evidently remarked again on Grabau's impoverished circumstances, because now Edward suggested that the young geology student might board at Roxbury and run errands for him for a few hours every day. While Grabau does not appear to have boarded with the Hales or served as Edward's messenger boy, from this point on he began to give natural history classes in the church and at the Hale House.

Hattie must have rued her lack of training in chemistry while she was on the geological field trip at Warsaw, because Edward replied: "It is indeed all the pities in the world that I did not teach you chemistry…twenty years ago…I know I did say, when I said that you ought to take up botany, that you ought to take regular lessons in chemistry; and I think there was some inquiry into classes at the Technology. But you and I could have made a nice little laboratory in what I call the Microscope room, or in the little room two stories above it. At least I could have told you how to use litmus paper, and how to create salt. Do you see, the real pleasure of it is that you come nearer to the foundation of things…"[33]

Following her return from Warsaw, Hattie again rented a cottage in Shelburne, on the northeastern edge of New Hampshire's White Mountains. As he anticipated his short visit there in September, Edward rejoiced, "<*Every day will go more lightly now*>. I shall take with me no end of work to be done in the summer house. If I write 4 hours a day 15 pages an hour, and you five 15 pages an hour that makes 135 pages say 16000 words, which is equal to seven sermons, or half a very short novel" (in shorthand at the end of another letter, he anticipated more amorous activities).[34] Hattie wrote in pencil on this envelope "Carrie Arranging for the Chicago trip." The only hint that Edward gave in his letters about this plan was the easily missed reference to his anticipation of a week in S (Shelburne) and a week in C (Chicago).

Unfortunately, bad weather during the Freeman children's holiday with Hattie kept them cooped up in the small house in Shelburne. But during the nearly six days that Edward was there (he

Wearing her usual white raiment, Sarah Jane Farmer sits beside the Great Tent at Green Acre, Eliot, Maine, in 1894 with religious leaders she had invited to participate in her effort to keep the World's Parliament of Religions going on a permanent basis (see over). To her right is the young Hindu, Swami Vivekananda, and to her left are the Armenian lecturer M. H. Gulesian and a rather glum-looking Edward Everett Hale.
Courtesy Eliot Bahá'i Archives, Eliot, Maine, No. 6474. Collections of Maine Historical Society.

seems to have stayed at a nearby hotel), they drove in a pony and trap to "the summit" and took a couple of other excursions. They also worked on the paper he would deliver before the World's Parliament of Religions in Chicago. But "in these six days, there has been the charm that we have not been in the least hurried," wrote Edward as he waited at Portland for his connection to Boston on September 10.[35] Two days later, he traveled to Chicago via Philadelphia, where he was joined by Arthur, arriving too late for the opening on September 11 of the first formal gathering of representatives of Eastern and Western spiritual traditions.

The star of the so-called World Parliament of Religions was the young Hindu guru Swami Vivekananda, who launched the proceedings in the Exposition's World's Congress Auxiliary Building (now the Art Institute of Chicago) with a passionate appeal for universalism and tolerance, greeted by thunderous applause. Edward concluded his short address, "Spiritual Forces in Human Progress," with his standard call for a permanent court of arbitration for world peace and his opinion that "the new religion is something new, Its name is Idealism."[36] He then attended the concurrent Unitarian Congress before turning his full attention to the World's Fair.

Like Hattie earlier in the year, Edward raved in his journal about the Fair's architecture and the effect of the electric lighting; but it was not just the miracle of electricity that lit up Edward's spirits. Hattie and Carrie joined him, probably on Saturday, September 23, when he noted in his diary that he called early at the Raymond Hotel, the hotel Hattie said she and Carrie stayed in when referring to their visit ten years later. For the next week, they explored every corner of the Fair together and, on their last day, September 30, after spending six hours there, they took a farewell circuit in an electric launch of the canals and the Court of Honor. Apparently, Edward had been extremely vague about his plans for his lengthy stay in Chicago before leaving home for Emily wrote Bertie and Greta in Paris on September 21 that "Papa has been at Chicago for more than a week, and will not be home for a fortnight more."[37]

Edward was struck once again by "the search lights streaming through the murky mist above, and the long lines of Electric lights marking the leading features of the great buildings." He noted their favorite exhibits without ever naming his companions. Topping the list was the La Rabida building, with its display of Spanish cultural treasures representing the civilization that Columbus supposedly brought to the Americas. Replicas of Christopher Columbus's three ships, which had sailed into the fairgrounds from Lake Michigan, were moored alongside. "The wonder is that they secured the things," remarked Edward about the Spanish treasures, and, indeed, diplomatic relations with Spain were already tense and would erupt into war less than five years later. Next on Edward's list were the giant Ferris wheel that they rode together ("You hardly know you are in motion, sitting in a glass room, but you get the balloon effect of the whole neighbourhood") and the fine arts show, where both Nelly and Phil's paintings were on display. Late that night, he caught a train to Iowa City to visit his son Jack (Edward Jr.) and Jack's new wife, Rose, while Hattie and Carrie returned to Boston.

During his stay at Iowa State University, Edward was a proud witness to his academic son's lecture on Hamlet. The interest he took in the studies and nascent careers of his children was remarkable and his letters are full of his love and support for all of them as individuals, although some of them, particularly Philip, apparently found his certitude intimidating. Edward's talent for inspiring so many to reach higher in life was noticed by his contemporaries. What does not seem to have been recorded to the same degree was the tremendous support he had from his staff, including Hattie, although he did worry that he might kill some of them with overwork.

Herbert D. Ward, who interviewed Edward in his home office in May for a major, generously illustrated profile, "Edward E. Hale. The Man with a Country," published in *McClure's Magazine* that September, tried to get to the bottom of the famous cleric's "power." "Where did Doctor Hale get the strength to carry through his hundred duties? —editing—writing—aiding public work and public and private charities—correspondence—for he is the busiest man in Boston, and his business increases upon him week by week in an appalling ratio." Edward only added to his growing mythology, claiming that writing a sermon took him no more than two hours: "I have no patience with the idea that it takes six days of grinding to write a sermon. What nonsense! A sermon consists of about two thousand five hundred words. I take a cup of coffee before breakfast

Deep in thought, and perhaps correcting proofs, Edward sits at his desk in his home study where he spent a large proportion of his time writing his books and articles. Here Hattie and his other secretaries would take dictation, including his vast correspondence, while Emily's portrait kept watch behind him.
Frontispiece to volume II of Edward Everett Hale, Jr.'s Life and Letters of Edward Everett Hale.

and write about six pages—that is, six hundred and fifty words. In the morning I dictate to my amanuensis one thousand five hundred words. I am intensely interested in the subject, and this takes only a quarter of an hour. In the afternoon I look it over and add five or six hundred words, and the sermon is done."[38] Anyone who has seen the sheaves of sermons partly in Edward's handwriting but mostly in Hattie's at the Andover-Harvard Theological Library will wonder how she might have reacted to such a throwaway characterization of her hard work, including the back and forth of ideas between them.

The *McClure*'s and other profiles contributed to Edward's growing national celebrity. But whatever he proclaimed to the press, he was becoming increasingly desperate to unyoke himself from parish work and the endless demands on his time. He was determined to reorganize the *Lend a Hand* magazine so that it was no longer a burden on him, financial or otherwise, and to cut back on his office appointments so as to spend more time in researching his various memoirs in the Boston Public Library and other archives with Hattie and in joining her on excursions, preferably in the "open air."

With his large family and hordes of visitors and callers at his Highland Street house, Edward often declared that the only place where he could really rest and "get his bearings" was the summer house in Matunuck. Hattie was again invited to join him there in June 1894 for a working holiday following his visit to Meadville Theological College in Ohio for commencement and the Middle States Unitarian Conference. He wrote from Meadville in excited anticipation, "We will go by that nice fast train which leaves at 1 p.m. How much we will crowd into those five days. We will write our 5000 words, 1000 a day, and then voyaging, and driving and walking and botanizing, and birds and geology, and *<love making and kissing will be all the pleasanter>*."[39]

On July 4, Hattie began a letter from a hotel in Joggins, Nova Scotia, to Edward, who was giving an Independence oration in Philadelphia that day, with a paragraph that gave a vivid sense of the rigors of the geological field trips encountered by Professor George Barton's mostly female students. She was sharing a room with her friend and fellow student Parnell Murray: "I begin this letter under horrible circumstances. I am sitting on the bed undressed, Miss Murray is undressing, & a man in the next room is singing & playing on an organ. Fancy it, eighteen of us women were up until half past eleven last night, & up at four this morning, & Mr. Barton does not think it proper in him to ask this man to stop. I shall do it myself if he continues & state the circumstances."[40]

They had crossed from Eastport, Maine, to St. John in dense fog, docking so late the night before that they were forced to remain on the steamship until their early morning train to Joggins. Edward replied from Matunuck that he was "horror-struck to know that there are 18 of you! It must be like a personally-conducted Cook party." He was grateful that she had not told him they were descending into a coal mine on a vertically sliding railroad until it was over. The Hales and their guests were enjoying a "day out of heaven…The sky and the sea and the pond so blue and the willow and the maple and the trees beyond so green. You remember it, for it is out of what I shall always think of as your window that I am looking…Matunuck is now associated <*more than ever with you and what you say and what you think and what you love*>." He continued this theme in another letter: "The long and the short of it is that <*we are absolutely spoiling each other*> for the humdrum of ordinary society," and enclosed a note from Susan with a flower she could not identify, wishing "Harriet could see it but dont know her address."

Edward had hoped that Hattie would return in time to spend a night with him in Portsmouth, New Hampshire, en route to one of his lecture engagements. He reminded her, however, that he had to be back at Matunuck by August 3 for their "great family party," which had even summoned Bertie and Greta home from Paris with their baby son Dudley. In fact, Hattie and Parnell Murray had extended their field trip with a few days in Quebec. A rare fragment of a letter Hattie wrote from there describes their visit to the geologically interesting Natural Steps and fossils above the Montmorency Falls. She enclosed a *Lobelia* for Edward to examine under his glass.[41]

Back together again in Shelburne in early September 1894, the couple worked on Edward's Council Report for the National Conference in Saratoga where he intended to announce his retirement from the chairmanship. This was the conference where the ethical and spiritual factions called a truce at last and agreed on a preamble to the conference constitution. Edward's letters to Hattie and Emily on September 27, make an interesting contrast in substance. To Hattie, who always encouraged him to describe his honors, he wrote: "They adopted a vote of thanks to me by a standing unanimous vote" and "I am petted and flattered by everybody here: and have enjoyed the week very much."

But he composed a more substantive account for Emily, who had lived through the intellectual divisions behind the schism of the last three decades: "You would never forget the closing moment. After the different leaders of any faction had said a word counseling the new formula one unanimous *Aye* went up from the crowded house. [Conference president Senator George F.] Hoar put the noes and all was still as death. He declared it unanimously voted—and people rose and cheered...The eternal words always come in place—'May the *peace* of God which *passeth* all *understanding*' is exactly what would come on a logic-splitting crowd, and had compelled them to *pass* their intellectual processes to a spiritual plane." As he reported in *The Outlook*, the revised preamble declared: "The Conference recognizes the fact that its constituency is Congregational in tradition and policy. Therefore it declares that nothing in this Constitution is to be construed as an authoritative text, and we cordially invite to our working fellowship any who, while differing from us in belief, are in general sympathy with our spirit and our practical aims."[42]

For whatever reason, Hattie, a member of the MIT Class of 1895, did not complete her courses to earn a degree and perhaps, as a so-called "special student" that was never her intention.[43] She may have found the Tech courses too demanding in comparison to the introductory courses of the Teachers' School of Science; she must also have realized that studying at that level would not allow her the flexibility needed for her regular and clandestine meetings with Edward and for her other interests. Whatever the reason, she had told Edward several times in 1894 about the plans she was making for an extended European trip in 1895.

"What a long time since we had done any letter writing. Now alas! it begins," wrote Hattie on February 20, 1895, just after arriving in Fryeburg, Maine, where she had joined an Appalachian Club outing to snowshoe in that corner of the White Mountains region. Now, as they faced long separations for a good part of that year, she compared letter-writing with the physical intimacy of the past several months of happiness together at Union Park: "<*I do not like it as well as sitting in your lap as you very well know. Then I can*> whisper <*all sorts of things in your ear and have a chance to kiss you in that little hiding place on your neck at the same time. To think no body* [sic] *in the whole world knows any thing* [sic] *about it*> but Mrs. Andrews & me!"[44] Her naivety or self-delusion was astonishing. But perhaps she felt that her generous plan to take her niece Carrie Freeman, who would turn eighteen that summer, on a five-month European tour would deflect any newly aroused suspicions or criticisms.

A few days later, Edward left on a trip to Philadelphia, Washington, and North Carolina, meeting up in New York with his old friend "Mac," William H. McElroy, editor of the *New York Tribune,* who was to be his traveling companion on this late winter break from the rigors of Boston's climate and the church season. In Washington, Edward stayed in the Connecticut Avenue mansion of his old friend Gardiner G. Hubbard, one of the founders of the Bell Telephone Company and the first president of the National Geographic Society. The Hubbards' deaf daughter Mabel was the wife of Alexander Graham Bell. Bell had written to Edward in 1894 asking if he would be a trustee for a fund to pay for the future college education of Helen Keller for which he enclosed an initial contribution of $1,000.[45]

"Mr. Hubbard says ladies *are* members of the Geographical Society, and he will be glad to see that you are put on the list," Edward wrote Hattie after departing Washington, and continued with an amusing observation: "I have much to tell you in long dark talks perhaps, <*when I have you on my knees*> about wealth and its uses, and its failures, as exhibited in the Hubbard palace. Think of hearing the telephone bell at 9 every evening. 'Oh! That is Alex's call.' Then you run to the long wire, and Alex Bell, who is at Madison or Chicago or wherever he happens to be, talks to you for 5 minutes. This in place of a letter from your sweetheart. But <*you and I must be hospitable*> as St. Paul says."[46] Edward disliked this new invention intensely.

From Hot Springs, North Carolina, Edward described a drive through George Vanderbilt's almost completed Biltmore estate near Asheville. The 250-room palace, still under construction on 125,000 acres, was modeled after the great French châteaux of the Loire Valley. Frederick Law Olmsted, who had laid out the grounds, gave Edward a personal tour of the "chateau." Edward explained that the Olmsted-Vanderbilt connection dated back to when Olmsted was farming on Staten Island as a young man on land adjacent to a farm owned by Vanderbilt's father, William H. Vanderbilt.[47] It was at that time that Olmsted had become engaged briefly to Emily Perkins of Hartford (Edward's future wife) following an earnest three-year correspondence, a fact that Edward either did not know or, more likely, did not care to mention to Hattie. Now Edward told

Hattie, largely in shorthand, that Olmsted had advised George Vanderbilt to buy more land and lead the way in forestry. By the time he finished, Vanderbilt owned about 125,000 acres on his Biltmore estate and at Mt. Pisgah. Gifford Pinchot, who would become a leader in the national forestry movement, became chief forester of Biltmore in 1891.

But now it was Hattie's turn to travel. Edward visited her one evening just before she left Boston. After he left, she wrote:

> <*God bless you. God bless you always for the dear words you said last night to me*> & I know they are all true. That I can be of <*help to you is now the real purpose of my life*>, I think you understand that very well. It began to seem real to me (I mean my going) as you left last night, & I could not help crying for awhile, as there are tears now in my eyes as I write. I sat up & worked writing etc. for an hour & went to bed at eleven <*with your dear old hat folded in my* arms>. I have…put it in the trunk with your old thick grey jacket. <*I kissed them both as I could not kiss* you>. But all that seems natural enough, for I remember years ago <*how I used to kiss your clothes*>…& the stair case (the winding one) <*at the old church before I*> dared <*to kiss you or indeed ever hoped to. How much the years have*> brought <*to me as well as to you*>.[48]

On April 13, as the *SS Werra* of the German Norddeutscher line made its stately way down the Hudson toward the open sea, Hattie wrote a letter to be carried back on the pilot boat and mailed at Hoboken, New Jersey. She and her niece Carrie were accompanied by Emma Cummings, the ornithologist and botanist who would be Hattie's principal traveling companion for the rest of her life. "I am now on the steamer," she wrote. "The tears came to my eyes as I walked over the wharf for I thought always of a day in November when you & I walked back together over it, & I there thanked God in my heart that I was going home with you instead of going over the waters with her." She was referring to their send-off of Judith Andrews on her long voyage to India in the fall of 1893. "How foolish I am to go!" she now described herself as thinking. "Why did I do such a thing! I will never do it again, certainly, while I have to go away & leave him."[49]

On Easter Sunday, April 14, Edward wrote a letter to await Hattie's arrival in Gibraltar. In her thoughtful way, Hattie had written an Easter note for Judith Andrews to give him. "I was not prepared for your note by Mrs. Andrews," he wrote. "I had known you would write a line from the ship. (I had not expected the nice long letter you did send). But when she gave me the note and pinned the pansies in I broke down." During such lengthy separations, letters were essential symbols of their love. "<*I always carry the last one with me in my pocket until the next one comes*>," wrote Hattie in 1889, "<*then every quiet moment that I am alone I take it and read it again and again…I slip my hand into my pocket and touch it, hold it that I may touch something that you had touched and so be your love*>."[50] To avoid unnecessary anguish over inevitably lost and delayed letters, they once again numbered their letters and sent a weekly telegram.

Crossing the Atlantic was always a time of anxiety for the one left behind. It was just as well that Edward only heard later about the severe weather the women encountered soon after they headed out to sea. "Miss Cummings & Carrie were sick, I was not, but I was light-headed. There was so much motion that our trunks & bags went all over the floor & had to be lashed…Some people were thrown down the gangway & injured, but I knew enough to keep my berth." As they approached the Azores, Hattie was relieved to report that, "If all goes well, we reach the Azores tomorrow. Miss Cummings has been sicker than ever before & only came to the table last night to dinner. Carrie came for the first time for lunch to-day." With his comfort and wellbeing always on her mind, she continued her long letter on their first Friday apart (their special day), "I hoped you used the door key for the first time & went in, sat at my desk & wrote your sermon and laid down for your nap."[51]

It was Edward who introduced Emma Cummings to Hattie. Hattie's enthusiastic comments about her, written from Gibraltar on April 23, indicate that the highly competent, well-traveled, but somewhat impecunious younger woman's travels with Hattie were made at Hattie's expense: "Miss Cummings is splendid. She does all the arranging, which I should not like to do, thinks of everything, does all the haggling about prices, is very ladylike and gracious, so she makes friends with people & is altogether perfect. She takes all the care, which I know would worry me & besides she is enthusiastic in her enjoyments. We mean to go from Tangier to Cadiz."[52] The two were becoming good friends, allied in temperament and scientific interests. Emma Cummings was one of Edward's most important legacies to Hattie.

Four days later, Edward confirmed that he was taking advantage of Hattie's hospitality in her absence. Following a series of parish calls in wet weather, he let himself into Union Park: "Then I took a little very hot whiskey & water, for fear of a chill. It was your whiskey & the good God's water. Then I lay down on your lounge, with your rug *Maude* over me, your lap tablet, and this nice sheet of paper, which will not weigh so terribly as the others do."[53] Edward Everett Hale, a well-known temperance advocate, who had resigned from Boston's St. Botolph Club when his co-founders refused to make it dry (a plaque in this most convivial of clubs records this fact), seems not to have been a stranger to whiskey or wine "for medicinal purposes."

And so the five-month-long back-and-forth of their letters began. Sometimes Hattie's letters read like travelogues. But her deep connection with the affairs of their church manifests itself in a veritable diatribe she sent him from Venice in response to the information that he and Minot Savage, minister of the Church of the Unity, were talking about uniting their churches: "I am not happy about it," she told him. Describing the very different atmospheres of the two churches, she continued:

> Yours has a religious atmosphere which I never can feel in his; his has the atmosphere of a lecture hall, where the speaker is to define his position & convince you by clear, logical argument...The very aspect of the two men, you in your gown, he in his frock coat, only symbolizes the two churches. And then the Lord's Supper, which he never administers, which I suppose he believes is a superstition & a relic of the past. What will you do about that? ...Do remember how much more your people love you than they can ever love Mr. Savage & do remember me, one among many, or <*first among all and how much I shall*> lose & <*shall*> grieve <*if you go away from your own*> place.

Minot J. Savage, a popular preacher and lecturer who had been minister of the Church of the Unity since 1874 and was a good friend of Edward, was proud of the fact that he was the first individual in the U.S. or Europe "who, while occupying a pulpit, in the regular course of his pulpit ministrations, frankly accepted evolution and Darwinism, and frankly attempted to reconstruct religious and theologic thinking and theory, and bring them into accord with this newer and higher revelation of God."[54] Even though Hattie had long been a student of the various theories of evolution, she felt that Savage had gone too far and lost the spiritual element in his preaching and his services. In his reply to Hattie's concerns, Edward assured her that the idea had been found to be impracticable, and "I have ceased thinking much about the matter, as you have guessed from my letters." "You are perfectly splendid when you rise to the acme of your wrath," he concluded after reading another of her diatribes five days later.[55] Changing demographics and politics in the city of Boston were continuing to undermine the viability of the big Unitarian churches there, causing Edward and colleagues such as Minot Savage increasing anxiety. In January 1896, Savage accepted an offer to share the ministry of the Church of the Messiah in New York with his old friend and mentor Robert J. Collyer, whom he was expected to succeed but never did.

But before this, it was time for the first conference on International Arbitration at Lake Mohonk, where Edward gave the powerful opening address, captivating the participants as he cried: "A permanent tribunal. I want us to urge first, second, last and always a permanent tribunal. That is the thing...which must be rubbed into the public mind." He made this call at Mohonk four years before the Hague Conferences and twelve years before Secretary of State Elihu Root declared it to be "a chief duty upon the American delegation to the Second Hague Peace Conference to propose such a tribunal." Writing from Room 35, Edward wrote Hattie in the French Alps, "I do not know how high above the clouds you will be when you read this. I am in one, on my little piazza, in the pretty *new* part of this house which you do not yet know."[56]

The Hales were looking forward to a reunion of their children at Matunuck. On July 24, 1895, Edward wrote happily from the Red

The Hales were always fond of family gatherings and here some of the family is gathered on one of the porches of the Matunuck house. Emily often appears in family photographs wearing costumes. Apart from Emily on the porch and very tall Edward and his architect son Bertie at right, the others may include Nelly, Edward Jr., and daughters-in-law Rose and Greta.
Hale Family Papers, Sophia Smith Collection, Smith College.

House: "Rob and Phil were here, Monday night Berty and Jack arrived in triumph. We rushed down the avenue, just after sunset, to welcome them, and they waved American flags from the Right & Left of the Wagon, and stuck out their heads, each with a *mask* on, which was the twin of the other's. Since then, you can imagine the jollity…It is very pretty and pleasant to see them all together: and George Clarke is here, who is a sort of brother to all of them. Arthur came on Saturday night, but had to go on Sunday night. He comes and goes on his wheel from Kingston. Indeed, from what I hear of the wheel in Europe, I shall expect to see you and Miss Cummings and my dear Carrie ride into Boston, on your wheels from New-York."[57]

Hattie responded from Salzburg, Austria, to his descriptions of that raucous Hale family reunion, "Those home letters of yours make me feel how much of your life goes on in which I have no part or share. Of course, it can not be otherwise." But she told him she was glad he had encouraged her to make this trip: "Yes! It was well that you let me come. I have had a great deal of pleasure…I believe few women love Nature as I do & that mountain & sky mean as much to others as to me. Certainly in these sights of uplifted mountains I have gained something in my Life which can never go out of it & which I believe few feel as I do. I care nothing about the development of man or of character, which I know so interests most people; but I do want to know how the world was made & I have seen it in part. I have given it up year after year because I would not be parted so far from you."[58]

But there was a specter haunting this summer of good times. Despite many advances in medical science by the end of the nineteenth century, the cause and effect of contaminated food and drink and the vector of infectious diseases were not yet fully understood. Water and milk were often suspect, and this may have been even more the case in a remote place like Matunuck, despite Susan's conscientious housekeeping. The Hales had already lost two young sons to severe bacterial diseases. Now, in mid-August, Edward reported the kind of ominous news that filled Victorians with fear: "We are very anxious about the life of our dear young friend George Clarke. You have hardly heard me talk of him. But he is one of whom my young people are so fond, and no one whom I was so glad to have in the house. He came here for his holiday. And as soon as he returned for work he broke down in bad typhoid. He lies now awaiting one of those terrible crises…I hardly know whether Edward, Phil or Robert need him or love him most. I should feel his death as a great personal loss." But on August 28, Edward could report that George had weathered the crisis: "It seems not to be the rampant typhoid form, but a long slow form, about which they suppose there is not critical danger I hope not. Do you know that typhoid proper is more dreaded by the Doctors when it attacks young men in the prime of life, between 20 and 35, than in any other cases?"[59]

Before it was possible for her to receive the letter about George Clarke, Hattie wrote Edward about a dream that seemed close to a premonition. In her dream, he was suddenly taken ill with a chill. As she ran for some wine and a hot water bottle, the confusion and her nightmarish fear woke her up. Carrie reminded her that it was fortunate she had not had that dream the first night in their latest lodging because of the girlish superstition that first night dreams come true. In the same letter, she responded to Edward's confession that he and Martha Adams had visited Niagara Falls together following the annual Chautauqua meeting. He hoped that Hattie would not feel jealous. Hattie assured him that she trusted Martha completely and was only glad that he had such a pleasant companion for that trip. But she continued with a well-worn theme: "I am rebellious that all your best times have to be apart from me, & then you write me of them. And all my best times have to be apart from you & then I write (what I can) about them to you. The number of questions in history, in politics, in literature that I want to ask you here is simply innumerable. Besides that I want you to share my enjoyment at the time I am enjoying it. I can not reproduce it some grey cold day next November."

Hattie reminded him that they had agreed to spend their customary fall holiday together for a few days in late October following the National Unitarian Conference in Washington, "somewhere where we can enjoy out of door life & natural scenery together...I hope you will think well of this," she continued, "but if you don't you don't & I can only accept, though with great bitterness of spirit."[60]

Edward and Hattie's fears and premonitions broke into hideous reality in September, when both Emily Hale and the Hales' youngest son Robert fell desperately ill with typhoid, possibly contracted from contaminated water at Matunuck.[61] Hattie returned to America on October 4 after nearly six months in Europe. As she recalled three years later: "Mrs. Freeman was on the wharf waiting for us, & my first words were to ask for your family, for Mrs. Hale & Robert were both sick & I had not heard for so long…I spent the night at W. Newton & went in the next day to the (Park) house to see you… We should have almost met on the side walk opp. the door, but I would not have it so <*for I wanted to run into your arms and*> so I ran up the steps first & opened <*the door and got inside before you came in and then I had myself so happily in your dear arms*>."[62]

Two days later, twenty-five-year-old Robert, a promising poet and writer and a radiant and affectionate personality, succumbed to a more rampant form of the disease that his friend George Clarke had survived. The letters that Edward wrote to friends and family over the next few days and his account of his son's death in his journal are heartbreaking: "How little I thought of what I was next to write here," he confided to his journal on October 8, the day of his beloved youngest child's funeral:

> His mother is upstairs, where she has lain for four weeks and so weak that they dare not tell her of his death…His fight with fever at the last was so terrible that I was not going to look upon his face again, so sad was the expression, almost of agony. But Phil told me I should see nothing of this, and it was true. As Phil said, it was just the look of interest in a new problem before him, and there was the dear smile on his face which belonged to his determination to solve that problem…Dear Phil said, 'You knew I confided everything to him, and I would take his advice about very little things'…Several of the boys were here last night, who are the pall-bearers of today. They have but one thing to say, and that is of his force of character and of his intense love for everybody…For myself, I am only so glad now that I have never thwarted what seemed his vague plans for study and for life. Low down in them, I am sure, was his wish to take care of me and his mother until we died.[63]

The Hales turned in on themselves in deepest mourning. Emily was prostrated with grief when she learned the truth. The *New York Times*, reporting on the opening of the National Unitarian Conference in Washington on October 21, declared, "Great regret is generally expressed that Dr. Edward Everett Hale has not been able to attend this year's conference on account of deep family afflictions."[64] There would be no fall excursion for Edward and Hattie that month or year; it was all Hattie could do to find the words to comfort Edward after such a searing loss.

9

The Toll of Depression

As Hattie supported Edward through terrible grief, the underpinnings of her own life were being eroded. The global economic depression that began in 1893 came to shatter Hattie's financial security and the independence she valued so highly. It was triggered by the McKinley Tariff Act, which had reduced U.S. revenues, and by Britain's unloading of American securities. The stock market fell sharply in May that year after months of anxiety over diminishing gold reserves. Mines and factories closed, and railroads failed. By year's end, unemployment stood at 3 million (an "army" of unemployed marched on Washington the following April), some 15,000 businesses and more than 600 banks had foundered, speculative investments disappeared, and family fortunes evaporated.

The following year, 1894, the Wilson-Gorman Tariff Bill canceled reciprocity treaties with Spain and Cuba, took sugar off the free list, and instituted a 40 percent tax on Cuban goods, devastating profits from Soledad, Hattie's cousin Edwin Atkins's 12,000-acre sugar plantation which had reached a high-water mark of one million dollars before the tariff bill became law. Following the poor grinding season of 1895, thousands of Cuban men were discharged, adding to already high unemployment, and fanning the flames of longstanding unrest among recently emancipated slaves into the insurrection that would contribute to the Spanish-American War three years later.

The tariff bill also laid taxes on woolen goods, adversely affecting profits at the Aetna Mills, her late father's textile mill (now part of Edwin's business empire). "You will know, perhaps before you read this, whether the Tariff will go through," Edward wrote her in late July 1894. "The battle is on Coal-Wood, Iron and Sugar. You Aetna people are cut down in the protection on manufactured goods from

A photograph from the Atkins family archive shows E. Atkins Company employees under the old slave bell at the Soledad plantation near Cienfuegos, Cuba, in 1895. Note the armed guard hired to protect the plantation and its workers from roving bands of angry insurrectionists.
From the Atkins Family Photographs, number 37-216. Courtesy of the Massachusetts Historical Society.

90 per cent, which the McKinley [Tariff of 1890] gave you, to 45 percent."[1]

In addition to devastated share values, Hattie's bonds would soon be cut in half. It is surprising that she was able to afford the five-month grand tour of Europe in 1895 but, from then on, Hattie's letters increasingly refer to the need to economize. Even so, she traveled West twice in 1896, the first time with the expectation she would be able to see Edward. Late in February, Edward joined Emily and Nelly in Santa Barbara, California, where Emily was recuperating from her life-threatening illness and devastating loss of Rob in the light-filled winter house of their wealthy Rhode Island friends, the Hazards of Peace Dale. In the Hales' absence, their architect son Bertie and Judith Andrews, determined to lift the Hales' spirits, were overseeing much needed renovations to their house.

Despite her reduced income, Hattie decided to join her friends Thomas and Elizabeth Watson, fellow students of geology, on their trip to the Grand Canyon. Thomas Watson, who had been Alexander Graham Bell's assistant at Boston University in inventing the telephone ("Mr. Watson—come here—I want to see you"), was the beneficiary of one tenth of the patents. That allowed him to retire before he was thirty. The Watsons' interest in rocks began on their honeymoon in Europe, particularly after seeing Vesuvius, "a place where rocks were actually being made!"[2] The couple enrolled as special students in Professor William Crosby's geology courses at Boston Tech in 1892, the year before Hattie. Hattie's friendships with the Watsons, Parnell Murray, Mary Dann, and Amadeus Grabau were rooted firmly in geology courses at Boston Tech.[3]

Five years earlier, Hattie had backed away from the idea of joining Edward in California and accompanying him home; this time, she acted on her impulse. Edward wrote his secretary on February 29, "Hattie writes me that she is to come as near us as Santa Fe and the Canon of Colorado."[4] That Hattie's Western trip was not preplanned with Edward is clear in his letter to her the following week: "As you approach me from day to day, I can make plans for meeting you somewhere. You are right in saying that it is too late for me to change my plans for going home. I have made positive engagements for the second week in March [he meant April] which I must hold to."[5] Ten days later, he wrote to her at Flagstaff, Arizona, care of the Watsons: "How near you are to me!...I close suddenly for the greater caution."[6]

Duly cautioned, Hattie wrote one of her open letters when she arrived in Flagstaff, two days after her forty-ninth birthday: "Dear Mr. Hale, We reached here yesterday afternoon, when I found a mail of eighteen letters waiting for me...We leave to-morrow morning for our trip to the Canon. It is a drive of eighty five miles & we shall take two days for it; the same to return; & we should certainly have three days there...How are Mrs. Hale & Nellie? I trust they are both well & happy in the surroundings which you describe as being so beautiful...With cordial regards to your family & much love to yourself, I am yours always, Hattie."[7]

In the meantime, Edward wrote urging Hattie to stay on in the West rather than returning to Boston's "beastly climate" with him. He told her he wanted her to have time to study and enjoy the scenery, geology, and botany of the Pacific Coast and the Ojai Valley region east of Santa Barbara but he certainly realized how it would look to suspicious Bostonians if he stepped off the train with her. He told her that he would "work like a beaver" in April so that they could be together for much of May. But his March 22 postscript headed "To be read first" indicated he had found a way to see her before returning home: "All the enclosed is superseded. All you have to do is to telegraph me before Wednesday noon where you shall be at S. Bernardino, and to wait there if you can, or at Redlands which is virtually the same thing, until Friday. I leave here at 8.30 Thursday & expect to be in San Bernardino that night." "Stick to your party at San Bernardino," he told her in another letter. "I will find you there or somewhere. And will give myself time to find you."[8]

On March 20, at "Cameron's Camp, Grand Canon," Hattie wrote a long and fascinating account of her expedition to the Grand Canyon with the Watsons: "Dear Mr. Hale, Here we are! We have really accomplished the object of our long travel. We spent last night 2500 ft. down in the canon & have this morning walked up three miles on a burro trail, for there is a mine being worked at that point... We are all dead tired at this moment, as we have until within a half hour been half starved. Mr. & Mrs. Watson are resting, stretched upon the ground in our tent. But I don't feel the need of lying down & so will begin now the tale of our adventures which have been many & unexpected. I will begin at the beginning, as we used to say."

This was 1896, thirteen years before the railroad was extended from Williams near Flagstaff to what had become Grand Canyon Village. Watson was misled by a circular advertising a hotel near the South Rim (it was not built until 1905!). He had also been in touch with the Le Baron outfitters in Flagstaff for two months but all they came up with was a rickety prairie wagon and horses, a young guide-driver-cook John—who, as they were to discover, was good-natured and helpful but inexperienced and no cook—and inadequate food, water, and cooking implements (they had to supply their own bedding).

The intrepid geologists set off through a fine forest of Ponderosa pines and skirted San Francisco Mountain, an extinct volcano white with snow.[9] Once on the open plain around Dead Man's Gulch they climbed down from the wagon to walk. That night, they stayed at a ranch well supplied with hay for the horses and water from a spring, but the yard was strewn with rubbish and the one-room cabin was filthy. A bed on stilts with straw and unclean blankets seemed certain to harbor lice and bedbugs so they decided to sleep in a row on the floor, wrapped up in their blankets with their feet to the fireplace. Things looked better when a friendly cowboy turned up and treated them to fresh, if dirty, beef cooked in lard, the last satisfying meal they had for several days. Cowboy and driver climbed a ladder to sleep in the upper room.

By lunchtime the next day, chilled by riding into the cold north wind all morning, they were glad to make a fire in another dirty cabin. "We cooked our dirty food & ate our dirty dinner & declared we were having a first rate time & were no 'tender feet.'" At sunset, they reached their journey's end, or so they thought. What had been billed as a hotel, turned out to be another log cabin. "No one there! locked!" John broke down the door only to find the cabin was piled high "with merchandise of various kinds." John wasn't sure if this was where they were supposed to spend the night so he and Watson set out on foot in opposite directions to see if they could find a more welcoming cabin. When John came back, he reported that the cabin he had found was secured with a Yale lock; breaking it open was "a penitentiary offense." Since it was rapidly growing dark and even colder and they had no lantern or candle to explore further, they made a fire of old boxes and barrels they found behind the cabin, warmed themselves up, and made a frugal supper. Then they unloaded the wagon so that the two women could sleep there, uncomfortably jammed together. Wrapped in his Navajo blankets, Watson stretched out under the stars on one of the doors they found in the cabin, apparently intended for the future hotel.

"It was a glorious night, not a breath of air!" reported Hattie gamely. "But oh! so cold! The little water left in our canteen froze. We were so stiff from our hard bed. Every bone in my body ached, & we all felt alike. I should have said there was no undressing but taking off our boots. I even left my gloves on…I did know enough not to bring a nightdress."

The next morning, they walked to "the 'rim' so called, close by, & [we] had our first view of the Grand Canyon—red rocks, blue shadows—a great distance, the nearer portions all barred with horizontal lines of stratification. One cannot describe the indescribable. We spent our forenoon walking & looking & wondering; then what a contrast! back to our dirty dinner! dried Graham bread, heavy & old, which I should only give to a dog at home; soaked in sweetened coffee, for all the condensed milk is sweetened. Then we packed up & started off four miles through the pine woods, to this Cameron's mining camp which is at the head of the trail."[10]

The log house at Cameron's camp was inhabited by eight miners but, fortunately, a better equipped camp than theirs had broken up two days earlier. A miner set up one of their tents for them and built a fire outside: "So we were warm & the starlight night was glorious." After an early breakfast the next morning, they set off down the trail to a stone house with a fireplace, cooking stove, and well stocked with supplies for the miners, who were absent. For the first time, they had a table, seats, and spoons, as well as canned tomatoes and fresh tough steak for lunch. They felt as if they had "struck ile" [oil]. While the men continued on down to the river, the women did some housekeeping and tried, very unsuccessfully, to make biscuits for breakfast the next morning.

With an introduction and lengthy additions to their experiences in the Canyon itself and their return trip (she had broken off her handwritten account before finishing), some diplomatic softening of her harshest indictments, and pseudonyms for the Watsons, Edward published Hattie's account of their adventure as "The Grand Canon of the Colorado (From a Staff Correspondent)" in the final, May 16 issue of his newspaper *Boston Commonwealth*.[11] Hattie began this published account: "We are just out from the Grand Canon of the Colorado, having had a week of great adventure and a glimpse of rough western life such as I hardly expected..." When claiming in this account that she would always think of it as the most adventurous of her travels, she could not have predicted the extent and frequency of her world travels in later years. Humor, not earnest Hattie's most prominent quality, sparkles through additions to the published account and it is probable that her light-hearted, witty editor had a hand in this. For instance, describing the "horrid" biscuits made by the privileged Boston women, "Myles [Watson] said it was not safe to throw them away, as it might cause an avalanche."[12]

Finding Edward's letters awaiting her at Flagstaff with the news that he was leaving Santa Barbara on Thursday, Hattie immediately wrote to him at Los Angeles, "To be called for at the Post Office": "We all leave here this afternoon. Mr. & Mrs. Watson...have a week in Southern Arizona. But I shall not go with them, for in that case I should miss you. I have been hesitating whether to say I will meet you at Los Angeles, San Bernardino or Redlands, but I have determined upon the last as in your letter you score it as if it were the most desirable...I shall go to Hotel Windsor, as Baedeker gives it, as the best. If the hotel has burnt, or is full or if for any reason I can not get in, I will communicate with you through the Post Office."[13]

As their telegrams kept passing each other with revised plans, it is a wonder that they succeeded in meeting up at all. On March 22, Edward confirmed in pencil after receiving one telegram: "P.S. Tuesday a.m. I held this when I got your telegram to which I have replied. I come to S. Bernardino Thursday & hope to find you that night! Joy, joy, joy!"[14] But meet up they did, staying briefly at the La Casa Loma Hotel in Redlands before Edward traveled back to Boston alone.[15] Judging by specific comments in Edward's letters that summer, the ardent pair almost certainly spent the night together.

A letter Hattie wrote Edward seven years later when she stayed in the same hotel with her friend Emma Cummings after they attended a scientific convention in San Francisco, seems to provide confirmation. "I remember so plainly everything <*about*> my visit here. I even knew my <*old room as I passed it. Do you wonder*>?" Edward, by then aged eighty-one and with his mind more on the passing of so many dear old friends, responded, "Think of it! Our dear Casa Loma! How well I remember sighting you on the side-walk, after missing you at our Hotel. I am afraid our dear Mr. Smiley shews some marks of his sorrow in his brother's death."[16]

By Easter, Edward was back in Boston, staying at Bertie's house while renovations continued at Highland Street. But Hattie remained in California another three weeks. She stayed in an expensive and unappealing hotel in downtown Santa Barbara while awaiting the arrival of the Watsons. "I miss Mr. Watson," she admitted, '& think I could travel happily with him, for he will go where there are objects of natural history & he is intelligent & full of interest about them. But as it is, I am tired of these hotels in these parallelogram town[s], & entirely <*apart from the joy of seeing you*> I am quite ready to come home, even if the sun does always shine here."[17] Mary Atkins recorded in her diary on April 25 that she was at the Union Park house "when Hattie arrived from her journey of 2 months in Arizona & California. Dr. Hale met her at the Station."[18] This was not the first time that Aunt Mary noted Edward's solicitude for her niece as well as the frequency with which she found him at Union Park when she called on Hattie, as if it was now taken for granted by members of the Freeman family.

Hattie was not home for long. On June 5, she described her scramble to pack her trunk and bid farewell to her many friends and family before leaving the next day for Colorado Springs with her new friend Mrs. Strong, another fellow geology student. They were to join a geological field trip into Middle Park led by William Crosby, their former professor at Boston Tech, which the Watsons, still in the West, had also promised to join. In the meantime, Edward was at Lake Mohonk with Martha Adams for the second annual peace conference, at which he again made one of the opening speeches. He used very similar phraseology in recounting his experiences there for his lawful and secret wives.[19]

All did not go according to plan when Hattie and Mrs. Strong arrived in Colorado Springs. They found that their party was scattered and the Watsons were staying at nearby Manitou Springs, probably because the cog railroad to the top of Pike's Peak originated there.[20] "The worst has happened," a devastated Hattie wrote Edward dramatically from there on June 16. "Mr. & Mrs. Watson left for Boston this morning, & we are stranded here."[21] Considering they had two young daughters and Watson's Fore River Ship and Engine Building Company was rapidly becoming one of the biggest shipyards in the country, the Watsons' wish to return home after two months' absence seems entirely reasonable. Apparently, the women were upset at the prospect of being left alone in the less than stimulating and reassuring company of Professor Crosby, who was growing very deaf. They expected the generous Watsons to organize and perhaps even underwrite their trips to the many geological sites in the area; certainly Hattie had made it clear that she found Thomas Watson a stimulating companion.

Three days later, things were looking up, although frustrated Hattie began her letter, "The devil. That is the way I am inclined to begin this letter rather than with the usual loving greeting. Everything seemed such a mess. To think that besides losing this trip, there is a chance more than that, a probability of losing Kelly's Island with Grabau, & Chautauqua with you." Hattie's nephew Frank Freeman, now a junior at Newton High School, would be working as Grabau's assistant that summer and Hattie had arranged to visit them both on her return journey, although Grabau had said he would be tied up with other people until late July. "And as for Chautauqua!" Hattie continued. "Isn't it hard! How many times have we tried for Mohonk & Chautauqua & nothing has ever come to pass. If it fails this time, I shall hate the name of both of those places."[22]

Despite their bad start, Hattie and Mrs. Strong began enjoying each other's company. The beautiful widow had confided that her surgeon husband, Charles P. Strong of Harvard Medical School, had died of blood poisoning after pricking his finger while performing an appendectomy. It was Mrs. Strong's first trip out West and everything delighted her. The two women made many enjoyable excursions with Professor Crosby and Hattie's letters reflected her renewed delight in the Colorado mountains. After reading about the women's climb up Pike's Peak, Edward wrote "I do not think you understand what a feat the summit is…You do not say any thing about difficulty of breathing…What you tell of the Alpine flowers is lovely."[23] As record-breaking temperatures made the East Coast unbearable, he urged her to stay on in the Rockies for as long as possible.

Meanwhile, instead of spending the first part of the summer at Matunuck, Edward and Emily visited Nelly and her companion, artist Gabrielle Clements, at their house and studio at Folly Cove on Cape Ann. Edward explained why they were increasingly more comfortable there than at "Susy's hotel," where, "in these later days, there are too many people for whom you do not very much care… Now at Folly Cove there is absolutely no one, day in or out but G.C. and her mother. About this I must confess, there is one drawback. Gabrielle gabbles the whole time. It is as bad as another person you and I know [he was referring to Mary Cobb]. I call her Gab Royale, the queen of Gabblers. She walks right into the room where I am writing or reading and goes at it. But she is a hard working artist, and is devoted all through the hours of daylight in her studio to a piece of decoration."[24]

From Boston, where he was spending a few days, leaving Emily with Nelly and Gabrielle at Folly Cove, Edward wrote Hattie a long, ardent letter, which he mailed to her in two parts. The first part reached her there before she left. The second, more sensual part did not and had to be forwarded to Union Park. He opened this second letter to "<*My darling child the dearest girl in all the world to me*>" with his transcriptions in Latin, English, and shorthand of the famous ode to a thousand kisses written by Catullus ("Edward") to his love Lesbia ("Hattie"). He described how they would spend precious time together if she passed through Boston, concluding: "<*There*> was <*never*> any <*Lesbia*> who <*had cheeks*> or <*lips*> or <*breath or soft loving features*> like <*my Hattie or had*> such <*a pretty way of showing her own dear boy how much he was to her*>. Someday I will succeed in <*showing her the*> same."[25]

Two days later, Edward repeated a proposal that they meet in Albany and then travel down the Hudson to Lake Mohonk, where they could spend a week together rather than in Boston. But

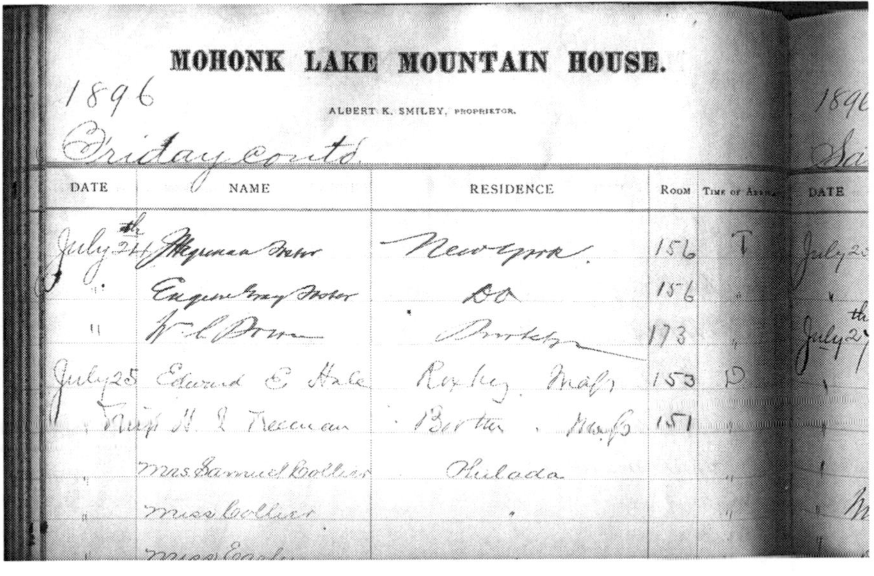
MOHONK LAKE MOUNTAIN HOUSE.

ALBERT K. SMILEY, PROPRIETOR.

1896

DATE	NAME	RESIDENCE	ROOM	TIME OF ARRIVAL
July 24th	[illegible]	New York	156	T
"	[illegible]	Do	156	"
"	[illegible]	[illegible]	173	"
July 25	Edward E. Hale	Roxbury, Mass	153	D
"	[illegible]	[illegible], Mass	151	
"	Mrs. Samuel Collier	Philada		
"	Miss Collier	"		

A page of the 1896 Mohonk Lake Mountain House register clearly shows that Edward signed in for both himself and Hattie on July 25 for adjoining rooms 153 and 151.
Courtesy of the Mohonk Mountain House Archives.

before Hattie agreed to meet Edward en route home, she evidently poured out her loneliness from Chicago where she was visiting Judith Andrews's youngest son Clement (Cle), librarian of the John Crerar Library of Science at the University of Chicago. Her *cri de coeur* elicited this heartfelt response from her lover: "As you say in your shorthand, or as you imply, we have <*so good a time when we are together that all separate life*> seems intolerable…When I am all sole alone, I begin to say <*why is she not here, why did I not go to find her, and why are we not together*>…I know it would be better not to say this or think it, but to go to work squaring the circles, or discovering perpetual motion, or doing something else <*if only it would put the*> impossible <*memory out* of> the way…I take a certain grim satisfaction when I see that <*in my loneliness I follow the lines of yours*> or that you in yours follow <*the lines of mine*>…<*how empty life seems without you*>." And again he repeated his hope that she would "feel like stopping at Albany and going down to L.M. with me."[26]

They did manage a week together at Lake Mohonk. The Mohonk Mountain House register shows that they checked in under their own names to adjacent rooms with a connecting balcony on Saturday, July 25. Edward and Nelly would share similar connecting rooms at The Maplewood in Bethlehem, NH, in late August, when he told Hattie, "We have two nice rooms on the first floor, opening into each other, not differing much from our rooms at Mohonk, but that there is no piazza."[27]

A few days after his return to Matunuck, Edward wrote: "It is very quiet here, very quiet, the least bit dull; but, as I am well aware, very good for me. It is rather hard <*after such a week as we had together*> when every moment was alive, and we never wished away time."[28] Since their stay at Mohonk was not incognito and Hattie recalled the delightful talk at the Smiley family's dinner table, their hosts evidently saw nothing illicit about the relationship of a highly respectable 74-year-old married Unitarian minister, for whom they had the greatest admiration, and his equally respectable middle-aged literary amanuensis with whom he was hard at work each day. But, of course, they were not aware of the passionate letters the pair had been exchanging before their arrival there.

Edward traveled to Boston from Matunuck on August 3 to see Hattie before she left with her niece Ethel for a week in Maine but his failure to write for the next ten days was, as always, wounding and worrying to her. Adding to her insecurity, Hattie had just spotted the evidence that Henrietta Pierce, her oldest friend in Union Park, was leaving and had not told her. "I am broken hearted & hurt" she wrote. "The sign 'For Sale,' is up at Etta's house & she has never written me of it. It is so bitter to feel that the love & confidence which you give to a friend whom you have known for years, is not returned. I suppose Miss Mary often feels pained in the same way by my attitude towards her."[29] However, Etta's sick old mother, whom she had nursed devotedly for years, had died the year before and the house had too many associations for this unselfish and deeply loyal woman, as she would admit to Hattie in a letter. A more likely motivation was the rapidly deteriorating neighborhood as more and more of the houses on Union Park were being converted into rooming houses to accommodate a new flood of immigration. Now the bulk of immigrants were coming from southern and eastern Europe; about 150,000 Italians, 80,000 Poles, and nearly 25,000 Lithuanians entered the Bay State between 1890 and 1910. At the same time, the Jewish population expanded from 4,000 around 1890 to around 40,000 by 1910.[30]

Soon after arriving at Isle of Springs, Maine, Hattie wrote one of her open letters to "Dear Mr. Hale," a sure indication that she had not heard from Edward for some time and that he might be with his wife. She and Ethel were staying in the hotel on this picturesque, 100-acre island of modest cottages and unspoiled natural beauty, a favorite resort for Unitarians at that time, and were spending a good deal of time with the Young family, "Mr. & Mrs., & the two daughters Lucy & Mrs. Patten."[31] Two days later, Hattie had begun another letter, certain that Edward must have lost the piece of paper with her address, when two of his letters arrived at last.

Hattie told Edward that she was keeping up with politics through the *Boston Evening Transcript* sent to her daily and was shocked to discover that her old friend Joshua Young was on the opposite side: "It seems as though Bryan's speech at Madison Square had lost the cause. Heaven grant it may be so! What do you think? Mr. Young 'is not sound'!" She was referring to "sound money," the gold standard of the Republican platform, and continued indignantly: "He has not made up his mind which way to vote, or if he will not avoid the responsibility by not voting at all. Then when he made some half apology & said I must not consider him a silverite. I was so unguarded as to say 'No! I should lose much of my respect for you if I did.' Then, that settled heavily on his mind, & I saw it was not the thing for me to say, & I apologized, or rather I said I ought not to have said it, & I was sorry I had, which was perfectly true, but I did not say but what I held to my statement, which I do."

Referring to the continuing severe economic depression, she concluded about Young, "You know he did not like Blaine personally, & so he either did not vote at all or voted for Cleveland, I forget which, & so helped to bring on the present disasters of the country. I can not see why adherence to a platform is not a much more important thing than adherence to a man. If everyone may bolt their party because he does not like the candidate selected, why! there would be inextricable confusion." This makes it clear that Hattie and Edward were on the same page politically. It always shocked Hattie when she discovered that some of her closest friends, such as the Reverend Young and Judith Andrews, were, or were suspected to be, Democrats.

Hattie was right. The acceptance speech for the Democratic nomination that William Jennings Bryan gave at Madison Square Garden on August 12 was a flop, a huge disappointment for his supporters after his dramatic barnstorming across the country. The speech was tarnished and brutally criticized for being addressed to the media rather than to the people and Bryan's campaign hit the skids the day that the scorching heat wave that killed almost 1500 people, particularly in the New York tenements, peaked. Despite Bryan continuing his ceaseless speechmaking, amounting to five hundred across twenty-seven states, William McKinley, the front porch campaigner, won the presidency by a margin of 271 to 176.

Hattie begged Edward to go to Matunuck rather than stay in Boston in the deadly heat but adopted a characteristically lighter tone when describing their adventures in nature along the cooler Maine seashore: "This morning we spent three hours in a row boat. Ethel & I row admirably together. Mrs. Young was in the stern guiding us. It was low tide & we kept us close to the rocks to see the sea urchins, looking like so many chestnut burrs, on the rocks. We brought home two & a star fish, & I now have them in a basin of salt water here in my room…How I do love the study of Natural History. I sometimes think it is the only thing in Life that really interests <*me besides my love for you*>."[32]

There was a reason for Edward's protracted silence. It seems that he had not informed Hattie that he had invited his longtime staffer and editor of the *Lend a Hand* magazine Minnie Whitman to Matunuck during the time when Hattie was becoming anguished (shades of the Sarah Farmer incident). As reported by Susan Hale in a colorful August 13 letter, marked "Private," to Edward's secretary Martha Adams, the two colleagues appeared at the Red House together late one Saturday night (could that have been the same Saturday that he parted from Hattie?) when Susan had already gone to bed. Their train from Boston broke down and, instead of going to a restaurant, "they sate [*sic*] 2 hours in the RR station at Providence… reading aloud 10 x 1 reports to each other." Susan was incensed to see that "the Chief was in a state of abject Devotion to the Lady. I was madder than thunder. I can't bear the sight of her, and never imagined seeing her under my Roof & Fig tree, but Lucretia (who hates her)" served them the ham that was intended for breakfast. Two of Susan's paying guests were away so Susan "popped Mrs. W. into their bed…there were 12 at breakfast…and nothing to eat, minus the Ham, but some pickled fish & an omelette…(oh, He took her after breakfast for a row on the Pond). Now he has asked me to invite her again before summer is over!"[33] Susan was relieved when her brother wrote that he was not coming down to Matunuck after all because he was preaching at Bethlehem in the heart of the White Mountains.

As previously mentioned, Susan was all too aware of her brother's often flirtatious relationships with women of intellect. She was also highly skeptical of Edward's various magazine ventures which universally lost money. In fact, Edward was facing yet another magazine failure and was contemplating having to let Minnie Whitman and Mr. Smith, his business manager, go. Minnie, a widow with five children, was among a handful of staffers who had been with him almost his entire tenure at the South Congregational Society. His "devotion" might be attributed to his guilt over her uncertain future.

Edward's tangled financial affairs, made far more critical by the state of the economy, were now the concern of his older sons. Six years before, Emily had expressed what many of Edward's friends and relations, including Hattie, were feeling, that the *Lend a Hand* magazine was a drain on his energy and financial resources (Minnie Whitman and a "typewriter" received salaries, he did not). While Emily had recognized that periodical publishing "may be in the blood" and "is your great pleasure," she reminded him that, since they were getting old, "isn't it better to draw in, and make your work simple and do nothing that is not really necessary. It makes me miserable to feel that this steady leakage is going on, in your strength, and in your income."[34] Susan had received a letter from Arthur on the subject and now wrote, "The important [thing] is to put off the Grand Opening at Highland Street as long as possible," and "Lucretia gave me a turn by saying she had received this week a new number of the Commonwealth!"[35] In January 1897, *Lend a*

Hand was absorbed by *Charities*, a new publication in New York, but the Lend A Hand Society's interests continued to be recorded from 1898 in the less ambitious *Lend A Hand Record*, with Minnie Whitman once more as co-editor with Edward.

Hattie was enjoying the company of her nieces Carrie and Ethel, nephew Frank, and teacher friend Carrie Shaw in her small rented house in Shelburne. Also staying with Hattie was her friend Parnell Murray, a science teacher at Boston's Girls' High School, whose account of the six-week course in embryology she had just completed at the Marine Biology Laboratory in Woods Hole filled Hattie with envy. However, Miss Murray told her that her landlady there, otherwise "a smart, shrewd lady," was disdainful of these new college educated professional women: "This woman could not understand why this class of women came down to do such work. She said with a lofty air, 'We have plenty of young women in town who can afford to sit in a rocking chair & read novels & amuse themselves. They don't go into any such work.' And she considered these towns girls as vastly superior & treated Miss Murray & all like her with a patronizing air. Doesn't that show the limitations in the life of our country people & the hopelessness of trying to wake them up."[36] These remarks smack of feminism but so very often did Edward's. Hattie's later opposition to woman suffrage, therefore, seems all the more surprising.

In her next letter, Hattie expressed her pleasure in the Freeman children's visit, remarking on how studious Ethel had become in contrast to her older sister Carrie, while Frank was amusing himself taking photographs. Parnell Murray's description of what she had learned that summer filled her with envy: "It makes me long to do some <u>work</u> in Natural History. I should be so much happier if I had more <u>work</u> in my life: something I had to do & could do. I believe that for unmarried women, who have to earn their living in some occupation which is congenial, & where the pay is so sure that they have no anxiety, that they are far happier than those who are living as I am. I feel as if I were playing with Life, & I am not satisfied. I am always making plans for my future, but they do not grow definite."[37]

Although Hattie never took a course at the Marine Biological Laboratory at Woods Hole, she was on its Corporation board for its first twenty years and Parnell Murray was not her only science teacher friend who studied there. This striking photograph of MBL students and faculty fishing for specimens in the harbor in the summer of 1895 reflects Hattie's many similar experiences at Alpheus Hyatt's summer school at Annisquam and later at the Bayville Summer School in Maine.
Courtesy of the Woods Hole Marine Biology Laboratory Archives.

This is one of the most revealing passages about Hattie's painful conundrum. She had concluded her studies at Boston Tech and now longed for a professional life but she wanted a life with Edward even more. Back in Matunuck after staying with some of his Boston parishioners at their summer resorts, Edward responded, as always, with great sympathy to Hattie's comments about her need for work. In shorthand, he told her he was thinking about her all the time, "and so think a great deal of what you say about regular work. I am sure you are right about it. You inherit your father's capacity for business and the consequent love of it…I do think when October comes, we can address ourselves seriously to see what daily work you can give yourself to, with its weekly compensation, not amateur work, but real work, at regular hours, where you lift in your place, such work as so many men and so many women do so ill."[38]

Facing the departure of all her guests, and having endured two weeks of bad weather, making her beloved hiking and outdoor mountain life impossible, the tone of Hattie's letters began to change. Lonely and worried about her finances and those of her friends, she was lapsing into depression, as she made clear in two letters in early September. She was nostalgic for the stimulating table talk at Mohonk: "How I wish I could hear some men talk. I hate my life here, in which I have absolutely no interest. I hope another year will not find me here. Think of the weather! I have been here fourteen days & have waked to <u>three</u> pleasant mornings…We have so often a dense fog, which clears soon after breakfast. The waking & looking out into such greyness instead of into sunshine chills me through & through. And such dampness & such smell of the Berlin pulp mills which seems to become more apparent under these circumstances…My loneliness in life seems to grow, & all I can do to battle with the sense of it, seems of no avail."[39] Edward also wrote that he had no one to talk to at Matunuck. His son Edward Jr. was mad about golf and played every day and Susan was too busy with housework and herding inefficient servants and demanding guests to sit and talk with him until late in the evenings. Emily, not the most stimulating conversationalist at the best of times, increasingly preferred to avoid the noise and chaos of "Susan's hotel," choosing to spend much of the summer with Nelly and Gabrielle Clements at Folly Cove.

When Hattie heard from Edward that he might not be able to arrive with her on September 15, as she had expected, and that it might be as late as the 22nd, when she was certain the weather would be cold and miserable, her depression deepened. The Freeman children were about to return to West Newton and she had put off other guests so that they could be alone together. "I beg of you to consider what this living here alone with Sophy & Mary can be with absolutely no neighbors, a great deal of grey weather, & worst of all, no work to do," she wrote. "If I had the work, all would be well, but I can not create it." Now Judith Andrews had put her Rutland Square house in the hands of a broker and, with her own income severely reduced, Hattie felt she could do nothing more than ask her to move in with her: "I doubt if I should have kept my home until now, except that <*it might be a second home to you*>, & I will not take anyone into <*it not even her without first asking you and making sure that you*> would <*come there with the same*> freedom <*that you do now*>. And I doubt <*if you would if she were there*>, though <*she more than any*> one else probably <*knows how much we love*>."[40]

Edward assured her that he would come to her house just the same and now rearranged his plans so as to be with her for nearly a week between September 11 and 17. Following his departure, she wrote, "I do not live over the visit very much. I will not permit myself to. The contrast is too sharp & I am afraid of getting blue by thinking of it." But a few days later, she admitted, "I look back upon your visit as an oasis in my life! How gladly I would live those days over again!" Naturally, she was delighted when he laid out a calendar for the winter in which he would spend two days a week with her: "<*Yes! I will spend Tuesday out of doors gladly so long as the*> weather will allow & when it <*does not we will be in some other place. So long as we are together and you will be with me all day I will do anything you wish and go anywhere you want*>. Oh, <*how glad I shall be to see you again*>."

As he tried to cheer her up, Edward had reminded Hattie that she was "one clear beam of sunshine across so many foggy lives." Hattie thanked him, told him she would try and make that help her but, in truth, she was only happy when she was with him. "The only sunshine I have is Sophy," she told Edward a few days later, "her unfailing cheerfulness which shows itself unconsciously & always is a perfect benediction. She is richer than I, richer in nature, that she can always have this inward sunshine, while I am so much dependent upon the outer sunshine."[41] There is no doubt that Hattie was acutely weather sensitive.

Despite her misery in her continuing self-imposed exile in dreary Shelburne, Hattie did not forget the significance of October 5 for the Hales, the one-year anniversary of Rob's death. Edward expressed gratitude for all her attempts to help him through his grief, telling her that he and his family were going through the day unsure what to say or do. He was due to attend opening ceremonies at Harvard, only too aware of all the memories this would bring flooding back of his youngest son's student days. Glued in a copy of the book the Hales had printed of Rob's best stories and poems, which Hattie gave her niece Ethel for Christmas that year, is a copy of the following letter to Edward from William Dean Howells:

> My dear Hale, I have read every line of Robert's book, both poetry & prose. The poetry is always good, the fine expression of a man who thinks with his feelings; but the prose amazes me. In your son has passed into silence one of the greatest gifts for fiction that the world has ever had the promise of. I might blame his work in some little things of method; some touches of subjectivity in the handling; but for infinitely the greater part all is as it should be & wonderful. How at his time of life did he know men & women so well? How did he know himself so well? Everything in his book is so sane, so just, so wise! He could have done <u>anything</u> if he had lived. I am amazed at his work, & I know the trade of fiction pretty well. What a loss![42]

By October 8, Hattie could bear Shelburne no longer and decided to drive in a coach and four with her latest guests fifty miles to Wonalancet on the southern edge of the White Mountains, leaving Sophie and Mary behind in Shelburne. There she hoped to find a more attractive house for the following summer. But she discovered there was no Catholic church in Wonalancet and she could not deprive her maids of their religion. In a letter to Hattie at Wonalancet, Edward described what it was about his wife that he found so hard to live with. It seemed to be her total self-absorption, her failure to listen to other people's stories or points of view, in particular her husband's. For a man who spent his days and his energy listening to his parishioners' problems and trying to find solutions, this must have seemed inhuman, but the Hales had been married for forty-four years and Emily may have wearied of her husband's domineering personality. Besides, they were very different people. Naturally, Edward contrasted Emily's thoughtless detachment and focus on herself and her ill health unfavorably with Hattie's warmth and extraordinary generosity to those less fortunate and to her family and friends—particularly to him! He told Hattie about a typical morning spent giving advice, convinced that most people forgot immediately what he suggested: "But do you know, I begin to think that this is not from lack of sympathy. It is that most people are deaf and hear nothing. And 9/10 of the others are wholly self-absorbed <*just like my wife*> and do not pay the slightest real attention to anything that is said."[43] In another letter, he described how his wife interrupted his story of an incident that day, subverting it into something quite different, and then walked away. Hattie, on the other hand, registered and reacted appropriately to everything he ever told her.

A letter like this was a siren call to Hattie. She turned her back on Shelburne and returned to Boston two weeks early, staying with friends until Union Park was reopened at the end of October. On October 16, Edward wrote in large letters, "The Last Letter!!!!!... Is it not wonderful <*is it not almost perfect that we have come to the end*>. We have not been perfectly <*good but we have been pretty good. And another time*> perhaps we shall bear <*it a little bit better*>." He attached a circular about the classes to be held that winter at the South Congregational Church, including "How our Part of the World was Made" by "Mr. A. W. Grabau of the Natural History Society and the Institute of Technology."[44]

Bemoaning the fact that she had had to stay away from Boston until late October year after year, Hattie wondered why she could not find a solution to this annual exile. It had made sense while her parents were still alive and Pepperell was their country residence but she had failed so far to find a suitable substitute, while her Union Park house, like most of the city residences of the elite, was closed down during the heat of the summer, as were the churches. But now, happily restored to Edward and her usual busy life in Boston, Hattie quickly emerged from her late fall blues. Above all, she was determined to raise sufficient funds from the wealthier ladies of the church so that Mrs. Andrews could pay her bills and stay in her own house. In this she was entirely successful.

The winter months were happy ones for Hattie as she and Edward resumed their usual routine of spending Tuesdays and Fridays together and sometimes more than that, meeting to do research in libraries such as the Boston Athenaeum and the new Boston Public Library, and enjoying outdoor excursions when the weather permitted. They were undoubtedly reassured by the election of Republican William McKinley in November following one of the most dramatic presidential campaigns in U.S. history. McKinley's policies promoting pluralism, industrial growth, and the gold standard seemed to guarantee that the depression would soon be over. Not mentioned in Hattie and Edward's letters that fall, however, was the worsening situation in Cuba. The insurrection there was supported by a New York-based Cuban Junta, many of them American citizens, which was having considerable success in arousing public sentiment against Spain. They were supported by the "yellow journalism" newspapers of William Randolph Hearst's *New York Journal* and Joseph Pulitzer's *New York World.* The Junta had arranged a mass meeting in Boston's Faneuil Hall on November 26, 1896, at which several leading citizens, including the Massachusetts governor and Edward Everett Hale, were advertised to speak. According to Edwin Atkins in his memoir *Sixty Years in Cuba,* he succeeded in getting several of the leading speakers to withdraw after the insurrectionists ordered the burning of all sugar estates in Cuba, and the meeting was abandoned.[45] It is likely that Atkins called on his cousin Harriet to change Edward's mind.

Edwin's mother Mary Atkins frequently noted in her diary that "Dr. Hale" was at Hattie's house when she visited her niece at this time. Hattie was busy with her own projects and friends. After working for hours on her "Widows Report" and a very long botanical letter to her S.H. pupil, she wrote to Edward one Sunday night in late November 1896, to tell him how happy she had been to see him at his communion service that morning: "It <*is so good to be*> so near <*you and to see every*> line <*in your face as well…If I could only throw my arms around your neck and say to every one. He is mine he is mine. And I am his. I have no other love besides his*>." Such strong feelings for a married minister would seem to indicate that Hattie had little thought for her own reputation. In the same letter, she went some way toward explaining why she was not bothered by public opinion: "I thank God that whatever thralldom I may be under, I am not under that: what people may think of me…I remember, almost from girlhood, having a sort of defiant attitude of what people might think of me; Oh! Dear! how different <*you are from the*> rank & file & <*the more I see of other people the more I*> realize <*I am more like you than like them. This is one*> reason besides others, <*why I love you so*> utterly & so completely."[46]

Their happy winter together came to an end in late February 1897 when Edward, with Emily and Nelly, accepted an invitation from retired Boston industrialist James W. Tufts to stay at the resort he was developing at Pinehurst, North Carolina, home of the future Pinehurst Golf Course. Pinehurst was yet another example of Hale's genius for inspiring ordinary people, including the newly rich, to humanitarian action. James Tufts, who had made a fortune manufacturing soda fountains and related products, was determined to make a philanthropic contribution by building a retreat where middle-class Americans could recuperate from the stresses and ailments caused by the Industrial Revolution. It was Edward who had told him about the curative powers of the North Carolina Sandhills and Tufts apparently planned his resort with Edward's assistance and encouragement.

As they had done before, Hattie and Edward left Boston together on a train to Worcester the morning of February 24, the first part of Edward's journey to North Carolina. There were only two other people in their carriage so they were able to relax like a married couple. The next day, she told him how fortunate they had been because the carriage was very crowded on her return journey. Despite looking forward to having a favorite aunt to stay with her, Hattie wrote, "I can not tell you how all the sense of expectation & anticipation has died out & how barren it all seems. <*Dear heart it is because you are not here to bring life and light to me*>." She had received the letter he wrote on the train and mailed in New Haven and concluded that it had been "4 months since I have really written <*you because we have been together all the time. Good bye dear heart. God keep us both safe for each other again*>."[47]

In early March, Hattie was getting ready for a trip to New York City and then to the Bahamas with Emma Cummings. The night before they left for New York, Hattie wrote, "I will not go to bed even at this late hour without writing you a few last words. Not a thing is in my trunk yet, though the bed, the 'Ah! quell joyeux' bed is quite covered with them." Her glancing allusion to the shared significance of her bed is a reminder that, on the eve of his seventy-fifth birthday and her fiftieth, Edward and Hattie were as physically drawn to each other as ever (his note wishing her bon voyage written the same day began "<*my own dear darling blessing of a dear darling child*>"). In the same letter, Hattie wrote that she was glad Edward would see the spectacular peach orchard at Pinehurst and she thought she would go there to see it for herself in March 1898, "& then keep on for Shortia."[48] She obviously had no idea that her world would collapse around her that year and that her search for the very rare *Shortia galacifolia* (Oconee Bells) in the Carolina Appalachians would be delayed another five years.

But for now, Hattie continued to live the life she had fashioned for herself since she became financially independent following her father's death nine years earlier, while always trying to economize. She and Emma sailed to Nassau late on March 11 after spending the day in the new wing of New York's Natural History Museum. Their vacation was an entire success in beautiful, if too hot, weather. The two naturalists largely kept apart from other American tourists, delighting in the colorful, exotic plants they only knew from glass houses in New England and observing and hearing the friendly, picturesque "negroes" on their daily rounds from their shared verandah high above the street. They took drives around the island and visited the coral reef, a prime objective.

In her first letter from Nassau on March 18, Hattie sang Emma's praises: "Miss Cummings is perfectly splendid as always. We have got on to the basis of Emma & Harriet…She is so interested in all the botany & has a good knowledge of it too, especially the trees." Hattie had her first experience riding a bicycle in tandem with the son of one of her widows, who was stationed in the Bahamas. In the meantime, Edward wrote from Pinehurst "Poor dear Nelly has been confined to her bed for six days…Her mother spends 2 or 3 hours in the bed every morning, and 2 every afternoon."[49] Hattie told him, "I have great <*long dreams of you*> every <*night and often of Mrs. Hale*>. But these last as you may guess are not pleasant. But they are so funny! For instance last night, I offered to go to walk with her & she immediately began to lean so hard on me that I could hardly move."[50]

On March 30, Hattie and Emma sailed for New York. On board the steamer *Santiago*, Hattie wrote Edward a gushing letter for his seventy-fifth birthday: "I thought of how Boston looked on the corner of School & Tremont Sts. seventy five years ago; & then I thought of all the stories of <*your*> childhood which you have told me, & then I tried to make those days as real as these days, & tried to live for a while in them."[51] Edward wrote Martha Adams on April 5 that he had celebrated his seventy-fifth birthday with Nelly in Washington and that his friend Samuel P. Langley, secretary of the Smithsonian, had taken them to see his most recent flying machine.[52]

Hattie was still in New York with Emma Cummings on April 11, Palm Sunday, before boarding the steamer to Boston the next night, when she wrote asking Edward to let her know what time she could expect to see him at her house on Tuesday. She told him she would be "waiting for the sound <*of your*> latch key." Instead, at 4.40 P.M. that day, after waiting for him all afternoon, she poured out her misery at his failure to appear, mostly in shorthand: "<*I know it is too late for you now and I have been waiting and hoping all the afternoon. I think this is as hard as being in*> Nassau <*and having you in*> Pinehurst…<*This is no home without you*>. Miss Mary <*is*> up stairs <*alone. I am*> down stairs <*alone…I do not care enough for her to have her in the same room with me…It will break my heart on Friday if you do not come early or if you have any engagement to take you away*>."[53]

Hattie knew that the Hale Club was hosting a birthday celebration for Edward that evening at the South Congregational Church. In view of the fact that he was accompanied in the receiving line by Emily and Lucretia Hale and Sarah Hooper, her older relation and longtime mentor at the SCC who Hattie often said would violently disapprove and intervene if she knew the true nature of her relationship with Edward, it is understandable that he could not break away. Long separations and the prospect of them were weighing on Hattie more and more and their stolen times together were never enough for her. After spending a day with Edward on April 16, she wrote, "<*Dearest I can not help sending you any little word of love. Because I have been with you all day I am now thinking of you all the time and what you said. How I wish we could live so day after day*>."[54] On April 29, Hattie's Aunt Mary Atkins died. Hattie must have felt

This letter, written mostly in shorthand, expresses Hattie's misery at Edward's failure to turn up at her house, as she had expected. It also shows her extraordinary penmanship. Her handwriting was round and clear and her shorthand forms were exquisitely rendered. Whenever she wrote long passages in shorthand, it indicated a higher level of intensity in her feelings, as in this case. Harriet E. Freeman to Edward Everett Hale, April 12, 1897. *Hale-Freeman special collection, Hale Family Papers, Manuscript Division, Library of Congress.*

the loss, since she and her father's sister had grown close following the death of Mrs. Atkins's husband Elisha. In June, Hattie's cousin Grace, who inherited most of her mother's money, gave Hattie the $200 remembrance Mary Atkins had left for her.

Edward and Hattie evidently saw much of each other following her return from Nassau but in mid-June the inevitable summer separation began again. Hattie wrote from Dublin, New Hampshire, where she was climbing Mount Monadnock with the Appalachian Club, sympathizing with Edward who was wearing himself out on Unitarian business in Omaha, Nebraska. She reminded him that they would spend all day the following Tuesday together so that "when you read this <*you will be only looking forward to have me run into your arms when you*> call Coo!! <*How I wish I*> could hear the dear sound now!" "My summer plans are very satisfactory," she continued; "indeed, that seems a cold word. They promise to be delightful & more than I dared hope. Still, I have not seen the place. I am taking it all on statement." She was proud of the admiration her young protégé Amadeus Grabau was earning from her mountaineering and amateur geologist friends in Dublin, Boston, and elsewhere: "Grabau, here as everywhere, makes friends with all whom he meets. He is to give a geological talk to-night & is to make diagrams for it."[55]

The Hales, meanwhile, were deeply involved in the dedication of the Robert Beverly Hale Library, built in memory of their adored Rob at the foot of the driveway to their Matunuck house. The library was Edward's idea and vision but Rob's close friend George Clarke acted as treasurer for the fundraising effort, oversaw the library's design and construction, and organized a special train and carriages for the Boston attendees.[56] Hattie knew only too well how emotional the day would be for the Hales, writing Edward from Union Park that afternoon (June 26): "my thought & heart goes back <*to you and what you are doing today*> & how many memories & broken hopes must keep to <*you. God keep us all who have such sorrows*>. Perhaps I can not understand yours No! I am sure I can not! <*But I*> know in part because I have lost Fred. <*But I*> would <*suffer again and suffer any time to save you from anything that*> might <*hurt you*>."[57]

The next day, June 27, Hattie traveled by steamer to Boothbay Harbor, Maine, to stay at the nearby summer school of the Teachers' School of Science at Bayville, now led by Amadeus Grabau. From there, she allowed herself to crow a little about "how much my expenditure of $160 a year in employing Grabau as guide & lecturer has done in starting people on lines of study which they could not have reached otherwise." For the Bayville course, Hattie hired a boat and boatman to be used for collecting samples. She and another student went out to fish up "sea treasures" early one morning: "We took up live sand dollars from the bottom. I never saw a live one before [she drew a sketch] & then as we pulled in one star fish, his stomach was turned inside out as he was feeding. It was a great mass of white gelatinous stuff in the centre. I had never seen that before. Then we get the lower forms of Bryozoa & Hydroids & watch them as their tentacles come out & wave."[58] Hattie was in her element.

By July 2, still at Bayville, Hattie was thinking forward to the house she would be renting at Amherst near the Agricultural College where she and Edward had so often studied trees in the botanical garden under the tutelage of Professor Samuel Maynard, the school's horticulturalist. Edward would be joining her and her nieces Ethel and Helen there for a few days after lecturing in Philadelphia. "When you pack for Phila, you pack for Amherst. Put in your black alpaca coat & your white suit. I have set my heart on seeing you dressed in the latter all the time that the weather is suitable. Also, if you can, put in anything that you would like to have read aloud. I shall put in for you Miss Bakers New Eng. Captives. I am sure you will enjoy that."[59] The Mark Twain-like white summer suit had been yet another gift from her.

Edward's four-day stay at Amherst was one of the happiest interludes for them both. She wrote after he left: "We like to keep you in fresh remembrance here, to make it seem as if you were here & had just left the room & were coming back in a moment…We don't clear up the parlor at all, but have it in a delightful state of disorder. Ethel & I both find it charming to do so. She has now many regrets that she did not sketch you & did not ask you what you think of women becoming ministers! Dear child! I don't know when she will have another chance. It seems to me that it will *<be a long time before I shall have a chance to kiss you and have my arms around you as I want to. Good bye dearest>*."[60]

* * *

Hattie had had the highest hopes for the summer house she rented at Holderness, New Hampshire, on beautiful Squam Lake (made famous by the movie *On Golden Pond*). But when she and her nieces, nephew Frank, and maids Sophie and Mary arrived there, they were appalled by its primitive accommodations and filth. There was not room for all of them in the house, let alone for Edward's expected visit. "Frank has taken eleven pictures of the garrets & rubbish around the house, "she wrote in disgust. "I wish I could send them to you in this; but we must wait for their development. He has just been to camp & seen the men & boys in their dress or undress. He says he wouldn't want Carrie & Ethel around where they would see them." She was paying the owner, Dr. J, who also owned the nearby camp, $350 for the place and wanted to wriggle out of the lease. She heard about an unoccupied cottage below where one of the hotels overlooking Big Squam Lake was located but when she discovered that the house had strong connections with Hartford, Emily's home town, she was certain that Edward would not want to run into these people. "My summer life becomes more & more a problem to me," she despaired. "In speaking to Dr. J of the guests I should have to give up in having no chamber for them, I spoke of you. He said in the most assured way, that when you came to Holderness that you were to visit in his camp, so he evidently thought he had relieved me of that difficulty. How would you like to sleep on a cot or wire bed, without sheets, wash out doors, go through the woods an untold distance to the W.C."[61]

With no viable alternatives at hand and her landlord disinclined to annul her lease, Hattie and her family decided to stay on at Holderness. Frank had recently graduated from Newton High School with high honors, had changed his name to Frederic William, and would begin his studies at Boston Tech that fall. To her surprise, their stay was happy, despite the poor accommodations, and when Edward visited, they made considerable progress on his book about his deceased college friend, the poet, critic, editor, and diplomat James Russell Lowell. But the epistolary record for the rest of 1897 is extremely sparse. On October 9, Edward wrote Hattie at Intervale, New Hampshire, just before she returned to Boston for the winter (the letter was forwarded to her there) telling her he would call on her as soon as he heard she was home. But Edward later told her doctor, Silas Weir Mitchell, that the breakdown that Hattie suffered in 1898 began that summer.

10

"For pity's sake"

"I hang <*my life*> absolutely <*upon you. I know it is not*> natural <*and perhaps not right but I can not help it. You hardly know how little*> else <*I have besides*>," wrote Hattie from Bermuda on March 16, 1898. She thanked him for the two letters and the birthday poem she had just received from him on the steamer that arrived from New York two days earlier. Deeply depressed, this was perhaps the closest she came in the surviving letters to admitting that her love for her much older, married minister was inappropriate and morally questionable. There is an astonishing lack of any such overt admission in the Reverend's letters; he had convinced himself and her that their relationship was "God-given and God-blessed."[1]

Hattie preceded her plaintive cry with a description in her clear, round handwriting of the unexpectedly dreary, cold weather in Bermuda, where she and her occasional companion Hortense Dudley were staying with the Joshua Youngs: "The days are uniformly grey, chilly, windy, & monotonous…We sit in doors on black haircloth furniture with shawls & sacks on to keep us warm. Or we walk down the white roads into the town for exercise & do not meet many people except negroes. Hortense & I go out & try to sketch just for an occupation, but with no sun, there is no light & shade, & we shiver in the greyness." Although she admitted she was sleeping better, she did not know how she was going to endure it for another two weeks.

Although this, like so many of Hattie's letters, is only partially dated and gives no place of origin, she mentioned that she was on an island and that LeFroy found interesting old documents in the library in the town nearby. Sir John Henry Lefroy (1819-1890), who was governor of Bermuda between 1871 and 1877, wrote *Memorials of the Discovery & Early Settlement of the Bermuda or Somer Islands, 1515-1586*, which Hattie must have studied before traveling to Bermuda herself.[2]

Because both Edward and Hattie were mostly in Boston the winter of 1897-1898, there are no letters that spell out the sequence of events that caused her to leave her house in Union Park at the end of February 1898. Edward's journal indicates that they worked together regularly on his sermons and correspondence during January. Having been together on January 25, their letters to each other the next day do hint that she had told him of her distress and her need for his sympathy and support. Her concluding shorthand says it all: "*<Darling you will love me always for now perhaps you know that I need you very very much>*."[3]

But Hattie was also preparing to give another geology lecture, most likely at the Boston Girls' High and Normal School, and was deep into her textbooks, wishing she had better access to the latest discoveries in scientific journals and papers. Edward, who had left her the day before to visit the Eliots in Cambridge, now told her "Eliot said your first lecture was very successful. He had not inquired *<about>* the second." His old college friend Samuel Eliot, who had been a longtime leader in the Boston public school system as well as trustee or director of many of Boston's leading cultural institutions, would also have encountered Hattie in his roles as chairman of the Society to Encourage Studies at Home and as president for twenty-six years of the Perkins School for the Blind where she had long volunteered. Edward had greatly admired Hattie's previous lecture and now assured her that, despite her longtime fear of speaking, "power of expression is one of your marked capacities."[4]

In the month before leaving for engagements in Philadelphia and Washington, Edward worked and lunched with Hattie at Union Park numerous times. In a letter mailed at New Haven on February 28 (Hattie noted on the envelope, "The last letter addressed to Union Park"), he wrote, "And I shall get a brave letter from *<my own child at Arthur's tomorrow>*. And I shall see her on the Trinidad—

Unitarian girl!…Wednesday morning I shall come on to New York to wave my handkerchief to my <*own sweetheart*>."[5] The *Trinidad* was a steamship that sailed between New York and Bermuda and "Unitarian girl" was a reference to Hattie's role assisting the Reverend Young in Bermuda.

It is hard to know if Hattie made a precipitous decision to close down her house and presumably stop paying the mortgage (the ugly specter of foreclosure) or whether she had been planning to do this for some time. The immediate problem seems to have been the collapse in the value of her bonds. In September 1898, the New England Loan and Trust Company went into receivership, the first step to liquidation, and Daniel O. Eshbaugh, its respected president, committed suicide a few days later. Perhaps like others who held bonds from this bank, Hattie had been lulled into complacency by Eshbaugh's long and very optimistic interview with the *New York Times* on the eve of the 1896 election which brought William McKinley to the presidency. Eshbaugh was certain that a majority of western farmers and property owners whose mortgages were held by his bank would vote for continuation of the gold standard which in turn would quickly return the national economy to prosperity. Instead, they voted for Bryan and bimetallism. In the wake of the election and despite Eshbaugh's optimistic assessment, the bond values declined precipitously and the final blow to the bank was a law suit brought by two major creditors. Hattie brought suit against the New England Loan and Trust Company in 1900.[6]

Although his letters to Hattie in Bermuda have not survived, Edward does seem to have kept writing to her, providing the emotional support that Hattie needed at this point. But, while she was suffering in Bermuda in March, Edward was having the time of his life in Washington. On March 7, he wrote Martha Adams that he was "in the seat at the head of the Table in the Committee Room of the Judiciary." His intimate friend Senator George F. Hoar was chairman of the Judiciary Committee and had decreed that "Dr Hale is to have all the privileges which the chairman has and more."[7] Hattie's response to Edward's boast that he had "opened the Senate with prayer" seems slightly tinged with sarcasm: "Was it not good for you to open the Senate! I am sure I am glad & proud enough of it, as all your friends must be, for I see that you are!"[8]

Edward must have felt himself to be at the center of a maelstrom. Following the sinking of the battleship Maine in Havana harbor on February 15, passions were whipped up by the yellow press of Hearst and Pulitzer. Although these newspapers insisted that the battleship had been blown up by the Spanish, historians are now certain that it was an accident. Hattie's cousin Edwin Atkins was in Cuba as usual that winter, struggling to keep his vast sugar plantation operational in the midst of threats from the insurgents, and lobbying Washington, as he had for three years, to support Cuban autonomy under continued Spanish rule. At first, as he wrote his wife Katharine on February 19, he thought that the *Maine* disaster might have been caused by insurgents trying "to cause trouble between the Governments" but had come to the conclusion that it was more likely to be accidental. A week later, however, he wrote: "The Maine disaster did not cause near the excitement here that it did North, and the universal sorrow manifested should strengthen relations were it not for certain d—d fools in Congress and our yellow journals which are tools of the New York Junta."[9]

President McKinley desired a peaceful resolution but, after he learned that Spain was negotiating to purchase two cruisers being built in England for Brazil, he asked Joseph G. Cannon, the powerful chairman of the House Appropriations Committee, to obtain funds for upgrading the U.S. military. McKinley and Cannon agreed that $50 million, taken entirely out of the Treasury's surplus, would suffice. Thus, on March 7, Cannon introduced the "Fifty Million Dollar Bill" for national defense. The next day, there was a brief debate in the House and the bill passed by a unanimous vote of 311 to 0. In the Senate, the measure passed by an equally lopsided margin of 76 to 0.

Susan Hale was staying at Washington's Grafton Hotel that winter, and, as she wrote William Weeden on March 13, she sat with Edward in the Senate Gallery on March 9 "when they passed the appropriation for $50,185,000. Wasn't it Luck! Intensely interesting…But I will tell you all about that scene at Matunuck. It will be my stock in trade all summer." She also attended a reception given for her brother by some Unitarians in Georgetown: "Everybody surprised to see me and disgusted at my Brevity. But I am due in 39 Highland Street, to serve the machine (and keep an eye on Lucretia) while Mrs. Hale and Nelly go to Pinehurst to join their Spouse and Parent."[10]

Opinion in the Senate was definitely turned in favor of U.S. intervention when, on March 17, Senator Redfield Proctor of Vermont, who had just returned from visiting Cuba with American Red Cross founder Clara Barton, gave a stirring speech in the Senate chamber. He thundered against "the spectacle of a million and a half people, the entire native population of Cuba, struggling for freedom and deliverance from the worst misgovernment of which I ever had knowledge." A prominent dissenter, however, was Senator George Hoar. In fact, he was to become one of the Senate's most outspoken opponents of the McKinley administration's increasing imperialism, denouncing the annexation of Hawaii that summer and bitterly criticizing the brutal Philippines-American War that began the following year.

As Edward waited for the telegram informing him when to expect Emily and Nelly's arrival in Washington, Hattie reminded him that she would be leaving Bermuda on March 30, arriving in New York on April 1, and begged him to have a letter waiting for her at home. "Home" was temporarily her niece Effie Ellis's boarding house at 176 Marlboro Street.[11] Knowing how Hattie was suffering, Edward's affectionate opening in a letter to Emily as she began the first stage of her journey to join him in Washington reads as if he was having it both ways, or hedging his bets: "Dearest, You will be 300 good miles nearer when this reaches you. Perhaps this is why I dreamed of you with such reality just now…I went last night to the most splendid party, . . It was the annual Social of the Geographical Society…I saw literally hundreds of people I shook hands with."[12]

After their vacation at Pinehurst, the Hales made the first of almost annual visits to Hampton Normal and Agricultural Institute in Hampton, Virginia, at the invitation of the school's principal, the Rev. Dr. Hollis B. Frissell. Hampton had been founded in 1868 by black and white leaders of the American Missionary Association to provide education for freed men and women. Booker T. Washington attended the school in the 1870s and, in 1878, the first Native American students arrived there. The Hales did not return from the Hampton Institute until April 8.

For the rest of April until early May the daybook catalogs an apparent resumption of Hattie and Edward's customary work and meetings at Hattie's new lodgings near the church but, shorn of the discreet nest that she had created for them both, Hattie felt their relationship would never be the same. On top of this misery, she must have been upset by events in Washington and in Cuba that month. Her cousin Edwin Atkins was in the capital on his way north from Cuba, meeting with "the President, Secretaries of State and Navy, and with many leading Senators. I talked as I never talked before, feeling that what I said might possibly turn the scales," he wrote his wife on April 3.[13] But his optimism was short-lived. Senator Proctor personally attacked Atkins's veracity on the Senate floor, claiming that he had evidence that Atkins received special favors from the Spanish government and had the U.S. Consul in Havana in his pocket. Atkins denied the charges in a press interview on April 19 but he had lost his influence in Congress. President McKinley reluctantly succumbed to pressure and signed the joint resolution to recognize Cuban independence on April 20. Spain broke off diplomatic relations with the U.S. the next day and declared war on April 24. The House responded with its own declaration of war on April 25, making it retroactive to April 21.

Although he was the head of Hattie's family, the beleaguered Edwin Atkins had no time or patience for her crying jags and nervous outbursts. He evidently asked his brother-in-law William Howell Reed to take charge. Edward was suffering from a particularly virulent influenza that spring and was also extremely worried about his older sister Lucretia who underwent major eye surgery on May 2. Not surprisingly, Hattie's deep depression is not mentioned in his journal. But, after seeing her in church on Sunday, May 8, Edward wrote her a deeply sympathetic but firm letter, knowing that her refusal to seek help was putting her at risk of being sent to the McLean Asylum by her worried relatives. Edward must have been no less concerned that she was confiding the real cause of her unhappiness to her closest friends: "<*Dear Hattie my own darling girl*> This is a love letter, but as Mr. Beecher says it is stern love & kindness," he began. "You must read it once a day, and must do what it says." He reminded her that she must conceal her sadness from everyone else except him: "Act just as you did in church this morning. Or as you did here last week at the party. Grant that it is acting. You must do it. You can do it. And because you love me, you will do it. Have I ever asked you to do anything for me, and you have refused? Do this I command, now, for the same reason."[14]

The same evening, he wrote to Silas Weir Mitchell, the celebrated Philadelphia neurologist who is believed to have treated several of the Beecher-Perkins women (including Harriet Beecher Stowe, Catharine Beecher, Charlotte Perkins Stetson, and perhaps even Emily Hale) for nervous exhaustion in the past. "I want your best professional advice," Edward began, and then proceeded to paint a revealing if somewhat dramatized portrait of Hattie as she had been before and since the black clouds of depression overcame her: "A near friend of Mrs. Hale's and mine is suffering terribly in hypochondria. She is about 50 years of age and I am told that the immediate Cause is what women call the 'turn of life.' But her Father and her Mother both died Insane. She broods over this, and, of course it endangers her own sanity. Her friends have not had power enough over her to make her follow any line of treatment. But <u>you</u> get the confidence of your patients, so I want to send her to Philadelphia that she may consult you." He described Hattie as "singularly well educated," an "admirable woman of business, with a real passion for Natural Science," a director of his charities for twenty years, and, as a volunteer, his "best amanuensis." But "<u>Now</u>, and since last summer, all this is overboard."

The rest of Edward's letter seems to exaggerate the extent and duration of Hattie's depression but he may have felt that doing so would increase the chance of Mitchell seeing her.[15] Edward seems to have been unaware that Dr. Mitchell and his second wife were agonized over the recent loss of their only child, their adored twenty-two-year-old daughter Maria Gouverneur Mitchell. Maria had succumbed on January 24 to diphtheria, the same dreaded disease that had killed Mitchell's first wife, by whom he had two sons. The Mitchells would commission renowned sculptor Augustus Saint-Gaudens to make a memorial sculpture of their daughter.

Edward obviously received a favorable response from Mitchell because on Saturday, May 14, his daybook reads: "The Ladies went off to Philadelphia and I called on Mrs. Andrews as she went down." Someone added in pencil. "This is H.E.F. and Mrs. Andrews, not the ladies of his own household." One week later, they were back in Boston for a week (Hattie stayed with her close friend Etta Pierce in Dorchester) after Mitchell agreed to take on Hattie as a patient. Edward continued to be unwell while they were away, writing to Hattie in Philadelphia, "Now I have sworn on all my gospels that I will not leave this house until I am well. No not if the Armada of Spain were thundering in the Roxbury ditch, as some people think it will."[16]

Hattie returned to Dr. Mitchell to begin treatment on May 24. Before she left, Edward wrote once again to Mitchell: "My friend [he had dropped the charade of her being a friend of his and Mrs. Hale's] leaves for Philadelphia tomorrow, with Mrs. Andrews, her next friend. I shall tell them to drive to your home, to ask where you will have them live…Miss Freeman will shew you a note from me, which I wrote to soothe her. It is all true enough; but she is in no sort destitute. She has been used to spending 7 or 8,000 dollars a year, and now has to satisfy herself with half that income. But 3500 dollars a year is not beggary."[17] However, Dr. Mitchell was charging each patient today's equivalent of $2,000 a month when Charlotte Perkins Stetson was under his care eleven years earlier.[18]

And so began one of the most revealing and, on Hattie's part, emotionally intense exchanges of letters of the couple's entire relationship. Judging by the short time that elapsed between the beginning of Hattie's treatment and her first letters to Edward and other Boston friends, Dr. Mitchell did not consider hers a serious case. If he had done so, he would have forbidden her to write at all. Within two weeks, she moved to a rest home in Media, a western suburb of Philadelphia, run by a Miss Pennington.[19] There Hattie was assigned a personal nurse-companion, a Miss Wise. At that time, Media was a popular summer resort for well-to-do Philadelphians with several large vacation hotels. William Dean Howells described the "vast, quiet house in a pleasant street" where his daughter Winifred was treated under Dr. Mitchell's supervision in 1888.[20]

On June 6, Edward wrote from Mt. Washington, about six miles outside Baltimore, where he was attending the annual meeting of a local Lend a Hand club and was to give a commencement address the next day. He had hoped to be able to stop off in Philadelphia to see her but, as he told her, he had to hurry back to a slew of engagements in Boston. Despite her many entreaties, Edward did not visit Hattie during her two months in Media. His frequent letters were invariably loving and supportive but he was apparently overwhelmed by his sister Lucretia's descent into blindness and dementia that summer and he and Emily had agreed to stay in Concord for Greta Hale's latest confinement. Since he also failed to take advantage of another opportunity to stop off en route to engagements, it is probable that he was reluctant to be closely associated in public with Hattie's breakdown. But on Sunday morning, June 12, he wrote, "I have the great joy of 2 <*letters from you one yours to me and one*> Mrs. Andrews's <*which she has lent me. Both of them make me happy though there is a sad*> vein <*in each of them because both of them show that you are really better whether you know it or not*>."[21]

On June 15, Hattie described the monotony of her days in Media and of the enervating heat: "This life in itself is enough to bring on nervous depression," she wrote, and then continued: "I had a letter from George [Whalley, the Freeman family's factotum] yesterday that was perfectly heartbreaking to me…For 33 yrs. & 6 months he has had the keys to the house & now for the first time, he has not got them. He goes & looks at the outside of the house to see if that is safe & poor Kate McIntyre does the same thing. I continually reproach myself with the injury I have done to other people who loved & trusted me, besides the unhappiness I have brought upon myself by such a step." Arrangements had been made for Mary and Sophie to spend the summer with a friend of Nelly Hale, a Miss Putnam, at her summer home in New Hampshire. Hattie now begged Edward to support her wish to return to Boston: "You like cheerful letters I know. But I do not see how I can write them. You know how much I have done for you. I came here in the first place to please you. I came here in the second place to please you. But I can not continue here at the expense at which I am living, even to please you. I sleep well at night now, except for the heat, & I have no nervous turns. And I must face your displeasure if needs be, & get back where there is less expense & cooler weather."[22]

Thinking that professional work would be the best antidote to her boredom and depression, Edward responded, "I have been thinking <*darling of mine*> that in the autumn <*you will want regular life just as you did last year*> and I mean to talk with Miss Murray <*and perhaps some of the other teachers*> about your having a regular class or classes in botany in the High School or the Normal School… I think you will like this, and <*as your affectionate friend and keeper*>

I shall not hesitate to say so."[23] That same day, she reported a visit by Dr. Mitchell: "The Dr. came out here on horseback last night on his way to his own country home beyond. He staid to supper for he is most friendly with the ladies who keep this house, who were once nurses…The Dr. said to me that the recovery from my form of nervousness was apt to be sudden. Do you know what that means? That I may go back at any time with only a schedule of directions, one of which I am sure will be, 'Control yourself.'"[24]

Silas Weir Mitchell was now seventy, handsome, white-haired, and charming. According to contemporary accounts, he had a commanding bedside manner and he was a good listener but, like Edward, he opposed woman suffrage and expressed serious doubts about women's colleges. His novels, which Edward and Emily read to each other, are often misogynist, displaying his general antipathy towards women of independent spirit by describing them in one biographer's words "either as repellent or as women who became submissive to their husbands once married."[25] Edward was certainly aware of his niece Charlotte's angry indictment of Mitchell's treatment in her short story "The Yellow Wall-Paper," and may even have influenced its publication in the *New England Magazine* (he handed over the editorship of that magazine to his younger associate Edwin Mead in 1889).[26] How could he, therefore, once again recommend that a woman whose independent and adventurous spirit he admired place herself under the control of a man whose understanding of intellectual women was directly opposed to her own ambitions and ideas? However, Hattie never complained about Mitchell in her letters to Edward, perhaps because his biases and interests were similar to his and she knew that Edward admired his writing.

Edward continued his usual round of engagements to preach and lecture that month and accepted invitations to stay with friends and colleagues. On June 20, he traveled west with Nelly to speak at commencement at Oberlin College where they stayed with his geologist friend George Frederick Wright and his wife. Then they journeyed on to Toledo and Detroit, concluding their excursion with what had become almost an annual visit to the widow of former President James Garfield at Lawnfield in West Menton, Ohio. From there, he wrote, "With this day ends this Western excursion…I am light-hearted all the time because you say you are so much better

This photograph of a portrait of Silas Weir Mitchell is in the papers of Charlotte Perkins Gilman. While Charlotte never retracted her opinion of Mitchell, and even embellished on it in later life, several scholars have come to his defense in recent years, providing evidence of his success with many patients and his insistence on the need for exercise and outdoor life for women whose indolence had contributed to their nervous ailments. These were not Hattie's problems, however.
Courtesy Schlesinger Library, Radcliffe Institute, Harvard University.

and I think the autumn will be wholly on the old lines. And I am making nice plans for you July & August and September."[27] The next day, Hattie wrote: "I struggle <*over your short hand and some of the dear words I can not make out…But I do work at them longer in hopes that I can make them out*>…My only treatment is the drip sheet & that I am getting so used to that in this warm weather it is more agreeable than not. Miss Wise is my constant companion, & I can only speak in her praise. I still feel that I do not need her, & her presence is a constant expense. Still, I must confess I should miss her. Don't despise me, but I have been learning some games of solitaire from her."[28] The drip sheet, a standard treatment in hydrotherapy, involved wrapping a sheet soaked in water around the patient and leaving him or her in a cocoon-like state while the sheet cooled.

Hattie traveled into downtown Philadelphia by trolley for regular consultations with Dr. Mitchell, reporting on June 29: "Yes! The Dr. did say on Saturday that any recovery was likely to be sudden. But Monday when I went in, he had heard from Ned [Edwin Atkins] that I was not to be 'permitted to return' while I was as nervous as when I left home & the consequence I am not allowed to leave. I am to be kept here in this heat & not allowed to see my friends." And she made a cry from the heart to Edward: "Do not, for pity's sake, leave me here…The terror of not being allowed to use your free will, & of going when & where you want! You know how I have always opened my home to other people. Mrs. Andrews, Etta, Hortense, & Hattie all say I can come to them. It is not the Dr. who says I can't go, except as Ned writes to him." And then the next day, "Can I ever have you at my table again? That is the worry & anxiety of my life, that those days when <*I can do something for you and you can kiss me in return have all gone*>."[29]

Although Hattie never referred to it in her letters from the clinic, the short-lived war in Cuba continued. Edward noted in his journal on July 4, "We felt badly enough about the news yesterday but to-day comes the tidings that Sampson has sunk the whole Spanish fleet."[30] Hattie, demoralized and lonely, could think of nothing else but her own unhappiness. Edward had asked his friend Professor George Frederick Wright of Oberlin College if Hattie might be able to assist him on a geological site later that summer but she told him: "I read the letters from Prof. Wright. I wish I could do the work; but I am sure you overestimate my attainments, & I can not do as well as you think I can. Do not be vexed with me for this…You know my old terror about not being able to talk. It is over me still, so much so that I am afraid to meet people, & that gives me a loneliness that you can not conceive of."

She told him that she thought that her loneliness, her feeling that she was alone in the world, was behind all her unhappiness and that she could no longer make decisions and stick to them the way she could just a year before. Rather than spending the rest of the summer working with Dr. Wright, she mentioned unfolding plans for her travel to Europe following her release on July 20. Hattie knew Emma Cummings was planning to see Edwin Atkins about this proposed convalescent trip (a change of scene following clinical treatment was part of Mitchell's rest cure) but she did not think Emma would go with her and, most of all she did not want her cousin to pay for the trip.[31]

Back in Boston, Lucretia Hale's condition was going from bad to worse: "The eye which was operated on refuses to heal, suppuration, inflammation, & sometimes horrid pain set in on successive days," Edward wrote. "This means, of course, that L cannot go to Matunuck while she has a daily visit from the Doctor. This means that Mrs. Hale or Nelly has to be here, and I do not like to leave either of them alone. But I shall go down tonight for Sunday and a few more days to Matunuck." Then the Hales were planning to go to Concord "to spend two or three weeks near the Bertys" for Greta's confinement before Edward returned to Boston for the fiftieth anniversary celebration of the "Association of Science." The day before, he had assured her, "*<pray do remember and understand that>* 1st 2nd and last *<I think of you all the time and what and how it will be when we are together again as God made us to be. I love you always and always and always>*."[32]

The short-lived war with Spain was over. "We have the great news of the surrender of Santiago, and I am so pleased," exulted Edward on July 14. "It is really a War carried on as I would have it. The sending all these people back is a master stroke. I believe I shall write a story of the poor native Cubans, whom the Spaniards reduced to slavery, and finally killed. They shall have a vision of the return of Spain to the other side of the Ocean, sent by a strong arm."[33] Here he makes it quite clear that he fundamentally disagreed with Edwin Atkins's views on the matter.

It would have been interesting to know if Hattie agreed with Edward on this point but she was oblivious to anything but her own situation, a far cry from her usual generous, thoughtful, outward-looking nature: "*<Shall you come on to see me off>*," she asked him in shorthand on July 17.[34] Edward had thought that Parnell Murray would be Hattie's traveling companion, even though he knew she preferred Emma Cummings. "Miss Murray has seen your cousin Ned," Edward wrote. "He even urged <*her to stay abroad all the winter with you*>. I laughed at this <*for I know you would never do that*>. But it seems <*Ned said that as to money you had a*> much better <*income than you know yourself*>. Much better is very strong."[35]

Hattie got her way and Emma Cummings agreed to accompany her to Europe, probably persuaded by Edward, who called on her in Marblehead. Hattie's friendship with Parnell Murray seems to have cooled from that point on and Emma Cummings became her traveling companion for the next twenty-five years. On July 22, Edward wrote from Matunuck: "<*I am so sorry not to come on to say good bye. But Miss Cummings will carry my last letter. Mrs.*> Andrews <*will give you my last kisses…*> Then there will come that horrid fortnight broken only by the telegram announcing your arrival, & then, letters every second day."[36] The two women sailed for Europe on July 27 and were still there in October. More than likely, Ned Atkins paid for their European sojourn. On their fifth day at sea, Edward wrote, "And we have sent to Spain the conditions of peace, and I really hope that you may hear at Southampton that the war is over… My favorite phrase is that we have picked up the stitches which were dropped after the defeat of the Great Armada."[37] But the Treaty of Paris of December 1898 set the United States further on the path to foreign imperialism, which many felt was unconstitutional and would cause nothing but problems for America. Spain ceded Puerto Rico and Guam to the U.S. as a war indemnity, along with the Philippines in return for $20 million. And Cuban sovereignty was recognized, exactly the opposite of what Ned Atkins had been lobbying for, although the U.S. would increasingly intervene if it did not approve of the Cuban government.

Running through all of Hattie's letters those months was her desperate fear that she and Edward would never work and love together again. Their physical relationship was much on her mind, as she wrote from The Hague in mid-August: "I dreamed <*of you last night. Such dreams do not come very often and I only wish I could make them real. In this dream I was in bed with you and had my arms around you as I have for so many times and*> alas! <*I*> fear <*I never shall again. The old days have gone. Will others as good ever come again*>." Realizing the risk of this revelation falling into the wrong hands, she worried that there might indeed be someone else who could translate their shorthand: "*To think that you and I are the only ones in the world who know this dear short hand*>. But how can you be sure <*that it*> has not been taught to anyone else, as <*you have*> kept it & taught <*it to me*>."[38] She was right to worry about the security of the shorthand, although she probably never knew that for certain.

It is not surprising that Hattie preferred Emma Cummings to Parnell Murray. The cultured and highly competent younger woman was not only proficient in several languages but was up to date in her knowledge of European art, history, and architecture in addition to being a naturalist on Hattie's level. She was obviously a sympathetic and tactful person, whose upbeat personality provided the perfect antidote to Hattie's lowered spirits. Hattie was pathetically dependent on Emma at the beginning of this trip as she explained her reaction to "the most uncomfortable experience" of being left behind on a station platform in Amsterdam for an hour and a half, without money and speaking only English, when the train door closed before she could board and Emma was carried away without her. But Emma had researched and planned well and Hattie's spirits lifted as they wandered from Holland to Belgium to France and, finally, to Italy.

Many of Hattie's descriptions in her long letters delighted Edward who was unusually bound to the domestic scene that summer. Greta gave birth to baby Margaret effortlessly but Lucretia's health worsened. On September 3, Edward wrote in his journal, "Everything came to a crisis last night, this morning. L had a regular contest with the two nurses, at 1 a.m. tho' she is really fond of both of them. Dr. G came round at once but he had to inject morphine and she has been under that all day." Two days later, he wrote his secretary Martha Adams: "Poor Lucretia ran down steadily, and fatally fast. For a week or more, she has known nothing & nobody, absolutely without a mind…Saturday p.m. in awful heat, we carried her to Waverley, to the McLean." Edward's reaction to McLean was classic: "My child, there is almost a horrible satire in that place, the McLean Asylum is the most charming home I ever saw. No shew palace in Europe or America which I have ever seen, is to be named in the same day. A prospect of 20 miles radius, the best private picture gallery within a hundred miles!"[39] No wonder that a 2001 history of "America's premier mental hospital" was titled *Gracefully Insane*.

In the meantime, Edward's devoted Hattie, who had been spared confinement in McLean, continued her protracted moan about losing her house and thus him: "My old life at home, with its eventful Tuesdays & Fridays seems so far away, as if it were a thing of another life. How can I make a new home? And shall I go to Mrs. Andrews's home. You <*would never come there as you came to mine… Tell me tell me what can I do to*> reconstruct <*that which I have broken… God bless and keep you dearest. And make you glad*> in spite <*of your*> anxiety <*about*> Miss Lucretia." Hattie spent hours in European hotels and pensions from August to October reminding him of what they had meant to each other. In this same letter from Paris, she wrote: "<*So many*> pages <*of paper have passed*> between us for <*so many many years. I carry your picture with me always. And the dear little silver*> box do you remember it." Apparently, one of the pieces of paper folded inside it had the words "To <*my own darling who wears my ring. Never woman loved man as you have loved me nor man woman as I have loved you and this my darling knows. She is mine and I am hers and we are as one only*>."[40] These words, she told him, were the most precious to her of all his tokens of love since she had lost his ring.

That same day, Edward wrote from Chocorua, New Hampshire, where he was spending a few days with Emily and Nelly. He told Hattie that he had been to Miss Putnam's to visit Mary and Sophie, who were glad to see him. He reported that they were well treated but seemed to be very lonely in a house hemmed in by woods and mountains and two miles from any other house. "They expressed great pleasure in your letters, asked eagerly when you come home, and were well pleased when I told them that I wanted you to have a smaller house, with them, and where you could easily go to the Natural History, to church, and to see your friends."[41] In other words, he wanted Hattie to stay in the Back Bay and not return to shabby Union Park, which was increasingly hard for him to reach with his gammy leg.

Again from Paris, Hattie told Edward at the end of a seven-page letter, much of it in shorthand, that her dreams of him were being spoiled, "<*For just as I am about to run into your arms Mrs.*

Hale comes in. I have> wakened twice <*with a kind of horror from such dreams*>."[42] She complained that she had not received a letter from him for eighteen days, the last was dated August 26. Edward, of course, was on holiday with Emily and Nelly in New Hampshire. A letter that Emily wrote to her son Jack (Edward Jr.) just eleven days later would have seriously distressed Hattie: "I came home last Saturday, and Papa and I have been alone together ever since, having quite a honey moon, and going somewhere together every afternoon. On Wednesday we went out to Waverly, to see poor Lucretia. It is a most lovely place and there really was nothing painful about seeing her. She was not in the least rational, but she had no painful fancies, and though she was planning about going away, did not beg to be rescued."[43]

But, in addition to keeping his wife happy, Edward was doing the best he could at holding together Hattie's circle of friends, family, and maids in her absence by calling on them and sending her news of them. Hattie also received many letters from her friends, family, and maids during her illness and convalescence. Her dear old friend, the Reverend Joshua Young, wrote to her in Genoa to thank her for her letter congratulating him on his seventy-fifth birthday. After describing the "lovely party" given for him by the ladies of his church, he touched on the one subject he knew she most wanted to hear about: "I see the name of Dr. Hale in the papers from time to time, and that he advised the young men of Harvard in his sermon recently to seek their associates among their superiors, and then gently reminded them that their <u>superiors</u> might be their 'brother blacks.' Large hearted and clear-eyed man!" In quaint, old-fashioned language, her country pastor, who was almost certainly aware that her illicit love for her city pastor was behind her unhappiness, gently counseled Hattie: "Allow me to say, don't delay, act promptly, under the direction of your friends and establish the new <u>home</u> as soon as possible, and as much as possible with the old surroundings, through the presences of those who have become, as it were, a very part of yourself, of your life."[44]

The same day, Hattie's "large-hearted man" wrote to her on the steamship *Kaiser Wilhelm* on which she and Emma traveled from Monaco to Genoa. He had just returned from spending the night at Wellesley with his friends the Reverend and Mrs. James Bram. The canoe trip he had hoped to take with their mutual friend Winthrop Lee from Wellesley to South Natick as part of his studies into the history of John Eliot's Indian bible for the Antiquarian Society was rained out. He told Hattie that Mrs. Bram asked him, "how it was that while other men of 75 are dried up and have lost their enthusiasm, I am fresh and young, and glad to take a canoe voyage." Instead of his rather lame reply, he told Hattie, "I ought to have said <*...that when I was between 50 and 60 years old I was drawn very near to a spirited accomplished woman who took it on her to see that I should not grow old*>. I could have said <*that she led me outside myself and from the cares of a home which was full of cares into a daily communion with*> Nature...I did say that diversity of occupation was the great necessity as people grow older and older <*but I did not tell her how in my kiss this*> diversity of occupation had been brought about."[45]

From Genoa, Hattie wrote her impressions of the casino at Monte Carlo, a description which shows she was recovering her natural curiosity and rational approach to life, concluding, "I had always supposed the Bank cheated, & allowing the new comers to win a little, fleeced them later. But in this, it hardly seems possible, as no human being could control the chance that would throw the ball into one compartment or another. We tried to see the point of the game, but failed entirely in learning why one won or lost." She had received a cablegram that morning from Howell Reed: "'Pleasant home Boston ready, Mary & Sophy awaiting you.' So it has come to pass," she told Edward, "& the home will be there."[46] She remarked in her next letter from Naples that her sister-in-law and the Reeds "did not write to ask me if I wanted it, or where it should be," continuing in shorthand, "<*Edward will you be bound to me and come there when I come back...* If I <*come back as the*> Prodigal <*son did will you not be as tender. I so often think of you as a kind of father to me as much as one I love so much. When I think of*> Father's desk in the sitting room & <*think of you as you sat there so much I*> blend <*you with him and you seem as a father*>."[47] Ten years earlier, Edward had suggested that he could advise Hattie like a father as she cast around for the direction she should take in life following her own father's death. A psychologist would no doubt make much of this father-daughter aspect of their relationship, including his persistence in calling her "my child."

In his last letter addressed to Hattie at Gibraltar, where he hoped to catch her before she embarked for America (the letter was returned to Highland Street), Edward confirmed that he knew all about Hattie's relatives' efforts to find her a new home and approved of their choice: "The place is admirably convenient for me. It will be curiously convenient for you <*to come here to go to church to go to*> lectures and to go everywhere. I think <*we shall enjoy the*> Park & Fenways <*as we have never done before*>...how soon all this writing and waiting will be over <*and I shall have my own girl in my own arms.*> We <*will enjoy this winter in ways we had never thought of before*>."[48]

Two and a half weeks later, Edward sent Hattie a letter to greet her as the *SS Kaiser Wilhelm* arrived in New York harbor, opening with his characteristic greeting after a long separation, the longest they had endured since her five-month sojourn in Europe in 1895: "Joy, joy, joy. Oh quell Gioia! Home again. Home again from a foreign land. How I wish I could be at Quarantine to see you!"[49] The family had taken an apartment for Hattie in the new six-unit Hotel Torrington at 384 Commonwealth Avenue, in the heart of Back Bay, and there Mary and Sophie awaited her return.[50] It was certainly very convenient for Edward but far too close to gossiping parishioners, as Howell Reed probably intended. With so many of his wealthiest parishioners living in fashionable and very proper Back Bay, Edward would now have to be more careful about his frequent calls on Hattie.

Hattie's sister-in-law, the other Harriet Freeman, delivered Edward's next note when she met Hattie off the boat in New York on November 1: "I have never seen the new home till this moment!" he had written. "I write at the dear old desk. Everything is charming, a great deal more than my fancy painted! <*Remember dear child it is my home as much as it is yours and if it pleases me why you will make it*> please you...Dear Carry is here in her element putting the last touches to everything."[51] Edward's journal for Saturday, November 5, reads: "So to Hatty's to dine, and dictated the sermon to her." The emotion of their reunion is not hard to imagine.

***

Hattie had suffered a serious breakdown and it would be a long time before she recovered her former self-confidence, decisiveness, and enterprising spirit. The course of that recovery can only be traced through Edward's letters and a few from Hattie's beloved "Marmee," Mrs. Andrews, since a newly cautious Edward must have destroyed Hattie's letters following her return from Europe. He may also have felt that they lacked the usual spirit and enterprise that he found so captivating. The fatherly tone of Edward's letters indicates Hattie's continuing psychological fragility. He did his best to encourage her to keep to a weekly schedule, much of it working or making outings with him. But it is hardly surprising that Hattie's spirits continued to be low. While Edward had urged her to remain involved with her Boston Society of Natural History, she had to tell her old friend Alpheus Hyatt that she could no longer underwrite the salary of a guide to its museum, as reported in *Appleton's Science Monthly*.[52] Perhaps as a result of family pressure, she transferred 37 Union Park on December 28, 1898, to Luther S. Phelps, who lived in the lodging house next door and was in real estate. At some point that winter, according to Alpheus Hyatt, Hattie gave eighteen geological specimens from British Columbia and Yellowstone Park to the Society's Lowell Collection.[53]

The following March, when the Hales were again at Pinehurst for a few weeks, Edward's letters were full of encouragement as Hattie vacillated about her plans for the summer. First she considered renting the house of the late Charles Babbidge, the Freeman family's onetime minister in Pepperell, then she debated returning to her spiritually uplifting mountains, this time in Tennessee. In both places, she apparently wanted to resume horseback riding. Edward supported all these ideas and also suggested she see if Dr. Wright again needed assistance in geological fieldwork. He was frustrated that her concern for Mary Cobb and for Mary and Sophie held her back from any of these plans to spend her summer in the "open air." Instead she decided to rent a house, large enough for her household and where Edward could come and see her with relative ease, in the suburb of Milton, an area with many beautiful gardens. The Hale family had spent their summers in Milton for several years until the Matunuck house was built for them.

On June 4, Hattie and Edward checked into Mohonk Mountain House, together with Nelly and Martha Adams, for the annual peace conference there. This time, Edward had adjoining rooms with his daughter, Martha was further down the corridor, while Hattie's room was on the third floor.[54] It is not known how long Nelly and Martha stayed on following the peace conference but Edward and Hattie worked there for ten days on the proofs of his *James Russell Lowell and His Friends*, a compilation of Edward's articles on Lowell in *The Outlook* magazine, and took many long walks around the lake, where she took a photograph of him.[55] Two months later, he gave her a copy of the book, hot off the Houghton Mifflin presses, inscribed "Hatty, from her friend and adviser, who assisted her in writing this book, July 20, 1899. Holderness, Lake Mohonk."[56]

Before leaving for Mohonk, Edward wrote to William Fowler, chairman of the trustees of his church, formally resigning as minister: "I have known, oh, for a long time, that the church needs a minister as well as a preacher. And nothing but the kindness of every member of the congregation has justified me in remaining so long in a charge where I have left so many of a minister's duties unfulfilled…the church ought to have a young and active minister."[57] It would take another eighteen months and several aborted attempts to persuade senior ministers to accept the post, before Professor Edward C. Cummings of Harvard was ordained and installed as associate minister in October 1900.

Edward had already begun writing about various aspects of his long life and career and now he applied himself in earnest to summing up his nearly eighty years. Early in August 1899, he told Hattie that Martha Adams had joined him at Matunuck to help him with that and various other writing projects: "We are pegging away on my Autobiography. There is twice as much needed as I had supposed. It will come down to about 1882 and then <*it will end abruptly by saying about this time his guardian angel stepped into his life and began to take care of him. And after this time what she did not do for him is not worth telling about and the reader is respectfully referred to her. But what her name is this book will not tell*>. Who can it be?"[58] More than a century later, that question is answered.

Edward and Susan Hale left Matunuck in mid-August to travel together to the annual Assembly at Chautauqua, New York.

In early June 1899, Hattie, who was becoming a master of the box camera, took a photograph of Edward on the pier below the great Mohonk Mountain House sitting on a pile of deck chairs to accommodate his long legs. This slightly bizarre image appeared in *Harper's Weekly* on February 6, 1904, with that magazine's announcement of Edward's arrival in Washington as chaplain to the U.S. Senate.
Harriet E. Freeman Papers, bMS 273, Andover-Harvard Theological Library, Harvard Divinity School.

Edward's descriptions of the weeklong events held in beautiful weather that year are those of a comfortably uncritical insider, with his usual touch of vanity, whereas Susan's characteristically clear-eyed comments to her friend Mrs. William G. Weld (ancestor of the governor of Massachusetts), written the same day, make a lively contrast to her brother's: "My dear, this is a most wonderful place, there are ten thousand people, truly that number, here this minute, and I saw them all at the Auditorium yesterday, at church, really an imposing scene, a great bowl of a place with sloping ranks of seats to contain these people, open to the air above, all woods and great trees, so it wasn't hot. A fine organ, a trained choir of one hundred voices or more, instruments…and the audience all singing 'Holy, Holy, Holy,' like mad." She continued with a description, in her usual colorful style, of the earnest bluestockings, or "shirt-waists," of which Hattie was one, although Hattie had not yet been to the main Chautauqua campus: "You know they are all here improving their minds, learning some darn thing or other, and hearing lectures and being very devout especially Sundays." She concluded, "It is all, in fact, extremely interesting, but Lord! I shall be glad to get out of it."[59]

After a quiet summer in Milton, Hattie, Mary Cobb, and Mary and Sophie moved to 53 Gloucester Street, a small house in Boston's Back Bay, where they stayed for just nine months until Hattie's income was fully restored. The winter was one of close cooperation with Edward as they worked together on his "Memories of the 19th Century" and New England history, spending many hours together at the Boston Public Library and the Massachusetts Historical Society. In March 1900, the Hales were again at the Hampton Institute. That month, Edward wrote numerous letters to Hattie who was staying at the Mountain House in Montclair, New Jersey. She had intended to spend a good deal of her stay riding horseback and taking long walks but poor weather made both difficult. Edward wrote her, when she had moved on to Washington, an account of his mother-in-law's funeral in Hartford on March 17. Mrs. Perkins died on March 14, the same day as her much younger half-brother the Reverend Thomas Beecher, at her son Charles's house aged ninety-four and nine months.[60] They were the last of Lyman Beecher's children.

By the spring of 1900, Hattie was keen to leave the cramped and noisy house on Gloucester Street. In a rare letter to have survived from this period, she wrote to Edward as he was traveling by train to a two-week lecture and preaching tour in the Midwest: "I was in the house all the morning yesterday writing, thinking <*of you*> crossing the country… <*I know how much you must be*> enjoying it. <*If only [I was] by your side…I remember how often I have taken those long*> western journeys across the plains. <*I love to sit in*> one of those Palace cars with a good book, & look at the landscapes gliding by. And <*I always loved to*> be at <*night in*> a sleeping car & then wake in the <*morning*> & lie & look at the world & in some way or other I always expect to find a different world from that upon which I closed my eyes." She wrote as if she thought she would never have those experiences again, proof that she still could not think outside the narrow box in which her depression confined her. She continued to look back rather than forward, confirmed by her mournful response to Edward's news that his train stopped at the Ayer railroad junction nearest Pepperell: "How well I remember those Sunday afternoons!! There was more than one of them when I drove down to meet you. Well may <*you say*> dear Pepperell! Would <*that my right hand*> had been withered before I signed away my birthright!"

Since the program for the November 1, 1899 unveiling of a memorial tablet to the Pepperell veterans of the Battle of Bunker Hill is glued into the pages of Edward's journal for Friday and Saturday, November 3 and 4, he must have joined Hattie in Pepperell for that ceremony. At a time when her spirits were still low, this would have made Hattie's loss of her ancestral home even more of a tragedy for her. The tablet was presented to the town by Mrs. Edith Prescott Walcott, a member of the Pepperell chapter of the Daughters of the American Revolution. This must have inspired Hattie to make her own application to the DAR, which had been founded in 1890.[61]

Hattie was determined to return to her longtime home in Boston's South End and now, with her bonds restored (creditors' claims, including Hattie's, against The New England Loan and Trust Company were heard that year), Hattie had the means to negotiate the transfer of 37 Union Park back to her. In fact, she had resumed responsibility for the $8,000 mortgage in an agreement with Luther Phelps the previous July, only seven months after transferring the property to him.[62] She told Edward that she had just written to inform Howell Reed of her decision. She must have known the wealthy Reeds with their Back Bay townhouse and their large house in the beautiful suburb of Belmont would disapprove of her moving back into a neighborhood which had become little better than a slum. By 1900, 85 percent of the houses in the Union Park area were multi-occupant boarding houses.[63] But by late June 1900, she and her household were back in her spacious, five-story brick house where she would remain with Mary and Sophie into the early 1920s. There she and Edward could more discreetly continue their long relationship as he approached his eightieth year.

That summer, Hattie, secure once more in her own shell and her own life, resumed her field trips and studies of natural history. In late May, she was back at the Agricultural College in Amherst studying with her old friend Professor Maynard. In July, she and Mary Cobb joined Amadeus Grabau at the School of Natural History in Bayville, Maine, and in August she rented a cottage at Kennebunk Beach where her family visited her. Before Edward left for Matunuck that summer, his sister Lucretia died. He wrote to Will Reed on June 12, "Our poor dear Lucretia is at rest…She had not recognized me for the last fortnight, she had not recognized any one…I do not think she suffered."[64]

Edward was always unfailing in his devotion to his sisters, another mark of his generally high principles when it came to family. On the other hand, while he seems never to have addressed in writing the hypocrisy of his or anyone else's extramarital affair, in fact he appeared to avoid the topic of sin altogether, he did like to expound on the virtues of devoted marriage. The most revealing example is the letter he wrote Martha Adams, his admirable secretary of thirteen years, on the eve of her marriage that summer to J. Freeman Leland, an apple farmer in Sherborn, Massachusetts, at which Edward was to officiate. This fatherly letter of advice gives the outward impression that his own marriage approached his traditionalist ideal, when in fact he must surely have been thinking of Hattie rather than Emily, or perhaps a combination of the two: "Life does not begin till you are married," he pronounced:

"Looking Backward," the title of Laura E. Foster's graphic commentary on the consequences for women of worldly ambition, plays on the title of Edward Bellamy's socialist utopian novel. Published in *Life*, at that time a magazine of general interest and humor and the home of Charles Dana Gibson's Gibson Girls, a male ideal of non-threatening and chaste early-twentieth-century American upper class womanhood, the image was a somber reminder of continuing social constraints.
From Life, *August 22, 1912. Library of Congress.*

> Till people are married, or engaged, it is very hard to preach about Love—about bearing each other's burdens...My one bit of advice, or injunction, that the bride and bridegroom shall have no secrets from each other comes in here. Love is a life outside oneself. It is the Life for which everyone is made, and without which everyone is incomplete. To think for an hour or a day, 'What will make myself happy?' is certain failure. Here comes in what you hear me say so often—that you must never give up the romance of it; and do not let him give it up...People suffer a great deal by not being demonstrative enough to each other.

For a man who had conducted a secret relationship behind his wife's back for sixteen years already, Edward's emphasis on the importance of not having secrets from each other is incomprehensible. However, we know that he suffered from his wife's coldness. Now he told dutiful Martha that she knew better than most how to carry out his mother's advice to brides, "Make yourself so useful to your husband that he cannot do without you." Basically old-fashioned in his ideas of the "proper" role of the so-called "Good Wife," he revealed his distaste for the personal ambitions of the "New Woman" of Martha's generation. He urged her to "think in his [her husband's] thoughts, wish with his wishes, dream in his dreams, as you plan in his plans and work with his purposes. So you get over that ghastly weariness which comes and ought to come with 'self-culture,' 'self-examination,' 'self-improvement,' and all the other damnables which follow on the lonely or selfish theories."[65] Hattie knew only too well what Edward expected from the perfect wife and did her best to fill that role, without receiving any of the benefits of lawful marriage, including emotional security and social recognition. Moreover, while he told her how much he admired her drive and competence, and benefited from both these qualities, he seemed at the same time to equate this level of personal ambition as a sure route to "loneliness." A period cartoon shows this was a common cultural attitude. No wonder Hattie was so conflicted.

As long as Edward lived, Hattie was forced to conceal her extraordinary devotion to him, except when they were alone together. In mid-August, before Edward was due to visit Hattie in Maine,

Judith Andrews wrote some motherly words of advice which show that she was well aware of the reality of Hattie's relationship with their longtime minister: "Keep up a brave heart, Girlee, keep back desponding words, keep down feelings of regret and hopelessness…Above all give your best friend a happy visit, do that much for one who has done so much for you…Even more caution than you sometimes need. Remember that strangers are around you who know nothing of you but have heard of Dr. Hale if they are not acquainted with him. Curious eyes will watch you." She urged Hattie, as she probably had done many times before, "do not wear your heart upon your sleeve."[66]

This letter is another sign that gossip had resumed and that greater caution than ever was needed. In fact, Edward now told Hattie to address him as "Fred Ingham, care of Miss Clark at Highland Street." Edward had originally invented Frederick Ingham as the narrator of his magazine stories when authorial anonymity was often the rule. Thus, Ingham was the harassed minister of "My Double and How He Undid Me" and the naval officer who was Philip Nolan's friend and confidant in "The Man without a Country." At least one scholar has suggested that Ingham was the image of the man that Edward would have liked to be.[67]

In his invention of Frederick Ingham as a double for himself, he seems to be an apt concealer of Edward's own double life. Edward told Hattie he had received her second Ingham letter "but now Mrs. Hale sometimes talks of going to Bar Harbour with me…If at the last moment she does, I must put off my visit to you until I come back from the East. But I suppose, I hope, that you mean to stay at K until the 1st of October." Edward's letter three days later recalls the deceptions involved in their plans for their assignation in Bethel, Maine, thirteen years earlier: "There is a fast train from Boston to Portsmouth at 3.15. I will take that and will rely on meeting you at Portsmouth…the boat for Greenacre does not go until 5.30. So I will wait in the Steam Railway station until 5.20, for you…I shall check one of my valises to Kennebunk, with the idea that we can go direct there from Greenacre on Monday."[68]

The "Miss Clark" to whom Hattie must now address her letters was Smith College-educated Abigail Clark, whom Edward had hired to replace Martha Adams. "The event of yesterday was that

Abby Clark came on…at 4.30 in the afternoon," Edward wrote from Matunuck in early August. "She turns out very nice, is diligent & intelligent, and learns fast. The only drawback…is that nobody can remember what she never knew; there are things like addresses, and people's names & all that which nobody but you & Martha Adams knows."[69] Abby Clark, a young woman of quick intelligence, ironic humor, and skill on the typewriter (Hattie always took dictation in longhand) was increasingly appreciated by Edward. She would become as indispensable to him as Hattie had been, as well as earning the trust of his wife and daughter, causing Hattie bitter pangs of jealousy in the last years of Edward's life. What would Hattie have felt if she had known that Edward taught both Martha Adams and Abby Clark the essential symbols of Towndrow's shorthand? "I will therefore make you a list of Towndrow arbitraries on the next page," he wrote Martha in March 1900. "You can keep it in sight and bid Miss Abigail do the same."[70] His handwriting was so interspersed with shorthand symbols that his secretaries could not decipher his writings without this key.

On October 7, 1900, Professor Edward Cummings of Harvard was ordained as associate minister of the South Congregational Church; Edward now became pastor emeritus. He expressed his enormous relief at passing on the burden in a letter to Martha Adams Leland, headlining this letter, "The First Day of Freedom!" "Dear Martha, I address to you the first note of this Historic Day. As I put on my pepper & salts, it occurred to me that I need Never put on a black coat again as long as I live."[71] Edward Cummings was the father of a preeminent twentieth-century poet, e e cummings (as he came to write his name), who was a week away from his sixth birthday when his father was ordained. Cummings had not been the first choice. Rev. William W. Fenn of the First Unitarian Church in Chicago, who would soon become a professor at Harvard Divinity School and later its Dean, and Rev. Samuel Atkins Eliot, son of Harvard's president and by now secretary and soon the first president of the American Unitarian Association, had declined the call.

Further evidence of Hattie's restored income came at Christmas when she showered gifts on the Hale family. She gave Edward a beaver (an elegant top hat made of beaver's fur), which apparently delighted the Hale women but him less so. After Christmas, she received notes from Emily and Nelly. "Dear Miss Freeman," began Emily, continuing with measured irony: "It really seems as if you could not have given presents, of late, to any one out of this family. I keep seeing beautiful things in the study, and saying, 'Why, wherever did this come from?' till finally I am sure the answer will be 'Oh, Hatty always gives me this'…But I did not mean to dwell on all your good deeds, only those to me, and the charming little Japanese (or Chinese) plate is what I personally have to thank you for." Nelly's note was far warmer: "Dear Miss Hattie, I can't tell you how delighted I am with my lovely new comb." She told her that she had lost the tortoise-shell comb that she loved on the train as she traveled to California with her mother, that she had tied her hair back with "very unattractive India-rubber" since then, and "now I feel…that I've made a great step in the road to elegance! Thank you once more most warmly, dear Miss Hattie, and a happy New Year to you."[72]

As preparations were being made across the country to celebrate the new century, Edward was invited as Boston's grand old man to open the city's ceremony on the night of December 31, 1900, from the balcony of the State House on Beacon Hill. A guard of honor from the Commonwealth Club came to escort Dr. Hale to the State House and he appeared on the balcony at a quarter to twelve. As far as the eye could see, the crowds stretched out below as some two hundred members of the Cecilia and the Handel and Hayden societies sang "Old Hundred." Then Edward, with Emily and Nelly close by, spoke the moving words of the Ninetieth Psalm in his deep voice, followed by the singing of the chorus Samuel Sewall had written for the first day of January 1701. At midnight, the bell of King's Chapel struck, Edward led the throngs in "Our Father which art in Heaven," and trumpets played "America."

Edward had told Hattie that if she came to the side door of the State House, he would meet her there and she could "go up with him to the balcony." However, as she later told a niece, "Although I started long before the hour, the nearest I could get was on the back side of the Shaw Monument" at the top end of Boston Common below the State House.[73] This is an apt metaphor for what would transpire within three years.

11

An Adventurous Life

With home, income, and self-confidence restored, Hattie was determined to resume her life of scientific exploration and adventure with Emma Cummings, using her long, descriptive letters to include Edward. First on her deferred list of geological and botanical discovery in 1901 was an expedition to find a route into the Dismal Swamp in Tidewater Virginia, a geological wonder formed when the Continental Shelf made one of its last shifts. But, in early February, in the midst of finalizing plans with Emma and Edward, Hattie was struck down with acute appendicitis. Her thoughts must have flown back to her brother Fred who had died of a ruptured appendix in 1887. That very year, Thomas G. Morton performed the first successful removal of an infected appendix in Philadelphia.[1]

Hattie undoubtedly suffered the usual symptoms of acute appendicitis—severe abdominal pain, vomiting, and fever, with the pain increasingly concentrated in the lower right side of her abdomen. She underwent surgery in mid-February on the eve of Edward's scheduled departure for New York, en route to his annual working vacation with Emily and Nelly at the Hampton Institute. The night before, Edward sent Hattie an encouraging note by special delivery, concluding in shorthand: "*<this is only to tell you how much I love you and how much every body loves you>*. And it is *<to say how thankful we are that the grave event will be over so soon>*."[2]

Edward was reluctant to leave Hattie but her doctor assured him that she would be on her feet again well before he returned to Boston in April. In New York on February 17, as he waited for

Emily to join him, he received an encouraging special delivery note from Mary Cobb with a loving message from Hattie. Two days later, his spirits were high after receiving a cheerful telegram from Frank Freeman and a note from Hattie in her own handwriting.[3] But she was not out of the woods yet. The pain and fever lasted for some time following the operation and an additional surgical procedure proved necessary. Through it all, she was very carefully nursed at home.

Hattie's life-threatening crisis deeply upset and worried Edward and regained for her the sympathy of Emily, who seemed to equate Hattie's health battles and psychological traumas with her own. Emily began a letter to Hattie by apologizing for failing to call by to get the latest update for her husband before she left Boston, and continued with a poignant insight into her state of mind during the years in which her husband's relationship with the younger woman was at fever pitch. "I am sure you know what real interest and sympathy all your friends have been feeling for you," she began her letter. She told Hattie that she had felt depressed for some time before Robbie died and she nearly died of typhoid, "But all that my friends said and wrote and did, while it seemed possible that I might die, made me feel that much more love had been given to me than I had dreamed of, and I have never since gone back to feel as I did before. I hope you may have the same experience, my dear."[4]

Emily's letter was a surprisingly kind if somewhat condescending expression of solidarity with the much younger woman who had deceived her for many years and indicates that Emily was well aware of Hattie's own struggles with depression. But Hattie was no hypochondriac. In fact, she was generally blessed with rude good health and physical strength and she was determined to resume her active, adventurous life. Indeed, she now seemed to be more assertive about her own priorities, although always insisting she was living vicariously for the aged and increasingly lame Edward.

As she recovered, Hattie, always fascinated by scientific or medical progress, regaled Edward and some of her closest friends with graphic details about appendectomies in general and her surgery in particular. At least one friend was repelled by this unsolicited information but Edward characteristically reveled in it, writing, "I cannot tell you with what interest I have read & read again your surgical letter <*and as you know you have been my teacher in*> science <*for the last 20 years but I never thought that you were to teach me about surgery from your own impression*>. I wait <*eagerly for tomorrow's letter which will tell me whether the improvement holds on*>."[5] Unfortunately, these letters are not in the collection. After Hattie went so far as to send Edward her appendix, he told her, "The precious little sinew is carefully treasured among the choicest <*of my possessions. To think that it was a part of you when it was so necessary that it should do its duty well*>!!!!"[6]

By that time, the Hales were in Washington, where Edward eagerly awaited Hattie's arrival with Emma Cummings on March 26 for a brief rendezvous en route to their revised destination of Charlottesville, Virginia. "<*[W]e shall have Tuesday together to do whatever you want to do*>. I shall have the day wholly free," he told Hattie.[7] He had told her that the general opinion in Washington was that it was not feasible to visit the Dismal Swamp before May at the earliest. Edward published Hattie's first letter from Charlottesville in which she described the spring birds that she and Emma heard and observed that morning so accurately and well that this anonymous letter heralds her growing passion for ornithology, one that was strongly influenced by Emma. She described a woodpecker, "a black and white fellow, jerking up the trunk of a tree." It was difficult to ascertain the amount of red in his coloring as he kept disappearing "tantalizingly" round the tree trunk. They decided he was a yellow-bellied sap-sucker, one of sixteen birds they identified that morning.[8]

In the meantime, Judith Andrews forwarded to Hattie in Charlottesville a letter she had received from Mrs. Helen Merriman of Intervale, about the possibility of renting a house adjacent to her property there belonging to a Miss Margaret Worcester who was planning to travel in Europe that summer. Thus began Hattie's long association with the upscale White Mountain resort of Intervale and in particular the various cottages she would rent on or adjacent to Stonehurst, the Merrimans' grand summer estate. Mrs. Merriman described this one as "a very nice house, simply and well furnished and in exquisite order. It is beautifully situated with an enchanting view, and has considerable land and a barn or shed. It seems to me <u>most</u> desirable, and will probably cost between $400 & $500."[9] The Merrimans had persuaded friends to buy land and construct summer residences on or around their property and were generous benefactors to the local community of North Conway.

The man behind the creation of Stonehurst, and Intervale's first summer resident, was Helen Merriman's father Erastus B. Bigelow of Clinton, Massachusetts, inventor of power looms, innovative carpet manufacturer, and published expert on tariff issues. He was a member of the founding committee in 1861 of Boston Tech (MIT). Helen, the Bigelows' only child, inherited the entire property of several hundred acres and a large, architect-designed house in 1879, five years after her marriage to the Reverend Daniel S. Merriman, pastor for twenty-three years of the Central Church in Worcester, Massachusetts. Helen and Daniel Merriman were munificent benefactors to many Worcester institutions, in particular the Worcester Art Museum.

Determined to see the Dismal Swamp before they left Virginia, Hattie and Emma traveled to Old Point Comfort at the very tip of the Virginia Peninsula at Hampton Roads. But, after crossing the mouth of the Chesapeake Bay by ferry, they encountered one road block after another in their attempts to reach Lake Drummond or the Dismal Swamp Canal. Lake Drummond, a large natural lake of unusually pure water essential to the ecology of the swamp, was certainly a priority destination for the two women, who knew the region to be a virtual laboratory of primeval forest and bird and wildlife. They had hoped to reach Lake Drummond by launch from the town of Suffolk north-west of the Swamp but that had been discontinued due to the silting in of the access stream. Refusing to accept defeat, they drove themselves by carriage back to Norfolk and took a train forty-five miles south to Elizabeth City, North Carolina. After spending the night there, the only women in a hotel filled with men attending court sessions, they were able to board a passenger boat very early the next morning on the Pasquotank River which connected with the Dismal Swamp Canal on the eastern edge of the Swamp. They hoped to reach Lake Drummond via a connecting canal.

As long as the boat remained on the river, the two naturalists were enchanted by the picturesque cypress trees and abundant bird life, but the canal proved to be a bitter disappointment. Part of the Intracoastal Waterway built in the late eighteenth century to provide protected passage for shipping during stormy winter months, it had only recently been reopened after an expensive dredging operation. The resulting mud deposits were very unsightly and had killed hundreds of cypress trees. Moreover, Hattie and Emma were now told that they could not reach Lake Drummond except by hiring a private launch at Norfolk.

An evocative photograph "Reflections in a Cypress Swamp"—both women were photographers—misleadingly dominates the last page of their account, which ends rather lamely and uncharacteristically for two intrepid adventurers and naturalists: "Thus ended our long-talked-of trip through the Dismal Swamp, which did not prove to be dismal at all."[10] They might have added "except for the devastation wrought by man" considering that commercial logging was well under way and would soon accelerate to the point where the swamp's virgin forest was entirely removed by the 1950s. But the seeds were sown for, within a year, Hattie and Edward would launch their efforts to rescue and preserve the forests of New Hampshire's White Mountains, Emma would lead a drive to preserve and plant trees in her home town of Brookline, and Hattie and Emma would throw their support behind the burgeoning nature conservancy movement. They would have been delighted to know that the Great Dismal Swamp National Wildlife Refuge was established in 1974. Lake Drummond is at the heart of its more than 112,000 acres and boat tours are given from the Dismal Swamp Canal to Lake Drummond. Apart from the other barriers they encountered, it was certainly a mistake for the two women to visit the region before the peak influx of migratory songbirds from late April to mid-May.

Hattie's illness apparently brought her, at least temporarily, back into the Hale family fold. In May, Edward noted a delightful drive he and Emily took with Hattie and a belated birthday party that Etta Pierce threw for him at which both Emily and Hattie were present. Later that month, he attended the annual arbitration conference at Mohonk with Nelly before he joined Hattie "by the assistance of 8 different vehicles" at the house of their good friends the Maynards at Amherst Agricultural College (today's University of Massachusetts at Amherst), arriving there late on Saturday evening, June 1. After Edward preached at Amherst's Unitarian church, the Maynards drove him and Hattie all over "this beautiful place" with its "matchless hemlock forests."[11] Edward caught a train back to Boston the following evening, while Hattie stayed on in Amherst for a few more days. The next day, Edward wrote her there, closing his brief letter, "Give my love to all *<and darling keep it all for yourself whom I love with all my heart>*."[12]

Edward joined Hattie at West Newton for Carrie Freeman's engagement party for her brother Fred and Lucia Proctor on June 10. As she and Edward wove their respective families ever closer together, it was certainly a happy time for Hattie who was enjoying the best of all worlds at last. Her troubles apparently behind her, she now had the freedom for scientific adventures with a like-minded and trusted female friend, the emotional security of a long term illicit relationship now almost regularized, her close relationship with her late brother's family, and the prospect of spending the summer in her beloved White Mountains.

Before Edward returned from a trip with Nelly to Ohio and Buffalo, New York (where they visited the Pan-American Exposition), Hattie departed for Intervale with Mary Cobb, Carrie Freeman, and, as always, Mary, Sophie, and the cat, assured that Edward would visit her there later that summer. In fact, Hattie and Edward had made several plans to be together during the summer months as they continued to work on his "Memories of the 19th Century." In early August, they spent two weeks together, beginning with Hattie's first visit to the annual Chautauqua Assembly (where Edward was slated to lecture on "American History in the Nineteenth Century"). They paid a visit to the Pan-American Exposition, and stayed at Lake Placid in the Northern Andirondacks. William Howland, publisher of *The Outlook* magazine, had a summer house there and he and Lyman Abbott, the magazine's editor-in-chief, had invited Edward to discuss publication of what would be titled "Memories of a Hundred Years."[13]

Edward made three separate visits to Intervale in September. He had been unsure until the last if he was going to be able to leave Emily who had been feeling very unwell during the final weeks at

Matunuck. However, Emily improved enough once they returned to Roxbury that he was able to travel to Intervale by September 2. On the train ride back to Boston on the 6th, stunned passengers, including Edward, were told at Portsmouth that President William McKinley had been shot point blank in the stomach by anarchist Leon Czolgosz in the Temple of Music at the Pan-American Exposition. McKinley was just six months into his second term. Bruised and bloodied by the enraged crowd, Czolgosz defiantly told police after his arrest: "I am an Anarchist. I am a disciple of Emma Goldman. Her words set me on fire."[14] After surgery to remove the bullets from his abdomen—although one could not be located—it seemed for a few days that McKinley would recover so Edward carried Hattie's invitation to Emily to join her husband when he returned on September 11 to Intervale. Reluctant to leave home again but grateful to be invited, Emily declined.

On September 14, Hattie and her guests received the shocking news that the President had died at 2:15 that morning, eight days after he was shot, from gangrene. As Edward wrote Emily two days later, "I feel horridly about the President. I have written to Bachelor [editor of *The Christian Register*] to recall my Leader which seemed to me trivial for a week of sorrow." Edward concluded his letter, "I have done mountains of work and am not displeased with it." On a lighter note, Edward told Emily that he and the rest of the party had enjoyed a lovely ride with Hattie the day before, followed by tea with Hattie's cousins the Thaxters, "he the son of [poet] Celia Thaxter...most agreeable young people, who are the next neighbours to the Edward Cummingses at Cambridge, and have very funny stories <*about*> the intimacy of their children." Edward was referring to the Thaxters' daughter Elizabeth (Betty), born after poet Celia Thaxter's death, whose childhood playmate was future poet e e cummings, son of Edward Cummings, the new minister of the South Congregational Society. Edward Estlin Cummings, who would acquire a libertine reputation, recorded years later, when Elizabeth Thaxter was a respectable married woman, that he and his childhood friend Betty stripped and examined each other's anatomy several times and were almost caught, an intimacy undetected by their parents.[15]

Strangely, Edward did not mention in this rather gossipy

letter that his former Harvard protégé Theodore Roosevelt was now president of the United States. On September 13, Roosevelt was hiking with a group of friends on remote Mt. Marcy in the Adirondacks when he spotted a ranger running toward them bearing a telegram with the news that the president had taken a turn for the worse. He raced through the night to Buffalo where he was sworn in as president in a friend's house. He assured the group gathered around him: "In this hour of deep and terrible national bereavement I wish to state that it shall be in my aim to continue absolutely unbroken the policy of President McKinley for the peace, prosperity and the honor of our beloved country." But TR was known to champion progressive causes such as child labor laws, food and drug regulation, conservation, railroad reform, and trust-busting.[16] Highly ambitious and always on the run, he had managed his ranch in South Dakota while recovering from the death of his first wife, was the volunteer colonel of the famous "Rough Riders" in the Spanish-American War in Cuba after resigning as secretary of the navy, and was governor of New York before accepting the vice presidential nomination. He had been a controversial choice as running mate from the point of view of McKinley loyalists the year before. In fact, McKinley's longtime political mentor Mark Hanna, now a senator from Ohio with presidential aspirations of his own, was horrified, declaring, "Now that damn cowboy is president!"

Edward led a memorial service on September 19 for the slain president at the South Congregational Church, which he described in a letter to Hattie: "The service today…was well nigh perfect. People crowded the church, men had to stand where they could. Phil said, what I felt, that they all read the responses <u>with a will</u> as if they were glad they could do something about it. The singing was admirable in the same way…I read [Secretary of the Navy John D.] Long's admirable appreciation of his friend (McKinley) and the rest of the address was what you have heard me saying all the week."[17]

After attending the Daniel Webster centennial celebration at Webster's alma mater, Dartmouth College in Hanover, New Hampshire, where he received an honorary Doctor of Laws and was thenceforth addressed as the Reverend Dr. Hale, Edward made a final brief visit to Intervale in late September. On his return home, he received surprising news from Amadeus Grabau, who was now an assistant professor of geology at Columbia University in New York. Grabau wrote that he and Mary Antin, Edward's promising eighteen-year-old Jewish immigrant protégé, intended to get married, and very soon. They wished Edward to perform an interfaith ceremony for them (Grabau was the son and grandson of German-born Lutheran ministers) at his Roxbury house on October 5 so that they could travel back to New York together before classes started at Columbia.

Edward and Hattie were aware that young Mary had joined a Hale House natural history field trip led by the geologist, who was thirteen years older, and that she had assisted him at the summer school in Bayville, Maine, for three weeks that summer. Young Mary had partly funded her studies at Boston's prestigious Girls' Latin School with the 1899 publication of *From Plotsk to Boston*, her collected letters to an uncle recounting her family's arduous journey from Russia to the United States five years earlier. A precocious student, she won the friendship and encouragement of several wealthy Jewish philanthropists while Edward gave her unfettered access to his library. But Grabau was a notorious flirt and Hattie and Edward thought that he was already engaged to be married to another young woman. "Do not feel that we are in too great a hurry," wrote Grabau in the letter Edward immediately forwarded to Hattie. "A new life is opening up for me here, and Mary will begin it with me. For her, too, the conditions will be better than before to continue her studies for I fully intend to let her develop without retardation. She will attend Barnard College, and fit herself for the work before her. We both have faith in the future." "I hate it," Edward admitted to Hattie. "I think it is the end of all that her friends hoped for from her. I think that to a considerable extent it compromises him. But...I shall marry them...I certainly do not want to give an idea that I am set against them in their future life."[18]

In a letter dated the day of the wedding, Edward told Hattie that he and Nelly buzzed around making the room where he was to perform the marriage attractive before Antin and Grabau arrived at 11 a.m. They were joined by a few of Grabau's friends, including his mentor Professor William Crosby of MIT and his wife, and by Mary's father. Edward did not mention her principal Jewish

Professor Amadeus Grabau of Columbia University's Geology Department in 1905, four years after his marriage to Mary Antin.
Courtesy Columbia University Archives.

benefactors in Boston, Lima and Jacob Hecht. In fact, her early marriage prevented Mary from graduating from the Girls' Latin School and she wrote to her principal correspondent, the British author and Zionist Israel Zangwill, a year after her marriage that "all her devoted wealthy friends and supporters had abandoned her." She guessed that her "intermarriage" was the cause, although she insisted "I have not changed my faith."[19]

There are no surviving letters from Hattie expressing her opinion about this unexpected marriage. She admired both the Grabaus and continued her friendship with the couple but her negative attitude toward interfaith and interethnic marriage, at least in her own family, would become clear. Both Amadeus Grabau and Mary Antin would build lasting reputations, he as a geologist of prolific scholarship and international standing, and she as a moving chronicler of her Jewish immigrant experience in *The Promised Land* (1912) and popular lecturer, but their marriage and Mary's sanity would not fare well in the long run.

In the meantime, Hattie's summer with Mary Cobb had convinced her that she could no longer tolerate the presence of her mindlessly loquacious companion in her house. Now there appeared to be a possibility that Miss Cobb could spend her declining years with relatives in Brewster. "The chance of freedom from Miss Mary is one which you must not lose," wrote the ever sympathetic Edward. "I would gladly pay her board at Brewster, as the best gift I could <*make to my own dear child*>. Be quite firm <*about*> that, though as I know you must have some one. Do <u>not</u> ask Mrs. Andrews, as you will be apt to do. You must not make yourself a nurse."[20] He hoped that Hattie could find a younger boarder, perhaps a Radcliffe girl, and named various friends who might have suggestions. If Hattie had asked Emma Cummings to live with her, as Edward had previously suggested, Emma must have made it clear she wished to remain with her family in Brookline. From now on, Hattie would live alone in her large house with the ever faithful Mary and Sophie, although her nieces would increasingly stay with her to attend cultural events in the city.

While her passion for botany and geology only increased, Hattie's close affiliations with Boston's scientific institutions were beginning to erode. Gradually, the pioneering but amateur efforts of the Women's Education Association to establish and underwrite scientific institutions that would educate women as well as men were overrun by a rising class of scientists with doctorates, almost exclusively male. Their emphasis on academic qualifications and professionalism succeeded in excluding the majority of women from employment at leading scientific institutions, from membership in professional societies, and from publishing in professional journals. The Boston Society of Natural History had been a home away from home for Hattie for many years but events were now loosening her ties with that once august institution. Hattie lost one of her greatest supporters when its curator Alpheus Hyatt collapsed and died unexpectedly on his way to a meeting at the BSNH on January 15, 1902. The Society now began its sad decline.[21] George Barton succeeded Hyatt as the head of the Teachers' School of Science. Another scientific institution led by Hyatt and underwritten by the Women's Education Association was the Woods Hole Marine Biological Laboratory of which Hattie was a founding corporation member for its first twenty years. However, there is no evidence that she ever studied there and, within a few years, she and other members of the WEA found their opinions ignored by the professionals as funding came from wider sources, such as the government and universities.

As a lifelong student, Hattie remained an assiduous attendee of lectures but she now broadened her choice of subject matter into the liberal arts while parlaying her scientific knowledge into independent study, field trips with Emma Cummings, and, most important, into activist support of forest and bird conservation. She also began joining a wider array of organizations, clubs, and societies, some of which reflected her increasingly conservative and traditional social attitudes, notably the Mayflower Society and the Daughters of the American Revolution.[22] She became an active member of Pepperell's Prudence Wright Chapter. That year, she also became a member of the exclusive Massachusetts Horticultural Society, along with Daniel Smiley, who had taken over management of the Mohonk Mountain House hotel and property, including its impressive gardens, and whose descendants still control and run the historic hotel today. Such ancestral, patriotic, and social societies reinforced the Yankee belief that the genuine Americans were those of old British origin.

But now, in early 1902, Hattie was determined to achieve another of her pre-1898 ambitions, to find one of America's rarest wildflowers growing in the wild. The French botanist André Michaux had made a collection of plants in America in about 1794. When Asa Gray visited Michaux's herbarium in Paris in 1839, he found a plant he did not know. Michaux's notes indicated that this mystery plant, which Gray named *Shortia galacifolia,* had been gathered in "les hautes montagnes de Carolinie." According to Hattie's account, it was Charles Sprague Sargent, professor of arboriculture at Harvard and the first director of Harvard's Arnold Arboretum, who, in 1886, found the leaves of a plant in the Carolina mountains the same day that he received a letter from Gray "bidding him rediscover Shortia and cover himself with glory." Sprague asked Frank E. Boynton of Highlands, South Carolina, and his botanist brother if they could find more specimens of the plant which Gray had confirmed was indeed Shortia.[23] When Hattie was in Highlands in 1893, that same Frank Boynton was her guide. She asked him then if he would guide her to the Shortia region and he promised to do so. She had told Edward in 1897 that she planned to pursue it in 1898; instead her life took a dark turn. Now she was more determined than ever.

Edward heard nothing from Hattie for several days after she and Emma left Asheville, North Carolina, for the mountains. Then, when the Hales were staying in Arthur Hale's bungalow in Baltimore, Edward received a box of *Shortia* from Hattie with no explanation. Naturally, he was delighted: "I shall pack the roots in moss in the hope of making them grow under my glass frame!" he wrote Hattie, continuing, "Mrs. Hale has determined that she must get home Sunday, and that she cannot go alone. This puts an end to all chances for my joining you at Norfolk."[24]

Two days later, Hattie's long letter describing finding *Shortia* growing en masse at Oconee in the White Water Valley (the plant is now known as Oconee Bells) reached Edward. As before, this would be the backbone of her published article, enhanced on this occasion by the historical facts suggested by Edward. "What a wonderful success you had, such as your courage and pluck deserved," he wrote from the Bungalow: "When the letter has gone its round, I shall print it in the Record. May I not? The only reason to be given, apparently why it was lost so long, is that until 1837 those Cherokee lands were as I suppose very little visited by Whites. And even now very few travelers for pleasure will do what you did. I think Michaux is the 1770 botanist. We will look up his Journals and find if this is his locality."[25]

After a thirty-mile drive with Frank Boynton in a "hack" driven by a local "colored boy," Hattie and Emma simultaneously spotted *Shortia's* characteristic leaves, including buds about to open into flower. Further on, in even damper ground where the sun could break through felled trees, they saw an abundance of flowers: "There is a single flower to each stalk, having five white petals, each delicately fringed…We got down on our knees, looked at them, touched them, but did not gather one. For all their abundance, we could not but remember their history, and we could not pick even one to have it fade and then be cast aside." Evidently, she overcame her scruples when it came to gathering plants for Edward. Hattie's photo of a bank of *Shortia* is featured on the last page of her article in *The Chautauquan*.[26]

Hattie returned to Boston in time to attend the grand, ticketed celebration of Edward's eightieth birthday at the recently completed Symphony Hall, a McKim, Mead & White architectural triumph. The Hale Club initiated the idea of a national celebration and Henry L. Higginson, wealthy founder of the Boston Symphony Orchestra, was chairman of the organizing committee. In March, *Harper's Weekly* had declared: "If he lives until April 3, Dr. Edward Everett Hale will be the recipient of natal-day honors such as no American man of letters ever received. Boston plans to make the day notable by a tribute of affection to her 'first citizen.'"[27]

Edward's oldest and closest friend, Senator George Hoar, gave the birthday address of which the most memorable sentence captures the reason Edward had the devotion of so many: "We bring you the heart's love of Boston, where you were born, and Worcester, where you took the early vows you have kept so well; of Massachusetts, who knows she has no worthier son, and of the great and free country to whom you have taught new lessons of patriotism, and whom you have served in a thousand ways."[28] In acknowledging this tremendous outpouring of affection, Edward, accompanied by his four sons, his daughter-in-law Greta, and his oldest grandson Dudley, told the gathering of nearly three thousand admirers that "if it had not been better said for me by others than I can say it for myself, I should say that I know no man who has so many friends in the world as I have."

Always in need of new experiences, and perhaps feeling underemployed, Edward accepted an invitation to be visiting chaplain to the undergraduates at the University of Chicago for the month of May 1902. With him went his new secretary Abigail Clark. Abby was proving to be a worthy successor to Martha Adams, who had given birth to her first child the previous fall. On May 10, Edward wrote Martha about Abby, "Her observation is exquisitely delicate & precise, and she sees through the diamonds, and prospectuses & fuss and features generally with admirably funny penetration."[29] Edward's duties in Chicago were not onerous, mainly chapels for the undergraduates, men and women, four days a week. Before long he was caught up in the high-level social whirl he adored. On May 9, for example, he described the elegant dinner given by the University's president "for the young Mr. Rockefeller, the son of the 'Founder' [who had given 17 million dollars to the University]. I knew young R. before, an interesting, intelligent, conscientious man. His new wife was a Miss Aldrich, a daughter of the somewhat eminent Senator from Rhode Island."[30]

John D. Rockefeller Jr. would become a major figure in the development of institutional philanthropy and gave over $537 million to myriad causes over his lifetime. Conservation was prominent among his wide range of interests and he purchased and donated land for many American national parks, including Grand Teton, Acadia, Great Smoky Mountains, Yosemite, and Shenandoah. His marriage on October 9, 1901 to Abby Greene Aldrich, daughter of Nelson W. Aldrich, chairman of the Senate Finance Committee, was the major society wedding of the Gilded Age. The Rockefellers would have six children, a daughter and the five famous Rockefeller brothers.

It was a summer for family landmarks. Edward and Emily's son Philip was the last to marry at age thirty-seven. Lilian Westcott was not his first love but he was none the less devoted to her.[31] He met the much younger and very talented Lilian Westcott at the school of the Museum of Fine Arts, Boston, when he was her professor. On June 11, 1902, Edward married the couple at her parents' house in Hartford; they left that evening for a honeymoon at Niagara Falls which the two artists found so inspirational they stayed on to paint together all summer long.

The next family event in a year full of them was Ethel Hale Freeman's graduation from Smith College in Northampton. Ethel, Hattie's second oldest niece and Edward's goddaughter, had shown intellectual promise from an early age. On June 17, Edward gave the commencement address, "The Educated Citizen," and the Smith College archives have preserved a couple of photographs of Edward with Hattie and Ethel taken that day. One of these shows Edward and Hattie on a path in the Smith botanical garden: a very tall old man dressed in clerical black and wearing his usual slouch hat stands next to a short and rather dumpy middle-aged woman whose flower bedecked hat shades her face into anonymity. In the other, taken after the commencement ceremony, Hattie's features are also obscured (see next page).

During their four days at Northampton, Edward and Hattie took several side trips, including visits to the Maynards at Amherst and a ride to Westhampton to see the house where Edward and his siblings had visited their grandparents in the 1820s.

Harvard commencement was next on the schedule of events. A carriage took Edward, Emily, Nelly, and Hattie to Class Day on June 20 before Edward attended commencement ceremonies on June 25. The highlight for him was the ceremony arranged by the Harvard chapter of Alpha Delta Phi at which President Theodore Roosevelt presented him with a gold medal in recognition of his eighty years and his work on behalf of their fraternity. Two days later, the Hales left for Matunuck.

In the meantime, Hattie, preparing to leave for another summer in Miss Worcester's cottage in Intervale, wrote Edward about her ambitious plans for a week-long hiking and camping trip to New Hampshire's Presidential Range, Mts. Adams, Jefferson, Madison, and Washington. "If all goes well, a week from to-day Frank, Emma Cummings, Edith Hull (my cousin), Vyron Lowe (the guide) &

myself will be walking from Ravine House to the Perch, the upper camp, taking a look at King's Ravine on the way." The morning after her party arrived from Boston, she told him that she was working on the proofs for her *Shortia* article: "You were right in galacifolia, it is one word without a break; & I am glad you called my attention to the 'without flowers.' There were no flowers in the Michaux specimen, that added to the perplexity, but there were ripened

Holding her box camera in one hand, Hattie bends solicitously over an exhausted-looking Edward among the crowd of graduates and their families behind College Hall of Smith College. Edward had just given the commencement speech.
Photograph by J. B. Walker, Smith College Archives, Smith College.

capsules, & I shall put that in & mail the proof to Chautauqua this morning."[32]

The adventures of Hattie's party in the high White Mountains that summer are well documented in letters Hattie wrote Edward, one of which he published in the Correspondence section of the *Record*, and a journal account kept by Emma Cummings. "Frank" Freeman—Hattie had not yet got used to calling him Fred—was a serious photographer with a superior camera and he took a series

A snapshot from a Weeden family album was taken on the Matunuck beach as members of the Hale and Weeden families and their friends celebrated Independence Day 1902. Edward sits apart from a group of women, including Emily, Rose, and Greta Hale, in a storm-battered shelter on the dunes. As he gazed out to sea, perhaps his thoughts were with Hattie and her party who were about to set off on their weeklong hike in the Presidential Range.
Courtesy of Austin Smith.

of striking photographs of this week-long hike. Writing the next day about the first day of their hike on July 9, Emma reported that they left the Ravine House at half past ten: "Each one carried a bag fastened by a leather strap over the shoulder containing all necessary articles for our camp life...The guide Mr. Vyron Lowe with a load of provisions went by another and more direct route to the camp called the Perch, on the western slope of Mt. Adams." After walking for seven hours, they "reached the 'Perch' about half past

About to embark from the Ravine House at Randolph for the hike to the Perch on Mt. Adams, Hattie, at second left, is greeted by her cousin Edith Hull while smiling Emma Cummings looks on. Holding his large camera case, young Fred Freeman towers over the three women. Not shown was Rayner Edmands, who was acting as their guide for the day, and most likely took this photograph.
From the album of Fred Freeman's photographs compiled by Hattie for guide Vyron Lowe. Courtesy of Alan Lowe.

five O'clock and found a cheerful fire and hot dinner nearly ready for us…we climbed 3000 feet yesterday." Heavy rain kept them confined to camp until late the following afternoon when they followed the Randolph Path to the summits of Mts. Adams and Jefferson before returning to the Perch.[33]

In a letter from the Perch written during the same heavy rainstorm, Hattie reminded Edward, "This is the anniversary of Fred's death, & you know I had just come down from Mt. Adams when I got the telegram which took me home. I was with Mr. Edmands then. He came up with us yesterday & I then reminded him that 15 years ago that same day, July 9th, we were on this mountain together."[34] Now Hattie told Edward, "On our way over & back we went over what is called the 'Gulfside Trail' above tree line, of course, where for half a mile, Mr. Edmands has made a path, laying the boulders flat & where there is a rise, placing them as steps. We call it the 'Sidewalk.' I can tell you it is fun skipping over it after the more toilsome boulder climbing." As well as being responsible for the Perch, Rayner Edmands was the first to build continuous, uniformly graded paths in the Presidential Range, always rising but never steeply, bearing in mind the cumbersome costume of lady walkers. However, about this time, conservation-minded AMC members began criticizing such environmentally intrusive paths in favor of blending with natural features. But, even though conservation of the White Mountain forests would shortly become a priority for Hattie, she also paid her guides, the Lowes, to continue building trails. Either Hattie or Edward struck personal sections in some of her letters, indicating an intention to use the descriptive passages for an article which appears not to have been published.

Back in Intervale, Hattie called for the first time on a neighbor, a Mrs. Harold Nichols, wife of a New York minister who was a keen mountaineer. Mrs. Nichols had begun campaigning at the highest level for forest preservation in the White Mountains: "She wrote to Roosevelt, asking that Congress take the whole Presidential range as a reserve, as they have just taken the mountains in South & North Carolinas [a misundertanding on Hattie's part, see chapter 13]…She was fired to do this because she heard that the slopes of Madison & Adams had passed into the hands of a lumber Co." Mrs. Nichols had received letters from Roosevelt and Gifford Pinchot, an early activist in the forestry movement who had been in charge of the forestry efforts at the Biltmore Estate when Edward visited there in 1895. Since 1898, he had been head of the Division of Forestry of the new National Forest Commission, later the U.S. Forest Service, in Washington and was now rising to national prominence under the patronage of President Roosevelt.

Hattie's pleasant party of hikers was breaking up and she and Fred were about to leave for a brief visit to Montreal, a graduation gift from his devoted aunt. Fred had graduated earlier that summer from MIT with a degree in mining engineering and metallurgy and was due to begin work on August 1 at the Aetna Mills: "On our return, Lucia Proctor the fiancée will come for her visit," Hattie continued her letter. "You & Mrs. Hale are to come the middle of the month." This was to be Emily Hale's first visit to Hattie in the White Mountains with her husband, an apparent watershed in the trio's complicated relationship. However, Hattie conveyed her anxiety about this potentially uncomfortable situation in shorthand ten days before the Hales' arrival: "<*I love you always Kit and sweetheart and long so much to see you. But Mrs. Hale will not let me stay and talk with you and put my hands upon you. I do not believe you know how hard it will be for me. But I hope she will feel like*> lying <*down and sleeping some of the time when you feel like*> being <*awake*>."[35]

Evidently Lucia did not measure up to Hattie's exacting standards. From her point of view, her nephew's choice of a bride was disastrous, although she admitted Frank was happy: "[W]hat on earth <*there is about her*> to attract a boy who has any sense <*I can not*> imagine...There is absolutely no companionship in her company for she knows absolutely <*nothing*>, has never been anywhere, so she has no experience to draw from. She has read <*nothing which is*> worth while. Besides, she is not strong, she can not walk. And she is very silly...If I had other nephews I should not feel so badly. But <*this is the only one*> & to <*think that in the* > future, <*if I ever want to see anything of him I have got to see her is*> any thing [*sic*] but pleasant."[36]

Hattie chose to join a scientific excursion to the West Coast with Emma rather than attend Frank's wedding the following May. But her pride in her twenty-two-year-old nephew shines through a letter she wrote after he began work at Aetna Mills: "Frank has begun his work, sorting wool, & finds it interesting…At first the wool all looked just alike to him, Australian & western & others. At the end of the first day, he could begin to see just a little difference & now he sees it more & more." Having grown up without a father, the young man enjoyed talking to his male colleagues: "Frank is stimulated to read the papers & be up to them in such knowledge."[37]

Before the Hales' arrival, Hattie made another attempt, with

Hattie was an expert driver and had taken Edward for drives in Boston's parks for years. Now the two old friends could escape the other guests for drives into the beautiful countryside surrounding Intervale.
From the album "Pictures of the Chief at Intervale To Abigail W. Clark from Harriet E. Freeman Christmas 1902." Hale Family Papers, Sophia Smith Collection, Smith College.

her guide Thad Lowe, to find alpine flowers near the summit of Mt. Washington. From the Summit House, she wrote Edward that she was disappointed to find so little, just geums (*Peckii*), *Arenaria Groenlandica,* mountain cranberry, and white *Castilleja*. That evening, she spent two hours in the office of the Mt. Washington newspaper *Among the Clouds*, looking at back numbers and conversing with the editor and publisher, Frank Burt, a West Newton resident whom she already knew. She told Burt that Edward had had two

Hattie's cat Buffie is the focus of Carrie and Ethel Freeman's and Edward's attention on the lawn in front of Hattie's rented cottage in Intervale.
From a copy of the album "Pictures of the Chief at Intervale To Abigail W. Clark from Harriet E. Freeman Christmas 1902." Harriet E. Freeman Papers, bMS 273, Andover-Harvard Theological Library, Harvard Divinity School.

White Mountain adventures in his youth that would be worth telling. Burt said he would be happy to call on Edward at Intervale and take his dictation. "But I told him you had an amanuensis engaged for the whole of your stay here," she wrote, concluding slyly, "What a good time I shall have as amanuensis!" Abby Clark also vacationed in the White Mountains that summer and Edward published two of the women's letters in the *Record*.[38] At this stage, Hattie was pleased that the younger woman shared their pleasure

Judging by the state of her dress and gloved hands, Hattie was fully engaged in one of her favorite pursuits, gardening, while Edward read under the trees. This photograph was discovered in the house of one of Hattie's great-nieces following her death and subsequently donated to join Smith College's large collection of Hale family papers. Of the few surviving photographs of Hattie, it comes closest to showing her features as a mature woman.
Hale Family Papers, Sophia Smith Collection, Smith College.

in the White Mountains. She compiled for Abby an album of photographs she took of Edward and her nieces during their stay with her that summer.[39]

Hattie need not have worried about how much she would see of Edward at Intervale. The perennially exhausted Emily spent much of her time resting and showed no interest in accompanying them and Hattie's nieces on their drives and expeditions, including a train ride up to Crawford Notch and back. In between these excursions, Edward and Hattie labored together outdoors in the pine woods patching in additions to the "Memories" series, preparing them for publication as a book.[40] Edward also dictated a long article for *Among the Clouds* about his 1841 adventure in Carter's Notch.

But the threatened desecration of the forests by indiscriminate lumbering on the northern slopes of the Presidential Range was on all their minds. Following the example set by Mrs. Nichols, Edward, Hattie, the Rev. Daniel Merriman, and Rayner Edmands met with her on her piazza on Sunday, August 30, to plan a public meeting to discuss strategy. On September 4, they met at Intervale House, joined by "Mr. Fisher" [of the Division of Forestry] and Abby Clark who traveled up from Boston to record the meeting. Pasted into Edward's journal that day is Abby's special dispatch to the *Boston Herald,* "To Save the Forests. Dr. Edward Everett Hale's Eloquent Address. Prof. Edmands of Harvard Also Pleads for Trees. Preserve Presidential Range Theme at the Intervale."[41] Edward agreed to head a committee to begin lobbying the federal government. A few weeks later, at a meeting of the New Hampshire Society for the Protection of Forests, steps were taken toward the establishment of a reservation in the White Mountain region. The society's forester, Philip W. Ayres, reported on his investigations into the state of the region's forests and presented numerous letters of support. A motion was presented "that the Society heartily cooperate with the committee appointed at Intervale, of which Dr. Edward Everett Hale is chairman, to present the subject before Congress," a motion that was unanimously adopted.[42]

Edward devoted his entire leader for the October 1902 edition of the *Record* to the urgent need for action to save America's forests from wholesale destruction by the rapacious lumber industry. He advocated federal government investment and enforcement of proper maintenance and protection of this precious resource. But his high hopes for action on saving the Presidential Range forests appeared to be dashed by a chaotic meeting in Boston on October 24 of the committee formed at the August meeting in Intervale. He described it as "a perfect Fiasco," concluding, "Of course I shall resign."[43] In fact, Edward, strongly backed and often goaded by Hattie, was to make forest preservation in the White Mountains one of his principal initiatives in the final years of his life (see chapter 13).

A month later, Edward returned to Intervale, this time without Emily, and he and Hattie made the trip together that retraced the steps of his 1841 experiences in the same area. In a biographical note abstracted from the fuller account in his diary, Edward recalled that "On Thursday, Oct. 9, 1902, the Ethan Allen Crawford of today rode me and Hatty Freeman to the creek of the house where Stilling my guide in that 1841 tramp then lived; and there Channing and I spent the night before we started. The house is now a ruin, doors, windows and chimneys taken out, and the ridge pole of the roof broken." "As it was a raw morning," Edward noted in his diary, "Crawford dressed me in his own coon skin coat, & I was thoroughly comfortable. In 1841, I wore the coat of his great-grandfather Abel, when my own was wet."[44]

Replete with happy reminders of his vigorous youth in the White Mountains and coddled by Hattie and her maids, Edward headed back to Boston to celebrate his fiftieth wedding anniversary on October 14 with Emily and their family and friends. On the train, he was accosted by Sarah Jane Farmer, "clad as always in her picturesque white merino shroud," who bent his ear all the way from Portsmouth with her latest revelations about "Bab" and "Babbism," as he liked to call Bahaism.[45] Farmer now enjoyed the friendship and munificent support of philanthropist Phoebe Hearst, mother of newspaper tycoon William Randolph Hearst, who had converted to the Bahá'i faith in 1898 and, after moving to Washington from California, hosted Baháist meetings in her grand house there. Farmer's previously ecumenical Greenacre-on-the-Piscataqua would become a center of Bahaism following her conversion. This resulted from a meeting with Abdu'l-Baha in Palestine (now Israel).[46]

Ten days later, Susan Hale sent a classic description of the golden wedding celebration to Emily's cousin Lucy Perkins in Hartford. She explained that she reached 39 Highland Street in time for the family lunch: "Here everything was in a pleasing confusion, doorbell ringing flowers pouring in (yours looked lovely) Yellow Chrysanthemums served by the cord like fire-wood with immense long stems, green leaves and puppy-dog petals, Nelly everywhere, looking very nice in her gray gown." "Parber" carved the chickens, giving Susan dark meat which she disliked but Edward, her favorite nephew, exchanged his white meat for hers, the new daughter-in-law Lilian held her husband's hand whenever she was not eating, and Bertie and his family arrived late to be slotted in around the table and fed. Then everyone went to change and rest before the celebration tea: "Pa retired but an odious Miss Fowler or Farmer rooted him out to press his hand…Telegrams from President and things poured in, all on yellow paper."

Susan suspected that Edward had invited everyone from the South Congregational Church: "It became in fact a dreadful seething mass," Susan continued. "The Weedens presented a Dreadful Crystal Clock, with Gobs of jewels round it…Altogether, Lucy, it was a very charming scene, so genial and cordial, so sans facon, you know, with the masses of flowers, the wobbling heads, and the nice gray haired men doing homage. And my Boys all so tall and strong and middle-aged. Arthur couldn't be there, he was tending the Strike."[47] As an executive of the Pennsylvania Railroad Company, Arthur Hale was involved in negotiations to settle the United Mineworkers of America strike against the operators of anthracite mines in eastern Pennsylvania (including his company).

"All went off well, so well that I was sorry that I did not let you come," Edward wrote Hattie that evening. Four days later, Emily wrote to thank Hattie for her flowers: "If I had not been so tired by the golden wedding that my head has been tired…ever since, I should have written to you, before, to thank you for the beautiful bouquet of golden marguerites and maiden hair. It was very much admired, and just the thing for the occasion. I am so very sorry that the mountains would not let go of you long enough for you to come. It really was just what we wanted it to be, so simple and home like, and no wedding follies about it."[48]

While Edward was spending more and more time officiating

at funerals or attending memorial services for old friends and parishioners, he must have envied Hattie and Emma as they planned another lengthy trip, this time to California with the American Ornithologists' Union (AOU), an excursion announced in *Science.* Led by C. Hart Merriam, famed naturalist and co-founder and current president of the AOU, the trip was timed to coincide with the Union's annual meeting in San Francisco on May 15 and 16.

Increasingly, Edward and Hattie's separations were due to Hattie and Emma's pursuit of naturalist adventures. However much he continued to encourage Hattie, Edward, who was becoming bored with the predictability of his Boston life following his retirement and the death of so many of his closest friends there, was undoubtedly envious of her freedom to set an independent course. It is understandable, therefore, that he described his own scientific adventures in Washington that spring in some detail. From boyhood on, he had a passion for technological experimentation and innovation which was reflected in some of his short stories. Today, NASA credits Edward Everett Hale with being the first to conceive of a manned space station in "The Brick Moon," a story published in the *Atlantic* in 1867. The following year, in "My Visit to Sybaris" also in the *Atlantic,* he described ubiquitous Jeep-like "steam wagons" long before they became practicable. Over the intervening years, Edward had maintained friendships with many leading scientists and inventors and now he, Emily, and Nelly were invited to stay with wealthy Mrs. Hubbard, widow of his longtime friend Gardiner G. Hubbard, organizer of the Bell Telephone Company (later AT&T) in 1877, and subsequently a founder of the National Geographic Society and the American Association for the Advancement of Science.

Hattie wrote "National Academy" [of Science] on the envelope of a letter Edward wrote her from the Hubbard mansion on April 23. The Academy had been founded by Louis Agassiz and Benjamin Pierce in 1863 as an elite, and many would say exclusionary, body of the nation's leading scientists ("If you were not a woman <*you would have been*> chosen into it," declared Hattie's loyal admirer). Agassiz's son Alexander, who was president of the NAS from 1901 to 1907, was yet another of Edward's well placed friends in Washington at that time. Agassiz invited him and Nelly to an opening event before the Academy's annual meeting at the Arlington Hotel and they traveled there in Mrs. Hubbard's brand new Studebaker Electric with her deaf daughter Mabel, Mrs. Alexander Graham Bell. "I was glad to introduce Nelly to so many distinguished men," Edward wrote, listing several of them, and then mentioned an interest of Hattie's: "Dr. Barker of Philadelphia had been reading a paper about the new metal Radium. The thing you say is that it Revolutionizes all Science. It knocks the Atomic theory rather high I believe."

Two days later, Edward and Nelly set off again in the chauffeur-driven Studebaker to call on Edward's old friend Samuel Langley, third secretary of the Smithsonian since 1887. Edward wrote of the Studebaker, "You must distinguish between Electric and those bad smelling naptha things which emit smell and steam. This takes on a box of fifty miles of power, and has immense Rubber tire wheels and is comfortable, and I am coming round to like it." But Edward wrote of Langley, "Poor fellow he is in wretchedly low spirits," no doubt because Langley was being thwarted in his attempts to reconstitute his "Aerodrome" for manned flight. His efforts would sink in two very public and humiliating crashes into the Potomac River before the end of the year. But Langley's contributions as a solar physicist had earned him many honors. Edward delighted in telling Hattie that "he shewed us & told us a great deal about his studies of the invisible end [of] the spectrum," before describing, with sketches, Langley's discovery of light variations within the color spectrum.[49]

During the Hales' latest stay in Washington, the Alexander Graham Bells gave a dinner party at which the talk was largely about other scientific developments which Edward knew would fascinate Hattie: "There is a good deal going on about utilizing Solar Heat…Langley says that the desirable thing is to establish on or near the line of the Equator say 25 heat stations, to absorb and use Sun-Shine, create Power & distribute it. They now carry Power by wire 150 miles from some Water Fall in California. I suppose you improve this so as to carry it 600 miles." Among Bell's innumerable interests was the possibility of manned and unmanned flight. He began experimenting with tetrahedral kites and wings constructed of multiple compound tetrahedral box kites covered in silk in 1898. The great inventor showed Edward one of these after dinner.[50]

Edward was reenergized by his stimulating encounters and experiences in the capital city, and enjoyed the milder climate there, which primed him for the offer which came his way less than three months later.

The day before her departure from Boston for the AOU trip, Hattie wrote saying that she had ordered a box of grapefruit at the Faneuil Street market to be sent to the Hales, "So <*you will be thinking of me as you*> eat them. <*But not only then you will always be thinking of me I am sure and you will never know whether you are*> really <*glad or sorry that I have gone as I can not tell whether I am glad or sorry that I am going…Good bye. You will remember how careful you are to be in every way. For I am your own sweetheart*>."[51]

Despite the fact that Hattie wrote long screeds to Edward from various points on this excursion, her surviving letters are spotty, even fragmentary. But Edward printed extracts of three of her letters in the *Record*. As they passed through Ohio in their special economy class AOU Pullman carriage, Hattie wrote, "Emma hears that Dr. C. Hart Merriam who is to conduct our party is a perfectly delightful man who knows trees especially well…I wonder if you know him. If you do, I wish we could have had a letter from you."[52] Merriam, chief of the U.S. Biological Survey in Washington, was now working on the published record of the findings of the 1899 exploratory voyage along the Alaska coastline led by railroad magnate E. H. Harriman. Merriam had helped Harriman organize this important scientific expedition by persuading leaders of all branches of scientific study to participate.

The AOU excursion's first stopover was in Chicago. Driving through the World's Fair Park with her hosts, Hattie reported that most of the buildings were now gone (they were destroyed by fire within nine months of the fair's closing) but she saw the "three little Spanish caravals which you & Carrie & I saw there in 1893" and the Raymond Hotel where they had stayed. This is the only reference in the letters to Hattie having been with Edward during the closing days of the 1893 Columbian World's Fair.

Edward published parts of Hattie's letters from the Grand Canyon. The AOU party presented Merriam with an Indian basket in gratitude for his leadership (he was already drawn to ethnography), then Hattie was among those who rode down a steep, narrow trail to the Colorado River. "I met here the young man stationed by the head of the Geological Department. I asked him a lot of geological questions and he answered them all. We are now in the carboniferous. We go down, down to the archaean, and then the contact line between granite and sedimentary is as plainly marked as if drawn by a ruler."[53]

During the AOU conference in San Francisco, Hattie and Emma were both elected to associate membership, thus officially beginning their long and loyal association with that organization. From the Yosemite Valley, where she and their small party of birders (and Hattie's friend Emily Cook of the Indian Bureau—not a birder) were camping in tents, Hattie indicated her growing admiration for Hart Merriam, who had now left the party: "I am sure he will always greet me cordially, whenever I may meet him again. I think that never, excepting yourself, have I ever met a gentleman so uniformly kind, helpful, attractive, wise in knowledge, simple, without a trace of conceit or self to be seen…He has been asked to many of the religious ceremonies of the Indians, & you know they never ask anyone to whom they are not very friendly." Today, Merriam is considered to have been a key transitional figure in natural history studies between those carried out by the older generation of less formally trained naturalists and the world of twentieth-century specialists. This goes a long way to explaining Hattie's comfort level with him.

In the same letter, Hattie referred to a landmark event of the week before, President Roosevelt's three-day visit to the Yosemite Valley with naturalist and wilderness preservationist John Muir, when the two men camped together overnight at Glacier Point.[54] Scottish-born Muir had discovered the Yosemite Valley as a young man and lived there for many years. His inspirational writings sparked the creation of Yosemite National Park in 1890 under California's jurisdiction. While traveling to Yosemite together on May 14, 1903, Muir told the President about state mismanagement of the valley and rampant exploitation of the valley's resources. Even before they entered the park, he was able to convince Roosevelt that the best way to protect the valley was through federal control and management.

When Hattie wrote her next letter from Yosemite, her own party's plans to spend a whole day at Glacier Point had been foiled by a dramatic change in the weather; the temperature had dropped overnight to 37 degrees and it snowed all morning, so instead she stayed in bed in the tent she shared with Emma, covered by six blankets, wearing a woolen nightdress, with a hot water bottle at her feet, writing her journal and many letters. When it stopped snowing that afternoon, she was able to explore her surroundings in all their whitened beauty because, practical as always, she had bought some rubber boots and rough workman's gloves in the local store. The other women had only linen skirts and shirtwaists for anticipated hot and dusty conditions. As usual on these expeditions, Hattie instructed Edward to "<*save my letters for me for I write more to you than in my journal*>."[55]

Hattie had apparently made plans for Edward to play a role in Fred Freeman's wedding at West Newton on May 25, described in the newspaper account Edward sent her as "one of the leading social events of the season." "Dear Ethel came for me as you had planned & took me to the station…[Rev. Julian C.] Jaynes took the whole service, my service exactly with 2 rings, until both rings were on. Then I announced them husband & wife…Then I addressed them both in a tone so low that the people should not hear."[56] Despite Hattie's scornful assessment of Lucia's lack of intellectual curiosity, she was, according to the newspaper account, a Wellesley graduate.

Hattie and Emma continued their California excursion through June, staying at Santa Barbara, Pasadena, and the La Casa Loma Hotel in Redlands, which naturally brought memories flooding back of her romantic interlude there with Edward in March 1896. She was delighted that the head waitress remembered her face from seven years earlier, remarking, "I remember so plainly everything about my visit here & even knew my <*old room as I passed it. Do you wonder*>?" She concluded her letter in shorthand, "<*If I do not dream of you tonight I shall not know what I can be made of…here with so many memories you are constantly in my mind…I shall be really happy only when I am in your arms again*>."[57] She and Emma walked up to the

Smiley brothers' grounds at Smiley Heights, which were open to the public, but their houses were largely shut up. Edward, who had recently returned from the latest international arbitration conference at Mohonk, replied that Albert Smiley was visibly saddened by the recent death of his twin brother Alfred at Redlands.[58]

From Los Angeles, Hattie described her delight in her visit to her cousin Charles Ellis, son of her mother's younger sister Harriet, who had died in 1860 at only thirty-eight: "He remembers Pepperell very well as a little boy, & wanted to talk much of that. He is but a year older than I, & we were the best of friends in younger life. I do not think he can be at all like his father [Charles Mayo Ellis], for he was always most amiable & lovable. He graduated in the class of 1865, & came out here around the Horn, for his health in 1868."[59] Together, they visited wealthy businessman and thoroughbred racehorse owner "Lucky" Baldwin's Santa Anita Stable. From there Hattie and Emma planned to travel south to Capistrano and San Luis Rey and again to Santa Barbara before returning to San Francisco via Monterey, and so home via stopovers in Salt Lake City and Colorado Springs. Small wonder that Edward, contrasting her experiences with the relentless and boringly predictable demands on him in Boston, exclaimed, perhaps a little enviously, "What an adventurous Life you have had."[60]

There was a National Education Association convention of 30,000 teachers, "Protestant and Catholic, white and colored," underway in Boston before Hattie's return. "The town is full of Teachers," reported Edward. "We had 600 of them at Church today."[61] Two days later, he hosted on Hattie's behalf a luncheon for some of the Indian Bureau teachers to meet local "Friends of the Indian." Edward managed to pull together a very compatible group with his new daughter-in-law Lilian acting as his hostess. Among the guests were Frank Wood of the Boston Indian Citizenship Committee and Dr. Hollis B. Frissell, president of the Hampton Institute, Mary Drury, president of the Boston Women's National Indian Association, and Mary Collins, "of the Sioux, the most distinguished Indian teacher here." Edward wrote Hattie a full description of the dinner, for which he paid because he enjoyed it so much:

> I made Miss Collins tell familiarly about her hospitals & the irrigation problems…I told about my Zuni's and the silver headed canes, I made Alice Longfellow tell how she was made a Princess of the Ojibwas, which she did with great fun, I made Grace tell about your Grandfather & the Choctaw Indians, we made Frissell talk about his Indian boys… I had an old letter of Roosevelt's about the Indians on his Ranch & his life among them. Miss Collins read us the beginning of the 7th of Matthew from the Sioux Bible, I shewed the Eliot Dictionary & we kept well up to high water mark.[62]

It must have seemed to Hattie that this happy state of affairs would continue for as long as Edward lived but the letter he passed on to her on July 27, 1903 from Matunuck shortly before she and the Hales set off for their month in Intervale together heralded a devastating blow to the pattern of their long relationship. Edward's old friend Senator George Hoar, a leading Unitarian, wrote urging him to accept nomination to become chaplain to the United States Senate. Edward reported that the Hale women were keen for him to accept. He did not tell Hattie that he had already telegraphed his acceptance to Senator Hoar.[63]

12

First Winters without Edward

"I do like to live in all the <*world*> rather than in Highland Street," wrote Edward from home on November 23, 1903, enclosing a letter of introduction for Hattie in Princeton.[1] His letters during Hattie's absence with Emma for the American Ornithologists Union meeting in Philadelphia and then in New Jersey indicate that he was finding his life in Boston increasingly dull in contrast to the intellectual stimulation that he had tasted most recently that spring in Washington. He remained pastor emeritus of the South Congregational Society but he longed to escape the routine civic and ministerial demands that continued to dog him. Now he could look forward to spending that winter in the capital's milder climate and cosmopolitan society.

Hattie continued to pursue her scientific interests during her two-week stay in New York later that month. There she saw a good deal of her former protégé Amadeus Grabau, now associate professor of geology at Columbia University, his young wife Mary Antin, now a special student at Barnard, and her old friend Mary Dann, science teacher at a large girls' high school in Brooklyn. Edward had spoken to "Mary Dann's 2500 girls," nearly all the children of immigrants, on November 5 and was moved by their singing of the national anthem, as he wrote Hattie.[2] Some weeks later, Grabau wrote Hattie, "When I think of what a good time we had that last Saturday, I can not regret that I had to leave you in such a hurry. I could scarcely thank you for all the good times during the two weeks and for your good hospitality. But then, I am used to being your debtor and I like to be. And so I am affectionately yours, Amadeus W. Grabau." In his long letter, the only one in the Library of Congress collection, Grabau must have shocked his opera-loving benefactor with his devastating critique of Wagner's *Parsifal*. Hattie probably gave him and his wife tickets for the second of three performances at the Metropolitan Opera, the first allowed outside Bayreuth. The reviewer for *The New York Times* applauded the performance of American soprano Marion Weed, who replaced the Bayreuth star Mme. Ternina at the last minute.[3]

While Hattie was away, Nelly traveled to Washington to find winter accommodation for herself and her parents. Then, on December 14, the Senate unanimously approved Edward's nomination. Sadly, Ruth Hoar, wife of the instigator of his nomination, died that month. On the eve of Edward's departure for Washington with Nelly, Edward's younger friend Professor Francis G. Peabody of the Harvard Divinity School, wrote: "It will make an interesting winter for you and the lucre is not to be despised. But you have a pretty unregenerate set of chaps to exert an influence on. I suppose you remember the remark of Francis Dana that 'you might as well try to put out hell by throwing snowballs into it, as to argue with a democratic majority,' and I fancy that the U.S. Senate is just about as susceptible to religious influences."[4] Edward's associates on the *Record*, explained his new honor as temporary, occurring "through the instrumentality of Senator Hoar, who, learning that Dr. Hale was to spend the winter in Washington, at once conceived the idea that his presence there should be utilized by the Senate to make him its chaplain."[5]

On January 4, 1904, the new Senate chaplain noted in his diary, "First day of service…I entered the Senate with the Secretary, and took the Vice-President's seat. Mr. [William P.] Frye [of Maine] who is acting President of the Senate came a minute after. He tapped with the gavel. I rose and the Senate rose. I read 'Wherefore we say Abba, Father,' and then repeated the Lord's Prayer."[6]

In a letter four days later, Edward described for Hattie a large supper party at the White House when he was seated at the president's table with Secretary of War Elihu Root, historian Henry Adams, and Jacob Schurman, president of Cornell University. Roosevelt apparently told him "he was glad to be President when I was Chaplain of the Senate! Does this satisfy you?" he teased Hattie. But he had found new ground for his propensity for name-dropping. In view of Emily's semi-invalidism, Nelly was to be Edward's hostess in Washington: "Nelly had yesterday a long searching interview with Mrs. Lodge, the wife of our Senator, about our Social Duties," he wrote. "I am pretty high in President Jefferson's System of social etiquettes, as it is left in his own handwriting in the State Department, and which these people care for more than they care for the 10 commandments. (I do not mean Mrs. Lodge who is ever so nice)." He signed off in shorthand, "*<I think of you about 100 times in every 60 minutes>*."[7]

In the meantime, suffering from one of her perennial "head aches" and overwhelmed as always, Emily wrote querulous letters from Roxbury to "Papa" in the apartment Nelly had found for them at 1717 20th Street: "I am beginning to look forward to the flat, as a refuge from all the things I can't do. Thank you for sending the bank card, and for your sympathy in my trouble. I never felt just so before. So many things to be paid and no way to get money!"[8] Abby Clark, who traveled to Washington with Emily before the end of January, continued to work as Edward's secretary there, accompanying him to the Capitol on days when the Senate was in session. Almost as soon as she arrived, Emily came down with a serious case of influenza which confined her in the apartment for the next three weeks.

Edward now poured out his hopes and plans for his Senate ministry in long letters to Hattie, most often on U.S. Senate letterhead, wondering about the degree to which he would be expected to be "a religious or moral adviser to the whole nation."[9] He also hoped to bring his influence to bear on public issues close to his heart: African-American education, international arbitration, and forest preservation. Hattie had never expressed any interest in Edward's passion for international arbitration and from now on he found himself at the center of various arbitration initiatives, particularly with the outbreak of the Russo-Japanese War in February 1904. Although he was removed from day-to-day operations of the *Lend a Hand Record* while he was in Washington, Edward continued as its editor until the end of his life, making it a forum for news and progress on all of these issues, but most of all for arbitration and peace. The 1904 issues include many articles about the annual Peace Congress which was to be held in Boston that October as well as progress on investigating the state of forests in the White Mountains.

Not surprisingly, the Hales began making new friends in addition to the large acquaintance they had already in Washington. Among them was Ellen Maury Slayden, the charming, intelligent, and witty wife of Congressman James L. Slayden of San Antonio, Texas, who was popular in Washington society. Extracts from her diary and letters, which were published as *Washington Wife*, include a colorful, gossipy letter she wrote to her sister on January 20, 1904, criticizing a White House reception. A society reporter in Texas printed this letter without Slayden's permission. Her frank reference to the president's insistence on inviting people of all ranks and color to his vast receptions and the inefficient way this one was organized threatened to get Mrs. Slayden and her husband into trouble. But, instead of being offended, the author president expressed admiration for her descriptive abilities.

"Among the interesting people" at the reception, Slayden wrote, "was 'the good gray head that all men know' of Dr. Edward Everett Hale, who is now chaplain of the Senate. His face is as wise and kind and humorous as old Dr. Herff's [*sic*?], and he shows the same gentle deference to the most insignificant acquaintance." She continued, "I suppose you noticed that Mr. Slayden had introduced a bill authorizing the President to offer his services in effecting arbitration between Russia and Japan. There is great interest in the matter here, and there is to be a mass meeting at one of the theaters tomorrow afternoon when Cardinal Gibbons, Andrew Carnegie, and Dr. Hale will speak."[10]

Unfortunately, in contrast to Edward's many long, informative letters from Washington, there are very few of Hattie's letters in 1904, a year in which she had her own interesting experiences. Perhaps Edward found it was more difficult to hide her letters in the cramped apartment than in his spacious study on Highland Street. In February, Hattie traveled to Cuba with her cousin Grace and Grace's husband Howell Reed to visit Edwin Atkins who spent winters overseeing his sugar plantation at Cienfuegos. Hattie's party stopped briefly in Washington where she was able to see Edward in his Senate office. On February 8, she wrote to him the morning after boarding a steamer at Tampa, Florida, that would carry their party to Havana. Their departure was delayed by fog which produced a phenomenon that Hattie delighted in describing, "a rainbow without prismatic color. It made two thirds of a circle, & was below us as we looked down from the upper deck & apparently about thirty ft. from us. Each one could see his or her own shadow but no other shadow; & behind my head for instance was a luminous point which indicated the sun. A gentleman of the party said it was an 'egotistical rainbow.'"[11]

Hattie was unaware at this point that her old friend Joshua Young, the Freemans' longtime minister at Groton, had died the day before at his retirement home in Winchester, Massachusetts. Young's memoir about his involvement in the funeral of John Brown was published two months later in *The New England Magazine*.[12]

In the absence of Hattie's letters from Cuba, it is fortunate that Edward chose to feature one of them in the *Record*, her clear and informative account of extracting sugar from cane on Edwin Atkins's plantation: "This is not a show place, as some of the plantations are, but where everything is brought to bear upon production… The great yellow-washed house faces the mill and the sugar-house. It is of stone, and was built by old Serria, the former owner, a hard cruel master in the old slave days, and terrible stories are told of him. But the ghosts of those old days are laid away, and the new civilization, which began here twenty years ago [with emancipation], has taken its place." She described the tremendous labor required to cultivate and harvest the five thousand acres of cane and deliver it to the processing plant, and the growing of sufficient food to support the workmen and their families, two thousand in number. "Twelve hundred tons of cane are ground here every day," she told him before describing the extraction process.[13] Hattie's interest in the production of raw sugar showed her to be very much her father's daughter. She tended now to recall her pride in his achievements as a trader and manufacturer rather than dwell on his last years of sad decline. By contrast, she never claimed any inherited characteristics from her mother, at least in her letters to Edward.

Hattie wrote her friend Etta Pierce that she was enjoying long horseback rides with Cousin Ned at Soledad. Hattie must have delighted in Edwin's explanations of the tropical research carried on at his Atkins Garden and Research Laboratory which he had established at Soledad in 1901. Interested in developing better strains of sugar cane through selection and breeding, he had consulted with Harvard University botanists and set aside eleven acres of land. He and an experienced plant breeder began to create a botanical garden and collected trees, shrubs, and plants from all over the tropical world.[14]

In fact, the situation on the plantation was far from bucolic. As Hattie described it a year later when Edward asked if Edwin would receive some of his friends:

> Ned's estate, Soledad, is fifteen miles from Cienfuegos & must be approached from there. Ned & his friends always go to the estate from there by water, & there is no conveyance save his own steam launch. That leaves Cienfuegos every morning for mails etc. & returns in the afternoon. So it serves very well for his friends to come up in the morning & return in the afternoon. You know there is no house, or any town, or any place which one could stay nearer the estate than Cienfuegos…He is very hospitable, as you know. I am sure he would be very glad to give any of your friends any advice; & certainly, he knows Cuba, root & branch. But I can say that if any American thinks to go out there & make a pleasant home especially for a lady simply for the pleasure of it, he has a very mistaken idea of Cuba.[15]

It was also potentially dangerous. The 1898 peace settlement with Spain recognized Cuba's independence but a congressional amendment exercising America's right to intervene in its internal affairs was adopted by Cuba's constitutional convention in 1901. Despite, the United States' formal end to its military occupation in May 1902, Cuba, the largest island in the Caribbean, quickly became a military and economic appendage of the United States. Many Cubans resented the rush by American citizens and colonists to make fortunes in this comparatively undeveloped island rich in agricultural land and nickel and to turn it into a tourist destination. By 1905, about 60 percent of all rural land was in the hands of foreigners. Soledad was plagued by insurgency attacks around the time of Hattie's visit, as Edwin Atkins's letter book shows. On February 29, 1904, he sent a telegram to a Mr. Squiers, U.S. Legation, Havana: "Incendiaries burning Soledad fields since yesterday, work stopped. Suggest you inform authorities. Atkins." Other letters around this time indicate that fires had been set in the center of various cane fields and a great deal of crop lost.[16] In 1906, when rebels assembled an army of 24,000 men and drove the Cuban president into resigning, President Roosevelt established a second provisional government in Cuba, which lasted only three years. However, U.S. marines had to be sent into the country a number of times over the next few years to protect U.S. interests, including sugar.[17]

Meanwhile, Edward observed the debates on ratification of the Panama Canal Treaty in the Senate. Senator Mark Hanna of Ohio had been the single most powerful advocate for locating the canal in the Columbian province of Panama, along the route of the abandoned French effort, rather than the route through Nicaragua previously favored by the Americans. With the help of massive maps, he succeeded in demonstrating that Nicaragua was dense with volcanoes, some of which posed a threat, and the site was switched to Panama. When Columbia failed to ratify the treaty, Panama broke away with U.S. support, and agreed on a Canal Zone. But Hanna, recently reelected, was absent during the Panama ratification debate, fighting a losing battle at home with typhoid. In the early evening of February 15, the former McKinley kingmaker who, according to Edward, was enormously well liked by his Senate colleagues, died. One of the senators told Edward that Hanna was "the most affectionate Man who ever lived." Edward poured out his and their sense of loss in his letter to Hattie as the news that Hanna was dying filtered through to the Senate floor.

Edward began that day by performing a duty of his new office, obviously arranged sometime before his arrival in Washington. He offered opening prayers on the occasion of Susan B. Anthony's eighty-fourth birthday at the 36th Annual Convention of the National American Woman Suffrage Association (NAWSA) running from February 11 to 17 in Washington's National Rifles' Armory Hall. Edward made his customary digs at the suffragist movement in his letter to Hattie the following evening: "I was to open the suffrage meeting with prayer & I found myself in a crowd of wild-cat women, locked out of the Hall, because it was in possession of the 'Executive Committee.'" His derogatory comment about veteran Unitarian minister and women's rights activist Antoinette Blackwell was probably intended to be humorous but comes across as patronizing, even rude: "You should have seen Anne Blackwell ship forth in a long ulster of imitation fur, coming down to her Feet, looking like an Omnibus driver on a stormy day, for fear people should think she was a woman. She was to read their instructions to Congress. Imagine my amazement when my niece Charlotte Stetson [now Gilman] tells me that she [Blackwell] was to address the Senate Monday afternoon. It turned out that this meant that she thinks she is to appear before the House Committee on Suffrage this morning."

Antoinette Blackwell was the first female minister of a recognized religious denomination whose better-known sister-in-law was suffrage leader Lucy Stone Blackwell. She did in fact speak at a hearing before the Senate Committee on Woman Suffrage following the NAWSA convention two years later. She was one of the very few pioneer suffragists who voted on November 2, 1920. In their official history, NAWSA underscored the irony of Edward Everett Hale's participation in the birthday of their illustrious co-founder: "Monday, February 15, Anthony's 84th birthday and it was a coincidence that in the morning of that day the convention should be opened with prayer by the Rev. Edward Everett Hale, chaplain of the Senate, a life-long opponent of woman suffrage. When he was invited to come he asked definite assurance that it would not be interpreted that he had changed his opinion."[18]

While Edward's views of suffragists remained unreconstructed, Hattie's opinions of the reenergized women's suffrage movement remained unclear from the letters at this point. However, it was likely that, like the majority of other women of her class in Boston, she belonged to the Massachusetts Association Opposed to the Further Extension of Suffrage to Women founded in 1895. In 1898, Mrs. Edwin F. Atkins and Susan Hale were members of that Association's standing committee.

In contrast to his reluctant appearance at the NAWSA convention, Edward was flattered to be asked to officiate at Mark Hanna's funeral on the Senate floor. "I have never seen a ceremony so <u>august</u> and so simple," he told Hattie. "Every seat filled. The different parties coming in, in order, and perfectly silent. I and the other chaplain were at the desk of the secretary in <u>front</u> of the President's[.] Right in front, twelve feet from me, were Roosevelt, <u>and</u> poor Mrs. Hanna. Desk and coffin utterly & completely covered with Flowers, and Ferns & Palms, a mountain of them."[19] But Hanna had left an important legacy. On February 23, Edward reported that the Panama Treaty was passed the day before "by the very strong vote of 60 to 19. The debate has been curious, disagreeable from some points of view but on the whole enlightening...we see more of the abominable intrigues of the French rascals, who began the canal and now propose to sell their work to us. The President has named an admirable commission to carry it through."[20] Ferdinand de Lesseps was the French developer of the Suez Canal who then promoted a similar plan to build a canal connecting the Atlantic and Pacific Oceans through Panama. The project was devastated by the challenging tropical topography and the crippling death toll from malaria and yellow fever, and was ultimately closed down due to insufficient capital and financial corruption. By December 1888, the Panama Canal Company was bankrupt and was liquidated two months later. In 1904, the United States bought out the assets of the company and resumed work with a different approach.

The education of blacks was one of the themes that Edward often returned to in his letters. Responding to one of Hattie's letters from Cuba in which she decried the godlessness of the black laborers on the plantation, Edward told her that Susy was reporting the same thing from Jamaica, where she was spending the winter. "I am pained to find great want of sympathy among the whites here [in Washington] for the blacks," he continued. "They are very eager to keep the Races apart, without being willing to take the inevitable consequences." More an advocate for African-American education than ever, Edward told Hattie he would be giving the oration at the inauguration of Dr. John Gordon as president of Howard College [University] while she was in Washington. But he followed with an opinion that showed him to be in direct opposition to Dr.

Gordon's views, expressed in his inaugural address on March 30, about the importance of sticking to Howard University's mission of providing higher education to blacks: "This was a college which with great enthusiasm was started in 18<u>65</u>, and named for General Howard, and has not succeeded," Edward wrote. "According to me, it has had too much Latin & Greek and <u>Hebrew</u>, and too little smithery and carpentry and common sense." His views were more in line with those of his friends Booker T. Washington of the Tuskegee Institute and Hollis Frissell of the Hampton Institute.[21]

Hattie and Edward were now longing for their reunion in Washington. He wrote her in New Orleans on February 28 to tell her about his plans for her visit: "It is only 15 days now until I shall rest my heart and my eyes with a sight of you! Oh! quell gioia!...I am planning, while you are here, to go down the River to the place, some miles <u>below</u> Mt. Vernon where Washington was born. Then I mean to take you <u>up</u> the river to the great Falls of the Potowmack (as the old books call the River), which people call equals to [the Rhine Falls at] Schaffhausen [Switzerland]...We will find enough to do and see and say, will we not!" His letter the next day must have relieved and delighted Hattie: "You need not distress yourself about my coming here another winter I shall not do that. I distress myself a good deal as to the succession. And it pains me a good deal that, beside Hoar, I have no person to advise with about it."[22]

Hattie arrived in Washington on March 18 after a few days in Chapel Hill, North Carolina, where she enjoyed many conversations about the botanical and geological characteristics of the region with her new correspondent Professor Collier Cobb (1862-1934), head of the geology department at the University of North Carolina, whom she first met briefly in 1893 when he was a student at Harvard.[23] On March 18, Hattie settled in at Washington's Hotel Normandie for a two-week stay. Wasting no time, Edward picked her up the next morning and they drove to the National Museum of Natural History to call on Dr. Merriam and Dr. Howard of the U.S. Biological Survey. "Both of them are vastly entertaining men," noted Edward in his diary. They lunched with friends, including Emma Cummings and Mary Dann, who had arrived for a conference of science teachers, and then attended Hart Merriam's "marvelous lecture on Alaska." Between scientific meetings, Edward and the "science ladies" enjoyed several more lunches together, including one at the elegant new Willard Hotel building ("Washington's first skyscraper"), which opened that year. The following Thursday, March 24, Edward and Nelly lunched with Hattie and then drove to the National Zoological Park.[24] The busy, happy two weeks ended on April 7 when Edward bade farewell to Hattie and Emma at the station as they left for a week in New York.

In New York, Hattie was apparently concerned as always with her array of philanthropic and conservation causes. She asked Edward to pursue certain influential sources of support for bird protection, including the Carnegie Trustees, for he replied the next day to assure her he was doing so. In the same letter, he told her about a couple of calls he had made on two diplomats caught up in the two-month-old Russo-Japanese War, perhaps in his role as a leading advocate for an international tribunal. They were Count Arthur Cassini, Tsar Nicholas II's ambassador, and Baron Kaneko, Imperial Japan's special envoy. Edward reminded Hattie that when Kaneko was a student at Harvard in the 1870s, he was "one of the boys who had to come to the S.C.C. and sit in the front pew." Kaneko, who became Japan's minister of justice in 1900, had been sent to Washington as a special envoy to enlist American diplomatic support to end the war. He succeeded in persuading President Roosevelt, his contemporary at Harvard, to help mediate a peace treaty. Edward now told Hattie that he expected to see Kaneko in Boston, "where I shall call you to help me in entertaining him."[25]

But Hattie's mood, having invited her former companion Mary Cobb for a stay at Union Park, was once again affected by the older woman's inane chatter which reminded her of the twelve long years she had endured it when "Miss Mary" was her lodger. Edward replied with empathy having just sat through Emily's tiresome babbling at the dinner table. But he reminded Hattie that "this sort of cramped talk" had not interfered with all their worthwhile activities across the years, including the "Larger Life" they had shared, and would continue to share.[26] Five days later, longing to resume compatible conversation with her soul mate, Hattie greeted the Hales' return to Highland Park with roses.

***

However glad Edward and Hattie were to be reunited, it was not long before the old man was on the move again. In late May, Arthur Hale arranged for his father, Nelly, and Howell Reed (who had written a book about the U.S. Sanitary Commission during the Civil War and was quite an authority) to tour the Gettysburg battlefields and attend the Memorial Day ceremony there at which President Roosevelt spoke. From Gettysburg, Edward and Nelly traveled to Mohonk for the tenth annual arbitration conference. Baron Kaneko gave an excellent speech, and Edward drew attention to the naval appropriations bill earlier that year for $100 million, of which $22 million was slated to pay for two new battleships. He pointed out that this was more than the valuation of Harvard's ninety plus buildings and the land they were built on. Another speaker reminded the august audience that the veteran peace activist now had the ear of senators in Washington. If Edward had truly believed he would not return to Washington, such comments began to help change his mind.

For the third year, Edward and Emily joined Hattie at Intervale, this time on August 2, as reported in an Intervale newspaper, which noted that "Dr. Hale undoubtedly holds the record among all living mountain climbers for the earliest visit to Mount Washington, which he climbed first in 1841." Edward's diary entries indicate a much quieter stay than in previous years. But, for the first time, their visit was reported by the *Boston Globe,* which gave the false impression that Emily had joined him and Hattie in outdoor life: "Rev. Edward Everett Hale, D.D., and Mrs. Hale are enjoying a visit of a month with Miss Hattie Freeman at her charming cottage at Intervale. They take frequent trips off together with their hostess, and a few days ago took luncheon with friends at the Mount Washington hotel."[27] Implying that the Freeman party had taken advantage of drives to all of them, the society columnist described the various scenic areas within easy reach of Intervale, raising the question of who had reported the visit and why. It might be seen as an attempt to further regularize the Hales' relationship with Hattie now that he was becoming a recognizable figure in the nation's capital, although it was common practice at that time to announce the arrival of prominent or wealthy figures in fashionable summer resorts.

Edward had worried in early July that he had not heard from his close friend Senator George Hoar for some time. There was a good reason; Hoar was on his death bed at his home in Worcester. On August 20, Emily wrote Nelly, "News that Mr. Hoar is dying will affect you deeply. Miss Freeman has done her best to prevent a sudden shock and I really think he [Edward] is none the worse in health and goes on as usual though this suspense is very hard upon him." Emily's description of her usual poor health gave the lie to the *Globe*'s report of her participation in outdoor life: "I am really afraid to do more than is necessary. I have so little strength, and my head is so bad. This news and the suspense makes it feel horribly."[28] The same day, Hattie, who was diverting Edward with happier memories of White Mountain exploits, wrote on his behalf to the head of the Gray Herbarium at Harvard to see if they had any of his correspondence with the late Asa Gray about the plants he brought back in "about 1850" from Mt. Katahdin. "He wishes to know if in any of the correspondence relating to the herbarium, any trace can be found of those plants, or of their names…Upon reflection, he thinks the trip may have been made as early as 1845."[29]

Hattie was very disappointed that Emma did not join her in Intervale after Edward's visit but Emma was caught up in the excitement of the impending publication of her pocket guide to New England birds which she co-authored with a wealthy Brookline neighbor and fellow amateur ornithologist Harriet E. Richards. When their initial title, *Baby Pathfinder to the Birds*, was disputed by another author, Edward advised Emma they should select a different title to avoid a law suit and they did so.[30]

Senator Hoar died at his home in Worcester on September 30, on the eve of the opening in Boston of both the thirteenth Universal Peace Congress, organized by Edward's close friend Edwin Mead, and the Council of the American Protestant Episcopal Church. Edward was devastated by the loss of his intimate friend of sixty years. On the opening day of the Peace Congress, Monday, October 3, he co-officiated at Hoar's funeral in Worcester's Church of the Unity, and delivered a eulogy as eloquent as the one Hoar had given for his eightieth birthday just two and a half years before. That day, Hattie wrote from Intervale with her usual thoughtfulness, "This is a day of such import & meaning to you that I can not think of anything else. I am living in imagination in all that is going on at Worcester. Who will go up with you? I hoped Howell might."[31] In fact, it was faithful Nelly who accompanied her father.

Edward had organized devotional meetings for the peace delegates, visiting prelates, and leaders of other denominations at the South Congregational Church each morning. It was a very challenging program for a man of his age, even if he had not been grief stricken. "There are a good many important people here," he told Hattie as the great men were arriving in Boston, naming a radical German critic of the New Testament and the bishop of Hereford, John Percival, "the only English Bishop who opposed the Boer War. I am to lunch with him today, at the 20th Century. If you had been here I should have asked you to go."[32] In his rousing opening speech, Secretary of State John Hay acknowledged that this latest peace initiative was happening at the same time the Russo-Japanese War was raging on the other side of the world and that it also coincided with the death and funeral of Senator Hoar, "our dear and honored co-laborer in this sacred cause." In response, Bishop Percival decried the competition for religious, dynastic, and national dominance as wrong-headed notions that had racked the earth with wars. Other major speakers included peace activist and Hull House founder Jane Addams, Julia Ward Howe, labor leader Samuel Gompers, and Booker T. Washington, who excoriated the rising incidence of "lynching" of blacks in the South.[33]

In his nightly accounts for Hattie of the concurrent conventions, Edward described the pageantry surrounding the Episcopalian conclave. As it drew to a close, he told her about the procession of bishops and other clergy: "There were ten thousand people in the street, mostly women, to see eighty men in white red and black robes march from Clarendon Street into Trinity Church with an escort of 20 choir boys & as many other clergy, no! more. Now you cannot say that any Religious Sentiment, and Love of God or passion for a larger life made them do that. It is simply Idolatry. It is simply bowing down before a Visible bit of outside, which does not have anything to do with Religion. Well! I took my station in the church where I could retire at the proper moment. And not expose anyone to Contagion."[34]

As lay and religious delegates began to leave town, Edward admitted, "In a way, I suppose it was as well that I had the absolute <u>rush</u> of the two conventions...I was not permitted to think my own thoughts or to have my own way in what, as you see, is so great a personal grief. The real thing to do would have been to go to Intervale and spend the week quietly with you. But this would simply have been a Sin. I am too much connected with the whole thing to do that decently!" Of the Peace Congress, he wrote, "To you privately, I will say that the Conference has <u>not</u> risen to the height which I hoped for...<u>But</u> John Hay's opening address would alone justify the whole occasion with its cost (30,000 dollars) and anxiety and worry."[35] The next day, he told her, "the five mornings at our church have saved me. Oh! a great deal. It was <u>my</u> plan, I was responsible. And it did more than I had foreseen. Actually to introduce the Baptist chief, Dr. Rowley, and the Episcopal Allen and the Methodist Bishop Mallalieu personally to each other, and to see them day by day grow into respect and regard for each other...There, of all the crowd, it was Rowley who brought the Jew Fleischer! Did I tell you how he read the Isaiah passages?"[36]

Rabbi Charles Fleischer of Boston's Temple Israel, like his predecessor Rabbi Solomon Schindler, was a Reform Jew who was born in Germany, although he was educated in New York. Schindler, who was appointed in 1874, was especially attracted to Boston's intellectuals, radicals, and Unitarian ministers and was determined to shed most of his congregation's Orthodox traditions and Americanize it. His powerful sermons drew large audiences which were "more than half Christian," according to the Darwinist Unitarian minister Minot Savage. By the mid-1880s, his congregation of "100 of the richest and most influential Hebrews in the city" was able to build a new temple in a still fashionable part of the South End. Among the speakers at the dedication were Edward Everett Hale, Minot Savage, and Phillips Brooks. But Schindler was moving too far away from traditional Jewish ritual and outraged his congregants when he advocated intermarriage with liberal Christians and preached the socialism of Edward Bellamy. He stepped aside and was replaced by Charles Fleischer, "an even more ardent Americanist," who was delighted to be greeted on arrival at the railroad station in 1894 by the Reverend Hale with the words, "Now my son, you too are one of the preachers of New England." Fleischer, a romantically handsome bachelor, soon became a star in Boston's intellectual and artistic circles and was admired by and was friends with liberals like Harvard's Charles W. Eliot.[37] But matters were to take a very different turn in the face of unrestricted immigration at the turn of the new century.

As always, Edward knew that Hattie was living through everything he was experiencing with him. As he told her: "It is a pleasure to remember that there is one person who cares a little whether I did what I tried to do or not, or whether I am preparing for an oration or for a death bed. <*It is that hard work of sympathy for my daily life which make me*> dread looking forward even for six hours and <*when I have you at hand I*> know that there is one person who cares whether I succeed or fail…When I got home last night at ten o'clock, the Salutation was 'Where have you been?'"[38] This reads like a man whose wife was quite detached or, more likely, was now struggling with loss of short-term memory. Although Edward makes few criticisms of his wife in the surviving letters, there are occasional indignant responses from Hattie which show the contrast between Emily's self-absorption and Hattie's loving care. "<*I think Mrs. Hale is a selfish thing to lie in bed and not get up and help you with your stocking when she knows how hard it is for you to get it on. I want to say she is a horrid pig*>," she began a letter after seeing him in Washington in January 1905.[39]

As soon as the conferences were over, Edward traveled to Ithaca, New York, to debrief two members of the Peace Committee who were unable to attend: Dr. Jacob Schurman, president of Cornell University, and Andrew White, chairman of the American delegation at The Hague, who had been expected to be the keynote speaker on "The Work and Influence of The Hague Court" but was ill. On his return from Ithaca, Edward began a letter to Hattie at Intervale, "<*My own darling Kit and sweetheart and wife and life*>, East Wind <*and guide and philosopher and friend*>."[40] He yearned for her to return to Boston before the end of the month so that they would have a month together before he left for Washington. None of his letters at this time explain why he did so but he had evidently bowed to friends in the peace movement who felt that he could use his influence on the senators. Nelly, whose artistic career and social life were already looking far more promising in Washington than in Boston, must also have urged him to continue there, if only for the sake of his health.

Hattie returned home on October 30 after stopping in Newburyport to comfort her ailing uncle Frank Howe. In a letter from her uncle's house, she told Edward about her developing plans for a six-month winter sojourn in Italy, a Grand Tour for Ethel. She knew that the weather would be best in the spring and summer, "but that is not the time that I want to be away. <*I think to be away when you are and at home when you are. 'Where thou goest I will go. And where thou stayest I will stay'*>. But even the beauties of Italy, even the help & benefit that I can be to Ethel in giving her this trip, <*does not*> in the least <*reconcile me to the parting from you*>."[41]

Although his letters continued to assure Hattie that he missed her terribly while he was in Washington, Edward's first letter on U.S. Senate letterhead in early December 1904 made it clear how much he enjoyed being a witness to the great debates on issues of the day: "I sit in the Senate chamber in the corner where you remember me, so that I may shake hands with old friends, and welcome the new ones. Today for the first time, the work of the Senate began and I heard the bill read which will become the basis of a great deal of debate, for restricting the number of members from the South, in those States where the Negroes are not permitted to vote…Everybody is as cordial as possible, even the 'Democrats' seem to me in good spirits. I have put 'Democrats' in quotation because it is such an absurd name by its derivation, for a party which makes a principle of abridging the right of suffrage to the [crossed out 'black ra'!] white race."[42]

The Jim Crow era was well under way. Since Reconstruction, there had been sixteen black representatives from the South but Republicans in Congress had been confronting since the 1880s the gradual disfranchisement of African Americans achieved in several Southern state constitutions. George H. White, the Republican representative from North Carolina between 1897 and 1901, had introduced a bill in 1900 making lynching a federal crime punishable by death, but it was ignored in the Judiciary Committee. Thus began a long struggle in Congress to enact federal anti-lynching legislation. In his farewell speech, White predicted that someday other blacks from his region would sit in Congress but no African Americans would be elected to Congress from the South again until 1972.

Hattie and Edward were not parted for long since they were both delegates to the American Forest Congress in Washington from January 2 to 6, 1905 as described in Chapter 13. Following her return to Boston, Hattie wrote that she was upset by a letter she had received from Lucy Young, daughter of the Reverend Joshua Young, who had died the previous February. Lucy felt that "the lessons that her Father taught so long at Groton are being set aside by Mr. [Pemberton H.] Cressey. He called a meeting at the Parish & gave them his views about the Communion Service. Either they did not have any, or they did not dare to state them for he had it his own way. And they had a service in which the table was set; & the bread & wine was not passed. You would not approve of that surely," she insisted. "But why did all those church members acquiese [*sic*] so readily?"[43]

Reverend Cressey was not the only younger Unitarian minister who was doing away with some of the traditions that Edward and Joshua Young espoused and practiced. Hattie's growing dissatisfaction with Edward Cummings's preaching style at the SCC grew to the point where she began trying out other churches. After attending a service in Brookline, she exclaimed in a letter to Edward: "Oh! what a different thing you would have made out of it. There was nothing spiritual about it; nothing to help one in a daily Life. You have given me a hunger for something better & now I can not be fed. I get my spiritual food every morning by reading one of the Senate Prayers & a selection from James Freeman Clarke. I really think it would be as well to give up going to Church entirely, & give that time to reading something that will quicken my spiritual Life as it is not quickened by the sermons I hear."[44] Edward responded by trying to explain the difference between religious and ethical approaches to preaching: "What you say about preaching involves a great mystery. It is a mystery which, according to me, is not unfolded or unveiled in the Divinity Schools. Au fond, that is the reason why I dislike them…I think that the business of a preacher, as distinguished from that of a Chief Justice or other Lawyer, is to help people accept or grapple with the difficulties or Mysteries, instead of trying to explain them away. Probably this ends in this, that you and I would value feeling, or inspiration, or the faculties born in us, innate, more than we value logic."[45]

In January 1905, a peevish note began creeping once again into Hattie's letters, and she expressed the jealousy she was feeling for Edward's secretary, Abby Clark. She must have noticed his growing fondness for this extremely competent younger woman, who evidently shared Edward's sense of humor, for now she wrote in shorthand: "<*I should be happier if I knew that you do not kiss her or let her kiss you. But you will make me no promise for all I am your own Kit. Now do not be angry because I say this. But remember it is not*> easy <*it is very hard for me to be here alone and know she is with you doing everything for you constantly*>."[46] She began reminding him of what they had meant to each other in the past, telling him that she kept a memento of their few times at Matunuck together. She had made photoprints of the snapshot that someone had taken of the two of them sitting in adjacent boats on the pond behind the Red House in September 1887, although she was surprised that some of her close friends did not recognize either of them in the photo (see page 120). When she sent it to Edward, he agreed with them.[47] In another undated January letter, Hattie told him that she had attended the annual meeting of the South Friendly Society. "To my mind, the whole thing is so interwoven with you & Mrs. Andrews, that it seems but a melancholy affair <*without*> either of you," she mourned, concluding "And so the affair is over, & I am still Treas… Perhaps I really do cling to it a little because it is the last tie to hold me to the dear old S.C.C. which has tender recollections for me for a whole life time."[48]

It cannot have helped Hattie's spirits that she was now living alone with Mary and Sophie, although she protested otherwise in a February letter: "This afternoon, I have been out to Miss Mary's, as I always go on Monday. When I came home & sat at my solitary supper, I was more than ever thankful that she was there & not here. I had rather be lonely, alone. How did I ever stand it so many years! And how much longer could I have endured it had she not had that ill turn which compelled a change? Yes! I am perfectly thankful that neither she nor Miss Noyes are here!"[49] Although she insisted that she did not miss her longtime lodgers, her letters increasingly show her need to fill every possible moment of her days to counter the loss of Edward's companionship. Now Hattie and Emma were planning their Florida excursion, following a five-day stopover in Washington for the inauguration in his own right of Theodore Roosevelt on March 4 (he had been elected by a landslide in November 1904). She hoped that Edward would preach at All Souls Unitarian Church there on March 5, "the anniversary, twenty five years, since my Mother's death, March 5, 1880." He replied that even if he could not change an engagement in Princeton, "we can have Saturday, Sunday, Monday, Tuesday, and Wednesday, all to ourselves."[50]

Edward was not able to avoid a prior engagement in Princeton and upset Hattie by failing to telephone her at her Washington hotel on his return and before she left for Florida with Emma. On March 12, he wrote to her at the Hotel Valencia in St. Augustine with his explanation and loving words for her fifty-eighth birthday, too late to stem the hurt feelings expressed in shorthand before she received that letter. Her spirits lowered, as they always were, by cold and torrential rain, and pained by his silence, she wrote: "<*I have been torturing myself in wondering what I could have done or said that you should be angry with me and would not write…The days have been very dreary to me since we parted now a week since. I have heard not one word from you in all this time*>…if this weather continues, I can never again have a pleasant thought of St. Augustine, any more than I can of Bermuda." Despite receiving his letter and birthday verses the next day, she began a cry of sadness that would become a recurrent and escalating theme in her letters: "<*Loving you as I do and parted from you as much as I have been for the last two years and may perhaps be in the future what have I to make me happy*>."[51] But then the sun shone once again on St. Augustine and she wrote from Ormond that they enjoyed exploring the old fort and other historic sites.

In Ormond Beach, Hattie met several acquaintances from a visit she had made nearly thirty years earlier, including Bradford Torrey, the New England nature writer. From that point on, Emma and Hattie went on excursions with Torrey and other birders and also took a two-day hundred-mile round trip on board the Hiawatha, a custom-built steamer, on the Ocklawaha River to the St. Johns

River between Palatka and Silver Springs. "The two nights have been marvelously bright & clear, & the stars so brilliant that we could see their reflections in the water," Hattie now wrote, telling Edward that "Mrs. Stowe took this trip, so many years ago, & her poetical description of it is used as a part of the advertisement on the pictured folder." She told him that the South African water hyacinth had invaded the narrow river and become a threat to navigation. This part of their Florida trip was such a success that they decided to stay on at least another week, and did not start the long train journey to New York until April 7.

On Edward's birthday, April 3, Hattie began a letter, "I cannot let this marvelous, wonderful, never-to-be-forgotten day go by without writing you. And I must write to you at Hampton & trust to its being forwarded." They had been to Oak Hill for two days to watch the herons fly in to roost in the evening. "They came mostly from the north, & as we saw them outlined against the sky, with long necks & legs dangling, they looked like Japanese pictures more than anything in real life…There were 1500 to 2000 herons in all. The Man clapped his hands, so we saw them all in the sky at once." On their ride home, they were enchanted to see Venus, Jupiter, Mercury, and Orion reflected in the water, while fireflies danced around them.

Their drive next day took them to deep woods with great oaks, tall and short palmettoes, magnolias in full bloom, and mulberries. On their way back, they tied up the horse and climbed up one of the mysterious shell mounds to watch large birds, including Great Blue Herons, sailing in the air above the coastline of low islands and winding inlets. A memorable day indeed. On April 6, the day before they left for New York, they hired a small steam launch and invited their friends to join them for a day of bird watching down the Halifax River. Despite that anticipated adventure, Hattie yearned to be with Edward, telling him in shorthand that she was beginning to forget how he responded to her conversation, the tone of his voice, his expression, "*<even your smile. Your laugh I can not hear. But then I seldom make you laugh. Why should I not forget somewhat in four months>*."[52]

The Hales left Washington for a brief holiday at Hampton Institute as Hattie and Emma traveled north to New York. Edward wrote from Hampton on April 7 and 8 to tell her that he was being pampered by the students and was enjoying "the Freedom from the irksome things of Washington. 1st and chiefly <*the conversation with intelligent men like*> Frissell and some of the <*others here*>. One feels <*this particularly at table*>. To have 3 <*times a day a really intelligent companion*> and <*to talk on the large subjects*> this after 5 <*months of mere chatter is something which you can comprehend*>. Perhaps I never sympathized enough with you, tho I always did <*know what pleasure*> Miss Dann <*brought to you*>." Hattie replied about the chatter at home, "<*I think if you ever*> showed <*that you did not enjoy it you might have something different*>."[53]

Even though the Hales returned to Boston in April, Hattie left even earlier than usual for the White Mountains. By late May, she was staying with her youngest niece Helen at the Eagle Hotel in Concord, New Hampshire, while Edward was busy with all the events of Anniversary Week. A few days later, he wrote to her at Intervale, "No! I will not be so tyrannical as to say that I want you to come back when I know that you enjoy every minute there, and that here you are annoyed & worried very often." She still went through the motions of asking his permission to leave on extended trips but that would change the longer he stayed in Washington. "As I told you I would consent to your going to Europe," he now told her. "You must not make me say that I want you to go. But I shall always be most careful not to say that I am wretched when you are away. But all this does not prevent me from saying how very very very glad I am when you come back."[54]

Hattie was at the Summit House on Mt. Washington when Edward wrote to tell her about the christening of Fred and Lucia Freeman's baby daughter Barbara on July 1: "She had on the christening dress which Fred wore and your Father. She was as sweet and even jolly as a dear child could be, came to me with perfect ease and enjoyed it all as much as any of us. My dear child, the whole was perfect, but that as you know we missed you and Ethel…Fred took two snapshots with the camera of me with her in my arms." Once again, Hattie chose mountain life over a marker in her nephew's growing family but she was pleased to receive a letter from Lucia describing the ceremony.

On July 5, Hattie registered her climbing party, including Emma, a cousin Edith Hull, and their guide Vyron Lowe, in the AMC message bottle on Boott Spur after sitting on Overhang Crag for an hour to enjoy the view: "A glorious, quiet Fourth for all of us, marred only by the recent news of the death of Secretary John Hay." But in a letter to Edward at Matunuck on July 8, she admitted that her long descent over the old Crawford Bridge was "'slow' for I think there never was a person who walked the mountains as slowly as I do. In the first place, to climb really makes me very leg weary & sadly out of breath, & then if there is anything beautiful, & there always is, I will stop to look at it, after having done all that hard work to get up where it is. I asked Vyron if he ever had a party who enjoyed mountain sights so much & he said promptly 'No! Never.'" But once again, she was disappointed to find they had come too late for the blooming of alpine flowers.

Later that month, unsure of when and if Edward would be joining her at Intervale, Hattie poured out her misery over their long separations in letters to Matunuck filled with anguished shorthand passages. "I am perfectly discouraged & disheartened with our correspondence. I think I shall only <*write you completely bored and bitter letters which may be printed in the*> newspaper. <*If ever I write anything from the heart anything from my*> real soul, you entirely ignore it, & never reply to it or even refer to it." In another, she complained: "<*I find it very hard to keep my faith with these long separations and our letters*>. I read in the paper that the President is to call the Session Nov. 11. That means <*that you will go again in about*> 3 <*weeks after my return to Boston*>. Another <*long absence, another*> series <*of letters which may only tell of the outside of our lives. I shall*> either <*die of grief*> or <*become*> indifferent; for there is no half way about it <*to me. 'I am not made of iron'*>."[55]

Two days later, writing from Edgartown on Martha's Vineyard where she was staying with friends, she responded with her characteristic sympathy to Edward's very worrying news from Matunuck that Emily was not well and their six-year-old grandson Nathan, Edward Junior's middle son, was very ill with fever and diarrhea: "I am very very sorry for the anxiety which comes to you with Mrs. Hale's condition & for the sickness of the little boy. I sincerely hope that he may not have anything so serious as typhoid." Edward had told her that neither Emily nor Nelly would allow him to travel on his own and it now seemed most likely that Nelly would accompany him to Intervale. Hattie responded: "I must say one thing. What will Nelly do for occupation? You know Mrs. Hale spent a good deal of time in 'looking at the ceiling,' as you said. Nelly won't do that. She will be doing something. <*If she is to do every-thing for you I must say that I shall have no pleasure in your visit. I want to write for you every morning as I always have. I want to read to you. I want to put on your slippers and your shoes*>. And the many other things of which I do not <*write*>. Cover <*you up when you lie down for your nap. I must have these*> privileges & pleasures <*if she comes*>. And I think you will let me. Can she not bring her paints?"[56]

Most of Edward's letters in this exchange are missing but he evidently told her of an additional worry which puzzled Hattie: "I can not think what it can be that you mean when you <*write about*> the insanity of some one which is an anxiety to you, whom I do not know of, & of whom you will not tell me <*more until you see me*>. That makes it quite a mystery. But I am very sorry & will wait." Since Edward would confess the following year that the least thing would upset Emily, it seems likely that her own illness and that of her little grandson, with all the memories of her beloved Rob's fatal battle with typhoid and her own ten years before, had tipped her temporarily over the edge.

Back at Intervale, after stopping at West Newton to see her family and at Union Park to collect two more trunk loads of household items to make her rental house more comfortable, Hattie wrote, "I am planning every sort of thing for your comfort & happiness, where you will sit at the table, what you will have to eat, which chair you will like best &c. There is a seat out doors under a beautiful pine tree, very near the house, & with no rise of ground where I <*am sure you will be very happy. You shall never*> rise from your chair to greet a visitor & you must never even speak of it in apology."[57] On August 15, Edward wrote from Highland Street that he and Nelly would be leaving for Intervale at last the next day and Nelly intended to make it an artistic visit. "Do not think me weak," he wrote. "But I am tired beyond words, and you must not mind if I spend three days in abject rest. Ride? Yes. But to talk comparatively little."

Edward and Nelly left for home on Sept. 2 after what seems to have been a successful holiday for all of them. It is difficult to understand, though, why Hattie stayed on in Intervale until the end of October even though she knew that the Hales would return to Washington two weeks later. On October 18, Edward wrote, "Nelly leaves us for Washington. She will spend tonight at Baltimore, and go to Washington in the morning to hunt up our Winter quarters." Acknowledging that Hattie was now bewailing his imminent departure even to the point of wishing they had never met, he continued, "Dear child, Do not compare our lives with what we can imagine possible, but compare them with what would have been had we never met. Do not say 'Would God we never had met.' You do not think so and it is not so. Suppose I had been spending my life in Alton Slevius [illegible], and you had never heard of me, or I had never heard of you."[58]

From now on, Hattie labored in her letters to recall for Edward their happy years at the South Congregational Church on Union Park Street, before its move to the Back Bay. But those days could never be recaptured; Boston was now a very different place. Political power was slipping rapidly out of the hands of the Unitarian, Brahmin elite, many of whom were leaving Unitarian churches for Episcopal or Congregational equivalents. In a letter written the day after the December 12 Boston mayoral election, Hattie revealed the ingrained animosity of the long dominant Protestants of Anglo-Saxon origin toward the rising Irish American Catholic political class. Ward Six Democratic boss John Francis (Honey Fitz) Fitzgerald, now remembered as a grandfather of President John F. Kennedy, had beaten Republican Louis Frothingham, the Harvard-educated, wealthy, blue blood speaker of the Massachusetts House of Representatives and brother of Edward's friend the Reverend Paul Frothingham: "Of course, you mourn the election of Fitzgerald over Frothingham. How deplorable! I was down town yesterday with Ned & so heard more talk than I often do. I had not realized how many of the business men of the city lose their vote by living in the suburbs. No one in Ned's office can vote, & in the Boston wharf property, where Ned is President & Mr. Moses Williams & [illegible] are leading men, the property paying a tax of $40,000 not one of the three can vote. Can such a wrong ever be righted."[59]

* * *

Italy now beckoned, a happy diversion for Hattie. On the eve of sailing from New York, she wrote to remind Edward that he had not yet sent her a letter of introduction to the American ambassador in Rome. She also enclosed pre-addressed envelopes for mail collection in Naples and Rome: "Use the Naples address first. We plan to be in Sicily all January & then in Naples for the first fortnight in February. After that Rome, for 3 weeks & we shall give directions there for forwarding."[60]

13

Preservation and Conservation

While Hattie's increasing feelings of unhappiness and loneliness due to Edward's prolonged absences in Washington permeate many of her letters at this time, these years also established an additional shared mission for them, the fight to win federal legislation to conserve the rapidly depleting forests in the White Mountains. Both Hattie and Edward had spent time over the years studying trees at the Agricultural College in Amherst, Massachusetts, under the tutelage of Professor Samuel Maynard, the school's horticulturalist, and Emma would serve on the tree-planting committee in her home town of Brookline for forty years. At the same time, Hattie and Emma became activists for bird preservation and Hattie lobbied for and contributed to efforts to preserve wildlife, particularly the American bison. All three of them were contributors to the birth of the national conservation movement.

The year before Hattie began urging Edward to attach his name and reputation to the cause of the White Mountain forests they both loved, the Society for the Protection of New Hampshire Forests was founded. Philip W. Ayres was appointed the Society's forester and charged with investigating the state of the region's forests. Also in 1901, North Carolina Senator Jeter Pritchard introduced a bill authorizing $5 million for establishing the Southern Appalachian Forest Reserve. But in the following decade, Congress rejected more than forty bills calling for national forests in the eastern United States. Again and again, political conservatives declared that the federal government lacked the constitutional authority to purchase private land and argued that states should be responsible for their own forests. Indeed, as early as 1878, Wisconsin had created a 50,000-acre forest preserve to protect the headwaters of major rivers and Pennsylvania took a similar initiative in the 1890s. The New York State legislature established the Adirondack Park in 1885, declaring the area "forever wild" in its constitution.

The champions of private property rights liked to point to what George Vanderbilt had been able to achieve just outside Asheville, North Carolina. In the 1890s, Vanderbilt quietly bought 600,000 acres of cut-over woodlands to add to his Biltmore Estate and ordered the state forester, Carl Schenck, later director of the Biltmore Forest School, to begin planting trees. The Biltmore Forest, which Edward saw in its infancy when Frederick Law Olmsted guided him through the estate in 1895, would become known as the Cradle of Forestry. Gifford Pinchot became chief forester of Biltmore in 1891. Five years later, he was appointed to the National Forest Commission and was charged by President Cleveland with developing a plan for managing the nation's Western forest reserves. In 1898, he became head of its Division of Forestry, renamed the U.S. Forest Service and moved to the Department of Agriculture in 1905. Pinchot was a guiding light of Theodore Roosevelt's conservation initiatives and one of Edward's most valuable contacts in Washington.

To circumvent the issue of states' rights, the Appalachian National Park Association and the Society for the Protection of New Hampshire Forests persuaded five southern states to pass legislation giving their consent to the purchase of land by the federal government. In 1903, the Appalachian Association began campaigning for a national forest preserve instead of a national park, emphasizing their changed focus with a new name, the Appalachian National Forest Preserve Association.[1]

President Roosevelt's reform agenda was well under way during his first two years in office with the passage of landmark Progressive legislation aimed at breaking up the "trusts," occasioned by the rampant consolidation of businesses which threatened to eliminate competition, and advances in the reform of women and child labor, wages and hours of work, and safety and health conditions in factories. A landmark in the development of western America, the Newlands Reclamation Act (1902) directed the proceeds from the sale of arid and semi-arid lands in the west toward the construction of dams and other reclamation projects. And then Roosevelt's program was met with unforeseen obstruction when Joseph G. Cannon of Illinois was elected House Speaker in November 1903. A fiscal conservative, the sixty-seven-year-old had, with the exception of two defeats, served in the House since 1870 and had been a tough-minded chairman of Appropriations.

Whatever he said to the contrary, Cannon considered himself to be the absolute ruler of the House and was determined to reestablish its preeminence in controlling the nation's purse strings. Friendly and gregarious, the cigar-chomping, spittoon-using Cannon was personally popular, but he was a champion of the status quo and despised all reform. For the next seven years, "Uncle Joe" maintained an iron grip on the House, operating through a small group of like-minded men who controlled the Rules, Ways and Means, and Appropriations committees. Following his election in his own right in 1904, Roosevelt tried to work with Cannon to move his program of reform forward but pro-business Cannon was obdurate in his determination to kill any such legislation in committee, amend it to death, or simply ignore it. Hattie would express her increasing dislike for this obstructionist force with powerful invective, although mostly concealed in her letters to Edward.

On the eve of Edward's departure for Washington in late December 1903, he printed in the *Lend A Hand Record* Hattie's letter bemoaning the destruction she had observed of the path to the Cascade camp: "For a mile we walked over a logged area, the pretty forest path simply a mass of mud. Forty men are at work now, and the force is soon to be increased to eighty…Constantly we heard the noise of the dynamite explosions, as rock is being blasted for the construction of roads on which to haul out the wood."[2] From now on, goaded by Hattie, Edward was to make forest preservation in the White Mountains one of his principal initiatives from his privileged seat in Congress.

In mid-April 1904, as his first congressional season in Washington was drawing to a close and he was not expecting to return for another, Edward wrote Hattie with his characteristic optimism, "We have got the New Hampshire Reservation into the [Senate] Bill...if we can get it through our House that will be a great Victory. And <*you must count that as one of your triumphs*>."[3] In fact, neither of them can have had the slightest idea at that stage of what a long and bitter struggle it would be to get the combined Appalachian and White Mountain bill passed into law. But the bill would become a major goal for a wide range of interests, including the lumber industry.

Forest and Irrigation featured a group photograph of those delegates to the American Forest Congress who had arrived in Washington by January 2 standing on the steps of the Navy Department. They were to attend a reception with the President at the White House that evening. As Hattie told Edward when she received her copy of the magazine, she and Helen could just be made out in this photograph by using a magnifying glass. Indeed they are standing together in the middle of a top row of this gathering of solemn-faced men and women.
Courtesy of American Forests.

Hattie and Edward were both delegates to the American Forest Congress in Washington between January 2 and 6, 1905. Its purpose was, as Edward reported in the *Record,* "to establish a broader understanding of the forest in its relation to the great industries depending upon it; to advance the conservative use of the forest resources for both the present and the future need of these industries; to stimulate and unite all efforts to perpetuate the forest as a permanent resource of the Nation."[4] Hattie represented the Massachusetts American Forestry Association and took her youngest niece, Helen, a budding arborist, with her. Edward represented the Massachusetts Association and the Appalachian Mountain Club. He noted in his diary that he and Emily—who must have been feeling well that day—"picked up the two H's [at the Grafton] & went to the crowded Forestry meeting on January 3." The next day, he presented a resolution favoring the establishment of a national forest reserve in the White Mountains. In a special session at the National Theater on January 5, President Theodore Roosevelt gave his much anticipated address on "The Forest in the Life of a Nation."

Attendance at the Congress, as reported by *Forest and Irrigation,* far exceeded expectations, averaging a thousand at its eight sessions. Delegates "included practically all persons engaged directly in forest work, the leaders in state forest associations, and an unusually influential lot of representatives from the railroad, lumbering, mining, irrigation, and grazing interests of the country."[5] Writing about the Congress in the *Record,* Edward remarked: "Here were seventeen hundred men…of marked intelligence, who had assembled to give a week to practical discussions on this great business. 'Where the America of 1999 shall be in the supply of wood.'" While the ratio of men to women was overwhelming at this first Congress, one of the speakers was Mrs. Lydia Phillips Williams, a delegate from Minnesota who was chairman of the forestry committee of the International Federation of Women's Clubs.[6] Hattie and Emma's efforts would increasingly be made in the guise of enlisting the support of the women's clubs of America.[7] All of these efforts were greatly strengthened by the creation that year of the U.S. Forest Service within the Department of Agriculture with Gifford Pinchot at its helm.

* * *

Although she remained closely involved with the forest conservation movement, Hattie had broadened her conservation focus to nature in general but particularly bird and wildlife protection. Back in Boston following the American Forest Congress, she wrote that Emma had received a letter from their landlord and guide in South Carolina's Oconee Valley, where they had found *Shortia galacifolia* in March 1902. "He says…the dear plant is still safe. But that thousands of acres in that vicinity have been sold to a Baltimore Lumber Co. & he fears for the future. He speaks with real tenderness of Shortia & of what a loss it would be if it should be killed." Then she poured out her anger and frustration at the depredations being inflicted on nature:

> Will not this invader, Man, spare anything! Has he no respect for any-thing that has ever been created on this planet, but thinks that everything was put here that he might turn it into dollars & cents. Here comes a cry to save Shortia! Another, to save the Buffalo! Another from a different direction, 'Against the destruction of White Herons & Red Ibises on the Lower Amazon.' It makes one sick to think that civilized man can be such an iconoclast & savage. I wish some one with a pen of iron & ink of venom would write an invective as would make the hunter stand & blush & at least be ashamed of himself, if he would not mend his ways. And Man, as an animal is the least interesting & beautiful of all these things he is destroying!"[8]

Hattie's own passionate invective should have been published not just hidden in a letter to Edward.

Hattie and Emma began their long and loyal association with the American Ornithologists' Union (AOU) when they traveled to California to attend the Union's annual congress in San Francisco on May 15 and 16, 1903 (see chapter 11). They were named associate members during that meeting. It was through her friendship with Emma that Hattie was first drawn to bird watching and protection.

Emma was working on a pocket guide to common water and game birds, hawks, and owls of New England with her neighbor Harriet E. Richards, an associate of the AOU. The book was to be illustrated from photographs taken by George Curtis of specimens at the Museum of Comparative Zoology at Harvard and the Museum of the Boston Society of Natural History. Meanwhile, ornithologist and photographer Herbert K. Job, who made many contributions to the text, was pioneering in photographing many of these water birds in their natural habitat. Hattie and Emma had observed his painstaking techniques in June 1900, as she wrote Edward.[9]

The first of the bird conservation movements, the Massachusetts Audubon Society, had been founded in Boston in 1896 by Harriet (Mrs. Augustus) Hemenway after she read a description of bloody massacres at egret rookeries. Harriet was the daughter-in-law of philanthropist and archaeologist Mary Hemenway, widow of a trader and owner of a sugar plantation in Cuba. She was a longtime and generous parishioner of the South Congregational Church. Mary had left an estate of $15 million at her death in 1894, including a bequest to further the education of women in science. Two years later, Harriet Hemenway and her cousin Minna Hall gave afternoon teas at which many of Boston's fashionable women pledged to boycott hats decorated with bird feathers. They then convened a more formal meeting of prominent men and women to form the Massachusetts Audubon Society, drafting William Brewster, curator of mammals and ornithology at Harvard's Museum of Comparative Zoology and the country's leading field ornithologist, to be its president. The movement spread quickly to most other states.

Another important figure in the burgeoning bird protection movement was William Dutcher, a member of the bird protection committee at the American Ornithologists' Union. He had formulated the AOU Model Law as a blueprint for state legislatures in 1886 and continued to lobby for the measure, particularly to halt the sale of plume birds in New York. In 1900, Congress passed the Lacey Act to prohibit the interstate shipment of wild species killed in violation of state laws. This was the first federal conservation legislation. At the same time, Dutcher was assembling a warden force to guard rookeries in key coastal states, from Florida to Oregon.[10] In 1905, Dutcher became president of the new National Association of Audubon Societies for the Protection of Wild Birds and Animals (National Audubon Society) in New York which Hattie proceeded to help with fundraising and spreading the word. She mentioned in January that a rich man had pledged a large sum to Dutcher to support bird protection activities and that she had invited the Society's new young traveling agent to tea and took him to a lecture by Ernest Baynes at the Natural History Society: "He is trying to do for the Buffalo, what Mr. Dutcher is trying to do for the birds. Save them from extermination!" "If you really want me to," she continued, "I can write an article about Mr. Dutcher's work for the Record. Of how many words?"[11]

That March, Edward published Hattie's article "Preservation of Birds" about the work of the newly incorporated National Audubon Society under Dutcher's leadership, with graphic examples of the scandalous slaughter and treatment of birds. This was the only article in the *Lend A Hand Record* bearing her name, although she clearly wrote several more anonymously about her conservation interests or provided the material for Edward to do so. In this case, she described the progress being made by the thirty-six existing state societies to make and enforce laws to protect threatened bird populations, blaming "unprincipled men who are willing to kill for money," but placing major responsibility on "Woman, in her foolish and selfish love for adornment." "To a bird lover," she continued, "to see aigrettes [egrets' feathers] on a woman's hat pretending to be beautiful or ornamental, is as if one saw an Indian wear a human scalp. All the women who are members of the Massachusetts Audubon Society, and there are three thousand of them, pledge themselves not to wear aigrette, breast, or wing feathers which mean the death of a bird." Hattie concluded her long and impassioned appeal with a call for donations to be paid to William Dutcher.[12]

In New York in early April, Hattie wrote Edward that she planned to read her article, which she had just received, to Mary Dann and Emma that evening. While they were there, Emma and Hattie visited the Bronx Zoo and the Natural History Museum, where they saw the recently installed brontosaurus. Then they took the just completed subway ("now one of the wonders of New York") up to 126th Street to call on William Dutcher at the new headquarters of the National Audubon Society. Reacting to Dutcher's reports of the Society's latest efforts for bird protection in Florida, Hattie wrote Edward: "How much more beautiful & interesting Life would be if all birds could be so protected from brutes of men... that they would not be afraid of us," with an indignant parenthetical, "(I suppose even Roosevelt would go gunning, as he is now going wolf hunting from just a love to kill)."[13] It was hard to comprehend how the president who was becoming synonymous with conservation causes could at the same time gun down wild animals for sport and as trophies. A few months later, one of the Society's game wardens in Florida was shot to death while trying to defend the herons from plume hunters. In the *Record*'s October issue, Edward responded to Hattie's distress about this murder. He—and she—called for donations to cover the trial in Florida.[14]

Hattie continued to funnel the latest intelligence to Edward for further articles in the *Record* about Dutcher's work and that of Ernest H. Baynes in founding the American Bison Society and rebuilding and protecting herds of the nearly eradicated buffalo native to the North American continent, another cause enthusiastically supported by the huntsman president. She complained that she had had no success in persuading Lyman Abbott to publish similar appeals in *The Outlook*.

Getting the word out about the devastated conditions of the New Hampshire forests was now paramount. During 1905, momentum gathered for an orchestrated campaign to inform and raise support beyond the existing pool of activists for forest preservation in New England. The fall 1905 issues of *Forest and Irrigation* featured articles by experts such as Philip Ayres and Edwin Start and advocates like former New Hampshire governor Franklin W. Rollins, now president of the Society for the Protection of New Hampshire Forests. These illustrated the current appalling conditions and explained the proposed solutions behind the various bills that were being considered by Congress. Edward was honored with a photograph as being "among the very first to advocate the establishment of a White Mountain Forest Reserve." No mention was made of Mrs. Nichols or Miss Freeman. Edward's article, "Our Eastern Forests," appeared in the November issue. Describing the urgency of the situation in the White Mountains," he wrote: "The present processes of lumbering strip every inch of the country of every shrub and tree which is larger than a blackberry bush. This means that in the snows of winter and the consequent freshets of spring the soil itself is carried away...You cannot sit back in your chair and say that the twenty-first century may take care of itself."[15]

Hattie was in Italy for the first half of 1906 so she relied on Edward's progress reports. A far smaller American Forest Congress was held in the "New Willard Hotel" on January 16 and 17 where the chairman, Secretary of Agriculture James Wilson, who was also president of the American Forestry Association, appointed several committees. Gifford Pinchot was to be chairman of Resolutions while Edwin Start and Philip Ayres were appointed to two committees each, the latter to the Committee on the Forest Reserve Bill. Called upon for a short address, Edward urged all public-spirited citizens to consider and advocate for "the proposed White Mountain and Appalachian Forest Reserves."[16] The amalgamated bill "For the Purchase of Two National Forest Reserves...The Appalachian Forest Reserve and White Mountain Forest Reserve" was before the 59th Congress and so lobbying for the bill was underway in earnest. Edward reported in the May *Record* that the "Bills" were introduced in the Senate on March 9. But on March 25, he told Hattie: "About the Forests Pinchot and Ayers [*sic*] still think we shall get our Bill through, and I find the Carolina gentlemen are hopeful. I do not share their hopes, though of course I share their wishes. The side I see is of a determination among the Leaders to make the session short; and I think our Affair, like the copy Right affair, will be thrown on to another year."[17]

Hattie and Emma renewed their efforts on behalf of the bill that fall. Among the general announcements at the beginning of the November 1906 issue of *Forest and Irrigation* is one headed "Of Interest to Women." It reads: "On November 13, Misses E. G. Cummings of 16 Kennard Road, Brookline, Mass., and Harriet E. Freeman, of 37 Union Park, Boston, Mass., called at the offices of the Forest Service and the American Forestry Association, in the interest of the White Mountain and Southern Appalachian bill. It is hoped, among other things, they may be able to enlist the women's clubs in this important measure." Back in Washington in December, Edward wrote: "I do not write you from step to step about Forests though I think of nothing else, some days. It does not look very encouraging to me. Our new Forester, Mr. Bass is here and I had a long talk with him. I have [talked to Representative John] Dalzell [of Pennsylvania] twice, who is, I think as much a <u>steerer</u> of the House as Cannon. I dined by the side of a leading member of the House Friday, and he had never heard of the matter at all, and I had to begin at the very beginning. That is the sort of thing which discourages you. But we have two good months before us."[18]

By this time, Hattie had convinced herself that the real villain in holding up the bill was Speaker of the House Joseph Cannon, who controlled the Rules Committee and, therefore, which proposed bills could come to the House floor for debate. In December, as lobbying efforts intensified, she told Edward about a meeting on forestry that she attended at Boston's progressive Twentieth Century Club, of which Edward was a co-founder. Edwin Start was the speaker in place of Philip Ayres who was in Washington. "Perhaps you have already seen Mr. Ayres…or you may see him & also Mr. Start who is ready to go at any moment when he can be of use. Your sympathy & hope for the Bill is well known…Of course, if you know of anything under the light of Heaven that you can do, you will do it." In another mid-December letter, she wrote: "I can hardly control my expression of contempt & vindictiveness towards him [Cannon]. You, as a man, look on both sides, as you say a woman can't, & so have no word of disapproval (that is putting it mild!) Mr. Start says to me that we dislike him because he will not look at this question as we do. But that he is popular in Washington & will certainly be elected Speaker for the next Congress."[19]

In a letter written in late December 1906, in which she told Edward about her decision to attend the annual congress of the American Association for the Advancement of Science (AAAS) in New York, having joined that prestigious organization with the support of her friend Amadeus Grabau, Hattie passed on what she had learned about the continuing destruction of the forests in the White Mountains during a brief visit to Intervale. On her return from Intervale, a colleague in the Massachusetts Forestry Association had "stated the political side of [the forestry bill] in a clearer way than it had ever been put to me before…The Speaker is steering the Republican Party. Forests, one way or the other, are nothing to him. If

N.H. were Democratic & the State was to be won for the Party by buying her Forests, he would do it. But the State is governed by the Boston & Maine. The more logging the more railroad traffic, & the two corporations play into each others hands." Congressman John W. Weeks of Massachusetts, who summered in the White Mountains and who had taken up the cause after being appointed by the Speaker to the House Committee on Agriculture, had telegraphed "Interview with Speaker Cannon does not indicate likelihood of consideration of Forestry Bill. We have not given up yet, however." "I have," exclaimed Hattie, "& it makes me half sick with unhappiness. The Glen Road & all about Glen Ellis Falls are likely to go this winter...I don't see how you can have one word of justification for Cannon. I think that to all who love Forests, he will be thought as much of an enemy to his country as Benedict Arnold or Jefferson Davis."[20]

At the AAAS meeting, Hattie met up with Grabau, Mary Dann, and University of North Carolina geologist Collier Cobb, another friend from her student days. She wrote Edward that his geologist friend Professor Charles H. Hitchcock of Dartmouth, who had named Mt. Hale after him and awarded him the L.L.D., "said his anger was against Gov. Harriman of N.H. who sold vast areas of N.H. forests to Lumber Cos. for $18,000. I did not ask him in what year. But you probably know."[21] Julius H. Ward, in his polemical article "White Mountain Forests in Peril" in the February 1893 issue of *Atlantic Monthly*, had blamed Governor Walter Harriman's decision in 1867 to sell 172,000 acres of forestland, including land in the White Mountains, to private speculators for $26,000.[22]

Once again, Edward's address at the Forestry Association's annual meeting was published in the January 1907 issue of *Forest and Irrigation*. But what must truly have set Hattie on fire against Speaker Cannon was Edwin Start's article "Why the Bill Hangs Fire: An Explanation and a Plea." Emphasizing that the bill had been advocated by all the important interests involved, "has met with no opposition from the Senate of the United States...has received the unanimous endorsement of a large and able committee of the House of Representatives...and has been repeatedly urged by the President in messages to Congress," he laid the blame at the feet not just of an obstructionist Speaker but also the inertia of the

American electorate: "The people in a democracy get from their representatives just what they insist upon having."[23]

To find that Speaker Cannon and his legislative entourage were on board a Caribbean cruise ship that she and Emma joined in March 1907 was more than Hattie could bear.

14

Filling the Gap

For Ethel Freeman, a devotee of Shakespeare's Italian plays as well as Italian music, literature, and art, Italy was sheer enchantment, stimulating her creative juices, just as Hattie had hoped. Since graduating from Smith College, Ethel was a student at Boston's Museum of Fine Arts as well as producing and acting in the Bard's plays for the Lend A Hand Society Drama Club. In addition to lengthy stays in Naples, Sicily, and Rome (where Hattie was presented to the Pope), the three women spent two weeks in Tunis, and shorter stays in Florence, Venice, and the Italian lakes, with day trips to countless picturesque hilltop towns. The women's Italian tour in the first half of 1906 is well documented in their letters to family members at home. Hattie wrote her-sister-in-law on February 13 about her cousin Edwin's generosity: "I wrote Ned when at Taormina, & shall write him again. I never forget that I am indebted to him for the great pleasure of this trip."[1]

A letter Hattie wrote Edward from Venice describes a high point: "How I wish you could be with Ethel & me now in our room…Our Hotel is on the Grand Canal." Their first-floor room overlooking the water was opposite Santa Maria della Salute: "On the opposite bank are boats stationed, brilliant with Japanese lanterns, & there singing goes on until midnight. Trovatore, Carmen, Bella Napoli, & all sorts of entrancing airs…Ethel is quite overcome by it…Here it is Desdemona & Portia who become real to her…it is impossible to put into language the growth, the awakening, the delight which she has had on this trip...she will certainly not be content long at home after this.[2]

In the meantime, Hattie's youngest niece Helen wrote her that Ethel's friend Arthur Berenson, one of art historian Bernard Berenson's three lawyer cousins, to whom she would become briefly engaged, had spent the evening with the Freemans at West Newton: "He is certainly a very interesting talker."[3] It is possible that Ethel met Arthur Berenson through Bernard's sister, Senda Berenson, who taught physical education and introduced many different sports at Smith College for twenty years until 1911.

Hattie had escaped Boston for now but the spiritual and cultural unease of the generation of Boston Brahmins who grew to adulthood during the industrial revolution following the Civil War had begun to manifest itself in unsettling ways, and not just in Boston. Shortly after their arrival in Italy, Hattie heard from several quarters that there had been a crisis of faith in Edward's own family. His second son, forty-two-year-old Union College English professor Edward E. Jr., had attended a series of sermons by a visiting British Presbyterian evangelist, Dr. W. J. Dawson, in Schenectady, and had decided to convert (his wife and sons were already Presbyterians). In mid-January, Edward told Hattie in Naples that Edward Jr. had spent most of a day with him and told him about "his Religious experiences."[4] On January 28, his son wrote, "Dear Papa, I became a member of the First Presbyterian Church on Thursday evening by appearing before the session and making a statement of my belief."[5]

In February, Edward and the rest of his family and the "elite" from the SCS were shocked and angered by Edward Jr.'s public announcement of his conversion and apparent denunciation of Unitarianism. Hattie's friends sent her the newspaper clippings, of which one, headlined "Dr. Hale's Sons New Light," quoted part of the son's explanation: "We all come to a place in our lives when we feel that there is something lacking in our life, and Christ speaks to us in that still, small voice, and if we accept him he brings us into the new life…Most of you are aware of the fact that I was a Unitarian, and that they are known as a sect which lays more stress on reason and intellect than on the heart. Who would have thought that I would have been led to accept Christ in a revival meeting in a Methodist church?"[6]

Hattie was so incensed by Edward Jr.'s apostasy and disloyalty that she wrote Helen Freeman from Sicily, "I wish the young man could have a letter of reproach from some Unitarian every day for the next year. I have written mine but do not mail it because if Mrs. Hale should ever know it…she would probably never let Mr. Hale visit me again…What a shame that he, of all others, who has his Father's name, should do it. How much more becoming had his name been Peter!"[7] But she must have decided to send the letter (although it has not been found among Edward Jr.'s papers) because Edward was apparently grateful for her action. He admitted in shorthand that he had been very wretched about it all but had not wanted to tell her so. He believed that the blame could be laid on the emotional barrenness of his son's married life: "To have such a person at the age of 40 speak to us as he does in that paper, is to shew that he was very badly brought up…You cannot say in Public, nor can you say, in kindness to him, what Susy says to me, very kindly, and very well that the poor boy has been dying 'for want of Love'…the real revelation is that the Presbyterian church is so far on its good behavior that it fairly bids for Unitarians, opening to them its gates, and making no fuss about creed."

He concluded, "When I read your letter to Edward, I was very glad you had written it, <u>and</u> sent it, <u>and</u> not submitted it to me."[8] In September, after telling Hattie that he no longer knew if Edward intended to give up his professorship at Union College and "study" in New York (apparently at the Presbyterian Union Theological Seminary) as he had mentioned six months earlier, he wrote sadly of the son to whom he had once been so close, "He does not give me his confidence which is the painful business to me."[9]

The Hales seemed to believe that Edward Jr. was unhappy in his marriage and yet he remained married to Rose to the end of his life and Edward generally spoke fondly of her in his letters. But there was growing alarm about the increase of divorce in the United States. President Roosevelt called for a National Congress on Uniform Divorce Laws in Washington between February 19 and 22, 1906. Forty-two governors sent 150 men (and very few women) to consult on this complex issue and Edward wrote Hattie, "as you see, of course, it is very important. I have to give more or less time to it."[10] In fact, he gave just the opening prayer, including these words:

"If the households are pure, the States will be pure; if the States are pure the nation will be pure, and thus shall we be that happy people whose God is the Lord." This seems reminiscent of his 1881 sermon on Unitarian Principles, in which he said "the Unitarian Church demands purity of character from those who belong to it," and particularly from its ministers. This vein of hypocrisy was seen again in his idealistic strictures for marriage sent to Martha Adams in 1900. But Edward Sr. did not relate his own marital discontent to that of his son and namesake, at least in his surviving letters to Hattie, where the idea of leaving Emily was never mentioned. Society remained deeply disapproving and punitive of divorce, particularly if one of the divorcees was or had been a minister.

A prime example of hypocrisy over sexual ethics at this time was that of Professor George D. Herron, a radical Christian Socialist who was minister of the First Congregational Church in Burlington, Iowa, before wealthy socialist Mrs. Elizabeth D. Rand endowed a chair of Applied Christianity for him at Iowa College. Herron fell in love with Mrs. Rand's daughter Carrie and eventually his wife sued him for divorce on the grounds of deserting her and their two children. The story of how this divorce and remarriage in 1901 were attacked by the American press and clergy is the subject of a chapter, "The Story of a Lynching," in muckraker Upton Sinclair's book *The Brass Check*. Sinclair argued that his friend had married too young and was "wretchedly unhappy," a repeat of the Henry Bernard Carpenter story of 1887-88. In Sinclair's view, Herron, "as one of the most popular radical orators in the country...was a dangerous man to the 'interests,' and here was the chance to destroy him." Edward's friend, the Reverend Newell D. Hillis, successor to Henry Ward Beecher and Lyman Abbott as minister of Brooklyn's Plymouth Church, "refused to shake hands with him, turning his back on him on a public platform." Another minister, Thomas Dixon, with similar views to Hillis, portrayed Herron as "a gorilla" in his novel *The One Woman*. Newspapers called Herron's marriage to Carrie Rand a "free love wedding," "just a say-so to be terminated at pleasure."

Herron highlighted this hypocrisy in his response: "The ethics of the legally and ecclesiastically enforced family make it possible for a man to live a life of monstrous wrong, of ghastly falsehood, even of unbridled lust, and yet be highly moral according to the standards by which we are judged."[11] Sinclair persuaded the couple to go abroad. Edward undoubtedly reacted to this case with tolerance, as he had to the revelations in 1887 that the Reverend Henry Bernard Carpenter was bigamously married and to a myriad other cases of parishioners and friends desperate to escape unhappy marriages. But once again it demonstrates Edward's hypocrisy when it came to his own personal life.

Two old friends died while Hattie was abroad. The first, on February 27, was Edward's brilliant scientist friend Samuel P. Langley, secretary of the Smithsonian Institution. Edward and Ulysses S. Pierce, Edward's deputy in the Senate chaplaincy, conducted Langley's funeral at Pierce's All Souls Unitarian Church: "Just the people I wanted were there, ranging from the Chief Justice and the President to the black men who swept out the Smithsonian Institute," Edward wrote Hattie. One of Langley's friends thought he had died of a broken heart, "not from the Failure of the Aeroplane," which another friend said did not fail, "but because he was so sensitive that he could not bear ridicule."[12]

Six months earlier, Edward had written an article for the *Record* defending "Mr. Langley's Aerodrome," concluding, "It is a pity to have to say that if one of the first scientific men of our time had not been too busy to wish to 'make money,'...the reader would have seen in the air before this time what he has not seen, as one and another of the aerodromes went out on its daily message above his head."[13] On December 17, 1903, just nine days after the failure of the second Langley Aerodrome test, Orville Wright quietly succeeded in piloting his and his brother Wilbur's simpler flying machine with a far lighter engine on the beach at Kitty Hawk, North Carolina. Langley's longtime supporter Alexander Graham Bell remained convinced that the Langley machine could fly. He encouraged Glenn Curtiss to persuade the Smithsonian to allow him to restore and modify the Aerodrome and it finally flew in 1914. Orville Wright was enraged when the Smithsonian displayed this modified machine as the first airplane capable of manned flight.

In late March, Hattie heard from several quarters that Mary Cobb had suffered another stroke on March 12 after two years of semi-invalidism following an initial stroke two years earlier. She died a week later. Recalling Miss Mary's unselfish dedication to the SCC Sunday school for many years, Edward wrote, "And indeed, indeed, though you have heard me say hard things about her, I am not such a fool as not to know her absolute loyalty to me and her unselfishness the moment the idea of Duty came in."[14] Despite her own ambivalence about her longtime companion, Hattie must have been reminded of the Freeman family's three-generation friendship with the Cobbs of Brewster. "I am sure we must all be grateful that there was so little lingering and so little suffering," she wrote her sister-in-law.[15]

1906 was the year of great earthquakes. In the same letter of April 14 in which she described the view from their room in Venice, Hattie mentioned the accounts they were reading of the eruptions of Vesuvius that had begun in May 1905, and which they must have observed when they were in Naples in February. The eruptions reached their climax on April 7 with lava fountains and earthquakes and a 40,000-foot eruptive column of ash and gas. At 5.13 in the morning of April 18, a devastating 7.8 magnitude earthquake struck San Francisco, California's most populated city at the time. Subsequent fires, many of them deliberately set, virtually obliterated its buildings. Ironically, the previous evening, the great Italian tenor Enrico Caruso, a native of Naples, starred in Bizet's opera *Carmen* in San Francisco's Grand Opera House, whose roof collapsed in the earthquake.

In a letter which Hattie later marked "San Francisco Earthquake," Edward described the involvement of two leading Unitarian friends in the relief operations. One of these was Major General Adolphus Greely, president of the standing committee of All Souls Unitarian Church and Edward's good friend, to whom he had introduced Hattie on her visit to Washington fifteen months earlier. Greely had been appointed commander of the Pacific Coast detachments of the U.S. Army just that winter and was now in charge of organizing security and relief operations. Another was Senator George C. Perkins of California, a self-made millionaire, who "moved in the Senate that 500,000 dollars be appropriated for the expenses of relief," and, as Edward wrote Hattie, told a friend that he would pay it himself if the Senate did not vote for it. "Whether he is worth two cents now, is I suppose doubtful," wrote Edward. "But he is brave and energetic as ever."[16]

Writing to Collier Cobb from Verona, Italy, on April 22, Hattie remarked of the two catastrophes: "Does it not seem to you that in the evolution of forces, it seems but right that the Creative Force should not have ordained Life on this planet until the eruptive forces had ceased? Such questions trouble me a great deal, & leave much that can not be answered."[17] So was Hattie, after all, a believer in "special creation"? Who or what was the "Creative Force" in her world view? That fall, Hattie researched and wrote one of her papers on the geological cause of the earthquake (as it was understood at that time) which she read to the Home & Country Club at her home and then passed on to Edward so that he would be well informed when talking to his scientist friends in Washington.

In the meantime, the Hales continued to be anxious about their architect son Bertie's fragile health. Shortly after arriving to take a rest cure in St. Moritz, Switzerland in January 1906, he contracted a severe case of influenza which kept him in bed there for two weeks. Then in May, the Hales heard that Bertie was in "a hospital" after suffering for three days from terrible pain in his kidneys. A recovering Bertie and his wife Greta would spend the July 4 holiday at Matunuck where the family was evidently shocked by his appearance. Edward wrote Hattie, "Greta goes this morning: poor child, she is sadly divided between her children in New Jersey and her husband here. He will stay with us for the present. It is a perfect place for rest." Emily, who was at Folly Cove with Nelly and Gabrielle, wrote Edward, "I am shocked to hear of Berty's having lost fifty pounds. I think there must be some mistake about it."[18] But they all must have wondered about the underlying cause of these severe health problems in a man of just forty. Had his wild youth at Harvard and as an architectural student at the Beaux Arts in Paris exposed him to some insidious infection? During their courtship in 1891, Bertie had told Greta about the severe headaches and problems with his eyes that he had suffered ever since his stint as a field archaeologist near Athens, Greece, in 1890. Passionately in love, Greta begged him then not to tell her father about his health problems for fear he would insist on a delay in their marriage.[19]

Hattie was always sympathetic about any reports of ill health or troubles in Edward's large family. Responding to her inquiries about Emily, he admitted in April that "the least thing upsets her, and so it does not do to make any arrangements for the future…we cannot leave her alone…She does not know why but she is Home-sick." Hattie and her party were due back in Boston at the end of May and Edward assured her "As long as you stay in Boston I shall stay there. The day you go to New Hampshire, I propose to go to Matunuck. How Emily will feel about this I do not know." On the subject of the Hales' August visit to Intervale, Edward wrote, "Simply, I should like to do just what we did last year. I am afraid you will not like to have Mrs. Hale. But that you must decide."[20]

Busying herself on her return to Boston by organizing her collection of Italian botanical specimens, Hattie sent one or two for identification to Harvard's Gray Herbarium, of which she was a subscribing member.[21] She also threw herself back into her work for the Fatherless and Widows Society. Edward wrote admiringly of this tireless work, reminding her that, "if you take such care of Mrs. Hildreth, and Bud [illegible], and Miss Holyoke and your 64 widows, you must remember that so you are acquitted from worrying about the Slum People, whom you do not like and whom, perhaps, you would not know how to help so well."[22] On July 11, from Matunuck, Edward referred once again to Hattie's growing xenophobia: "I have been thinking that you would escape your 'Furriners' if we had carried out our old plan, and U had a house on the 99 acre lot here. I have not seen a person not of the American type since I came here 8 days ago. Negroes, Indians, Yes! But no Eye-Talians, Irish, Germans or Russians!"[23]

Hattie, who had longed to leave the exclusive Back Bay and return to her house in Union Park six years before, had been shocked to find that her once peaceful, orderly, homogeneous neighborhood was now a noisy, crowded slum. She became interested in the Immigration Restriction League founded in 1894 by three Harvard graduates who opposed the influx of "undesirable immigrants." Initially, the League disseminated information and statistics about the floodtide of humanity filling up cities like Boston through books, pamphlets, meetings, and numerous newspaper and journal articles. Another influence on Hattie may have been the writings of economist and statistician Francis A. Walker, president of MIT from 1881 to 1897. Walker directed the U.S. Censuses of 1870 and 1880 which indicated that the ethnic composition of America was undergoing a radical change. By 1887, he had decided that the "foreign element" was behind the growing confrontation between capital and labor. At the same time, several other intellectuals and Harvard professors, including two of Hattie's favorite instructors, Darwinist John Fiske and geologist Nathaniel S. Shaler, began in the late 1880s to denounce foreign influences on their own Anglo-Saxon or Teutonic American culture, profoundly influencing their students. Throughout this period, the leading voices for continuing democracy and tolerance were those of Edward Everett Hale and Harvard's president Charles W. Eliot.

But, in 1901, the IRL began adopting increasingly racialist language under the leadership of its firebrand co-founder Prescott F. Hall. Astoundingly high immigration statistics in the earliest years of the twentieth century (the number in 1905 exceeded one million and kept growing the following two years) brought more and more politicians and intellectuals to Hall's side. His publication "Selection of Immigration" and Senator Henry Cabot Lodge's article "Efforts to Restrict Undesirable Immigration" in *The Century* magazine in January 1904 fueled public angst and radicalized many policy makers. In the meantime, Senator William P. Dillingham of Vermont spearheaded restriction as chairman of the Senate Commission on Immigration. Even President Roosevelt sent a message to Congress in 1904 that only the "right kind" of immigrant could ensure the nation's health, although advising Congress to avoid discrimination on the basis of national origin or religious beliefs.

While Hattie was staying in Northeast Harbor, Maine, in July 1906, she exchanged letters with Edward about immigration. She was collecting relevant literature and now he said that he would send or bring to her at Intervale transcripts of Massachusetts Congressman August P. Gardner's forceful speeches in the House of Representatives on the need for restricting immigration. Gardner was the son-in-law of Senator Henry Cabot Lodge, a longtime friend of Edward. Edward told Hattie that the solution he favored differed from Gardner's and proceeded to describe a quota system:

"It seems to me that early in the year, say in January a Report could be prepared here by experts, from different States, as to the number of foreigners wanted that year…This could be proclaimed, here and in Europe. Our Emigration Offices in Europe, of whom we have a competent number, would then give out <u>numbered</u> permits…and when they had given out 1,000,000…or 750,000 if that were the number agreed upon no more should be received that year."

There were two counteracting problems, as Edward saw it: "For all such plans the difficulty is that the well organized steamship companies make a great deal of money by bringing the largest number possible…<u>and</u> that on the whole <u>employers</u> in the large cities, do not want to scatter the emigrants. Rents, and wages both would be affected if we could send 50,000 people out from the older Boston, and really well meaning people…do not want to reduce Rents in Boston or to raise Wages." Edward's opinions were part of the currency of debate on the proposed immigration act in the Senate, debates which Edward, who had been suggesting solutions to immigration problems since the 1840s and 1850s, certainly watched with great interest and discussed with many of his friends in the Senate. He continued to update his readers on immigration issues in the *Record*, always seeking to find a midpoint between the extremists of either side. [24]

On the subject of extremes, it was a short leap from immigration restriction to the "pseudoscience" of eugenics. That year, 1906, Wilbur M. Hays, assistant U.S. secretary of agriculture and president of the American Breeders Association, announced the formation of a Committee on Eugenics "to investigate all proper means of influencing heredity with the idea of encouraging the increase of families of good blood, and of discouraging the vicious elements in the cross-bred American civilization." Formed in 1903 by scientists and professional plant and animal breeders to promote the study of heredity in their fields, the ABA became the first national, membership-based group to promote eugenics research in the United States and educate the public.[25]

Hattie's apparent interest in this twisting of Darwin's theory of "survival of the fittest" and the recently rediscovered lessons of Gregor Mendel's 1860s discoveries in plant genetics fit right in with her longtime studies of various theories of evolution and now her targeted xenophobia. In December 1908, she reported that her nephew had heard Harvard President Charles W. Eliot speak before the Economics Club: "Fred thought he [Eliot] was drawing in his horns a little on unlimited emigration, which he has heretofore advocated. The conditions now are getting to be too overwhelming." She wondered if Edward had received "the last publication of the Restriction Emigration League, 'Eugenics, Ethics & Emigration' by Prescott S. [*sic*] Hall. Have you? And have you read it? It is worth while. You may remember I made you a Life Member."[26] By that time, six months before Edward's death, the eugenics movement had captured the enthusiasm and support of many liberal Protestant clergymen, including Edward's friend Newell D. Hillis, minister of Brooklyn's Plymouth Church.[27] There is no evidence in Edward's letters to Hattie that he subscribed to this already controversial pseudoscience.

Although he remained intellectually engaged in leading issues, particularly the eastern forests reservation bill, Edward was increasingly frail physically. On August 3, 1906, he, Nelly, and Ethel Freeman traveled together to Intervale while Emily stayed at home. This stay was very quiet; Edward took slow walks in the meadow in front of the Red House, sat on a chair in the pine grove dictating letters to Hattie, or she read to him while Nelly and Ethel painted his portrait.[28]

Edward promised Hattie that he would return to Intervale toward the end of September but once again Emily's own frailty put paid to that idea, as he wrote Hattie on September 14: "I must give up, and you must all thought of our coming next week or the next. It is all what women (and their Doctors) call <u>Nerves</u>. But that is a reality, as much as smoke is…Every time when I even suggest the subject, she trembles, as if I proposed her going to the guillotine. Not because it is Intervale. I think she would rather go there, than almost anywhere…When she arrived here from Matunuck, you would have said she had come from a battle-field." He concluding despairingly, "She spends almost all the time on the Sofa or in Bed. I surrender to this unwillingly enough, as you may guess." The next day, he repeated his frustration: "I am home sick for the Red House, the Piazza, Moat and the valley up or down. Indeed you have guessed from my letters that we are pretty stupid here."[29]

Edward passed on worrying news he had heard from Howell Reed about renewed insurgency problems on the Atkins's Soledad plantation, including the theft of two hundred of their horses. Whatever her level of concern for her Cousin Edwin's plight in Cuba, Hattie did not respond to this news in her surviving letters. As described in chapter 13, the issues which most exercised her during these years were the preservation of New Hampshire forests and birds and wildlife.

Hattie must have been both surprised and disappointed when, shortly after the Hales' return to Washington for a third winter, Edward remarked, "When I came, I thought seriously that I might resign on the first of January though I did not say that even to you. Pierce and my own Senators talked me out of that, and for the present I shall say no more about my succession." Feeling bored and lonely before the congressional and social season was underway in Washington, he tried to pin Hattie down to attending a "grand Archaeological Meeting" there in early January: "The one thing I look forward to is your visit and you say nothing about it…Pray come, as early as you can, and stay as late as you can." Two days later, he tried again: "Of course if you like to go to Mr. Foster's party I shall go with you, and so to the President's…All the Departments are at work as much in the Recess as if Congress were at work. Be sure to let me know by what train you come so that I may meet you."[30] He was dismayed when she decided not to attend this meeting. "Now, really, there is not so much on this programme to interest me, as I expected. Seriously, do you think it is worth my coming on to it?" she asked. Perhaps she realized that his family dynamics, particularly Emily's neediness, would make it unlikely that he could spend much time with her. As he put it, "never was Life so much interrupted as mine."[31] Instead, she promised that she would come to Washington in March for a longer visit. As things turned out, Hattie may have looked back on this watershed decision with regret.

Instead of Washington, Hattie suddenly decided to travel at the end of the year on her own to New York to attend the annual meeting of the American Association for the Advancement of Science, as described in chapter 13. Back in Boston, she signed up for lectures on a wide range of subjects, continued her volunteer work with the Woman's National Indian Association and the Fatherless and Widows Society, and joined several more clubs and professional groups, telling Edward that the list of her memberships was now surprisingly long. She admitted to what was driving her across all fronts that winter: "Why am I doing so many things? Simply that I may not have time to think of myself. Mrs. Andrews says, 'You are doing too much, you must stop or you will break down.' Honestly, I believe it never comes to her mind of what a hole in my life your leaving here makes for me & that I am simply trying to fill it up... Not one of my near friends has ever had the apprehension to say to me that although it might be the best thing for you, she was sorry for me."[32] This was classic sublimation.

Despairing of the South Congregational Church under Edward's professorial associate minister, Hattie continued to look for another spiritual home, experimenting by attending Reform Jewish services at Temple Israel to hear the liberal Rabbi Charles Fleischer preach: "I went to Rabbi Fleischer's service again yesterday, with pleasure & profit. He is giving a course on the Old Testament, 'Face to Face with the Bible,' he calls it. He said yesterday 'It is said God made Man in His Image. But each one of us make God in our image, as we make our conception of Him, according to our own spiritual mindedness.' He also said 'In the fullness of time we shall understand why love gives us sorrow as well as happiness.' My mind dwelt much on that."[33] Now in his twelfth year at Temple Israel, Fleischer was about to move his wealthy congregation to a brand new, custom-designed-and-built Moorish-style tabernacle on Commonwealth Avenue. Edward Hale attended the dedication ceremony. There Fleischer would reintroduce Sunday services, preaching to audiences composing almost as many non-Jews as Jews.

Hattie probably continued to attend regularly to hear Fleischer preach but, following his public announcement that he admired Emerson more than he did Moses, he began to feel it was time for him to leave the Temple. When Rabbi Emeritus Solomon Schindler preached a sermon in 1911, he remarked that it had been a mistake to try and make Jews more like Gentiles. Fleischer riposted that he did want to make Jews more like Gentiles and hoped to fuse all

Americans into a new people, in other words the melting-pot theory. He left to establish Boston's first community church, the Sunday Commons, a nonsectarian religion for persons of all backgrounds.[34] By this time, it was becoming clearer that Hattie did not subscribe to assimilation of all races, ethnic groups, and even creeds.

In the meantime, Hattie's preferred minister was enjoying the Washington social whirl once again, having attended a party at the White House, with other receptions and meetings to look forward to. Emily was usually confined to the house with palsy and some mental confusion, so that it was Nelly who was his social companion and hostess. Nelly had also opened a Washington studio and accepted many portrait commissions. The oldest son, Arthur, and his wife lived nearby, and Susan was often there during the winter. Edward was stimulated by the many important issues being debated in the Senate and his friendships with men and women of intellect. But Hattie, facing the reality of bitter cold and ice in Boston and feeling very alone in her large house as she approached her sixtieth birthday, began to snipe at him: "Well! How are Tuesdays & Fridays with you? <*The same as other days or is there still some*> poetry & romance <*to them*>?" Then, pressing the guilt button a little harder, she wrote, "It certainly is surprising when you have to be so careful of yourself here that you can do so much there…I hope you won't be scornful any more when people ask you if you have had a pleasant winter in Washington. You would certainly find a winter here irksome & tiresome in comparison."[35]

Early in February, Hattie reached a real low in a wrenching letter in which she told him that she had made her booking with Emma and another birding friend for a month-long Caribbean cruise departing New York on March 5. She had decided it was hopeless to expect to see much of him if she came to Washington. His days as he described them were too broken up and, "You would not or could not come to see me in my hotel, & it really might be a disappointment or even an annoyance such as my two former visits to Washington were." But "what will you do after the 4th of March, when your duties end?" she asked. "Probably stay on there, because now it is Nelly's home, & she will want to stay. I shall be here in April & May & then go to Intervale, or somewhere early in June," and then she came to the point: "I have lingered here in Boston many Junes <*because I would not leave you*>. But now, much has changed <*you have left me four winters. You can not*> expect <*me to feel just the same as I did before*>. And I feel that I must have June in the exquisite beauty of the country, instead of the commonplace-ness of Union Park. If you are here in April & May, <*we will make the most of it*>. But the later <*you return*> in April, <*the less we shall see of each other*>."[36]

In mid-February, Hattie enjoyed a visit by her close friend Mary Dann. Together, they visited many favorite haunts and old friends, including their retired Boston Tech geology professor William H. Niles. Then Hattie and Ethel Freeman decided to throw a joint birthday party at Union Park in early March since Hattie would be away on her sixtieth birthday: "The party was charming but no credit to me! My nieces did it all. While conversation was going on, all stopped to listen to distant music which came nearer & nearer as the girls came down stairs, singing their Italian songs & dressed in their Italian costumes." After a standup supper, they all returned to the parlor where the nieces played out "two excellent charades. The back parlor was the stage, & the sliding door made excellent curtains. The first was Panama, in honor of our [planned] visit there… The other charade was Cousin Grace…Grace was quite touched by it." Now, as Hattie packed two trunks upstairs, she told Edward, "We leave for New York tomorrow at three O'clk."[37]

Already despising House Speaker Joseph Cannon as she did, Hattie's shock was palpable when she discovered that he and a congressional party were on board when they joined their cruise ship, the S.S. Bluecher. She began her first letter by expressing her delight in the man who would be sitting next to her at her table throughout the cruise, a Mr. Hanscom of New London, Connecticut, "who is constructor & designer, perhaps I should say the architect of great naval ships of war. He designed the Maine, also the two great steamers of the Pacific Ocean, The Dakota & The Minnesota. He is'nt [*sic*] at all a war like man, but very mild & gentle. We think alike on Forestry, Emigration, Indians & War Ships. So I told him we ought to go into partnership." But her comments about Cannon were uniformly negative and strongly tinged with Brahmin snobbery. "Fortunately he is not much to be seen. At the table he sits far at my back, & his chair is on the other side of the deck." All the passengers had been invited to a reception to meet the Speaker the night before, but "Of course, neither Emma nor I went."

Hattie and Emma were always among the passengers who took advantage of excursions wherever they moored, including a train ride to Caracas through the mountains from the Venezuelan port of La Guaira, where, as Hattie described it, "the mountains rose directly up from the sea, perfectly familiar to me from a picture that Father had."[38] Back on board ship, Hattie and her friends heard Cannon speak (he was being encouraged by his friends to run for the presidency in 1908): "It was but cheap oratory," was Hattie's predictable reaction. As for the principal intent of the Congressional party, "There are men on board who say [they] are going down to Panama 'to kill Roosevelt,' to make an inspection [of work on the canal] which may be unfavorable," she reported.[39] In her next letter, Hattie explained that, because the ship had been put in quarantine for six days due to an outbreak of yellow fever in the Venezuelan port, the party had been held on board all day in blistering heat on arrival in Colon harbor. The outraged passengers were released the following morning to travel through the Canal Zone on two special trains, one for the Congressional delegation, the other for the tourists. "The train was run back on siding for us to see the work done," was all that Hattie had to say about the immense work of digging the channel.

As the Bluecher steamed along the north shore of Cuba heading to Havana, Emma Cummings and another woman in the Boston party requested an interview with the seventy-one-year-old House Speaker to discuss the forestry bill. Characteristically obdurate, Hattie refused to join in, although sitting close enough to overhear Cannon's rejection: "The Appalachian Bill is all up…He cares nothing for forests. He said if this appropriation were made for N.H. all the states would want the same for their forests & for everything else. He didn't seem to know or care anything about water supply, or flow of rivers, or the washing away of the soil." She concluded, in disgust, "Observe, Cannon now has increase of salary, by allowing a Bill to come up which provided for it! With a party like this on board one is not apt to have their respect for Government increased."[40]

Hattie's letter describing a near disaster in which she and Emma were involved at Nassau in the Bahamas apparently never reached Edward but Congressman J. Hampton Moore gave a gripping account in his lively and informative book about the Caribbean expedition, *With Speaker Cannon*.[41] The old tender that was transporting groups of passengers back to the ship after they been stuck on shore due to severe weather almost foundered when returning with the last group of about 150, including Hattie, Emma, and the Speaker and his party. "Everyone was on deck to welcome us after our absence of three days!" Hattie wrote in another letter. "After I was on board, I learned more of our peril, from those who saw us from the Ship, especially from Mr. Hanscom."[42]

Hattie stayed on in New York for a few more days after the Bluecher docked on April 7. There she received Edward's letter informing her that the Merrimans had agreed to rent their Intervale property to the new British ambassador, Edward's friend James Bryce, for the summer. Three days later, Hattie wrote that she had got "the situation from Ethel, who called on Mrs. Merriman last week. She was at a dinner company with Prof. [William] James, Cambridge. He leaned across the table & said to her, 'do you want to rent your house this summer?' She said, 'Certainly not! My grandchild is to spend the summer with me.'" The Merrimans' son, a history instructor, later professor, at Harvard, and his wife would have four children. "It seems that Mr. Bryce had appealed to Prof. James to find him a suitable place for the summer. And on further interviews the Merrimans considered it more favorably…The Embassadors [*sic*] had always been to the seashore, & she felt they should know the beauty of our mountains."

Hattie felt sorely done by as she found out that two of the cottages she would have preferred for the summer were now to be rented to members of the British Legation. Instead, she had been backed into taking the despised Red House (not to be confused with the Red House in Matunuck). Thoroughly upset, she declared, "this will be my last summer at Intervale. So far as I can foresee & plan for my own life in the future, I shall go abroad in the summer of 1908."[43] But everything turned out better than she could have hoped. She was able to rent a larger and more attractive house and sublet the Red House to a single man from the embassy.

On April 16, en route to Boston, Edward and Nelly attended the dedication of Bertie's most important building to that point, the Engineers Building on New York's 40th Street, which his proud father called "a great triumph." Bertie's reputation was growing since his design for the new Post Office building in New Orleans had recently won out over entries from some of America's leading architects. On Sunday, April 20, an exhausted Edward wrote in his diary: "Victoria Victoria! Libertas libertas! Home Home! No more fatigue. No more distress. Never, never to make any more appointments to do anything or to say anything." The next day, Sunday, he stopped by Union Park where he and Hattie "overhauled drawer No. 1 of the old college papers." And so, for a few weeks, they resumed their former life of work, drives, and lunches together.

Two months later, Hattie wrote from Intervale, "Here I am in Mrs. Currie's house. It is perfectly charming & I am in rapture that I am to live here in these lovely surroundings for four months, June 20—Oct. 20, with practically no break." She had been very relieved to escape the city because, "The warm days & nights which came at the last before I left Boston, made the people of my neighborhood swarm in the streets. At the same moment, there was a hurdy-gurdy going in front, & a phonograph in the back of the house. It seemed as if I should go crazy. This peaceful quiet, with only the songs of the birds, is Heaven in comparison." She was expecting Emma and Edith Hull the next day. Generous as always, she told Edward to expect an express delivery from Pierce's of "3 bottles of sherry, 2 boxes ginger, 1 jar prunes, 1 lb salted peanuts, 1 lb salted pecans, 1 box chocolate peppermints." Five days later, she exulted that there was a piano in the house and that Dr. Currie's library was filled with books on early church history and the classics, and had a lounge chair, an open fireplace, and "a W.C. close by," providing every comfort for Edward. In the meantime, "Our valises are packed & we go at 2.30 to the Summit by train, & Vyron will meet us there."[44]

Susan Hale was unwell that summer, not helped by the grind of catering for her brother and a succession of guests. She and Edward were relieved when Nelly and Emily arrived from Folly Cove with a new cook. Responding to this news, Hattie wrote: "So, you have all your 'women folks,' <*the 3 who in life are nearest you. I hope in hav-*

ing them you do not forget her who should be nearest you but is not>." She was still trying to meet up with Mrs. Bryce, "Whereas I have called & received a call in return from Lady Isabella Howard, but as she is an Italian & Catholic, I do not think we shall be very intimate." Lady Isabella Howard was in fact a daughter of the British Earl of Newburg but her family lived in Rome. Her husband, Esmé Howard, the new chargé d'affaires, was a member of one of the leading British Catholic families, the Norfolks.

On Monday, August 5, Edward and Nelly made the annual train journey to join Hattie. Edward's diary pages for August are blank but he wrote on September 2: "We had almost perfect weather at Intervale…The house is perfectly planned…quite high above the Intervale, in the edge of the pine forests which surround the 'Embassy.' I think we went to ride every day but two…One Sunday we lunched at the Embassy…I saw Mr. & Mrs. Bryce, Mr. Howard & Lady Isabella Howard [and five others] a good deal, in the most absolutely informal way. Everyone of those 9 is a simple, unaffected & agreeable person." By the time Hattie returned to Boston on October 20, there was little more than a month before the Hales set off once more for Washington.

There are almost no letters from that winter, with the exception of one from Hattie on which she had pasted the top of his letter of January 6, 1908, which he had opened with his long familiar "My dear child." "Please don't address me as above," complained an infuriated Hattie. "If you do, I shall be as 'put out' as you were with me when I addressed you as 'My dear Chief.' You address Mrs. Andrews, Martha Brooks, Annie Cummings & many others in this way & I do not want to be classed with them in your estimation." She concluded with a nice dig in shorthand, "<*Always be sure that I love you and that I am always your own Kit not your dear child with*> 1000 <*other*> children!"[45] Now aged sixty, it was long overdue for Hattie to rebel against this infantilizing sobriquet. Once again, social and intellectual Washington had a strong hold on the Hales, with the probable exception of Emily. In January and April that year, both Edward and Nelly were profiled by the magazine section of *The Washington Times*.[46]

Even though just one of Edward's 1908 letters survives and

Hattie's only begin in May, the usual back and forth continued. Hattie was undoubtedly involved in the intense lobbying campaign to get the Appalachian-White Mountain bill out of the House Judiciary Committee and onto the House floor for a vote that year. She may have been among the delegation of Massachusetts citizens that appeared on April 25 before the House Committee on Agriculture's hearings on the bill, stopping off in Washington on her way south for a spring vacation with Emma. That Committee's chairman was Congressman John W. Weeks who, although appointed by Speaker Cannon, was in favor of the bill, or one resembling it. It may also have been Hattie who provided Edward with a report of a paper given by the chairman of the Appalachian Mountain Club's real estate trustees that spring on the forest reservations held by that conservation-minded club, of which nine were in New Hampshire.[47]

On May 12, Hattie wrote from Chapel Hill, North Carolina, where she was visiting her friend Collier Cobb. She and Emma had just arrived from Wilmington, where they explored Lake Waccamaw and the Green Swamp, notable for their unusual geology and rare bird and wildlife. Professor Cobb greeted Hattie with two letters from Edward. The first one she opened brought the happy news of the birth of Philip and Lilian Hale's daughter Nancy: "Now I suppose Lilian will be prettier than ever & be dearer than ever to your eyes. And I expect it will do a wonderful lot for Phil too," wrote Hattie. But she remained fixated on the obstructionism of Joseph Cannon, who was running for the presidency that year (he received just 58 votes at the Republican Convention in Chicago in June to Secretary of War William Howard Taft's overwhelming tally of 702). "It seems as though on every side there is a rising feeling of outrage against Cannon, entirely apart from our own personal feeling about his wriggling with our Appalachian Bill...Howell said it would be worth the defeat of the Republican party to get him out of the way."[48]

Hattie remembered that Edward would be opening "the White House Conference" with prayer that day. In fact, it was the following day, May 13, when the three-day Conference of Governors called by President Roosevelt opened at the White House. Chief Forester Gifford Pinchot was the prime mover for the conference which was to become a seminal event in the history of conservationism. The meeting was attended by governors of states and territories, members of the Supreme Court and Cabinet, scientists, and various national leaders and philanthropists, such as Andrew Carnegie, and resulted in the setting up of a presidential Commission on the Conservation of Natural Resources. Edward gave the invocation and was undoubtedly present for Roosevelt's opening address, "Conservation as a National Duty," but he and Abby left Washington together that afternoon for the train journey home. In the June *Record*, Edward reported once again that the Sixtieth Congress had adjourned "without providing for the purchase by the nation" of New Hampshire's White Mountain Reserve. He blamed this partly on the lack of interest by representatives from the rest of the country in funding the acquisition of lands in the original states.[49]

Not long after her return to Boston from Virginia, Hattie packed once again for Intervale, despite her assertion the year before that she would not return there in 1908. She must have arrived in time for the tragic news that on June 18 every building in the summit colony on Mt. Washington was burned and destroyed, with the exception of Tip-Top House, where she had often stayed, and two barns. She is unlikely to have ventured to the summit that summer. In the meantime, Edward must have felt torn between the needs of his wife and his sister. He spent July in Matunuck with Susan, whose poor health continued to worry him, while Emily, at home in Roxbury with Nelly, wrote Edward many short letters complaining about the stifling heat. Nonetheless, he wrote Hattie on July 18 that he was looking forward to joining her with Nelly on August 5, while reminding her of his own physical limitations: "I am afraid I have not let you know how closely my Lameness and the fast Breathing which belongs to it keeps me still. You must expect a life much limited by such conditions. I can walk down to the Library at the Foot of the Avenue and after resting there can walk back again. But that is quite a Feat."[50]

Edward's diary entries for his stay at Intervale with Hattie, Carrie, and Ethel Freeman are almost illegible. His handwriting, always difficult, was even a challenge for Hattie to decipher in his final years. However, he reported in the September *Record* that the New Hampshire Forestry Association met on August 5 at Intervale "and gave a part of two days to the consideration of the crisis which awaits the New England forests. Governor Rollins presided, and there was a satisfactory attendance of gentlemen and ladies." A letter he wrote Emily a week later is quoted in *Life and Letters*: "We are going to-day after our regular drive to a reception at the Merrimans. Alas, there are no nice Bryces there!...Our customs are very regular. We drive in the morning, I am apt to take a short nap before dinner; a longer nap follows dinner and then two hours or more on the piazza. There are a few callers...In the evening there is almost always music and I am in bed by nine o'clock. You must not be anxious about me. I sleep well, eat well, and wonder to think that seven days are gone since I saw you."

As a parting gift, Edward gave Hattie a copy of *The Soul of the Bible*, a selection of readings from the Old and New Testament made and edited by his deputy in the Senate (and successor a year later) and minister of All Souls Unitarian Church in Washington. Edward wrote the introduction to his faithful colleague's book and inscribed this copy: "H. E. Freeman: Aug. 26th, 1908, Intervale. I have left the green Ribbon where the book opened in the morning as the [illegible phrase]. You make this the home [?] for all of us."[51]

The Freemans were getting ready to celebrate the ordination of Helen's fiancé, Harold Arnold, in early October. "I shall go to West Newton direct," Hattie wrote from Intervale on October 1, "& remain there until Sunday morning, when you will see me at Church, & I will then go home with you. You do not tell me what I want most to know, if you are to preach & if there is to be a communion service which you conduct. But I take this for granted. Otherwise, you will not see me there."[52] In another letter, Hattie explained her skittishness about turning up at the South Congregational Church. Although she had agreed to continue as treasurer for the South Friendly Society, she felt increasingly alienated from the Cummings regime and from Abby Clark. She had evidently been complaining to Edward again about Edward Cummings's conduct of the church, an attitude she shared with Edward's other longtime lieutenant Judith Andrews, and seems to have felt she was *persona non grata* there: "I felt sure you would hardly reply to the other matter, & from the point of view of pure Congregationism...you can be justified. I will try never to refer to it again, & I hope Mr. Cummings' name will never pass between us again. But I have a great sense of injustice, which is blinded by sorrow, when I think how he has forced me to leave your Church, & your Secretary has forced me to leave your Study, the two places which I did love as much as my own Home." With characteristic pathos, she concluded: "Do not think of coming out to West Newton to-morrow, as you wrote you possibly might, you will not see me until after the Communion Service Sunday when <*we will meet*> as acquaintances <*for I will not kiss you there again*>."[53]

Harold Arnold's ordination was the spur that made Susan Hale drop a corner of the heavy veil that concealed the Hale family's attitude to Hattie's long relationship with her brother. Perhaps she saw Hattie as coercing the shaky old man to travel unnecessarily, although Susan's remarks show he was always eager to escape the too quiet house with Nelly. Writing to one of her friends from 39 Highland Street, she marveled at her brother's enduring spirit: "I never saw such a family, always on the rampage after ordinations, weddings, funerals, any Old Lark. This means Pa and Nelly, for Ma and I creep to our respective holes as soon as they leave the house, and only poke our noses out for meals." Then she related how her brother and Nelly had traveled by train to Bridgewater, Rhode Island, to attend an ordination ceremony for a young Providence man named Arnold, and said, in her characteristically sharp way, "This was all on account of the fiancé of Young Master Arnold who is a niece to the Ex-concubine Harriett [*sic*] Freeman." This letter was published in a collection of Susan's letters selected by her friend Caroline Atkinson; however, Miss Atkinson omitted the damaging sentence.[54]

The Hales endured another blow on November 10, 1908, with the news of Bertie's death at his home in New York. His *New York Times* obituary gave the cause of death as "nervous disorders, after a long illness."[55] Bertie's symptoms had increased to troubles with his heart, for which, following the advice of his doctor, he had traveled twice that year to Bad-Nauheim in Germany for the water cure. On June 25, Bertie wrote from there to Greta at their country house in Logansville, New Jersey, fully aware of the seriousness of his condition: "If I ever come home again…I think we will spend May &

June at Logansville so as to have the roses and the vegetables—and then we will come on here for perhaps July and August. We'd take Margie and Dudley and will stop in Paris."[56]

Helen Freeman, who for years had spent the birthday she shared with Edward's late brother Nathan with the Hales, called on them earlier than usual with a gift to find the anxious old couple fielding telephone calls with varying reports of Bertie's condition. Edward and Emily were too frail to attend their son's funeral but two letters Edward wrote Helen Freeman over the next two to five days show his usual courage (none survive from Hattie, although his gratitude for her solicitude shows that she wrote many): "All the children, Edward, Phil & Nelly were able to be together at their brother's funeral. And now I have more of my children on the other side than here. I saw Greta, that is Berty's wife, for five minutes yesterday. Dear child, she is brave, I dare not say wise, because she made no plans nor told me of any."[57]

Thoughtful as always, Hattie visited Bertie's grave in Newburyport to lay a wreath two or three weeks after his burial and wrote a full report from there for Edward. She called in on the Marquand aunts at Curzon's Mill and was told stories about two of Bertie's sons (the children had been sent to stay at Curzon's Mill during their father's final illness) which she felt would warm Edward's heart.[58] The principal of the local school had been reluctant to allow Bertie's small son Robert Beverly (named after his late uncle) to attend there temporarily during his father's final illness until his aunt told him that the boy's grandfather was Edward Everett Hale. Delighted at this connection, the principal told her he was the nephew of the late Henry Bellows, one of Edward's closest friends and colleagues, and he took in young Robbie.[59] When the same aunt asked Bertie's oldest son Dudley, whom Edward adored, to walk with her a little, he excused himself, saying "No! I can't leave Uncle Phil. He feels so very lonely that I think I had better stay with him."[60] Poor Philip, always a very sensitive man, had now lost two of the brothers who were closest to him.

The Hales returned to Washington a little earlier than usual that year. On November 29, Edward wrote Hattie that their freight and boxes had arrived safely, Mrs. Hubbard and other friends had called by with flowers and gifts, and the Senate would not meet until a few days later. Hattie threw herself into her winter activities again. Extracts from a mid-December letter show the range of her interests. She had been disappointed by the weak temporizing of "the President's letter on Woman Suffrage…But I do wish he would stop talking about women bearing children. Does he believe in polygamy? For in no other way can the surplus woman population have husbands and children." Roosevelt would continue railing from his "bully pulpit" about "race suicide," resulting, as he saw it, from the unwillingness of selfish upper class women to undertake pregnancies: "The worst evil," as he saw it, was "the greater infertility of the old native American stock especially in the North East."[61]

Indian rights continued to be high on Hattie's range of causes. In an undated late November letter, she had referred to the sufferings of the women and children of the Navaho men imprisoned at Fort Huachuca for the past year without trial for refusing to send their children to school, remarking bitterly, "Truly the Stars & Stripes seems to me but a dirty rag, while it covers such iniquities as the U.S. have practiced on the Indians." Now, following "a stirring Indian meeting on Friday morning…We have sent 50.00 to the women & children, 46 of them, who are in a terribly destitute & suffering condition because of the imprisonment of their husbands… Things are moving, though you take so little interest in them." She enclosed a report of a recent conversation she had had with Hart Merriam, who had told her "that the U.S. had made Treaties with the Indians which were entirely disregarded in a few years." Clearly, American Indians were excluded from her xenophobia, although none of them had invaded her neighborhood—they were corralled on reservations. "And Forestry is moving too," she continued. Edwin A. Start, editor of the newsletter of the Massachusetts Forestry Association, had tabulated all of Cannon's actions, or lack of same, on the forestry bill. And, finally, "I spend all to-morrow at work on my Widows Report, which I read on Wednesday. This is my 18th now & my fright is all over about it now, when at first I used to dread it so much."[62]

As Christmas approached, Hattie reminded Edward of all the Christmas afternoons he had spent with her and her household in her back parlor, "making merry over the giving of the presents. I can not believe that we shall ever spend such another Christmas." Three days before Christmas, she told him, "I think of my Pilgrim ancestors & all their winter hardships a great deal in these days! If I had not been in Belmont [with her Atkins relations] I should have gone Sunday afternoon to hear Mr. Frothingham's address, Arlington St. Church, to the Mayflower Society." She invited Miss Holyoke, a single working woman and former parishioner of the old South Congregational Church, to spend Christmas Eve with her: "I knew she would have her Christmas Eve alone in a lodging house, & so I asked her here for the night. Her enjoyment was great beyond words." The two women steeped themselves in memories of their former minister on what she could not have known, but might have guessed, would be his last Christmas. As she finished her long letter, she told him that she was "going to the Jewish Temple for Rabbi Fleischer's Saturday morning service. This is the Feast of the Hanuka [*sic*]…"[63] This would certainly have been in "Solomon's Temple" as the 1,000-seat tabernacle on Commonwealth Avenue was known.

If Edward missed his years of dividing his attentions at Christmas between Hattie and her circle and his own family, there are no letters to confirm it. He was happy in the circle that his family had closed around him in Washington, and with his new friends there. One of these, Ellen Maury Slayden, gives a charming picture of that family group in Nelly's N Street house in early January 1909, when she joined Susan, Nelly, Gabrielle Clements, and Miss Putnam for tea, "a delightful party of New England spinsters," as she called them: "I had heard of Miss Susan's unusualness from friends in Mexico, but the half had not been told. When Miss Nellie asked her to pour the tea, she thumped down in her chair, and gave a little extra bounce before she began to pull up her sleeves so hurriedly that I thought her next move would be to pound the teacups into atoms. But what a wonderful old woman she is, and not old either. She is so free from prejudice, social, political, sectional. She said it cost like the devil to stay at the Grafton and you couldn't keep a cat."

Then Nelly took the visitors through "to shake hands with 'Papa,'" describing an exchange which demonstrates the old man's humor and ability to charm friends into helping with research for his many journalistic and literary projects: "The doctor was seated in a long chair with a very ugly pillow back of his shaggy head, but his grip and his voice are always surprising. He had enjoyed my answer to his note some days ago asking if I could get him some data about the earthquake in Mexico in 1838. Books failing me, I had rung up Mr. Godoy at the embassy and gotten an excited reply, 'No! An earthquake in Mexico? No, I have not heard of it! When?' News travels slowly there."[64] Ellen Slayden never mentioned Emily in her diary entries about the Hales.

Hattie's attitude toward women's suffrage activists finally becomes clear in a letter she wrote Edward after attending the annual meeting of the Women's Education Association at Mrs. Augustus (Harriet) Hemenway's house in the Back Bay. Mrs. Francis H. Williams was in the chair, pro tem. "She is a fierce Suffragist," Hattie told him, "absolutely sharp & bitter, criticized Prof. Lowell because in his address to his students, he said they had the future of the making of the country 'as if there were no women'! She looks like a little spitfire when she talks about it." Hattie was overjoyed when their mutual friend Elizabeth Kidder, whom they called "the Princess," was elected president. Among the women Hattie named as present were Katharine Loring, Lucy Lowell, and Sarah Crocker, all of whom had been inspirational or shared in Hattie's quest for higher education.[65]

Despite missing Edward, Hattie had the means and the will to enjoy life. She told him she was off to Pepperell for the day and then the following week "to Intervale for a glimpse of winter & some snow shoeing," with her cousin Edith Hull. "What concerns you most," she continued, "I have definitely engaged my rooms at The Grafton for March 1, for Inauguration week." However, Helen Freeman was not sure if she could join her so close to her wedding. "In case she does not go, I shall bring my other dear Helen, Helen Dodd." As for her plans to return to Europe, "I have not taken my passage yet…But there is no reason that I should not go, except <*that I*> leave <*you*>." She planned to go for six months this time and plunged the guilt shaft deep this time: "Perhaps the thought of you being here in Boston six months <*without me strikes the same sick dead feeling that it does to me to be here*> 6 six <*months without you*>…

My mind will not & can not take in what it means, for it seems to me that I come to the end, come to a wall. So, all the more do <*I hope that in the*> 2nd <*week of March we may happily plan*> to renew <*our old*> life <*together as far as may be possible*>."[66]

On another January Sunday, Hattie reported, "I have had some painful duties…in which I should have your sympathy, as I was acting according to your wishes. I have been destroying some of your letters. It is a very hard task! What do you do with mine! I don't think it is respectable to tear them up & put them in a waste basket."[67] So she burned them in the fireplace of her back parlor. This may explain the paucity of Edward's letters in the final year of his life. Since there are no letters from him about Bertie's last illness and death, perhaps these are the ones he asked her to destroy, or perhaps they related to Emily's dementia or some Senate controversy. But Hattie was to discover that Edward kept an extraordinary number of her letters.

Edward had offered to get Hattie and the two Helens tickets to view the inauguration at the Capitol but she preferred to view the parade, telling him that her hotel had secured tickets for them on the stand opposite the White House. From there, she would "have no compunction of leveling my opera glass at Mr. Taft. But don't you feel a sort of pang at losing Mr. Roosevelt?" she asked, "I do!"[68] The inauguration of William Howard Taft would be a bitter-sweet occasion for the Freemans and Hales, all of whom were devoted to Theodore Roosevelt. Roosevelt, long a sincere admirer of his former undergraduate chaplain and father of his classmate Arthur Hale, had used Edward's immunity to criticism to further Taft's election in the face of attacks on his Unitarianism. In one letter to Taft, he suggested mentioning that Chaplain Hale of the Senate was also a Unitarian and that there was not "in all the United States a man more revered by the clergymen of every denomination, a man with whom every true Christian must feel eager to be associated in Christian brotherhood."[69]

Hattie had hoped for mild weather but Edward noted in his diary that they awoke on inauguration day to a heavy snow storm. Edward went to the Capitol with his grandson Dudley and Nelly "at 9:10…But my own service, the first act of the new V.P. [former Congressman James S. Sherman] did not come until 12:10…Mr.

Fairbank's farewell was very cordially received and Mr. Sherman's inaugural."[70] The next morning, he and Nelly returned to the Capitol where, again according to his diary, "We had an unusual randan in the Vice President's room with some Sherman grandchildren." After lunch, he "called for the Hatty party at the Grafton." From then on, Edward's diary is filled with many meetings, lunches, and drives with them.

Happiest of all for Hattie was the Monday morning, March 8, that they spent alone together, "way beyond the Capitol." "We called at Glacier Wright's publishing office, where they print the journal of archaeology," Edward recorded, continuing: "After some shopping we called on Greeley (General) at the War Office."[71] On Hattie's birthday, March 13, two days before they returned to Boston, she and Helen Dodd went to supper with the Hales and on one of the Sundays, Hattie and Helen Freeman attended All Souls to hear Edward preach. As Hattie wrote Helen after his death, "I am sure Mr. Hale never preached after that Sunday we heard him in Washington! And do you remember how quickly he came from the pulpit directly to us, to greet us, with such a sweet smile! How glad I am now, that I went & that I was able to give such a beautiful time to you & to Helen Dodd!"[72]

Edward celebrated his eighty-seventh birthday on April 3 quietly in the house on N Street. Hattie sent him a book about the Moon and a box of truffles, for which he thanked her in letters of the 4th and 5th. That night he became acutely ill. He told her in a brief letter on Easter Sunday that he had been overcome by one of his painful bowel attacks, was on a liquid diet and very weak. He concluded, "There is one person who loves me and understands me and believes in me and more <*important…loves me with her whole heart and soul…as I do her*>."[73] Edward was too ill in Washington to attend Helen Freeman's wedding on Easter Monday.[74] He wrote Hattie that day: "Write me about the wedding which is going on as I write." Hattie appeared to be planning to return to Washington to see him again before she left the country. "I hate to say it," he told his former collaborator on sermons, "but you must not expect to hear me preach. Sam hardly lets me go to the Senate, and I know I shall not be able to. It is as much disappointment to me as to you. I am very weak! Do not worry however."[75]

By April 22, Edward's doctors felt he was strong enough to return to Boston with Abby: "Dear Mrs. Hubbard sent her magnificent auto to take us to the marble station," where Abby found a "rolling chair" to carry him to their train. They arrived at South Station at 8:13 the next morning. "Here was Phil with a wheel chair for me, and I took 37 inches from my car to his. So I was luxuriously carried to dear Cook's carriage…to bring me to the same old 39 Highland St, to which I brought Emily and the Baby Bob in the autumn of 1870" [actually December 1869].[76]

The journey was very hard on the sick old man and he noted three days later that "no one was permitted to see me & I was permitted to see nobody." This must have been agonizing for Hattie, who had just four days left before she was due to leave Boston with Emma for the start of their long European trip. But Edward's doctor and the Hale family relented and allowed Hattie to take the invalid for a short drive on Thursday, April 29. His description in his diary is heart-warming:

> This is the great day of history. Kings & Prophets have waited for it & did without the sight. All the Same it has come & has gone which means that Hatty took me to drive. I opened the door of the house & let her in. She brought in her own hand [artist Benjamin] Champney's picture of Carter Notch which she had bought for me at the sale of his pictures in mid winter…she & I did have a perfect regulation drive in Franklin Park. Home again in 40 minutes & before I see her she is to go to England & through half the Continent of Europe. I have promised to write 3 times a week & I am never to write <*about*> anything but myself. How cross she will be <*about*> this limitation before the 7 months are over.[77]

Edward died at 3 a.m. on June 10, less than two weeks after addressing a "plea for closer unity between the Unitarian and Trinitarian wings of the Congregational body," at the annual American Unitarian anniversary week in Boston.[78] Emily, Nelly, and Abby were with him to the end. Abby wrote to Martha Adams Leland that morning: "Oh Martha—Our poor Chief is gone! Can you realize it. I can't & I write at his desk in the study while his dear body is on the couch. He has been growing weaker & weaker day by day for almost a fortnight. Dr. Temple told me the end was near. And told me of people of whom he was thinking & that I must write in the morning to say that he thought of them. Your name was first. He died quite without pain this morning, just as the clock struck 3. Mrs. Hale, Miss Nelly, Phil & I were here as well as the nurse. Oh, it is a mercy he is gone. But I think I shall never see light again."[79]

So was Martha really the first? Could Edward really have managed to keep up the deception to his dying breath? Hattie received the news of his death in London. Although she certainly wrote him her usual long, descriptive, loving letters during those last weeks, none of them survive, and if he did indeed write to her three times a week, those letters are also missing. Since he had become too weak to wield a pen in his final days, Abby was in charge of his correspondence and his diary entries. It was Abby who located Hattie's surviving letters in Edward's study, and, at Hattie's request and following Edward's instructions, as she told Nelly, she who boxed them up and returned them to their author.

15

Life after Edward

Extraordinary accolades followed the announcement of Edward's death. "Dr. Edward E. Hale Dead: Revered Author, Preacher and Reformer Called Home at an Early Hour This Morning," blazed *The Boston Globe*. The newspaper devoted two pages to "Boston's first citizen," including photographs of "The Loved Chaplain of the United States Senate" and "World-Honored Advocate of Peace," at home and in his study. The Los Angeles *Times* headlined its obituary, "Long Noble Life of Toil is Ended...Nation Mourns His Death." *The New York Times*, while acknowledging his influence and asserting that "he stands in the public mind for gentleness and, on the whole, for 'sweet reasonableness,'" was objective in its opinion about his literary reputation, which it felt—correctly as it turned out—would not long outlive him, with the exception of "The Man Without a Country." Tributes poured in to Emily from President Taft, Senator Lodge, and Mark Twain. Governor Eben S. Draper of Massachusetts lauded her late husband's "goodness, great-heartedness, and broad-minded judgment of men of all creeds and classes."[1]

Then followed the appreciations in magazines with which Edward had been associated. *Forest and Irrigation,* which was briefly renamed *Conservation: Forests, Waters, Soils and Minerals,* honored Edward with his portrait on the cover of the August edition, apotheosized by the open wings of an American eagle sitting on conifer branches and ears of wheat. The magazine printed his address at the Forest Congress that January. Albert Shaw in *Review of Reviews,* called him "a more truly national personage, in his knowledge and sympathies, than were any of the other New England thinkers and leaders." His friend and colleague in the peace movement, Edwin Mead, who had succeeded him as editor of the *New England Magazine,* called him "the most naturally and naively religious soul I ever knew." There were several tributes in *The Outlook,* which had published a good deal of Edward's writings over his final years. Thomas Wentworth Higginson, in his warm and perceptive appreciation, recalled his old college friend's "peculiar and attractive personality," "extraordinary versatility," and "exhaustless energy." But he also remarked that his "impetuous temperament," brought on him "the criticism of men of less talent but more accurate habits of mind," noting later that, "His undeniable habit of rather hasty and inaccurate statement sprang from his way of using facts simply as illustrations." Along these lines, he concluded, "This man's busy existence may not always have run in the accepted grooves, but its prevailing note was Love. If the rushing stream sometimes broke down the barriers of safety, it proved more often a fertilizing Nile than a dangerous Mississippi."[2]

On June 16, impetuous Edward's greatest and most potentially dangerous love wrote to her niece Helen from London: "I am sure you are thinking of me, & of the great loss which will never be filled in this Life. But for him, I will not permit myself to grieve, when I realize the limitations which were surrounding him more & more. His last letter tells me how he spent most of the time on his 'quarter deck' a little bit of a piazza which he had built out at the rear of his Study & once he wrote when there, 'Alas! It is not dear Intervale.' How much dearer that place will always be to me now, because of him!" She concluded, "I hardly need to suggest it, but I hope you will go to see Mrs. Hale before you leave for your July & August vacation. She is always especially fond of you, & I hope you will not fail to do this."

That same day, Helen wrote a condolence letter to Emily Hale, including a surprising statement. Expressing her heart-felt sympathy, she wrote of her aunt's special friend, "The world says that, in his greatness, he belonged to it, but I know that first of all he belonged to you and you alone." Surely Helen and her sisters must have guessed the truth about their aunt's relationship with Edward? For instance, in a long letter to Helen from Berlin in August, Hattie thanked her and Harold for their letters of sympathy in her loss. "It seems as though I could write forever about him, as I could tell story after story if I could have a sympathetic listener," wrote Hattie. "Everything about him is so sacred to me, that I could not tell them otherwise...How often he said 'it is good to be loved.' But I think he had no conception of the love that was given him."[3] Was she thinking of herself as she wrote those words?

Hattie's housekeeper Mary Driscoll wrote her regular misspelled letter to Hattie on July 23, expressing her empathy as someone who had helped her mistress give Edward every domestic comfort over many years: "...everything that Dr Hale did was fine and you were fortunate in having the grate pleasure of his company so mutch and it was so nice to have him with you at Intervale and he loved to go their and visite you we will all miss him but I trust our lose will be his gain in paridise Sophie is well and sends love buffie [the cat] is well and loves pork kidney...I am afectionely Mary Driscoll." The same day, her sister-in-law in West Newton, the other Hattie Freeman, wrote along similar lines, although her response indicates that Hattie had poured out her true feelings to her: "I have no doubt that your watchful, tender care prolonged his life and so he could give these last beautiful years, not only to his family and his friends, but send his help and influence throughout the nation."[4]

Despite her great sadness, Hattie enjoyed her latest European trip with Emma. From Vienna in September, she wrote Helen: "I remember that, when a child, you would mildly boast that you had an aunt who knew everything. I must say I have always had a drive to learn facts, & it is still fresh upon me here. Happily, I have a companion who shares that interest, & is quite abreast of me, & I must say, put us together, we do know piles in history, art, archaeology, botany & several other subjects which make Life more interesting."

They stayed longest in Berlin, where they visited all the museums and picture galleries, the Kaiser's palace, and saw the treasures that archaeologist Heinrich Schliemann had brought back from the excavations of Troy. They also followed in the footsteps of the great Protestant reformers, such as Martin Luther and John Huss.

Hattie found eight letters waiting for her in Vienna, including one each from her friends from geological studies, "Miss Murray, Mr. Watson, and Dr. Grabau," all undoubtedly writing to commiserate about their shared loss. But she told Helen that her "real grief is that I hear nothing from Nelly Hale."[5] While she had written Nelly every ten days since she ceased to hear from her father, she had received just two letters from Nelly. Can she really have expected more than that? After all, Nelly must have felt overwhelmed in the aftermath of her father's death, not the least being with the care of her confused old mother.

Abby Clark wrote many letters to Nelly as she helped the Hales sort out Edward's affairs. With her father gone, Nelly had no interest in staying on in the cavernous house in Roxbury, another neighborhood whose demographics had changed drastically since the Hales moved there in 1869, and lost no time in putting it up for sale. She took her mother to Folly Cove for the summer, leaving Abby in charge of clearing the house and organizing Edward's books for sale.[6]

There was already discussion about who should write Edward's biography. Edward himself had wished his friend Edwin Mead to do this. However, while Abby was visiting Susan at Matunuck in August, she wrote Nelly that William Weeden, looking "ghostly pale"—he died in 1912—had walked up to the house to say he intended to write to Nelly that she, Abby, should write all or part of his friend's biography. "I tried to make him understand what my wish was, simply to be of service to you," but she did not know if she had convinced Weeden. "Even if I had the skill to do the blessed work," Abby continued, "I couldn't undertake to have my name appear if for no other reason, that it would wound poor Miss Freeman's sensibilities, & she has a right to have her feelings consulted." She told Nelly that Etta Pierce had already insisted that Hattie should be the one to write the entire biography and that Hattie would herself claim precedence over Abby. "I was glad enough to say that the whole thing must be left to you & Mr. Mead & no one else. I think Mr. Weeden must be slightly out of his mind," Abby concluded.

In September, Abby told Nelly that Judith Andrews had got "an awful bee in her bonnet about Hatty Freeman & me. She wants

Hatty to write to me 'a letter of sympathy and gratitude.' Well, I don't want Hatty to write me any kind of letter. It's so ludicrous one can't be seriously bothered about it." It seems that Judith Andrews was upset about the estrangement and rivalry between Edward's two principal secretaries but rational Abby, who found Mrs. Andrews' emotional sentimentality distasteful, concluded, "Goodness, how did your sainted Father & my Chief keep peace with all these freaks!" Abby forwarded a letter from Hattie, in which Hattie had presumably asked her to return her letters to Edward. "My worst enemy need never wish me worse than to have made up that box of letters for the poor soul," protested Abby. "It was so sickening, somehow. But I've done it, for I know your Father would wish them to go back to her at once—Indeed, he told me so. Perhaps they will be a comfort to her. I should think they might be."[7] It is hard to believe that Abby, who was well versed in Towndrow's shorthand, could resist reading some of the letters before returning them to Hattie.

Minnie Whitman of the Lend A Hand Society, who had begun working at the SCC Sunday school at the old Castle Street church forty-eight years before, wrote Hattie in Berlin in early August to thank her for sending her $30 so that she could take a brief holiday. "Perhaps you know the old house & the dear old study are for sale. The sign is up and as soon as maybe, others will call the old place theirs and the work of devastation and probably rebuilding will go on. Nelly and Mrs. Hale go to Washington in the autumn… The Chief's Lend A Hand Society will stand, I hope for all time and I trust it may always be as free from the 'red-tape system' as he planned and desired it to be. It is his memorial."[8] Indeed, the Lend A Hand Society is still actively engaged in philanthropy in Boston. The Roxbury house was quickly sold and, on October 19, the *New York Times* reported: "E. E. Hale's Estate $40,932." Among his assets were 126 shares of American Sugar Refinery and 20 shares of Atchison, Topeka & Santa Fe Railroad common—both curiously related to Atkins business interests. Could they have been a gift from Hattie? If so, they would now help support Emily Hale.

In Washington, Nelly continued making art and apparently kept an eye on some of her late father's causes. Sometime following her return to Boston in October, Hattie evidently wrote Nelly deprecating the decision to rewrite the Boston city charter, replacing the eight-member Board of Aldermen and an unwieldy Common Council of seventy-five representatives, three from each of the city's twenty-five wards, with a nine-member Common Council elected at large for two-year terms. Worst of all, the mayor's term would extend to four years and would ensure veto power. While this had been an initiative of a Finance Committee appointed to investigate reports of Mayor Fitzgerald's scandalous "payroll graft," instead it sealed the Irish Catholic Democratic control of the city that Edward and Hattie had feared. The irrepressible "Honey Fitz" Fitzgerald won the mayoral election of January 1910 with a plurality of 1,402 votes. On February 4, Nelly answered Hattie, "I did feel dreadfully about the Boston City Election, and now I am much interested, as you may imagine, in the Ballinger-Pinchot hearings."

Gifford Pinchot had become convinced by the previous summer that President Taft's newly appointed secretary of the interior Richard Ballinger intended to "stop the conservation movement." Pinchot presented Taft with a 50-page report accusing Ballinger of an improper interest in his handling of coal field claims in Alaska. Then, in January 1910, Pinchot openly rebuked Taft, and asked for Congressional hearings into the propriety of Ballinger's dealings. Taft promptly fired Pinchot, but from January to May, the U.S. House of Representatives held hearings on the controversy. While Ballinger was cleared of any wrongdoing, he was criticized from some quarters for favoring private enterprise and the exploitation of natural resources over conservationism. Nelly had been attending these hearings and told Hattie that their mutual friend Gifford Pinchot would be interrogated that afternoon by the joint committee regarding the "Interior and Forestry investigation."[9]

The Forestry Bill for which Hattie and Edward had fought for so long was threatened by Pinchot's firing but things began to look up when Hattie's despised enemy, the obstructionist House Speaker Joseph Cannon, was stripped in March 1910 of his control of the Rules Committee, the source of his power over legislative priorities. The House passed the Weeks Act, as it had become known, on June 24, 1910, less than five months before losing control to the Democrats in the November mid-term elections. After delays, negotiations, and filibustering, the Senate passed the Appalachian-White Mountains Forest Reservation Bill on February 15, 1911, and it was signed by President Taft on March 1, 1911. Now the federal government was authorized to appropriate funds for the acquisition of lands and forest reserves and some 30,000 acres were purchased as the first parcel toward the proposed 698,000-acre White Mountain National Forest.[10] Edward would have greeted this news with a triumphant "Victory! Victory! Victory!" letter to Hattie.

Hattie's continued work in support of Indian rights and nature conservation and her love of American art can be glimpsed in a long letter she wrote in early January 1910 to C. Hart Merriam, whom she increasingly admired and turned to for advice on behalf of her interests, particularly American Indian land rights. Merriam retired that year as chief of the U.S. Biological Survey to concentrate on projects funded by Mrs. Edward Harriman (she granted him $12,000 a year for life), including studying and assisting Native American tribes in the western United States. The landholdings of the Yuma Indians of California and the beautiful Hetch Hetchy Valley in Yosemite National Park were both threatened by the U.S. Reclamation Service's plans to dam the Hetch Hetchy River. Hattie asked Merriam if he could recommend that the Women's National Indian Association should petition Congress to grant each Indian ten acres rather than the five acres they had been offered. "Pardon this long letter," she concluded. "I can only say as an apology that it is always a great pleasure to me to talk to you; & as I can not do so in person, I have done it on paper."[11] The damming of the Hetch Hetchy Valley in Yosemite National Park was and continues to be a major environmental controversy. Following the earthquake of 1906, San Francisco applied to the U.S. Department of the Interior to gain water rights to Hetch Hetchy, provoking a seven-year environmental struggle with the Sierra Club led by John Muir. The Raker Act of 1913 permitted the flooding of the valley, a blow from which Muir never recovered. He died two years before construction of the dam began.

Another letter of April 1911 to Merriam indicated that Hattie and Emma had attended the annual meeting of the American Ornithologists' Union in Washington the previous November. Hattie's letters to Merriam over the following decade confirm the extent of her travels with Emma and the deepening of their friendship with Merriam and his sister Florence Bailey and her husband, with whom Hattie and Emma would share birding experiences. Florence was a pioneering ornithologist who introduced the popular idea of field guides for bird identification while her husband Vernon Bailey was a field naturalist and long-time collecting partner of Merriam. Likewise, Hattie intensified her correspondence with geologist Collier Cobb, telling him in February 1910 that she had begun a course at Radcliffe on meteorology under Professor Robert De Courcy Ward.[12]

Hattie received a long letter from Mary Dann in March 1910 describing the memorial service for Edward that she had attended at the Brooklyn Institute of Arts and Sciences where he had frequently lectured. Hattie had evidently sent her a ticket and would surely have attended if she could. Principal speakers were Professor Franklin W. Hooper, director of the Brooklyn Institute, a chemist and geologist who shared many of Hattie's scientific memberships, and the Reverend Ulysses S. Pierce, Edward's successor as chaplain to the U.S. Senate.[13] Hattie took every opportunity to remind others about Edward, including selecting some of his prayers to be printed in *The Christian Register*. When a committee of Edward's friends commissioned sculptor Bela Pratt, a student of Augustus Saint-Gaudens and a longtime instructor at the School of the Boston Museum of Fine Arts, to sculpt a statue of Edward Everett Hale, Hattie was a generous subscriber. According to the *Boston Globe* of November 9, 1910, she had recently donated $100 to the Rev. Edward Everett Hale Fund which had reached a total of more than $13,000 by that date.

Susan Hale, the last of her generation of siblings, died at Matunuck on September 17, 1910. Perceptive as she was of human nature, she had certainly understood almost as well as Judith Andrews the true nature of her brother's relationship with Hattie; besides, he had probably confided his feelings to her. Shortly before sailing home after spending the winter in a Cannes hotel with her nurse-companion Mary Keating, Susan suffered a stroke. As he told his brother Jack, Arthur received a cable from Mary Keating from Naples dated April 29: "Sailing. Miss Hale had slight shock Sunday affecting left hand. Secretly. Mary." "I don't know quite what to think," admitted Arthur, "but the 'secretly' is encouraging."

There was a back and forth between Arthur and Jack about whether Susan should be allowed to return to Matunuck or stay with Mary in Arthur's New York apartment. But strong-willed Susan insisted on returning to her own home in Matunuck, where she sank rapidly, fiercely protected from unwanted visitors by Mary. Rose, Jack's wife, was allowed to see Susan briefly in July, telling her husband, "I saw Susan for a few moments, looking very shrunken & pathetic; but very plucky."[14] Jack, Susan's favorite nephew, now Edward E. without the "Junior," wrote the charming and insightful introduction to *Letters of Susan Hale* published in 1918.[15]

Hattie delayed going overseas again with Emma until late 1911. She may have been reluctant to leave the seriously ailing Judith Andrews. Her passport application, dated November 22, 1911, and witnessed by Emma, noted that she intended to travel for no more than one year.[16] On December 11, 1911, she wrote Helen from their ship as they neared Gibraltar, "You may know that wherever I go, I always carry with me several parcels of Dr. Hale's letters. I read them when far away & near to home, & always find infinite companionship in them. In that which I opened to-day, I find so much that is valuable to Ministers, & their wives, that I have copied it for Harold & you & now enclose it" (it was Edward's 1905 letter with his view of the mysteries of preaching). She told Helen that "Dr. Grabau" had come to the steamer to see them off before they sailed from New York: "I am most happy to say, he is now recognized by men of the highest scientific authority & associates much with them. And his wife, Mary Antin, is now recognized in literary circles; & not only that, but her writings, published in The Atlantic Monthly, add much to their income. I rejoice greatly in the achievements of both."[17] She ended by sending her love to Harold and Freddie and "the Bird," presumably an expected second baby.

Hattie was referring to the *Atlantic Monthly*'s serialization of Mary Antin's autobiography *The Promised Land*, which transformed the young woman into a public figure. Another of her articles, "A Woman to Her Fellow-Citizens," published in *The Outlook*, further embraced the "melting pot theory," chided restrictionists who hoped to limit immigration, and promoted Theodore Roosevelt's presidential candidacy. It caught the former president's eye and he suggested they meet at the offices of *The Outlook*. They became friends and correspondents. Roosevelt had decided to challenge his old friend President William Howard Taft for the presidency after Taft became more conservative and turned against many of Roosevelt's progressive ideals. Failing to win adequate support from the Republican Party, Roosevelt and his supporters established a third party, the Progressive Party. This became known as the Bull Moose Party early on when the irrepressible Roosevelt kept referring to himself as a "bull moose." After surviving an assassination attempt in October 1912, he boasted that "It takes more than that to kill a bull moose." Antin threw herself into campaigning for Roosevelt but the election was won by Democrat Woodrow Wilson. Edward Everett Hale Jr., ran for Congress in this election but lost.

Antin became a popular lecturer on open immigration and a new cause, her support of Zionism. The archives of the Immigration Restriction League at Harvard's Houghton Library includes a copy of a letter written by an unidentified IRL staff member to Hattie on December 9, 1912, six months after she returned from her trip to Egypt and Europe with Emma: "Replying to yours of Saturday, I have not read Mary Antin's book, but should suppose it would have quite a little effect, as all books setting forth the melting-pot theory do...I should not be at all surprised to find that this book was part of the general plan of campaign which the Jews have been making for the past ten years on the subject of immigration...I think that in the course of two or three years the eugenic work which is being done by the American Breeders Association and others will tend to off-set the melting-pot doctrine."

The writer, who may have been IRL co-founder and president Prescott F. Hall, intimated that financier and Zionist Jacob Schiff was behind the campaign to support Jewish immigration to the United States from Russia and to rewrite the history of Jewish immigration. He recommended that Hattie read works by Houston Stewart Chamberlain and Dr. Alfred P. Schultz that advocated racial purity. Chamberlain was a German anti-Semitic writer and son-in-law of composer Richard Wagner, who influenced Hitler. Birth control, sterilization, and the regulation of marriage for the preservation of racial purity had become the ultimate goals of the Immigration Restriction League.[18]

This letter, and her membership in nativist societies such as the

Daughters of the American Revolution and the Mayflower Society, appear to confirm Hattie's anti-Semitism, at least when it came to her own family. According to E. Digby Baltzell, an acclaimed historian of America's upper classes, the "newly rising tide of anti-Semitic and anti-immigrant sentiment...gradually infected much of old-stock America between 1881, when the pogroms against the Jews began in Russia, and the final closing of the gates against unrestricted immigration in America in 1924."[19] Mary Macomber Leue, who was close to Hattie's niece Ethel Hale Freeman, was told by her that she was forced by her mother, and by inference her aunt—the two Harriet Freemans—to break off her brief engagement to Arthur Berenson, a lawyer cousin of the eminent art historian, and return his ring.[20] There are hints in Hattie's 1909 letters that Hattie contributed to a compensatory painting holiday in Italy for Ethel the winter of 1908-1909.

Hattie and Emma's principal destination from January to early March 1912 was Egypt and Hattie's letters to Collier Cobb from a tourist boat on the Nile, on which they spent seven weeks, and from Cairo, provide colorful and geologically informative accounts of their experiences, including stays at Assam (which she spelled Assouan), site of the future great dam, and Luxor, with excursions by donkey to most of the great archeological wonders. She kept Professor Cobb informed of the latest achievements of her scientific circle and she told him about her meeting with Thomas Watson and his wife, who were also spending the winter in Egypt. With the end of her long correspondence with Edward, she had turned her energies to cementing her friendships with and encouraging, and sometimes financially supporting, the exploits of her scientific friends. From Egypt, the two women sailed with their party to Athens and Constantinople, and then traveled north to Bremen, Germany, via beauty spots in Austria and Bavaria and several German cities whose trees and parks they greatly admired, to rejoin their steamship for the return voyage to Boston. On arrival in New York, Hattie spent four days with the Grabaus and their four-year-old daughter Josephine in their rented house in West Chester County where she and Grabau poured over the vast manuscript for his *Principles of Stratigraphy*, published the following year.[21]

Soon after Hattie's return, she left to spend yet another summer in Intervale but would certainly have attended the funeral of Judith Andrews, who died on August 29, 1912, at her home on Rutland Square. Mrs. Andrews's obituary in the *Boston Transcript* described her as Edward Everett Hale's onetime "right hand." Her letters to Hattie across the years, many of which Hattie retained with the love letters, made it clear that her first loyalty, apart from that to her own three sons, was always to Hattie and their "Chief." If she had felt any warmth toward Emily, this staunchly upright woman would not have been so encouraging of their relationship.

Hattie returned home to a situation which caused the Freeman family great anxiety. It is possible that Fred Freeman, who had risen to treasurer and general manager of Aetna Mills, crossed swords with Edwin Atkins over policy, perhaps relating to brewing labor problems: in 1913 the Mill's weavers came out on strike against pay cuts and demanded restoration to $15 a week.[22] But the reason Atkins gave for Fred's dismissal was his alleged infidelity with a Miss Lewis whom he visited on Sundays in Gloucester where she was staying with her mother while his wife Lucia and three children were absent all summer on Nantucket Island. Hattie wrote Helen and Harold to report on her meeting with Alice Palmer, a friend who worked as social secretary for the Boston Legal Aid Society, to which Hattie was a subscriber.[23] Miss Palmer advised Hattie that it would be useless for Fred to meet with his uncle, as he had proposed. Miss Lewis would have to be present at any such meeting to provide the evidence that Fred needed and, since Atkins was about to depart for Cuba, it was unlikely to occur until he returned. In any case, Miss Palmer felt that this was only an excuse to oust Fred from the business.

Knowing Hattie's pride in the company her father had built, it must have been a bitter blow to her. In January 1909, she had told Edward that Fred, "with Edwin Atkins's approval, is adopting the policy of making finer grade goods, at higher prices. There are fewer mills in the country which can do this, as it requires more the knowledge of experts. But Fred's education, & training & brain power leads him into the higher lines." "The Aetna Mills is really a personality to me," she concluded.[24] Although Hattie felt that

Fred's behavior was unwise, she sympathized with him: "Really, I suppose Lucia's personality has become so intolerable to Fred, that he welcomed any opportunity that separated them."

Hattie was told that Edwin's son Robert, who worked with his father, remarked on hearing about Fred's alleged infidelity: "Well! I wonder what the Aunt in Egypt will say to this when she returns!" Feisty as always, Hattie prayed that Fred would be vindicated and could bring a charge of libel against his uncle, "But the power of Gold," she told the Arnolds, "is so strong in this world that I dare not hope for so much." In fact, Fred left Aetna Mills, was divorced by Lucia, moved to Portland, Maine, and married Madeleine Jean in December 1915. Since the Freeman family's finances were tied in with the Atkins Company, some kind of financial accommodation must have been reached. Fred Freeman published under the pseudonym of Will Ourcadie a volume of his Portland sketches and another of political caricatures of local notables: *Sketches in and about Portland, Maine* (1917) and *Mother Goose Comes to Portland* (1918). He also drew several posters and cartoons in support of woman suffrage during those years, presumably because his new wife was a supporter herself, which must have further shocked his anti-suffrage family. He founded a successful rug-hooking business and was always a great favorite of Hattie's. He outlived his devoted aunt but, according to descendants of Helen Hunt Arnold, Fred became an alcoholic and eventually committed suicide.[25]

As Hattie struggled to defend her nephew, preparations were being made to install the Hale statue inside the Charles Street gate of Boston Public Garden. On Thursday, May 22, 1913, the unveiling exercises began with a service at the Arlington Street Church. Former Massachusetts governor and U. S. secretary of the navy John D. Long gave the opening address, followed by former President William H. Taft and Edward's close friend the Reverend Dr. James De Normandie. After the service, these men walked down Arlington Street to the Public Garden where they were joined by Mayor John F. Fitzgerald, who, in one of life's ironies, gave a long appreciation of Hale in accepting the statue for the city. According to a newspaper account, special dispensation was given for Mrs. Hale to be driven to the site in a carriage accompanied by Nelly, a Dr. Mary Hobart, and Miss Abigail Clark, "for many years the devoted secretary of

Bela Pratt's very effective statue just inside the Charles Street entrance to the Boston Public Garden is a reminder of its subject's fleeting fame. But the statue must have been a favorite place of contemplation and communication for the previously unknown woman who arguably loved Edward Everett Hale best of all.
Photograph by Deb Stallwood.

Dr. Hale." Thousands of citizens, among whom presumably was Hattie, watched eight-year-old Edward Everett Hale III, one of Bertie's sons, cut the cord which held the Stars and Stripes in place over the statue, assisted by his five-year-old cousins Nancy Hale, Philip's daughter, and Elsa Diederich, Arthur's granddaughter.[26] Convention reigned and Hattie's extraordinary devotion of four decades could not be publicly acknowledged, another blow to her, even if accepted.

Nine months later, newly inaugurated mayor James Michael Curley gleefully mocked Proper Boston by threatening mischievously to sell its sacrosanct Public Garden and use half the money to fund public gardens for other less privileged parts of the city. He also threatened to put a water-pumping station under the Boston Common as well as public toilets for the convenience of visitors. He had already broken with Brahmin tradition the day before by holding his inaugural festivities in Tremont Temple where 2,500 of his supporters saluted the second Boston-born Irish American mayor. "The day of the Puritan has passed; the Anglo-Saxon is a joke; a new and better America is here," Curley boasted. Brahmins must learn, he said, that "the New England of the Puritans and the Boston of rum, codfish, and slaves are as dead as Julius Caesar."[27] It is easy to imagine sainted Edward on high, relieved to have departed the scene and yet chortling over this comeuppance—but Hattie would have been among those having apoplectic fits.

Perhaps Emily Hale was too far gone to understand this insult. After quarter of a century of semi-invalidism, she died at the age of eighty-four on May 24, 1914, at the Brookline house she shared with Nelly, although her reported residence on the death certificate was Nelly's little house in Washington, D.C. The cause of death was congestive heart failure.[28] Emily was buried alongside her husband at Forest Hills Cemetery. She left her estate to Nelly. Emily never made a public mark but her devotion to her family shines through all her letters. On the other hand, Susan and Lucretia's letters over the years occasionally mentioned their resentment of Emily. They found her cold and distant—"cruel, hard even"—and always quick to make it clear she preferred her own family, the Beechers and Perkinses, to Edward's siblings. But they agreed that she "had a hard row to hoe. Nine children, and always ill. Being a Beecher seemed to support her."[29] Despite intimations that she might have suffered from dementia in her final years, Emily's letters in the last two years of Edward's life are lucid, if shaky in penmanship.

That winter, Hattie wrote an astonishingly vehement letter to Collier Cobb in which she made her feelings about uncontrolled immigration and her opposition to woman suffrage abundantly clear. She had heard, presumably from her fellow travelers in immigration restriction, that there were "three to four millions of 'unstarted people'" in the mountains of North Carolina and that "this large core of true English stock may be developed in to the best material for the future. At the present rate of their inroads, in 1950 70% of the population will be foreign...We feel ourselves in a precarious condition here, with the increasing power & assertiveness of the Roman Catholic church under the lead of a clever diplomatic cardinal." Enclosing printed materials produced by the Massachusetts Association Opposed to the Further Extension of Suffrage to Women for their campaign which was used to persuade men to vote against suffrage in their state's November 2, 1915, referendum, Hattie continued:

> We are feeling the danger of Woman Suffrage, & the best women in the State are organized against it. How any sober minded person, in the face of our overwhelming foreign population, can advocate an enlargement of the suffrage, I do not understand. But quite apart from that, I consider it absolute nonsense on biological grounds. I don't think it is worth the argument & I can say most cordially with Dr. Hale, it is the greatest humbug of the age. But as between women, it is getting to be a line of social cleavage & the two camps stand well apart.[30]

Hattie's anti-suffrage stance stemmed largely from her fear, shared by many from her background, that the voting power of newcomers to America would double through female enfranchisement and thus threaten the behavior patterns, status, and security of old stock Americans. At the same time, as a member of the elite leadership of the world of women's clubs and charity associations, whose support, encouragement, and companionship she had enjoyed all her adult life, she feared that she and they would lose these formal and informal social networks. A number of organizations had been founded in the face of renewed suffrage activism, starting with the Massachusetts anti-suffrage association in 1895. Between 1896 and 1915-16, the membership had grown from 560 to 16,443. Membership of the male anti-suffrage association, founded the same year with the misnomer Man Suffrage Association, included Harvard President Charles W. Eliot, Harvard professor John Fiske, and railroad executive Charles Francis Adams Jr. All were friends of Edward but it is not known if he was also a member.

Massachusetts men voted overwhelmingly against suffrage in the 1915 referendum. In Boston alone, the anti-suffrage margin of victory was 21,000 votes, of a total of 83,000 cast. But 1915 and 1916 were the high-water marks of anti-suffragism. Just four years later, on June 25, 1920, Massachusetts became the eighth state to ratify the Nineteenth Amendment. Hattie's reaction is unknown but many anti-suffragists ceased their resistance without overt displays of bitterness.[31]

Collier Cobb must have expressed a very different view about immigration since Hattie responded in her next letter: "We should never look at the Immigration Problem from the same point of view, because of the difference in our environment. With your surroundings, you can have no idea of our conditions, where to see an American in street cars or in public places is almost the exception. I am living with foreigners as much as if I were abroad. But we never touch; we have no common interest; & I think that is one of the many dangers of this country; we are a heterogeneous population. If you doubt it, come here & see."[32] Judging by the surviving letters, her correspondence with Professor Cobb began tailing off at this point. Feeling as she did, it was not surprising that Hattie looked forward to her long summers away from Boston. Having apparently turned her back on more strenuous summers in the White Mountains, perhaps following the death in 1913 of Daniel Merriman, Hattie rented a house for the summers of 1914 and 1915 in the picturesque and thoroughly homogeneous New Hampshire town of New Ipswich. From there, she wrote to the Gray Herbarium to ask them to confirm if the specimen that she enclosed from her garden was *Aster oblongifolius*.[33] But her memories of New Hampshire summers with Edward remained strong and she gave a granite bird bath in memory of Edward to the famous "bird village" of Meriden, New Hampshire, home of her friend, naturalist and bison preservationist Ernest Harold Baynes.

The summer of 1916, Hattie and Emma set off for another ambitious overseas adventure, a four-month trip to the Far East. Although the Great War was raging in Europe, it did not affect shipping from the West Coast. Writing on June 25 from a hotel in San Francisco to Hart Merriam, who spent the summers there, Hattie told him that they had expected to sail on the *Nippon Maru* the day before, "But there is a strike by the dockmen & the steamer can not be loaded…There are fifteen of us here under the charge of Dr. H. H. Powers who is to conduct us for a month's travel in Japan & a month in Northern China." Instead, Powers was hoping to get them on a Canadian ship sailing from Vancouver. If they could have anticipated the delay, they would have liked to see Merriam but Hattie told him that they had been able to see Alice Eastwood, the self-taught botanist and curator of the botany collections at the California Academy of Sciences who had rescued 1,497 of its botany specimens from the San Francisco fire. Hattie and Emma were due to return from Japan on October 11 and, while Emma had to return at once to Boston, Hattie intended to stay on the West Coast through November, and hoped that she and Merriam could meet then.[34]

But the Hale biography had been languishing. Apart from commissioning various friends of Edward's to write essays about aspects of his career, Edwin Mead appeared to have made no progress by 1915 and retired from the project, claiming ill health. In April, Abby Clark called on the publisher, Little, Brown, where an editor told her that they could not possibly proceed with Edwin Mead's plan to turn the project over to a minister friend of his to complete. She was not surprised to hear that, telling Nelly, "My dear, no-body would ever read a dozen pages, couldn't indeed. Dull doesn't express it. He [the Little, Brown editor] says its [*sic*] got to be Life & Letters with an emphasis on the Letters" and expected that Nelly would be the sole author, with which Abby heartily agreed. In the meantime, Arthur Hale passed on Nelly's opinion that each of the surviving children should write a chapter and that Abby Clark should be the editor.[35] Instead, it was decided that Edward Jr. would compile the book with chapters by Nelly on her travels with their father.

That July, Calvin Stebbins, the author of one of the essays commissioned by Mead, wrote Abby Clark to ask her what had become of the Hale book: "I hear nothing from Mr. Mead, and more than that he doesn't answer my letters. Some one told me that the whole subject has been passed over to Mr. Hale's Presbyterian son. If so, I want my manuscript." Stebbins continued about Edward's longtime comrade-in-arms in peace activism. "I hope the war has not made Mr. Mead sick. There are a certain class of men who think if they can bring about a disgraceful peace the Kingdom of God will be just outside the door." Abby forwarded the letter to Nelly telling her that she had written to Stebbins to let him know that the publishers had decided on a change of plan following Mead's retirement from the project and that he could retrieve his manuscript from Mead.

In another letter to Nelly telling her that she was sending their father's papers to Edward Jr. as he found he needed them, Abby mentioned that she had run into Mrs. Howell Reed, whose husband had died in 1914: "She is a very sad looking little lady & I believe she's nearly dying of grief, though why naturally passes all my powers of imagination."[36] Clearly, Abby was dismissive of most of her former chief's old guard in the church, including William Howell Reed. Grace Atkins Reed, who had relied heavily on her husband, died in 1920.

Edward Jr. labored over the enormous volume of papers that Abby sent him in Schenectady, keeping notes of his progress in reading his parents' letters, and often citing the "Freeman MSS" and "Freeman Memorandum (Summer 1904)," although only fragments of these survive with his papers. Frequently, in the notes Edward Sr. had dictated to Hattie at Intervale, he muddled the dates, and she does not appear to have corrected them, the first duty of a good editor. The younger Edward numbered Hattie's contributions and entered extracts from them in his running calendar of the letters, giving the impression that he was in correspondence with Hattie throughout the process of compiling *Life and Letters*.

Edward's notes as he read his parents' letters are often revealing. He appears to have been determined to place his parents' relationship at front and center of his selection. After noting an extract from a letter his father wrote his mother on February 14, 1883, "There were times, when on a Sunday your father would go round to the P.O. to see if there were a letter to you from me. But I am afraid those days of romance are now over [and that this will wait till Monday]," their son wrote, "I don't believe they were ever over to judge from his letters." He was not to know that his father was already losing his heart to Hattie that year. But after reading his mother's aggrieved letter as her errant husband was heading off to join Hattie in Maine in October 1887, their son noted only, "A summer trip to Maine!"

Overwhelmed by the quantity of letters he had to read, Edward Jr. noted in despair one day, "It takes three or four hours of the closest application to do a year, & is very hard on the eyes" (he has my sympathy). His next entry read, "By the next week I had almost broken down & stopped till today Feb. 12. That is terrible. But I really was quite a wreck and stayed so for quite a while. Not much better now." Apparently, many of the discarded authors, including Stebbins, had relented and given Edward permission to use portions of their essays in his account.[37]

Abigail Clark's role in *Life and Letters* was major. She arranged all the papers for Edward and also provided a typed outline for him. She named and explained Towndrow's shorthand for him, knowing that he would encounter it throughout his father's papers.[38] In the meantime, she published her own account of Edward's early life in six issues of *The Christian Register*, which also published Calvin Stebbins's three-part account of Edward's Worcester years and Bradley Gilman's four-part account of Edward in Europe.[39] It seems probable that Nelly had brought about a reasonable rapprochement between Hattie and Abby and some of Edward Sr.'s friends in the interest of completing the book. On December 6, 1917, Abby wrote Nelly, "I do want to shout for joy over the 'life,' which came yesterday. More than ever I feel sure the Lord's hand was in Mr. Mead's illness, sinful though it may be to utter such sentiments. I think the whole thing is charming & delightful as it can possibly be. And I think its [*sic*] wonderful the way Edward has brought such order & symmetry & beauty out of that chaos of papers I sent him."[40]

Certainly, the family and the inner circle of friends were pleased that Emily Hale was portrayed as a devoted and much loved wife and mother. There is no mention anywhere in *Life and Letters* that Emily was a semi-invalid from the mid-1880s for the rest of her life. Edward Jr. had succeeded as a "keeper of the family flame." Later biographers took the lead from Edward Jr. in asserting that the Hales' marriage was unusually happy, clouded only by the loss of several children. But the first objective biographer, Jean Holloway, reported evidence that diary entries and even letters of an intimate nature relating to Emily Hale may have been removed from his father's papers by Edward Jr. during the course of writing *Life*, and it appears that Hattie's contributions to the biography were also removed.[41]

Bradley Gilman, himself a prolific and popular biographer who had been proposed by Edward's surviving children to rewrite the biography, was not so kind about *Life and Letters*, in fact he was disappointed. He declared in the *Harvard Theological Review*, "This biography should have appeared at least a half-dozen years ago in order to meet the public's interest at flood tide. Dr. Hale died in 1909, and this volume bears the date 1917. In those eight intervening years many of his associates have died, and the world has moved on, forgetfully, so that the book will not receive so wide a reading as it deserves." While Gilman found *Life and Letters* "readable," he felt it would have been far livelier and captured more of his friend's magnetic personality "if its author had not almost wholly eliminated incidents and anecdotes." He felt that the son's stated intent to avoid criticism and evaluation of his father's work was "an unfortunate and unfruitful position for a biographer to take. The result of it is that the book seriously lacks warmth and color," declared Gilman. "There is never a line of enthusiasm for the eminent and brilliant father."[42]

In fact, Edward Sr.'s literary style was soon caught up in a devastating riptide of stereotypes—the "genteel tradition" and "Indian Summer"—as Modernists, including a younger generation of Harvard graduates such as T. S. Eliot and e e cummings, came to scorn Boston society and culture and most of liberal New England literature. Only nonconformists escaped the critique of the old-fashioned, idealistic side of the cruel World War I watershed. As Van Wyck Brooks expressed it, "The culture of the nineteenth century had gone to seed, and the young were bent on destroying it, root and branch. It was futile, it was incoherent, it was full of cant. It was so much sentimentality, priggishness and 'slop.'"[43]

In the unlikely event that Hattie ever shared any of her letters from his father with Edward's son, he did not quote from them. While he thanked her in his preface to volume one for placing at his "disposal a number of books of reminiscence and remark taken down by her from my father in his later years," the only roles he gave Hattie in three brief references were as his father's amanuensis, the old friend with whom he stayed in Intervale late in life, and one of his friends who took him for drives in his final weeks.[44] But Hattie evidently used her letters as a touchstone for Edward's beliefs and their love for the rest of her long life and she did share several of them with her nieces. During World War I, she sent a couple of his letters to her niece Ethel to read. "These two letters were written with little interval of time & you may like them. They tell of the expectation & then the coming of Berty's baby, who is the Margaret now Freshman at Wellesley & they tell of the Peace which closed our short War with Spain & shows his great joy over it. How often I ask myself what would be his attitude in the present world conditions."[45]

She may well have wondered. Peace activist and social reformer that he was, Edward would certainly have been sympathetic to the radical pacificism and socialism of John Haynes Holmes, Unitarian minister of the Church of the Messiah in New York City and successor there to Edward's good friend Minot J. Savage. The day after Reverend Holmes pronounced war "an open and utter violation of Christianity," President Woodrow Wilson requested from Congress, on April 2, 1917, a declaration of war on Germany. When Holmes proposed a resolution in favor of "the ministry of reconciliation, the preparation of peace, the establishment of social justice, [and] the proclamation of God's law" at a meeting of the General Conference of Unitarians in Montreal that September, he was opposed by Conference president William Howard Taft. Instead, the former president moved a resolution attesting to the sense of the Conference that the "war must be carried to a successful issue to stamp out militarism in the world." The American Unitarian Association soon declared that any opposition to the war effort like

Holmes's was treason while AUA President Samuel Atkins Eliot wrote that he expected disloyal ministers to be dismissed. In 1918, the AUA Board moved to deny financial aid to any church whose minister "is not a willing, earnest, and outspoken supporter of the United States in a vigorous and resolute prosecution of the war." The board of Holmes's church supported their minister's freedom to preach as he felt called but, of the fifteen active Unitarian pacifist ministers, only six remained in their pulpits at the end of the War.[46]

Another outspoken intellectual who fell afoul of majority American opinion during the Great War was Amadeus Grabau. There was a violent backlash against Americans of German descent, particularly those who expressed sympathy with Germany's cause or its culture. According to Alan Mazur, one of his biographers, Grabau's "vociferous defense of Germany, and his disruption of the [Columbia geology] department" led to his dismissal from Columbia University in 1918. This blow was preceded by the breakdown of his marriage with Mary Antin caused by their utterly opposed world views. Antin never recovered her equilibrium and was mentally fragile and struggled to write for the rest of her life. Grabau, although increasingly crippled with rheumatoid arthritis, was rescued professionally by his former students from China, who recommended him to head the new department of paleontology at Peking National University. Through all their travails, the Grabaus were generously supported financially and practically by their loyal friend Thomas Watson. Since Grabau also requested loans from William Crosby, his longtime benefactor and former professor at MIT, it is probable that Hattie was among those old friends who helped him to pay off his debts and fund the journey to China. There are no records to confirm this and Mazur says that Watson paid the entire $1,000 loan requested by Grabau.[47]

Hattie continued to travel far and wide with Emma Cummings well into her seventies, including trips to British Columbia and Glacier Park and two more extended overseas trips. They remained extraordinarily loyal to the American Ornithologists' Union, attending almost every annual meeting, including those on the West Coast.[48] Hattie's passport application of August 16, 1920 was for cruises to Honolulu and Japan that year and to South

America the following year. Departing from San Francisco in late September 1920, they disembarked at Honolulu on October 26. Some of her surviving books show that she studied Hawaiian plant life and geology as well as those of the Philippines, presumably another stopping off point. In 1921, they took a three-and-a-half-month Raymond & Whitcomb cruise down the west coast of South America from Panama to Valparaiso, Chile, and then crossed the Andes by train through Argentina and on to São Paulo and Rio de Janeiro, Brazil, where they boarded the *SS Vestris* for the return cruise to New York. Hattie wrote from the *Vestris* to Mr. Robinson of the Gray Herbarium in May, describing examples of trees and plants they had observed during their travels in the hope he could confirm their identifications.[49]

Hattie remained in her Union Park house with faithful Mary and Sophie until 1922. The 1920 Census shows that 37 Union Park was surrounded by lodging houses filled with working class Americans and Canadian, European, and Armenian immigrants. Next door in No. 39 lived a family of four and no less than eighteen lodgers.[50] Only Hattie kept up the old style of the neighborhood before she moved first to Boston's venerable Hotel Vendome and then to 258 Mt. Vernon Street, West Newton, to live with her unmarried nieces Caroline and Ethel Freeman.[51] Carrie was a Girl Scouts official and Ethel Hale Freeman had taught drama at Smith College and now taught in local private schools. Helen Arnold, who lived in Roxbury with her family and seems to have been closest to Hattie's mold, was an avid arborist and horticulturalist and active in literary circles.

Presumably, Hattie was in Boston for the centenary celebration of Edward's birth on April 3, 1922, once again at a capacity-filled Symphony Hall, where Senator Henry Cabot Lodge, fresh from the Naval Disarmament Conference, gave a thirty-minute address. He avowed "admiration mingled with both reverence and affection" for his friend, reminding the audience of Edward's long labor for international arbitration. Joseph Chamberlin wrote a many-faceted appreciation for the *Boston Evening Transcript*, quoting extensively from letters Edward wrote to his onetime secretary Martha Adams Leland, which she had made available to him.[52] He mentioned Edward's lifelong use of "a system of shorthand, antiquated, pre-Pitman," which must have caught Hattie's eye.[53]

In August 1922, the Hale family celebrated Edward's centenary, the fiftieth anniversary of the Red House, and the twenty-fifth anniversary of the founding of the Robert Beverly Hale Library. The steps of that small local library provided a stage for the commemorations since the Red House had passed out of the family's possession following Susan Hale's death in 1910. Nelly spoke about her father and Edward Jr. spoke about his brother Robert. Philip, Lilian, and Nancy Hale, and Edward's wife Rose were all there. Someone gave Hattie a newspaper account of this family celebration.

The 1920s were tragic for the Atkins family. First there was Grace's death in 1920 and then, in January 1923, Edwin's younger son Ted, who was running the Soledad plantation, was killed along with his two young sons and their governess when the small seaplane in which they were flying from Key West to Havana lost power and crashed with full force into the sea. His wife, who was pregnant with a daughter, the nanny, the pilot, and two crew members were rescued and survived. But Edwin Sr. never recovered from this loss. A further blow was the breakdown of his older son Robert's marriage. Edwin died in 1926, the year of Robert's divorce. Like his cousin Fred Freeman before him, Robert left the company at that point, moved to New York, became a broker and investor in theatrical productions, and remarried. His five children from his first marriage grew up on the Belmont property which was eventually donated to the Massachusetts Audubon Society.[54]

Despite her rift with the Atkinses, all this must have saddened Hattie. But her spirits were undoubtedly lifted by the passage of the Immigration Act of 1924, the Johnson-Reed Act. This new law limited the annual number of immigrants who could be admitted from any country to 2 percent of the people from that country already living in the United States in 1890, down from the 3 percent that the Immigration Restriction Act of 1921 allowed, thus further restricting immigration from Southern and Eastern Europe. These quotas remained in place until 1965.[55]

In 1929, the year of the devastating Stock Market crash, the South Congregational Society was dissolved following its 1925 merger with the First Church, precipitating the sale and eventual demolition of the Church building at Newbury and Exeter Streets. Hale's successor, Edward C. Cummings, had been fatally injured in a car accident in 1926. The Aetna Mills, which had flourished into the 1920s, suffered losses of one and a half million dollars, resulting in the consolidation of its operations in Fitchburg. The Watertown plant, which still stands, was auctioned.[56] And, in a final blow, the collections of Hattie's beloved Boston Society of Natural History were dispersed that same year. Perhaps this was all too much for her to bear.

The 1930 Census shows eighty-three-year-old Harriet Freeman living in a Newton boarding house for eight female lodgers, five of them over seventy, run by the Carvell sisters with two resident servants.[57] Since both Ethel and Carrie were working and Ethel spent the summer months at her farm in northwestern Massachusetts, they may have decided that their aunt would do best in an old people's home. She died there early in the morning of December 30, 1930, after a short illness and her impressive obituary appeared that evening in the Brahmins' favorite newspaper, the *Boston Evening Transcript*. Her claim in her obituary to be closely associated with Edward Everett Hale was read by a generation living in a very different world from the one they had enjoyed together. Hattie was buried next to her parents in Mt. Auburn Cemetery in Cambridge—and so she and Edward remained separated in death, their story forgotten.

Epilogue:

Concealing Is Revealing

Edward Everett Hale's relationship with Harriet Freeman contravened his own and his society's moral precepts, but nothing, not even Henry Ward Beecher's sexual scandal and the prospect of similar recrimination, deterred him. While Hale himself was remarkably tolerant of other people's moral weaknesses and his liberal theology was humanitarian and nonjudgmental (he was a Unitarian after all), the pillars of his church, his family, and his wider Unitarian friendships upheld his stature as a bastion of moral rectitude. His need for Hattie's love and companionship is human and understandable, but how could he persist at the same time in promoting exemplary moral standards to his congregation and to the nation?

The consequences of exposed adultery in the nineteenth century were dire, but today there are stringent and punitive rules against relationships that cross ethical boundaries between ministers, politicians, doctors, psychiatrists, teachers, or other caring professionals and their parishioners, patients, constituents, or students—or between any person of authority and an employee. There are many examples of contemporary infractions and resulting scandals, but one seems curiously reminiscent of the Hale-Freeman story. The Reverend Dr. F. Forrest Church, the Stanford and Harvard-educated son of Senator Frank Church, was senior minister of the liberal Unitarian Church of All Souls in Manhattan's affluent Upper East Side (the church of two of Hale's closest friends where he often preached). Forrest Church, who died tragically early of cancer in 2009, could be compared to Edward Everett Hale. This high profile, charismatic, and dedicated minister, author or editor of twenty-five books, newspaper columnist, and frequent guest on radio and television, also initiated important welfare programs in New York City. Thus, many in his congregation were shocked in 1991 when he announced from the pulpit that he was divorcing his wife of twenty years. Only subsequently did he admit to his board his involvement in a sexual affair with a female parishioner who was active in the administration of his church. A former board member distributed an open letter to church members as they exited the church contending that Dr. Church had violated the Code of Professional Practices of the Unitarian Universalist Ministers Association, which forbids sexual relations with members of a congregation or their spouses. A parishioner commented at the time, "A love affair and a divorce—it happens. What really touches my heart and soul as well as my intellect is the revelation of extreme dishonesty." Church was contrite. He was given a vote of confidence by the majority of his parishioners; divorced his wife; and married his lover. Together they devoted another eighteen years to their Church. The Reverend Church turned his failure into "endless capacity for empathy and compassion," as reported in his obituaries.[1]

This outcome would probably have been impossible in the nineteenth and early twentieth centuries for a man in Edward's position, as the examples of the Reverends Carpenter and Herron have shown. But the Reverend Beecher's charisma became a salvage mechanism for his career, if not his reputation, and perhaps that charismatic quality and his unbounded humanity would have secured support for Edward. He credited Hattie with giving him new life and convinced and/or deluded himself that his relationship with her was "God-given" and "God-blessed." For two decades, they considered their commitment to each other solid as marriage, even if it could not be announced to the world. He even gave her a ring and hair from his beard. And inside the privacy of her house, their relationship reached a level of intimacy that gave each of them great joy. But Edward never mentioned in the surviving letters any possibility of divorce, and neither did Hattie—or his wife.

As for Hattie, she would have done anything for this man she had adored since childhood, an attachment she admitted at a time of deep depression "was not right." But could Edward be accused of using Hattie as long as it suited him, benefiting from her unswerving devotion and the material and emotional comfort she provided, while taking advantage of her willingness to abide by the rules he and society set for their relationship? Edward certainly caused Hattie to feel increasingly abandoned, even discarded, after he left for Washington with Emily and Nelly. He seemed to think that all the happy times they had had for many years and the work they had done together should be enough for her, while he continued to lead a stimulating life in the nation's capital, safely re-ensconced in the bosom of his family. But Edward surely would not have been nominated by his admiring friend Senator George F. Hoar to be chaplain of the U.S. Senate if this relationship had become known. Edward knew he could continue to rely on Hattie's loyalty and discretion even while her anguish became unendurable to her.

If the Hale family suspected a romantic and physical relationship, as Susan Hale's use of the euphemistic term "concubine" implies in a letter to a friend, did Edward ever explain and justify that relationship to his wife and family? Did Emily or the Hale family try to end or curtail the affair? While I have found no overt proof of either, the trajectory of the relationship following Edward's nomination to his highest office seems to indicate that his family "circled the wagons" to shield his reputation and their fragile mother's feelings. Even if she had wanted freedom from her dominant husband, Emily Hale was trapped by strict societal convention, her ill health, and precarious family finances. And she seems to have understood and regretted the role she played in distancing her husband, as she told her daughter. Hale and his wife were certainly fond of each other, although they had increasingly less in common. He was also a remarkably concerned and involved father to his daughter and five surviving sons, and a loving, admiring, and protective brother to his two surviving unmarried sisters. In fact, it might be said that he probably got the best of everything.

While Harriet Freeman's life was certainly richer because of her intimate relationship with one of the era's most fascinating men, was she shackled by the discretion that her own and her paramour's status required? Did her emotional dependence on Edward limit her own potential? He expressed that concern himself early in their relationship. She was certainly aware that many other women of her privileged background, intelligence, and financial means (Jane Addams, Frances Willard, and Lilian Wald, for example—none of whom married) were breaking free from societal constraints to establish unprecedented institutions for reform. And Hattie envied her friends, like Mary Dann and Parnell Murray, who had pursued the same studies as her and became fulltime teachers of science. Was she so inculcated in Proper Boston strictures that she lacked the will or the insight to break free? Certainly, she always hoped, until the reality of the Washington years, that Edward would be able to spend more time with her.

While Hattie told Edward that she had never minded what other people thought of her, she seemed to go out of her way later in life to cement her status as the descendant of old Yankee stock, and her comments about people from less privileged or other ethnic and racial backgrounds often hint at snobbery and racism. A very complicated mix of scientific inquiry and social conservatism, she supported the anti-suffrage and immigration restriction movements. Yet she was a kind and loyal mistress to her two Irish Catholic servants and spent years lobbying for the rights of American Indians.

In this age when Tweets, e-mail, and cell phones have replaced letter writing, it is more difficult to conceal an extramarital affair or other covert activity. Again and again, men—generally men in positions of authority or trust—are forced to face relentless and embarrassing media scrutiny while their wives stand staunchly (and sometimes temporarily) by their sides. This has become a cliché. The incredible discretion of Edward Everett Hale and Harriet Freeman kept him on the right side of the angels and spared Emily Hale the limelight. But Nancy Hale, who was a baby when her grandfather died, apparently heard from her elders about this "special" friendship. A serious writer who was intrigued by family mythology, she published an insightful memoir about growing up with her parents, Philip and Lilian Hale, and her aunt Nelly—all artists—and made notes for a never written psychological memoir of her great-uncle Charles Hale, which would certainly have contained much speculation about his older brother, her forceful grandfather. The family rumor about Harriet Freeman must have tempted her imagination, as discovery of the code in the letters stimulated my curiosity. On the Freeman side, Hattie's great-niece Harriet McKissock, whose mother Helen Hunt Arnold was persuaded by Nancy Hale to donate a number of Hale-Freeman letters containing shorthand to Smith College, wondered in her 1997 notes on the collection: "Q. Was Aunt Harriet (H.E.F.) MORE than an intellectual companion?"[2]

Concealing is nearly always revealing.

Postscript

Some months after publication of the first edition of this book, another serendipitous discovery was brought to my attention. Hattie donated several family treasures to various Boston institutions. Among these was a piece of the lining of the flag that some believed was carried by Pizarro during the conquest of Peru, which Hattie's father had "appropriated" when he was in Caracas in 1837. Hattie donated this to the Boston Athenaeum, as recorded by Charles Knowles Bolton, librarian of the Athenaeum from 1898 to 1934, in his diary for June 15, 1915: "Miss Harriet E. Freeman called. She is very homely, vivacious and ubiquitous, 'a Hale Unitarian of 40 years standing' who now attends the cathedral on Tremont Street." Hattie delivered the flag morsel on October 7, 1915, and Bolton wrote that "she told me much about Edward Everett Hale whom she knew for forty years," followed by five paragraphs on what she told him, confirmation of Hattie's continuing obsession with Hale.

Bolton's reference to the Episcopal Cathedral Church of St. Paul reminded me of a letter on Cathedral letterhead from its rector, the Reverend Henry Goddard, which I found tucked in front of Hattie's copy of Hale's novella *In His Name*. In this letter, dated May 9, 1916, Goddard told her he had called on her twice when she was out, was very sorry to miss her, and was disappointed that a meeting prevented him from accepting her invitation to attend the play in which her niece was performing. He had returned the book which he had found "wonderfully, exquisitely beautiful."

Hattie had complained to Hale for some years before his death about the way some of the younger Unitarian ministers, including Edward C. Cummings, had departed from some of the more traditional Christian practices, such as communion, and her dislike of Cummings's dry, ethical preaching style. When Rabbi Charles Fleischer left Temple Israel in 1911 to establish the Sunday Commons, a nonsectarian religion for persons of all backgrounds, it ran counter to Hattie's growing distaste for melting-pot initiatives. And so Edward Everett Hale's most devoted disciple appears to have found a new spiritual home in the Episcopal Church, following in the footsteps of so many Boston Brahmin Unitarians.[1]

Notes

1. A Parish Call

1. Edward Everett Hale (EEH), Roxbury, MA, to Harriet E. Freeman (HEF), Union Park, Boston (UP), March 7, 1884. Special Correspondence, Edward Everett Hale and Harriet E. Freeman, 1884-1909, Hale Family Papers, Manuscript Division, Library of Congress (SLOC).
2. Edward Everett Hale, "The Man Without a Country," *Atlantic Monthly*, December 1863, and reprinted in multiple formats over the next seventy-five years.
3. Suffolk County Registry of Deeds, December 25, 1861, Libro 808, fol. 117-119, and April 29, 1862, Libro 811, fol. 148; Atkins et al, indenture, April 28, 1862, and Freeman et al to Atkins Trustee, indenture, January 28, 1868. Suffolk County Registry of Deeds, Libro 924, folios 305-308. All accessed through microfilm at the New England Historic Genealogical Society, Boston, 10/16/12.
4. William Dean Howells, *The Rise of Silas Lapham* (first published Boston, 1885; from Rockville, MD: Arc Manor, 2009 edition), 20.
5. All drawn from Hattie's letters to Edward in which she reminisced about her childhood, as well as his memories of what she had told him.
6. The present mill (now Farley-White Aetna Mills) was built in the 1880s. Water-wheels still supplied part of the power but use of water power gradually decreased. Thelma Fleishman, *Charles River Dams* (Charles River Watershed Association, 1978), 24.

2. The Freemans and the Hales

1. I am grateful to family historians Helen Atkins Claflin, Katharine Wrisley Claflin Weeks, and Robert Freeman Weeks for the very full

information on the Freeman and Atkins families in *A New England Family* and *A New England Family Revisited*. However, there is no information on Hattie's own family, beyond William F. Freeman's trading partnership with Elisha Atkins, and on Hattie herself because their interest in the Freemans ends with their ancestor Mary Freeman Atkins, Hattie's aunt.

2. George Harlan Lewis, *Edmund Lewis of Lynn, Massachusetts, and Some of his Descendants* (Essex Institute, 1908), 106-107. "The large yellow house that until recently stood across Elm Street from Town Hall was the Lewis Estate. This stately Federal-style mansion was constructed in 1819 for Squire James Lewis, a Billerica-born lawyer and prominent public citizen…A 1990s-style suburban house now stands on its site." See Ronald Karr, "Main Street: Pepperell's Highway of History," Pepperell Historical Commission http://www.pepperell-mass.com/historical/MainSt.html consulted 10/12/12.
3. Writing about the birthday party she was to share with her niece Ethel Hale Freeman in 1907, Hattie told Edward: "This will make up for the party I lost when I was a little girl. Did you ever hear of that? It was when we lived in Edinboro St. I came home & said I was going to have a party on my birthday & that I had invited all the girls & boys. I had done this <*without*> consulting my Mother, & the consequence was I had to go & tell them all they couldn't come. In those days when I had a party, the parlor velvet carpet was covered with white cotton, so we could dance better on the smooth surface. I loved the general upsetting which it made. Shouldn't think my activity would have made me a terror to my Mother! I think that was the reason I was sent to boarding school at Pepperell." HEF, UP, to EEH, Washington, DC, [February 27, 1907]. Box 25, undated, SLOC.
4. On March 7, 1859, an Irish Catholic boy at the Eliot School in Boston refused to read the Ten Commandments from the Protestant King James Bible. A week later, he again refused and was severely whipped on the hand by the assistant principal. Four hundred boys left the school that and the next day. The incident attracted intense national interest and sparked the creation of Catholic parochial schools in Boston and across the nation. [Wikipedia, consulted 9/20/12]
5. Caroline Crosby Freeman, "Sunny Days," bound album of botanical watercolors, ca. 1866. Boston Athenaeum; Freeman, "Happy Hours," ca. 1866. Private collection; Freeman, Civil War scrapbooks. American Antiquarian Society, Worcester, MA. List of books borrowed by William F. Freeman in 1871, from "Borrowed Books" ledger, Prints and Photographs Dept., Boston Athenaeum.
6. Elisha Atkins built two adjacent houses, 35 and 37, on Commonwealth

Avenue, both designed by Nathaniel Bradlee. But the Atkins lived in No. 37, a house so large that it was divided into 22 apartments in 1930 although it has been restored to a single-family residence in recent years. See Bainbridge Bunting, *Houses of Boston's Back Bay: An Architectural History 1840-1917* (The Belknap Press of Harvard University, 1967), Appendix A, 422.

7. Principal sources for social history, land reclamation, and architecture of Boston: William A. Newman and Wilfred E. Holton, *Boston's Back Bay: The Story of America's Greatest Nineteenth-Century Landfill Project* (Boston: Northeastern University Press, 2006); Bunting, *Houses of Boston's Back Bay*; Frederick C. Jaher, "Boston," chapter 2, *The Urban Establishment: Upper Strata in Boston, New York, Charleston, Chicago and Los Angeles* (Urbana, IL: University of Illinois Press, c. 1982); Betty G. Farrell, *Elite Families: Class and Power in Nineteenth Century Boston* (New York: State University of New York, 1993).
8. Van Wyck Brooks, *The Flowering of New England 1815-1865* (Boston: E. P. Dutton & Co., 1936), 485.
9. Both these houses were demolished during site preparation for building two grand hotels, the Tremont House and the Parker House.
10. See Edward Everett Hale, *A New England Boyhood* (New York: Cassell Publishing Co., 1893).
11. Thomas W. Higginson, *Carlyle's Laugh and Other Surprises*, (Boston, 1899), 160-161. Quoted in Jean Holloway, *Edward Everett Hale A Biography* (Austin: University of Texas Press, 1956), 34.
12. Quoted in Conrad Wright, *A Stream of Light: A Sesquicentennial History of American Unitarianism* (Boston: Unitarian Universalist Association, 1975), 47.
13. Quoted in John R. Adams, *Edward Everett Hale* (Boston: Twayne Publishers, 1977), 20.
14. Charles Mayo Ellis, *An Essay on Transcendentalism*, 1842. The reputed author's essay provided a basic overview of contemporary Transcendentalist beliefs on a range of topics such as "Art," "Religion," and "Criticism." Tiffany K. Wayne, *Encyclopedia of Transcendentalism* (New York: Facts on File, 2006), 93.
15. See miscellaneous letters to Harriet Freeman and others; "Tarry at Home Travel," *New England Magazine*, Vol. 1 (November 1889), 337; EEH, *Tarry at Home Travels* (New York: Macmillan, 1907), 67.
16. Edward Everett to Sarah Preston (Everett) Hale, January 2, 1843, Massachusetts Historical Society. Quoted in Holloway, *Hale*, 61.
17. Edward Everett Hale, "My Reminiscences," *Woman's Home Companion*, Vol. 36, Nos. 3 and 5 (March and May 1909).
18. Edward Everett Hale, *Memories of a Hundred Years* (New York: Macmillan, 1902), Vol. II, 142, 151.

19. Edward Everett Hale, *A Tract for the Times: or, How to Conquer Texas Before Texas Conquers Us*, Boston, March 17, 1845, reprinted as "Freedom in Texas," *Works*, VI, 221-36.
20. *Proceedings of the Boston Society of Natural History*, August 20, 1845, II, 54, quoted in Holloway, *Hale*, 81. Phanerogamia was a former primary division of plants comprising those having reproductive organs.
21. EEH, *Letters on Irish Emigration*, 1852, 58. Quoted in Adams, *Hale*, 87.
22. Holloway, *Hale*, 104-107; Edward E. Hale, *Kanzas and Nebraska* (Boston: Phillips, Sampson, 1854).
23. EEH's assessment of Frederic Dan Huntington's achievements at the South Congregational Church, quoted in Edward Everett Hale, Jr., *The Life and Letters of Edward Everett Hale* (Boston: Little, Brown, 1917), vol. I, 282.
24. *The Elements of Christian Doctrine and its Development*. Five sermons preached before the South Congregational Society, Boston, in January, February, and March 1860 and printed at its request (Boston, 1860).
25. See "Ninety Days Worth of Europe," chapter 13 of EEHJr., *Life and Letters*, vol. 1, 293-318.
26. See Records of the South Congregational Church, 1823-1887 (SS 12), South Friendly Society. R. Stanton Avery Collections, New England Historic Genealogical Society.
27. EEH, Island Heights, NJ, to HEF, Altamonte, FL, March 9, 1890. Hale Family Papers, Sophia Smith Collection, Smith College (HFP-SSC). In his reminiscences of EEH, his friend Lyman Abbott recalled: "The attempt to follow emancipation with National aid to education, after a vigorous and at first hopeful struggle, failed. Dr. Hale's interest in that attempt, in which Senator [George F.] Hoar was a leader, is interpreted by himself in the following letter." He then quoted EEH's opinion that it was the New York *Nation* that killed the national education plan. "...but for them, we should have had for twenty years, a thorough system of education at the South supported by the National Treasury." Lyman Abbott, "Snap-shots of my contemporaries: Edward Everett Hale—an American Abou Ben Adhem," *The Outlook*, Oct. 26, 1921; American Periodicals Series Online, 300.
28. Conrad Wright, *The Liberal Christians: Essays on American Unitarian History* (Boston: Beacon Press, 1970), 83.
29. EEH, "The National Conference of Unitarian Churches," *Christian Examiner* 78 (1865), 427, quoted in Wright, *Stream of Light*, 64.
30. See Jon H. Roberts, *Darwinism and the Divine in America: Protestant Intellectuals and Organic Evolution, 1859-1900* (Madison, WI: The University of Wisconsin Press, 1988).
31. Gray's review of Darwin's *Origin of Species* appeared in the *Atlantic*

in July 1860. The split between evolutionists and creationists (a modern term) is as deep as ever, a fact acknowledged by the reprinting of Gray's review in Atlantic.com on August 31, 2011. See also P. J. Croce, "Probabilistic Darwinism: Louis Agassiz vs. Asa Gray on Science, Religion, and Certainty," *Journal of Religious History*, Vol. 22, issue 1, February 1998, 35-38.

32. Hale had also written and published prolifically in several genres during these years, particularly for the *Atlantic*. These included "The Brick Moon," 1867 (Hale is acknowledged by NASA to be the first to conceive of a manned orbiting space station). In his Utopian fable *Sybaris and other Homes* (1869), Hale imagined the people driving automobiles, parking as many as sixty-five of them outside church on Sunday. These he saw as steam cars, propelled by engines driven by petroleum. This was thirty years before the advent of automobiles! (quoted from Joseph E. Chamberlin, "Boston's Great Pastor-at-Large," *Boston Evening Transcript*, April 1, 1922). See also Alexander MacDonald, "The Brick Space Station," in *The Long Space Age: An Economic Perspective on the History of American Space Exploration* (Balliol College, Oxford dissertation, 2012, provided by the author).

33. *The Lord's Supper and Its Observance* by Lucretia P. Hale (Boston, 1866), inscribed "Hattie Freeman, with the best love of E.E.H. Dec. 28, 1868" and *The Elements of Character* by Mary G. Chandler (Boston, 1854), inscribed "Hatty E. Freeman with the love of E.E.H March 3, 1870." These books and many others were donated by a dealer, along with the Harriet E. Freeman papers, to the Andover-Harvard Theological Library, Harvard Divinity School, and have been cataloged for the Library.

34. "Often my father did not get home to dinner; if he was kept downtown on business he would lunch at one or another place, and perhaps spend the afternoon making parish, and other calls, and doing various things, getting home for supper which we had at half-past six. After supper he generally retired to the study. My mother used to read aloud to us children in the parlor—few recollections of childhood are more definite or more beautiful than those readings—but during those years my father was rarely in the parlor in the evenings. Frequently he was at some public affair, speaking at some meeting, as he often did, or lecturing now and then in Boston and elsewhere, or at a club meeting where he might have been for dinner." EEHJr, *Life and Letters*, vol. 2, 141.

35. Nancy Hale, *The Life in the Studio* (Boston: Little, Brown, 1969), 127; Nancy Hale to Harriet McKissock, June 4, 1974. HFP-SSC.

36. HEF, Newton, MA, to EEH, Roxbury, Sept. 21, 1870. This letter, along

with other letters preceding the Special Correspondence of Edward Everett Hale and Harriet E. Freeman, 1884-1909, is filed in the General Correspondence section of the Hale Family Papers at LOC (GLOC).

3. Panic, Church, and Science

1. HEF, Waterville, NH, to EEH, Pasadena, CA, February 15, 1891. SLOC.
2. EEH, Waterville, NH, to Emily Hale, Boston, MA, August 2, 1868. Quoted in EEHJr., *Life and Letters*, II, 92.
3. David Reed (1790-1870) was the founding proprietor and editor for more than forty-five years of the *Christian Register*, which was devoted to the advocacy of liberal Christianity. He was also a founder of the South Congregational Church and its oldest officer at the end of his life. See David Reed: Heralds of a Liberal Faith www.harvardsquarelibrary.org/Heralds/David Reed.php
4. Ironically, Hale was also in Chicago the previous November, shortly after the Great Fire there, when he toured the burned out areas and met with religious and lay leaders at relief headquarters. EEH diaries, November 1871 and November 1872. Edward Everett Hale Papers, 1832-1909 (SC12555) from the collection of the New York State Library Manuscripts and Special Collections, Albany, NY (NYSL).
5. "We have received and read 'The New and The Old,' the latest born of the magazines. We salute it in the language of the response of the witches to the invocation of Macbeth: First Witch—All *Hale*! Second Witch—All *Hale*! Third Witch—All *Hale*! It will have to encounter the keen rivalry of the *Atlantic* and *Galaxy*, but we trust that it will prove Greater than both, by the *All-Hale* thereafter." *Western Monthly*, III (January 1870), 80. Quoted in Holloway, *Hale*, 179.
6. "The Wilson Committee—Mr. Elisha Atkins' Testimony," *The New York Times*, January 26, 1873.
7. William Howell Reed, *Reminiscences of Elisha Atkins* (Privately printed, Cambridge, University Press, 1890), 142-147.
8. "A Letter from Elisha Atkins," *The New York Times*, May 30, 1876.
9. Until 1873, the Hale family rented a house in Milton where the Kidders had their country estate and Emily and Edward often stayed at the Kidders' seaside house in Beverly. In addition to the generous annual bonus that Kidder gave Edward, he also paid the Harvard fees of the Hales' most academically promising son, young Edward E. Hale Jr.
10. "Thurs. July 31 73 To Providence at 2 with Katy Kennedy, Mary Quink, the four little boys and Bruno [the dog]." EEH journal, 1873. NYSL.
11. EEHJr., *Life and Letters*, II, 187. Weeden, Bellows, and Hale were col-

leagues in the U.S. Sanitary Commission during the Civil War and then in the post-Civil War efforts to establish a stronger centralized organization for the independent Unitarian churches; Hale and Hedge were longtime co-editors of the *Christian Examiner;* and Weeden and Hale were closely allied in *Old and New.*

12. Holloway, *Hale,* 198.
13. This account of the Beecher-Tilton scandal relies heavily on chapters 12 and 13 of Debby Applegate's brilliant Pulitzer Prize-winning biography of Henry Ward Beecher: Applegate, *The Most Famous Man in America: The Biography of Henry Ward Beecher* (New York: Doubleday, 2006), 391-456.
14. See Applegate, 422, and Adams, *Hale,* 116 and 136, note 44.
15. EEHJr., *Life and Letters,* II, 230.
16. Harry was not the first of the young Hale brothers to die. He was born just as his older brother, Charles Alexander (Charlie), died of diphtheria on March 17, 1868. Little Charlie was named after two of his father's favorite brothers.
17. In trying to understand her subject, Holloway made much of Edward's youthful uncertainty about whether to become a minister or a writer.
18. On November 6 and 17, 1873, Edward noted in his diary that he called on William F. Freeman, a rare occurrence. Perhaps this was when Freeman called on his pastor's help in talking his strong-willed daughter out of her wish to attend Vassar. More than twenty years later, Edward reminisced, "You know that I do not much like sending girls to college. I am not sure that you have forgiven me that I advised against your going to Vasser. How terrible you would have been! I believe you would have worn spectacles!" EEH, Little Boar's Head, NH, to HEF, Shelburne, NH, September 2, 1894. SLOC.
19. Margaret W. Rossiter, *Women Scientists in America* (Baltimore: The Johns Hopkins University Press, 1982), vol. 1, "Struggles and Strategies to 1940," 13.
20. In the late 1870s, Alice James, the brilliant but chronically ill sister of William and Henry James, began working with Katharine Loring, who led the history department for the S.H., and the two women became close friends, eventually living together in London until Alice James's death. See Jean Strouse, *Alice James: A Biography* (Cambridge, MA: Harvard University Press, 1980).
21. See *Society to Encourage Studies At Home* (Cambridge, MA: Riverside Press, 1897). Harriet Freeman is listed as a correspondent for two years in Appendix A, List of Correspondents who Served Two Years or More, 184.

22. Rossiter, *Women Scientists*, 30-31.
23. "The Rev. Edward Everett Hale. His Methods of Work. The Story of the Man Without a Country." "From the Boston Herald." *New York Times*, May 6, 1880.
24. HEF, Quebec, Canada, to EEH, Matunuck, [late July/early August 1894] Undated miscellaneous fragment, Box 25, SLOC.
25. HEF, Ormond, Florida, to EEH, Washington, March 1905. SLOC. [Emma and she are about to take the 2-day Ocklawaha trip] "I wanted to take it when I was here with Mother in 1878. But she was not able to take it; & I could not go alone & leave her alone; so I did not go." In 1890, Edward presented to the American Antiquarian Society, Worcester, Massachusetts, on behalf of Hattie, her mother's fifteen scrapbooks compiled day by day during the Civil War. *Proceedings of American Antiquarian Society*, 1890, 50.
26. See Nancy Hale's notes for a never realized novel based on Charles Hale's life. She must have heard about Charles's embarrassing behavior at the dinner table from her father, Philip, and her Aunt Ellen. Nancy Hale Papers, Sophia Smith Collection (NHP-SSC).
27. Mary Cobb was the sister-in-law of a close friend of her father's in Brewster, Freeman Cobb. Cobb (1830-1878) led a colorful life, making his fortune in Australia when he established at age twenty-two with a partner Cobb & Company, a carrying and coach company, which made him a fortune. His name became synonymous with "coach" in Australia. Having sold the company, he returned to America in 1856, married his cousin Annette Cobb, Mary's sister, and lived grandly in Brewster until he lost his large fortune in banking investments. In 1871, Cobb moved his family to South Africa where he died insolvent. Sometime after his impoverished family returned to America, Hattie's father apparently offered Mary a home. Despite the differences in their ages and temperaments, Hattie remained loyal to Mary Cobb and to her family, whose friendship with the Freemans had endured for three generations.
28. "To Miss H. E. Freeman," February 14, 1882. EEH Journal. NYSL.
29. EEH, Matunuck, to HEF, Milton, MA, August 8, 1899. SLOC.
30. This letter, dated April 3, 1882, along with other letters preceding the special collection of Hale-Freeman letters dated 1884-1909, is filed with General Correspondence in Box 13 of the Hale Family Papers at LOC (GLOC). Since Hattie said she always kept this letter, it is likely that the pre-1884 letters belong with the special correspondence with EEH.
31. *Ten Times One is Ten: The Possible Reformation, A Story in Nine Chapters by Col. Frederic Ingham*, 1881, inscribed on two facing pages: "One of

ten copies given by me to My Own Ten Edward E. Hale. 'My own Ten' means the Ten persons nearest me in the work & pleasure of Life.' Hatty Freeman With the grateful love of Edw. E. Hale April 10, 1882." Andover-Harvard Theological Library, Harvard Divinity School (AHTL).

32. HEF, western shore of Lake Superior, to EEH, Matunuck, July 24, 1890. GLOC.
33. EEH, Madrid, to HEF, Pepperell, MA, June 13, 1882. GLOC.
34. *In His Name: A Story of the Waldenses* by EEH (Boston: Roberts, 1881) Inscribed by Hale "Hattie E. Freeman March 13, 1883 with all good wishes & prayers for her birthday from the author." AHTL.
35. Edwin F. Atkins, *Sixty Years in Cuba: reminiscences of Edwin F. Atkins* (Privately printed at Riverside Press, Boston, 1926), 81-82.
36. June C. Erlick, "Mission to Cuba," *The Boston Globe Magazine,* March 14, 2000, 16-17, 23–26.
37. Christopher Harris, "Edwin F. Atkins and the Evolution of American Cuba Policy, 1892-1902," 4–5. Published at www.kislakfoundation.org/kislak_prize.html
38. EEH, Queenstown, Ireland, to HEF, UP, May 6, 1883. GLOC.
39. EEH, St. Germain en Laye, France, to HEF, UP, June 7, 1883. GLOC.
40. Alfred G. Mayer, "Alpheus Hyatt, 1838-1902," *The Popular Science Monthly*, Vol. 78 (February 1911), 129-146; Robert S. Shrock, "Alpheus Hyatt," in *Geology at MIT: A History of the First Hundred Years of Geology at the Massachusetts Institute of Technology* (Cambridge, MA: The MIT Press, 1977), Vol. 1, 215-220. For Hattie as a member of the corporation board of the Marine Biological Laboratory see donors lists in annual reports of the Woods Hole Marine Biological Laboratory, 1887-1907.
41. Cyril Aydon, *Charles Darwin: His Life and Times* (Philadelphia: Running Press, 2008), 285.
42. EEH, Washington, to HEF, UP, January 17, 1886. GLOC.
43. EEH, Roxbury, to HEF, Pepperell, October 3, 1883. GLOC.

4. Romantic Love

1. EEH, "Wisconsin, on the rail," to HEF, UP, January 29, 1884. SLOC.
2. EEH, Roxbury, to HEF, UP, March 7, 1884. SLOC.
3. EEH, Roxbury, to HEF, UP, April 3, 1884. SLOC.
4. EEH, Ohio, Illinois, to HEF, Pepperell, May 14, 1884. SLOC. See Bruce G. Charlton, "Editorial Preface to the English translation of *Goethe's correspondence with a child* by Bettina von Arnim, 1837." www.hedweb.com/bgcharlton/preface-bettina.html Consulted on 8/10/11.
5. EEH journal, Sunday, June 15, 1884: "Train to Ayer Junction. Hatty

Freeman meets me and we drive to Pepperell. Monday, June 16: Drive in the morning to River [by] the trotting park. P.M. Call on Dr. Babbidge [the Freemans' retired minister] and Mrs. Jewett. Writing in evening on the inventions. Tuesday, June 17, Drive in morning to [blank] Train at [blank] for Boston. Home at 10." NYSL.

6. Emily Hale, Peekskill, NY, to EEH, Roxbury, June 20, 1884. HFP-SSC.
7. EEH, Matunuck, to HEF, Pepperell, June 27, 1884. SLOC. Gottfried Ephraim Lessing (1729-1781), a major figure of the Enlightenment era, was a German writer, philosopher, dramatist, and art critic.
8. Emily Hale, Peekskill, NY, to EEH, Matunuck, July 1, 1884. HFP-SSC.
9. Applegate, *Henry Ward Beecher,* 462-464.
10. See "James Freeman Clarke," ch. 3, Francis G. Peabody, *Reminiscences of Present-day Saints* (Boston, New York: Houghton Mifflin, 1927), 41-64. According to George S. Merriam in his "Reminiscences of Edward Everett Hale," *The Outlook,* November 12, 1910: "When James Freeman Clarke—his brother in spirit, though almost antithetical in temperament and fighting usually in the same ranks—when Clarke and many others of his friends went over to Cleveland . . . in 1884, it was a grief to him [Hale]."
11. EEH, Matunuck, to HEF, Pepperell, July 3, 1884. SLOC.
12. Emily Hale, Peekskill, NY, to EEH, Matunuck, July 3, 1884. HFP-SSC.
13. EEH, Brunswick, Maine, to HEF, Pepperell, July 10, 1884. SLOC.
14. EEH, Coney Island, to HEF, Pepperell, July 14, 1884. SLOC.
15. See "Gray's Manual of Botany, 1st edition 1848," part of the Harvard University Botany Libraries' Asa Gray Bicentennial website: http://www.hugh.harvard.edu/libraries/Gray_Bicent/manual. htm and Elizabeth B. Keeney, *The Botanizers: Amateur Scientists in Nineteenth-Century America* (Chapel Hill: University of North Carolina Press, 1992), 34.
16. EEH journal, July 26-30, 1884. NYSL.
17. EEH, Matunuck, to HEF, Pepperell, August 4, 1884. SLOC.
18. EEH, Matunuck, to HEF, Pepperell, August 23, 1884. SLOC.
19. EEH, Matunuck, to HEF, Pepperell, September 5, 1884. SLOC.
20. EEH, Roxbury, to HEF, Pepperell, September 28, 1884. SLOC.
21. EEH, Matunuck, to HEF, Pepperell, September 3, 1884. SLOC.
22. EEH, Matunuck, to HEF, Pepperell, August 30, 1884. SLOC.
23. EEH, Matunuck, to HEF, Pepperell, August 25, 1884. SLOC.
24. EEH, Matunuck, to HEF, Pepperell, September 1, 1884. SLOC.
25. EEH, Matunuck, to HEF, Pepperell, September 7, 1884. SLOC.
26. Emily Hale, Matunuck, to EEH, Roxbury, October 15, 1884. HFP-SSC.
27. EEH, Matunuck, to HEF, Pepperell, September 3, 1884. SLOC.
28. Francis G. Peabody, Cambridge, to EEH, Roxbury, May 8, 1884. Edward Everett Hale Papers, AHTL. Peabody was the brother-in-law of Harvard president Charles W. Eliot.

29. EEH, Saratoga, NY, to HEF, Pepperell, September 24, 1884. SLOC.
30. EEH, Roxbury, to HEF, Pepperell, September 29 and October 1, 1884. SLOC; Thomas Towndrow, *A Complete Guide to Stenography, or An entire new system of writing short hand* (New Haven and New York, 1832).
31. Emily Hale, Roxbury, to EEH, Saratoga, September 23, 1884. HFP-SSC.
32. The tensions between Irish Catholic immigrants and the existing Anglo Protestant community in Boston's North End had erupted into the Eliot School Rebellion in 1859. This may have prompted Hattie's parents to remove her from the local Boston school and send her to boarding school in Pepperell. See Chapter 2, 26.
33. Barbara Miller Solomon, *Ancestors and Immigrants: A Changing New England Tradition* (Cambridge: Harvard University Press, 1956), 48 *passim*; 84 85.
34. Emily Hale, New Haven, to EEH, Roxbury, December 12 and 16, 1884. HFP-SSC.
35. Edward Everett Hale, *The Unitarian Principles* (Boston: American Unitarian Association, n.d.), No. 51, Fourth Series, 12-13.
36. EEH, Roxbury, to HEF, Pepperell, September 28, 1884. SLOC.
37. The Mrs. Adams who received EEH and party that day was Abigail, wife of Charles Francis Adams (1807-1886), third and only surviving son of President John Quincy Adams. In 1870 Charles Francis Adams Sr. built in Quincy the first memorial presidential library in the United States, to honor his father. The Stone Library includes over 14,000 books written in twelve languages. The library is located in the "Old House" at Adams National Historical Park in Quincy, Massachusetts.
38. EEH, Washington, to HEF, UP, February 15, 1885. SLOC.
39. EEH, Washington, to HEF, UP, February 9 and 10, 1885. SLOC. Theodore Dwight was U.S. State Department librarian from 1875-1888; then, from 1888-1892, was in charge of the Adams family archives and secretary and proofreader for Henry Adams during his completion of the *History of the United States*. Between 1892 and 1894, he was librarian at the Boston Public Library.
40. EEH, Washington, to HEF, UP, February 25, 1885. SLOC.
41. Holloway, *Hale*, 224.
42. Emily Hale, Roxbury, to EEH, ?, February 24, 1885. HFP-SSC.
43. William Weeden, "Reminiscences," original manuscript copybook at Rhode Island Historical Society. Photocopy of typescript by Rockwell K. DuMoulin at Center for the Study of Hale Family Art, Matunuck, RI. Courtesy of Austin Smith; EEH, Matunuck, to HEF, UP, August 6, 1896: "In the afternoon, I went down to call on William. But this is always rather hard now. We are not to each other what we were, and

we try hard to pretend we are." EEH, Matunuck, to HEF, UP, July 17, 1903. SLOC.

44. EEH, Matunuck, to HEF, UP, June 23, 1885. SLOC.
45. EEH, Matunuck, to HEF, Pepperell, July 17, 1885. SLOC; Emily Hale, Roxbury, to Ellen D. Hale, Paris, France, May 25, 1885. HFP-SSC.
46. For an 8-minute video about the restoration and family association see: http://www.youtube.com/watch?v=OZQyPpgJsFk7feature=chan nel page The EEH quotes were taken, misleadingly, from his letters to Hattie and the final photo shows him with Hattie in 1902.
47. EEH, Roxbury, to HEF, Pepperell, August 12, 1885. SLOC. He also told Hattie that he had written a letter of sympathy to Helen Hunt Jackson's widower. Helen and Edward became good friends when she wrote articles for his *Old and New* in the 1870s.
48. Written for young people, these papers were printed in 1886 in *The Chatauquan*. In 1903, they were reprinted in book form under the title *How to Live*, for which Edward wrote an introduction. EEH, *How to Live* (Boston: Little, Brown, 1903).
49. EEH, Mayfield, New York, to HEF, Pepperell, August 18, but postmarked August 26, 1885. SLOC.
50. EEH, Matunuck, to HEF, Pepperell, August 22 and 29, 1885. SLOC.
51. EEH, Beverly Farm, near Marblehead, to HEF, Pepperell, September 11, 1885. SLOC.
52. EEH, Roxbury, to HEF, Pepperell, September 15, 1885. SLOC.
53. EEH, Roxbury, to HEF, Pepperell, September 16, 1885. SLOC.
54. The inscribed book, part of the Freeman Collection, is in the Andover-Harvard Theological Library. Mt. Watatic (1,832 ft.) is on the border of Massachusetts and New Hampshire fifteen miles from Pepperell.
55. EEH, Roxbury, to HEF, Pepperell, October 9. 1885. SLOC. There is no indication why William Freeman was asking for that address but he may at that stage have recognized the state of his health and the need for sheltered care.
56. Decades later, she told her niece Ethel in an inscription to the copy of *Ten Times One Is Ten* she gave her that "'The Loyal Wife' on page 51 is my story of Mrs. Bowen."
57. EEH, Roxbury, to HEF, Pepperell, October 27, 1885. SLOC.
58. EEH, Coney Island, to HEF, Plymouth, Mass, July 19, 1885. SLOC.
59. EEH, Boston, to HEF, Pepperell, October 27, 1885. SLOC.
60. Suzette (Bright Eyes) LaFlesche (1854-1903), an Omaha Indian, was educated at the Hampton Institute in Virginia.
61. EEH, Bridgeport, Conn., to HEF, UP, January 26, 1886. SLOC. Henry Kidder, described in his *New York Times* obituary as "the foremost member of the church of the Rev. Dr. Edward Everett Hale, being a

Trustee of that church for many years," who was also President of the American Unitarian Association, died on January 28, 1886. Two of his sons, his second wife (daughter of the president of Meadville Theological College in Ohio), and his Boston physician were at his bedside when he died. A self-made man, Kidder became Boston's leading banker and most benevolent citizen.

62. EEH, Philadelphia, to HEF, UP, February 9 and 10, 1886. SLOC.
63. EEH, Roxbury, to HEF, UP, March 23, 1886. SLOC.
64. EEH, Roxbury, to HEF, UP, April 4, 1886. SLOC.
65. EEH, Swampscott, MA, to HEF, Pepperell, July 16, 1886; EEH, Matunuck, to HEF, Pepperell, July 19, 1886. Both SLOC.
66. EEH, Roxbury, to HEF, UP, [December 28, 1886]. SLOC.

5. Loss and Liberation

1. Applegate, *Beecher*, 465-467. Catharine Beecher had died in 1878, James Beecher shot himself to death in 1886. Thomas Beecher, whom Edward despised, attended but refused to accompany the family to the graveyard, saying "I'm not going to traipse all over Brooklyn behind a corpse."
2. EEH, Altamonte Springs, FL, to HEF, UP, March 23, 1887. SLOC.
3. EEH, Palatka, FL, to HEF, UP, March 10, 1887. SLOC.
4. EEH, Roxbury, to HEF, UP, by hand, [April 7 1887]. SLOC.
5. EEH, Roxbury, to HEF, UP, April 18, 1887. SLOC. The reception was in honor of Edward's colleague and good friend Minot J. Savage, minister of Boston's Church of the Unity, with whom he often exchanged pulpits.
6. EEH, South Congregational Church, Boston, to HEF, UP, May 5, 1887. SLOC.
7. EEH, Roxbury, to HEF, UP, May 11, 1887. SLOC.
8. See "Dr. Carpenter's Troubles: The Story of his two marriages told," *New York Times*, February 14, 1888. According to a brief profile in *The Poets of Maine* (1888), Carpenter wrote a series of literary papers for the Boston *Sunday Globe* while he was in Europe. Bernard Carpenter did not have much longer to live. After returning to America, he was beginning to establish himself as a popular lecturer when he suffered a fatal stroke at the Hotel Sorrento on Maine's Mt. Desert Island. See "Sudden death of a minister. The Rev. Henry Bernard Carpenter falls dead while dressing," *New York Times*, July 18, 1890.
9. EEH, Worcester, MA, to HEF, Asheville, NC, written "10 minutes after good bye" on May 24 but postmarked Boston, May 26, 1887. SLOC.
10. EEH, Ithaca, NY, to HEF, Asheville, NC, [May 28, 1887]. SLOC. EEH, Ithaca, to Emily Hale, Roxbury, May 28, 1887. NYSL.

11. See Van Wyck Brooks, *New England: Indian Summer 1865-1915* (New York: E. P. Dutton, 1940).
12. EEH, Providence, RI, to HEF, West Newton, MA, July 11, 1887. SLOC.
13. EEH, Matunuck, to HEF, Pepperell, August 15, 1887. SLOC.
14. This may have been the assembly that Hale called a "horse show" of packaged lectures arranged for "popular effect." In a letter criticizing an assembly he attended in New Hampshire, he told Methodist minister Jesse L. Hurlbut (a leader of religious education at Chautauqua for fifty years) that he had witnessed "a concert, a temperance lecture, woman's rights address, a reading from Shakespeare, a normal class—but no Chautauqua." He singled out for criticism the distribution of special diplomas for the completion of courses saying that this should be centralized at Chautauqua, New York. EEH to Jesse L. Hurlbut, July 17, 1889, quoted in Andrew C. Rieser, *The Chautauqua Moment: Protestants, Progressives, and the Culture of Modern Liberalism* (New York: Columbia University Press, 2003), 207-208.
15. This copy print in several duplicates survived in the papers purchased in the late 1990s from a dealer by the Andover-Harvard Theological Library, Harvard Divinity School. These papers, books, and photographs all relate to Edward Everett Hale but their origin was unknown until the author's article about the Hale-Freeman letters was published in the *Journal of Unitarian Universalist History* in December 2008. The collection is now cataloged online as the Harriet E. Freeman Papers (bMS 273), AHTL.
16. HEF, UP, to EEH, Roxbury, May 29 for July 10, 1892. SLOC.
17. EEH, Matunuck, to Emily Hale, Roxbury, August 29, 1887. NYSL.
18. EEH, Roxbury, to HEF, Pepperell, September 7, 1887. SLOC.
19. EEH, Boston [written en route from Matunuck], to HEF, Pepperell, September 14, 1887. SLOC.
20. Someone wrote in pencil in Edward's journal for September 6, 1887, "Enter Martha." The General Correspondence section of the Hale Family Papers at LOC also includes many letters to Martha Adams from Edward which help fill in the chronological record.
21. EEH, Roxbury, to HEF, Pepperell, September 14, 1887. SLOC.
22. Emily Hale, Roxbury, to EEH, Matunuck, September 12, 1887. HLP-SSC.
23. EEH, Boston, to HEF, Pepperell, October 3, 1887. SLOC. William Boyd Carpenter (1841-1918), Bishop of Ripon since 1884, was Bernard Carpenter's middle brother. He became a star of the Church of England, knighted for his long tenure as bishop and as court chaplain first to Queen Victoria, then to Kings Edward VII and George V.
24. EEH, Roxbury, to HEF, Pepperell, October 6, 1887. SLOC.

25. EEH, Boston, to HEF, Pepperell, October 5, 1887. SLOC.
26. EEH, West Bethel, Maine, to Emily Hale, Roxbury, October 11, 1887. NYSL.
27. EEH, Roxbury, to HEF, Pepperell, October 16, 1887. SLOC.
28. EEH, Boston, to HEF, Pepperell, November 1, 1887. SLOC.
29. EEH, Roxbury, to HEF, UP, December 25, 1887. SLOC.
30. Books transferred from the Harriet E. Freeman collection to the library of Andover-Harvard Theological Library (AHTL).
31. HEF, UP, to EEH, Washington, [December 1908]. SLOC.
32. EEH, Roxbury, to HEF, UP, December 29, 1887. SLOC.
33. Rayner Edmands, Helen's widower, never remarried but continued to live in the spacious house he had built with his wealthy wife on Garden Street in Cambridge, which he eventually donated in her name to Radcliffe College.
34. "Lectures on Natural Science," Copy of circular issued December 1887 [dated incorrectly 1888] in First Annual Report of the Marine Biological Laboratory, 1888. MBL Archives, Woods Hole, MA.
35. Edward had given her *The Micrographic Dictionary; A Guide to the Examination and Investigation of the Structure and Nature of Microscopic Objects* by J. W. Griffith and Arthur Henfrey (1860), inscribed, "On her birthday. To the first botanist of her time from the last. March 13. 1888. E.E.H. to H.E.F." AHTL.
36. EEH, North Shaftsbury, VT, to HEF, UP, March 13, 1888. SLOC.
37. EEH, Atlanta, GA, to HEF, UP, April 10, 1888. SLOC.
38. EEH, Roxbury, to HEF, Colorado Springs, [April 30, 1888]. SLOC.
39. EEH, Manhattan Beach, NY, to HEF, Pepperell, July 8, 1888. SLOC.
40. EEH, Boston, to HEF, Colorado Springs, June 9, 1888. SLOC.
41. EEH, Matunuck, to HEF, Colorado Springs, July 2, 1888. SLOC.
42. EEH, Matunuck, to HEF, Colorado Springs, July 11, 1888. SLOC. A dried specimen of these forget-me-nots is archived in Box 34 of the Hale Family Papers. SLOC.
43. EEH, Matunuck, to HEF, Pepperell, August 5, 1888. SLOC.
44. EEH, Matunuck, to Emily Hale, ?, August 7, 1888. NYSL.
45. EEH, Chautauqua, to HEF, Brewster, August 25, 1888, forwarded Aug. 29. SLOC.
46. EEH, Boston, to HEF, Pepperell, [Aug. 29, 1888]. SLOC.
47. EEH, Roxbury, to HEF, Pepperell, October 4, 1888. SLOC. Edward's day book notes on Friday, September 28, "Children's Mission to Pepperell"; on Sunday, September 30, "To Groton to Preach for Mr. Young. To Cambridge evening service in the chapel. I preach. Sleep at Peabody's." Whether it was in Pepperell, Groton, or Cambridge, they were certainly together that weekend.

6. The Protégés: Charlotte Stetson (Gilman) and Helen Keller

1. Helen Lefkowitz Horowitz, *Wild Unrest: Charlotte Perkins Gilman and the Making of the "Yellow Wall-Paper"* (Oxford University Press , 2010), 23-26.
2. Horowitz, *Wild Unrest*, 55-56.
3. Monday, February 21, 1887: Writing until 9 a.m.; to Philadelphia where I call on Dr. Weir Mitchell, etc. Back in Boston Feb 23. EEH diary. NYSL.
4. Diary of Charlotte Perkins Stetson, February 26, 1887. Charlotte Perkins Gilman Papers, Schlesinger Library, Harvard. Accessed online http://pds.lib.harvard.edu/pds/view/13726670?n=22&p
5. *Proceedings of the Boston Society of Natural History*, 1890, 248-249.
6. HEF, Colorado Springs, to Alpheus Hyatt, Boston, May 15, 1888. Archives of the Boston Museum of Science.
7. EEH, Roxbury, to HEF, Colorado Springs, May 31, 1888. SLOC. Edward's employment of the word "miracle" to describe Helen's progress under the tutelage of Annie Sullivan was prescient in view of the title of the award-winning 1962 movie *The Miracle Worker*.
8. EEH, Harvard College, to HEF, Colorado Springs, June 7, 1888. SLOC.
9. *Lend A Hand Record*, April 1903, 26-27.
10. EEH, Roxbury, to HEF, Colorado Springs, June 9, 1888. SLOC.
11. The photo was donated to the New England Historic Genealogical Society of Boston by Thaxter Spencer in June 2007. See Matthew M. Burke, "Brewster scene of historic photograph," *Cape Cod Times*, March 6, 2008.
12. Helen Keller, Boston, to Mrs. Kate Adams Keller, Alabama, September 24, [1888], in Helen Keller, *The Story of My Life*, Part II. Letters (1887-1901). *The Story of My Life,* © 2011 American Foundation for the Blind. All rights reserved. http://www.afb.org/mylife/book.asp?ch=P2Let13&select=1#1 Consulted August 26, 2012.
13. Horowitz, *Wild Unrest*, 177-186.
14. EEH, Pasadena, CA, to HEF, UP, February 24, 1891. "No. 15 California." SLOC. Emily had written Edward that January from Philadelphia, where she was checking on Nelly's health, asking him to send her the *New England Magazine* "with Charlotte's article in it, and the Nationalist with her first poem." Emily Hale, Philadelphia, to EEH, Roxbury, January 5, 1891. HFP-SSC.
15. M.D., "Perilous Stuff," *Boston Evening Transcript*, April 8, 1892, in Julie Bates Dock, *Charlotte Perkins Gilman's "The Yellow Wallpaper" and the History of Its Publication and Reception* (University Park, PA: The Pennsylvania State University Press, 1998), 107.

16. Charlotte Perkins Gilman Papers, Schlesinger Library, Harvard. Newsclippings, Divorce, 1892. Accessed online <http://pds.lib.harvard.edu/pds/view/13163457>

7. Romance and Deception

1. HEF, UP, to EEH, Roxbury, February 27, [1889]. Box 25 Undated [or more accurately, in this case, inadequately dated]. SLOC. Estes & Lauriat, a publisher with a bookstore on Washington Street, went out of business under that name in 1898. Hattie was probably referring to the Chestnut Hill Reservoir which was created in 1870 to supplement Boston's water needs.
2. Suffolk County Registry of Deeds, Libro 1878, folio 535-536, May 25, 1889.
3. HEF, UP, to EEH, Washington, March 1, 1889. Box 25. SLOC.
4. "Miss [Ida] Noyes has been to the meeting this afternoon in regard to Day Nurseries....There were people there opposed to Day Nurseries… Miss Noyes has been brought up to believe in kindergartens & Day Nurseries as she believes in the Bible, & she was amazed to hear any other view presented." HEF, UP, to EEH, Washington, DC, February 27, 1889. SLOC.
5. John R. Adams, "James Freeman Clarke," in his chapter on Hale's "Friends and Acquaintances," *Hale*, 21-22.
6. EEH, Matunuck to HEF, UP, April 18, 1889. SLOC.
7. George H. Barton was also Instructor in Determinative Mineralogy and Geology at Boston Tech (MIT), 1886-1892, and Instructor in Geology when Hattie was a special student at Boston Tech between 1891 and 1894. Alpheus Hyatt asked Barton to take over direction of his Teachers' School of Science in 1891. See "George Hunt Barton (1852-1933)," in Robert R. Shrock, *Geology at M.I.T. 1865-1965*, I, 301-324.
8. HEF, UP, to EEH, Roxbury, May 30, 1889. Box 25. SLOC.
9. Ibid May 30, 1889.
10. "How many tales of cruelty I listened to, how many backs scarred by the slave driver's lash & some not healed, I looked upon, how many poor scared creatures I secreted in cellars or garrets until the danger was past I cannot tell, only this I did again and again, both while living in Boston and in Burlington…" Joshua Young to Wilbur H. Siebert, the prominent Underground Railroad historian, in a letter dated April 21, 1893. Wilbur H. Siebert Papers, Ohio History Center, Columbus, Ohio.
11. Young wrote at least one article for Hale's *Old and New*, "Ephesus of the Church History," Vol. 6, 1872, 538-546. This may have been one of

the dull theological articles Hale was forced to include by his partner, the American Unitarian Association.

12. EEH, Matunuck, to HEF, Belmont, June 15, 1889. SLOC.
13. EEH, Matunuck, to HEF, Belmont, June 16, 1889. SLOC. Hattie does not appear to have written her autobiography. Instead, she assisted Edward in writing various versions of his memoirs. The first was *A New England Boyhood,* first published in serial form in the *Atlantic Monthly* in 1892 and then as a book in 1893.
14. HEF, Belmont, to EEH, Matunuck, June 16, 1889. SLOC.
15. HEF, Eastport, Maine, to EEH, Matunuck, [ca. June 25, 1889]. SLOC. Boston Tech's George Barton was an expert on glaciers.
16. EEH, Harvard University letterhead, postmarked Boston, to HEF, Grand Menan, New Brunswick, June 27, 1889. SLOC.
17. HEF, UP, to EEH, Matunuck [July 11, 1889]. SLOC. This was George Frederick Wright's *The Ice Age in North America, and Its Bearings Upon the Antiquity of Man* (1889). Wright was a Christian Darwinist in Asa Gray's mold and the book was largely based on his 1887 Lowell Institute lecture series which Hattie is likely to have attended at the Teachers' School of Science.
18. HEF, Mohonk Lake House, New Paltz, NY, to EEH, Matunuck, July 14, 1889. SLOC. According to Mohonk's 1889 register, Hattie checked in on July 12, 1889, and was assigned Room 134 which is on the lake side of the central building built in 1888. However, she told Edward she was in Room 173. I am grateful for the assistance of the Mohonk Mountain House Archives in identifying the rooms in which Hattie and/or Edward stayed.
19. HEF, Mohonk, to EEH, The Weirs, NH, July 25, 1889. SLOC.
20. HEF, Saratoga, NY, to EEH, Matunuck, July 31, 1889. SLOC.
21. HEF, Brewster, MA, to EEH, Matunuck, August 17, 1889. SLOC. Louis Agassiz's last work arguing against Darwin's theory, "Evolution and the Permanence of Type," appeared in the *Atlantic Monthly* shortly after his death: *Atlantic Monthly*, vol. 33 (1874), 92-101.
22. EEH, Matunuck, to Emily Hale, ?, August 28, 1889. NYSL.
23. Susan Hale, Olana, NY, to "J.B." (EEHJr), [Cornell University, Ithaca, NY, where he was an assistant professor of English literature], October 28, 1889. HFP-SSC. This is the only known case where Susan called Jack "J.B." but the letter is filed with others to EEHJr., she calls his father "Parber" in other letters to him, she refers to the $100 J.B. paid for his stay, and a letter two years later indicates that they often bandied the word "concubine" in the amusing letters they wrote each other. Juxtaposing "concubine Farmer" with "his lawful wife" when referring to Jack's mother seems disrespectful, although neither Susan nor Lucretia were fond of Emily.

24. HEF, Pepperell, to EEH, Roxbury, October 1, 1889. SLOC.
25. EEH, "Tarry at Home Travel: On the Nissitisset," *New England Magazine*, Vol. 9.4 (December 1890), 529-535. For some reason, this was published a year later than he had originally intended.
26. HEF, Pepperell, to EEH, Roxbury, October 17, 1889. SLOC.
27. HEF, Pepperell, to EEH, Roxbury, October 25, 1889. SLOC.
28. *The Unitarian*, November 1889. See also George W. Cooke, *Unitarianism in America: A History of its Origin and Development* (Bibliobazaar, 2006, originally published 1902), 225-229.
29. HEF, Pepperell, to EEH, Roxbury, November 3, [1889]. Box 25. SLOC.
30. HEF, Pepperell, to EEH, Roxbury, November 14, [1889]. Box 25. SLOC.
31. HEF, Altamonte, FL, to EEH, Island Heights, NJ, March 9, 1890. SLOC.
32. HEF, Louisville, KY, to EEH, Roxbury, March 20?, 1890. SLOC.
33. EEH, Island Heights, NJ, to HEF, Altamonte, FL, March 9, 1890. HFP-SSC; Emily Hale, Pepperell, to EEH, Roxbury, September 19, 1890. HFP-SSC. See also note 68.
34. Denwood Thompson's play "The Old Homestead" is an American classic based on the playwright and actor's childhood memories of Swanzey, New Hampshire. It first opened in Boston in April 1886. Hattie must have wished Carrie to see the play to get an understanding of New England, personified for Hattie by her Lewis antecedents on the New Hampshire border.
35. HEF, Victoria Hotel, New York City, to EEH, Roxbury, May 6, 1890. SLOC.
36. EEH mentioned one example of a rare book in the Parker/Crosby/Lewis/Freeman library when, perhaps at William Freeman's request, he wrote to Mr. Whitney of the Library of Congress asking for information about a particularly interesting imprint: *A Thankfull Remembrance of Gods Mercy. In an Historicall Collection of the great and mercifull Deliverances of the Church and State of England, since the Gospel began here to flourish, from the beginning of Queene Elizabeth. Collected by Geo: Carleton, Doctor of Divinity and Bishop of Chichester* (London…1627). Thorvald Solberg who was the first Register of Copyrights at the Library, reported that this book was not then at the Library of Congress but the Freemans may have sold it at some stage since it is now in its Rare Book collections. EEH, Matunuck, to HEF, Pepperell, July 26, 1883. GLOC.
37. EEH, Matunuck, to HEF, Brewster, July 11, 1890. SLOC.
38. EEH, Matunuck, to HEF, Brewster, July 14, 1890. SLOC.
39. Box 34, Miscellaneous Memorabilia, of the Hale Family Papers at the Library of Congress includes two folders with multiple small envelopes containing ear locks and hair clippings, mostly dated from 1886

through the 1890s and an additional one dated 1902. Many of the very small envelopes have printed at one end "If not found, return to Edward E. Hale, 30 Highland Street, Roxbury." Hale wrote billets doux in shorthand on many of the envelopes.

40. HEF, Brewster, to EEH, Matunuck, July 12, 1890. SLOC. See photographs on page 116 in *Images of America: Brewster* (Arcadia Publishing for The Brewster Historical Society, 2002).
41. HEF, Brewster, to EEH, Matunuck, [July 14, 1890]. Box 25. SLOC.
42. HEF, Montreal, to EEH, Matunuck, July 20, 1890. SLOC.
43. HEF, [shores of Lake Superior], to EEH, Matunuck, July 23, 1890. SLOC.
44. HEF, [western end of Lake Superior], to EEH, Matunuck, July 24, 1890. SLOC.
45. Judith Andrews, Boston, to HEF, Snow Hill, Alabama, March 6, 1904. SLOC.
46. EEH, The Red House, Matunuck, to HEF, Tacoma, WA [marked Raymond Excursion], July 25, 1890. SLOC.
47. Emily Hale, Roxbury, to HEF, UP, December 27, 1900. SLOC.
48. EEH, Milton, MA, to HEF, Hotel Ryan, St. Paul, MN, August 24, 1890. SLOC.
49. EEH, Roxbury, to HEF, UP, January 1, 1891. SLOC.
50. EEH, Marietta, GA, to HEF, UP, February 5, 1891, "no. 3 California." SLOC. To alleviate Hattie's anxiety about him, Edward agreed to number his letters and send her a weekly telegram.
51. EEH, Sanderson, TX, en route to Tucson, AZ, to HEF, UP, February [?], 1891. "No. 11 California." SLOC.
52. Emily Hale, Roxbury, to EEH, [California], February 8, 1891. HFP-SSC.
53. HEF, UP, to EEH, Pasadena, CA, February 25, 1891. SLOC.
54. HEF, Waterville [Valley, NH], February 18 [1891]. SLOC.
55. HEF, Boston, to EEH, Pasadena , March 8, [1891]. SLOC.
56. HEF, UP, to EEH, Ojai Valley, CA, March 10 [1891]. SLOC. Edward had given explicit directions to Nelly about research on Columbus in Washington archives. EEH, Roxbury, to Ellen Day Hale, Washington, January 21, 1891. HFP-SSC.
57. EEH, Ojai Valley, CA, to Martha Adams, Boston, March 14, [1889] 1891. GLOC.
58. HEF, UP, to EEH, California, March 10, [1891]. SLOC.
59. EEH, San Francisco, to HEF, UP, March 20, 1891. SLOC.
60. Ellen Day Hale, "Journey to California, 1891," Ch. XXXIII, in Hale, Jr., *Life and Letters*, II, 347.
61. EEH, San Francisco, to HEF, UP, [March] 20, 1891. SLOC.

62. HEF, UP, to EEH, San Francisco, March 26, [1891]. SLOC. The miracles to which Hattie apparently refers are those described in Joshua 10:12-14 and 2 Kings 20:11, as well as the immaculate conception of Jesus and resurrections of Lazarus and Jesus described in the Gospels.
63. HEF, Intervale, NH, to EEH, Roxbury, October 3, 1904. SLOC.
64. HEF, UP, to EEH, San Francisco, March 18, [1891]. SLOC.
65. The letters of Emily Hale from T. S. Eliot were deposited at Princeton University, to be closed to researchers until 2020.
66. HEF, UP, to Alpheus Hyatt, Boston Society of Natural History, April 5, 1891. Archives of Boston Science Museum.
67. EEH, Roxbury, to HEF, "Please deliver on board" [the Britannic], September [12] 20, 1891. SLOC.
68. *The Unitarian*, 1891, 476 passim. This volume of *The Unitarian* includes an eight-page review of Edward's biography of James Freeman Clarke by the Rev. J. T. Sunderland of Ann Arbor, Michigan, who thought it should have been fuller and longer. "One finds himself constantly coming to matters about which he wants to know more, interesting & important parts of Dr. Clarke's life & work which are left almost a blank." Sunderland made a strong argument for what made Clarke's church stand apart, 252–260.
69. EEH, Roxbury to HEF, Poindexter House, Intervale, NH, October 27, 1891. SLOC.

8. Separations and Tragedy

1. "Dr. Hale at Seventy," *The Unitarian*, Vol. 8.5 (May 1892), 215.
2. EEH, Roxbury, to Ellen Day Hale, San Francisco, CA, April 4, 1892 in EEH Journal, April 4, 1892. NYSL. Nelly must have added this letter to her father's journal.
3. EEH journal, April 18, 1892. NYSL.
4. The dates in his journal for early May are confusing. They place him in Pepperell, and both he and Emily wrote letters to Bertie and Greta in Paris from Pepperell on May 5, 1892, but there are also records to show that Edward and Hattie were present in Boston at the annual meeting of the Lend a Hand clubs the afternoon of May 5. Emily Hale and EEH, Pepperell, to Herbert and Margareta Hale, Paris, France, May 5, 1892. Hale-Marquand Papers, Courtesy of the Trustees of the Boston Public Library/Rare Books.
5. Susan Hale, San Francisco, to EEHJr., Halle, Germany, April 3, 1892. EEHJr. Papers, NYSL. In this colorful, over-the-top letter, Susan, who would enjoy a far more successful trip to California the following year, wrote in disgust: "I loathe and hate California, and passionately

long to be out of it, and I'm going to write a work called 'Unitarians & how they undid me.' For all the good money I made was outside their Damnomination (Good joke)…strange to say, I may come back to this accursed spot another year, for I have made a great reputation here & by keeping clear of Unitarians, I am sure to make a lot of money…Now in spite of the above you must know that this same devilish March I have had a delightful time."

6. Susan Hale, Boston, to EEHJr., Halle, Germany, May 10, 1892. EEHJr., NYSL.
7. The numerous geological subjects at Boston Tech were organized into a definite curriculum leading to a Bachelor of Science degree in 1890. Professor William H. Niles was the first head of the Department of Geology. Robert R. Shrock, *Geology at M.I.T. 1865-1965*, vol. I, 12. Hattie was a special student in biology and geology at Boston Tech, Class of 1895, between 1892 and 1894.
8. HEF, UP, to EEH, Roxbury, June 3, 1892; EEH, South Congregational Church, Boston, to HEF, Yellowstone, June 19, 1892. Both SLOC.
9. Emily Hale, Roxbury, to Ellen Day Hale, California, May 22, 1892. HFP-SSC.
10. EEH Journal, May 17, 18, and 21, 1892. NYSL. The Perry Street Conference was probably an Associated Charities meeting.
11. HEF, UP, to EEH, Roxbury, May 27 and June 7, 1892. SLOC.
12. EEH, Matunuck, to HEF, Duluth, Minnesota, No. 4, June 10 or 11, 1892; EEH to HEF, Yellowstone, forwarded several times, June 20, 1892; EEH, Roxbury, to HEF, Yellowstone, June 20 and 21, 1892. All SLOC.
13. EEH, Roxbury, to HEF, Butte, Montana, June 22, 1892. SLOC. Jean Holloway was the only one of Edward's biographers to note a significant diminution of his creative powers in his fifties, which she attributed to a mid-life crisis about the direction he had taken in life. She noticed a return of purpose and serenity when he was in his early sixties, exactly when his special relationship with Hattie began. Holloway did not have access to the love letters which remained in private hands until the late 1960s.
14. EEH, Roxbury, to HEF, [Lake Superior en route to Yellowstone], June 12, 1892, and to Butte, Montana, June 22, 1892. Both SLOC.
15. William Howell Reed, Belmont, MA, to HEF, Yellowstone, June 29, 1892. SLOC. Edward Jr. (Jack) was a newly minted Doctor of Philosophy.
16. EEH, London, to HEF, UP, July 19, 1892. SLOC.
17. EEH, Exeter, England, to HEF, UP, forwarded to Shelburne, VT, July 23, 1892. SLOC.

18. EEH, Paris, to HEF, UP, forwarded to Brewster, Cape Cod, August 6, 1892. SLOC. EEH's journal for this trip is in the Harriet E. Freeman Papers, AHTL, and includes several pen and ink sketches of Giverny landscapes. On August 10, noting that he had received and mailed letters to Hattie and to Martha Adams, he wrote "I think nothing much happens here."
19. EEH, *East and West: A Story of New-Born Ohio* (New York: Cassell, 1892), inscribed copy transferred from the Harriet E. Freeman Collection in the Manuscript division to the library. AHTL. Edward copied one of the sketches he made at Bethel in October 1887 and pasted it with a Gorham sketch into his journal for September 12 to 15, 1896. NYSL.
20. Thomas Starr King, *The White Hills: Their Legends, Landscape, and Poetry* (Boston: Crosby and Ainsworth, 1868 edition), 245-316.
21. Julius H. Ward, "White Mountain Forests in Peril," *Atlantic Monthly*, 71 (February 1893), 247-255. Quoted in Christopher Johnson, *This Grand & Magnificent Place: The Wilderness Heritage of the White Mountains* (Durham, NH: University of New Hampshire Press, 2006), 175.
22. EEH, Portland, Maine, to HEF, Shelburne, NH, October 5, 1892. HFP-SSC.
23. EEH, Roxbury, to HEF, Shelburne, NH, October 31, 1892. SLOC.
24. EEH, Philadelphia, to HEF, UP, November 18, 1892. SLOC.
25. EEH, Matunuck, to HEF, Duluth, Minnesota, June 10 or 11, 1892. SLOC.
26. EEH Journal, January 26, 1893. NYSL.
27. Susan Hale contributed to the Women's Building; Nelly and Philip exhibited paintings in the Fine Arts Palace.
28. EEH, poem to HEF on back of invitation to luncheon at the Union League Club, Chicago, February 21, 1893. EEH Journal for that day. NYSL.
29. HEF, Chicago, to EEH, Roxbury, Tuesday afternoon [May 16?] and May 20, 1893. Both SLOC.
30. Erik Larson, *The Devil in the White City: Murder, Magic, and Madness at the Fair that Changed America* (New York: Random House, Vintage, 2003), 251, 269-273.
31. EEH, Amherst, to Emily Hale, Roxbury, June 5, 1893. NYSL.
32. "Professor Edward Everett Hale, Jr., of Iowa University was married this afternoon at the old Shay farmhouse, Waterford, Conn., to Miss Rose Perkins, 2nd dau. of Prof. Maurice Perkins of Union Coll. The ceremony was performed by the Rev. Edward Everett Hale, father of the groom, assisted by the Rev. George Alexander of the Fifth Avenue Presbyterian Church, New York." *New York Times*, June 16, 1893.
33. EEH, Matunuck, to HEF, Warsaw, NY, August 9, 1893. SLOC.

34. EEH, Matunuck, to HEF, Warsaw, NY, August 18 and 25, 1893. SLOC.
35. EEH, Portland, Maine, to HEF, Shelburne, Sunday [September 10, 1893]. SLOC.
36. EEH, "Spiritual Forces in Human Progress," in John H. Barrows, ed., *The World's Parliament of Religions* (Chicago: Parliament Publishing Company, 1893), I, 340. Jenkin Lloyd Jones was a leading force behind the World's Parliament.
37. Emily Hale, Roxbury, to Herbert and Margareta Hale, Paris, September 21, 1893. Hale-Marquand, Courtesy of the Boston Public Library/ Rare Books.
38. Herbert D. Ward, "Edward E. Hale. The Man with a Country," *McClure's*, I.4 (September 1893), 291-301. The *McClure's* profile was preceded in July 1893 by "A Gifted Writer: Home Life of Edward Everett Hale," a lengthy profile in San Francisco's *The Morning Call*.
39. EEH, Meadville, OH, to HEF, UP, June 13, 1894. SLOC.
40. HEF, Joggins, Nova Scotia, to EEH, Philadelphia, July 4, 1894. SLOC. A typescript report on the excursion is in the MIT Archives (T-N/C949).
41. EEH, Matunuck, to HEF, Windsor, Nova Scotia, [June] July 10, 1894; to Eastport, Maine, forwarded to St. John, Nova Scotia, July 19, enclosing Susan's July 3 letter; and to Hotel Frontenac, Quebec, July 23, 1894; HEF, Chateau Frontenac, Quebec, to EEH, Matunuck, [late July 1894], undated Miscellaneous fragment [Box 25]. All SLOC.
42. EEH, Saratoga, NY, to HEF, Shelburne, NH. SLOC; and EEH, Saratoga, to Emily Hale, Roxbury, September 27, 1894, quoted in EEHJr., *Life and Letters*, II, 367; EEH, "The Unitarian Conference," *The Outlook*, October 6, 1894, 559.
43. Per the MIT Institute Archives and Special Collections, Harriet E. Freeman was a special student in Biology in 1891 and 1892 and in Geology in 1893 and 1894. E-mail communication, March 20, 2013. She did not earn a degree. Fax from Office of the Registrar, MIT, November 18, 2009.
44. HEF, Fryeburg, Maine, to EEH, Roxbury, February 20 [1895]. SLOC.
45. Alexander Graham Bell, Cape Breton, Nova Scotia, to EEH, Roxbury, April 21, 1894. Box 35-25. HFP-SSC.
46. EEH, Asheville, NC, to HEF, UP, March 5, 1895. SLOC.
47. EEH, Hot Springs, NC, to HEF, UP, March 8, 1895. SLOC.
48. HEF, UP, to EEH, Roxbury, [April 5, 1895]. SLOC. The hat was donated with the Harriet Freeman collection to the Andover-Harvard Theological Library.
49. HEF, Hoboken, NJ, to EEH, Roxbury, April 13 [1895]. SLOC.
50. EEH, Roxbury, to HEF, Gibraltar, April 13, 1895; HEF, Hoboken, NJ, to EEH, Roxbury, April 13, 1895, postmarked April 17; HEF, Brewster, MA, to EEH, Matunuck, September 2, 1889. All SLOC.

51. HEF, On board the Werra, to EEH, Roxbury, [April 18-21, 1895]. SLOC.
52. HEF, Gibraltar, to EEH, Roxbury, April 23, 1895. SLOC.
53. EEH, UP, to HEF, Gibraltar, April 27, 1895. SLOC.
54. Minot J. Savage, *The Irrepressible Conflict between Two World Theories* (Boston, 1892, 8-9,11. Quoted in Roberts, *Darwinism and the Divine in America*, 1988, 194.
55. HEF, Venice, to EEH, Roxbury, Mary 31, 1895; EEH, Matunuck, to HEF, London, June 18, 1895; EEH, Boston, to HEF, London, forwarded to Chamonix, France, June 23, 1895. All SLOC.
56. Larry E. Burgess, *Mohonk: Its People and Spirit: a History of One Hundred and Forty Years of Growth and Service* (New Palz, NY: Mohonk Mountain House, 2009), 49; EEH, Mohonk Mountain House, to HEF, London, forwarded to Chamonix, France, June 5, 1895. SLOC. Mohonk Mountain House has preserved in its archive nearly all the hotel registers, a revealing source for some of Edward's and Hattie's stays there.
57. EEH, Matunuck, to HEF, Innsbruck, Austria, July 24, 1895; EEH, Matunuck, to HEF, Paris, August 17, 1895. Both SLOC.
58. HEF, Salzburg, Austria, to EEH, Matunuck, August 11, 1895. SLOC.
59. EEH, Matunuck, to HEF, Paris, August 17 and 28, 1895. Both SLOC.
60. HEF, Nuremberg, Germany, to EEH, Matunuck, August 22, 1895. SLOC.
61. Susan subsequently had the water in Wash Pond tested and it was found to be pure.
62. HEF, Avignon, France, to EEH, Roxbury, October 4, 1898. SLOC.
63. Extracts from EEH's journal, October 8, 1895, quoted in EEHJr., *Life and Letters*, II, 361-363.
64. "Unitarian Leaders Meet...Everett Hale Unavoidably Absent," *New York Times*, October 22, 1895.

9. The Toll of Depression

1. EEH, Matunuck, to HEF, Quebec, July 27, 1894. SLOC.
2. Alan Mazur, *A Romance in Natural History: The Lives and Works of Amadeus Grabau and Mary Antin* (Syracuse, New York, 2004), 52.
3. Watson established a highly successful shipping company, earned an MS in geology at Union College (1919) and a Ph.D in engineering (1921), and was even a Shakespearean actor during long periods of leisure. He was a very generous friend to the Grabaus when they fell on difficult times, helping them with loans and advice. See my chapter 15, 391.
4. EEH, Santa Barbara, CA, to Martha Adams, Boston, February 29, 1896. GLOC.

5. EEH, Santa Barbara, to HEF, UP, March 2, 1896. SLOC.
6. EEH, Santa Barbara, to HEF, Flagstaff, Ariz., March 12, 1896. SLOC.
7. HEF, Flagstaff, AZ, to EEH, Santa Barbara, March 15, 1896. SLOC.
8. EEH, Santa Barbara, to HEF, Hotel Windsor, Redlands, CA, March 15 to 22, 1896, postmarked at Redlands March 26, 1896. SLOC.
9. Most likely Humphreys Peak, tallest of the volcanic San Francisco Peaks north of Flagstaff.
10. This trail, which today is the Bright Angel Trail, was originally used by the Havasupai Indians and had been recently improved by prospectors. One of the miners, Ralph Cameron, realizing that the tourist trade was more profitable than mining, bought out his partners and took control of the trail, which he extended from Indian Garden to the river and began to charge a toll of $1 per person for its use.
11. Edward had become financially entangled with the weekly newspaper and there was a constant struggle to pay printers' bills. His financial advisers insisted on him "cutting loose from 'The Commonwealth'" altogether. See Holloway, 226-227.
12. She enclosed the oil-smeared manuscript in a preprinted envelope to Rev. Edward E. Hale, Mission Hill, San Bernardo, marked "If not found, return to 3 Hamilton Place, Boston" but gave it to him when she saw him in Redlands. SLOC.
13. HEF, Flagstaff, AZ, to HEF, Los Angeles, CA, March 23, 1896. SLOC.
14. EEH, Santa Barbara, CA, to HEF, Hotel Windsor, Redlands, CA, March 22, 1896. SLOC.
15. Redlands, settled in 1888, became a popular wintering spot for wealthy East Coast residents and from the 1880s to the 1950s, the heart of the largest navel-orange producing region in the world. Albert and Alfred Smiley, proprietors of Hattie's beloved Mohonk Mountain House, were known as Redlands' "patron saints." They paid to have the city's public library built in 1898. Hattie recalled years later that they were warmly greeted by Albert Smiley at Smiley Heights, his summer residence.
16. HEF, La Casa Loma, Redlands, CA, to EEH, Roxbury, June 9, 1903; EEH, Exeter, NH, to HEF, San Francisco, forwarded to Pacific Grove, CA, June 13, 1903. Both SLOC.
17. HEF, Santa Barbara, to EEH, Roxbury, [April 1896]. Box 25 Undated miscellaneous fragments. SLOC.
18. Mary Atkins diary, Atkins Family Papers, Massachusetts Historical Society.
19. EEH, Lake Mohonk Mountain House, to HEF c/o Mr. Cle W. Andrews, Librarian at John Crerar Library, Chicago, June 4, 1896, SLOC; and EEH, Mohonk, to Emily Hale, Hartford, same day, quoted in EEHJr., *Life and Letters of Edward Everett Hale*, II, 384-385.

20. The company that built and ran the cog railroad—still the highest in North America—was founded in 1889, the year after Hattie's previous climb up Pike's Peak, and was open to tourists by 1891.
21. HEF, Colorado Springs, to EEH, June 16, 1896. SLOC.
22. HEF, Colorado Springs, to EEH, Matunuck, June 21, 1896. SLOC.
23. EEH, Boston, to HEF, Alta Vista Hotel, Colorado Springs, July 2, 1896. SLOC.
24. EEH, Folly Cove, to HEF, Colorado Springs, July 8, 1896. SLOC.
25. EEH, Roxbury, to HEF, Colorado Springs, July 9, 1896, in two mailings, the second forwarded to UP. Both SLOC.
26. EEH, Boston, to HEF, co/ Cle Andrews, Crerar Library, Chicago, July 11, 1896; EEH, Folly Cove, Cape Ann, to HEF, c/o Amadeus W. Grabau, Buffalo, NY, July 16, 1896. Both SLOC.
27. Mohonk Mountain House register, July 25, 1896. "Edward Everett Hale, Boston, Room 151; Miss Harriet E. Freeman, Boston, Room 153"; EEH, Bethlehem, NH, to HEF, Shelburne, NH, August 23, 1896. SLOC.
28. EEH, Matunuck, to HEF, UP, August 6, 1896. SLOC.
29. HEF, UP, to EEH, Matunuck, August 11, 1896. SLOC.
30. Thomas H. O'Connor, *The Boston Irish: A Political History* ((Boston: Back Bay Books, 1995), 152.
31. HEF, Isle of Springs, ME, to EEH, Bartlett, NH, August 13, 1896. SLOC.
32. HEF, Isle of Springs, ME, to EEH, Matunuck, August 17 [1896]. Box 25. SLOC. The deadly heat wave killed almost 1500 people, particularly in the tenements of New York. Bryan's political campaign hit the skids in New York on the same day, August 12, that this heat wave peaked.
33. Susan Hale, Matunuck, to Martha Adams, Boston, August 13, 1896. GLOC.
34. Emily Hale, Beverly, MA, to EEH, August 10, 1890. HFP-SSC.
35. Susan Hale, Matunuck, to Martha Adams, August 23, 1896. GLOC.
36. HEF, Shelburne, to EEH, Little Boar's Head, NH, August 25, 1896. SLOC. In the Marine Biological Laboratory Annual Report for 1896, Parnell S. Murray, Teacher in Girls' High School, Boston, is listed as Student in Embryology 1 (Course Preparatory to Investigation). Courtesy of Marine Biological Laboratory Archive, Woods Hole, MA.
37. HEF, Shelburne, to EEH, c/o Mr. William H. Fowler [head of the SCS Standing Committee], Little Boar's Head, North Hampton, NH., August 28, 1896. 1896. SLOC. That day, Edward wrote to her from Bartlett, the destination he had mentioned to Susan. He was doing the rounds of his Boston parishioners' summer resorts.
38. EEH, Matunuck, to HEF, Shelburne, undated letter [late August/early September 1896]. SLOC.
39. HEF, Shelburne, to EEH, Matunuck, September 3 and 7, 1896. Both SLOC.

40. HEF, Shelburne, to EEH, Matunuck, September 9, 1896. SLOC.
41. HEF, Shelburne, to EEH, Roxbury, Sunday and Thursday [September 20, 24, 30 (Box 25), and October 2, 1896]. All SLOC.
42. See *Six Stories and Some Verses* by Robert Beverly Hale, with the inscription: "Ethel Hale Freeman with the best love of Aunt Harriet. Christmas 1896." AHTL. Glued on the following page is the duplicated letter to EEH from William Dean Howells, New York, November 27, 1896.
43. EEH, Roxbury, to HEF, Wonalancet, NH, October 15, 1896. SLOC.
44. EEH, Roxbury, to HEF, Wonalancet, October 16, 1896. SLOC.
45. Atkins, *Sixty Years in Cuba,* 211.
46. HEF, UP, to EEH, Roxbury, Sunday night 9.30 P.M. [Late November, 1896]. SLOC.
47. HEF, UP, to EEH, Pinehurst, NC, February 25, 1897. Box 25. SLOC.
48. HEF, UP, to EEH, Pinehurst, Monday evening [March 8, 1897?]. Box 25. SLOC.
49. EEH, Pinehurst, to HEF, Nassau, Bahamas, March 16, 1897, postmarked March 18. SLOC.
50. HEF, Nassau, to EEH, Pinehurst, March 21, 1897. SLOC.
51. HEF, On board Santiago, to EEH, Washington, DC, April 3, 1897. SLOC.
52. After nine years of unremitting effort and expense, Langley's Aerodrome No. 6 had flown 4,200 feet, staying aloft over one minute, the previous November. By this time, Langley thought that he had concluded his work with flying machines. Unfortunately for Langley, his renewed efforts with an enlarged, engine-driven, piloted airplane in the early nineteen hundreds as the Wright Brothers drew closer to success met with disaster and ridicule.
53. HEF, UP, to EEH, Roxbury, April 12 [1897]. Box 25. SLOC. She and Emma had met up with him briefly in New York as he returned from Washington to Boston.
54. HEF, UP, to EEH, Roxbury, April 16 [1897]. Box 25. SLOC.
55. HEF, Dublin, NH, to EEH, Roxbury, June 20 [1897]. SLOC.
56. On a flyer announcing details for the dedication ceremony which Edward sent Hattie, he wrote "I invented this, but Geo. Clarke did it." This library was the site of a centennial celebration of Edward's birth on April 3, 1922. The Hales had the volume of Rob's writings reprinted for this occasion, Robert Beverly Hale, *Six Stories and Some Verses* (Boston, 1897). Copyright Philip Hale.
57. HEF, UP, to EEH, Roxbury, June 26, 1897. SLOC.
58. HEF, Bayville, Maine, to EEH, Matunuck?, [June 28,1897]. SLOC.
59. HEF, Bayville, to EEH, Roxbury, July 2, [1897]. Box 25. SLOC. She was

referring to Charlotte A. Baker's *True stories of New England captives carried to Canada during the old French and Indian Wars*, published that year.

60. HEF, Amherst, to EEH, Matunuck, July 22, 1897. SLOC.
61. HEF, Holderness, NH, to EEH, Matunuck, [August 16, 1897]. Box 25. SLOC.

10. "For pity's sake"

1. EEH, Boston, to HEF, Pepperell, October 4, 1888. SLOC.
2. HEF, [Bermuda, to EEH, Washington], Wednesday, March 16 [1898]. Box 25. SLOC.
3. HEF, UP, to EEH, Roxbury, January 26, 1898. SLOC.
4. EEH, Cambridge, to HEF, UP, [January 26, 1898]. SLOC.
5. EEH, en route to Philadelphia, to HEF, UP, February 28, 1898. SLOC.
6. "All not Bound to Silver: What Daniel O. Eshbaugh says of some Western States," *The New York Times*, July 26, 1896; "Mortgage Concern Fails: Otto T. Bannard is Appointed Receiver for the New England Loan and Trust Company," *The New York Times*, September 27, 1898; "Daniel O. Eshbaugh Dead: New England Loan and Trust Company President Found Drowned in the North River," *The New York Times*, October 2, 1898.
7. EEH, Washington, to Martha Adams, Boston, March 7, 1898. GLOC.
8. HEF, Bermuda, to EEH, Pinehurst, NC, March 16, [1898]. Box 25. SLOC.
9. Edwin Atkins, Soledad, Cuba, to Katharine Atkins, Belmont, MA, February 19 and 26, 1898. Quoted in Edwin F. Atkins, *Sixty Years in Cuba*, 274.
10. Susan Hale, Washington, DC, to William Weeden, Providence, RI, March 13, 1898. NYSL.
11. See Bunting, *Houses of Boston's Back Bay*, 415. Effie Ellis appears to have leased the house from its original owner Eben Jordan, who also owned five adjacent buildings, but, according to the insurance atlases of 1922, she had succeeded in buying it.
12. EEH, Washington, to Emily Hale, [New York?], March 17, 1898. NYSL.
13. Atkins, *Sixty Years in Cuba*, 279.
14. EEH, Roxbury, to HEF, 176 Marlboro Street, Boston, May 8, 1898. SLOC.
15. EEH, Roxbury, to Silas Weir Mitchell, Philadelphia, May 8, 1898. Silas Weir Mitchell Papers. Courtesy of the College of Physicians of Philadelphia. The two letters related to Hattie are filed under Literary Correspondence.

16. EEH, Roxbury, to HEF, 1605 Summer Street, Philadelphia, May 16, 1898. SLOC.
17. EEH, Roxbury, to Silas Weir Mitchell, Philadelphia, May 23, 1898. Mitchell Papers, College of Physicians of Philadelphia.
18. Horowitz, *Wild Unrest*, 138.
19. This Miss Pennington might have been Mary Engle Pennington (1872-1952), who moved to Philadelphia at an early age, was admitted to the University of Pennsylvania in 1890, and earned her Ph.D. in 1895. She became director of the Clinical Laboratory at the Women's Medical College of Pennsylvania. Alternatively, it is possible that this clinic was the Brookwood Sanitarium on North Ridley Creek Road in Media, which was "established in 1898 for the care of women suffering from nervous and mental diseases...under individual control and maintains 25 beds. Dr. S. Elizabeth Winter is the medical superintendent." Charles Palmer, editor, *A History of Delaware County, Pennsylvania*, Vol. I (Harrisburg, PA: National Historical Association, 1932), 191.
20. Horowitz, *Wild Unrest*, 137.
21. EEH, Roxbury, to HEF, Media, PA, June 12, 1898. SLOC.
22. HEF, Media, to EEH, Roxbury, June 15, 1898. SLOC.
23. EEH, Roxbury, to HEF, Media, June 19, 1898. SLOC.
24. HEF, Media, to EEH, Roxbury, June 19, 1898. SLOC.
25. Horowitz, *Wild Unrest*, 128.
26. Charlotte Perkins Stetson, "The Yellow Wallpaper," *New England Magazine* 5, January 1892. See Horowitz, 128, 189-190, and my chapter 6.
27. EEH, Menton, Ohio, to HEF, Media, June 26, 1898. SLOC.
28. HEF, Media, to EEH, Roxbury, June 27, 1898. SLOC.
29. HEF, Media, to EEH, Roxbury, June 29 and 30, 1898. Both SLOC.
30. The North Atlantic Squadron under the command of Rear-Admiral William T. Sampson, but led by Rear Admiral Winfield Schley during Sampson's temporary absence ashore, destroyed all the Spanish vessels that tried to escape the blockaded Santiago Harbor the morning of July 3, 1898.
31. HEF, Media, to EEH, Roxbury, July 6, 1898. SLOC.
32. EEH, Roxbury, to HEF, Media, July 8 and 9, 1898. SLOC.
33. EEH, Matunuck, to HEF, Media, July 14, 1898. SLOC.
34. HEF, Media, to EEH, Matunuck, July 17, 1898. SLOC.
35. EEH, Matunuck, to HEF, Media, July 18, 1898. SLOC.
36. EEH, Matunuck, to HEF, Media, July 22, 1898. SLOC.
37. EEH, Matunuck, to HEF, Amsterdam? [envelope is missing], August 1, 1898. SLOC.
38. HEF, The Hague, to EEH, Matunuck, August 16, 1898. SLOC.
39. EEH, Roxbury, to Martha Adams, Sherborn, MA, Sept. 5, 98. GLOC.

40. HEF, Paris, to EEH, Roxbury, September 9, 1898. SLOC.
41. EEH, Chocorua, NH, to HEF, Paris, September 9, 1898. SLOC.
42. HEF, Paris, to EEH, Boston, September 12, 1898. SLOC.
43. Emily Hale, Roxbury, to Edward E. Hale Jr., September 23, 1898. EEHJr., NYSL.
44. Joshua Young, Groton, MA, to HEF, Genoa, Italy, October 5, 1898. SLOC.
45. EEH, Roxbury, to HEF, London, October 5, 1898, forwarded to Genoa, SLOC.
46. HEF, Genoa, Italy, to EEH, Roxbury, October 11, 1898. SLOC.
47. HEF, Naples, to EEH, Roxbury, October 13, 1898. SLOC.
48. EEH, Roxbury, to HEF, Gibraltar, October 14, 1898, forwarded to Roxbury. SLOC.
49. EEH, Roxbury, to HEF, SS Kaiser Wilhelm, New York City, October 31, 1898, forwarded to Roxbury. SLOC.
50. Bunting, *Houses of Boston's Back Bay*, 429.
51. EEH, "In the new home," Hotel Torrington, 384 Commonwealth Avenue, Boston, to HEF, New York, [Nov. 1 1898]. SLOC.
52. "Among the agencies employed by the Boston Society of Natural History for making itself a vehicle of instruction to the public has been the employment of an educated man and teacher to the museum, who should also give lectures there. The salary of this officer has heretofore been provided by the bounty of Miss Harriet E. Freeman, but she has been obliged to discontinue her contribution, and the curator is now seeking other means of maintaining a suitably qualified assistant," in "A Natural History Society as a School," *Appleton's Popular Science Monthly*, 1899, 281.
53. Suffolk County Registry of Deeds, Freeman to Phelps, December 28, 1898. Libro 2584, folio 279; "Botany," *Proceedings of the Boston Society of Natural History*, Vol. 28, 1899, 48.
54. Register for Mohonk Mountain House, June 4, 1899. Mohonk Mountain House Archives.
55. Hattie's photo appeared in *Harper's Weekly*, February 6, 1904, 195.
56. Edward Everett Hale, *James Russell Lowell and His Friends* (Boston and New York: Houghton, Mifflin and Co., 1899). AHTL.
57. EEH, Lake Mohonk, NY, to William P. Fowler, Boston, May 15, 1899. Quoted in EEHJr., *Life and Letters*, II, 371-2.
58. EEH, Matunuck, to HEF, Milton, MA, August 8, 1899. SLOC. Interestingly, both of the major Hale biographies tail off noticeably from the early 1880s for the remainder of his life. The Hale-Freeman letters were not available to the first three Hale biographers but Hattie would provide extensive notes to Edward's son Jack who compiled *Life and Letters of Edward Everett Hale.*

59. Susan Hale, Hotel Athenaeum, Chautauqua, NY, to Mrs. William G. Weld, Boston, August 14, 1898. Quoted in *Letters of Susan Hale* (Boston: Marshall Jones, 1919), 346-348.
60. EEH, New York and New Haven RR, to HEF, Montclair, NJ, forwarded to c/o Mrs. E. R. Astruder, 4 Lafayette Square, Washington, DC. March 17, 1900. SLOC.
61. HEF, 53 Gloucester Street, Boston, to EEH, en route to Midwest, April 17 [1900]. Box 25. SLOC; *Programme of the Unveiling of the Memorial Tablet presented to the Town of Pepperell by Mrs. Edith Prescott Walcott November 1, 1899* can be found online.
62. Suffolk County Registry of Deeds, folio 2617, folio 495, Phelps to Freeman, July 3, 1899. For a Fee of $1, Phelps agreed to return 37 Union Park with its mortgage of $8,000 and taxes for that year. Harriet E. Freeman vs. The New England Loan and Trust Co. et al—Quiet title; 37 Union Park belonging to Luther S. Phelps transferred to Harriet E. Freeman, about 2040 sq. ft. 4-story brick house," in "Real Estate Matters," *Boston Daily Globe,* May 30, 1900. Perhaps the house was leased to a tenant in the interim.
63. Per John Freely, *Blue Guide Boston and Cambridge* (New York: W. W. Norton, 1994), 229-230.
64. EEH, Roxbury, to William Howell Reed, Belmont?, June 12, 1900. GLOC.
65. EEH, Pittsfield, to Martha Adams, July 1, 1909, included in a tribute marking the hundredth anniversary of EEH's birth, "Boston's Great Pastor-at-Large," by Joseph E. Chamberlin in *Boston Evening Transcript,* April 1, 1922.
66. Judith Andrews, Boston, to HEF, Kennebunk Beach, Maine, August 19, 1900. SLOC.
67. See John R. Adams, "Frederick Ingham and Other Doubles," in his *Edward Everett Hale* (1977), 45-48.
68. EEH, Matunuck, to HEF, Kennebunk Beach, August 20 and 23, 1900. Both SLOC.
69. EEH, Matunuck, to HEF, Kennebunk Beach, August 7, 1900. SLOC
70. EEH, Hampton, VA, or Washington, DC, to Martha Adams Leland, Sherborn, MA, March 1, 1900. GLOC.
71. EEH, Roxbury, to Martha Adams Leland, Sherborn, MA, October 8, 1900. GLOC.
72. Emily Hale, Roxbury, to HEF, UP, December 27, 1900; Ellen Day Hale, Roxbury, to HEF, UP, December 27, 1900. Both SLOC.
73. HEF, Berlin, to Helen Hunt Arnold, August 17, 1909. HFP-SSC.

11. An Adventurous Life

1. As more and more surgeons performed appendectomies, diagnosis and operative techniques improved. But the dangers were often as great for the surgeons as for the patients in those pioneer years. Hattie's friend Mrs. Strong had lost her surgeon husband, Charles P. Strong of Harvard Medical School, when his finger was pricked while he was removing an infected appendix and he quickly succumbed to acute septicemia, for which there was no cure in pre-antibiotic days.
2. EEH, Roxbury, to HEF, UP, "Tuesday p.m., 7 o'clock," [February 13, 1901]. SLOC.
3. Although her nephew had changed his name by deed poll in 1897 to his father's name Frederic William Freeman, Hattie continued to call him Frank until his marriage in 1903.
4. Emily Hale, Hampton, to HEF, UP, February 23, 1901. SLOC.
5. EEH, Hampton, to HEF, UP, March 4, 1901. SLOC.
6. EEH, Washington, to HEF, UP, [March 21, 1901]. SLOC.
7. Ibid. Edward took the women to see philanthropist Phoebe Hearst's pictures at her grand Washington house on March 27.
8. [HEF], "Bird Friends," *Lend a Hand Record,* May 1901, 7-8.
9. Judith Andrews, Boston, to HEF, Charlottesville, VA, March 28, 1901, enclosing letter from Helen Merriman of Intervale NH, March 27, 1901. SLOC.
10. Harriet E. Freeman and Emma G. Cummings, "Dismal Swamp and How to Go There," *The Chautauquan,* Vol. 33 (August 1901), 515-518. In their "Essay on the Literature of the Dismal Swamp," Peter C. Stewart, Paul W. Kirk, Jr., and Harold G. Marshall reference this "charming account" by "two enterprising New England women," as Hattie and Emma called themselves, noting the limitations of their expedition and their "audacity to advise people on how to find the Dismal Swamp." In Kirk, *The Great Dismal Swamp* (Charlotte: University of Virginia Press, 1979). They were probably referring to the great literature that preceded Hattie and Emma's limited, if charming, account (Thomas Moore's 1803 ghost ballad "The Lake of the Dismal Swamp," Henry Longfellow's 1842 poem "The Slave in the Dismal Swamp," and Harriet Beecher Stowe's 1856 best-selling novel *Dred: A Tale of the Great Dismal Swamp*).
11. EEH Journal, June 1-3, 1901. NYSL.
12. EEH, Boston, to HEF, c/o Professor Maynard, Amherst Agricultural College, June 4, 1901. SLOC.
13. *The Outlook,* formerly *The Christian Union,* which Abbott co-edited with Henry Ward Beecher from 1876 to 1881 and whom he succeeded

as pastor of Brooklyn's Plymouth Church, published several of Edward's reminiscences in serial form over the final years of his life.

14. Quoted in Scott Miller, *The President and the Assassin: McKinley, Terror, and Empire at the Dawn of the American Century* (New York: Random House, 2011), 304.
15. EEH, Intervale, to Emily Hale, Roxbury, September 16, 1901. NYSL.
16. Miller, *President and Assassin*, 331-332.
17. EEH, Roxbury, to HEF, Intervale, September 19, 1901. SLOC.
18. EEH, Roxbury, to HEF, Intervale, September 29, 1901, enclosing letter from Amadeus Grabau, New York, September 27, 1901. SLOC.
19. Evelyn Salz, editor, *Selected Letters of Mary Antin* (Syracuse, NY: Syracuse University Press, 2000), 4.
20. EEH, Roxbury, to HEF, Intervale, October 5, 1901. SLOC.
21. See Richard I. Johnson, "Rise and Fall of the Boston Society of Natural History," *Northeastern Naturalist*, Vol. 11.1 (2004), 81-108. JSTOR 3858546. The BSNH became in 1946 the Boston Museum of Science and the original Back Bay building is now a flagship store of Restoration Hardware.
22. Hattie's application for membership in the DAR was accepted on August 21, 1903 (Application 44435) on the basis that her maternal ancestor Lemuel Parker "assisted in establishing American Independence, while acting in the capacity of 'private, corporal, sergeant.'" Courtesy Archives of the Daughters of the American Revolution; *Boston Daily Globe*, January 4, 1903.
23. According to Charles F. Jenkins, "Asa Gray and His Quest for *Shortia galacifolia*," *Arnoldia*, 2 (1946), 18-28, it was a 17-year-old North Carolinian boy, George Hyams, who rediscovered Shortia in May 1877. Eighteen months later, Hyams' father sent the specimen to a friend in Rhode Island who in turn sent it on to Asa Gray at Harvard. A triumphant Asa Gray wrote to a botanist friend on October 21, 1878, "No other botanist has the news." Gray, his wife, and three botanist friends, including Charles S. Sargent, traveled south the following spring to see the plant growing in the wild for themselves, with meager success, so Sargent renewed the search in 1886, two years before Asa Gray's death. Gray's successor at the herbarium, Sereno Watson, told Edward in 1889 that they had Shortia in their collections (see my chapter 6).
24. EEH, Baltimore, to HEF, Charleston, SC, March 24, 1902. SLOC.
25. EEH, Baltimore, to HEF, Fayetteville, NC, March 25, 1902. SLOC. EEH did not publish her letter in the *Record*, probably because he and Hattie decided it merited wider circulation.
26. Harriet E. Freeman, "How Two Women found the Shortia," *The Chautauquan*, 35 (August 1902), 490-495.

27. "Edward Everett Hale," *Harper's Weekly*, March 22, 1902, 365.
28. George Frisbie Hoar, *Autobiography of Seventy Years* (New York: Charles Scribner's Sons, 1906), II, 448.
29. EEH, Chicago, to Martha Adams, Sherborn, MA, May 10, 1902. GLOC.
30. EEH, Chicago, to HEF, UP, May 9, 1902. SLOC.
31. While he was studying art in Paris between 1887 and 1892, Philip lost his heart to a young woman, Katharine Kinsella, who kept him on a string even while she spent part of a summer with him and his family at Matunuck. Susan Hale, always a good judge of character, suspected that Katharine was playing her nephew along and took a dislike to her. Later, Phil was briefly engaged to artist Ellen Reed.
32. HEF, UP and Intervale, to EEH, Matunuck, July 1 and [about July 7, 1902]. These two are among many inadequately dated or undated, but nonetheless important Hattie letters that the LOC archivists relegated to Box 25. SLOC.
33. From Emma Cummings' journal account, Randolph, NH, July 9-13, 1902. SLOC.
34. HEF, The Perch, to EEH, Matunuck, "No. 2 letter from Harriet Thursday," July 10, [1902]. Box 25.SLOC.
35. HEF, Intervale, to EEH, Matunuck [about July 18 and about August 8, 1902]. Box 25 Undated. SLOC.
36. HEF, Intervale, to EEH, Matunuck, about July 26, 1902. Box 25 Undated Misc. fragments. SLOC.
37. HEF, Intervale, to EEH Matunuck, August 8, [1902]. Box 25. SLOC.
38. Appalachian Mountain Club archives, August 5, 1902; HEF, Summit House, to EEH, Matunuck, August 5, 1902. SLOC; "Correspondence. Coos Co., N.H.," *LAH Record*, September 1902, 18-19. Frank Burt took over *Among the Clouds* from his father Henry M. Burt who edited and printed the paper from 1877 to 1884.
39. Photograph album titled by Hattie "Pictures of the Chief at Intervale To Abigail W. Clark from Harriet E. Freeman Christmas 1902." AHTL. There is another album with photographs taken at Intervale in the Ethel Hale Freeman Papers, Smith College Archives.
40. Volume 1 of *Memories of a Hundred Years* was published at the end of 1902 and Edward gave Hattie a copy for Christmas. His inscription read in part, "But you have read it long before, though it is but just now 'published.' Copy or proof, you have read it all, and more of the copy was in your hand writing than in that of any of the rest of us." EEH, *Memories of a Hundred Years*, 2 vols. AHTL.
41. *Boston Herald*, September 4, 1902.
42. "For the Protection of New Hampshire Forests: An Important Meeting of the State Forest Association," *Forestry and Irrigation*," October 1902, 397.

43. EEH, Roxbury, to HEF, Intervale, October 14 and 24, 1902. SLOC.
44. EEH, Journal, October 8 and 9, 1902 and a note in Biographical MS Box 41, NYSL; EEH, "My First Ascent of Mount Washington," *Among the Clouds*. Season of 1903. AHTL.
45. EEH, Roxbury, to HEF, Intervale, October 12, 1902. SLOC.
46. For a fascinating account of Farmer's experiment at Green Acre and the divisions caused by her conversion to the Bahá'í faith, see Leigh Eric Schmidt, *Restless Souls: The Making of American Spirituality from Emerson to Oprah* (San Francisco: HarperSanFrancisco, Division of Harper Collins, 2005), 17, 185-213.
47. Susan Hale, Olana, Hudson, NY, to Lucy Perkins, Hartford, CN, October 24, 1902. GLOC.
48. Emily Hale, Roxbury, to HEF, Intervale, October 18, 1902. SLOC.
49. EEH, W. Washington, to HEF, UP, April 23 and 25, 1903. Both SLOC.
50. EEH, W. Washington, to HEF, UP, April 26, 1903. SLOC. Bell's tetrahedral wings were named *Cygnet I, II* and *III*, and were flown both unmanned and manned (*Cygnet I* crashed during a flight carrying its pilot) in the period from 1907 to 1912.
51. HEF, UP, to EEH, Baltimore, Friday morning [May 1, 1903]. SLOC.
52. HEF, somewhere crossing Ohio, to EEH, Roxbury, Sunday morning [May 3, 1903]. SLOC.
53. "America: Grand Canon," *LAH Record*, June 1903, 26-27.
54. HEF, [Yosemite, CA], to EEH, Roxbury, [May 20, 1903]. Box 25 Undated Misc. fragment. SLOC.
55. HEF, Yo Semite [*sic*], to EEH, Roxbury, May 21, [1903]. SLOC.
56. EEH, Roxbury, to HEF, San Francisco?, May 25, 1903. SLOC.
57. HEF, Redlands, CA, to EEH, Roxbury, June 9, 1903. SLOC.
58. EEH, Exeter, NH, to HEF, San Francisco, June 17, 1903. SLOC.
59. HEF, Los Angeles, to EEH, Roxbury, ca. June 13, 1903, Box 25. Undated miscellaneous fragment. SLOC.
60. EEH, Roxbury, to HEF, Colorado Springs, July 5. 1903. SLOC.
61. Ibid. See also "Teachers' Convention," *LAH Record*, August 1903, 18-19.
62. EEH, Roxbury, to HEF, [Colorado Springs], July 7, 1903. SLOC.
63. In the copy of his *Prayers in the Senate* that Edward gave Hattie on November 20, 1904, he wrote, "I was chosen to this office by the Unanimous vote of the Senate. The request was sent to me by Telegraph. I answered "Such a Request is a Command." AHTL.

12. First Winters without Edward

1. EEH, Roxbury, to HEF, Philadelphia, November 23, 1903. HFP-SSC.

2. Hattie was in Groton for the installation there of her young protégé the Reverend Pemberton Cressey, previously the minister of the Unitarian church built and endowed by the Merrimans in North Conway, near their summer house in Intervale. EEH, New York, to HEF, Groton, November 5, 1903. SLOC.
3. Amadeus Grabau, New York, to HEF, UP, January 14, 1904. SLOC; *New York Times*, January 8, 1904.
4. Francis H. Peabody, Cambridge, MA, to EEH, Roxbury, December 30 1903. NYSL. Quoted in Holloway, *Edward Everett* Hale, 251.
5. "Office Notes," *LAH Record*, January 1904, 19.
6. EEH, Washington, to HEF, UP, January 4, 1904. SLOC.
7. EEH, Washington, to HEF, UP, January 10, 1904. SLOC.
8. Emily Hale, Roxbury, to EEH, Washington, January 25, 1904. HFP-SSC.
9. EEH, Washington, to HEF, UP, March 3, 1904. SLOC.
10. Ellen, Maury Slayden, to her sister, January 20, 1904, in Slayden, *Washington Wife: Journal of Ellen Maury Slayden from 1897-1919* (New York: Harper & Row, 1963 edition), 54-55.
11. HEF, "On board the Olivetti, the little steamer which in summer goes between Boston & Bar Harbor. 11 a.m," to EEH, Washington, February 8, 1904. SLOC.
12. Joshua Young, "The Funeral of John Brown," *The New England Magazine*, Vol. 30, April 1904, 229-243, with photographs.
13. "Correspondence. America. Cuba," *LAH Record*, April 1904, 13-14.
14. In 1919, Atkins created an endowment fund and turned the management of the Garden over to Harvard University to continue its work in economic botany for Cuba's benefit. The acreage increased during Atkins' lifetime and when his son-in-law William H. Claflin became president of the Soledad Sugar Company, the garden's name was changed to the Atkins Institution of the Arnold Arboretum. Fidel Castro nationalized Soledad and the botanical garden which continues as the Jardín Botánico de Cienfuegos. See E. D. Merrill, "The Atkins Institution of the Arnold Arboretum, Soledad, Cienfuegos, Cuba," *Bulletin of Popular Information Arnold Arboretum Harvard University* (December 13, 1940), 66, 68, 70.
15. HEF, UP, to EEH, Washington, [February 1905]. SLOC.
16. Edwin F. Atkins Letterbook, 26 Feb-27 Apr 1904. Atkins Family Papers, Vol. II.30. Massachusetts Historical Society.
17. Miller, *President and Assassin*, 335-336.
18. Elizabeth Cady Stanton, Susan B. Anthony, Ida Husted Harper, editors, *A History of Woman Suffrage*, vol. 5 (1900-1920), 98-99.
19. EEH, 1717 20 St., Washington, to HEF, Cuba, February 19, 1904. SLOC. He made a sketch showing seating around Hanna's coffin.

20. EEH, Washington, to HEF, c/o W. H. Reed, New Orleans, February 23, 1904. SLOC.
21. EEH, Washington, to HEF, Cuba, February 23 and 26, 1904. SLOC. Edward was also a strong supporter of former slave Jennie Dean's Manassas Industrial School for Colored Girls.
22. EEH, Washington, to HEF, UP, [March 1, 1904]. SLOC.
23. HEF, Soledad, Cienfuegos, Cuba, to Collier Cobb, Chapel Hill, February 19, 1904, and HEF, UP, to Collier Cobb, May 14, 1904. Collier Cobb Papers, Southern Historical Collection, Wilson Library, University of North Carolina at Chapel Hill (UNC).
24. The National Zoo was created by an 1889 Act of Congress for "the advancement of science and the instruction and recreation of the people." In 1890, it became part of the Smithsonian. Plans for the zoo were drawn up by Edward's friend Samuel P. Langley, third secretary of the Smithsonian, William T. Hornaday, noted conservationist and head of the Smithsonian's vertebrate division, and landscape architect Frederick Law Olmsted, Emily's first fiancé.
25. EEH, Washington, to HEF, UP, April 14, 1904. SLOC.
26. EEH, Washington, to HEF, UP, April 16, 1904. SLOC.
27. "Table Gossip," *Boston Daily Globe*, August 28, 1904.
28. Emily Hale, Intervale, to Nelly, Folly Cove, August 20, 1904. HFP-SSC.
29. HEF, Intervale, to Benjamin L. Robinson, Gray Herbarium, Cambridge, MA, August 20, 1904. Gray Herbarium Archives, Harvard University.
30. Edward told Hattie in July that Emma had asked his advice about the controversy surrounding her first choice of a title for her little book which had already been claimed by another author. "I also think that Emma's Bird Book for instance, would be a better name," he wrote. EEH, Matunuck, to HEF, Intervale, July 15, 1904. SLOC. Published first as *Baby pathfinder to the birds . . . a pocket guide to one hundred and ten land birds of New England* (Boston: W. A. Butterfield, 1904), it was reissued in two illustrated volumes by the same publisher as *Baby Bird Finder* (1904-6).
31. HEF, Intervale, to EEH, Roxbury, October 3, 1904. SLOC.
32. EEH, Roxbury, to HEF, Intervale, October 1, 1904. SLOC.
33. *Official report of the thirteenth Universal peace congress: held at Boston, Massachusetts, U.S.A., October third to eighth, 1904* (Boston: The Peace Congress Committee, 1904).
34. EEH, Roxbury, to HEF, Intervale, October 4 and 7, 1904. Both SLOC.
35. EEH, Roxbury, to HEF, Intervale, October 8, 1904. SLOC.
36. EEH, Roxbury, to HEF, Intervale, October 9, 1904. SLOC.
37. E. Digby Baltzell, *Judgment and Sensibility: Religion and Stratification* (New Brunswick, NJ: Transaction Publishers, 1994), 243—244.

38. EEH, Boston, to HEF, Intervale, October 12, 1904. SLOC.
39. HEF, UP, to EEH, Washington, "Saturday 5 p.m." [January 1905, following Forestry meeting in Washington]. Box 25 undated. SLOC.
40. EEH, Roxbury, to HEF, Intervale, October 19, 1904. SLOC. A few months later, Hattie told him, "You know it was Miss Mary who first called me an 'East Wind.' On my last call, she was so surprised & interested & somewhat excited when I told her what I had been doing & what I was going to do, that when I left she said she felt as if she had had a 'shower bath.'" HEF, Groton, MA, to EEH, Washington, [January 1905]. Box 25. SLOC.
41. HEF, Newburyport, MA, to EEH, Roxbury, Saturday 7 a.m. [October 28, 1904]. Box 25. SLOC.
42. EEH, U.S. Senate, Washington, to HEF, UP, December 7, 1904. SLOC.
43. HEF, UP, to EEH, Washington, [mid January 1905]. Box 25 undated. SLOC.
44. HEF, UP, to EEH, Washington, Sunday, n.d. [mid-February 1905]. Box 25 undated. SLOC.
45. EEH, Washington, to HEF, UP, February 15, 1905. SLOC.
46. HEF, UP, to EEH, Washington, [January 15?, 1905]. Undated Misc. fragment. Box 25, SLOC, dated as response to EEH's letter of 1/13/05 and the upcoming lecture on 1/18/05 by buffalo conservationist Ernest Harold Baynes at the BSNH that Hattie mentions in her letter.
47. This copy print is in the Harriet E. Freeman Papers, AHTL.
48. HEF, UP, to EEH, Washington, Friday morning [January 1905]. Box 25 Undated. SLOC.
49. HEF, UP, to EEH, Washington, [February 1905]. SLOC.
50. EEH, Washington, to HEF, UP, February 20, 1905. SLOC.
51. HEF, The Valencia, St. Augustine, FL, to EEH, Washington, DC, March 15 and 16, [1905]. Both SLOC.
52. HEF, Ormond, FL, to EEH, Washington, Sunday, March 19, [March 21, 23, 26, April 3 and 8], 1905. All SLOC.
53. EEH, Hampton, VA, to HEF, New York, April 8, 1905. SLOC. HEF, Bretton Hall, NY, to EEH, Hampton, VA [April 9, 1905]. Box 25. SLOC.
54. EEH, Roxbury, to HEF, Intervale, June 4, 1905. SLOC.
55. HEF, Intervale, to EEH, Matunuck, [July 25, 1905]. SLOC.
56. HEF, Edgartown, Nantucket, to EEH, Matunuck, July 26, 1905. SLOC.
57. HEF, Intervale, to EEH, Matunuck, [August 3?, 1905]. Box 25 Undated. SLOC.
58. EEH, Roxbury, to HEF, Intervale, October 18, 1905. SLOC.
59. HEF, UP, to EEH, Washington, n.d. [ca. December 13,1905, misfiled with Feb./Mar. 1905 letters]. SLOC.
60. HEF, Murray Hill Hotel, New York, to EEH, Washington, December 19, 1905. SLOC.

13. Preservation and Conservation

1. I have drawn most of the background on the struggle to establish eastern forest preserves from the history section of the U.S. Forest Service website: http://foresthistory.org. Consulted 8/12/2013.
2. "Correspondence. White Mountains, N.H.," *LAH Record* (*LAHR*), December 1903, 22.
3. EEH, Washington, to HEF, UP, April 14, [1904]. SLOC.
4. "Correspondence. Washington," *LAHR*, January 1905, 10.
5. From "American Forest Congress Held at Washington, D.C. January 2 to 6," *Forest & Irrigation* (*F&I*), Vol. XI, January 1905, 3.
6. "Forestry," *LAHR*, May 1905, 3.
7. "American Forest Congress," *F&I*, Vol. XI, January 1905, 4. The article also includes cartoons of leading attendees, among them "Dr. Edward Everett Hale," and a List of Delegates, including HEF and EEH.
8. HEF, UP, to EEH, Washington, [mid-January 1905]. Box 25 undated. SLOC.
9. In June, 1900, Hattie had described for Edward a day she and Emma spent with bird photographer Herbert K. Job. She explained Job's painstaking technique for taking photos of nesting Florida shore birds. HEF, Gloucester Street, Boston, to EEH, Roxbury, June 8, 1900. SLOC.
10. See Jennifer Price, "Hats Off to Audubon," *Audubon Magazine*, December 2004. Adapted from the chapter "When Women Were Women, Men Were Men, and Birds Were Hats," in Price, *Flight Maps: Adventures with Nature in Modern America* (New York: Basic Books, 1999). (http://archive.audubonmagazine.org/features0412/hats.html)
11. HEF, UP, to EEH, Washington, Friday morning [January 1905]. Box 25. SLOC.
12. Harriet E. Freeman, "Preservation of Birds," *LAHR*, March 1905, 11-14.
13. HEF, New York, to EEH, Hampton, [April 8 and 9, 1905]. SLOC.
14. EEH, "Herons and Aigrets," *LAHR*, October 1905, 18.
15. *Forest and Irrigation*, 1905 articles: photograph of EEH, 397; and Philip W. Ayres, "Reasons for a National Forest Reservation in the White Mountains," September 1905, 421-427; Edwin A. Start, "A White Mountain Forest Reserve: Its Immediate Need, and Its Relation to the National Forest Reserve Policy," October 1905, 450-452; Edward Everett Hale, "Our Eastern Forests," 495-498; Franklin W. Rollins, "A Forest Reserve in the White Mountains: Reasons Why the East as Well as the West Should have Forest Reservations," 512-516, and H. J. Robertson, "Best Use of the White Mountain Region," 529-531, all November 1905.

16. "Meeting of the American Forestry Association," *F&I*, January 1906, 1.
17. *LAHR*, May 1906, 11; EEH, Washington, to HEF, Italy [no envelope], March 25, 1906. SLOC.
18. EEH, Washington, to HEF, UP, December 17, 1906. SLOC.
19. HEF, UP, to EEH, Washington, December ?, 1906. SLOC
20. HEF, UP, to EEH, Washington, Thursday evening, [late Dec. 1906]. Box 25. SLOC.
21. HEF, Manhattan Hotel, New York, to EEH, Washington, Monday evening [December 31, 1906] and Tuesday morning [January 1, 1907]. Box 25 Undated. SLOC.
22. However, researcher Iris Baird found that the sale of state-owned land was "much more obscure and confusing than Ward and others present it." See Christopher Johnson, *This Grand & Magnificent Place: The Wilderness Heritage of the White Mountains* (Durham, New Hampshire: University of New Hampshire Press, 2006), 172 and note 6.
23. EEH's address "Looking to the Future," and Edwin Start's "Why the Bill Hangs Fire: An Explanation and a Plea," *F&I*, January 1907, 24-25 and 29-31.

14. Filling the Gap

1. HEF, Rome, to Harriet M. Freeman, West Newton, MA, February 13, 1906. Ethel Hale Freeman Papers, Smith College Archives.
2. HEF, Venice, to EEH, Washington, April 14, 1906. SLOC.
3. Helen Freeman, West Newton, to HEF, Rome, February 6, 1906. SLOC.
4. EEH, Washington, to HEF, Naples, January 18, 1906. LOC.
5. EEHJr., Schenectady, NY, to EEH, Roxbury, January 28, 1906. HFP-SSC.
6. Newspaper clipping, possibly from the Boston *Evening Transcript*, ca. late Jan., early Feb. 1906, enclosed in a February 5, 1906 letter from Miss Perkins to Gertrude Pease and passed on by Mrs. Pease to HEF in Italy. SLOC.
7. HEF, Taormina, Sicily, to Helen Freeman, West Newton, February 7 [1905] 1906. EHF-SSC.
8. EEH, Washington, to HEF, Sicily?, March 17, 1906. SLOC.
9. EEH, Roxbury, to HEF, Intervale?, September 18, 1906. SLOC.
10. EEH, Washington, to HEF, Rome, February 18, 1906. SLOC. According to *Proceedings of the National Congress on Uniform Divorce Laws*, February 19[-22], 1906. Consulted online.
11. "Rev. Dr. Hillis Attacks Prof. George D. Herron: Says that He is Either a Coward or a Monster," *The New York* Times, April 24, 1901; "Prof. Herron is Married: Miss Rand Becomes the Wife of the Socialist. They

will Live on a Farm Where Other Socialists Will Aid Them in Their Propaganda," *The New York* Times, May 28, 1901. Upton Sinclair, "The Story of a Lynching," Ch. XX, *The Brass Check: A study of American Journalism*, 1919. Sinclair concluded, "I wonder which is the more disagreeable phenomenon, sexual license or venal hypocrisy."

12. EEH, Washington, to HEF, Naples, [first page missing, but attached to envelope dated February 5, 1906]. SLOC.
13. "Mr Langley's Aerodrome," *LAH Record*, September 1905, 3-5.
14. EEH, Washington, to HEF, Florence, March 20, 1906. SLOC.
15. HEF, Florence, to Harriet M. Freeman, West Newton, April 5, 1906. EHF-Smith.
16. EEH, Washington, to HEF, Florence, forwarded to Milan, April 24, 1906. SLOC.
17. HEF, Verona, Italy, to Collier Cobb, April 22, 1906. Cobb Papers, UNC.
18. EEH, Matunuck, to HEF, Intervale, July 6, 1906. SLOC; Emily Hale, Folly Cove, to EEH, Matunuck, July 8, 1906. HFP-SSC.
19. Margareta (Greta) Marquand, New York City, to Herbert D. Hale, Roxbury?, November 20, 1891. Hale-Marquand Papers, Courtesy of the Trustees of the Boston Public Library/Rare Books.
20. EEH, Washington, to HEF, Florence, April 26, 1906. SLOC.
21. HEF, UP, to B. L. Robinson, Gray Herbarium Archives, June 12 and 26, 1906. Gray Herbarium Archives, Harvard University.
22. EEH, Roxbury, to HEF, UP, July 1, 1906. SLOC.
23. EEH, Matunuck, to HEF, Intervale, July 11, 1906. SLOC.
24. EEH, Matunuck, to HEF, North East Harbor, Maine, July 21, 1906. SLOC; "Aliens in the United States," *LAHR*, May 1907, 6; "Immigration," *LAHR*, April 1908, 15.
25. Christine Rosen, *Preaching Eugenics: Religious Leaders and the American Eugenics Movement* (Oxford University Press, 2004), 35-36.
26. HEF, UP, to EEH, Washington, December 26, 1908. SLOC.
27. Rosen, *Preaching Eugenics*, 85-90.
28. Two examples of these portraits are in the Harriet E. Freeman Papers at the Andover-Harvard Theological Library, Harvard Divinity School.
29. EEH, Roxbury, to HEF, Intervale, September 14 and 15, 1906. Both SLOC.
30. EEH, Washington, to HEF, UP, December 17, 1906. SLOC.
31. EEH, Washington, to HEF, UP, December 22, 1906. SLOC.
32. HEF, UP, to EEH, Washington, January 6, 1907. SLOC.
33. HEF, UP, to EEH, Washington, January 19, 1907. Box 25. SLOC.
34. Baltzell, *Judgment and Sensibility*, 245-246.
35. HEF, UP, to EEH, Washington, [January 14, 1907]. Box 25 Undated. SLOC.

36. HEF, UP, to EEH, Washington, Wednesday evening [early February 1907]. Box 25 Undated. SLOC.
37. HEF, UP, to EEH, Washington, March 3, [1907]. SLOC.
38. HEF, "On board the Bluecher," Port de Spain, Trinidad, March 15, 1907, and "Latitude of Cuba," n.d. Saturday afternoon [ca. March 17, 1907], both to EEH, Washington. SLOC.
39. HEF, "On board the S.S. Bluecher [en route to Kingston, Jamaica], to EEH, Washington, March 19, 1907. SLOC.
40. HEF, "On board S. S. Bluecher. Off the coast of Cuba," to EEH, Washington, "Holy Thursday 07" [March 28, 1907]. SLOC.
41. J. Hampton Moore, *With Speaker Cannon through the Tropics* (Philadelphia: The Book Print, 1907), 346-352.
42. HEF, "On board S.S. Bluecher, to EEH, Hampton, April 6, 1907. SLOC.
43. HEF, New York, "Monday evening" [April 7, 1907] and Boston, April 10, [1907], to EEH, Washington. Box 25, SLOC.
44. HEF, Intervale, to EEH, Matunuck, [June 20, 1907]. Box 25 Undated. SLOC.
45. HEF, UP, to EEH, Washington, [after January 6, 1908]. SLOC.
46. "Chaplain Hale Young Old Man," *The Washington Times*, January 12, 1908, Magazine Section, 4; "Ellen Day Hale," *The Washington Times*, April 12, 1908, Magazine Section, 7.
47. "Appalachian Reservations," *LAHR*, May 1908, 4.
48. HEF, Chapel Hill, NC, to EEH, Washington, May 12, 14, [after 14], 19, 1908. All Box 25. SLOC.
49. "New England Forestry," *LAHR*, June 1908, 1-3,
50. EEH, Matunuck, to HEF, Intervale, July 18, 1908. SLOC.
51. "Forestry," *LAHR*, September 1908, 8; EEH, Intervale, to Emily Hale, Roxbury, August 12, 1908. Quoted in EEHJr., *Life and Letters*, II, 406. Ulysses S. Pierce, *The Soul of the Bible*. Introduction by EEH (Boston: American Unitarian Association, 1908). AHTL.
52. HEF, Intervale, to EEH, Roxbury, Sunday morning, [October 1?, 1908]. Box 25. SLOC.
53. HEF, Intervale, to EEH, Roxbury, September 23 and October 1, 1908. Both SLOC.
54. Susan Hale, Roxbury, to Carla [Atkinson], October 15, 1908. Special Collections, University of Rhode Island, Kingston, R.I. See *Letters of Susan Hale*, edited by Caroline P. Atkinson, with an introduction by Edward E. Hale Jr. Caroline Atkinson published the ex-concubine letter but omitted that phrase, 443-4. I am grateful to Joan Youngken for drawing my attention to the original letter.
55. Obituary, "Herbert D. Hale," *New York Times*, November 11, 1908. Bertie's Newburyport death certificate, entered incorrectly as November

12, gave the cause of death as cancer of the liver. Massachusetts, Town & Vital Records, 1620-1988. Ancestry.com.

56. Herbert D. Hale, Bad-Nauheim, Germany, to Margareta Marquand Hale, Logansville, NJ, June 25, 1908. Hale-Marquand, Papers, Courtesy of the Trustees of the Boston Public Library/Rare Books.
57. EEH, Roxbury, to Helen Freeman, West Newton, November 15, 1908. HFP-SSC.
58. Curzon's Mill was to figure prominently as "Wickford Point," as were Bertie's widow and children, in Greta's cousin John Marquand's satirical novel of the same name.
59. This Robert Beverly Hale became a noted artist and curator of American art at the Metropolitan Museum of Art.
60. HEF, Newburyport, MA, to EEH, Roxbury, Sunday afternoon [day after Thanksgiving 1908]. Box 25. SLOC. Greta Hale married architect John Oakman, who was six years younger, in 1910. He adopted her five children by Bertie and their daughter Renée was born in 1911.
61. Quoted in Jean H. Baker, *Margaret Sanger: A Life of Passion* (New York: Farrar, Straus and Giroux, 2011), 41.
62. HEF, UP, to EEH, Washington, n.d. [November 1908] and Sunday morning n.d. [mid-December 1908]. Both Box 25. SLOC. Roosevelt's letter to Lyman Abbott on woman suffrage from the White House, November 10, 1908, was reprinted in *The Remonstrance,* a quarterly publication of the Massachusetts Association Opposed to the Further Extension of Suffrage to Women.
63. HEF, UP, to EEH, Washington, December 26, [1908]. SLOC.
64. Slayden, *Washington Wife,* January 8, 1909, 116-117.
65. HEF, UP, to EEH, Washington, January 14, 1909. SLOC.
66. HEF, UP, to EEH, Washington, January 11, 1909. SLOC.
67. HEF, UP, to EEH, Washington, "Sunday evening," n.d. [Jan. 1909]. SLOC.
68. HEF, UP, to EEH, Washington, [late February 1909]. Box 25 undated misc. fragments. SLOC.
69. Adams, *Edward Everett Hale,* 110. The letter in question is dated Oyster Bay, August 28, 1908.
70. March 4, 1909, entry in EEH's diary. Quoted in EEHJr., *Life & Letters,* II, 407-8
71. "Glacier" Wright was the same George Frederick Wright who was a longtime friend of Edward's and whose writings were greatly admired by Hattie. He and his son, Frederick B. Wright, co-edited the archaeology journal *Records of the Past*. Hattie became a member of the Archaeological Institute of America that year.
72. HEF, London, to Helen Freeman Arnold, June 16, 1909. HFP-SSC.

73. EEH, Washington, to HEF, Roxbury, "Easter Sunday a.m." [April 11, 1909]. SLOC.
74. Helen Freeman Arnold's daughter, Harriet McKissock, thought that her parents had been married by Hale but he was only able to send Helen a message from his sick bed in Washington.
75. EEH, Washington, to HEF, UP, April 12, 1909. SLOC.
76. EEH Journal, April 22, 1909. NYSL.
77. Benjamin Champney (1817-1907) was the founder of the White Mountain School of painting whom Hattie and Edward had visited at his Intervale studio on several occasions.
78. Holloway, 259.
79. Abigail Clark, Roxbury, to Martha Adams Leland, Sherborn, MA, June 10, 1909. GLOC.

15. Life after Edward

1. *The Boston Globe*, June 10, 1909; *The New York Times* and *The Springfield Daily Republican*, June 11, 1909. Another Massachusetts newspaper, *The Springfield Daily Republican*, declared "No one will forget him who has lived in his day." *The Washington Herald* reported "Senate Eulogizes the Life of Hale." *The San Francisco Call*'s headline was "Nation Mourns the Death of Rev. E. E. Hale" and *The Salt Lake Herald*'s was "Famous Divine Called Beyond." Hattie's friends must have collected obituaries for her since most of these can be found in the Harriet E. Freeman Papers at the Andover-Harvard Theological Library.
2. Albert Shaw, "Edward Everett Hale," *Review of Reviews*, July 1909; Edwin D. Mead, "Edward Everett Hale," *New England Magazine*, Vol. 40 (July 1909), 526; Thomas Wentworth Higginson, "Edward Everett Hale," *The Outlook*, June 19, 1909.
3. HEF, London, to Helen Hunt Arnold, Bridgewater, RI, June 16, 1909; Helen Hunt Arnold, Bridgewater, to Emily Hale, Roxbury, June 16, 1909 (there is no condolence letter from Hattie in this file); HEF, Berlin, to Helen Hunt Arnold, August 17, 1909. All HFP-SSC.
4. Mary Driscoll, UP, and Harriet M. Freeman, W. Newton, to HEF [sent to London and forwarded to Berlin and then Copenhagen], July 23, 1909. Both SLOC.
5. HEF, Vienna, to Helen Arnold, Bridgewater, September 4, [1909]. HFP-SSC.
6. Hattie appears to have purchased at least two books at the sale of Edward's library: a leather-bound *Commonwealth of Massachusetts Manual for the Use of the General Court: containing the Rules and Orders of the Two Branches* (Boston: Write & Potter, 1876), with "Charles Hale"

embossed in gold on the cover, and Hale's copy of the Constitution. AHTL.

7. Abigail Clark, Matunuck, to Ellen Day Hale (Nelly), Folly Cove, August 11, 1909; Clark, Cambridge, to Nelly, Folly Cove, Friday p.m. [September? 1909]; Clark, Cambridge, to Nelly, Folly Cove, Saturday [September? 1909]. All HFP-SSC.
8. Minnie Whitman, Boston, to HEF, Berlin, Germany, August 3, 1909. SLOC.
9. Ellen Day Hale, Washington, to HEF, UP, February 4, 1910. HFP-SSC.
10. Randall H. Bennett, *The White Mountains: Alps of New England* (Charleston, S.C.: Arcadia, 2003), 129.
11. HEF, UP, to C. Hart Merriam, Washington, January 3, 1910. C. Hart Merriam Papers, Bancroft Library, Berkeley, CA.
12. HEF, UP, to Collier Cobb, May 6, [1910]. Cobb Papers, UNC.
13. Mary Dann, Brooklyn, NY, to HEF, UP, March 23, 1910. HEF-AHTL.
14. Arthur Hale, New York, to EEHJr., Schenectady, NY, April 30, 1910; Rose Hale, Matunuck, to EEHJr., Schenectady, July ?, 1910. EEH Papers, Box 20, NYSL.
15. Hattie's copy of this book is now at the Andover-Harvard Theological Library. The original letters can be examined in the archives of the University of Rhode Island.
16. Harriet E. Freeman, U.S. passport application, November 22, 1911. Ancestry.com. U.S. Passport Applications, 1795-1925.
17. HEF, on Norddeutscher Loyd, Bremen, to Helen Arnold, [Roxbury], December 11, [1911]. HFP-SSC.
18. Unidentified writer [perhaps Prescott F. Hall], Immigration Restriction League, Boston, to HEF, UP, December 9, 1912; Immigration Restriction League (U.S.) Records (MS Am 2245), Houghton University Library, Harvard University.
19. Baltzell, *Judgment and Sensibility*, 246.
20. Conversations and e-mail exchanges with Mary Macomber Leue who continues to live in Ethel Hale Freeman's former farm, Journey's End, near Ashfield in northwestern Massachusetts, which she inherited from Ethel. Leue's mother and Ethel, who became friends through their performances for the Lend A Hand Dramatic Club, bought the farm while Ethel was teaching drama at Smith College and turned it into a vacation-home for working girls from the Boston mills. See chapter 3 of Mary Macomber Leue's *Trying to Get it Right This Time: My Reminiscences:* <http://thoughtsnmemories.net/thoughstnmemories_html/myremspref.htm>
21. HEF, S.S. "Arabia," January 7, 1912; Cairo, February 21, 1912; D. George Washington of the Norddeutscher Lloyd Bremen line, June

4, 1912, and Boston, June 28, 1912; Intervale, September 22, 1912, and Newburyport, MA, Thanksgiving, to Collier Cobb provide lengthy accounts of her activities that year. Cobb Papers, UNC. Emma evidently sent a selection of her photographs from this trip to the National Geographic Society, hoping for publication in the magazine. These can be viewed at www.corbisimages.com/Search#pg=emma+g+cummings

22. Maud deLeigh Hodges, *Crossroads on the Charles: A History of Watertown, Massachusetts* (Canaan, NH: Phoenix Publishing for the Watertown Free Public Library, 1980), 156.
23. According to the *Annual Report of the Boston Legal Aid Society*, 1912, Hattie paid dues that year of $10.
24. HEF, UP, to EEH, Washington, January 11, 1909. SLOC.
25. HEF, UP, to Helen and Harold Arnold, [West Roxbury?], January 14, [1913]. HFP SSC. This letter and others and a rare photograph of Hattie were discovered by Hattie's great-niece Holly Sawyer in her mother's house after her death and donated to the Sophia Smith Collection at Smith College. Fred Freeman's second wife was called Madeleine, as noted on his draft registration form U.S., World War I Draft Registration Cards, 1917-1918. The Marriage of F. W. Freeman and Madeleine Jean at Portsmouth, NH, on December 10, 1915, appears in "New Hampshire Marriages and Divorces." Both Ancestry.com.
26. "The Picture That Is in the News of the Day," *The Boston Herald*, May 23, 1913; unidentified and undated newspaper clipping. HEF-AHTL.
27. O'Connor, *Boston Irish*, 187-188.
28. Massachusetts Vital Records, 1911-1915 [online database, www.americanancestors.org April 11, 2012], volume 1914/25 Death, 59.
29. Nancy Hale, "notes for 'Charlies hope.'" Nancy Hale Papers-SSC.
30. HEF, Boston, to Collier Cobb, Chapel Hill, NC, February 21, 1914. Cobb Papers, UNC.
31. Thomas J. Jablonsky, *The Home, Heaven, and Mother Party: Female Anti-Suffragists in the United States, 1868-1920* (Brooklyn, New York, 1994), xxiv, 13, 54.
32. HEF, Boston, to Collier Cobb, Chapel Hill, NC, March 19, [1914]. Cobb Papers, UNC.
33. HEF, New Ipswich, NH, to [Benjamin L. Robinson, curator], Gray Herbarium, Cambridge, October 4, 1915. Archives of the Gray Herbarium, Harvard. The Barrett House in New Ipswich was used as a setting for *The Europeans*, a 1979 Merchant & Ivory film.
34. Harriet E. Freeman, U.S. Passport Application, June 5, 1916. U.S. Passport Applications, 1795-1925. Ancestry.com.; HEF, Colonial Annex Hotel, San Francisco, to C. Hart Merriam, San Francisco, June 25 [1916]. Merriam, Bancroft, Berkeley. Professor Powers was a sociolo-

gist and expert on the Far East who had been forced off the faculty of Stanford University in 1898 by Mrs. Stanford after she was offended by a talk he gave to the students "of a religious nature."

35. Arthur Hale, New York, to Edward and Philip Hale, April 16, 1915. HFP-SSC.
36. Calvin Stebbins, Boston, to Abigail Clark, Boston, July 16, 1915, forwarded to Nelly at Folly Cove, and Clark, Boston, to Nelly, Folly Cove, September 14 [1915]. HFP-SSC. Calvin Stebbins had studied theology with Edward in the 1860s, and Abby thought he might be Horatio Stebbins's brother.
37. EEH Papers, Box 41, NYSL. When Edward Everett Hale Jr. died in 1932 in Schenectady, New York, his widow was uncertain what to do about the mass of Hale papers in his study. Instead of offering them to Harvard or another Boston repository, she donated or sold them to the nearby New York State Library in Albany.
38. Abigail Clark's notes on EEH's shorthand. EEH Papers, Box 41. NYSL.
39. Abigail Clark, "Edward Everett Hale," *The Christian Register*, June 1, 8, 15, 22, 29, July 6, and 13, 1916; Calvin Stebbins, "Edward Everett Hale in Worcester," July 20, 27, August 3, 1916; Bradley Gilman, "Dr. Hale in Europe," August 10, 17, 24, 31, 1916.
40. Abigail Clark, Boston, to Nelly, ?, December 6, 1917. HFP-SSC.
41. Holloway, *Edward Everett Hale*, 97, footnote 1 re the absence of correspondence from Edward's courtship of Emily Perkins: "The diary which contains this entry [of their first meeting] has evidently been removed, as has all material of an intimate nature dealing with Emily Perkins Hale." However, Hale's son in the *Life and Letters* (I, 234) mentions the Journal entry of October 31, 1851, and a previous meeting at Dwight Foster's.
42. Bradley Gilman, "Review of 'The Life and Letters of Edward Everett Hale,'" *The Harvard Theological Review*, vol. 12, no. 1 (January 1919), 132-135.
43. Brooks, *New England Indian Summer*, 518.
44. Hale Jr., *Life and Letters*, I, ii, II, 356-357, 393, 409.
45. HEF to Ethel Hale Freeman, n.d. [1916]. SLOC.
46. "John Haynes Holmes," *Dictionary of Unitarian & Universalist Biography* online: http://www25.uua.org/uuhs/duub/articles/johnhayneshholmes.html. Consulted 8/13/2013.
47. Professor Alan Mazur, whose wife is descended from Amadeus Grabau's brother John, told me that he never came across any letters between Grabau and Harriet Freeman during the course of his research. Mazur, *Romance in Natural History*, 215-216.

48. The women's travels and their loyalty to the AOU are mentioned in Emma Cummings's obituary. See *Biographies of members of the American Ornithologists' Union by T.S. Palmer and others.* Reprinted from 'The Auk,' 1884-1954. Washington, 1954. Emma Cummings (1856-1940) was the author of *Baby Bird Finder* and *Brookline Trees*. She lived most of her adult life in Brookline, Massachusetts, serving for forty years on the local "Committee on Planting Trees."
49. Harriet E. Freeman, U.S. Passport Application, August 20, 1920. Ancestry.com. *U.S. Passport Applications, 1795-1925*; Harriet E. Freeman, passenger on S.S. Maui, arriving Honolulu, October 26, 1920. Ancestry.com. *Passenger Lists of Vessels Arriving or Departing at Honolulu, Hawaii, 1900-1954*; Harriett [*sic*] E. Freeman and Emma Gertrude Cummings on "List of United States Citizens on board S.S. 'Vestris,'" departing Rio de Janeiro April 25, 1921, and arriving New York, May 11, 1921. Ancestry.com. *New York Passenger Lists, 1820-1957*; HEF, "On board S.S. 'Vestris,'" to Benjamin L. Robinson, Gray Herbarium, May 10, 1921. Archives of Gray Herbarium. Several of the books in the Harriet E. Freeman Collection purchased by the Andover-Harvard Theological Library of the Harvard Divinity School indicate the level of botanical and geological research that Hattie did before embarking on her travels.
50. Fourteenth Census of the United States, 1920—Population, Union Park, Boston, Suffolk County, Massachusetts. In 37 lived Harriet Freeman, Head and owner, 72; Sophie Russell, 58, Maid, Ireland; Mary Driscoll, 63, Housekeeper, Ireland.
51. The address given in a listing of the Officers and Committees of the American Ornithologists Union, 1925
52. Martha Adams Leland's letters from EEH are in the General Correspondence section of the Hale Family Papers at the Library of Congress (GLOC).
53. "Senator Lodge Extols Ideals of Dr. Hale," *Boston Globe*, April 4, 1922; Joseph E. Chamberlin, "Boston's Great Pastor-at-Large," *Boston Evening Transcript*, April 1, 1922; newspaper clipping of unknown origin, August 1922.
54. Weeks and Weeks, *A New England Family Revisited*, 122-128.
55. Jablonsky, *Home, Heaven*, 57.
56. According to Leo Collins, in his *This is Our Church, the First Church in Boston, 1630*-2005 (Boston: Northeastern University Press, 2005), several of the SCC windows and the Kimball organ were incorporated into the First Church's Edward Everett Hale Memorial Chapel. However, that church building, its fifth, was gutted by fire in March 1968. A new

concrete and steel building was built inside the original exterior on the Marlborough Street site, again including an Edward Everett Hale Chapel. Nothing from the SCC building remains, however, in the new chapel; Fifteenth Census of the United States, 1930—Population,

57. Hodges, *Crossroads*, 157.

Epilogue: Concealing is Revealing

1. Peter Steinfels, "Pastor's Conduct Divides East Side Congregation," *New York Times*, October 7, 1991; Church's obituaries in *New York Times*, September 27, 2009 and *Washington Post*, September 29, 2009, both reference this failure and how he used it to further humanize his sermons and his pastorate.
2. Nancy Hale, Notes re "Charlies hope." Nancy Hale Papers, SSC; Harriet McKissock, Rowayton, Conn., 1997. Sophia Smith Acquisitions Files. More related letters turned up in Mrs. McKissock's house following her death and were donated to join the Hale Family Papers at Smith.

Postscript

1. Diary of Charles Knowles Bolton, June 15 and October 7, 1915. Boston Athenaeum (I wish to thank Catherina Slautterback for bringing these diary entries to my attention). Henry Goddard, Boston, to HEF, UP, May 9, 1916, letter found in the front of Edward Everett Hale's *In His Name: A Story of the Waldenses* (1881) given by EEH to HEF in March 1883 and now in bMS 73/1—Items removed from books owned by Harriet Freeman. Harriet E. Freeman Papers, AHTL.

Bibliography

Previous Hale Biographies

Hale, Edward Everett, Jr., *The Life and Letters of Edward Everett Hale*, 2 vols. (Boston: Little, Brown, 1917)

Holloway, Jean, *Edward Everett Hale: A Biography* (Austin: University of Texas Press, 1956)

Adams, John R., *Edward Everett Hale* (Boston: G. K. Hall, 1977)

Selected Works by Edward Everett Hale

A Man without a Country (multiple imprints)

A New England Boyhood (New York: Cassell, 1893)

How to Live (Boston: Little, Brown, 1903)

If Jesus Came to Boston (Boston: Lamson, Wolffe, 1895)

James Freeman Clarke: Autobiography, Diary and Correspondence (Boston: Houghton Mifflin, 1891)

James Russell Lowell and his Friends (Boston: Houghton, Mifflin, 1899)

Kanzas and Nebraska (Boston: Phillips, Sampson, 1854)

Memories of a Hundred Years, 2 vols. (New York: Macmillan, 1903)

Tarry at Home Travels (New York: Macmillan, 1907)

The Unitarian Principles (Boston: American Unitarian Association, n.d., No. 51, Fourth Series)

Other Works

Ahlstrom, Sydney E., *A Religious History of the American People* (New Haven: Yale University Press, 2004)

Amory, Cleveland, *The Proper Bostonians* (New York: E. P. Dutton, Parnassus, 1984)

Applegate, Debby, *The Most Famous Man in America: The Biography of Henry Ward Beecher* (New York: Doubleday, 2006)

Atkins, Edwin F., *Sixty Years in Cuba: reminiscences of Edwin F. Atkins* (Privately printed at Riverside Press, Boston, 1926)

Atkinson, Caroline P., editor, with introduction by Edward Everett Hale Jr., *Letters of Susan Hale* (Boston: Marshall Jones, 1918)

Aydon, Cyril, *Charles Darwin: His Life and Times* (Philadelphia: Running Press Books, 2008)

Baker, Jean H., *Margaret Sanger: A Life of Passion* (New York: Hill and Wang, 2011)

Baltzell, E. Digby, *Judgment and Sensibility: Religion and Stratification*. Edited and introduction by Howard G. Schneiderman (New Brunswick, NJ: Transaction Publishers, 1994)

Barrows, John H., editor, *The World's Parliament of Religions* (Chicago: Parliament Publishing Company, 1893)

Beam, Alex, *Gracefully Insane: Life and Death inside America's Premier Mental Hospital* (New York: Public Affairs, 2001)

Bell, Millicent, *Marquand: An American Life* (Boston: Little, Brown, 1979)

Bennett, Randall H., *The White Mountains: Alps of New England* (Charleston, SC: Arcadia, 2003).

Brewster Historical Society, *Brewster, Images of America* series (Charleston, SC: Arcadia, 2002)

Brooks, Van Wyck, *The Flowering of New England 1815-1865* (New York: E. P. Dutton, 1936)

Brooks, Van Wyck, *New England: Indian Summer 1865-1915* (New York: E. P. Dutton, 1940)

Bunting, Bainbridge, *Houses of Boston's Back Bay: The Architectural History 1840-1917* (Cambridge: The Belknap Press of Harvard University, 1967)

Burgess, Larry E., *Mohonk: Its People and Spirit: A History of One Hundred and Forty Years of Growth and Service* (New Palz, NY: Mohonk Mountain House, 2009)

Chamberlin, Joseph E., *The Boston Transcript: A History of Its First Hundred Years* (Boston: Houghton Mifflin, 1930)

Claflin, Helen A., *A New England Family* (privately printed, Belmont, MA, 1956)

Collins, Leo, *This is Our Church, the First Church of Boston, 1630-2005* (accessed through Google Books).

Cooke, George W., *Unitarianism in America: A History of its Origin and Development* (Bibliobazaar, 2006)

Crawford, Mary C., *Romantic Days in Old Boston* (Boston: Little, Brown, 1910)

Crocker, Kathleen and Jane Currie, *Chautauqua Institution, 1874*-1974, Images of America series (Charleston, SC: Arcadia, 2001)

Deutsch, Helen, *The Psychology of Women*, Vol. I, *Girlhood* (New York: Grune & Stratton, 1944)

Dock, Julie Bates, *Charlotte Perkins Gilman's "The Yellow Wall-paper" and the History of Its Publication and Reception: A Critical Edition and Documentary Casebook* (University Park, PA: The Pennsylvania State University Press, 1998)

Farrell, Betty G., *Elite Families: Class and Power in Nineteenth-Century Boston* (Albany, NY: State University of New York Press, 1993)

Fox, Richard Wightman, *Trials of Intimacy: Love and Loss in the Beecher-Tilton Scandal* (Chicago: University of Chicago Press, 1999)

Gilman, Charlotte Perkins, *Our Androcentric Culture, or the Man Made World* (print on demand, 2013)

Gosling, F. G., *Before Freud: Neurasthenia and the American Medical Community,1870-1910* (Urbana and Chicago: Chicago University Press, 1987)

Hagan, William T., *The Indian Rights Association: The Herbert Welsh Years 1882-1904* (Tucson, Arizona: University of Arizona Press, 1985)

Hale, Nancy, *The Life in the Studio: An Affectionate Recollection of Some Singular Parents* (Boston: Little, Brown, 1957)

Hayden, Deborah, *Pox: Genius, Madness, and the Mysteries of Syphilis* (New York: Basic Books, 2003)

Hodges, Maud deLeigh, *Crossroads on the Charles: A History of Watertown, Massachusetts* (Canaan, NH: Phoenix Publishing for the Watertown Free Public Library, 1980).

Horowitz, Helen Lefkowitz, *Rereading Sex: Battles over Sexual Knowledge and Suppression in Nineteenth-Century America* (New York: Random House, Vintage, 2003)

Horowitz, Helen Lefkowitz, *Wild Unrest: Charlotte Perkins Gilman and the Making of "The Yellow Wall-Paper"* (Oxford: Oxford University Press, 2006)

Howe, Helen, *The Gentle Americans: Biography of a Breed* (New York: Harper & Row, 1965)

Howells, William Dean, *The Rise of Silas Lapham* (Rockville, MD: Arc Manor, 2009)

Hudson, Judith Maddox, *Peaks and Paths: A Century of the Randolph Mountain Club* (Randolph, NH: Randolph Mountain Club, 2010)

Jablonski, Thomas J., *The Home, Heaven, and Mother Party: Female Anti-Suffragists in the United States, 1868-1920* (Brooklyn, New York: Carlson Publishing, 1994)

James, Henry, *The Bostonians* (New York: Random House, Modern Library, 2003)

Johnson, Christopher, *This Grand & Magnificent Place: The Wilderness Heritage of the White Mountains* (Durham, NH: University of New Hampshire Press, 2006).

Keeney, Elizabeth B., *The Botanizers: Amateur Scientists in Nineteenth-*

Century America (Chapel Hill, NC: The University of North Carolina Press, 1992)

King, Thomas Starr, *The White Hills: Their Legends, Landscape, and Poetry* (Boston: Crosby and Ainsworth, 1868 edition)

Larson, Erik, *The Devil in the White City: Murder, Magic, and Madness at the Fair that Changed America* (New York: Random House, Vintage, 2004)

Longsworth, Polly, *Austin and Mabel: The Amherst Affair and Love Letters of Austin Dickinson and Mabel Loomis Todd* (New York: Farrar, Straus, Giroux, 1984)

Lystra, Karen, *Searching the Heart: Women, Men, and Romantic Love in Nineteenth-Century America* (New York: Oxford University Press, 1992)

Lyttle, Charles H., *Freedom Moves West: A History of the Western Unitarian Conference 1852-1952* (Providence, RI: Blackstone and Unitarian Universalist Historical Society, 2006)

Marquand, John P., *The Late George Apley* (Boston: Back Bay, Little, Brown, 2004)

Marquand, John P., *Wickford Point* (New York: Time-Life Books, 1966)

Mazur, Alan, *A Romance in Natural History: The Lives and Works of Amadeus Grabau and Mary Antin* (Syracuse, New York, 2004)

Miller, Scott, *The President and the Assassin: McKinley, Terror, and Empire at the Dawn of the American Century* (New York: Random House, 2011)

Moore, J. Hampton, *With Speaker Cannon through the Tropics: A Descriptive Story of a Voyage to the West Indies, Venezuela and Panama* (Philadelphia: The Book Print, 1907)

Newman, William A., and Wilfred E. Holton, *Boston's Back Bay: The Story of America's Greatest Nineteenth-Century Landfill Project* (Boston: Northeastern University Press, 2006)

O'Connor, Thomas H., *The Boston Irish: A Political History* (Boston: Back Bay Books, 1995)

Peabody, Francis G., *Reminiscences of Present-day Saints* (Boston, New York: Houghton Mifflin, 1927)

Reed, William Howell, *Reminiscences of Elisha Atkins* (Privately printed, Cambridge, University Press, 1890)

Remini, Robert V., *The House: The History of the House of Representatives* (New York: Library of Congress, Smithsonian Books, Collins, 2006)

Rieser, Andrew C., *The Chautauqua Moment: Protestants, Progressives, and the Culture of Modern Liberalism* (New York: Library of Congress, Smithsonian Books, Collins, 2006)

Roberts, Jon H., *Darwinism and the Divine in America: Protestant Intellectuals and the Organic Evolution 1859-1900* (Madison, WIS: The University of Wisconsin Press, 1988)

Rose, Phyllis, *Parallel Lives: Five Victorian Marriages* (New York: Random House,Vintage, 1984)

Rosen, Christine, *Preaching Eugenics: Religious Leaders and the American Eugenics Movement* (Oxford University Press, 2004)

Rossiter, Margaret W., *Women Scientists in America*, Vol. I, *Struggles and Strategies to 1940* (Baltimore: Johns Hopkins University Press, 1982)

Salz, Evelyn, editor, *Selected Letters of Mary Antin* (Syracuse, NY: Syracuse University Press, 2000)

Sandweiss, Martha A., *Passing Strange: A Gilded Age Tale of Love and Deception Across the Color Line* (New York: The Penguin Press, 2009)

Schmidt, Leigh Eric, *Restless Souls: The Making of American Spirituality From Emerson to Oprah* (San Francisco, CA: HarperSanFrancisco, 2005)

Shrock, Robert R., *Geology at M.I.T. 1865-1965*. Vol. 1 *The Faculty and Supporting Staff* (Cambridge, Mass: The MIT Press, 1977)

Slayden, Ellen Maury, *Washington Wife: Journal of Ellen Maury Slayden from 1897 -1919* (New York: Harper & Row, 1962).

Society to Encourage Studies at Home, *Society to Encourage Studies at Home* (Cambridge: Riverside Press, 1897)

Solomon, Barbara Miller, *Ancestors and Immigrants: A Changing New England Tradition* (Cambridge: Harvard University Press, 1956)

Strouse, Jean, *Alice James: A Biography* (Cambridge: Harvard University Press, 1999)

Strouse, Jean, *Morgan: American Financier* (New York: Harper Perennial, 2000)

Thomas, Evan, *The War Lovers: Roosevelt, Lodge, Hearst, and the Rush to Empire, 1898* (New York: Little, Brown, 2010)

Towndrow, Thomas, *A Complete Guide to Stenography, or An entire new system of writing short hand* (New Haven and New York, 1832)

Tyng, Dudley, *Massachusetts Episcopalians 1607-1957* (Rhode Island: Delmo Press, 1960)

Weeks, Katharine Wrisley Claflin, and Robert Freeman Weeks, *A New England Family Revisited* (privately printed)

Whiting, Lilian, *Boston Days* (Boston: Little, Brown, 1912)

Wineapple, Brenda, *White Heat: The Friendship of Emily Dickinson & Thomas Wentworth Dickinson* (New York: Alfred A. Knopf, 2008)

Wright, Conrad, *A Stream of Light: A Sesquicentennial History of American Unitarianism* (Boston: Unitarian Universalist Association, 1975)

Wright, Conrad, *The Liberal Christians: Essays on American Unitarian History* (Boston: Beacon Press, 1970)

Index

Index Notes:

EEH refers to Edward Everett Hale.

HEF refers to Harriet Elizabeth Freeman.

EBH refers to Emily Baldwin Perkins Hale.

Page numbers in italics refer to photographs.

Abbott, Lyman 268, 331, 340, 404n27, 434n13
Abdu'l-Baha 288
abolition of slavery 36–37, 148. *See also* slaves and slavery
Adams, Abigail 95, 411n37
Adams, Charles Francis, Jr. 184, 385
Adams, Charles Francis, Sr. 411n37
Adams, Henry 298, 411n39
Adams, John Quincy 37, 95, 411n37
Adams, John R. 31, 147, 260, 403n13, 404n21, 407n14, 417n5, 432n67, 444n69
Adams, Martha: as amanuensis 120, 123, 127, 253; correspondence with EEH 167, 216, 227, 235, 247, 257, 261, 340, 366–67, 392, 414n20, 449n52; family 257–58, 261, 277; travels with EEH 120, 201, 210, 253
Adams National Historic Park 411n37
Addams, Jane 148, 310, 398
Adirondack Park, New York 324
adultery scandals 3–4, 58 59, 82, 380–81, 395–96, 398
Aerodrome 291, 341, 428n52, 442n13
Aetna Mills 20, 124, 203–4, 283, 284, 380–81, 394, 401n6
African-Americans 305–6, 313–14. *See also* slaves and slavery
Agassiz, Alexander 290–91
Agassiz, Elizabeth Cary 64
Agassiz, Louis 47, 64, 75, 76, 152–53, 290, 418n21
Agricultural College, Amherst 257, 268, 323
airplane invention 227, 341, 428n52
Aldrich, Abby Greene 277
Aldrich, Nelson W. 277
Alexander, George 423n32
Alice James: A Biography (Strouse) 407n20
"All not Bound to Silver" *(New York Times)* 429n6
All Souls Unitarian Church, Chicago 79
All Souls Unitarian Church, Washington D.C. 145, 341, 342, 365 *See also* First Unitarian Church, Washington D.C.

Alpha Delta Phi, Harvard College 31, 287
"Alpheus Hyatt" (Shrock) 409n40
"Alpheus Hyatt, 1838-1902" (Mayer) 409n40
amanuenses (secretaries) of EEH: Abigail Clark 260–61, 277, 299, 357; Carry Tallant 100; Mary Edes 67, 71, 77, 98, 99, 100. *See also* Adams, Martha; Freeman, Harriet Elizabeth "Hattie," and EEH
"America: Cuba" (Freeman) 301, 437n12
"America: Grand Canon" (Freeman) 292–93, 436n53
American Antiquarian Society 35, 402n5, 408n25
American Association for the Advancement of Science 333–34, 348
American Bison Society 331
American Breeders Association 346, 378
American Forest Congress 314, *326*, 326–28, 332, 369–70, 440nn1–7
American Forestry Association 327, 332, 441n16
American Indian politics. *See* Indian politics, American
American Missionary Association 237
American Ornithologists' Union (AOU) 290, 292–93, 297, 328–29, 375, 391, 449n51
American Philosophical Society 125
American Protestant Episcopal Church Council 309
American Sugar Refinery 373
American Unitarian Association (AUA) 36, 44, 47, 54, 79, 94, 111, 115, 157, 261, 366, 390–91, 412n61, 418n11
American Wool Company 96–97
Ames, Oakes 54–55
Amherst Agricultural College 257, 268, 323
Among the Clouds 285, 287, 435n38, 436n44
Anagnos, Michael 135, 136
Ancestors and Immigrants: A Changing New England Tradition (Solomon) 411n33, 446n18
Andover-Harvard Theological Library, Harvard Divinity School 8, 70, 190, 405n33, 412n54, 414n15, 415n30, 424n48, 442n28, 445n1, 446n15, 449n49
Andrews, Clement 213, 427n19
Andrews, Judith W.: death 380; on Edward Cummings 358; on EEH and HEF 196, 221, 260, 349, 372–73, 376, 380; finances 221, 223; health 377; HEF and 73, 161–63, 239; politics 157, 216; South Friendly Society work 62–63, 121, 165; visit by EEH 85
animal conservation. *See* bird conservation; bison conservation
Annisquam marine zoology laboratory, Massachusetts 74, 75, 219
Anthony, Susan B. 303, 304, 438n18
anti-lynching legislation 313
Antin, Mary 135, 271–73, 297, 377, 378, 391, 434n19
Antioch College 46, 146
anti-suffrage movement 304, 313, 384–85. *See also* suffrage movement

AOU. *See* American Ornithologists' Union (AOU)
Appalachian Mountain Club (AMC) 77, 103, 106, 166, 193, 229, 282, 327, 356
Appalachian National Forest Preserve Association 324
Appalachian National Park Association 324
Appalachian-White Mountains Forest Reservation Bill 182, 324–25, 331–33, 356–57, 374–75
Applegate, Debby 59, 407nn13–4, 410n9, 413n1
Appleton's Journal 53
Appleton's Popular Science Monthly 252, 431n52
arbitration and peace movement. *See* peace movement, world
Arlington Street Church, Boston 114, 171, 381
Arnim, Bettina von 80, 409n4
Arnold, Harold 358, 359, 377
Arnold, Helen Hunt Freeman. *See* Freeman, Helen Hunt (niece of HEF)
Arnold Arboretum, Harvard College 182, 275, 437n14
"Asa Gray and His Quest for *Shortia galacifolia*" (Jenkins) 275, 434n23
Associated Charities 38, 46, 101, 125, 422n10
Aster oblongifolius 385
Atchinson, Topeka & Santa Fe Railroad 373
A Thankfull Remembrance of Gods Mercy (London, 1627) 419n36
Atkins, Chet 72–73
Atkins, Edwin F. "Ned" (cousin of HEF): Cuban politics and 236–37, 238; death 393; family 23, 146; Fred Freeman and 380; interests associated with 373; on *Maine* battleship disaster 236; *Sixty Years in Cuba* 72, 224, 409n35, 428n45; supporting HEF 244, 337; textile mill business 203–4; visit by HEF 300–303. *See also* E. Atkins Company, Cuba; Soledad plantation, Cuba
Atkins, Edwin F. Jr. "Ted" 393
Atkins, Elisha (uncle of HEF): business 25–26, 203–4; Freemans and 16, 23, 119; health 124, 125; Union Pacific Railroad 54–55, 56, 73, 406n8. *See also* E. Atkins Company, Cuba
Atkins, Grace. *See* Reed, Grace Atkins (cousin of HEF)
Atkins, Helen. *See* Edmands, Helen Atkins (cousin of HEF)
Atkins, Katharine 146, 236
Atkins, Mary Elizabeth Freeman (aunt of HEF) 24, 25, 119, 125, 146, 171, 210, 224, 227–29, 402n1
Atkins, Robert 381, 393
Atkins & Freeman trading business 25–26
Atkins Garden and Research Laboratory, Soledad 302, 437n14
Atkins Institution of the Arnold Arboretum, Harvard College 427n14
Atkinson, Caroline 359, 443n54
Atlantic Monthly: on creation-evolution controversy 47, 153, 404n31, 418n21; EEH in 14, 34, 41, 176, 290, 405n32, 418n13; on forest preservation 181–82, 334, 423n21; Mary Antin in 377; on

New England logging industry 181–82, 423n21
AUA. *See* American Unitarian Association (AUA)
Audubon Magazine 440n10
Audubon Society, National 329–31, 440n10
Autobiography, Diary, and Correspondence [of James Freeman Clarke] (Hale) 147, 159, 160, 417n5
Autobiography of Seventy Years (Hoar) 276, 435n28
Aydon, Cyril 409n41
Ayres, Philip W. 287, 323, 331, 332, 333, 440n15

Babbidge, Charles 175, 252, 409n5
Baby Bird Finder (Cummings) 309, 329, 438n30, 449n48
Back Bay, Boston 17, 28, 109–11, 120, 169–70, 251, 402n6, 403n7, 434n21. *See also* Boston
Bahá'í faith 187, 288, 436n46
Bailey, Emma 115
Bailey, Florence 376
Bailey, Vernon 376
Baird, Iris 441n22
Baker, Charlotte A. 230, 429n59
Baker, Jean H. 444n61
Ballinger, Richard 374
Baltzell, E. Digby 379, 439n37, 443n34, 446n19
Bancroft, George 32, 96
Baring, Thomas 104
Barton, Clara 237
Barton, George Hunt 75, 147–48, 175, 191, 274, 417n7, 418n15
Battle of Bunker Hill 256
Baynes, Ernest Harold 330, 331, 386, 439n46
Bay State Sugar Refinery Company 73
Beecher, Catharine (aunt of EBH) 19, 413n1
Beecher, Edward 19
Beecher, Eunice 59, 111
Beecher, Henry Ward (uncle of EBH) 3, 19, 58–59, 84, 91, 111, 117, 434n13
Beecher, James 413n1
Beecher, Lyman (grandfather of EBH) 18–19, 58, 255
Beecher, Thomas 255, 413n1
Bell, Alexander Graham 74, 135, 194, 205, 291, 341
Bell, Mabel 135, 194, 291
Bellamy, Edward 139, 258, 311
Bellows, Henry Whitney 41, 44, 58, 67, 360
Bell Telephone Company 167, 194, 290
Bennett, Randall H. 446n10
Berenson, Arthur 338, 379
Berenson, Bernard 338
Berenson, Senda 338
"Best Use of the White Mountain Range" (Robertson) 440n15
Bethel, Maine 120-122, 123
biblical miracles of Christianity 169, 421n62
Bigelow, Erastus B. 266
Biltmore Estate, Asheville 194–95, 283, 324
Biltmore Forest School 324
Bingham, John A. 55
bird conservation: Audubon Society 329–31, 440n10; *Baby Bird Finder* (Cummings) 309, 329, 438n30, 449n48; HEF and 79, 156, 265–67, 274, 293, 307, 316, 317, 376, 386; photography 440n9; rise of 328–31. *See also* American Ornithologists' Union (AOU)

"Bird Friends" (Freeman) 265, 433n8
bison conservation 323, 330, 331, 439n46
Blackwell, Antoinette 304
Blackwell, Lucy Stone 304
Blaine, James G. 55, 56, 73, 82, 84, 96, 215
Blizzard of 1888, New England 126–27
Blue Guide Boston and Cambridge (Freely) 432n63
"bluestocking" women 103, 153, 255. *See also* women's rights and education
Board of Charities 38
Boston: Brahmins 82, 321, 338, 351, 383, 394; ethnic politics and Irish immigration 20, 28, 34, 37–38, 91, 109, 214–15, 321, 344–45, 374, 383, 404n21, 411nn32–33, 411nn32–33, 427n30, 447n27; Great Fire (1872) 53–54; land reclamation project 28; as literary capital of America 117; New Year's and new century's celebration 262; public schools 43, 64–65, 91; religious institutions 18–20, 23, 198, 311, 321, 349 (*See also specific names*); settlement history 23, 25. *See also specific neighborhoods*
Boston Association of Ministers 33
Boston Athenaeum 27, 224
Boston Commonwealth (Hale) 209, 217, 426n11
Boston Daily Advertiser 18, 29, 39, 41–43, 67
Boston Daily Globe 308, 369, 376, 432n62, 434n22, 438n27, 445n1, 449n53
Boston Dyewood & Chemicals Company 20, 26
Boston Evening Transcript 8, 143, 215, 338, 380, 392, 394, 405n32, 416n15, 432n65, 441n6, 449n53
Boston Globe Magazine 409n36
Boston Herald 65, 121, 143, 287, 408n23, 436n41, 447n26
Boston Indian Citizenship Committee 295
The Boston Irish (O'Connor) 427n30, 447n27
Boston Legal Aid Society 380, 447n23
Boston Miscellany of Literature and Fashion 35
Boston Museum of Fine Arts 278, 337, 376
Boston Museum of Science 434n21
Boston Post 59
Boston Public Garden 381, 382
Boston Public Library 64, 91, 191, 224, 255, 411n39
Boston Public School and Committee 43, 64–65, 91
Boston's Back Bay: The Story of America's Greatest Nineteenth-Century Landfill Project (Newman and Holton) 403n7
"Boston's Great Pastor-at-Large" (Chamberlin) 392, 405n32, 432n65, 449n53
Boston Society of Natural History (BSNH) 34, 75, 135, 252, 274, 330, 394, 431n52, 434n21; Museum 28, 74, 329
Boston Symphony Orchestra 276
Boston Technical Institute (MIT) 28, 64–65, 75, 125, 170, 266, 417n7, 422n7. *See also* Massachusetts Institute of Technology (MIT)

Boston Wharf Company 25
The Botanizers: Amateur Scientists in Nineteenth-Century America (Keeney) 410n15
botany: Alice Eastwood and 386; economic 302, 437n14; EEH's study in 82, 85, 86, 128; forget-me-nots 129, 415n42; HEF's study in 74, 82, 85, 97–98, 105, 128–29, 151, 192, 226, 285, 344; phanerogamia plant division 34, 404n20; works about 85, 98, 410n15, 415n35. *See also Shortia galacifolia* (Oconee Bells)
Bourke, John C. 112–13
Boutwell, George S. 55
Boynton, Frank E. 275, 276
Bradford, William 23
Bradlee, Nathaniel J. 14–15, 28, 402n6
Brahmins, Boston 82, 321, 338, 351, 383, 394. *See also* Boston
Bram, James 128, 129, 249–50
The Brass Check (Sinclair) 340, 442n11
Brewster, Elder William 23
Brewster, William 329
Brewster Weir, Massachusetts 160–61
"The Brick Moon" (Hale) 290, 405n32
"The Brick Space Station" (MacDonald) 405n32
Bronx Zoo, New York City 330
Brookline Trees (Cummings) 449n48
Brooklyn Institute of Arts and Sciences 376
Brooks, James 55
Brooks, Martha 95, 166, 355
Brooks, Phillips 46, 109, 121, 183–84, 311
Brooks, Van Wyck 30, 389–90, 403n8, 414n11, 448n43
Brookwood Sanitarium, Media 240, 430n19
Brown, John 148, 301, 437n12
Bryan, William Jennings 215–16, 235, 427n32
Bryce, James 353, 355, 358
Bryce, Mrs. James 355, 358
buffalo conservation 323, 330, 331, 439n46
Bull Moose Party 378
Bunting, Bainbridge 402n6, 403n7, 429n11, 431n50
Bureau of Indian Affairs 151, 293, 295
Burgess, Larry E. 425n56
Burnham, Daniel 184
Burns, Anthony 32
Burt, Frank 285–86, 435n38
Burt, Henry M. 435n38
Bushway, Phoebe 13
Byatt, A. S. 1

California Academy of Sciences 386
Calvinism 18, 36, 58
Cameron, Ralph 206, 208, 426n10
Cannon, Joseph G. 236, 325, 333–35, 351–53, 356, 361, 374, 443n41
Cape Cod. *See specific places*
Cape Cod Times 416n11
Carlyle's Laugh and Other Surprises (Higginson) 403n11
Carmen (Bizet) 342
Carnegie, Andrew 146, 300, 307, 357
Carpenter, Emma Bailey 115, 413n8
Carpenter, George O. 173, 176
Carpenter, Henry Bernard 114–15, 121, 340–41, 413n8, 414n23

Carpenter, William Boyd 114, 121, 414n23
Caruso, Enrico 342
Cassini, Arthur 307
Castro, Fidel 72–73, 303, 437n14
Catholicism and immigrants 19–20, 26, 28, 91, 146, 222, 321, 355, 374, 402n4, 411n32
Central Church, Worcester 266
The Century magazine 95, 345
A Century of Dishonor (Jackson) 104, 412n47
Chamberlain, Houston Stewart 378
Chamberlin, Joseph E. 392, 405n32, 432n65, 449n53
Champney, Benjamin 366, 445n77
Chandler, Mary G. 405n33
Channing, Grace 134, 139, 143, 167
Channing, William Ellery 32, 36
Channing, William Francis 32, 34, 134, 167
Charities (Hale) 218
Charles Darwin: His Life and Times (Aydon) 409n41
Charles River Dams (Fleishman) 401n6
Charles River history 20, 28, 401n6
Charlton, Bruce G. 409n4
Chatto (Chiricahua Indian subchief) 112
Chauncy Hall 27, 84
Chautauqua assemblies 99, 111, 112, 118, 129–30, 201, 211, 253–55, 268, 414n14
Chautauqua Literary and Scientific Circle 99
The Chautauqua Moment (Rieser) 414n14
The Chautauquan 99, 276, 412n48, 433n10, 435n26
Chicago: Great Fire (1871) 406n4; World's Fair (1893) 184–85, 188–89, 292, 423n30
Chiricahua Apache land rights 112–13
Choate, Rufus 33–34
Christian Examiner 45, 47, 407n11
Christianity: biblical miracles in 168–69, 421n62; morality and 38–39, 44–45, 76, 116, 148, 158–59, 184, 311, 364, 390. *See also specific denominations*
Christian Register 269, 376, 388, 406n3, 448n39
Christian Union 434n13
Church, F. Forrest 395–96
Church, Frank 395
churches. *See specific names*
Church of All Souls, New York City 44, 395
Church of the Disciples, Boston 44
Church of the Messiah, New York City 198, 390
Church of the Unity, Worcester 34, 197–98, 309, 413n5
Cienfuegos. *See* Cuba; Soledad plantation, Cuba
Circular for Ten Times One (Hale) 71–72, 102
Civil War 11, 41, 103, 149. *See also* United States Sanitary Commission
Claflin, Helen Atkins 401n1 (chap. 2)
Claflin, William H. 437n14
Clark, Abigail W.: as amanuensis 260–61, 277, 286, 287, 299, 357, 381–83, 436n41; on EEH biography 372–73, 386–87, 388; handling EEH estate 366–67, 372–73; HEF's dislike of 315, 358

Clark, Harriet Mower. *See* Freeman, Harriet Mower Clark "West Newton Hattie" (sister-in-law of HEF)
Clarke, Edward 63
Clarke, George 199, 200–201, 229, 428n56
Clarke, James Freeman 36, 44, 45, 74, 82–83, 89, 128, 147, 314, 410n10. *See also Autobiography, Diary, and Correspondence* [of James Freeman Clarke] (Hale)
Clay, Henry 33
Clements, Gabrielle 212, 220, 362
clerical. *See* amanuenses (secretaries) of EEH
Cleveland, Grover 82–84, 91, 96, 135, 184, 215, 324, 410n10
Cobb, Annette 408n27
Cobb, Collier: about 306, 334; correspondence with HEF 343, 356, 376, 379, 384, 385
Cobb, Freeman 408n27
Cobb, Mary: about 408n27; death 341–42; as HEF's companion 67, 73, 95, 97–98, 101–2, 106, 118, 125–26, 146, 150, 152, 164, 257, 263, 268; HEF's dislike of 152, 212, 273, 307, 315; Helen Keller and 135–37; living with HEF 252, 255, 273, 307; working for EEH 95, 99, 123
Cobb & Company 408n27
code-breaking 3, 5–6
Colfax, Schuyler 55
Collins, Leo 450n56
Collins, Mary 295–96
Collyer, Robert J. 198
Columbian World's Fair (1893) 184–85, 188–89, 292, 423n30
Columbia University, New York City 26, 271, 297, 391
Columbus, Christopher 167, 184, 189, 420n56
Commission on the Conservation of Natural Resources 357
Commonwealth Bank, Boston 25
Commonwealth Club, Boston 262
Commonwealth of Massachusetts Manual for the Use of the General Court 446n6
A Complete Guide to Stenography, or An entire new system of writing short hand (Towndrow) 411n30
Compromise of 1850 37–38
Comstock, Anthony 60
Comstock Law (1873) 60
Coney Island mental hospital 80, 84–85
Conference of Governors (1908) 356–57
Congregational Church of the Unity, Worcester 34
Congregationalism 18, 36
Conner, Camilla (daughter-in-law of EEH and EBH) 151, 154
"Conservation as a National Duty" (Roosevelt) 357
conservation efforts. *See specific types*
Conservation: Forests, Waters, Soils and Minerals 369. *See also Forest and Irrigation*
Cook, Emily 293
Cooke, George W. 419n28
Copperheads 14. *See also* Democratic Party
Cornell University 107, 116, 117, 298, 312
correspondence schools in America 64. *See also* Society to Encourage Studies at Home (S.H.)
"A Course of Practical Ethics" (Hale) 99

Cradle of Forestry 324. *See also* forestry movement
Crawford, Ethan Allen 288
creation-evolution controversy. *See* evolution-creation controversy
Crédit Mobilier scandal 54–55, 82
Cressey, Pemberton H. 314, 437n2
criminal conversation (adultery) 59
Croce, P. J. 404n31
Crocker, Lucretia 63, 64, 74
Crocker, Sarah 363
Crosby, William O. 75, 205, 210–11, 271, 391
Crossroads on the Charles (Hodges) 447n22
Cuba: Christianity in 305; economic botany in 302, 437n14; incident with HEF (1907) 353; politics 72–73, 203, 224, 236–37, 246, 302–3; Spanish-American War (1898) and 236–38, 245
Cuban Junta 224, 236
Cummings, Edward C. 253, 261, 269, 314, 358, 393–94
cummings, e e (Edward Estlin) 261, 269, 389
Cummings, Emma Gertrude *281*; about 8, 247, 449n48; forest preservation 332; living with HEF 273; ornithological interests 328–29; travels with HEF: (1895) 195–97; (1897) 225–27; (1898) 245–51; (1901) 263–67; (1902) 275, 280–82, 290; (1903) 292–95; (1904) 306–7; (1905) 316–19, 330; (1907) 351–53; (1908) 356; (1909) 371–72; (1910) 375; (1911-1912) 377, 378, 379–80; (1916) 386; (1920-1922) 391; works by 265–67, 309, 329, 433n10, 438n30, 449n48
Curley, James Michael 383
Curtis, George 329
Curtiss, Glenn 341
Curzon's Mill, Newburyport, Massachusetts 174, 360, 444n58
Custer, George Armstrong 160
Custer, Elizabeth Bacon "Libby" 160
Cuvier, Georges 76
Cygnet I, II, III 436n50
Czolgosz, Leon 269

Dalzell, John 333
Dana, Francis 298
Dann, Mary 186, 205, 297, 306–7, 318, 330, 334, 351, 376, 398
DAR. *See* Daughters of the American Revolution (DAR)
Dartmouth College, New Hampshire 25, 270, 334
Darwin, Charles 46–47, 75–76, 153, 404n31, 409n41. *See also* evolution-creation controversy
Darwinism and the Divine in America: Protestant Intellectuals and Organic Evolution, 1859-1900 (Roberts) 404n30, 425n54
Darwinism *vs.* Creationism. *See* evolution-creation controversy
Daudet, Alphonse 115
Daughters of the American Revolution (DAR) 256, 274, 379, 434n22
David Rockefeller Center for Latin American Studies, Harvard University 73
Davis, Isabella 102
Dawes, Henry L. 55
Dawes Severalty Act (1887) 103, 104
Dawson, W. J. 338
Dean, Jennie 438n21

Democratic Party 14, 37, 38, 91, 313. *See also* Republican Party
De Normandie, James 128, 381
depression, mental. *See* mental health
depressions, economic 54–56, 203–4, 215, 393
Destiny of Man Viewed in the Light of his Origin (Fiske) 76
The Devil in the White City (Larson) 423n30
Dickens, Charles 3
Dickinson, Austin 3
Dickinson, Mary 102, 103
Dictionary of Unitarian & Universalist Biography 448n46
Diederich, Elsa (great-granddaughter of EEH and EBH) 383
Dillingham, William P. 345
diphtheria, deaths from 61, 183, 239
Dismal Swamp, Virginia 263, 265, 266–67, 433n10
"Dismal Swamp and How to Go There" (Freeman and Cummings) 265–67, 433n10
divorce: examples of 66, 115, 143, 377, 381, 393, 396; societal perceptions of 66, 143, 339–41
Dixon, Thomas 340
Dodd, Helen 363, 365
Draper, Eben S. 369
Dred: A Tale of the Great Dismal Swamp (Stowe) 433n10
drip sheet treatment 243–44
Driscoll, Mary (maid of HEF) 146, 157, 220, 222, 241, 248, 251, 257, 273, 371, 392
Drury, Mary 295
Dudley, Hortense 150, 233, 244
Dutcher, William 329–31
Dwight, Theodore F. 96, 411n39

earthquakes: in Italy 342; in Mexico 363; in San Francisco 342–43, 375
East and West: A Story of New-Born Ohio (Hale) 181, 423n19
Eastwood, Alice 386
E. Atkins Company, Cuba 26, 28, 72–73, 124, 203, 409nn–35–6. *See also* Atkins, Edwin F. "Ned" (cousin of HEF)
Ecole des Beaux Arts, Paris 180, 343
economic botany in Cuba 302, 437n14
economy, U.S.: depressions 43, 54–56, 203–4, 215, 393; scandals 54–55, 82
Edes, Mary 67, 71, 77, 98, 99, 100, 102
Edmands, Helen Atkins (cousin of HEF) *13,* 52, 103, 125, 415n33
Edmands, J. Rayner 103, 117, 281, 282, 287, 415n33
Edmund Lewis of Lynn, Massachusetts, and Some of his Descendants (Lewis) 402n2
"The Educated Citizen" (Hale) 278
education initiatives: former slave 44, 438n21; women's (*See* women's rights and education)
"Edward E. Hale. The Man with a Country" (Ward) 189–90, 424n38
Edward Everett Hale (Adams) 31, 260, 403n13, 407n14, 417n5, 432n67, 444n69
"Edward Everett Hale," *Harper's Weekly* article 276, 435n27
Edward Everett Hale A Biography

(Holloway) 58, 96, 403n11, 404n20, 404n22, 406n5, 407n11, 411n41, 422n13
Edward Everett Hale House, Matunuck. *See* Matunuck, Rhode Island house
Edward Everett Hale Memorial Chapel 450n56
"Edwin F. Atkins and the Evolution of American Cuban Policy, 1892-1902" (Harris) 409n37
"Efforts to Restrict Undesirable Immigration" (Lodge) 345
"egotistical rainbow" 301
Egypt: Charles Hale in 43, 53; HEF's travels in 379
The Elements of Character (Chandler) 405n33
The Elements of Christian Doctrine and its Development (Hale) 39, 404n24
Elijah Cobb House, Brewster 137
Eliot, Charles W. 64, 296, 312, 345, 347, 385, 410n28
Eliot, John 250
Eliot, Samuel 31, 64, 150, 234
Eliot, Samuel Atkins 261, 391
Eliot, T. S. 170, 389, 421n65
Eliot School Rebellion (1859) 26, 402n4, 411n32
Elite Families: Class and Power in Nineteenth Century Boston (Farrell) 403n7
Ellis, Charles (cousin of HEF) 295
Ellis, Charles Mayo (uncle of HEF) 26, 32, 295, 403n14
Ellis, Effie (niece of HEF) 237, 429n11
Ellis, Harriet Lewis (aunt of HEF) 26
emancipation of slavery. *See* slaves and slavery
Emerald Necklace parks, Boston 91
Emerson, Ralph Waldo 31–32, 45, 349
Encyclopedia of Transcendentalism (Wayne) 403n14
Erlick, June C. 73, 409n36
Eshbaugh, Daniel O. 235, 429n6
"Essay on Classification" (Agassiz) 76
Estes & Lauriat, Boston 145, 417n1
ethnic politics and immigration 20, 28, 34, 37–38, 91, 109, 214–15, 321, 344–45, 374, 383, 404n21, 411nn32–33, 411nn32–33, 427n30, 447n27
"Eugenics, Ethics & Emigration" (Hall) 347
eugenics movement 76, 346–47, 378, 442n25
Everett, Alexander (uncle of EEH) 18, 29, 35
Everett, Edward (uncle of EEH) 18, 29, 33, 37, 39
Everett, Sarah Preston. *See* Hale, Sarah Preston Everett (mother of EEH)
Everett, William (cousin of EEH) 39
evolution-creation controversy 46–47, 75–76, 133, 152–53, 198, 343, 346, 404nn30–31, 418n21, 425n54. *See also* Darwin, Charles

Farley-White Aetna Mills 401n6
Farmer, Moses G. 167
Farmer, Sarah Jane 153–54, 187, 216, 288, 418n23, 436n46
Farrell, Betty G. 403n7
Fatherless and Widows Society, Boston 344, 349, 361
feminism. *See* women's rights and education

Fenn, William W. 261
Fifty Million Dollar Bill (1898) 236–37
fires, historic: Great Boston Fire (1872) 53–54; Great Chicago Fire (1871) 406n4
First Church, Boston 35, 393
First Church of Chestnut Hill, Newton, Massachusetts 170
First Congregational Church, Burlington, Vermont 340
First Congregational Church, New York City 44
First Unitarian Church, Chicago 261
First Unitarian Church, Orange, New Jersey 170
First Unitarian Church, Washington D.C. 33 *See also* All Souls Unitarian Church, Washington D.C.
Fish, Hamilton 53
Fiske, John 76, 345, 385
Fitzgerald, John F. "Honey Fitz" 20, 321, 374, 381
Fleischer, Charles 311–12, 349, 362
Fleishman, Thelma 401n6
Fletcher, Alice C. 104
Flight Maps (Price) 440n10
The Flowering of New England: 1815-1865 (Brooks) 30
Folly Cove, Gloucester, Massachusetts 212, 220, 343, 354, 372
Fore River Ship and Engine Building Company, Braintree, Massachusetts 211, 425n3
Forest and Irrigation 326, 327, 331, 332, 334, 369, 436n42, 440n5, 440n15
Forest Hills Cemetery, Boston 383
"The Forest in the Life of a Nation" (Roosevelt) 327
Forest Reserve Bill 332
"A Forest Reserve in the White Mountains" (Rollins) 440n15
forestry movement: American Forest Congress 314, *326,* 326–28, 440n5, 440n7; Appalachian-White Mountains Forest Reservation Bill 182, 324–25, 331–33, 356–57, 356–57, 361, 374–75, 374–75; articles on 440n2, 440n15, 440nn5–7, 441n16; Gifford Pinchot and 195; in *Lend a Hand Record* 327, 332, 356, 357, 440n2, 440n4, 440n6, 441n17, 443n47, 443n49, 443n51; opponents 374; rise of 181–82, 267, 323–25; in White Mountains 282–83, 287, 331–32, 436n42. *See also* logging industry
forget-me-nots 129, 415n42
Fort Huachuca, Sierra Vista, Arizona 361
Fort Marion, St. Augustine, Florida 112–13
Foster, Laura E. 258
Fowler, William P. 253
Franklin, Benjamin 95–96
Franklin in France (Hale and Hale) 95–96, 106–7, 125, 127
"Freedom in Texas" (Hale) 404n19
Freely, John 432n63
Freeman, Barbara (great-niece of HEF) 318
Freeman, Betsy (grandmother of HEF) *24*
Freeman, Bradford (uncle of HEF) *24*
Freeman, Caroline "Carrie" (niece of HEF) *285*; about 66, 84, 392, 394; Helen Keller and 137; travels with HEF 146, 152, 159,

185, 187–89, 193, 195–96, 200, 218, 268, 292, 357, 419n34
Freeman, Caroline Crosby Lewis (mother of HEF) 11, 19, 25–26, 27, 49, 63, 65–66, 85, 408n25
Freeman, Edmond (ancestor of HEF) 23
Freeman, Ethel Hale (niece of HEF) *285*; about 7, 66, 84, 392, 394; EEH and HEF letters 390; engagement of 379; Helen Keller and 137; schooling of 278, 337; travels with HEF 152, 214–17, 218, 230, 313, 337–38, 347, 357, 379, 446n20
Freeman, Frank Clark (nephew of HEF) *281*; about 66, 433n3; Aetna Mills and 380–81; death 381; family 283, 294, 318, 447n25; Grabau and 211; HEF and 152, 218, 264, 280–81, 284; on immigration 347; schooling 84, 283; works by 381
Freeman, Frederick (great-uncle of HEF) *24*
Freeman, Frederick William (brother of HEF): about 11; business 27, 124; death 117–18, 119, 263, 282; family 50, 66, 146; health 84
Freeman, Frederic William. *See* Freeman, Frank Clark (nephew of HEF)
Freeman, Harriet Elizabeth "Hattie" *13, 281, 286, 326*; about 8–9, 52, 114, 397–98, 400; Amadeus Grabau and 170–71, 252, 257, 333, 334, 372, 377, 379, 431n52; ambivalence toward humanity 169–70, 224–25; on American Indian politics 361, 375; Appalachian Mountain Club and 77, 103, 106, 166, 193, 327, 356; bird conservation 79, 156, 265–67, 274, 293, 307, 316, 317, 328–31, 376, 386, 433n10; botanical work 74, 82, 85, 97–98, 105, 106, 128–29, 151, 192, 226, 285, 344; on C. Hart Merriam 293; childhood 19, 23, 26–27, 402n3; condolence letters to 371; on creation-evolution controversy 47, 75–76, 343, 405n31; DAR and 274, 434n22; death 394; dislike for Joseph Cannon 325, 333–35, 351–52, 356, 361, 374; EBH and 262, 264, 312; on EEH, Jr.'s crisis of faith 338–39; EEH biographies and 3, 387, 390; EEH's books purchased by 446n6; father of 63, 106, 122; finances 5, 6, 154–55, 203, 226, 240, 256, 261–62, 381, 397–98; forest preservation 287–88, 331, 333–34, 352, 356; on Frank/Fred Freeman 283–84; on freedom 146, 200, 256, 268, 315; on frivolous women 162, 169–70, 307; geological work 252; gifts to Hale family 289, 292, 415n35; health 263–64; intelligence 81–82, 410n7; on interesting men 162–63; Joshua Young and 156–57, 233, 249; on Lucia Proctor 283; on marriage 103; Mary Cobb and 67, 73, 77, 97–98, 106, 123, 151, 307, 315, 408n27; mental health 6, 220–21, 232, 238–41, 252, 256; moving to Back Bay, Boston 251, 252–53, 255; on naturalism *vs.* Christian symbolism 168–69; on nature 328; Nelly Hale and 367, 372;

obituary 8, 394; parochial work 123–24; on politics 215–16; relationship with parents 65–66, 84–85; science education 64–65, 74–75, 149, 170, 175, 186, 193, 230, 376, 417n7, 422n7, 424n43; selling Pepperell estate 154–55, 160, 419n36; South End, Boston home 16–18; on spirituality 314; on stuttering 244; on suffrage 363, 384–85; as teacher 64–65, 234, 241; Vassar College and 63, 407n18; works by 161, 209, 265–67, 275–76, 279, 330, 412n56, 433n10, 435n26, 440n12; writing 65, 149, 418n13; as xenophobe 344, 346–47, 350, 355, 378–79, 384

Freeman, Harriet Elizabeth "Hattie," travels: (1885) 97–98; (1886) 106; (1887) 115, 119; (1888) 127–28; (1889) 150; (1890) 159, 161–62; (1891) 171; (1892) 175, 180; (1893) 185; (1894) 191, 192; (1895) 193, 195–97; (1896) 205–12, 214–17; (1897) 226–27, 229; (1898) 233, 245–51; (1900) 257; (1901) 265–67; (1903) 290, 292–95, 297, 436n53, 437n2; (1905-1906) 313, 316–19, 322, 332, 337–38; (1907) 350, 351–53; (1909) 364, 371–72; (1911-1912) 377, 378, 379–80; (1916) 386; (1920-1922) 391–92

Freeman, Harriet Elizabeth "Hattie," and EEH *279, 284*; avoiding scandal 117, 128–29, 193, 251, 260, 396–98; canoeing together *120*, 155–56; confessing love 105–6, 157–58, 166–67, 171, 177, 178–79, 195, 224–25, 371; defining relationship 80, 126, 233, 250, 312; depression without 220–21, 244; developing feelings 51–52, 68–69, 71–72, 73–74, 79–82, 83–84; dreams 248–49; gifts 68, 85, 105, 126, 163, 230, 261–62, 265, 275, 354, 365; grief support 105, 107, 122, 128, 202, 222–23, 229, 309–10, 360; initial meetings 11, 20–21; last visit (1909) 366; letter (1884) 92–93; losing closeness 244, 245, 246, 248; on missing each other 115, 196, 200, 201, 210, 316, 317, 319, 348–49, 350–51; rebelling against 355, 358–59, 363–64; on saving correspondence 161–62, 165, 364, 367; shorthand 90, 247; visits (1882) 67; visits (1884) 85–86, 87–88; visits (1885) 98–99, 100; visits (1887) 113, 118–20, 123–24, 125–26; visits (1889) 155–56; visits (1892) 181; visits (1893) 185–89; visits (1894) 191–92; visits (1896) 209–10, 213–15; visits (1897) 225, 230–31; visits (1899) 253; visits (1900) 260; visits (1901) 268; visits (1902) 278–82, 284–88, 412n46; visits (1904) 306; visits (1906) 347; visits (1908) 357–58; visits (1909) 364–65, 366; working together 3, 62–63, 101–2, 111, 123–24

Freeman, Harriet Mower Clark "West Newton Hattie" (sister-in-law of HEF) 84, 117, 146, 251, 337, 371, 379

Freeman, Helen Hunt (niece of HEF) *326*; about 7, 392; Hales and 360, 370; health 155; letters from HEF 371; travels

with HEF 152, 230, 318, 327, 365; wedding 363, 365, 445n74
Freeman, John 23
Freeman, Lucia Proctor 268, 283, 294, 318, 380–81
Freeman, Madeleine Jean 381
Freeman, Mary Elizabeth. *See* Atkins, Mary Elizabeth Freeman (aunt of HEF)
Freeman, Sara Maria (aunt of HEF) *24*
Freeman, William (grandfather of HEF) 16, *24*, 25
Freeman, William Frederick (father of HEF) *24*; business 20, 23, 25, 124; EEH and 63, 65, 84–85, 127–28, 130, 136, 407n18; family 50; health 80, 84–85, 101, 117–18, 412n55; HEF and 63, 106, 122, 146; library books checked out by 27; mental health 80, 84–85
Freeman family *24*; ancestral home of 137; EEH and 63, 65–66, 84–85, 125; HEF and 159, 160–61, 187, 218, 230–31, 273; Helen Keller and 137. *See also specific persons*
Free Religious Association 45
French Canadian immigration to Boston 34
Friends of the American Indian conferences 151
Frissell, Hollis B. 237, 295, 296, 306, 318
From Plotsk to Boston (Antin) 271
Frothingham, Louis 321, 362
Frothingham, Paul 321
Fugitive Slave Law (1850) 148
Fullum, Abel 30, 107, 288

Gandhi, Mahatma 116
Gardner, August P. 345
Garfield, James A. 55
Garrison, William Lloyd 159
gender relations. *See* women's rights and education
General Allotment Act (1887) 103
General Conference of Unitarians (1917) 390
Geological Survey of New Hampshire (1841) 32
Geology at M.I.T. (Shrock) 417n7, 422n7
Geronimo 113
Gibson, Charles Dana 258
Gilded Age 43, 54, 63–65
Gilman, Bradley 388, 389, 448n39
Gilman, Charlotte Perkins (niece of EBH) *142*; about 133–34, 416nn1–2; family 19, 304; mental health 111, 134–35, 137; writing 139–41; "The Yellow Wall-paper" 242, 430nn18, 430nn25–26
Gilman, Daniel Coit 74
Gilman, Houghton (nephew of EBH) 143–44
Gilman, Catherine "Katy" (sister of EBH) 19
Goethe, Johann Wolfgang von 80, 409n4
Goethe's correspondence with a child (Charlton) 409n4
Goldman, Emma 269
Gompers, Samuel 310
Goodale, George L. 125
Gordon, John 305–6
Grabau, Amadeus W. about 449n47; marriage 271–73; schooling 230; support from HEF 135, 170–71, 186, 211, *272*, 297–98, 425nn2–3; supporting HEF 377; teaching 223, 229–30,

257; travels with HEF 257, 333, 334; visits with HEF 379, 431n52; against World War I 391
Grabau. Josephine 379
"The Grand Canon of the Colorado (From a Staff Correspondent)" (Freeman) 209
Grand Canyon, Arizona: (1896) 206–7; (1903) 292–93, 436n53
Grand Opera House, San Francisco 342
"Granite Hill" (Freeman) 161
Grant, Ulysses S. 54
Grant administration corruption 54–56
Gray, Asa 34, 46–47, 76, 151, 404n31; *Shortia galacifolia* and 275–76, 434n23; works by 85, 98, 410n15
Gray Herbarium, Harvard College 151, 309, 344, 385, 447n33
The Great Dismal Swamp (Kirk) 433n10
Great Dismal Swamp National Wildlife Refuge 267
Greely, Adolphus 342, 365
Green Acre-on-the-Piscataqua, Maine 153, *187,* 288, 436n46
Greenleaf, Frederic 35
Griffith, J. W. 415n35
Gulesian, M. H. *187*

Hale, Alexander (brother of EEH) 29–30, 35, 407n16
Hale, Alexander (son of EEH and EBH) 39
Hale, Arthur (son of EEH and EBH): about 39; EEH and 99, 124, 188, 275, 289, 350; on EEH biography 386–87; health 61; marriage 151; at Matunuck 86, 199; on Nelly Hale 164; railroad business 184, 289; on Susan Hale 376–77, 383
Hale, Camilla Conner (daughter-in-law of EEH and EBH) 154, 350
Hale, Charles (brother of EEH) 28, 29–30, 35, 41, 43, 53, 61, 67, 407n16, 408n26
Hale, Charles Alexander (son of EEH and EBH) 39, 407n16
Hale, Edward (not EEH) 90, 107, 114, 165–66, 169–70
Hale, Edward Everett, civic work: at Chautauqua 99, 111, 112, 118, 124, 129–30, 168, 201, 253–55, 414n14; commencement ceremonies 278; Doctor of Laws, Dartmouth College 270; forest preservation 287–88, 323, 325–27, 331–34; on immigration 345–46; inspiring philanthropy in others 225; on international peace movement 299–300, 308; as lecturer 77, 83, 150, 153, 191, 224, 240, 376; Massachusetts Society for Promoting Good Citizenship 91; opening the new year 262; on presidential politics 82–83, 224, 410n10; on race relations 305–6, 438n21; on Roosevelt 364; U.S. Sanitary Commission work 149; on women's rights and education 59–60, 142–43, 147, 149, 304, 333
Hale, Edward Everett, literary works 65, *190;* Autobiography 253, 431n58; *Autobiography, Diary, and Correspondence* [of James Freeman Clarke] 147, 159, 160, 417n5; *Boston Commonwealth* 209, 217, 426n11;

"The Brick Moon" 290, 405n32; *Charities* 218; *Circular for Ten Times One* 71–72, 102; "A Course of Practical Ethics" 99; *East and West: A Story of New-Born Ohio* 181, 423n19; "The Educated Citizen" 278; *The Elements of Christian Doctrine and its Development* 39, 404n24; *Franklin in France* 95–96, 106–7, 125, 127; "Freedom in Texas" 404n19; "Herons and Aigrets" 331, 440n14; *In His Name: A Story of the Waldenses* 56–57, 72, 124, 409n34; "History of the Pacific Ocean and its Shores" 68; *History of the United States, written for the Chautauqua Reading Circles* 124; "Home Again" 102; *How to Live* 412n48; "The Human Washington" 111; *James Russell Lowell and His Friends* 253, 431n55; *Kanzas and Nebraska* 38, 404n22; *Lend a Hand* 99, 101–2, 103, 107, 112; *Letters on Irish Emigration* 37; *Life of Columbus* 167; "The Man without a Country" 2, 14, 96, 260, 369, 401n2; *Memories of a Hundred Years* 34, 268, 287, 403n18, 435n40; "Memories of the 19th Century" 255, 268; *Mr. Tangier's Vacation* 102, 112; "My Double and How He Undid Me" 2, 260; "My Friend the Boss" 102, 107; *My Reminiscences* 403n17; "My Visit to Sybaris" 290; *A New England Boyhood* 176, 403n10, 418n13; *Ninety Days' Worth of Europe* 39, 404n25; *Old and New* 47, 48, 53–54, 56, 58, 101, 407n11; "Our Eastern Forests" 331, 440n15; *Philip Nolan's Friends* 60; *Prayers of the Senate* 436n63; "Spiritual Forces in Human Progress" 188, 424n36; *Stories of Invention told by Inventors and their Friends* 101; *Sybaris and other Homes* 405n32; "Tarry at Home Travel" 32, 155, 403n15, 419n25; *Tarry at Home Travels* 32, 403n15; *Ten Times One Is Ten* 47–48, 69, 408n31; *A Tract for the Times* 34, 404n19; "The Unitarian Conference" 192–93, 424n42; *The Unitarian Principles* 94, 411n35

Hale, Edward Everett, parochial work: as chaplain at University of Chicago 277; as chaplain of U.S. Senate 6, 296, 298–300, 303–5, 347, 436n63; christenings 318; at Church of the Unity 34–35; on divorce 339–41; funerals 67, 270, 305, 309, 341; last sermon 365; ordaining ministers 358; on preaching 314–15; Rabbi leaders and 311–12; reformist activities 43–47; on retiring 88–89, 120; at South Congregational Church 65, 88, 120, 122–24, 253; training 20, 23, 32–33; Unitarian Conferences 79, 88, 164, 171, 183, 192–93; weddings 271, 278

Hale, Edward Everett, personal life *12, 42, 70, 187, 199, 254, 280, 285*; about 2, 6–7, 11, 20, 69, 370; ancestors 29; biography 2, 3, 372, 386–89; birthdays 173–74, 226, 227, 276, 365, 421n1; botanical interest 82, 85, 86, 128; as celebrity 129,

189–91, 355, 443n46; Charlotte Perkins and 139; childhood 30; children (*See specific names*); death 365–67; father of 41; finances 29, 41, 58, 88, 102, 191, 194, 217; Freeman family and 63, 65–66, 84–85, 125, 127–28, 130; health 168, 238, 239–40, 357; Helen Keller and 128, 133, 135–37; on interesting conversation 318; on Lucretia's death 257; on marriage 257–59, 271; memorials of 376, 381–83, *382*, 392–93, 450n56; Minnie Whitman and 216–17; obituaries 369–70, 445nn1–2; profiles published about 189–90, 424n38; relationship with EBH 18, 36, 69–71, 173–77, 222–23, 237, 288–89, 340–41, 358; relationship with family 48, 189, 198–99, 354, 405n34; schooling 30–32; science interests 290–92; sketchwork 180, 181, 423n18, 438n19; as temperance advocate 197

Hale, Edward Everett, and HEF *279, 284*; avoiding scandal 117, 128–29, 175–76, 179, 251, 396–98; canoeing together *120*, 155–56; confessing love 105–6, 157–58, 171, 176–77, 182–83, 191, 212, 213, 268, 299, 365; defining relationship 80, 126, 233, 250, 312, 439n40; developing feelings 51–52, 68–69, 71–72, 73–74, 79–82, 83–84; gifts 68, 69, 80, 95, 124, 253, 358, 415n35, 435n40, 436n63; Greek erotica 178; grief support 117–19, 124, 130–31, 182, 183; on HEF's intelligence 183; on HEF's life 295; on HEF's mental health 238–39, 240–41; hypocrisy of relationship 94–95, 121–22, 257–59, 340–41; initial meetings 11, 20–21; last visit (1909) 366; letter (1884) 92–93; locks of hair 160, 420n39; losing closeness 244, 245, 246, 248; on missing each other 115, 163, 196, 318, 348–49; naming HEF in Autobiography 253; organizing correspondence 161–62, 165, 294; poems 68, 184, 233, 408n28; renewed purpose 422n13; on saving correspondence 364, 367; shorthand 90, 247; visits (1882) 67; visits (1884) 85–86, 87–88; visits (1885) 98–99, 100; visits (1887) 113, 118–20, *120*, 123–24, 125–26; visits (1889) 155–56; visits (1892) 181; visits (1893) 185–89; visits (1894) 191–92; visits (1896) 209–10, 213–15; visits (1897) 225, 230–31; visits (1899) 253; visits (1900) 260; visits (1901) 268; visits (1902) 278–82, 284–88, 412n46; visits (1904) 306; visits (1906) 347; visits (1907) 354; visits (1908) 357–58; visits (1909) 364–65, 366; working together 3, 62–63, 101–2, 111, 123–24

Hale, Edward Everett "Jack," Jr. (son of EEH and EBH): about 39; crisis of faith 338, 441n6; EEH and 8; family 189; *Franklin in France* 95–96; *The Life and Letters of Edward Everett Hale* 38, 48, 60–61, 168, 253, 387–89, 404n23, 404n25, 405n34, 406n2, 407n11, 407n15, 421n60,

431n58; at Matunuck house 86, 220; political run by 378; on Robert Beverly Hale 393; schooling 107, 116, 406n9, 422n15; Susan Hale and 289, 377, 418n23; wedding 186, 423n32
Hale, Edward Everett, III (grandson of EEH and EBH) 383
Hale, Ellen Day "Nelly" (daughter of EEH and EBH) *40*; about 6, 39, 52, 289; as celebrity 355, 443n46; on EEH 312–13, 393; at EEH memorial 381–83; Hale estate 367, 372, 383; health 73–74, 164–65, 226; *The Life and Letters of Edward Everett Hale* 168, 372, 386–87, 421n60; living in Washington D.C. 350, 362, 364–65; researching for EEH 60–61, 167, 420n56; schooling 68, 73, 83, 86, 101, 149; science and 290–91; travels (1876) 60–61; travels (1884) 83, 86, 101; travels (1890) 159; travels (1891) 167; travels (1893) 184, 423n27; travels (1897) 225, 227; travels (1898) 242; travels (1899) 253; travels (1901) 267–68; travels (1904) 298–99, 307, 308, 310; travels (1905) 320–21; travels (1906) 343; travels (1907) 347, 354, 355, 362, 364–67; travels (1908) 357, 359, 360; work 175, 350
Hale, Emily (daughter of other Edward Hale) 170, 421n65
Hale, Emily Baldwin Perkins (wife of EEH) *40, 62, 199, 280*; about 2–3, 6; on Charlotte Perkins 416n14; childhood 19; children 39 (*See also specific names*); death 383; death of EEH 366–67; family role 48; at Folly Cove 220, 372; grief of Kidder's loss 105; grief of Robert's loss 202; health 48–49, 61, 83, 91–94, 166, 173–74, 180–81, 201, 205, 264, 268–69, 299, 319, 320, 344, 347, 350, 357; HEF and 163, 262, 264, 312; letter from Helen Freeman 370; mother 90, 117; Olmstead and 41, 194; portrayal in EEH biography 48, 388–89, 448n41; relationship with EEH 18, 36, 39, 69–71, 173–75, 173–77, 222–23, 249, 288–89, 358, 384, 397; travels 52, 56, 79, 80, 154, 179–80, 225, 283, 308; writing of 81, 82, 88–89, 98, 159
Hale, Enoch (grandfather of EEH) 29
Hale, Henry "Harry" (son of EEH and EBH) 39, 61
Hale, Herbert Dudley "Bertie" (son of EEH and EBH): about 39, 87; death 359, 444n55; family of 192, 289, 383; health 343; schooling 180; wedding 174; work 354
Hale, Herbert "Dudley" Jr. (grandson of EEH and EBH) 192, 360, 364
Hale, Lilian Westcott (daughter-in-law of EEH and EBH) 277–78, 289, 295, 356, 393
Hale, Lucretia P. (sister of EEH): about 29–30; death 257; dislike for EBH 383, 418n23; dislike for Minnie Whitman 217; health 238, 241, 245, 247, 249; at Matunuck 57, 64; supporting EEH 8; work 43, 53, 102; works by 43, 405n33

Hale, Margaret (granddaughter of EEH and EBH) 247, 360, 390
Hale, Margareta "Greta" Marquand (daughter-in-law of EEH and EBH) 174, 180, 192, 241, 245, 247, *280,* 343, 359, 360, 444n60
Hale, Nancy (granddaughter of EEH and EBH) 7, 49, 356, 383, 393, 398, 405n35, 408n26, 450n2
Hale, Nathan (ancestor of EEH) 29
Hale, Nathan (brother of EEH) 29, 30–31, 35, 41, 53
Hale, Nathan (father of EEH) 18, 29, 35, 37, 41
Hale, Nathan (grandson of EEH and EBH) 319
Hale, Philip (son of EEH and EBH): about 39, 86, 360; at EEH's death 366–67; family of 356, 383, 393; marriage 277–78, 434n31; schooling 160, 180; travels 184, 423n27
Hale, Robert (ancestor of EEH) 29
Hale, Robert Beverly (grandson of EEH and EBH) 360, 444n59
Hale, Robert Beverly (son of EEH and EBH) 39, 48, 86–87, 154, 201–2, 222, 428n42; death of 201–2; Library in honor of 229, 393, 428n56
Hale, Rose Perkins (daughter-in-law of EEH and EBH) 186, 189, *280,* 339, 393, 423n32, 448n37
Hale, Sarah (sister of EEH) 29, 35
Hale, Sarah Preston Everett (mother of EEH) 18, 29, 33, 35
Hale, Susan (sister of EEH) *42;* about 29–30, 362; on California 175, 422n5; at Chautauqua 253–55; death 376–77, 393; on EBH 383, 418n23; on EEH and HEF 119, 154, 179, 359, 376, 443n54; Hale family and 74, 288–89; health 354, 357; on Jamaica 305; running Matunuck house 57, 83, 153–54, 212, 220, 418n23; on Sarah Farmer 154, 418n23; supporting EEH 8; travels 68, 184, 423n27; on Washington politics 236; on women's suffrage 304; work 43, 102
Hale family *199, 280;* birthdays 276–77; celebrations 173–74, 186, 192, 288–89, 392–93; Charlotte Perkins Gilman and 133–34; finances 97; gatherings of 136, 151, 175, 343, 362–63; handling EEH estate 367, 372; HEF and 261–62, 267; Helen Keller and 135–37; politics 82; reunions 198–99, 212; tragedies 61, 201–2, 359–60. *See also specific persons*
Hale-Freeman letters: about 1–8; examples of *92–93, 228;* fate of 366–67, 373
Hale House at Harvard College 171, 186, 276
Hall, Minna 329
Hall, Prescott F. 345, 347, 378, 446n18
Hampton Normal and Agricultural Institute, Virginia 44, 237, 255, 295, 306, 412n60
Hanna, Mark 270, 303, 305
Harper's Weekly *254,* 276, 431n56, 435n27
Harriman, Edward H. 292
Harriman, Mrs. Edward 375
Harriman, Walter 334
Harris, Christopher 409n37
Harrison, Benjamin 130, 145

Hartford Female Seminary 19
Harvard College: Alpha Delta Phi 31, 278; Arnold Arboretum 275; Board of Overseers 46; commencement 278; Everett family and 29; Frederic Dan Huntington and 38–39; Gray Herbarium 151, 309, 344, 385, 447n33; Hale family and 87, 406n9; Houghton Library 7, 378; Medical School 433n1; Museum of Comparative Zoology 76, 329; professors 46–47, 125, 345, sugar cane research 302, 437n14; theology 18; women's education 63–64
Harvard Divinity School 107; Andover-Harvard Theological Library 8, 70, 190, 405n33, 412n54, 414n15, 415n30, 424n48, 442n28, 445n1, 446n15, 449n49; EEH at 30–32; professors 89–90, 261; Ralph Waldo Emerson's 1838 address 31; Unitarianism and 31, 36
Harvardiana 31
Harvard Theological Review 389
"Hats Off to Audubon" (Price) 440n10
Havemeyer, Henry 73
Hawthorne, Nathaniel 59
Hay, John 310, 311, 319
Hazard, Caroline 137–39
Hazard, Rowland 137–39
Hearst, Phoebe 288, 433n7
Hearst, William Randolph 288
heat wave (1896), New England 216, 427n32
Hecht, Jacob 273
Hecht, Lima 273
Hedge, Frederick 47, 58
Hemenway, Harriet 329, 363
Hemenway, Mary 329
Henfrey, Arthur 415n35
heredity, law of (Mendel) 75
Herford, Brooke 114, 171
"Herons and Aigrets" (Hale) 331, 440n14
Herron, George D. 340, 443n11
Hetch Hetchy River, California 375
Higginson, Henry L. 276
Higginson, Thomas Wentworth 31, 36, 37, 117, 370, 403n11, 445n2
Hillis, Newell D. 340, 347, 442n11
A History of Delaware County, Pennsylvania (Palmer) 430n19
"History of the Pacific Ocean and its Shores" (Hale) 68
History of the United States (Adams) 411n39
History of the United States, written for the Chautauqua Reading Circles (Hale) 124
A History of Woman Suffrage (Stanton, Anthony, Harper) 304, 438n18
Hitchcock, Charles H. 334
Hitler, Adolf 378
Hoar, George Frisbie 96, 235, 237, 276, 296, 306, 309–10, 397, 404n27, 435n28
Hoar, Ruth 298
Hobart, Mary 381
Hodges, Maud deLeigh 447n22
Hollis Street Church and Society 16, 109–11, *110*, 114–15, 121, 122–23
Holloway, Jean 58, 61, 96, 389, 403n11, 403n16, 404n20, 404n22, 406n5, 407n11, 407n17, 411n41, 422n13
Holmes, John Haynes 390–91

Holmes, Oliver Wendell 86
Holton, Wilfred E. 403n7
The Home, Heaven, and Mother Party (Jablonsky) 447n31, 449n55
Hooker, Isabella Beecher (aunt of EBH) 19, 111
Hooper, Franklin W. 376
Hooper, Sarah 41, 49, 227
Hornaday, William T. 438n24
Horowitz, Helen Lefkowitz 135, 416n13, 416nn1–2
Hotel Normandie, Washington D.C. 306
Hotel Torrington, Boston 251
Hotel Vendome, Boston 392
Houghton, Mifflin and Co. 253
Houghton Library, Harvard University 7, 378
Houses of Boston's Back Bay: An Architectural History: 1840-1917 (Bunting) 402n6, 403n7, 429n11, 431n50
Howard, Esmé 355
Howard, Isabella 355
Howard University 305–6
Howe, Francis A. (uncle of HEF) 26, 158, 167, 313
Howe, James Lewis 158
Howe, Julia Ward 117, 310
Howe, Mary Lewis (aunt of HEF) 26
Howells, Elinor 116
Howells, William Dean 17, 115, 116, 141, 222, 240, n428n42
Howells, Winifred 116, 240
Howland, William 268
"How Two Women found the Shortia" (Freeman) 435n26
Hubbard, Gardiner Greene 74, 194, 290
Hubbard, Mrs. Gardiner 290–91, 361–62, 366
Huidekoper, Elizabeth 100, 363
See also Elizabeth Kidder
Hull, Edith (cousin of HEF) *281*, 319, 354, 363
Hull House, Chicago 148
"The Human Washington" (Hale) 111
Huntington, Frederic Dan 38–39, 404n23
Hurlbut, Jesse L. 414n14
Huss, John 371
Hyams, George 434n23
Hyatt, Alpheus 74–75, 76, 125, 135, 170, 252, 274, 409n40, 417n7

The Ice Age in North America, and Its Bearings Upon the Antiquity of Man (Wright) 151, 152, 418n17
Images of America: Brewster (Brewster Historical Society) 420n40
immigration: Boston ethnic politics and 91, 214–15, 411nn32–33; Johnson-Reed Act (1924) 393; United States 344–47, 378–79. *See also* Irish immigration and Boston ethnic politics; race relations
Immigration Act (1924) 393
Immigration Restriction Act (1921) 393
Immigration Restriction League (IRL) 344, 345, 347, 378, 446n18
Indian Industrial School, Pennsylvania 113
Indian politics, American: Bureau of Indian Affairs 151, 293, 295; land rights 103–4, 112–13, 361, 375; organizations supporting 102, 103, 151, 295, 349, 375; works about 230, 429n59
Indian Rights Association (IRA) 103–4, 112

infidelity. *See* adultery scandals
Ingham, Frederick, (character) 2, 260
In His Name: A Story of the Waldenses (Hale) 56–57, 72, 124, 409n34
insanity. *See* mental health
International Arbitration, Mohonk conferences 152, 198
International Federation of Women's Clubs 327
Intervale, New Hampshire 171, 265–66, 268–69, 270, 282, 284–88, 308–9, 318–20, 344, 347, 353, 354, 357, 363
Intracoastal Waterway, Virginia 267
inventions: airplane 227, 341, 428n52; fire-alarm telegraph 167; power looms 266; Studebaker Electric car 291; telephone 167, 205; tetrahedral kites and wings 291–92, 436n50
Iowa State University 189
IRA. *See* Indian Rights Association (IRA)
Irish immigration and Boston ethnic politics 20, 28, 34, 37–38, 91, 321, 374, 383, 404n21, 411nn32–33, 427n30, 447n27. *See also* Eliot School Rebellion (1859)
The Irrepressible Conflict between Two World Theories (Savage) 425n54
Italy: Mount Vesuvius eruption (1906) 342–43; Venice 337
Jablonsky, Thomas J. 447n31, 449n55
Jackson, Helen Hunt 104, 412n47
Jaher, Frederick C. 403n7
Jamaica, Christianity in 305
James, Alice 407n20
James, Henry 407n20
James, William 353, 407n20
"James Freeman Clarke" (Peabody) 410n10
James Russell Lowell and His Friends (Hale) 253, 431n55
Jardín Botánico de Cienfuegos, Cuba 437n14
Jaynes, Julian C. 294
Jean, Madeleine 381
Jenkins, Charles F. 434n23
Jewish immigration 378. *See also* immigration
Jews, Reform, in Boston 45, 311, 349
Jim Crow era 313–14. *See also* slaves and slavery
Job, Herbert K. 329, 440n9
John Crerar Library of Science, Chicago 213
Johns Hopkins University 74
Johnson, Christopher 441n22
Johnson, Richard I. 434n21
Johnson-Reed Act (1924) 393
Jones, Jenkin Lloyd 79, 424n36
Jordan, Eben 429n11
Journal of Unitarian Universalist History 414n15
Judgment and Sensibility (Baltzell) 379, 439n37, 443n34, 446n19

Kaneko, Baron 307, 308
Kansas-Nebraska Act (1854) 38
Kanzas and Nebraska (Hale) 38, 404n22
Keating, Jack 376–77
Keating, Mary 376–77
Keating, Rose 377
Keeney, Elizabeth B. 410n15
Keller, Helen 128, 133, 135–37, *138, 140,* 173, 194

Keller, Katharine 133, 135
Kelley, William D. 55
Kennedy, John F. 321
Kennedy, Rose Fitzgerald 20
Kennedy, William Sloane 95
Kidder, Elizabeth 100, 363
Kidder, Henry 39, 56, 104–5, 163, 176, 406n9, 412n61
Kidder, Nathaniel 163–64
Kidder, Peabody & Co. 104
Kidder family 56–57, 100
Kimball, Helen 52
King, Martin Luther, Jr. 116
King, Thomas Starr 16, 119, 121, 181, 423n20
The Kingdom of God is Within You (Tolstoy) 116
Kinsella, Katharine 435n31
Kirk, Paul W., Jr. 433n10
Kit (nickname between EEH and HEF) 106, 107, 113, 283, 312, 315, 355

La Casa Loma Hotel, Redlands 209–10, 294
Lacey Act (1900) 329
LaFlesche, Suzette Bright Eyes 104, 412n60
Lake Drummond, Virginia 266–67
Lake Mohonk, New York. *See* Mohonk Mountain House, New York
"The Lake of the Dismal Swamp" (Moore) 433n10
land rights, Indian 103–4, 112–13, 361, 375. *See also* Indian politics, American
Lang, B. J. 65
Langley, Samuel P. 227, 291, 341, 428n52, 438n24
language of love. *See* shorthand, Towndrow's
Larson, Erik 423n30
Latin School, Boston 30, 32
Le Conte, Joseph 152–53, 168
"Lectures on Natural Science" (Woods Hole Marine Biological Laboratory, 1887) 415n34
Lee, Winthrop 250
Lefroy, John Henry 234
Leland, Martha Adams. *See* Adams, Martha
Lend a Hand (Hale) 99, 101–2, 103, 107, 112, 162, 164, 217–18
Lend a Hand Record: Abigail Clark's work in 286; on Aerodrome 341, 442n13; on bird conservation 330, 331; EEH's duties on 299–300; on forest preservation 287, 327, 332, 356, 357, 440n2, 440n4, 440n6, 441n17, 443n47, 443n49, 443n51; HEF's work in 276, 280, 292–93, 301, 325, 330, 433n8, 434n25, 436n53, 440n2; on immigration 346, 442n24
Lend A Hand Society 218, 337, 373, 446n20
Lesseps, Ferdinand de 305
Lessing, Gottfried Ephraim 82, 410n7
Letters of Susan Hale (Atkinson) 255, 377, 432n59, 443n54, 446n15
Letters on Irish Emigration (Hale) 37
Leue, Mary Macomber 379, 446n20
Lewis, Caroline Crosby. *See* Freeman, Caroline Crosby Lewis (mother of HEF)
Lewis, George Harlan 402n2
Lewis, Harriet. *See* Ellis, Harriet Lewis (aunt of HEF)
Lewis, Harriet Parker (grandmother of HEF) 25

Lewis, James "Squire" (grandfather of HEF) 25, 402n2
Lewis, Mary. *See* Howe, Mary Lewis (aunt of HEF)
Lewis, Samuel Parker (uncle of HEF) 49, 66
The Liberal Christians: Essays on American Unitarian History (Wright) 404n28
libraries: Andover-Harvard Theological Library 8, 70, 190, 405n33, 412n54, 414n15, 415n30, 424n48, 442n28, 445n1, 446n15, 449n49; Boston Public Library 64, 91, 191, 224, 255, 411n39; first presidential 411n37; Houghton Library 7, 378; John Crerar Library of Science 213; New York State Library 406n4, 448n37; Robert Beverly Hale Library 229, 393, 428n56; The Stone Library 411n37; U.S. State Department 95–96, 411n39
Library of Congress: Hale Family Papers 406n36, 408n30; Hale-Freeman Papers 3, 7; Rare Books collections 419n36
Life 258
The Life and Letters of Edward Everett Hale (Hale) 38, 48, 60–61, 168, 358, 404n23, 404n25, 405n34, 406n2, 407n11, 407n15, 431n58, 443n51; compiling 386–89; HEF's involvement in 387, 390; review 389
The Life in the Studio (Hale) 49, 405n35
Life & Letters (Agassiz) 152
Life of Columbus (Hale) 167
Little, Brown and Company 386
Lodge, Henry Cabot 345, 369, 392, 449n53
logging industry: of New England 181–82, 287, 325, 331–32; of Virginia 267. *See also* forestry movement
Long, John D. 270, 381
Longfellow, Alice 295
Longfellow, Henry Wadsworth 181, 433n10
Longfellow, Samuel 32, 151, 181, 182
Looking Backward (Bellamy) 139
"Looking Backward" (Foster) *258*
"Looking to the Future" (Hale) 334, 441n23
The Look Out: A Monthly Magazine 161
Loring, Frederick Wadsworth 53
Loring, Katharine 363, 407n20
Los Angeles Times 143, 369
Lowe, Thad 285
Lowe, Vyron 281, 282, 319, 354
Lowell, James Russell 31, 117, 231, 363
Lowell, Lucy 363
Lowell Collection, Boston Society of Natural History 252
Lowell Institute 65
Lowell Institute Lecture Series 53, 418n17
lumber industry. *See* forestry movement; logging industry
Luther, Martin 371

Macbeth (Shakespeare) 406n5
MacDonald, Alexander 405n32
Maine battleship disaster 236
Manassas Industrial School for Colored Girls 438n21
Manifest Destiny 33, 76
Man Suffrage Association 385
Manual of the Botany of the Northern United States (Gray) 85, 98, 410n15

"The Man without a Country" (Hale) 2, 14, 96, 260, 369, 401n2
Margaret Sanger (Baker) 444n61
Maria Mitchell Society 63
Marine Biological Laboratory. *See* Woods Hole Marine Biological Laboratory, Massachusetts
Marquand, John 444n58
Marquand, Margareta. *See* Hale, Margareta "Greta" Marquand (daughter-in-law of EEH and EBH)
marriage, societal perceptions of 66, 143, 339–41. *See also* divorce
Martineau, James 56
Massachusetts American Forestry Association 327, 333, 361
Massachusetts Association Opposed to the Further Extension of Suffrage to Women 304, 384
Massachusetts Audubon Society 329, 393
Massachusetts Emigrant Aid Company 38
Massachusetts Historical Society 53, 204, 255
Massachusetts Horticultural Society 274
Massachusetts Institute of Technology (MIT) 28, 64, 345, 417n7, 424n43 *See also* Boston Technical Institute
Massachusetts Society for Promoting Good Citizenship 91
Matunuck, Rhode Island house 57; EEH and HEF at 107, 118–20, 185, 412n46; fate of 393; maintaining 83, 97; Minnie Whitman at 216–17; restoration of 3, 5, 98–99, 412n46; Robert Beverly Hale Library 229, 393, 428n56; vacationing at 85, 98, 99, 106–7, 128–29, 175, 198–99, *199*, 212, 220, 343
May, Abby 74
Mayer, Alfred G. 409n40
Mayflower Society 274, 362, 379
Maynard, Samuel 186, 257, 268, 323
Mazur, Alan 391, 425nn2–3, 449n47
McClure's Magazine 189–90, 424n38
McElroy, William H. 194
McKenzie, Alexander 46
McKim, Mead & White 276
McKinley, William 216, 224, 236, 269–70
McKinley administration 235–37
McKinley Tariff Act 203
McKissock, Harriet 49, 399, 445n74
McLean Asylum 247
Mead, Edwin D. 91, 143, 309, 370, 372, 386–87, 388, 445n2
Meadville Theological College 100, 191
Media rest home 240–41, 430n19
medical progress 263, 264–65, 433n1
melting pot theory 350, 377, 378. *See also* immigration
Memorials of the Discovery & Early Settlement of the Bermuda or Somer Islands, 1515-1586 (Lefroy) 234
Memorials of the History for Half a Century of the South Congregational Church 65
Memories of a Hundred Years (Hale) 34, 253, 268, 403n18, 431n58, 435n40
"Memories of the 19th Century" (Hale) 255, 268
Mendel, Gregor 75, 346

mental health: of Charles Hale 67; of Charlotte Perkins Gilman 134–35, 137; of Emily Hale 61; of HEF 6, 220–21, 232, 238–41, 252, 256; of Mary Foote Perkins 134; perceptions of 143; of William Freeman 80, 84–85; of Winifred Howells 240
Merriam, C. Hart 290, 292–93, 306–7, 361, 375, 386
Merriam, George S. 410n10
Merriman, Daniel S. 266, 287, 385
Merriman, Helen 265–66
Messrs Chandler and Waters 41
Metropolitan Museum of Art, New York City 444n59
Metropolitan Opera, New York City 298
Mexico earthquake (1838) 363
Michaux, André 275, 276
The Micrographic Dictionary (Griffith and Henfrey) 415n35
Miller, Scott 434n14, 434n16
Minneapolis Journal 143
The Miracle Worker (film) 416n7
"Mission to Cuba" (Erlick) 73, 409n36
Missouri Compromise (1822) 38
MIT. *See* Massachusetts Institute of Technology (MIT) and Boston Technical Institute
Mitchell, Maria 63
Mitchell, Maria Gouverneur 239
Mitchell, Silas Weir *243*; treating Charlotte Perkins Gilman 134–35, 139–41, 240; treating Harriet Freeman 144, 232, 239–40, 242; treating Winifred Howells 116, 240; treatments 243–44
Mohonk: Its People and Spirit (Burgess) 425n56
Mohonk Mountain House, New York: HEF at (1885) 97–98; HEF at (1889) 151–52; EEH and HEF at (1896) 213–14; EEH and HEF at (1899) 253; International Arbitration conferences 198, 253, 267, 295, 308; Smileys and 274
Moore, J. Hampton 353, 443n41
Moore, Thomas 433n10
morality and Christianity 38–39, 44–45, 76, 116, 148, 158–59, 184, 311, 364, 390
The Morning Call 424n38
Morton, Thomas G. 263
The Most Famous Man in America: The Biography of Henry Ward Beecher (Applegate) 59, 407nn13–4, 410n9, 413n1
Mother Goose Comes to Portland (Freeman) 381
Mount Katahdin, Maine 34, 309
Mount Washington, New Hampshire 32, 106, 285, 318, 357
Mount Watatic, Massachusetts-New Hampshire 101, 412n54
Mr. Tangier's Vacation (Hale) 102, 112
Muir, John 293, 375
Murray, Parnell 115, 171, 191, 218, 245–46, 372, 398
Museum of Comparative Zoology, Harvard College 76, 329
Museum of Fine Arts, Boston 278, 337, 376
Museum of Science, Boston 434n21
Museum of the Boston Society of Natural History 28, 74, 329
"My Double and How He Undid Me" (Hale) 2, 260
"My Friend the Boss" (Hale) 102, 107

My Reminiscences (Hale) 403n17
"My Visit to Sybaris" (Hale) 290

NASA (National Aeronautics and Space Administration) 290, 405n32
National Academy of Science (NAS) 290–91
National American Woman Suffrage Association (NAWSA) 303–4
National Association of Audubon Societies for the Protection of Wild Birds and Animals 329–30
National Audubon Society 329–31, 440n10
"The National Conference of Unitarian Churches" (Hale) 45, 404n29
National Education Association 295
National Forest Commission 283, 324
national forest movement. *See* forestry movement
National Geographic Society 194, 237, 290, 447n21
Nationalist 139
National Museum of Natural History, Washington D.C. 306
National Zoological Park, Washington D.C. 307, 438n24
Natural History Museum, New York City 330
nature conservancy movement 267, 323. *See also* forestry movement; *specific focus*
Navajo tribe imprisonment 361
NAWSA (National American Woman Suffrage Association) 303–4
A New England Boyhood (Hale) 176, 403n10, 418n13
A New England Family (Claflin) 401n1 (chap. 2)
A New England Family Revisited (Weeks and Weeks) 401n1 (chap. 2), 449n54
New England Historic Genealogical Society of Boston 137, 416n11
New England Indian Summer (Brooks) 414n11
New England Loan and Trust Company 235, 256, 429n6
New England Magazine 143, 155, 242, 301, 370, 416n14, 419n25, 445n2
New England weather: Great Blizzard (1888) 126–27; heat wave (1896) 216, 427n32
New Hampshire Forestry Association 357
New Ipswich, New Hampshire 385, 447n33
Newlands Reclamation Act (1902) 325
Newman, William A. 403n7
New North Church, Boston 19–20
New York Journal 224, 236
New York State Library Manuscripts and Special Collections 406n4, 448n37
New York Sun 54, 56
The New York Times: on Daniel O. Eshbaugh 235, 429n6; on EEH 65, 408n23; on EEH estate 373; by Elisha Atkins 406n8; on Metropolitan Opera's *Parsifal* 298, 437n3; obituaries 202, 359, 369, 412n61, 425n64, 444n55, 445n1; on scandals 55, 59, 114, 406n6, 413n8, 442n11, 450n1
New York Tribune 194
New York World 224, 236

Nichols, Mrs. Harold 282, 331
Niles, William H. 125, 351, 422n7
Nineteenth Amendment to the United States Constitution. *See* suffrage movement
Ninety Days' Worth of Europe (Hale) 39, 404n25
North American Review 32
Northeastern Naturalist 434n21
North End, Boston 18–20, 26, 91, 411n32. *See also* Boston
Notman, James 70
Noyes, Ida 146, 315, 417n4

Oakman, John 444n60
Oakman, Renée 444n60
O'Brien, Hugh 91
Oconee Bells. *See Shortia galacifolia* (Oconee Bells)
O'Connor, Thomas H. 427n30, 447n27
Old and New 47, 48, 53–54, 56, 58, 101, 407n11, 418n11
"The Old Homestead" (Thompson) 419n34
Old St. Stephen's Church, Boston 19–20
Olmsted, Frederick Law 18, 41, 91, 184, 194–95, 324, 438n24
The One Woman (Dixon) 340
On Golden Pond (film) 231
On the Border with Crook (Bourke) 113
On the Origin of Species (Darwin) 46, 75, 76, 126, 404n31
opera 42, 136, 298
ornithology. *See* bird conservation
Ourcadie, Will 381
"Our Eastern Forests" (Hale) 331, 440n15
The Outlook 192–93, 253, 268, 331, 370, 377, 424n42, 434n13, 445n2
Painter, Charles C. 104, 112
Palmer, Alice 380
Panama Canal, Panama 303, 305, 352
Panama Canal Company 305
Panama Canal Treaty 303, 305
Pan-American Exposition (1901) 268, 269
Panic of 1873 54–56
Papist revival in United States 37–38
Parker, Harriet. *See* Lewis, Harriet Parker
Parker, Lamuel 434n22
Parker, Theodore 32, 36, 45
Parkman, Francis 19, 182
Parsifal (Wagner's opera) 298
"Pastor's Conduct Divides East Side Congregation" (Steinfels) 450
Peabody, Francis G. 89–90, 298, 410n28
peace movement, world: Congress 300, 309, 310–11, 438n33; international court of arbitration 145, 188; Kaneko and 307; World's Parliament of Religions 187–88, 424n36; World War I and 390–91
Peking National University, China 391
Pennington, Mary Engle 240, 430n19
Pennsylvania Railroad Company 289
Pepperell, Massachusetts home 25–26; selling 154–55, 160, 419n36
Percival, John 310
Perkins, Catherine. *See* Gilman, Katy (sister of EBH)
Perkins, Charles E. (brother of EBH) 19

Perkins, Charlotte. *See* Gilman, Charlotte Perkins (niece of EBH)
Perkins, Emily Baldwin. *See* Hale, Emily Baldwin Perkins
Perkins, Frederick Beecher (brother of EBH) 19, 53, 111, 115, 133, 139, 141
Perkins, George C. 342
Perkins, Lucy A. (sister-in-law of EBH) 90
Perkins, Lucy M. (niece of EBH) 289
Perkins, Mary Foote (mother of EBH) 3, 19, 48, 81, 90, 112, 117, 127–28, 134, 255
Perkins, Rose. *See* Hale, Rose Perkins (daughter-in-law of EEH and EBH)
Perkins, Thomas (nephew of EBH) 133
Perkins, Thomas Clap (father of EBH) 19
Perkins School for the Blind 135, 234
The Peterkin Papers (Hale) 43
Pettaquamscutt Historical Society 99
phanerogamia plant identifications 34, 404n20
Phelps, Luther S. 252, 256, 431n53, 432n62
philanthropy 277, 373. *See also specific organizations*
Philip Nolan's Friends (Hale) 60
Phillips, Mr. and Mrs. Moses 34
Pierce, Benjamin 290
Pierce, Hattie 52
Pierce, Henrietta "Etta" 16, 52, 146, 214, 239, 267
Pierce, Samuel S. 16, 52
Pierce, Ulysses S. 341, 348, 358, 376, 443n51
"Pike's Peak frock" 129
Pinchot, Gifford 195, 282–83, 324, 327, 332, 356, 374
Pinehurst, North Carolina 225, 226, 227, 236–37, 252
Pitman, Isaac 90
plants. *See* botany
Plymouth Church, Brooklyn, New York 58–59, 82, 340
The Poets of Maine (1888) 413n8
Polk, James K. 33
Popular Science Monthly 76, 133, 409n40
Possession (Byatt) 1
Powers, H. H. 386, 448n34
Pratt, Bela 376, 382
Prayers of the Senate (Hale) 436n63
Preaching Eugenics (Rosen) 442n25
Presbyterians, Unitarians relationship with 338–39
Presbyterian Union Theological Seminary 339
preservation efforts. *See specific focus*
"Preservation of Birds" (Freeman) 330
The President and the Assassin (Miller) 434n14, 434n16
presidential politics 82–83, 224, 235, 270, 410n10. *See also specific presidents*
Price, Jennifer 440n10
Prince, Mercy 23
Principles of Stratigraphy (Grabau) 379
Pritchard, Jeter 323
"Probabilistic Darwinism: Louis Agassiz *vs.* Asa Gray on Science, Religion, and Certainty" (Croce) 405n31
Proceedings of the Boston Society of Natural History 135, 416n5

Proceedings of the National Congress on Uniform Divorce Laws 442n10
Proctor, Lucia. *See* Freeman, Lucia Proctor
Proctor, Redfield 237, 238
Programme of the Unveiling of the Memorial Tablet presented to the Town of Pepperell by Mrs. Edith Prescott Walcott November 1, 1899 432n61
Progressive Party 378
The Promised Land (Antin) 273, 377
"A Protest against American Slavery" (petition, 1845) 36 37
Prudence Wright Chapter, DAR, Pepperell, Massachusetts 274

Rabbi leaders in Boston 311–12, 349
race relations 305–6, 313–14, 344. *See also* immigration; slaves and slavery
Radcliffe College 64, 137, 376, 415n33
Radicals in Unitarianism 45. *See also* Transcendentalism
railroad industry: in New England 28, 34, 35, 54–56; stock 373
Raker Act (1913) 375
Ramona (Jackson) 104
Rand, Avery & Company 72, 125, 127
Rand, Carrie 340
Rand, Elizabeth D. 340
Raymond & Whitcomb 392
"Reasons for a National Forest Reservation in the White Mountains" (Ayres) 440n15
Record. See Lend a Hand Record
Records of the Past (Wright) 365, 445n71
"Red and White on the Border" (Roosevelt) 104
Red House. *See* Matunuck, Rhode Island house
Redlands, California 209–10, 426n15
Reed, David 53, 406n3
Reed, Ellen 435n31
Reed, Grace Atkins (cousin of HEF) 53, 111, 146, 185, 229, 296, 300–301, 387, 393
Reed, William Howell (cousin-in-law of HEF): about 52–53; death 387; EEH and 257; on EEH and HEF 179; on Elisha Atkins 55, 406n7; HEF and 116, 185, 238, 251, 257, 300–301; on Soledad plantation 348; South Congregational Church work 62, 111, 165; on U.S. Sanitary Commission 308
reformism: religious 43–47, 45, 311, 349, 371; social 36, 43–44, 58–60, 103–4, 116, 147, 324–25
religion and morality. *See* morality and Christianity
religious institutions: Boston 18–20, 23, 198, 311, 321, 349; World's Parliament of Religions 187–88, 424n36. *See also specific names*
"Reminiscences" (Weeden) 96–97, 411n43
"Reminiscences of Edward Everett Hale" (Merriam) 410n10
Reminiscences of Elisha Atkins (Reed) 55, 406n7
The Remonstrance 444n62
Republican Party 37, 56, 82, 333–34, 378. *See also* Democratic Party
Restless Souls (Schmidt) 436n46
Restoration Hardware, Boston 434n21

Review of Reviews 370, 445n2
Rhode Island School of Design 133
Rhone Valley, France 56
Richards, Ellen Swallow 63, 64
Richards, Harriet E. 309, 329, 438n30
Richards, Robert 64
Rieser, Andrew C. 414n14
"Rise and Fall of the Boston Society of Natural History" (Johnson) 434n21
The Rise of Silas Lapham (Howells) 17
Ritchie affair 169–70
Robert Beverly Hale Library, Matunuck 229, 393, 428n56
Roberts, Jon H. 404n30, 425n54
Robertson, H. J. 440n15
Robinson, Benjamin L. 392, 438n29, 442n21, 447n33, 449n49
Rockefeller, Abby Greene Aldrich 277
Rockefeller, John D., Jr. 277
Rollins, Franklin W. 331, p440n15
A Romance in Natural History: The Lives and Works of Amadeus Grabau and Mary Antin (Mazur) 425nn2–3, 449n47
Roosevelt, Theodore: on assassination attempt 378; on Cuba 303; election 316; on Ellen Maury Slayden 300; at Gettysburg 308; as hunter 331; on immigration 345; conservation initiatives of 282–83, 324–25, 356; on Panama Canal 305; relationship with EEH 104, 270, 278, 298–99, 364; on suffrage 361, 444n62; supporters of 377–78; on Uniform Divorce Laws 339; Yosemite and 293
Root, Elihu 198, 298
Rosen, Christine 442n25
Rossiter, Margaret W. 63, 65, 407n19, 408n22
Russell, Sophie (maid of HEF) 146, 157, 220, 221, 222, 241, 248, 251, 257, 273, 392
Russo-Japanese War (1904) 307, 310

Saint-Gaudens, Augustus 239, 376
Salt Lake Herald 445n1
Salz, Evelyn 434n19
Sampson, William T. 244, 430n30
San Francisco Call 445n1
San Francisco earthquake (1906) 342–43, 375
The Sarah Farmer Inn, Maine 153
Sargent, Charles Sprague 182, 275, 434n23
Savage, Minot J. 74, 113, 197–98, 311, 390, 413n5, 425n54
Sawyer, Holly 447n25
scandals, adultery 3–4, 58–59, 82, 380–81, 395–96, 398
Scarlet Letter (Hawthorne) 59
Schenck, Carl 324
Schiff, Jacob 378
Schindler, Solomon 263, 311, 349
Schliemann, Heinrich 371
Schmidt, Eric 436n46
Schultz, Alfred P. 378
Schurman, Jacob 298, 312
Science (magazine) 74, 290
science, women in 63–65, 74, 273–74, 329, 407n19, 408n22. *See also* women's rights and education
scientific developments at turn of century 290–91. *See also* inventions
Scofield, Glenn W. 55
Scribner's Monthly 58

secretaries of EEH. *See* amanuenses (secretaries) of EEH
Selected Letters of Mary Antin (Salz) 434n19
"Selection of Immigration" (Hall) 345
Sewall, Samuel 262
Sex in Education (Clarke) 63
S.H. *See* Society to Encourage Studies at Home (S.H.)
Shakespeare, William 337, 406n5
Shaler, Nathaniel S. 345
Shaw, Albert 370, 445n2
Shaw, Carrie 218
Sherman, James S. 364–65
shorthand, Towndrow's: about 90; letter in *92–93, 228*; manual of 6, 411n30; others who knew 247, 261, 388
Shortia galacifolia (Oconee Bells) 151, 226, 275–76, 279, 328, 434n23, 435n26. *See also* botany
Shrock, Robert R. 409n40, 417n7, 422n7
Siebert, Wilbur H. 417n10
Sierra Club 375
"Similar Cases" (Gilman) 139
Sinclair, Upton 340, 442n11
"Six of One by Half a Dozen of the Other" (Loring) 53
Six Stories and Some Verses (Hale) 222, 428n42, 428n56
Sixty Years in Cuba: reminiscences of Edwin F. Atkins (Atkins) 72, 224, 409n35, 428n45, 429n9, 429n13
Sketches in and about Portland, Maine (Freeman) 381
"The Slave in the Dismal Swamp" (Longfellow) 433n10
slaves and slavery: abolition of 36–37, 148; Anthony Burns 32; in Cuba 72, 301; education of former 44, 438n21; Fugitive Slave Law 148; treatment of 417n10
Slayden, Ellen Maury 300, 362–63, 437n10, 444n64
Slayden, James L. 300
Smiley, Albert 151, 210, 295, 426n15
Smiley, Alfred 151, 210, 295, 426n15
Smiley, Daniel 274
Smith, Gerrit 148
Smith College, Northampton 7, 278, 338
Smithsonian Institution 291, 341, 438n24
"Snap-shots of my contemporaries: Edward Everett Hale - an American Abou Ben Adhem" (Abbott) 404n27
social service movement, international 47–48
Society for the Protection of New Hampshire Forests 287, 323, 331, 436n42
Society for the Suppression of Vice 60
Society to Encourage Studies at Home 407n21
Society to Encourage Studies at Home (S.H.) 64, 133, 234, 407n20
solar physics 291
Solberg, Thorvald 419n36
Soldiers and Sailors Monument, Boston 148–49
Soldiers Memorial Society 44
Soledad plantation, Cuba 72–73, *204,* 300–303, 348, 393, 437n14. *See also* E. Atkins Company, Cuba
Soledad Sugar Company, Cuba 301–3, 437n14

Solomon, Barbara Miller 411n33, 446n18
The Soul of the Bible (Pierce) 358, 443n51
South Congregational Church and Society, Boston: building 14, *15, 110*; classes 223; dissolution 393, 450n56; EEH's retirement 253; fiftieth anniversary of 65; integration of Hollis Church and 109–11, 114–15, 122–23; memorial services 67, 270, 310; ministers 11, 38, 90, 107, 165, 261, 314, 413n8 (*See also* Hale, Edward Everett, parochial work); Ritchie affair 169; work of 404n26
South End, Boston 14, 16–17, 109–11. *See also* Boston
Southern Appalachian Forest Reserve 323
South Friendly Society 38, 41, 46, 62–63, 126, 358
Spanish-American War (1898) 203, 236–38, 244, 245, 270, 390, 430n30
Spencer, Herbert 75–76, 133
Spencer, Thaxter 137, 416n11
"Spiritual Forces in Human Progress" (Hale) 188, 424n36
Springfield Daily Republican 445n1
Stanton, Elizabeth Cady 58, 60
Start, Edwin A. 331, 332, 333, 334, 361, 440n15
Stebbins, Calvin 387, 388, 448n36, 448n39
Stebbins, Horatio 168, 448n36
Steinfels, Peter 450n1
Stetson, Charlotte Perkins. *See* Gilman, Charlotte Perkins
Stetson, Katharine 134, 139
Stetson, Walter 134, 137, 139, 143
Stock Market Crash (1929) 393
Stonehurst estate of the Merrimans 265–66
Stone Library, Quincy, Massachusetts 411n37
Stories of Invention told by Inventors and their Friends (Hale) 101
The Story of My Life (Keller) 136, 137
Stowe, Harriet Beecher (aunt of EBH) 18, 19, 47, 53, 59, 82, 433n10
A Stream of Light: A Sesquicentennial History of American Unitarianism (Wright) 403n12
Strong, Charles P. 433n1
Strong, Mrs. Charles P. 210–11
Strouse, Jean 407n20
Studebaker Electric car 291
suffrage movement 58, 59–60, 218, 242, 258, 304, 361, 381, 384–85, 444n62, 447n31. *See also* women's rights and education
sugar plantations in Cuba. *See* Soledad plantation, Cuba
sugar trade, Boston 25, 26, 28
Sullivan, Anne "Annie" 133, 135–37, *138, 140*, 416n7
Sumner, Charles 37
Sunday Commons, Boston 350
Sunday Globe 413n8
Swallow, Ellen. *See* Richards, Ellen Swallow
Sybaris and other Homes (Hale) 405n32

Taft, William Howard 356, 364, 369, 375, 378, 381, 390
Tallant, Carry 100
"Tarry at Home Travel" (Hale) 32, 155, 403n15, 419n25
Tarry at Home Travels (Hale) 32, 403n15

Tate & Company 25
Teachers' School of Science 65, 75, 193, 230, 274, 417n7
telephone invention 167, 205
Temple Israel, Boston 311, 349, 362
Ten Times One Is Ten (Hale) 47–48, 69, 408n31
Ten Years War, Cuba 72
Ternan, Ellen 3
tetrahedral kites and wings 291–92, 436n50
Thaxter, Celia 269
Thaxter, Elizabeth "Betty" 269
Thayer, Eli 38
The Hague 145–46, 198, 312
theological disputes: naturalism *vs.* Christian symbolism 168–69; Unitarians and 36, 44–45, 47, 184. *See also* morality and Christianity
This Grand & Magnificent Place (Johnson) 441n22
This is Our Church (Collins) 450n56
Thompson, Denwood 419n34
Thoreau, Henry David 34
Ticknor, Anna Eliot 63–64
Ticknor, George 64
Tilton, Elizabeth 58–59, 117
Tilton, Theodore 58–59
Titus, Catharine 49
Today: A Boston Literary Journal 35
Todd, Mabel Loomis 3
Tolstoi Club at Harvard College 171
Tolstoy, Lev Nikolayevich "Leo" 116
Tomalin, Claire 3
Torrey, Bradford 316
Torriente, Ramon 72
Towndrow, Thomas 6, 90, 411n30. *See also* shorthand, Towndrow's
A Tract for the Times (Hale) 34, 404n19
trading industries in 19th century, Boston 25, 26, 28
Transcendentalism: defining 32, 403n14; Green Acre-on-the-Piscataqua 153; and Unitarianism 31, 44
Treaty of Paris (1898) 246
Trollope, Anthony 56
True Stories of New England captives carried to Canada during the old French and Indian Wars (Baker) 230, 429n59
Trying to Get it Right This Time (Leue) 446n20
Tucker, Lyman 121
Tufts, James W. 225
Tuskegee Institute, Alabama 306
Twain, Mark 369
Twentieth Century Club 310, 333
Tyler, John 33
typhoid disease: Emily Hale with 201, 264; George Clarke with 200–201; Mark Hanna with 303; Mary Edes with 100; Nelly Hale with 73; Robert Beverly Hale with 201–2, 320

Uncle Tom's Cabin (Stowe) 18
Underground Railroad 148, 417n10. *See also* slaves and slavery
Union College, Schenectady, New York 53
Union Pacific Railroad 28, 54–55, 56, 184
Union Park, South End, Boston 14, 16, *17*; demographic changes, 1890-1910 214–15, 427n30; home of HEF 164, 235, 256–57, 432n62

The Unitarian 173, 419n28, 421n1
"Unitarian Christianity" (Channing) 36
Unitarian Church, Newburyport 174
Unitarian Church of All Souls, New York City 395–96
"The Unitarian Conference" (Hale) 192–93, 424n42
Unitarian Conferences 45, 79, 88, 90, 183, 188, 191–93, 390, 404n29
Unitarianism: in 1850-60s Boston 18–20; hierarchy within 53; ministers against World War I 390–91; Presbyterianism *vs.* 338–39; Ralph Waldo Emerson's address (1838) 31; reform 44–47; theological disputes within 157, 184, 419n28; Transcendentalism and 31. *See also* American Unitarian Association (AUA)
Unitarianism in America: A History of its Origins and Development (Cooke) 419n28
"Unitarian Leaders Meet…Everett Hale Unavoidably Absent" 425n64
The Unitarian Principles (Hale) 94, 411n35
Unitarian Universalist Ministers Association 396
United Mineworkers of America 289
United States: Census 345; economy 43, 54–56, 54–56, 184–85, 203–4, 215, 393; foreign imperialism 246; government conservatism 325; immigration politics 344–47, 378–79; papist revival in 37–38; Spanish-American War (1898) 203, 236–38, 244, 245, 270, 390, 430n30
United States Biological Survey 292, 375
United States Congress: corruption within 54, 236, 238, 302, 334–35, 374; lobbying 282, 287, 304, 313–14, 323, 325–29, 332, 345, 356–57, 374–75; political acts by 38, 60, 103, 313, 339, 390
United States Department of State, archives 95–96, 125
United States Department of the Interior 375
United States Forest Service 283, 324, 327, 440n1
United States Reclamation Service 375
United States Sanitary Commission 41, 44, 149, 308, 407n11
Universal Peace Congress 300, 309, 310, 438n33
University of California at Berkeley 168–69
University of Chicago 277
University of Massachusetts at Amherst 268
University of North Carolina at Chapel Hill 306
The Urban Establishment: Upper Strata in Boston, New York, Charleston, Chicago and Los Angeles (chap. 2, Jaher) 403n7
USS *Maine* disaster 236
Vallandigham, Clement 14
Vanderbilt, George 194–95, 324
Vanderbilt, William H. 194
Vassar College, Poughkeepsie 63, 407n18
Vendome Hotel, Boston 174
Venezuela 352
Venice, Italy 337
Vesuvius eruption (1906) 342–43
Vivekananda, Swami *187,* 188

Wagner, Richard 298, 378

Walcott, Edith Prescott 256, 432n61
Wald, Lilian 398
Waldensian Protestant sect in France 56
Walker, Francis A. 345
Waltham Watch Company 84
Ward, Herbert D. 189–90, 424n38
Ward, Julius H. 182, 334, 423n21
Ward, Robert De Courcy 376
Ware, Henry 36
Washington, Booker T. 237, 306, 310
Washington Herald 445n1
Washington Post 450n1
Washington Times 355, 443n46
Washington Wife: Journal of Ellen Maury Slayden (Slayden) 300, 437n10, 444n64
Watson, Elizabeth 205–8, 211, 379
Watson, Sereno 150–51, 434n23
Watson, Thomas 205–8, 211, 372, 379, 391, 425n3
Wayne, Tiffany K. 403n14
weather, New England: Great Blizzard (1888) 126–27; heat wave (1896) 216, 427n32
Webster, Daniel 30, 37, 270
Webster, Edward 35
Weed, Marion 298
Weeden, William B. 47, 57, 58, 96–97, 236, 372, 411n43
Weeden family 119, *280*, 289
Weeks, John W. 334, 356
Weeks, Katharine Wrisley Claflin 401n1 (chap. 2)
Weeks, Robert Freeman 401n1 (chap. 2)
Weeks Act (1910) 374
weirs, fish 160–61
Weld, Mrs. William G. 255
Wellesley College, Wellesley, Massachusetts 139, 249–50, 294, 390
Welsh, Herbert 112–13
Westcott, Lilian. *See* Hale, Lilian Westcott (daughter-in-law of EEH and EBH)
Western Monthly 406n5
Whalley, George (servant of HEF) 68, 146, 241
"What Is It?" (Freeman) 161
Whig Party 29, 37, 38, 82
White, Andrew 312
White, George H. 313
The White Hills: Their Legends, Landscape and Poetry (King) 181, 423n20
"A White Mountain Forest Reserve" (Start) 440n15
"White Mountain Forests in Peril" (Ward) 182, 334, 423n21
White Mountain National Forest 375
White Mountains, New Hampshire: Appalachian-White Mountains Forest Reservation Bill 182, 287, 323, 324–25, 331–33, 356–57, 374–75, 436n42; EEH and HEF visits 122–23, 181, 320; EEH visit 32; HEF visits 51–52, 186–87, 278–82, *284*, 285–86; logging industry 181–82; tragedy at 357. *See also* *specific locations*
The White Mountains (Bennett) 446n10
White Mountain School of Painting 445n77
Whitman, Minnie 161, 164, 216–17, 373
"Why the Bill Hangs Fire" (Start) 334, 441n23
Wickford Point (Marquand) 444n58
"Widows Report" (Freeman) 224
wildlife preservation. *See* bird conservation; bison conservation

Wild Unrest: Charlotte Perkins Gilman and the Making of the Yellow Wall-Paper (Horowitz) 416n13, 416nn1–2
Willard, Frances 148, 398
Willard Hotel, Washington D.C. 307
Williams, Francis H. 363
Williams, Lydia Phillips 327
Williams, Moses 321
Wilson, Henry 55
Wilson, James 332
Wilson, Woodrow 378, 390
Wilson Committee, Crédit Mobilier scandal 55, 406n6
Wilson-Gorman Tariff Bill (1894) 202
Winter, S. Elizabeth 430n19
Wise, Isaac Mayer 45
With Speaker Cannon through the Tropics (Moore) 353, 443n41
Woman's Christian Temperance Union (WCTU) 148
Woman's Laboratory, Boston Technical Institute 64–65
"A Woman to Her Fellow-Citizens" (Antin) 377
Women and Economics (Gilman) 144
Women's Auxiliary Conference 157
Women Scientists in America (Rossiter) 63, 65, 407n19, 408n22
Women's Education Association of Boston 63–65, 75, 274, 363
Women's Home Companion 403n17
Women's National Indian Association (WNIA) 102, 103, 295, 349, 375
women's rights and education *258*; charitable clubs for 102; and child custody 66; in relationships 257–59; in science 63–65, 74, 218, 273–74, 329, 407n19, 408n22; Silas Weir Mitchell on 242. *See also* suffrage movement
"Women's Work for Women" 102
Wood, Frank 295
Woodhull, Victoria 58, 60, 111
Woodhull & Claflin's Weekly 60
Woods Hole Marine Biological Laboratory, Massachusetts 75, 125, 218, *219*, 274, 415n34
Worcester, Margaret 265, 278
Worcester Art Museum, Worcester, Massachusetts 266
World's Fair (1893), Chicago 184–85, 188–89, 292, 423n30
World's Parliament of Religions (Barrows) 424n36
World's Parliament of Religions, Chicago 187, 188, 424n36
World War I 390–91
Wright, Conrad 403n12, 404n28, 404n29
Wright, Frederick B. 445n71
Wright, George Frederick "Glacier" 151, 242, 244, 365, 418n17, 445n71
Wright, Orville 341
Wright, Wilbur 341

xenophobia. *See* ethnic politics and immigration

yellow journalism newspapers 224, 236, 289
Yellowstone National Park 162, 175
"The Yellow Wall-Paper" (Gilman) 139–41, 242
Yosemite National Park 293, 375
Youmans, Edward L. 76

Young, Joshua: death 301; HEF and family of 156–57, 233, 249; politics of 147, 148–49, 215–16, 417n10, 418n11
Young, Lucy 314
Youngken, Joan 443n54
Yuma tribal land rights 375

Zangwill, Israel 273
Zionism 378

CPSIA information can be obtained at www.ICGtesting.com
Printed in the USA
BVOW05*1756180914

366424BV00001B/1/P